WOMEN AND MEDIEVAL LITERARY CULTURE

Focusing on England but covering a wide range of European and global traditions and influences, this authoritative volume examines the central role of medieval women in the production and circulation of books and considers their representation in medieval literary texts, as authors, readers, and subjects, assessing how these change over time. Engaging with Latin, French, German, Welsh, and Gaelic literary culture, it places British writing in wider European contexts while also considering more distant influences such as Arabic. Chapters cover topics including book production and authorship; reception; linguistic, literary, and cultural contexts and influences; women's education and spheres of knowledge; women as writers, scribes, and translators; women as patrons, readers, and book owners; and women as subjects. Reflecting recent trends in scholarship, the volume spans the early Middle Ages through to the eve of the Reformation and emphasises the multilingual, multicultural, and international contexts of women's literary culture.

CORINNE SAUNDERS is Professor of Medieval Literature in the Department of English Studies, Durham University. Her third monograph, *Magic and the Supernatural in Medieval English Romance*, was published in 2010. Recent co-edited books include *The Life of Breath in Literature, Culture, and Medicine: Classical to Contemporary* (2021) and *Visions and Voice-Hearing in Medieval and Early Modern Contexts* (2020). She is Editor for English Language and Literature for the journal *Medium Ævum*.

DIANE WATT is Professor of Medieval English Literature at the School of Literature and Languages, University of Surrey. Her books include *Women, Writing and Religion in England and Beyond, 650–1100* (2019), *Medieval Women's Writing: Books by and for Women in England, 1100–1500* (2007), *Amoral Gower: Language, Sex and Politics* (2003), and *Secretaries of God: Women Prophets in Late Medieval and Early Modern England* (1997). She has edited and co-edited several books and is joint Editor-in-Chief of *The Palgrave Encyclopedia of Medieval Women's Writing in the Global Middle Ages* (launched in 2022).

WOMEN AND MEDIEVAL LITERARY CULTURE

From the Early Middle Ages to the Fifteenth Century

EDITED BY
CORINNE SAUNDERS
Durham University

DIANE WATT
University of Surrey

Shaftesbury Road, Cambridge CB2 8EA, United Kingdom

One Liberty Plaza, 20th Floor, New York, NY 10006, USA

477 Williamstown Road, Port Melbourne, VIC 3207, Australia

314–321, 3rd Floor, Plot 3, Splendor Forum, Jasola District Centre, New Delhi – 110025, India

103 Penang Road, #05–06/07, Visioncrest Commercial, Singapore 238467

Cambridge University Press is part of Cambridge University Press & Assessment, a department of the University of Cambridge.

We share the University's mission to contribute to society through the pursuit of education, learning and research at the highest international levels of excellence.

www.cambridge.org
Information on this title: www.cambridge.org/9781108835916
DOI: 10.1017/9781108869485

© Cambridge University Press & Assessment 2023

This publication is in copyright. Subject to statutory exception and to the provisions of relevant collective licensing agreements, no reproduction of any part may take place without the written permission of Cambridge University Press & Assessment.

First published 2023

Printed in the United Kingdom by CPI Group Ltd, Croydon CR0 4YY

A catalogue record for this publication is available from the British Library.

A Cataloging-in-Publication data record for this book is available from the Library of Congress.

ISBN 978-1-108-83591-6 Hardback

Cambridge University Press & Assessment has no responsibility for the persistence or accuracy of URLs for external or third-party internet websites referred to in this publication and does not guarantee that any content on such websites is, or will remain, accurate or appropriate.

Contents

List of Illustrations	*page* viii
List of Contributors	x
Acknowledgements	xv

    Introduction   1
    Corinne Saunders and Diane Watt

I PATRONS, OWNERS, WRITERS, AND READERS IN ENGLAND AND EUROPE

1. 'Miserere, meidens': Abbesses and Nuns   27
   Elaine Treharne

2. Creating Her Own Story: Queens, Noblewomen, and Their Cultural Patronage   50
   Mary Dockray-Miller

3. Woman-to-Woman Initiatives Between English Female Religious   65
   Mary C. Erler

II CIRCLES AND COMMUNITIES IN ENGLAND

4. *Ancrene Wisse*, the Katherine Group, and the Wooing Group as Textual Communities, Medieval and Modern   83
   Michelle M. Sauer

5. Syon Abbey and the Birgittines   104
   Laura Saetveit Miles

6. What the Paston Women Read   124
   Diane Watt

III HEALTH, CONDUCT, AND KNOWLEDGE

7. Embracing the Body and the Soul: Women in the Literary Culture of Medieval Medicine   141
   Naoë Kukita Yoshikawa

8. Gender and Class in the Circulation of Conduct Books   160
   Kathleen Ashley

9. Women's Learning and Lore: Magic, Recipes, and Folk Belief   179
   Martha W. Driver

10. Women and Devotional Compilations   206
    Denis Renevey

IV GENRE AND GENDER

11. Lyrics: Meditations, Prayers, and Praises; Songs and Carols   229
    David Fuller

12. 'It satte me wel bet ay in a cave / To bidde and rede on holy seyntes lyves': Women and Hagiography   250
    Christiania Whitehead

13. Tears, Mediation, and Literary Entanglement: The Writings of Medieval Visionary Women   269
    Liz Herbert McAvoy

14. Convent and City: Medieval Women and Drama   285
    Sue Niebrzydowski

15. Women and Romance   299
    Corinne Saunders

16. Trouble and Strife in the Old French *Fabliaux*   324
    Neil Cartlidge

17. Chaucer and Gower   342
    Venetia Bridges

V WOMEN AS AUTHORS

18. Marie de France: Identity and Authorship in Translation   379
    Emma Campbell

19. Julian of Norwich: A Woman's Vision, Book, and Readers   400
    Barry Windeatt

20. The Communities of *The Book of Margery Kempe*   420
    Anthony Bale

21. Christine de Pizan: Women's Literary Culture
    and Anglo-French Politics   438
    Nancy Bradley Warren

22. Beyond Borders: Women Poets in Ireland, Scotland,
    and Wales up to *c.* 1500   457
    Cathryn A. Charnell-White

General Index   478
Index of Manuscripts   486

Illustrations

1.1.	Opening of Psalm 61. Salisbury Cathedral Library, MS 150, folio 60 v.	*page* 37
9.1.	'Sator Arepo' Magic Square. Nicolai de Lyra, *Tabula in Libros Veteris Ac Novi Testamenti*. Cologne: Johann Koelhoff, the Elder, not before 1480, sig. t8 r.	181
9.2.	Tau cross. Multipurpose Prayer Roll. New York, The Morgan Library & Museum, MS Glazier 39, fol. 7 r.	183
9.3.	Birth girdle. New Haven, Beinecke Rare Book and Manuscript Library, Takamiya MS 56.	184
9.4.	Annunciation, Flemish artist. Sarum Book of Hours. MS Glazier 9, fol. 11 v. New York, The Morgan Library & Museum.	187
9.5.	Mandragora (Mandrake). Matthaeus Platearius, *Compendium Salernitanum*. MS M.873, fol. 61 v. New York, The Morgan Library & Museum.	189
9.6.	Hunting rabbit. Gaston III Phébus, Count of Foix, *Livre de la Chasse*. MS M. 1044, fol. 79 v. New York, The Morgan Library & Museum.	191
9.7.	Songe of a woman shepherde. *Kalender of Shepherds*. Paris: Antoine Vérard, 1503, sig. g1 v.	195
9.8.	Battle with a Snail. *Compost et kalendrier des bergiers*. Paris: Guy Marchant, 1496, sig. n1 v.	198
19.1.	Christ before Herod. Panel painting; Norwich, *c.* 1400–1425. The Fitzwilliam Museum, Cambridge.	405
19.2.	Instruments of the Passion, Bohun Psalter and Hours, showing the side-wound bottom centre. Bodleian Library MS Auct. D.4.4., f. 236 v.	408

19.3.	Saints enfolded in God's robe; historiated initial of All Saints as Crucifix-Trinity. The Ranworth Antiphoner, f. 271 v.	409
19.4(a) and (b).	Shrine of the Virgin. German, *c.* 1300.	411
21.1.	Christine de Pizan. From Henry Pepwell's 1521 edition of *The Book of the City of Ladies* STC (second edn)/7271.	450

Contributors

KATHLEEN ASHLEY is Distinguished Professor (emerita) at the University of Southern Maine. She has published many articles and books on literature, art, ritual, performance, and social history of the medieval and early modern periods.

ANTHONY BALE is Professor of Medieval Studies at Birkbeck, University of London. He has published widely on late medieval English religion and culture, including a translation of *The Book of Margery Kempe* (Oxford University Press, 2015) and a biography, *Margery Kempe: A Mixed Life* (Reaktion, 2021).

VENETIA BRIDGES is Associate Professor of Medieval Literature at Durham University. Her research focuses on the themes of reception and adaptation throughout the Middle Ages, with a particular interest in classical material. She has published widely on manuscript history, the Troy legend, and Alexander the Great, and is currently working on a study of the history of high medieval literature in the later Middle Ages.

EMMA CAMPBELL is Associate Professor/Reader in the School of Modern Languages and Cultures at Warwick University. She has published on a broad range of medieval French texts prior to the fourteenth century, including major traditions such as saints' lives and bestiaries. She is the author of *Medieval Saints' Lives: The Gift, Kinship and Community in Old French Hagiography* and co-editor of *Rethinking Medieval Translation: Ethics, Politics, Theory* and of *Troubled Vision: Gender, Sexuality and Sight in Medieval Text and Image*. Her book on medieval translation and untranslatability is forthcoming with Oxford University Press.

NEIL CARTLIDGE is Professor in the Department of English Studies at the University of Durham. He is the author of *Medieval Marriage: Literary Approaches 1100–1300* (D. S. Brewer, 1997), *The Owl and the Nightingale: Text and Translation* (Exeter University Press, 2001), and *The Works of*

Chardri (State University of New York, Binghamton, 2015). He has also edited two collections of essays: *Boundaries in Medieval Romance* (D. S. Brewer, 2008) and *Heroes and Anti-Heroes in Medieval Romance* (D. S. Brewer, 2012).

CATHRYN A. CHARNELL-WHITE is an early modernist based at Aberystwyth University. Her research focuses on various forms of identity in Welsh literature of the period: self, gender, regional, and national. She is also an editor and literary translator, and edited the first comprehensive anthology of Welsh-language women's poetry up to 1800: *Beirdd Ceridwen* (Cyhoeddiadau Barddas, 2005).

MARY DOCKRAY-MILLER is Professor of English at Lesley University, Cambridge, MA, where she teaches undergraduate classes in English literature and medieval studies. She is the author of *The Books and the Life of Judith of Flanders* (Ashgate, 2015) and *Public Medievalists, Racism, and Suffrage in the American Women's College* (Palgrave Macmillan, 2017).

MARTHA W. DRIVER is Distinguished Professor of English and Women's and Gender Studies at Pace University, New York City. A co-founder of the Early Book Society for the study of manuscripts and printing history, she writes about illustration from manuscript to print, book production, women and books, and the early history of publishing.

MARY C. ERLER is the author of *Women, Reading and Piety in Late Medieval England* (Cambridge University Press, 2002) and *Reading and Writing During the Dissolution: Monks, Friars, and Nuns 1530–1558* (Cambridge University Press, 2013). She co-edited *Women and Power in the Middle Ages* (University of Georgia Press, 1988) and *Gendering the Master Narrative: Women and Power in the Middle Ages* (Cornell University Press, 2003). Recently, she has published the article 'Syon at 1500: Observant Reform?' (*Viator* 51.1).

DAVID FULLER is Emeritus Professor of English at Durham University. He is the author of monographs on Blake, Joyce, and Shakespeare; co-author of literary treatments of the sacraments; editor of texts by Marlowe (Clarendon), Blake (Longman), and the *Pearl*-poet (Enitharmon); and co-editor of two collections: *The Arts and Sciences of Criticism* (Oxford University Press, 1999) and *The Recovery of Beauty: Arts, Culture, Medicine* (Palgrave Macmillan, 2015). His most recent books are *Shakespeare and the Romantics* (Oxford University Press, 2021) and the co-edited collection *The Life of Breath in Literature, Culture and Medicine*

(Palgrave Macmillan, 2021). He is currently working on a book on Shakespearean ballets (Bloomsbury, forthcoming).

LIZ HERBERT MCAVOY is Professor Emerita at Swansea University and Honorary Senior Research Associate at the University of Bristol. She has published widely in the areas of medieval women's writing, mysticism, and the anchoritic life.

LAURA SAETVEIT MILES is Professor of British Literature at the Department of Foreign Languages, University of Bergen. She researches medieval women's writing, visionary literature, monastic cultures, and gender/queer theory, and her prize-winning monograph *The Virgin Mary's Book at the Annunciation: Reading, Interpretation and Devotional in Medieval England* was published in 2020 by D. S. Brewer.

SUE NIEBRZYDOWSKI is Professor of Medieval Literature at Bangor University. She has published widely in the areas of medieval women's writing and gender and devotion, including *Bonoure and Buxum: A Study of Wives in Late Medieval English Literature* (Peter Lang, 2006). She has also edited or co-edited a range of volumes, including *Medieval Drama: The Yearbook of English Studies*, volume 43 (2013) and *Middle-Aged Women in the Middle Ages* (D. S. Brewer, 2011).

DENIS RENEVEY is Professor of Medieval English Language and Literature at the University of Lausanne. He has published eleven books as author or co-editor, and more than forty articles and book chapters, most of them in the field of late medieval religious literature. His most recent publications include, as author, *Devotion to the Name of Jesus in Medieval English Literature, c. 1100–c. 1530* (Oxford University Press, 2022) and, as co-editor, *Late Medieval Devotion to Saints from the North of England: New Directions* (Brepols, 2022).

MICHELLE M. SAUER is Chester Fritz Distinguished Professor of English and Gender Studies at the University of North Dakota. She specialises in Middle English language and literature, especially women's devotional literature, and publishes regularly on anchoritism, mysticism, hagiography, queer/gender theory, monasticism, the history of sexuality, and Church history.

CORINNE SAUNDERS is Professor of Medieval Literature in the Department of English Studies, and Co-Director of the Institute for Medical Humanities, Durham University. Her third monograph, *Magic and the Supernatural in Medieval English Romance*, was published in

2010. Recent co-edited books include *Middle English Manuscripts and their Legacies* (Brill, 2022), *The Life of Breath in Literature, Culture, and Medicine: Classical to Contemporary* (Palgrave Macmillan, 2021), *Visions and Voice-Hearing in Medieval and Early Modern Contexts* (Palgrave Macmillan, 2020), and *Romance Re-Written: The Evolution of Medieval Romance* (D. S. Brewer, 2018). She is Editor for English Language and Literature for the journal *Medium Ævum*.

ELAINE TREHARNE is Roberta Bowman Denning Professor of Humanities and Professor of English at Stanford University, where she specialises in medieval literature, archival and manuscript studies, and text technologies. She has published numerous books and articles on early British literary cultures, including *Perceptions of Medieval Manuscripts: The Phenomenal Book* (Oxford University Press, 2021). She is a Fellow of the Society of Antiquaries, the Royal Historical Society, the English Association, and the Learned Society of Wales, and she is a Trustee of the National Library of Wales.

NANCY BRADLEY WARREN is Professor of English at Texas A&M University. She is the author of numerous books and articles on medieval and early modern religious cultures. Her current research considers the legacies of medieval female spiritualities in the early modern Americas.

DIANE WATT is Professor of Medieval English Literature in the School of Literature and Languages at the University of Surrey. Her main research and teaching interests are in the areas of medieval literature, women's writing, and gender and sexuality. Her most recent book is *Women, Writing and Religion in England and Beyond, 650–1100*, published by Bloomsbury Academic in 2019.

CHRISTIANIA WHITEHEAD is a privat-docent and Swiss National Science Foundation Senior Research Fellow at the University of Lausanne on the team project 'Reconfiguring the Apophatic Tradition in Late Medieval England'. She specialises in monastic and devotional writing for women, insular hagiography, allegory, and lyric. Her recent books include *The Afterlife of St Cuthbert: Place, Texts and Ascetic Tradition, 690–1500* (2020), and the co-edited essay collections *Middle English Lyrics: New Readings of Short Poems* (2018) and *Saints of North-East England, 600–1500* (2017). A new co-edited volume of essays, *Late Medieval Devotion to Saints from the North of England*, was published in 2022.

BARRY WINDEATT is Fellow and Keeper of Rare Books at Emmanuel College, Cambridge. His interests include Chaucer in his European context, the English literature of contemplation, and the interface between textual and visual culture in medieval England. His parallel-text edition of the short and long texts of Julian of Norwich's *Revelations of Divine Love* was published in 2016, and his translation of the *Revelations* appeared in 2015. He is completing a cultural history of medieval East Anglia.

NAOË KUKITA YOSHIKAWA is Professor of Medieval English Literature and Culture at Shizuoka University, Japan, and was recently Leverhulme Visiting Professor at Swansea University (2019–20), collaborating with Liz Herbert McAvoy. She edited *Medicine, Religion and Gender in Medieval Culture* (D. S. Brewer, 2015), and, with Anne Mouron, co-edited *The Boke of Gostely Grace: The Middle English Translation, A Critical Edition from Oxford, MS Bodley 220* (Liverpool University Press, 2022), with the assistance of Mark Atherton.

Acknowledgements

We have incurred many debts in the preparation of this collection of essays. Our first is to our authors, without whose contributions the volume would not exist. We are especially grateful to them for their patience and generosity, and their commitment to the project over a long period. The completion of the volume coincided with the COVID-19 pandemic, which inevitably caused major interruptions and disruptions across our research community and put considerable strains on all those involved in the book.

The project had its origins in the meetings of the Leverhulme Trust–funded International Network 'Women's Literary Culture and the Medieval English Canon' that ran from 2015 to 2017, and we are grateful to the trust for their generous support (grant number: IN-2014–038), as well as to all those who contributed to the workshops held at Chawton House Library and the University of Boston, and to the conference held at the University of Bergen in 2017. We owe a special debt to Lynette Kerridge for her excellent organisation of these events and support of the project.

We are also grateful to the University of Surrey Faculty of Arts and Social Sciences (Academic Disruption Fund) and School of Literature and Languages, University of Surrey, for their financial assistance, and to the Department of English Studies and Faculty of Arts and Humanities, Durham University, for their support. Corinne Saunders' research is also supported by a Wellcome Development Award to Durham University's Institute for Medical Humanities (grant number: 209513/Z/17/Z).

We owe a special debt to Michael Baker, for his role as editorial assistant and his extraordinary work in preparing all aspects of the typescript, including the index. He has, as ever, been the most painstaking of copy-editors, and it has been a constant pleasure to work with him. We are grateful also to our editor at Cambridge University Press, Emily Hockley, whose inspiration this volume was, for her support, and to George Laver and the production team for their assistance, in particular, Liz Davey, Bharathan Sankar, and our copy-editor, Helen B. Cooper.

Introduction

Corinne Saunders and Diane Watt

Named women authors in the medieval period may seem to the modern reader disappointingly few, remarkable exceptions that break the rule of a firmly male literary culture. In England, they comprise Marie de France in the twelfth century and Julian of Norwich and Margery Kempe more than two centuries later. Yet female authorship extends far beyond these names. To English names we might add the Continental women whose writings were widely circulated, adapted, or translated, in particular Christine de Pizan in the fifteenth century, but also, although the early fourteenth-century Middle English version did not carry her name, Marguerite Porete, burnt at the stake for heresy in 1310 for the beliefs presented in her radical treatise *Mirror of Simple Souls* (*c.* 1300), St Catherine of Siena, whose *Dialogue* was translated into Middle English in the mid-fourteenth century, St Bridget of Sweden, whose revelations were translated in the 1340s, and the twelfth-century female physician Trota of Salerno, to whom a group of treatises on women's medicine widely circulated in England and the Continent was attributed. Other names hover on the margins: the anonymous 'Nun of Barking', the twelfth-century author of an Anglo-Norman life of Edward the Confessor, and Clemence of Barking, who translated the life of St Catherine of Alexandria (perhaps the same woman); Juliana Berners (*fl.* 1460), thought by some to have been the prioress of Sopwell Abbey, to whom *The Book of Hawking, Hunting, and Blasing of Arms*, also known as *The Boke of St Albans*, a collection of prose and verse treatises, is attributed; and Eleanor Hull, who translated a series of devotional works into English in the fifteenth century, also at Sopwell. The network grows larger still when letter writers such as the Paston women, writing in the second half of the fifteenth century, are added. Even this list, by no means comprehensive, gives some indication of the range of works by or attributed to women that were in circulation in England in the later Middle Ages.

As scholarship over the last three decades has also shown, modern notions of authorship are often reductive. Women's writings may be collaborative in different ways: through amanuenses, through translation and adaptation, but also through women's historical and literary relationships with the men who wrote their lives, as, for example, in the cases of Jacques de Vitry, bishop of Acre, the confessor and follower of Mary d'Oignies (*c.* 1170–1213) and author of her Latin life, and of the anonymous twelfth-century monk of St Albans (most likely Robert de Gorron, monk and subsequently abbot of St Albans),[1] whose *Life of Christina of Markyate* so vividly indicates personal knowledge of her. Marguerite Porete was closely associated with the German theologian and mystic Meister Eckhardt (*c.* 1260–*c.* 1328), celebrated for his work with and influenced by pious lay groups such as the beguines, communities of women in cities of northern Europe who adopted religious lives without entering established orders, and who included, as well as Porete, the thirteenth-century visionary poets Mechthild of Magdeburg and Hadewijch of Brabant.[2] And in a strikingly collaborative female relationship, Christine de Pizan's *Ditié de Jehanne d'Arc* (1429) is not only addressed to but in part shapes the influence and positive reception of Joan through its powerful, hagiographic presentation of her.[3]

Women's names, then, ripple out, connecting with others and reaching far across time and place. Perhaps most crucially, however, women's literary culture includes other intersecting and powerful networks: women are not only writers and collaborators in writing, but also patrons, readers, and subjects of texts. Their networks extend from Britain to the Continent and beyond. Evidence concerning women reading must be pieced together from wills and other historical records, and from literary references: it is not plentiful, but it is revealing of an active literary culture which included different communities of readers and different kinds of reading – silent and aloud, individual and to group audiences, meditative and for entertainment. As D. H. Green emphasises, despite the injunction of St Paul against the education of women and their exclusion from the medieval universities, several theologians, including in the fifth century St Jerome, not generally known for his sympathetic views of women, and, in the thirteenth century, Vincent of Beauvais, encouraged women reading, and hence the education of young women. By the fifteenth century, the French nobleman Geoffroy de la Tour Landry could strongly criticise resistance to teaching women to read. Green stresses the active models of both the Virgin and St Anne, often depicted as reading, and offering influential models for both religious and lay aristocratic women. Green emphasises crucial developments in the course of the Middle Ages: 'the extension of literacy from religious life to the lay world, where it could also be practised by men, but more commonly by women', and 'the domestication of literacy, its expansion from the monastery to the household, particularly in the education of the young in reading and the laywoman's use of prayer books and devotional reading matter in the home as well as in church'. He also emphasises the promotion of the vernacular, and hence of books in the vernacular, connected with the rise of women readers.[4]

Many of the essays in this volume discuss the sophisticated engagement of women in different kinds of religious community with books and reading, including with French and Latin as well as English books. The abbeys of Barking (founded in the seventh century by St Erkenwald; a Benedictine foundation from the tenth century) and later Syon, the Birgittine house founded in 1415, provide celebrated examples where women read and translated works from Latin into the vernaculars of Anglo-Norman and then English. Lay women also might be active and learned readers. Green offers examples of fifteenth- and sixteenth-century women such as Margaret Beaufort, mother of Henry VII, and Anne Stafford, Countess of Huntingdon, reading and studying in their chambers, but also reading to others or arranging public readings.[5] Felicity Riddy explores a pattern of spiritual teaching among women through her analysis of examples such as that of Margaret Sylemon, Prioress of Nuneaton (1367–86), whose copy of Robert Grossesteste's *Château d'amour*, left by her to the priory, is described in her will as owned both by her and her pupils, 'et discipulas suas'. If nunneries formed 'reading communities, their members teaching one another, sharing books and discussing them together', so too may lay groups of women have formed informal reading networks.[6] The household records of aristocratic vowesses such as Cecily, Duchess of York, mother of Edward IV, describe the reading of holy works at dinner, emulating, as with Margaret Beaufort, the practices of nunneries.

Devotional books were owned by women, bequeathed, and exchanged between religious communities and by laywomen.[7] Riddy offers an extended series of examples of donations and bequests of devotional works from the late thirteenth to the sixteenth century. They include bequests to priories and to individual nuns, as well as to laywomen. Carol Meale teases out a suggestive series of associations of holy books with women in late medieval England, beginning with an image of the seal of Margaret, Lady Hungerford and Botreaux (1462–78), which depicts a kneeling woman looking down at a book: Margaret bequeathed her mass books and other holy books, including to her granddaughter her matins book, while her father-in-law left to her a French book of saints' lives. Lady Margaret la Zouche left her 'best Primer' to her granddaughter in 1449, and, similarly, Anne Harding, wife of John Lord Scrope of Bolton, left her primer to her goddaughter in 1498. Not all bequests were made by gentry and aristocracy. Beatrice Milneth, the widow of a wealthy merchant, for instance, left her sister Anne Burgh an impressive bequest of religious books in 1448, including a French gospel of Nicodemus. Meale offers a variety of further examples of bequests in late medieval England.[8]

The active engagement of women with secular writing is clear both through the evidence of the texts themselves and through extra-textual records. Romances repeatedly refer to ladies reading books, both devotional and secular, and reading and writing letters; Chaucer's *Troilus and Criseyde* famously describes one of Criseyde's ladies reading the *Siege of Thebes* aloud to her (II.82–4), as well as the exchange of letters between Troilus and Criseyde. While wills and other records most often mention devotional books, such as psalters and books of hours, the work of Meale and others has demonstrated that they included many other categories. In the late fourteenth century, Eleanor de Bohun left a significant library to her children which, as well as devotional works, included chronicles, Giles of Rome's *De regimine principum*, and 'the Bohun ancestral romance of the "chivaler a cigne"' (the knight of the swan).[9] Alice Chaucer's estate papers record that a series of manuscript books was taken from her castle in Suffolk to her home in Oxfordshire in 1466, which included, as well as holy books, Christine de Pizan's *Book of the City of Ladies* and a French romance. Meale suggests that the arms of Joan Neville (d. 1462) on Hoccleve's *Regiment of Princes* with those of her husband may imply that she acquired it. The evidence of surviving wills, like the works themselves, suggests that Arthurian romances were especially popular among women readers. As well as the numerous romances, spanning classical, French, and Arthurian subject matter, owned in the fourteenth century by Isabella of France, wife of Edward II, Meale offers a range of other late medieval English examples, including in particular of the romances of Lancelot and Tristan. Isabel, Duchess of York, for instance, left a Lancelot romance to her son at the end of the fourteenth century, while a Lancelot was left to Isabella Eure, member of a northern gentry family, in 1435 by the spiritual chancellor of the bishop of Durham. Elizabeth la Zouche left copies of both romances to her husband in 1380, and Margaret Courtenay, Countess of Devon, left in her will of 1390/1 romances of Tristan, Merlin, and Arthur of Britain to her two daughters and another woman respectively. In the fifteenth century, Elizabeth of York signed a manuscript previously belonging to Richard III and containing part of the prose romance of Tristan, while a copy of the romance of Tristan was left to Joan Beaufort, Countess of Westmoreland (d. 1440), by her brother, Thomas, Duke of Exeter. Meale's examples include, as well as other Arthurian works, some non-Arthurian romances (discussed further by Saunders in this volume). Though examples are less numerous than for holy books, women certainly left romances to other women, again suggesting reading networks of family and friends.[10] Secular works were also owned and read by nuns, for example in Syon Abbey and the Benedictine nunnery of Amesbury.[11]

As well as owning, women commissioned books, both sacred and secular. Eleanor of Aquitaine and Marie de Champagne represent celebrated twelfth-century examples: both promoted writing in the vernacular, including history and romance. Wace's *Roman de Brut* is associated with Eleanor by Laʒamon, while Benoît de Sainte-Maure praises her as a patron. It is tempting to connect other romances written at the English court of Eleanor and Henry II with her, including Thomas's *Tristan*. Chrétien de Troyes' *Erec et Enide* may also be connected with their court, while the prologue to his *Le Chevalier de la charrette* claims it is written at Marie de Champagne's request. Also in the twelfth century, A *Life of St Margaret of Scotland* was written for Margaret's daughter Matilda, wife of Henry I. Not all patronage was royal. The St Albans Psalter was presented to Christina of Markyate sometime after she founded and became prioress of Markyate in 1145; probably commissioned by Geoffrey de Gorron, abbot of St Albans, as her *Life* is likely to have been, it directly addresses Christina. A *Life of St Lawrence* was written for an anonymous twelfth-century woman. Eleanor de Bohun commissioned the 'Edinburgh Psalter' (National Library of Scotland, MS Advocates 18.6.5) in the late fourteenth century. Meale also makes the tantalising suggestion that Eleanor was actively involved in her husband Thomas, Duke of Gloucester's acquisition of books for his celebrated library.[12] In the fifteenth century, Alice Chaucer may have been involved in the commission of a copy of John Lydgate's *Siege of Thebes* (British Library Arundel MS 119), as well as perhaps being the patron of Lydgate's poem *The Virtues of the Mass* and his translation of Guillaume Deguileville's *Pélerinage de la vie humaine*. Other women were patrons of individual religious works by Lydgate, including Eleanor de Bohun's daughter and granddaughter. Elizabeth Berkeley, the first wife of Richard Beauchamp, Earl of Warwick, was the patron of a verse translation of Boethius' *Consolation of Philosophy* by John Walton (1410), while her daughter, Margaret Talbot, not only owned devotional books but also commissioned Lydgate's *Guy of Warwick*, the protagonist of which was the legendary ancestor of the Earls of Warwick. In the same period, Osbern Bokenham wrote at least some of his female saints' lives for women patrons. Of his *Legends of Holy Women*, the Life of Mary Magdalen states it was commissioned by Isabel Bourchier, Countess of Eu, sister of Richard, Duke of York, and that of Elizabeth of Hungary by Elizabeth de Vere, Countess of Oxford; four more are dedicated to women.[13] The Vernon manuscript (Oxford, Bodleian Library, Eng. Poet. MS a. 1, 1390–1400) contains numerous works written for women, including Aelred of Rievaulx's *De insititutione inclusarum*, written for his sister, a nun; works by Richard Rolle written for female recluses; and the first book of Walter Hilton's *Scale of Perfection*, originally written for a woman, as well other works concerning female piety.[14] It seems likely that the collection was made for a community of nuns or devout laywomen. Such instances demonstrate an active culture of patronage by women that includes the commissioning of both secular and religious writing, and close engagement with composition and translation, as well as a more general topos of female readership.

Women's literary culture connects with and may overlap with male literary culture: women engaged actively with and collaborated with learned circles of men. These circles were frequently clerical, as is suggested by the examples of Meister Eckhardt and of the priest-confessors who acted as amanuenses for Birgitta of Sweden and Margery Kempe; in Norwich Kempe had access to a lively clerical and intellectual circle. Circles could also be courtly – as is suggested, for example, by the role of the husband in the conduct book *Le Ménagier de Paris* (c. 1393), who instructs his young wife in the skills of both hunting and hawking, offering a context for the knowledge of women that makes the attribution of *The Book of St Albans* to Dame Juliana Berners credible. Joan of Arc's letters reached beyond France to England and are addressed to Henry VI and John Duke of Bedford. Marie de France's address to Henry II or perhaps his son suggests the engagement of the court of Henry and Eleanor of Aquitaine with courtly writing. Christine de Pizan's close relationships with her patrons – Louis I of Orleans, Philip the Bold of Burgundy, and his son, John the Fearless – and the direction of her writings to noblemen and princes, provide clear evidence of shared literary culture.

In part, then, this book also offers a corrective to the notion that medieval women's literary history represents a tradition distinct from that of men. Simultaneously to work on women's writing, considerable research has been undertaken in the last several decades into the literary contexts of male writers, their working practices, and their relationships with scribes, patrons, and audiences. All have been subject to close and necessary scrutiny, as have the connections between England and the

Continent. Yet, while there have been numerous informative studies of women or gender in the work of male medieval writers, these are not typically connected to women's literary culture. There has been extensive work too on the representation of women across different literary genres, and in relation to literary and cultural history. All these strands have too often existed in parallel rather than being brought together. But, as the essays in this volume on major genres and on the writing of Chaucer and Gower suggest, a truly comprehensive exploration of women's literary culture must also take account of the treatment of women within literary works, both in terms of generic conventions and the engagement of male authors with women as subjects. We can never recover the responses of female readers, nor, as Melissa Furrow has emphasised in relation to romance, can we assume there was a single characteristic response.[15] The treatment of women as literary subjects, however, indubitably played a part in shaping the literary culture in which they also participated.

The very nature of that culture is multilingual and inclusive. Essays in this volume, therefore, engage with English, French, and Latin works, and look beyond, for example, to German, Welsh, and Scottish Gaelic literary culture. The book places writing within Britain in a wider European context, including, for instance, early English women missionaries in Francia, and it emphasises the multilingual and multicultural contexts of women's literary culture, looking beyond England to consider wider British, European, and more distant (including Arabic) influences. Essays explore book production and authorship; reception; linguistic, literary, and cultural contexts and influences; women as readers; and women as subjects. The volume is structured by topic, but individual sections and essays also consider chronological developments. Crucial questions recur across the volume. How were books produced and circulated? What was the role of women in these processes? What were the linguistic and cultural contexts of these works? How important were European and global traditions and influences? How are women represented, whether as authors, readers, or subjects? How does this change over time?

Patrons, Owners, Writers, and Readers

The first three essays focus on powerful, literate, and often multilingual women in England and Scotland, queens and abbesses, noblewomen and nuns, and on the literary and learning communities that they fostered and to which they contributed. Such women are often, wrongly, thought of as exceptional, but in fact, throughout the Middle Ages and across Europe, far from being marginal, elite women were at the heart of politics, society, and literary culture. Elaine Treharne's study of medieval nuns and abbesses as scribes focuses on manuscript evidence from post-Conquest England, especially in relation to changing institutional ownership. Looking initially at an early-twelfth-century legal manuscript from St Paul's London (Cambridge, Corpus Christi College, MS 383), Treharne draws our attention to short texts that were subsequently added to it by one 'Matilda' for the benefit of a female audience. Matilda's exact identity is unknown, but she was clearly educated and almost certainly was a nun, possibly from Barking Abbey. Similar additions are made to another manuscript (London, British Library, Cotton MS Vespasian D. xiv) which contains homilies and saints' lives, this time by an 'ancilla' or nun, who inserted prayers that she had authored herself sometime in the late twelfth century. Again, the scribe and writer may have been a nun at Barking, possibly associated with Abbess Mary Becket. These findings are so important because, as Treharne points out, there is very little proof of women's scribal activity in medieval England (in contrast with, for example, Germany and the Low Countries); hitherto scholars have assumed that manuscripts are written and glossed by men. Treharne outlines the sorts of evidence that could be considered to assign more anonymous scribal activity to women, concluding that medieval women scribes are everywhere, but to find them we need to read between the lines.

Mary Dockray-Miller's chapter shifts our focus from religious to secular women, although, as she observes, the two categories were often not distinct from one another in the Middle Ages. Dockray-Miller outlines the importance of queens and noblewomen as 'makers' of literary culture from the ninth to the sixteenth centuries, when they played key roles as patrons and book owners. Women such as Emma of Normandy and Edith of Wessex, both involved in the production of historical narratives that they commissioned, were not isolated from their counterparts on the continent but were very much part of a wider Northern European network of culturally sophisticated aristocrats. Further evidence of the importance of understanding continental connections when considering elite women's literary cultures is provided by Judith of Flanders, who joined the royal court in England and commissioned four highly ornate Gospel Books. As Dockray-Miller explains, women's literary and religious cultures often overlapped, as is also illustrated in the examples of Margaret of Scotland; her daughter Matilda, who married Henry I of England; her granddaughter Matilda, who married the Holy Roman Emperor Henry V; and her sister-in-law Adela, Countess of Blois. Dockray-Miller contends that

Eleanor of Aquitaine, who is probably the most well-known example of a medieval literary patron, is not, therefore, the exception that she has often been considered. Rather, her activities have to be understood in terms of a widespread culture of aristocratic women's cultural patronage that extends as far as Georgia, and from the Byzantine to the Mughal Empires, as is evidenced by the activities of Queen Tamar of Georgia, Anna Comnena, and Gulbadan Banu Begum.

In contrast to the studies by Treharne and Dockray-Miller of women as scribes and authors, patrons and book owners, Mary C. Erler's chapter focuses more specifically on the education of religious women, figured in terms of horizontal and vertical learning, in England at the very end of the Middle Ages. Erler's analysis highlights connections between women rather than the more widely discussed relationships between women and their male spiritual advisors. Exploring the sorts of texts that were obtained by women leaders of the late medieval women's houses, including the powerful English Birgittine abbey of Syon, Erler notes that the superiors acquired works relating to the religious rule of life and also other devotional texts, and were concerned with obtaining texts that would enable their communities to understand their life and governance. Erler argues that such works were not obtained for private study but would have been shared with the nuns via the vertical learning of refectory and other communal readings. Alongside this, more traditional horizontal learning or hierarchical instruction also took place in women's houses: nuns were expected to emulate their elders, and the elders in turn to offer guidance, including in relation to their reading, to which the exchange of books between nuns was essential. Finally, Erler finds evidence of more formal convent instruction, framed in compassionate and supportive terms.

Circles and Communities in England

The second group of essays focuses on literary communities, networks, and wider circles, whether religious (the critical tradition of *Ancrene Wisse* and its related texts; the textuality centred on Syon Abbey) or secular (the reading of the women in the Paston family). Michelle M. Sauer's chapter focuses primarily on the modern reception of *Ancrene Wisse*, and, by implication, the larger so-called *Ancrene Wisse* Group of which it is a part. *Ancrene Wisse*, or the *Guide for Anchoresses*, an anonymous thirteenth-century Middle English text written for a group of three anchoresses in the West Midlands, survives in a significant number of manuscripts, and its place within the literary tradition of medieval women in England seems uncontroversial. However, as Sauer explains, nineteenth- and twentieth-century editors of the *Ancrene Wisse* and related works, most of whom were men, tended to focus on the linguistic significance of these texts, paying little attention to their gendered devotional context. They also placed much greater emphasis on speculation concerning the identity of the male author of *Ancrene Wisse* than on examining the role of its immediate audience – the three anchoresses themselves – in shaping the work addressed to them. Women scholars working on the *Ancrene Wisse* Group have, in contrast, tended to be more aware of the importance of the material in relation to the history of women's anchoritism and more open to the possibility of women's authorship of some of the works within this group. Sauer argues that *Ancrene Wisse* had an expansive direct and indirect influence not only on later texts but also on women's devotional traditions, which, she suggests, may even have extended beyond England.

The rich textual history of Syon Abbey, the only English house of St Birgitta of Sweden's Order of St Saviour (discussed by Erler in relation to her larger consideration of the learning of late medieval nuns), is Laura Saetveit Miles's focus. Although there is limited evidence of English Birgittine nuns authoring their own texts, Miles demonstrates the myriad influences St Birgitta, Syon Abbey, and its community of nuns as well as monks had on women's literary culture in fifteenth- and early-sixteenth-century England. While the significance of Syon within the late medieval English cultural landscape cannot be overemphasised, like Dockray-Miller Miles challenges ideas of exceptionalism, arguing that its (textual) community is also representative of the intricacies of women's literary culture. As Erler has also shown, Syon women were certainly engaged in the commissioning of texts, and Miles demonstrates that this was not limited to the superiors but extended to aristocratic lay women with close ties to the abbey. Furthermore, the Syon community, led by Abbess Elizabeth Gibbs, was quick to exploit the new technology of printing, also supported by the patronage of wealthy noble women, such as Lady Margaret Beaufort. However, as Miles observes, the textuality of the abbey expanded beyond these powerful women to include the wider community of Syon nuns, and beyond England into continental Europe.

Diane Watt turns to the domestic circle of the Paston family, to explore the unique insights into the lives and book ownership of a late medieval gentry family offered by its fifteenth-century correspondence. The archive includes many letters written by women, although the most prolific of the correspondents, Margaret Mautby Paston, was almost certainly unable to write, and probably unable to read, calling upon her sons, servants, and chaplain to act as her scribes. Her letters and those of other Paston women demonstrate that having limited or no literacy skills did not necessarily prevent access to literary culture. Indeed, the Paston correspondence offers ample evidence of women owning, inheriting, bequeathing, lending, and borrowing books, which were regularly exchanged within extended familial and friendship networks. Watt extends previous research through her consideration of three Paston women – Agnes Berry Paston, her daughter-in-law Margaret Mautby Paston, and Margaret's daughter Elizabeth Paston (Yelverton) – and the books that were in their possession or that they may have read. Putting the evidence concerning book ownership provided by wills, for example, alongside that of letters provides intriguing insights into the spirituality and influence of women, and the value they placed on devotional and moral works. While Watt demonstrates that devotional books could have powerful everyday relevance, she also shows that the Paston women's reading included secular romance, the interest of which may have been as much political as personal. The reading interests of such women, then, extended far beyond the narrowly domestic.

Health, Conduct, and Knowledge

The third section of the book sustains this theme of expansive reading. It addresses textual evidence of the education and knowledge of women, beginning with their understanding of health care and medical matters, moving on to conduct books written by and for women, and then to a surprising range of arts, including chivalry and hunting, which might now be more typically connected with medieval men. The section concludes with women's contributions to the genre of the devotional compilation. Naoë Kukita Yoshikawa's chapter addresses women and medicine in the Middle Ages, especially works concerning the female body and reproduction. Noting the roles and models of religious and laywomen such as the twelfth-century physician Trota of Salerno in the care of the body and soul, she identifies positive representations of the female body in the mystical writings of, for example, the thirteenth-century nuns of Helfta and Mechthild of Hackeborn. In contrast to later gynaecological works such as the *Secreta mulierum* (*Secrets of Women*), which were often deeply misogynistic, Yoshikawa suggests that Hildegard of Bingen's medical texts ascribe a redemptive quality to women's reproductive processes. Most medical treatises were, however, not written for women, and even those women involved in health care, including midwives, had little access to them. The *Trotula* or *Trotula* ensemble, a compendium on women's medicine taking its name from Trota herself and first brought together in the twelfth century, was widely disseminated and translated as a whole and in parts. Although the early Latin versions were addressed to women, in its later incarnations the *Trotula* ensemble was owned largely by men. Nevertheless, there is some evidence of female readership and actual audiences of women, as is illustrated by a late Middle English translation of the *Trotula* entitled *The Knowing of Woman's Kind in Childing* and by another fifteenth-century Middle English text, *The Sickness of Women*. Yoshikawa concludes that the translation of medical treatises about women into the vernacular did increase women's access to this important form of textual knowledge.

Kathleen Ashley's chapter traces the development across time, class, and gender of an important medieval moral genre: the guide to conduct. While most early examples were written by men, one famous example was composed by a Carolingian noblewoman for her son: Dhuoda's *Liber manualis*. Not all such works were addressed to boys or men. The French king Louis IX's *Enseignemenz* (*Teachings*) provided advice for both his son and daughter. In the fourteenth and fifteenth centuries, the readership of conduct books expanded to include the middle classes. Indeed, as Ashley observes, Suzanne, the daughter of Anne of France, Duchess of Bourbon, had printed a work her mother had written for her so that it could reach a wider audience of women. The conduct works of Christine de Pizan illustrate the growing popularity of the genre, and although they primarily (but not solely) focus on the aristocracy, Christine de Pizan certainly assumed that the lower classes would learn from the examples set by those who followed her advice. Geoffrey de la Tour Landry's *Le Livre du Chevalier de la Tour*, written in the late fourteenth-century for his three daughters, differs from the previous examples in that it has a major focus on marriage rather than life at court, thus appealing to a wider readership. In the same period, *Le Ménagier de Paris* provides an example of a work addressed to a bourgeois audience that anticipates the development of 'household anthologies', which include conduct literature.

Taking up some of the same issues concerning healing and care as Yoshikawa, Martha Driver focuses on esoteric forms of knowledge very different from the religious learning addressed by Erler. Starting with the early Middle Ages and offering a broad survey through to the start of the early modern period, Driver examines a range of charms, incantations, prayers, talismans, amulets, recipes, and remedies. Many of these were certainly used for and sometimes by women, such as charms on birthing scrolls or girdles. Some examples are unexpectedly found in Books of Hours owned by women, though Driver's main sources include medical treatises and recipe books. Her discussion reveals the unexpectedly wide range of areas of expertise ascribed to medieval women, as is illustrated by Christine de Pizan's writings on warcraft and chivalry, and the guide to hunting, hawking, and heraldry attributed to Dame Juliana Berners (*The Book of St Albans*). Finally, Driver looks at the extremely varied and encyclopaedic advice available to women found in the compendium known as *The Kalender of Shepherds* (c. 1490), an important source of folk belief. Her chapter, like Yoshikawa's, demonstrates that medieval women's lore was much more diverse than the conduct books of the period suggest.

The final chapter in this section, by Denis Renevey, explores the roles of women in relation to late medieval devotional compilations. While compilations, arrangements of texts, or extracts from them, sometimes in translation or with substantial adaptation, provide crucial evidence of manuscript transmission and literary activity, the full extent of women's roles relating to them has not yet been assessed. Renevey examines the question of female subjectivity, considering the ways that female personae might serve as models for both male and female readers. Some late fourteenth- and early-fifteenth-century compilations address both men and women, while employing the topos of the female religious reader to depict the exemplary Christian life for all. Other works offer specific connections with female, particularly aristocratic readers, both secular and religious. The imagery of a luxurious bed in *Disce mori* (*Learn to Die*), for example, may offer intriguing evidence of the wealthy previous life of its probable recipient, Dame Alice, a vowess connected with Syon Abbey; *Book to a Mother* explicitly addresses the mother of the author, a widow perhaps interested in joining a religious community while also addressing a lay public. As well as adapting anchoritic material, compilations took up the spiritual teachings offered by Richard Rolle's vernacular writing. *Disce mori*, for example, both uses Rolle's texts and imitates the dynamics of Rolle's relations with his female readers, while also including a more general lay readership. Women's writings such as the *Revelations* of Birgitta of Sweden play an important part too in compilations. Though evidence is scant, the example of Eleanor Hull suggests that women also acted as compilers. As well as a French commentary on the Psalms, Hull translated and compiled a series of meditations, making sophisticated literary choices. Compilations, then, demonstrate both the range and complexity of women's involvement in devotional literary culture and the wider significance of the female subject for devotional writers, male and female, in later medieval England.

Genre and Gender

Both devotional and secular writing suggest that the relationship between genre and gender is played out across the medieval period in varying, sometimes ambiguous ways that are as likely to challenge as to affirm modern assumptions. As David Fuller's chapter demonstrates, this variety is particularly evident in the medieval lyric, a highly flexible genre including forms as diverse as meditations and prayers, songs, and carols, and spanning the twelfth to the fifteenth centuries. Both secular and sacred, popular and learned lyrics offer insights into attitudes to women and creative engagements with gender. Sacred lyrics find special inspiration through the figure of the Virgin Mary in her various forms, from suffering mother to heavenly queen. As Fuller suggests, such lyrics may both speak vividly to female readers and seem distanced from the lives of actual women, and, as with compilations, straightforward readings are likely to be simplistic. The context of virginity may be as relevant to male as female religious readers, while Marian lyrics may address complex theological questions in sophisticated ways, including through the conventions of *fin' amor*. Romance conventions are also taken up in secular lyrics, as are conventions familiar from *fabliaux* and anti-feminist satire: women speakers are repeatedly used to voice male stereotypes. The question of whether women in lyrics speak for themselves is therefore complicated. Fuller's analysis of the several poems attributed to women draws attention to the paucity of evidence and suggests the potential reductiveness of connecting the woman's voice with female authorship. The challenges of reading the woman's voice are brought into sharp relief by the 'Findern' manuscript, a fifteenth- and early-sixteenth-century provincial miscellany which includes the names of five women, who, it has been argued, composed and copied a number of the lyrics written in it. The work raises complex questions concerning the relationship between art and life, experience and imagination, persona and author. Such questions resonate through this volume, illuminating the richness and complexity of the connections between medieval women and literary culture, connections that call into question simple assumptions concerning relations between author, voice, and reader, and between convention, genre, and gender.

Just such richness and complexity are evident in Christiania Whitehead's exploration of women as writers, subjects, and readers of hagiography from the late seventh to late fifteenth centuries within the trilingual context of English literary culture. As with compilation, hagiography has a specific relevance for female readers engaged with the ideals and circumstances of pious lay life. Its models, however, are strikingly contrasting, comprising both the perfected virgin martyr and the powerful abbess. The accounts of Hilda, Æthelburga, and Æthelthryth in Bede's *Historia* are supplemented by the depictions of female sanctity and powerful female agency in works connected with the eighth-century Anglo-Saxon mission to the Germanic peoples, in particular the *vitae* of Willibald and Winnebald by the English nun Hugeburc of Heidenheim and the *vita* of Leoba by Rudolf of Fulda. Sophisticated literary skill is notably demonstrated by the hagiographical writing of Hrotsvitha, Canoness of Gandersheim. Whitehead goes on to discuss regulated communities of reading and writing in the long twelfth century, as hagiographical composition diversifies linguistically and reaches new audiences. Bede's abbesses lead a long textual life, joined by more recent examples such as Queen Margaret of Scotland and Christina of Markyate. While the *Vie seinte Audrée* perhaps composed by Marie de France (discussed further in this volume by Emma Campbell) rewrites the life of Æthelthryth probably for a secular, courtly audience, the anonymous 'Nun' and Clemence of Barking – perhaps the same author – write for and from explicitly monastic contexts, venerating both the virgin martyrs and the Anglo-Saxon abbesses. The early Middle English lives of the virgin martyrs in the Katherine Group, by contrast, are designed for a well-born group of anchoresses in the West Midlands, treating their subjects as empowering forebears but offering striking contrasts to anchoritic life. Whitehead shows that the lives of women saints continued to be popular reading in the fourteenth and fifteenth centuries in both lay and religious contexts. Benedictine compilations give notable prominence to the lives of female saints, while vernacular collections offer varying models for female sanctity, including northern saints and virgin martyrs, but also use newer, more experimental modes of sanctity drawn from the Continent, such as those of the Beguine women Elizabeth of Spalbeek, Christina Mirabilis, and Marie d'Oignies, important models for lay women looking beyond insular traditions. As many of the essays in this volume demonstrate, the tension between traditional and more recent models of holiness is both creative and disruptive, energising notions of female sanctity across the medieval period for audiences and authors.

Liz Herbert McAvoy returns to the importance of the community, or textual community, addressed in the second section, in her chapter on women visionaries. McAvoy adopts Karen Barad's terminology of dynamic *intra-actions* to describe the lives and writings of visionaries in the European High and later Middle Ages, taking as her starting point the complex and manifold spiritual female entanglements across space and time that are described in *The Book of Margery Kempe*. McAvoy traces such intra-actions back through Mechthild of Hackeborn and the nuns of Helfta in the thirteenth century to Hildegard of Bingen in the eleventh, and forwards to the later fourteenth century and Julian of Norwich. McAvoy also identifies the influence of Mechthild on *A Revelation of Purgatory*, written in the early fifteenth century by an anchoress of Winchester, and on the writings of Birgitta of Sweden, with which Kempe was familiar. Fascinatingly, McAvoy concludes that these interwoven spiritual connections between women are mirrored in the knotted patterns of manuscript patronage and ownership, noting, for example, the co-existence in one manuscript of Julian's work with the Middle English translation of *The Mirror of Simple Souls* by the radical French beguine, Marguerite Porete.

Sue Niebrzydowski explores such intra-actions from a different perspective in her consideration of women's involvement in medieval drama. In addressing this challenging topic, Niebrzydowski traces a remarkable and little-known series of medieval women dramatists, from Hrotsvitha of Gandersheim in tenth-century Germany, who wrote plays about the early Christian martyrs (also discussed by Whitehead), through Hildegard of Bingen and her *Ordo Virtutum* (*Play of the Virtues*) in the twelfth century, to Katherine Sutton, Abbess of Barking in the late fourteenth century, who composed liturgical dramas for Holy Week. These women dramatists are located within the wider context of medieval convent performances in England and Europe, and, as the recurrence of names and places in this volume suggests – Hrotsvitha, Hildegard, Barking – within active and influential networks of devotional literary culture. Religious women were not only the authors of such productions, but also actors, directors, and costume makers, and their convents provided the play space. Laywomen sometimes also contributed, for example by donating the fabric needed for liturgical performances. By contrast, as Niebrzydowski points out, the evidence of women's participation in drama outside the convents is often speculative or conjectural. Although the performance of the lost Chester pageant of 'our Lady thassumpcion' was linked to the wives and widows of the city, this is the only definitive English example of women associated with a Corpus Christi production. Other fragmentary evidence indicates the involvement of lay women in a range of dramatic forms, from saints' lives, interludes, and morality plays to processions and pageants. Although we can sketch only its outlines, women appear to have made a significant contribution to this influential and long-lived genre, in both its elite and its popular forms.

Corinne Saunders turns to the secular genre that has most often been associated with women – that of medieval romance – but also challenges the notion of romance as women's genre. Certainly, we know that women were patrons, owners, readers, and even writers of courtly romances; Marie de Champagne and Marie de France illustrate this point. However, the picture is complex: romances were often addressed to mixed audiences and read publicly rather than privately, and, as Saunders argues, it is impossible to know for certain how women responded to the romance narratives that they encountered. By focusing on three central romance themes – love and consent, virtuous suffering, and magic and enchantment – Saunders explores the imaginative spaces that female protagonists inhabit and the agency they demonstrate, and suggests how these might connect to ideals of Christian virtue, to the constraints imposed on women by chivalry, and perhaps to the lived experiences of medieval women. The chapter draws examples from a range of Middle English romances, from *Sir Orfeo*, *King Horn*, and *Havelok the Dane*, to *Sir Gawain and the Green Knight*, to Thomas Malory's *Morte Darthur* at the very end of the period. She concludes that medieval romance is the locus of both dialogue and debate about women and their place in medieval society and culture.

Such debate is further explored by Neil Cartlidge, whose chapter addresses the genre seemingly most antithetical to romance and, perhaps, least sympathetic to women. Yet as with most generalisations, the truth is more complex. *Fabliau* too deals in the extraordinary and marvellous, in what is literally 'fabulous', if in terms very different from romance. As Cartlidge argues, the brutal, caricatured, often obscene or plain-speaking humour of *fabliaux* means they cannot be read as commenting directly on the treatment of women or as reflecting general attitudes to gender. Their distortions, however, mean that they are responsive to theoretical analyses that foreground the burlesque. The *fabliau* 'Berengier au long cul' ('Berengar Longbottom'), for example, works through defamiliarisation and absurdity, resisting comfortable moral readings regarding either the wife's or the husband's behaviour – though, as with many *fabliaux*, the wife is also given a forceful voice and role. Cartlidge offers a new perspective on a manuscript usually celebrated for its collection of lyrics, London, British Library, Harley 2253, through his analysis of four Old French *fabliaux* found together in it. The most concentrated gathering of *fabliaux* in any extant English manuscript, the group offers a representative selection of the genre, depicting and undercutting sexual desire, violence, and humiliation by taking them to extremes that are both uneasy and absurd. Conceits are often male but are also ridiculed and undercut, and women are both victims and startlingly inventive aggressors. As Cartlidge shows, such works play creatively and troublingly with attitudes to language and shame/honour cultures, marriage, sexuality, and desire. Through often dazzlingly inventive, absurd, and distorted extremes of plot, character, and dialogue that celebrate neither gender, the *fabliaux* speak, perhaps, to the everyday, married lives of their audiences, male and female, in ways that create communities of their readers through shared laughter.

Venetia Bridges takes as her subject the two most influential English authors of the later medieval period, Geoffrey Chaucer and his contemporary John Gower, to analyse the roles of women within their corpus, both as subjects and as extra-textual readers. What does femininity enable in their works, and how – and what – do women mean? Bridges emphasises the embeddedness of both Chaucer and Gower in long-established and international textual cultures: the works of both engage actively with trans-European literary traditions and multilingual networks in sophisticated, complex, and self-aware ways. Central to Bridges' analysis is the notion of a hermeneutic that constructs women and femininity in ethical terms, as bound up with notions of vice and virtue. In this sense, Chaucer as well as Gower is 'moral'. Bridges explores questions of voice, agency, and genre across Chaucer's works to demonstrate the intimate connection of femininity with questions of reading and interpretation: *The Canterbury Tales*, *Troilus and Criseyde*, and the *Legend of Good Women* provide celebrated subject matter, while the dream visions raise new questions of interpretation and ethics, authority, emotion, and desire. For Gower too, as Bridges shows, ethics are a central focus, arising out of political, theological, and philosophical subject matter, but also from the fictional matter of the *Confessio amantis*. Women are 'ethical signifiers', and treatments of femininity open onto moral and political debates. The final part of Bridges' chapter explores presentations of women treated in common by Chaucer and Gower, illuminating their ideological priorities and contrasting practices of poetic *translatio studii*. For both, women's presence proves a complex, powerful, but often ambiguous textual phenomenon.

Women as Authors

This final section of the volume turns to the subject of women as named authors – and to figures who have received extensive scholarly attention. As this volume has argued, the fact that named female authors are few and far between does not translate straightforwardly into a paucity of women's literary culture in the Middle Ages. It does, however, place a peculiar burden on those whose names are recorded. As Emma Campbell's chapter clearly demonstrates, even in these cases questions of authorship are not straightforward. The writer today known as 'Marie de France' is placed among the earliest named women authors in French and in England, yet all we really know about 'Marie' is her name and that she may have written three, perhaps four, late twelfth-century works in Anglo-Norman French (c. 1160–90). The lack of evidence means we cannot be certain the same author composed all of the works conventionally ascribed to her. What, Campbell asks, might it mean to see 'Marie' less as an exceptional female author and more as exemplifying a multilingual culture of women's writing and translation? The notion that 'Marie de France' might indicate not one but several women authors opens up tantalising possibilities, challenging easy assumptions about women's literary culture and foregrounding the concept of collaborative networks of writing and translation that has been central to this volume. A critical focus on Marie as unique downplays the reliance of the works attributed to her on translation of different kinds, and their connection to an Anglo-Norman literary culture in which women were active participants. This culture includes the network of female saints discussed earlier by Whitehead, with which the author of the vernacular life of St Audrey (perhaps Marie) actively engages. Campbell explores too the networks and translations depicted within Marie's works, and the ways in which these comment on the processes of composition and transmission to which translation is central. Women's literary culture, Campbell argues, challenges traditional notions of authorship: it is characterised by collaboration, translation, intertextuality, and multilingualism.

Julian of Norwich's *Revelations of Divine Love* offer insights of a very different kind into female authorship, illuminated by Barry Windeatt. Of this figure too, we know very little, though external evidence, in particular Margery Kempe's account of the meeting between the two women, clearly identifies her as an anchoress celebrated for her holiness and spiritual guidance. Her *Revelations* comprise 'the stunningly independent and original testimony of a medieval English woman author' (400), the first woman to use English who can be identified. The two extant texts of the *Revelations* offer distinctive witnesses to medieval women's literary culture. The shorter version, almost certainly earlier, is explicit about its female authorship, but, Windeatt argues, reflects no particularly female approach. The longer version, by contrast, is the inverse, suppressing all reference to female authorship but developing a uniquely woman-centred exposition of deep theological sophistication that itself suggests extensive learning perhaps gained through the lively religious circles of Norwich; the revelations may also respond to visual and material culture. Female bodily experience becomes the way into spiritual understanding, and the topos of Christ as mother is central to Julian's theology. As Windeatt emphasises, especially remarkable is the self-enclosed quality of her writing, which creates less an inter- than an intratextuality – a feature that also may illuminate Julian's practices of composition; the two versions indicate ongoing and animated processes of vision, contemplation, writing, and rewriting. The afterlife of Julian's *Revelations* sustains that process of editing, as the short text finds its way into an anthology while excerpts of the Long Text are woven into a florilegium probably for nuns, and it is post-medieval communities of nuns too that ensure the survival of Julian's book. Even within the context of exile on the Continent and, later, flight from revolution, Julian's revelatory theology and spirituality are reanimated, her work copied and preserved by ongoing networks within women's literary culture.

The following chapter, by Anthony Bale, demonstrates that questions of collaboration and intertexuality are central to any consideration of *The Book of Margery Kempe*, which perhaps more than any other work challenges notions of authorship even while its authorial voice speaks so vividly. Recent scholarship on the *Book* and its contexts has shed new light on its historicity and its production, including the scribe (Richard Salthouse of Norwich) of the *Book*'s sole surviving manuscript witness. At the same time, international influences on Margery Kempe's piety and devotional practices, resulting from Kempe's travels to Europe and beyond across her life, including to Gdansk, Jerusalem, and Konstanz, have come to the fore. The *Book* itself presents Kempe as an outsider, repeatedly repudiated by communities, and as disruptive, a 'queer' influence. Yet collaboration is central, manifest in the presentation of Kempe's relationship with her priest-confessors and guides and the *Book*'s production through her two amanuenses, in her identification with a network of holy women and spiritual authorities, and in her startlingly intimate conversations with the Lord, the Virgin, and the saints. Bale recovers three earthly communities with which Kempe and her *Book* successfully engaged: Franciscan, Birgittine, and monastic, considering questions of literacy, education, and cultural prestige. He shows the indebtedness of Kempe's experience in the Holy Land to her integration into the Franciscan-led pilgrimage community, where she ultimately gained a high and holy reputation. Birgittine communities and patronage networks in Rome and at Syon, Bale demonstrates, also shaped Kempe's spiritual experience, while in Norfolk, a textual community including preachers and confessors formed around her. It is notable that, following Kempe's death, manuscript annotation and printing history suggest a community of engaged readers who responded affectively to her spirituality. Once again, women's literary culture proves to be made up of a complex web of communities, networks, collaborations, and intertexts that extend far beyond the lifetime of the individual author.

Nancy Bradley Warren expands the topic of women's literary culture to take in the highest political spheres of France and England in her consideration of the influence and reception of the writings of Christine de Pizan, whose life and career were inextricably caught up in the Anglo-French conflict of the Hundred Years' War. Warren begins from Christine's negotiations for the return of her son, sent to England as a companion to the son of John Montagu, Earl of Salisbury, a supporter of Richard II, and after Richard's deposition taken into the court of Henry IV, whom Christine distrusted as unsympathetic to France. As part of her negotiations, she dedicated and sent to Henry IV a copy of *L'Epistre d'Othéa* (1400), written for her son, while her autobiographical *L'Avision Christine* records that Henry tried to persuade her to come to his court to enhance its literary culture. Warren explores the shifting significance of the *Othéa* in the course of the fifteenth and sixteenth centuries to exemplify wider political shifts and changing attitudes to Christine as an author. Valued both as a didactic treatise on chivalry and virtue and as a prestigious French courtly work, the book was translated into English by Stephen Scrope, but Scrope also reduced female agency and power, changes that reflected wider cultural anxieties concerning female lineage and virtue in the context of Lancastrian claims to the throne. Warren connects Christine with two other powerful women: Joan of Arc, whose victory at Orléans is celebrated in Christine's *Ditié de Jehanne d'Arc*, and Margaret of Anjou, Henry VI's powerful French queen, who owned a copy of Christine's *Le Livre de fais d'armes et de chevalerie*, and who connected herself to Joan. By reworking Christine's treatments of women to reduce their political power and independent wisdom, translators of Christine's works also, Warren argues, contained the political threats represented by powerful women – military, intellectual, and in royal lineages. Strikingly, depictions of Christine as author shift her context from the court to the cloister, reaffirming traditionally gendered views of women even while her works continued to be circulated, translated, and printed in England, playing an important role in men's and women's literary culture.

Finally, Cathryn A. Charnell-White looks beyond England to the wider context of the British Isles. She addresses three fifteenth- and early-sixteenth-century women writers who composed erotic and satiric verse: the Welsh poet Gwerful Mechain, and the Scottish Gaelic poets, Iseabal Campbell, Countess of Argyll, and her daughter Iseabal Ní Mheic Cailéan. Adopting what she terms an archipelagic feminist approach, Charnell-White locates these women within the broader context of late medieval bardic culture in Ireland, Scotland, and Wales. As was the case with many of the women discussed in the early chapters of this volume, these three poets were all of high social status and extremely well connected through their families. Gwerful Mechain's poetry was very highly regarded in her own time, and a significant body of her work remains. Far fewer poems by Iseabal Campbell and Iseabal Ní Mheic Cailéan survive, but, like Mechain's, they were written to be performed before a specific audience. Charnell-White demonstrates that the poetry of Mechain and Campbell playfully reappropriates and subverts the formulaic misogynism typical of the male-authored verse in their bardic or coterie groups. Like Christine de Pizan, Mechain and Iseabal Ní Mheic Cailéan both respond to the sort of anti-feminist motifs characteristic of the European tradition of the *querelle des femmes* and also found within their own circles. In so doing, these poets challenge courtly ideals of women as chaste, silent, and obedient and present female sexuality in empowering terms.

Across this volume, empowerment and authority of different kinds, within both lay and religious spheres, within and beyond literary texts, are recurrent themes. Women's voices resonate far beyond the small number of women named as authors, and those resonances call into question our notions of writing and of literary culture. Women are readers, owners, and patrons, as well as writers. They read, exchange, and write books within circles and communities of different kinds, in England and beyond, extending across Britain and Ireland, and to Europe. Their literary, cultural, and political networks are powerful, connecting with clerical and lay intellectual and aristocratic circles. Their work is multilingual, rooted in practices of translation, adaptation, and collaboration. Their spheres of knowledge extend far beyond the obvious, from health, conduct, and wisdom to the arts of war and chivalry. It is no surprise that the intersections of genre and gender are complex and ambiguous, and that for male writers women become focal points for debates concerning love and sexuality, vice and virtue. Medieval women's literary culture is multifaceted, collaborative but with far-reaching influence and the power to challenge, shape, and change ideas of gender, reading, and writing, from its own time to the present.

Notes

1. Katie Ann-Marie Bugyis, 'The Author of the Life of Christina of Markyate: The Case for Robert De Gorron (d. 1166)', *The Journal of Ecclesiastical History* 68.4 (2017), 719–46.
2. See further Bernard McGinn (ed.), *Meister Eckhart and the Beguine Mystics: Hadewijch of Brabant, Mechthild of Magdeburg, and Marguerite Porete* (New York: Continuum, 1994).
3. See further Nancy Bradley Warren, 'Christine de Pizan and Joan of Arc', in *The History of British Women's Writing Volume 1: 700–1500*, ed. Liz Herbert McAvoy and Diane Watt (Houndmills: Palgrave Macmillan, 2012), 189–97 (190).
4. D. H. Green, *Women Readers in the Middle Ages* (Cambridge: Cambridge University Press, 2007), 257.
5. Green, *Women Readers*, 116.
6. Felicity Riddy, '"Women Talking About the Things of God": A Late Medieval Sub-Culture', in *Women and Literature in Britain, 1100–1500*, ed. Carol M. Meale (Cambridge: Cambridge University Press, 1993), 104–27 (108–9).
7. See on women's education Green, *Women Readers*, 84–99.
8. Carol M. Meale, '"alle the bokes that I haue of latyn, englisch, and frensch": Laywomen and Their Books in Late Medieval England', in *Women and Literature in Britain*, ed. Meale, 128–58 (128–32).
9. Meale, 'Laywomen and Their Books', 136.
10. Meale, 'Laywomen and Their Books', 139–41.
11. Nancy Bradley Warren, 'Chaucer, the Chaucer Tradition, and Female Monastic Readers', *The Chaucer Review* 51.1 (2016): 88–106.
12. For this and much of the detail noted here, see Meale, 'Laywomen and Their Books', 136.
13. See Diane Watt, *Medieval Women's Writing: Works by and for Women in England, 1100–1500* (Cambridge: Polity Press, 2007), 72 and 81–3.
14. See Riddy, '"Women Talking About the Things of God"', in *Women and Literature in Britain*, ed. Meale, 106–7.
15. Melissa Furrow, *Expectations of Romance: The Reception of a Genre in Medieval England* (Cambridge: D. S. Brewer, 2009), 5–6.

Further Reading

Dinshaw, Carolyn, and David Wallace, eds. (2003). *The Cambridge Companion to Medieval Women's Writing*, Cambridge: Cambridge University Press.

Finke, Laurie A. (1999). *Women's Writing in English: Medieval England*, London: Longman.

Green, D. H. (2007). *Women Readers in the Middle Ages*, Cambridge: Cambridge University Press.

Krug, Rebecca (2002). *Reading Families: Women's Literate Practice in Late Medieval England*, Ithaca, NY: Cornell University Press.

Loveridge, Kathryn, Liz Herbert McAvoy, Sue Niebrzydowski, and Vicki Kay Price, eds. (2023). *Women's Literary Cultures in the Global Middle Ages: Speaking Internationally*, Woodbridge: Boydell and Brewer.
McAvoy, Liz Herbert, and Diane Watt, eds. (2012). *The History of British Women's Writing Volume 1: 700–1500*, Houndmills: Palgrave Macmillan.
Meale, Carol M., ed. (1993). *Women and Literature in Britain, 1100–1500*, Cambridge: Cambridge University Press.
Wallace, David (2011). *Strong Women: Life, Text, and Territory 1347–1645*, Oxford: Oxford University Press.
Watt, Diane (2007). *Medieval Women's Writing: Works by and for Women in England, 1100–1500*, Cambridge: Polity Press.
Watt, Diane (2019). *Women, Writing and Religion in England and Beyond, 700–1100*, London: Bloomsbury.
Wogan-Browne, Jocelyn (2001). *Saints' Lives and Women's Literary Culture, 1150–1300: Virginity and Its Authorizations*, Oxford: Oxford University Press.

I

*Patrons, Owners, Writers, and Readers
in England and Europe*

CHAPTER I

'Miserere, meidens'
Abbesses and Nuns

Elaine Treharne

Cambridge, Corpus Christi College, MS 383, is an early twelfth-century English manuscript with a contemporary provenance of St Paul's, London.[1] In the hands of two scribes, it contains Old English law codes issued originally in the reigns of pre-Conquest kings; other legal texts, such as *Gerefa* (a colloquy about the duties of a reeve); and a charm against the theft of cattle. Later corrections to these texts, the addition of a version of the West Saxon genealogy, and a list of 'scipmen' at St Paul's demonstrate sustained use of and interest in the manuscript in the decades following its production, particularly by scribes concerned with texts centred on London. The small manuscript (*c*. 186 mm × 118 mm) testifies to the continued use of English within an institutional context after the Conquest in 1066; it demonstrates the longevity of the life of a utilitarian legal volume at a time when there was a keen interest in early English law;[2] and it hints at the movement of books and their erstwhile ownership by successive intellectually engaged readers.

That 'ownership' of medieval volumes need not imply permanence of location or homogeneity of use is amply illustrated by books in this early period. In order to avoid theft, some institutions (and individuals) inscribed their names as proof of ownership and anathema against potential thieves. In a significant majority of cases, though, 'ownership' of a book that was held institutionally was a temporary phenomenon. While numerous passers-through in books left traces of their activities in minor annotation or the inscription of just a name, others seemed to take up the mantle of temporary ownership with confidence and a high level of expertise. How these later readers and writers intervened in the leaves of the medieval volume is of great significance, not only to reveal levels of understanding and envisaged uses of the book but also to provide evidence for the existence of women scribes and poets, where more commonly there seems to be none.

Matilda

From its place of origin to its provenance by the mid-twelfth century of St Paul's, London, it seems certain that Corpus 383 moved institution again in the late twelfth or early thirteenth centuries. Written into the manuscript are several short texts that were written by at least one woman: Matilda *soror*. At folio 24r, Matilda reveals that she is 'Matildis Bey' soror ma*gist*ri Rob*er*ti bey' de Abbend[...]', and this tantalising biographical information is amplified by French and Latin texts inserted, probably in her hand, at folios 40v to 42v and folio 60v. This same scribe also wrote the French didactic poem I have entitled 'La Seisine' ('Possession') at folio 12r of the manuscript.[3]

The short Latin and French texts at folios 40v to 42v that I have titled 'Directions for the Troubled' are a dozen instructions to anyone struggling with various problems, advising them to say phrases from the Psalms to ward off evil or protect themselves:[4]

> **Folio 40v**
> Qui in inopiam decidit, dicat 'Iudica me Deus, et discerne causam meam'. Contre desturbers quant vos levez matin, si dirrez vi feiz: 'Deus in nomine tuo [sa]lvum me fac.'
>
> (Let those who fell into want, say, 'Judge me, O God, and distinguish my cause'. Against distress when you rise in the morning, say six times 'Lord, in your name, help me.') (Psalm 42:1 and 53:3)
>
> Qui chet en adversite del secle, die iii feiz deuant a[?] croiz a genoilz: 'Deus venerunt gentes.'
>
> (Whoever is a wretch in adversity at any time, say three times, while kneeling before the cross: 'Oh God, the heathens have come.') (Psalm 78:1)
>
> Qui deit pleider a plus huit[?] e sei die a ses genoilz: 'Miserere mei Deus.'
>
> (Whoever must plead more than eight [times?] should say on their knees: 'Have mercy on me, God.') (Psalm 50:3)

This sequence of guidance for those in need or suffering adversity is general in application and specific in remedy and suggests that the speaker is in a position of pastoral care that is informal. The various maladies or threats cover a wide range of circumstances:

> **Folio 41r**
> Qui deit bataille fere, die x feiz on aucun porlu: 'Eripe me de inimicis meis, 7 exaudi Deus. Orationem meam cum deprecor.'

(Whoever wants the battle to be done, say ten times in any position: 'I will call on the Lord, who is worthy to be praised, so shall I be saved from my enemies. Hear my prayers when I pray.') (Psalm 142:9 and 63:2)

Qui est en adversite, die: 'Exaudi, Deus, orationem meam et ne despexeris, et miserere mei, Deus, sanctum collocavit me homo.'

(Whoever is in adversity, say: 'Hear, O God, my prayer, and despise not my supplication, and have mercy on me, God, a man has set me as a saint.') (Psalm 54:2 and possibly 142:3)

Qui est en volente de peche fere, die: 'Deus misereatur nostri', et prie Deu od lermes kil lu dovist compungcium 7 il serat delivre.

(Whoever wants the power of sin to be diminished, say: 'God be merciful unto us' and pray God with tears that he will have compassion on you and he will set you free.) (Psalm 66:2)

Folio 41v
Qui est environe denemis, die x feiz: 'Exurgat Deus et dissipentur inimici eius.'

(Whoever is surrounded by enemies, say ten times: 'Let God arise, and let his enemies be scattered.') (Psalm 67:2)

Si poeste de deable est en home, die: 'In te, Domine, speravi non confundar in eternum.'

(If the power of the devil is within a person, say: 'In you, O Lord, I have hoped, let me never be put to confusion.') (Psalm 30:2)

Qui grant chose ueout comencer, est ende sei devant lauter, et die v feiz: 'Deus in adiutorium meum intende.'

(Whoever wishes to have something granted to begin or end, go in front of the altar and say five times: 'O God, come to my assistance.') (Psalm 69:2)

The scribe seems to be recalling from memory their knowledge of the Psalms. At folio 42r, there is a loose rendition of the opening of Psalm 24: 'Ad te, Domine, levavi', a Psalm usually said to pray for grace against one's enemies:

Folio 42r
Qui veout son desir en ben a complir, die x feiz: 'Ad te, levavi. Deus meus, in te confide; non erubescam.'

(Whoever wants their desire to be completed, say ten times: 'To these, I raise up. O my God, in you I put my trust; let me not be ashamed.') (Psalm 24:2)

Qui est entristor seit lendemein al sacrement de la messe, et die, 'Domine Deus, salutis meae.'

(Whoever is sad on the morrow at the sacrament of the mass, say: 'Oh Lord, the God of my salvation.') (Psalm 87:2)

Qui troble seveit, die od gemissemenz: 'Domine, refugium factus es nobis.'

(Whoever is in trouble, say while moaning: 'Lord, you have been our refuge.') (Psalm 90:2, with the singular 'meum' here pluralised)

Folio 42v

Qui dit ces two vers a sun moriant, salme nenterat mie en enfern: 'O Domine, quia ego servus tuus; ego servus tuus et filius ancille tue. Dirrupisti vincula mea: tibi sacrificabo hostiam laudis, et nomen Domini invocabo.'[5]

(Whoever says these two verses as they are dying, the Psalm will protect them from entering hell: 'O Lord, for I am thy servant: I am thy servant, and the son of thy handmaid. Thou hast broken my bonds: I will sacrifice to thee the sacrifice of praise, and I will call upon the name of the Lord.') (Psalm 115:16–17)

In addition to these Psalm-led 'Directions', at folio 51v on the top left of the writing grid, the scribe has written 'domino meo' and this same hand appears again at folio 60v: 'v feit diet "Miserere meidens"' ('Five times say, "Have mercy [on your] handmaidens"'). That this brief prayer specifies 'meidens', in English, only serves to add to the evidence that the manuscript was in the hands of women and that these texts added in the thirteenth century were specifically aimed at women's spiritual guidance and for women to enact such guidance for and among themselves.

Who this poet and spiritual advisor, Matilda, might have been is not known at present, though she herself claimed to be the 'sister of Magister Robert' of, probably, Abingdon.[6] The final entry at folio 60v, advising women to seek the mercy of God, together with the sequence of apotropaic Psalm-based prayers, suggests she is a religious woman writer with straightforward access to this second-hand book that is distinctly institutional in origin. Was this Matilda a nun or an obedientiary at a religious house that had a working relationship to St Paul's in London? Certainly, it is known that women's abbeys and priories (as with men's houses) obtained books from donors. What makes Corpus 383 particularly interesting is that it is a non-devotional, non-liturgical, English vernacular manuscript. It may have been no longer required by St Paul's and thus given to an affiliated institution of women religious as reading material.

Perhaps a woman's house proactively sought reading materials (*any* reading materials) in the vernacular specifically? Either way, it ended up in the hands of a woman who may or may not have paid close attention to the Old English law codes, but she certainly turned temporary ownership of the volume to her own literary and spiritual advantage, as well as to the devotional and spiritual advantage of other religious women perhaps under her care.

The vibrant cultural setting in which a poem such as 'La Seisine' might have been written cannot yet be proven, but there are known connections between St Paul's, London, where the manuscript was, and the nearby prestigious abbey for Benedictine women at Barking. Guillaume Adgar, a chaplain whose work was paid for by St Paul's, may also have been chaplain at Barking. In the second half of the twelfth century he compiled *Le Gracial*, a collection of Marian miracles that he translated from Latin to French for 'Dame Mahaut', possibly the abbess of Barking. He shows himself to be keenly aware of the need to provide vernacular religious texts for English and Norman female audiences, then.[7] Perhaps adding to evidence for the link between Barking and St Paul's, Corpus 383 might have been one of any number of manuscripts acquired by Barking for the religious community there. It is a striking coincidence in respect of Corpus 383's 'Matilda' that 'Mahaut' is the same name as 'Maud' or 'Matilda', and that Barking's well-known later-twelfth-century abbess was Adgar's Maud/Matilda (Henry II's daughter), who may have become abbess around 1175 and who died in 1198. Searching for any other 'Matilda' at Barking into the thirteenth century yields two potential nuns who both became abbesses: Maud/Matilda, daughter of King John (who died in 1252) and, less plausibly, Maud/Matilda de Leveland (who died in 1275). While these two figures are almost certainly too late from a palaeographical perspective, they were of elite status, and undoubtedly educated, like so many of the nuns at Barking throughout its history. There is little reason to think any of the Matildas incapable of writing lyrical poetry and religious guidance, and when I say 'writing' I do mean physically inscribing the manuscript, trained in the skill of penpersonship, as well as having the imaginative and creative capacity to compose texts.

Ancilla

The name 'Matilda' at folio 24r does make the evidence for identifying a woman scribe and author here as firm as one might hope for. Matilda's presence in this manuscript changes the functionality of the book, as well as indicating movement in its location and a shift in its intended readership, clearly other women needing succour. This is not the only such example from the period. London, British Library, Cotton MS Vespasian D. xiv, a mid-twelfth-century English homiletic and hagiographic manuscript written at Christ Church, Canterbury, also found its way to the hands of a woman religious: an 'ancilla' who composed a prayer to the Virgin Mary and a prayer to St Thomas, sometime in the late twelfth century.[8] Unlike Matilda, writing in the margins of Corpus 383, filling in blank spaces with her own poetry and protective microtexts, the 'ancilla' took up all the space at the beginning of Vespasian D. xiv, at what is now folio 4r. The mid-twelfth-century scribe began the homily *De initio creaturæ* from the First Series of *Catholic Homilies* by the Old English homilist, Ælfric (d. 1010), on folio 4v, leaving a blank recto – an opportunity for creative intervention by the later user of the manuscript.[9] Onto this empty leaf at folio 4r, the woman scribe wrote two prayers: the first to the Virgin Mary and the second to St Thomas Becket:

Oratio de Sancta Maria matre Domini

O dulcissima Domina Maria, pietatis et misericordie, respectum tue dulcedinis ad me digneris convertere; et per gaudium angelice salutationis redde mihi leticiam divine miserationis. Ut bonus Iesus filius tuus, qui mihi pro peccatis meis iuste irascitur, per amore tuo mihi misere pie repropitiari dignetur. Quatinus per te misericordissima absoluta meorum vinculis peccatorum, ego ancilla tua te dominam meam leta et gaudens ita salutare possim in perpetuum. 'Ave Maria, gratia plena, Dominus tecum. Benedicta tu in mulieribus.'

Prayer to St Mary Mother of God

(O most blessed lady Maria, full of compassion and pity. Deign to turn your sweetness to me; and by an angelic greeting restore to me the joy of divine compassion, so that your good son, Jesus, who, is rightly angered with me because of my sins, may deign to be graciously reconciled with wretched me through your love. By that, through you, most merciful, might I be freed from the bonds of my sins, so that I, your handmaid, may live happy and joyful, to greet you, my mistress in eternity. 'Hail Mary, full of grace, the Lord is with you. Blessed are you among women.')

Oratio de Sancto Thoma

Deus qui beatum Thomam archipresulem, ab exilio revocatum, in ecclesia propria gladio occumbere voluisti, praesta quaesumus ut fidei constantia roborati, superatis hostium visibilium minis et invisibilium insidiis,[10] eius meritis et precibus periculum anime devitemus. Per dominum nostrum Iesum Christum.[11]

Prayer to St Thomas
(God, who wished blesséd Thomas, archbishop, having been recalled from exile, to succumb to swords in his own church, grant, we pray, that we, strengthened by constancy of faith, having overcome the dangers of enemies both visible and invisible, may avoid danger to the soul by his merits and prayers. Through our Lord Jesus Christ.)

George Younge has suggested compellingly that the writer of these prayers was a nun at Barking.[12] He shows that the prayer for Becket 'corresponds precisely with the incipit of a collect assigned to the fourth canonical hour for the feast of Becket's martyrdom (29 December) in the *Ordinale* of Barking Abbey (*c.* 1400).'[13] He further links the prayer specifically with the appointment of Mary Becket, Thomas Becket's younger sister, as abbess at Barking in 1173, suggesting that Vespasian D.xiv itself moved to Barking Abbey at this time, too.[14] Notably, Mary Becket has been proposed as the real woman behind the persona Marie de France, author of the *Lais*, *Fables*, *Espurgatoire Seint Patriz* and *Vie seinte Audrée*.[15] In her suggested identification, Rossi shows Mary Becket/Marie to have been an exceptionally learned woman. Following the exile of her brother, she and the Becket family were also exiled, and Mary's circle effectively included all those scholars who surrounded her brother Thomas Becket: men such as John of Salisbury, Walter Map, and Herbert Bosham. In the possible identification of Mary with Marie de France,[16] it is of great interest to acknowledge, then, that Marie's own scholarship included a detailed knowledge of English sources – a reminder of the potential uses of manuscripts such as CCCC 383 late in the post-Conquest period. It is tempting, indeed, to follow this thread and to see in the possible interlibrary movement of Vespasian D. xiv from Christ Church Canterbury to Barking a deliberate acquisition of English manuscripts by Barking. This exemplifies the appreciation by that abbey's women religious of the potential of the vernacular as a source of learning and inspiration.

Marginal Note I

It seems essential to interrupt the scholarly narrative of suggestions and connections here to acknowledge that in Vespasian D. xiv and Corpus 383 we are witnessing medieval religious women's literary culture in the making. Not only do the marginalia in these two manuscripts represent a dynamic multilingual creativity by women (prayers *are* creative, historically and theologically resonant texts, usually underutilised by contemporary scholars), but they are texts written by women scribes, something there is no reason to doubt. As such, both scribal efforts require analysis to show what they reveal about textual practices in the respective religious institutions at the respective times of production: the end of the twelfth century for Vespasian D. xiv's *ancilla*, and perhaps 1200–30 for the Corpus 383 sequence of French and Latin interpolations.

In the case of Matilda's writing in Corpus 383, its marginality might dictate her choice of script: a hybrid form of semi-formal *textura* and *documentaria* that was absolutely current in the first half of the thirteenth century, just as Anglicana script was emerging. In her signature at folio 24r, Matilda's fluent handwriting contains features most seen in charter-hands: looped **d**, long **r**, long **s**, and split ascenders, but it is only semi-cursive. Her longer entries at folios 12r, 40v to 42v, and 60v have the chiaroscuro typical of documentary and early Anglicana hands, with a backward leaning aspect, and thick strokes on some letters, such as round-backed **d** and **s**, but without the embellishments that characterise the script later in the thirteenth century. The contemporaneity of the hand, its regularity, and the scribe's sustained respect for the previously ruled writing grid into which these additions are entered bespeaks a well-trained and bookish writer – one who understands the significance of *mise-en-page*, and whose lack of disruption to the look of the folio (with the exception of folio 60v, where the phrase is in the left margin because the lower margin is a curved end-piece of membrane) indicates an appreciation of earlier scribes' efforts to produce a well-made book.[17]

Cotton Vespasian D. xiv's woman scribe has a whole recto to herself upon which to inscribe the prayers to Mary and to Thomas Becket. Her writing is distinctly formal: a calligraphically expert early Gothic *textura formata semi-quadrata*, seen commonly in Psalters, Books of Hours, and other Latin liturgical books from the late twelfth century onwards. Its formality is underscored by the plummet ruling providing generous interlinear spacing and a precise line-count; the corrections made after careful reading, which might suggest revision rather than emendation; the relative lack of abbreviation; and the otiose decorative stroke on the headstroke of **t**. The two prayers are rubricated with red ink, though the rubrics have had to be inserted into spaces not designed for them, and the miniated initials **O** and **D** opening the prayers testify to the desire for ease of discoverability on the folio. All these features indicate a well-trained scribal context for the production of these two prayers, emerging from a writing environment used to working with liturgical books.

As such, these two religious scribe-authors offer remarkably rare evidence for women as contributors to English medieval textual production.

In the case of Matilda, the *name* makes her role reasonably assured; for 'ancilla', there is no reason to suppose that 'ego' is not the scribe herself. That both women writers were religious women seems certain, given the nature of the manuscripts and the texts they wrote. These books represent donated vernacular codices into which these women inscribed themselves articulately in Latin, French, and, for one or two words, English. That scholars might profitably attend closely to the marginal then (whether marginal to the main writing block as in Vespasian D. xiv, or upon the margins of the folios themselves as in Corpus 383) is clear: there are more women to be found on the edges of manuscripts.

Scribal Competence

There are many problems to overcome in the discovery of a fuller story of women authors and scribes within religious institutions in England. Unlike their sisters on the European continent, and especially Germany, English women participants in scribal culture are notable by their absence from the record. The record, as we have inherited it through the interpretations of earlier scholars, however, must be questioned and challenged.

There are several significant opportunities to rehabilitate women manuscript producers and users. The principal model has been clearly laid out by Diane Watt in her exemplary and paradigm-shifting work on women authors in the earlier medieval period.[18] In *Women, Writing and Religion*, Watt considers male medieval writers' *overwriting* of women authors: the claiming of women's words and their subsumption into male-authored works. Compounding this suppression is the tradition of modern and contemporary scholarship in which academic researchers necessarily find themselves; here, not only do those responsible for the writing of long histories of literature dismiss 'out of hand the relevance of the medieval and early modern', but they also 'reify certain ideas of "authorship" and "literature"' that often exclude anonymity, or early women, or the complexity faced by medievalists, who must engage with early texts that exemplify collaborative authorship or forms of literature (like the prayers or directions I have already discussed) that are considered unworthy of sustained study.[19]

As if this were not sufficient, the absolute default of scholarship to assume maleness of origin is a crushing blow for premodern women's textual production – and this despite our knowing that women were permitted, perhaps even expected, to write. Pamela Robinson highlights all the evidence she can find for books produced by women, noting that even in the *Rule of St Gilbert*, nuns were given permission to write service books, but little else without the Master's Permission: 'Libri tamen ad divinum officium scribi permittuntur.'[20] Institutions and religious orders varied significantly in their regulations, their resources, and their personnel throughout the medieval period, but the male default in the copying of books is demonstrated with dramatic effect in the otherwise brilliant work of Celia and Kenneth Sisam in their edition of Salisbury Cathedral Library, MS 150, the tenth-century, damaged Salisbury Psalter.[21] This stunning manuscript is the victim of a double-edged sword: it is a Psalter, and thus of limited literary or historical interest, and it is not yet available in open-access digital form, so its form and contents are comparatively inaccessible to international scholars. In their introduction to the volume, published in the 1950s, the editors discussed the probable place of origin of Salisbury Cathedral Library, MS 150, as well as the make-up of the manuscript, its history, and its language. They, and subsequent scholars, have accepted that the manuscript was produced in tenth-century Shaftesbury, perhaps around 975, before reaching Salisbury later in the medieval period. Since Shaftesbury, like Barking, was one of the four major royal female abbeys in pre-Conquest England (with Wilton and Nunnaminster, Winchester),[22] there is every reason to assume that a manuscript produced at the abbey was done so because of the desire of the nuns, if not completed through their actual labour. Of interest to this proposal is the tinted drawing at folio 60v (see Illustration 1.1), where the beginning of Psalm 61 is 'Nonne deo subjecta erit anima mea' (with a later Old English gloss, 'Hu nu underþeod byþ sawel min'). To the left of the opening verse, a female figure in a dark orange robe with a white veil stands with her right hand extended towards three intertwined dragons, the tail of one of which is curled around her legs. This nun-dragon figure forms the 'N' of the Latin word 'Nonne', here meaning 'Not?'[23] But there is surely an obvious visual and aural echo of Latin 'nunna' and Old English 'nunne' (nun) here, perhaps prompting the scribe-artist to draw herself into the narrative of the Psalms. Moreover, as the Psalm (61) calls for the resilience of the faithful in the light of attack, the miniature nun's posture of steadfastness and demonstrated resistance echoes the desire of the supplicant to remain unmoved by assailants.

    Given the evidence about this manuscript, it is interesting to note that throughout the 75-page introduction to the Salisbury Psalter edition, the pronoun the editors use for the scribe of the manuscript is masculine. There seems to be little genuine possibility in their minds that the main scribe of the Psalter could actually be a nun. This demonstrates the inevitability in scholarship that the default scribe in premodern manuscript

'Miserere, meidens': Abbesses and Nuns 37

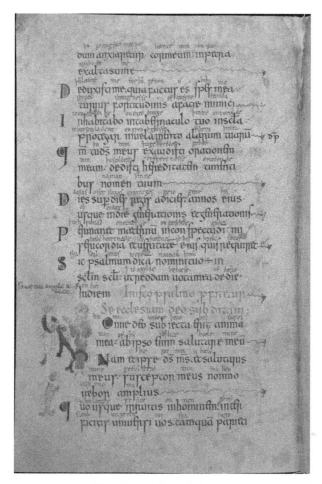

Illustration 1.1 Opening of Psalm 61. Salisbury Cathedral Library, MS 150, folio 60v. © Photo Cambridge University Library and Salisbury Cathedral Library, reproduced with permission of the Dean and Chapter of Salisbury Cathedral.

production is male even when the place of origin is a nunnery. Presumably, the scholarly explanation for a male scribe but a female institutional localisation would be the presence within the precincts of a chaplain for the nuns: a male confessor, a male mass-priest. These, and other officials, were present, undoubtedly. Denying the nuns any agency in the libric life of their own establishments, however (when other evidence from charters and elsewhere suggests a meaningful role for abbesses, their obedientiaries, and some of the nuns), is how the voices of women continue to be displaced and subsumed. Thus, Celia and Kenneth Sisam provide a fine and detailed examination of the original scribe of the Salisbury Psalter, discussing their efforts to adhere to a plan for the manuscript's layout, and suggesting that 'the scribe was his own illuminator'.[24] The language that is used of the production intimates a slight disappointment in the scribe's expertise: while the shapes of the decorated initials, for example, are 'drawn with remarkable precision and infinite variety of design', the colours are 'crude tints, dull reds . . . Nowhere is gold used. The delicate tracery of the designs is somewhat disguised by this rough painting.'[25] The lack of deluxeness that this book represents might go some way to explaining how few art historians have paid attention to it, too.

That the book was made for, and even by, a woman is hinted at throughout the introductory study to the Sisam edition itself. The End-Prayer, the editors note, shows forms that were altered from 'famulum tuum' to 'famulam tuam'. 'Evidently', they comment, 'the psalter was being used by a woman, presumably a nun',[26] but this is neither commented upon further nor returned to. I would like to suggest, employing Diane Watt's courageous model, that we speculate: that we permit the possibility, at least, that the manuscript was planned and executed by a Shaftesbury nun, perhaps around the time of Edward the Martyr's burial at the abbey in 979, and that it remained in situ in Shaftesbury until at least the thirteenth century.[27]

There are several key points to note in ascertaining the characteristics of (potentially) women's scribal work in the medieval period: one is that women scribes often adhere to scripts that are not inventive or particularly novel. This is important. It is a feature noted by Alison Beach in her groundbreaking work *Women as Scribes*. Beach comments in relation to hands from south Germany in the twelfth century, many of which are unequivocally women's, that there is a 'clear tendency to resist the new'.[28] This adherence to more conventional models of handwriting, then, suggests a certain conservatism in writing – a feature of women's writing to which I will return. It is worth stating in this regard that the tenth-century scribe of the Salisbury Psalter, according to Celia and Kenneth Sisam, demonstrates a script that 'shows no clear influence of the [new] foreign style' introduced into southern English monasteries as a result of the Benedictine Reform.[29]

The second point is that the hands of scribes who may be women are not always the most skilled calligraphic expositions, and it is the 'good' hand, the 'beautiful' exponent of script that is valued by most manuscript historians.[30] This leads to the ignoring or derogation of inexpert scripts – something that should be noted in the invisibility of women scribes. These two observations – the conservative and the calligraphically mundane – are, in one way, attributes that complement each other. We know very little about scribal training in general prior to the fourteenth century, but it is pragmatic to assume that many women writers could not access the levels of training or professional expertise available to most of their monastic and clerical brothers. This point is well borne out in the editors' description of the main post-Conquest glossator of the Salisbury Psalter, who glossed most of the manuscript, except for the Athanasian Creed where glosses were provided by the original tenth-century scribe, and some of the glossed words on folios 41v and 75v. The main Old English glossator worked on the manuscript around the first quarter of the twelfth century. Assuming, as we should, that the Salisbury Psalter was still at Shaftesbury at this time, there was clearly motivation to gloss all the Psalms in English, even at the point that English had lost its status as an authorised language of textual production. In their discussion of this scribe's work, Celia and Kenneth Sisam acknowledge that *this* scribe 'may have been a nun' who 'wrote a hand of advanced type'.[31] While the hand is described as 'advanced' in its use of Caroline forms of high **s**, **f**, and **r** in the vernacular, 'advanced' turns out not to be a compliment, for this woman's hand is described later in the same paragraph as giving the 'general impression of eleventh-century work. But in the latter pages the characteristics of the following century are unmistakable: the letters slope, the forms are degenerate, and the finishing of strokes is slovenly.'[32]

While for a moment (on page 14) the scribe is recognised by the editors of the Salisbury Psalter as possibly being a nun, by page 17 the same glossator is systematically pronominalised as male. This does at least suggest that the persistent derogation of the scribe's work as 'careless', 'slovenly', 'ignorant', 'unintelligent', 'struggling', and 'erratic' is not wholly gender based.[33] It may be because of this assessment of the poor quality of the Salisbury scribe and her gloss that she has attracted so little attention in the last sixty years from scholars beyond the work of a few Psalter specialists, where she does not feature prominently.[34] It is time perhaps to reappraise the work of this writer in the context of post-Conquest English, particularly post-Conquest English created by and intended for women, though there is little space to do full justice to the gloss or to the manuscript here.

Marginal Note II

The excellent scholarly work undertaken by Celia and Kenneth Sisam in their editing and close analysis of Salisbury Cathedral Library, MS 150 highlights specific and critically important aspects of studying scribes who are potentially religious women: namely, the burden of proof to identify women scribes in religious institutions, the perceived proficiency of their writing, and the received textual status of their work. Veronica O'Mara demonstrates how difficult it is to find evidence for women scribes in England, especially in comparison with the relative abundance of material to be discovered from the medieval period in Germany and the Low Countries.[35] O'Mara highlights the old-fashioned libraries of women's nunneries, the difficulty in determining the levels of literacy of women, and the absence of colophons.[36] She focuses her investigations on ownership of books and on prayers added to books with connections to female religious institutions. In this meticulous and determined research, the burden of proof to ascertain female scribal activity is exceptionally high – perhaps impossibly high. Even where, for example, there is a woman's inscription in a manuscript, it is (rightly) asserted that 'it is equally possible that a chaplain or spiritual director ... wrote this manuscript for Matilda [and] added the latter's ownership inscription'.[37] At no point would scholars doubt male attribution when there is a man's name in a margin or at the centre of an ownership inscription. What evidence for women's writing would be sufficient? Could we not always begin our *first* exploration of unlocalised or unattributed manuscript and documentary production (by far most manuscripts) with the question 'Was this written by a woman?' When there is no evidence to say it was written by a woman, is there actually any evidence that it was written by a male scribe?

Why Not Women?

Evidence for women scribes might emerge more comprehensively by focusing not only on books, but also on other forms of textual production. Palaeographers' judgements of low proficiency or lack of expertise in writing could be a diagnostic tool for identifying some women scribes. In Pamela Robinson's excellent exploration of a scriptrix at Nunnaminster in the twelfth century, she has a nun who signed her scribal stint in Oxford, Bodleian Library, MS Bodley 451, copying Smaragdus' *Diadema monachorum*. Here, the writing is 'neat, very upright', tidy and careful, resulting in a 'handsome volume', but other women's hands in the same manuscript are, as Robinson says, 'larger, less regular' and 'large and clumsy'.[38] Size and regularity of script become important in assessing whether a religious woman might be responsible for copying texts. Here, though, scholars must revise the persistent diminution of writing that does not match up to perceived standards of excellence in calligraphic presentation. On that basis, much writing that could be by a woman will be 'less good than'. This is well illustrated by a recent essay in which Julia Crick discusses London, British Library, Cotton MS Galba A. xiv, 'a small, charred, poorly written' eleventh-century manuscript.[39] This book is of contested origin, but Crick suggests it could reasonably be assigned to a religious house for women or a house that at least had female associates in the west or southwest of England. What is notable in this essay is the sustained criticism of the scribes' efforts in copying the manuscript. Crick labels the hands 'undisciplined', 'bizarre', 'crude', 'uncouth', 'ignorant of good scribal practice but ... deliberately following unusual conventions', 'large', and 'outrageously large'.[40] While as a scholar I struggle with subjective and pejorative labels for script, and while male scribes (such as Wulfstan, Archbishop of York) are equally capable of writing with calligraphic inexpertise,[41] the identification of large and irregular hands, and of hands that are not confidently written, is an excellent starting place for asking if the hand might not be a woman's. This is to turn negative appraisal by an aesthetically impelled palaeographical analysis into a positive prospect for potential identification.

Two thirteenth-century Mortuary Rolls can provide substantial evidence that scholars might begin to look for women scribes where there is inexpertise (as a positive feature) and within less prestigious forms of textual production than the liturgical or literary manuscript. London, British Library, Egerton MS 2849, parts I and II, and Cambridge, St John's College, MS N.31 are two near-contemporary rolls that commemorate Lucy de Vere, Prioress of Castle Hedingham, who died in 1225 and Amphelisa, Prioress of Lillechurch, who died between 1208 and perhaps 1214.[42] Both rolls can be palaeographically and contextually dated to pre-1230, with St John's N. 31 being a few years earlier than Egerton 2849.

Between them, the commemorative *tituli* of these two rolls provide scribal evidence for almost 400 individual religious houses in England and Wales in the first half of the thirteenth century, and for the hands of almost 500 scribes. St John's N. 31 is three times more extensive than Egerton 2849, but Egerton is a deluxe, illustrated roll, headed by a remarkable sequence of illustrations of the life and death of Lucy de Vere. Within these two rolls, many of the major abbeys and priories founded before 1230 are represented, and this means that for these houses there are several lines of Latin script testifying to the promise for their ongoing commemoration of the prioress. While it is impossible to prove who, specifically, wrote the *tituli* for the respective institutions, there is usually no evidence to suggest that women in the various houses were not capable of completing the formulaic written response to the prioress' deaths. Numerous occasions on the membranes of the two rolls allow for the testing of the theory that women's writing, as a result of a lack of access to sustained training and professional practice, is less calligraphically proficient than a monk's or canon's writing could be. The entry for the Benedictine nunnery at the Holy Sepulchre, Canterbury, for example, at folio 5r of Egerton 2849/2, is considerably larger than the entries that surround it.[43] The script is written in a black ink over four lines in a relatively assured Gothic semi-formata, but in contrast with the hands around it (Christ Church, St Gregory's, St Augustine's, Canterbury), it is somewhat old-fashioned and mannered. That said, immediately above Christ Church's entry, another female Benedictine house – Davington – is penned in a brown ink, in a rounded semi-cursive script, employing new features such as the long round-backed **d**, barred initials, and looped ascenders. Still relatively large, this entry's expert hand would belie its female scribe. This Davington entry is unlikely to be a woman writer, though, since it is in the same hand (but not the same script) as the entry that precedes it by three lines, written by a scribe from the male Benedictine institution of St Saviour's, Faversham, half a mile away from Davington Priory.

Again, a quick glance at folio 6r of Egerton 2849/2 shows that the writing of the sixth entry on that image immediately stands out as one of two larger, less cursive or documentary hands on the membrane. This is the entry for Nunnaminster, which is written in a rather unconfident Gothic rotunda with wavering downstrokes, similar in form to the hands that wrote Stanford University Libraries Special Collections, Codex MS 0877, a prayerbook from *c.* 1200, owned in the fifteenth century by Queen Elizabeth Woodville and Elizabeth of York. The hand of the scribe representing St Mary and St Eadburga's in Winchester is calligraphically competent, which is certainly not how the St Eþelflæd's, Romsey, entry could be described. This three-line *titulus* is decidedly old-fashioned, with its **d+e** ligature and uncrossed *nota* being much more common in the second half of the twelfth century than decades of the thirteenth. The scribe's pen is not well cut, and the control of the ink flow is irregular, as is the straightness of the writing along the ruled line. Interestingly, in this woman's hand the Old English graph, **þ** (thorn), appears, and at the end of the *titulus* the nun takes the opportunity to commemorate members and associates of Romsey: Judith, Mathilda, Ada, and Nichola (or Nicholas?). Romsey's *titulus* can be compared with the one immediately following, though, for a sharp contrast in the expertise of women's textual production. That *titulus* is Wilton Abbey's three-line commemoration, and it is written in an entirely contemporary cursive charter hand, illustrating very recent features, including looped uncial **s**, a sweeping crossed Tironian *nota*, and the broken **ct**-ligature. This entry, perhaps inspired by Romsey above it, also chooses to seek prayers for institutional sisters – Lucia, Alicia, and Cecilia – *sororibus nostris*.

From this brief investigation of a handful of entries in the Mortuary Roll of Lucy of Hedingham, there is variety in the proficiency and currency of what are probably women's hands. One can see in the scribes of women's houses characteristics of scripts that are usually derogated by palaeographers and writing that certainly inclines towards a larger size. Further research will clarify whether these characteristics can be broadly used as a diagnostic for women's writing, but the more significant point here is that many of these women's religious institutions seem to have been capable of producing scribes to write a *titulus* for the *breviators* as they circulated between these establishments seeking commemorative remarks. This is a starting point in reappraising the presence of religious women scribes: nuns for whom writing was an everyday practice, even when they may have had little sustained training to professionalise their work.

Making a Mark

Just as there is a fascinating world of religious women scribes to discover through Mortuary Rolls, so other less well-studied documentary evidence attests to the presence of literate women in the business of the church in the High Middle Ages. And while most of the examples I have discussed thus far cannot be individually traced writers, all are religious women – nuns and quite likely obedientiaries within their respective institutions. My final example of where scholars can look to determine literacy among women focuses on those elite aristocratic women who entered nunneries later in life (such as Lucy de Vere herself, who was not only the founder of Hedingham, but its first prioress too).

In a manilla envelope in Salisbury Cathedral Archives is a set of small pieces of medieval membrane, dating to the thirteenth and fourteenth centuries. These are rare survivals of the common practice of the Profession of Obedience by the heads of religious houses to the bishop in whose diocese their house was subject. One of these small pieces of vellum is the profession of Ela, Countess of Salisbury, and Abbess of Lacock Abbey, which she founded. In 1229, Ela, wife of Henry II's illegitimate son, William Longespée (d. 1226), began the process of establishing a nunnery in Lacock, Wiltshire. She initially intended this institution to be Cistercian, but when it was formally founded it was as an Augustinian convent. Ela laid the ceremonial foundation stone (after the new building's completion) in 1232, and the first prioress – Wymarca – took up her position. Some years after the foundation, in 1238, Ela became a nun and entered the abbey. In 1239 or 1240, she became abbess, a role that seems always to have been intended for her, given that Wymarca had held the only position of prioress since the abbey's establishment. When Ela made her profession of obedience to Robert de Bingham, bishop from 1229 to 1246 of the new cathedral at Salisbury, the confirmation of this process was written onto a very small slip of vellum. The wording is similar to other professions, such as that of John and Robert, successive abbots of the abbey of West Langdon, to the Archbishops of Canterbury between 1205 and 1249.[44] Ela's profession reveals that:

> Ego Ela, ecclesie de Lacoc electa Abbatissa, profiteor Sancte Sarrisburiensi ecclesie, tibique, Pater Roberte, eiusdem ecclesie Episcope, tuisque successoribus in ea canonice substituendis, canonicam obedienciam et subiectionem. +[45]

> (I, Ela abbess elect of the church of Lacock, declare to the holy church of Salisbury and to you, Father Robert, bishop of the same church and to your successors to be canonically substituted in it, canonical obedience and submission. +)

This small slip of membrane, written in a proficient Gothic *textura*, is testimony to the larger community's service of blessing the abbess, which followed the confirmation of her election by the bishop. After Ela's profession had been written and the mark of the cross was made by her, the slip was folded too swiftly since the cross that she wrote is now perfectly offset on the opposite side of the fold. The profession was then sewn into or onto a larger document – perhaps a register – in such a way that its six lines could be unfolded and read.

The provision of the mark of the cross might seem like evidence for assuming that Ela, Abbess of Lacock, could not write her name. Marks of the cross are often seen as evidence for partial or minimal literacy. However, comparable Professions of Obedience by abbots, such as that of Benedict Abbot of Torre in the fourteenth century, also end by the possible signing of the document: 'Et idem Abbas manu propria se subscripsit.' Not all abbots do more than indicate their authenticating cross: 'quam manu propria signo crucis confirmo +'.[46] Among present-day scholars, there would never be a question about the literacy of those abbots who only sign the cross. In other words, every scrap of evidence for *women's* ability to write, to wield a quill confidently (as Ela's steady cross suggests she could), must be considered testimony to their competent literacy. It is likely, and especially so given Ela's administrative experience in running vast estates before becoming a nun, that she was highly literate and had the ability not only to read, but also to write.

Marginal Note III

Women are everywhere in medieval cultures of literacy: they are present as scribes, as readers, as advisors, as annotators, inscribing themselves into the record. But they are often on the margins of the manuscript, or at the edge of text on a slip of vellum. They are in between the lines, they may not reveal their names, they may be a sequence of religious women working through time in one manuscript, but they are there. The burdens of proof that scholarship has traditionally placed upon those who seek women writers and readers make the discovery of these medieval women almost impossible. The derogation of scribes who might be women, and the lack of value attributed to texts that are not 'original', historical, or literary (like Psalters or Prayers) perpetuates the diminution of historical women's endeavours. It also suppresses the efforts of present-day scholars who seek to reveal these medieval women. But women scribes and readers are everywhere, and that assumption should be the basis for ongoing research. Rather than merely assuming that the text was created by or for men, we might first ask of medieval writing, 'Was this written or read by women?'.

Notes

1. On this manuscript, see Thom Gobbit, 'CCCC 383', in Orietta Da Rold, Takako Kato, Mary Swan, and Elaine Treharne, *The Production and Use of English Manuscripts, 1060 to 1220* (Leicester: University of Leicester, 2010; 2nd ed., Stanford University: em1060.stanford.edu); Kathryn Powell, 'The "Scipmen" Scribe and Cambridge, Corpus Christi College 383', *Heroic Age* 14 (2010): www.heroicage.org/issues/14/powell.php.
2. On which, see Patrick Wormald, *The Making of English Law: From King Ælfred to the Twelfth Century* (Oxford: Blackwell, 1999).
3. I discuss Matilda in my *Perceptions of Medieval Manuscripts: The Phenomenal Book* (Oxford: Oxford University Press, 2021), 98–105, where my focus is principally on trying to identify this religious woman and her poem, 'La Seisine', which is a short avian fable discussing the merits of the nightingale and the thrush.
4. The short verses are very lightly edited here to expand abbreviations and modernise <v> for <u>. The Psalm references are to the Vulgate version.

5. On this same folio in the top right margin, what appears to be the same hand writes 'Gif hwo', an English note, and, above it, 'A he' omnis homo premium'[?].
6. Treharne, *Perceptions of Medieval Manuscripts*, 98–9.
7. Emma Bérat, 'The Authorship of Diversity: Communal Patronage in *Le Gracial*', in *Barking Abbey and Medieval Literary Culture: Authorship and Authority in a Female Community*, ed. Jennifer N. Brown and Donna Alfano Bussell (Woodbridge: Boydell for York Medieval Press, 2012), 210–32 (223–7).
8. See Elaine Treharne, *Living Through Conquest: The Politics of Early English, 1060 to 1220* (Oxford: Oxford University Press, 2012), 157–8; and George Younge, 'An Old English Compiler and his Audience: London, British Library, Cotton MS Vespasian D. xiv' in *English Manuscripts Before 1400*, ed. Orietta Da Rold and A. S. G. Edwards, English Manuscript Studies 17 (London: British Library, 2012), 1–26.
9. This manuscript is digitised in full and openly accessible at the British Library's digital manuscript repository: www.bl.uk/manuscripts/FullDisplay.aspx?ref=Cotton_MS_Vespasian_D_XIV. It is possible simply to enter the shelfmark into the browser search engine and be taken straight to the manuscript's description and imaging.
10. This phrase is found also in a prayer to St Mary for the soul's peace attributed to St John of Damascus: 'In Maria invenimus propitiatorium nostrum, eripiens nos a futuris terribilibus suppliciis, et liberans nos ab omnibus minis et insidiis hostium visibilium, et invisibilium.' See José Calasanz de Llevaneras, *Compendium iuris canonici: Beatae Mariae Virgini dicatum* (Rome: Fridericus Pustet, 1905), 439.
11. Transcribed, translated, and very briefly discussed in *Living Through Conquest* (157), but silently edited here.
12. George Younge, 'Placing English in the Twelfth-Century Renaissance: The Canterbury Anthology and English Literature, c. 1066–1200' (unpub. DPhil thesis, University of Cambridge, 2012), 155–7. This thesis was completed after the publication of *Living Through Conquest*; Younge and I worked on these texts simultaneously and independently.
13. Younge, 'Anthology', 155.
14. Younge, 'Anthology', 156–7.
15. Carla Rossi, *Marie de France et les érudits de Cantorbéry*, Recherches littéraires médiévales 1 (Paris: Éditions Classiques Garnier, 2009). This is a reference I owe to Younge, 'Anthology', 156. See also Carla Rossi, *Marie, ki en sun tens pas ne s'oblie; Maria di Francia: la Storia oltre l'enigma* (Rome: Bagatto Libri, 2007), and Carla Rossi, 'The Surviving Iconography of Marie Becket', in *La Fucina di Vulcano: Studi sull'arte per Sergio Rossi*, ed. Sergio Rossi (Rome: Lithos, 2016), 37–44.
16. See further Emma Campbell's contribution to this volume (Chapter 18).

17. The entire manuscript is digitised at The Parker on the Web repository at parker.stanford.edu/parker. The manuscript shelfmark ('383') in the search box will display the codex.
18. Diane Watt, *Women, Writing and Religion in England and Beyond, 650–1100*, Studies in Early Medieval History (London: Bloomsbury Academic, 2020).
19. See Introduction in Watt, *Women, Writing and Religion*, 1–20 (6, 9, and passim).
20. Pamela R. Robinson, 'A Twelfth-Century Scriptrix from Nunnaminster', in *Of the Making of Books: Medieval Manuscripts, their Scribes and Readers. Essays Presented to M. B. Parkes*, ed. Pamela R. Robinson and Rivkah Zim (Aldershot: Scolar Press, 1997), 81, citing the Rule.
21. Celia Sisam and Kenneth Sisam (eds.), *The Salisbury Psalter, edited from Salisbury Cathedral MS. 150*, Early English Text Society O.S. 242 (London: Oxford University Press, 1959).
22. On which, see Sarah Foot, *Veiled Women*, 2 vols. (Aldershot: Ashgate, 2000). Daphne Stroud, 'The Provenance of the Salisbury Psalter', *The Library* 6 (1979), 225–35, also discusses Wilton as a possible place of origin for the Salisbury Psalter, associating the manuscript specifically with St Edith.
23. 'Nonne Deo subjecta erit anima mea? Hu nu underþeod byþ sawel min?' Shall not my soul be subject to God? (Psalm 61:2).
24. *Salisbury Psalter*, 2–3.
25. *Salisbury Psalter*, 3.
26. *Salisbury Psalter*, 6.
27. Later liturgical annotations in the manuscript suggest it continued in monastic use until the thirteenth century. See *Salisbury Psalter*, 6, §10; and 11.
28. Alison I. Beach, *Women as Scribes: Book Production and Monastic Reform in Twelfth-Century Bavaria* (Cambridge: Cambridge University Press, 2004), 132. See also Karin Schneider, *Gotische Schriften in deutscher Sprache: I. Vom späten 12. Jahrhundert bis um 1300* (Wiesbaden: Reichert 1987), 249. This conservatism identified by Beach and Schneider in German institutions may be an identifying component of women's writing in the premodern period, though again, Matilda and 'ancilla' in this discussion seem entirely contemporary, if rather formal, in the expression of their model scripts.
29. *Salisbury Psalter*, 8.
30. See Elaine Treharne, '"The Good, the Bad, the Ugly": Old English Manuscripts and Their Physical Description', in *The Genesis of Books: Studies in the Scribal Culture of Medieval England in Honour of A. N. Doane*, ed. Matthew Hussey and John Niles (Turnhout: Brepols, 2012), 261–83.
31. *Salisbury Psalter*, 14, §29.
32. *Salisbury Psalter*, 14, 16.
33. For these descriptions, see *Salisbury Psalter*, 16–21.
34. Phillip Pulsiano (ed.), *Old English Glossed Psalters: Psalms 1–50* (Toronto: University of Toronto Press, 2001); M. J. Toswell, *The Anglo-Saxon Psalter*, Medieval Church Studies 10 (Turnhout: Brepols, 2014), esp. 130–9.

35. Veronica O'Mara, 'Nuns and Writing in Late Medieval England: The Quest Continues', in *Nuns' Literacies in Medieval Europe: The Kansas City Dialogue*, ed. Virginia Blanton, Veronica O'Mara, and Patricia Stoop, Medieval Women: Texts and Contexts 27 (Turnhout: Brepols, 2015), 123–47; and Veronica O'Mara, 'The Late Medieval English Nun and her Scribal Activity: A Complicated Quest', in *Nuns' Literacies in Medieval Europe: The Hull Dialogue*, ed. Virginia Blanton, Veronica O'Mara, and Patricia Stoop, Medieval Women: Texts and Contexts 26 (Turnhout: Brepols, 2013), 123–47.
36. O'Mara, 'Nuns and Writing: The Quest Continues', at 126–9.
37. O'Mara, 'Nuns and Writing: The Quest Continues', at 138–40, discussing London, British Library, Additional MS 10596.
38. Robinson, 'A Twelfth-Century Scriptrix from Nunnaminster', 73–93 (76, 90).
39. Julia Crick, 'An Eleventh-Century Prayer-Book for Women? The Origins and History of the Galba Prayer-Book', in *Writing, Kingship and Power in Anglo-Saxon England*, ed. Rory Naismith and David A. Woodman (Cambridge: Cambridge University Press, 2018), 281–302.
40. Crick, 'An Eleventh-Century Prayer-Book', 287, 289. A parallel hand in London, British Library, Cotton Tiberius A. iii, folio 179r is described as 'huge, ugly, and peppered with majuscule letters' (288).
41. See Catherine Karkov and Elaine Treharne, 'The Presence of the Hands: Sculpture and Script in the Eighth to Twelfth Centuries', in *Medieval English and Dutch Literatures: the European Context. Essays in Honour of David F. Johnson*, ed. Larissa Tracy and Geert H. M. Claassens (Woodbridge: Boydell and Brewer, 2022), 127–50.
42. The Rolls are edited and mapped in Jean Dufour (ed.), *Recueil des Rouleaux des Morts (VIIIe siècle–vers 1536)*, 4 vols. (Paris: Diffusion de Boccard, 2005). The Rolls are the focus of a major digital project, *Medieval Networks of Memory*, directed by Elaine Treharne and Mateusz Fafinski. London, British Library, Egerton MS 2849 is fully digitised: www.bl.uk/manuscripts/FullDisplay.aspx?ref=Egerton_MS_2849/2.
43. See the specific folio in the digitised manuscript, cited in n. 42.
44. C. Eveleigh Woodruff, 'Some Early Professions of Canonical Obedience to the See of Canterbury by Heads of Religious Houses', *Archaeologia Cantiana* 37 (1925), 53–72 (70–1).
45. Salisbury Cathedral Archives, Chapter, Press II/19.
46. F. C. Hingeston-Randolph (ed.), *The Register of Bishop Grandisson Bishop of Exeter (AD 1327–1369)*, 2 vols. (London: George Bell, 1897), II.1002.

Further Reading

Beach, Alison I. (2004). *Women as Scribes: Book Production and Monastic Reform in Twelfth-Century Bavaria*, Cambridge: Cambridge University Press.

Blanton, Virginia, Veronica O'Mara, and Patricia Stoop, eds. (2015). *Nuns' Literacies in Medieval Europe: The Kansas City Dialogue*, Medieval Women: Texts and Contexts 27, Turnhout: Brepols.

Brown, Michelle P. (2001). Female Book Ownership and Production in Anglo-Saxon England: The Evidence of the Ninth-Century Prayerbooks. In *Lexis and Texts in Early English: Papers in Honour of Jane Roberts*, ed. Christian J. Kay and Louise M. Sylvester. Amsterdam: Brepols, 45–68.

Conrad-O'Briain, Helen (2008). Were Women Able to Read and Write in the Middle Ages? In *Misconceptions About the Middle Ages*, ed. Stephen Harris and Bryon L. Grigsby. New York: Routledge, 236–9.

Haines-Eitzen, Kim (2012). *The Gendered Palimpsest: Women, Writing, and Representation in Early Christianity*, Oxford: Oxford University Press.

Radini, A., M. Tromp, A. Beach, et al. (2019). Medieval Women's Early Involvement in Manuscript Production Suggested by Lapis Lazuli Identification in Dental Calculus. *Scientific Advances* 1, 1–8.

Robinson, Pamela R., and Rivkah Zim, eds. (1997). *Of the Making of Books: Medieval Manuscripts, their Scribes and Reader: Essays Presented to M. B. Parkes*, Aldershot: Scolar Press.

Smith, Lesley, and Jane H. M. Taylor, eds. (1995). *Women, the Book, and the Godly: Selected Proceedings of the St Hilda's Conference*, Woodbridge: D. S. Brewer.

Thompson, Sally (1991). *Women Religious: The Founding of English Nunneries after the Norman Conquest*, Oxford: Clarendon Press.

Watt, Diane (2020). *Women, Writing and Religion in England and Beyond, 650–1100*, Studies in Early Medieval History, London: Bloomsbury Academic.

CHAPTER 2

Creating Her Own Story
Queens, Noblewomen, and Their Cultural Patronage

Mary Dockray-Miller

A survey of the literary culture of queens and noblewoman in medieval Europe demonstrates the consistent and multiple ways that these aristocratic women created their own stories through patronage of and engagement with a wide variety of literacies and texts. Secular aristocrats participated in and created textual cultures in ways that both overlapped with and differed from those of the abbesses and nuns discussed by Elaine Treharne in Chapter 1. It is important to note that many medieval women who were queens and noblewomen were also abbesses and nuns at different stages of their lives; I will focus here on the literary cultures created by these women when they were in their secular roles.

Amy Livingstone and other feminist scholars have argued against the 'exceptional woman' model of historical analysis, showing that medieval 'women's power was normative rather than extraordinary'.[1] Heather Tanner, Laura Gathagan, and Lois Huneycutt echo this point when they ask 'How many "exceptional" women in positions of authority does it take before powerful elite women *become* the rule?'[2] These scholars are working against assumptions about medieval women's political and social power prevalent in twentieth- and twenty-first-century historiography and culture; from more serious publications like biographies of Eleanor of Aquitaine to TV shows such as the BBC's *The White Queen* (2013), medieval women with power are presented as anomalies who are interesting because of their irregularity. Those sorts of assumptions have also been operative in work on women's engagements with textual cultures, as Corinne Saunders and Diane Watt make clear in their Introduction to this volume. The exceptional secular aristocratic woman was instead the one who did *not* use literacy and textuality as tools of her personal and public expression.

Like Livingstone, Therese Martin argues against such assumptions of female exceptionalism, although Martin's focus is on artists and patrons rather than on political or military power. Martin asks 'how many so-called exceptions must there be before we decide that a new rule is in order?'[3] Instead of exceptions, Martin sees a 'pattern' of women engaged with the making of art; she uses the term 'maker' to refer to women who participated in a variety of roles in the process of artistic creation. Martin's analysis of the medieval use of the term *fecit* ('she made') shows that both patrons and artists were active in the 'making' of an art object[4] – she sees women actively engaged in the production of art as patrons, designers, facilitators, and owners, in addition to more modern understandings of 'maker' roles of sculptors, painters, and weavers/embroiderers.

Throughout this chapter, I will draw on Martin's term 'maker' to refer to many of the queens and noblewomen who used textuality in their secular lives. Queens and noblewomen were important makers of literary culture throughout the Middle Ages as they asserted social and political power and shaped aesthetic trends to create their own stories – stories which have largely been lost in traditional historiographic and critical focus on men. Representative aristocratic women are discussed here in roughly chronological order, indicating the ongoing nature of this literary culture throughout the Middle Ages

While most scholarship on medieval women's literary cultures tends to focus on the later Middle Ages, examples are readily available from the earlier part of the period. The royal courts of Wessex and Mercia in the ninth and tenth centuries provide a multigenerational female genealogy of secular women engaged with textuality. Discussions of King Alfred's education and translation programme often allude to the perhaps apocryphal story of King Alfred's childhood triumph in a literacy contest as a potential indicator of his early interest in written texts. The prize in this contest was a book of Old English poetry provided by his mother, Osburh.[5] In addition to information about Alfred's early interest in vernacular poetry, that narrative provides an early example of a literate, book-owning aristocratic woman displaying her literary prowess and her wealth in the public setting of the royal court. Osburh's daughter-in-law Ealhswith (the wife of Alfred, d. 902) is a probable owner of the 'Book of Nunnaminster', British Library, Harley MS 2965, a religious anthology of Gospel extracts and prayers that includes (in Old English) boundary-descriptions of land owned by Ealhswith and given to Nunnaminster, the women's religious house in Winchester.[6] Ealhswith's daughter Æthelflæd (d. 918) patronised the 'Mercian Register', the segment of the *Anglo-Saxon Chronicle* cataloguing and celebrating Æthelflæd's achievements as 'Lady of the Mercians' and defender of Mercia against Viking incursion.[7] Each of these three women – Osburh, Ealhswith, Æthelflæd – qualifies as a 'maker' in Martin's terms; while each of them has received historiographical attention in the past twenty years, their lineage as makers shows the routine use of textuality by queens and noblewomen in England before the Norman Conquest.

That Conquest was one crucial event in an extended period of cross-Channel communication and interaction. Elizabeth Tyler has argued that the multilingual, textually astute noblewomen of the northern European aristocracy were the bedrock of a 'literary culture that was created and shared throughout England, Normandy, Northern France, Flanders, and the Empire'.[8] That literary culture was multilingual and also generically diverse: women were engaged with history, poetry, hagiography, chronicles, and devotional texts. Since they are so numerous, it is difficult to include more than passing reference to each of these women in a chapter this brief.

Emma of Normandy's patronage of her *Encomium Emmae* in the early 1040s is emblematic of much of this culture. The text demonstrates an attempt by the twice-widowed queen with two living sons, one by each royal husband, to reduce tensions and assert her prominence and legitimacy at the royal court. The text provides a narrative of events that has been termed 'garbled, one-sided, and incomplete'[9] as well as an 'improvised and often confused though never unsophisticated exploration of the boundary between history and fiction'.[10] While the *Encomium*'s editors refer to the 'encomiast' as the agent who decided on the content, valence, and focus of the text, Emma was a maker of the text as well, quite possibly the primary maker, as she commissioned it and defined its purpose and scope. The triumphant illustration on the frontispiece shows the 'encomiast' presenting the book to Emma and her sons; it draws on traditional iconography of the Virgin at the Nativity,[11] aspirationally presenting the Queen Dowager as the dominant force for goodness and plenty in an English kingdom actually riven by war, assassination, and rivalry.

Emma's daughter-in-law Edith, Queen to Emma's son Edward the Confessor, followed a similar path in her production of the *Vita Edwardi Regis*. Edith's text is titled a *Vita*, but it is much more like Emma's *Encomium* than a standard hagiography;[12] it is clear that the creators of the *Vita* knew the *Encomium Emmae*.[13] The text was created over a period of about two years, and events unforeseen at its conception changed its purpose and content substantially during that time. The *Vita* was originally devised as a celebration of Edith's extended, royal-adjacent family, probably in early 1065; she is acknowledged as the patron and director of the project from its early sections, fitting perfectly into Martin's definition of a maker. Recent lexical analysis with digital tools indicates that Edith's voice and phrasing are probably preserved in sections of the text that are especially celebratory of Edith, her brothers, and her father,[14] indicating that Edith was deeply involved in the production of the text. The Northern Rebellion and subsequent rupture between her brothers (autumn 1065), the death of her husband Edward (January 1066), the Battle of Stamford Bridge between her brothers (September 1066), and the Norman Conquest (October 1066) led to a reconfiguration of the prosimetric text into a lament for the loss of peace and a celebration of Edward's holiness. In early 1067, the widowed queen and her team of scribes, prose writers, copyists, and a poet (with individuals probably filling more than one of those roles at a time or in sequence) had to revise some of the earlier work and produce new prose sections that reflected the text's post-Conquest purpose. Like Emma's *Encomium*, Edith's *Vita Edwardi* does not meet modern standards of historical accuracy. However, it certainly does achieve its purpose of providing Edith an outlet to create and control the narrative of her family's place in recent history, as the *Vita* supplies a selective and editorialised version of events leading up to the Norman Conquest.

Edith's contribution to women's literary culture created a unique text, extant in only one manuscript. Edith's sister-in-law, Judith of Flanders, created no texts *ex nihilo*; instead, she used religious books and other art objects to assert her status and piety in a variety of politically fraught situations.[15] Daughter of Count Baldwin IV of Flanders, Judith was in her late teens when her first marriage in 1051 to Tostig Godwinson (brother to Queen Edith of England) took her to England with the intention of strengthening diplomatic ties between England and Flanders. As Lady of Northumbria and a royal courtier, Judith established her position through patronage and gifts to religious institutions. While she controlled no land, she was able to assert her identity as a wealthy, pious patron through gifts of deluxe statues, relics, and altar ornaments. Notably, Judith also commissioned the only extant group of gospel books from pre-Conquest England that can be securely identified to a single patron; all four present deluxe evangelist portraits and elaborate decoration that demonstrate the visual as well as textual components of medieval literary culture.

Two of these books include frontispiece donor portraits; both showcase Judith's stylish fashion sense as well as her piety (New York, Pierpont Morgan Library, MS M.709, f.1 v and Fulda, Hessische Landesbibliothek, Cod. Aa.21, f.2 v). The well-known portrait made in England, an image of Judith kneeling at the foot of the cross, depicts her in a high-status gown with flowing sleeves similar to the dress worn by the Virgin Mary above her; Judith's presence at the crucifixion provides both devotional focus and status statement. The second portrait was made on the Continent, definitely after Judith and her husband Tostig fled to Flanders in late autumn of 1065, and probably after his death in September of 1066. This less well-known portrait depicts Judith presenting her book to Christ, declaring her literate and literary devotion to Him. While her gown in the Fulda portrait is not as ornate as that in the Morgan Library, it too presents her dressed in deluxe fabrics with gold embroidered borders. Like the Morgan portrait, the Fulda portrait has both social and religious functions, asserting her high social status and her deep religious devotion.[16] Judith's second marriage, to Welf IV of Bavaria in 1070, made her the Lady of Ravensburg; she died in 1094, a respected matron. The endleaves of the gospel book now in Fulda enumerate items she left to Weingarten Abbey, where she is still celebrated as a dedicated and lavish patron.

The elaborate gold treasure bindings of all of her books (only the two covers at the Morgan are extant) similarly declared the wealth and status of their owner. Judith could have used the books in both private and public spaces, in her personal chapel and in grand cathedrals on feast days, reading the selections from Gospel texts and meditating on the deluxe imagery. One of the books, now at the library at Monte Cassino, was probably Judith's personal book that she used most frequently; sometime in the last quarter of the eleventh century, she gave it as a diplomatic gift to the Empress Agnes during Welf's participation in the political and religious machinations of the Investiture Controversy. The illustrations in that book are unusual enough that they suggest she had some design input: the zoomorphic evangelist symbols, the irregular border motifs, and the decorative animals are striking in their difference from those of the more conventional decorations in her manuscripts now at the Morgan.[17]

While only these four books remain, the extensive list of relics, books, and objects that Judith bequeathed to Weingarten, coupled with the mentions of her gifts and patronage in the English sources, demonstrate that her commissioning of religious books and other devotional items asserted her identity as a powerful and wealthy player on the international stage.[18] Judith's endeavours were obviously successful – every medieval text that mentions her, from the *Anglo-Saxon Chronicle* to the *Vita Edwardi* to Symeon of Durham's *Libellus*, emphasises her piety and Christian charity. Her work as maker created and maintained her public persona.

Piety such as Judith's was a celebrated trait for an aristocratic woman. While some level of religious devotion was expected, hers was unusual enough to be noted in written sources that rarely mention women, especially women who are not royal. Judith must have been acquainted with the royal and pious woman known to history as St Margaret of Scotland, since Margaret's and Judith's time at the English court overlapped from 1057–65. Celebrated during and after her life for her piety and Christian charity, Margaret was a cosmopolitan noblewoman of the eleventh century: born in Hungary to an exiled English prince and a Hungarian noblewoman, she came to England with her family in 1057, when she was about twelve years old. She was educated at Wilton Abbey, where she acquired some Latin literacy to complement her already impressive multilingualism. She fled to Scotland with her family after the Norman Conquest. Her marriage to King Malcolm of Scotland in 1069 was by all accounts a success: they worked well together as a royal couple and had eight children who lived to adulthood. Margaret of Scotland was acknowledged as a saint; she was venerated locally and then officially canonised by Pope Innocent IV in 1250.[19]

Margaret's literacy formed an integral part of her piety and her queenship; her *Vita* celebrates her 'religious zeal for the holy volumes' and praises her for reading to her illiterate husband as part of their joint devotions.[20] The *Vita* also tells the miraculous story of Margaret's personal gospel book, which was dropped in a river by an inattentive attendant; it was later retrieved from the bottom of the river and 'the brightness of the pages and the form of the letters remained untouched'.[21] That book (Oxford, Bodleian Library, MS Lat liturgy f.5) includes a later poetic addition identifying it as the queen's book saved from the river. The poem does not name Margaret specifically but refers to her as the 'holy queen' in the present tense, indicating that she was still alive when the book was returned to her and the poem inserted on f.2 r.[22] Rebecca Rushforth suggests that the book was made at Wilton, possibly by a woman; its texts include extracts from the Gospels that show an interest in the Virgin Mary and other women who were part of Christ's ministry.[23] As such, Margaret's gospel book was made for a multilingual woman (if not Margaret herself, then for another Wilton resident), possibly by a woman, with texts focused on women integral to the origins of Christian belief – it is eminently representative of the idea of 'medieval women's literary culture', and thus it is entirely appropriate that the modern discovery of the manuscript's connection to Margaret of Scotland as the unnamed 'holy queen' was made by Lucy Hill, who was only twenty-two when she read the poem and made the connection just after the Bodleian Library purchased the book from Sotheby's for only six pounds in 1887.[24]

Like the textual genealogy of the women of the royal houses of Mercia and Wessex in the early medieval period, a Scottish-Norman-continental genealogy connects the textual expressions of Margaret's descendants and extended kin networks, demonstrating a series of women who emulated each other in literary patronage and literacy practices. Margaret's *Vita* was commissioned by her daughter Matilda, known as Matilda of Scotland to differentiate her among the plethora of Matildas throughout western Europe in the High Middle Ages. Matilda of Scotland thus helped to create her mother's story as well as her own as she patronised the valorisation of her mother's holy and royal life. Matilda married Henry I, King of England, in 1100 and so was Queen of England as well as Duchess of Normandy until her death in 1118; Matilda's recent biographer has argued that 'Matilda of Scotland succeeded at queenship to an extraordinary degree because the political structures of her day allowed her the opportunity to do so and because she was herself skilled at manipulating those structures'.[25]

Part of that success was her literary patronage – in addition to her mother's *Vita*, Matilda is remembered more generally as a patron of books and music.[26] She corresponded with numerous prominent churchmen, including the poet Hildebert, bishop of Lavardin, who wrote three poems for her.[27] More specifically, the earliest manuscript of the Anglo-Norman *Voyage of St Brendan* names her as its patron (that manuscript, designated C in editorial discussion, is Oxford, Bodleian Library, MS Rawlinson D 913, f.85, a single folio containing only the first 310 lines of the poem). Later manuscripts invoke Adeliza, second queen of Henry I.[28] William of Malmesbury provides the most effusive praise of Matilda's literary engagement in the letters that preface his *Gesta Regum Anglorum*; while she died before it was completed, she was the initial patron of this eminently canonical, monumental, and crucial work of historiography. William states that Matilda 'among her other virtues never ceased to support good literature and advance those who were devoted to it'.[29] He also notes that 'her sainted mind had devoted so much attention to the business of literary studies'.[30]

William also invokes a female genealogy of literary culture when he dedicates the completed *Gesta Regum* to the daughter of Matilda of Scotland, another Matilda – this one termed 'Empress Matilda' by virtue of her first marriage to Henry V, Holy Roman Emperor. In the text's second prefatory letter, addressed to Empress Matilda, William declares 'the greatest possible affection for your imperial majesty, and with the offer of this book on the history of the English kings, the writing of which we arranged on our lady's [Matilda of Scotland's] instructions, we entrust ourselves and all that is ours to your royal patronage'.[31] The editors of the *Gesta Regum* date these letters to 1124–6, probably 1126.[32]

Empress Matilda was also the second-choice dedicatee of another important historical text, the *Song of the Princes of Canossa* by the Italian monk Donizo; this encomium is known in modern times as *Vita Mathildis*, although it is not technically a hagiography.[33] The monks at Canossa initially dedicated the celebratory history to the formidable Countess Matilda of Tuscany to entice her patronage of their monastery (the entire second half of the *Song* focuses on Matilda's achievements, while the first book enumerates those of her ancestors). It was finished just after she died in 1115 and hastily rededicated to the Empress Matilda, at that moment married to Emperor Henry V, one of Countess Matilda's important allies.[34] The Countess commissioned one known deluxe gospel book (New York, Morgan Library, MS M 492) and probably others; she supported a number of monastic authors, as remarked in the *Song/Vita Mathildis*. Part of the Countess's exercise of immense political and military power was patronage of books and texts that furthered the establishment of her status throughout Europe. Empress Matilda's subsequent receipt of the *Song* and of the *Gesta Regum* ten years later reinforces the essential nature of textual culture in a powerful medieval woman's assertion of her position.

At about the same time, Adela, Countess of Blois, was actively patronising poets and historians as part of her establishment of her powerful, glittering court. The sister-in-law of Matilda of Scotland and aunt of Empress Matilda, Adela has been termed a 'female Lord' by her biographer, as she ruled when her husband was away on Crusade and after his death.[35] Adela was the dedicatee of the poem 'Adelae Comitissae', written between 1099 and 1102 by Baudri, abbot of Bourgueil and poet of the Loire School.[36] The poet hopes for both praise and reward from his patron: in the beginning of the extended ekphrastic celebration of Adele's bedchamber, Baudri notes that 'She has an ear for verse and takes an interest in books. / Also, she's well aware that the poet deserves his stipend' (ll. 38–9). Baudri states as well that 'She herself has a lively talent for writing poems' (l. 41); while Otter notes that none of Adela's poems has survived, texts by other poets and correspondents confirm her literary patronage and hint as well at authorship.[37] Tyler sees Baudri constructing Adela in the text so that he is 'making his patron his co-creator … he still figures her as a collaborator in this exploration of fictionality'.[38] More conventionally, the preface to Hugh of Fleury's 1109/10 *Historia ecclesiastica* addresses Adela, its patron, 'both as a ruler and as learned women'.[39]

Adela's political power, sophisticated education, and patronage of the literary arts is something of a precursor to the much more famous case of Eleanor of Aquitaine (*c.* 1122–1204), who was similarly powerful, educated, and literary. Indeed, Eleanor is probably the original 'exceptional' medieval woman, the subject of numerous biographies and films. Her life lends itself to popular assumptions about the Middle Ages: a beautiful, wealthy heiress, she was married to both the King of France and the King of England; her second husband held her under house arrest for fifteen years; she emerged back into public life to act as regent for her sons.[40] An integral part of this mythology is Eleanor's patronage of and contributions to the 'courts of love' and troubadour poetry that flourished in France and England through the twelfth century (Rosenberg's 1937 biography is the most emblematic of this narrative; its subtitle is *Queen of the Troubadours and of the Courts of Love*[41]). Recent scholarship, more circumspect about Eleanor's literary patronage, moves beyond what Jean Flori terms 'the theory of Eleanor as a patron, surrounding herself at Poitiers with a broad court of educated men, troubadours, poets and romancers', to see her instead as performing 'an important role in the Plantagenet court's system of literary patronage'.[42] Eleanor was thus part of a female aristocratic culture that routinely commissioned, patronised, encouraged, and participated in literary expression, rather than an exceptional innovator of textual culture. The cinematic narrative of her political and marital life, not her literary patronage, led to modern culture's erroneous perception of her as exceptional.

On the other side of Europe at the same time, Queen Tamar of Georgia (r. 1184–1213) ruled over a Georgian 'golden age' that included the production of the Georgian national epic, *The Knight in the Panther Skin*. Huneycutt credits the queen regnant for the country's peace and prosperity: 'During Tamar's reign Georgia reached the height of its commercial importance, military power, and territorial extent.' She also notes that Tamar used 'textual and visual media' to craft and promote her image.[43] The prologue to *The Knight in the Panther Skin* praises Tamar as its patron and primary audience – it also refers to her as 'King' and plays with the dissonance of the masculine noun and subsequent female pronouns. Rustaveli, the poet, says 'Behold the sun of our King Tamar – bright of face and dark of hair. / I do not know how I shall hymn her praises. Do I dare to dare?' (ll. 10–11).[44] A few lines later, the poet notes his task as 'to sing her Kingly praises' (l. 17). As did Eleanor and a myriad of noblewomen before her, Tamar asserted herself in and through literary culture to establish her status as a learned, important, powerful woman worthy of praise.

Like Tamar of Georgia, Anna Comnena practised Orthodox rather than Roman Christianity, and she too created her own story, notably composing the *Alexiad*, 'one of the most commonly read and widely available

Byzantine histories'.[45] While the *c*. 1148 *Alexiad* focuses on the life and deeds of her father, the Byzantine Emperor Alexios, Anna's first-person voice is very prominent throughout, especially in the text's prologue and conclusion. While previous critics and historians have commented negatively on Anna's 'hysterical and unreasonable' emotion in her text, especially her narratives of the deaths of her husband and her parents, recent feminist scholarship has connected her style to that of classical lamentation.[46] Leonora Neville shows how Anna 'played with the boundaries of the genre [history]' to confirm and subvert assumptions about women writers: 'When caught in the act of the male gendered activity of history writing, her enactment of female lamentation shows that indeed she was not an aberrant woman.'[47] In her forced retirement from active participation in politics and court life, Anna definitively created her own story as well as that of her extended family, glorifying her father and husband, with herself as actor and author in the process.

All of these queens and noblewomen exemplify the ordinary nature of this aristocratic female exploitation of literature and textuality. These examples simply multiply throughout the High and Late Middle Ages, throughout Europe and beyond. Matilda Plantagenet, Eleanor of Aquitaine's oldest daughter, who married Henry the Lion, King of Germany, in 1168, made her mark with personalised psalter and gospel books; the gospel book includes a praise poem of Matilda and her husband.[48] Marie, Countess of Ponthieu (d. 1250), patronised romance texts that praised her both overtly and obliquely for her fortitude and determination.[49] Isabella of France, queen consort, queen regent, and queen dowager of England (d. 1358), owned and commissioned a wide variety of books, both secular and devotional, and saw 'the production and use of books as a part of her roles as queen, wife, and mother'.[50] An enormous number of extant psalters and books of hours are known to have been owned and used by European noblewomen as part of their religious devotions as well as assertions of social status.[51] For example, the Psalter-Hours of Mary de Bohun (Oxford, Bodleian Library, MS Egerton 3277), commissioned by Joan Fitzalan for her daughter, 'is simultaneously a precious, personal devotional relic and a tangible, public symbol of their family, wealth, and privilege'.[52] Such books often included coats of arms and/or devotional portraits to emphasise the secular prestige of their lay owners and users. These books owned by and made for lay aristocratic women included texts in various vernaculars as well as Latin.[53] Dame Eleanor Hull (d. 1460), whose minor-nobility family served the Lancastrians for generations, even translated a number of devotional texts from French into Middle English after she was widowed.[54]

While arguably an early modern rather than a medieval noblewoman, Lady Margaret Beaufort (d. 1509), mother of Henry VII, also translated devotional texts from French to Middle English: the *Imitation of Christ* (Book 4) and the *Mirror of Gold for the Sinful Soul*, which were published in the first decade of the sixteenth century and popular enough to go through multiple printings.[55] Like many of the other women noted here, she owned deluxe, personalised Books of Hours (Cambridge, St John's College, MS N.24; London, British Library, MS Royal 2 A.xviii). She also commissioned texts in French and English from printer William Caxton, thus providing a bridge from the medieval to the early modern for aristocratic secular women's literary culture.

Just a few years before the printing of Lady Margaret Beaufort's translations, another powerful, older, royal woman was also using textuality to advance her own and her family's causes: Gulbadan Banu Begum, widowed aunt to Mughal King Akbar, responded to her nephew's call for written history of her brother and father (his father and grandfather) by composing the *Ahval-i Humayun Badshah*, also called the *Humayunnama* (1587), a narrative of their reigns focused, to some extent, on the women of the house. Now extant in only one manuscript (London, British Library, Or.166), the Begum's text 'takes us through the complex set of relations in which women of the nobility were involved in the domestic sphere, pointing to the public political affairs that were necessarily conducted here as well as in the courts'.[56] The manuscript is in Persian, although it uses many Turki words; the Begum was evidently very comfortable in both.[57] She presents her text in the first person, providing personal details ('I got into my litter and went and paid my duty to my royal father'[58]) as well as information and narratives about power struggles among the prominent families at court, including the extended sections of the royal family. Gulbadan Banu Begum, whose hajj in 1578 is recorded in both Mughal and European texts,[59] belies in many ways the colonialist view of the *haram* as socially and culturally sequestered and impotent.[60] Ruby Lal notes that 'Gulbadan's [writing] process would be located very much in the harem', raising intriguing questions about the writing process for this literate and literary noblewoman.[61] Would her scribes and copyists also have been women of the harem? Did she compose and/or dictate different sections in different languages? What was the literary and textual culture of the harem, and how did it differ from that of the court at large? Gulbadan Banu Begum's *Humayunnama* allows us to ask those questions, although the answers are far from evident.

This chapter began in ninth-century Wessex and ends in sixteenth-century India, showcasing a selection of the aristocratic women who acted as makers of texts as part of their social, political, marital, and cultural activities. This literary culture allowed these women to create their own stories, whether explicit narratives about themselves and their extended families or other texts that made more indirect statements about their makers' personalities, politics, religious beliefs, aesthetic preferences, and social statuses. In her analysis of northern Europe in the eleventh century, Tyler argues for 'the leading role that royal women, rather than royal men, played as literary patrons'.[62] This point could be applied more generally to the entire medieval European period. As Elaine Treharne argues in Chapter 1, the masculinist mindset of modern scholarship about the Middle Ages assumes a male default for creators of textual culture: patrons, commissioners, artists, writers, scribes, copyists, and others. The literary cultures of the noblewomen surveyed here contribute to the dismantling of these sorts of assumptions. Like the abbesses and nuns who were often their biological kin as well as spiritual sisters, secular aristocratic women routinely – not exceptionally – acted as agents and makers in their literary cultures, indicating the regular importance of textuality in a noblewoman's portfolio of power and influence.

Notes

1. Amy Livingstone, 'Recalculating the Equation: Powerful Woman = Extraordinary', *Medieval Feminist Forum* 51.2 (2015), 17–29 (29).
2. Heather J. Tanner, Laura Gathagan, and Lois Huneycutt, 'Introduction', in *Medieval Elite Women and the Exercise of Power, 1100–1400: Moving Beyond the Exceptionalist Debate*, ed. Heather Tanner (New York: Palgrave Macmillan, 2019), 1–18 (2).
3. Therese Martin, 'Exceptions and Assumptions: Women in Medieval Art History', in *Reassessing the Roles of Women as 'Makers' of Medieval Art and Architecture*, ed. Therese Martin (Leiden: Brill, 2012), 1–33 (1).
4. Martin, 'Exceptions and Assumptions', 2–4.
5. Asser, *Asser's Life of King Alfred*, ed. William Henry Stevenson (Oxford: Clarendon Press, 1904), chs 22 and 23, 19–20.
6. Michelle Brown, 'Female Book Ownership and Production in Anglo-Saxon England: The Evidence of the Ninth-Century Prayerbooks', in *Lexis and Texts in Early English: Studies Presented to Jane Roberts*, ed. Christian Kay and Louise Sylvester (Amsterdam: Rodopi, 2001), 45–67.
7. See Pauline Stafford, 'The Annals of Æthelflæd: Annals, History and Politics in Early 10th-Century England', in *Myth, Rulership, Church and Charters: Essays in Honour of Nicholas Brooks*, ed. Julia Barrow and Andrew Wareham (Burlington, VT: Ashgate, 2007), 101–16; see also Tim Clarkson, *Æthelflæd: The Lady of the Mercians* (Edinburgh: John Donald, 2018).

8. Elizabeth M. Tyler, *England in Europe: English Royal Women and Literary Patronage, c. 1000–c. 1150* (Toronto: University of Toronto Press, 2017), 17.
9. Alistair Campbell and Simon Keynes (eds.), *Encomium Emmae Reginae*, 2nd ed. (Cambridge: Cambridge University Press, 1998), lvii.
10. Tyler, *England in Europe*, 99.
11. Catherine Karkov, *The Ruler Portraits of Anglo-Saxon England* (Woodbridge: Boydell, 2004), ch. 4, 119–56.
12. Frank Barlow (ed. and trans.), *The Life of King Edward Who Rests at Westminster*, 2nd ed. (Oxford: Clarendon Press, 1992), xix.
13. Tyler, *England in Europe*, 151.
14. Mary Dockray-Miller, Michael Drout, Sarah Kinkade, and Jillian Valerio, 'The Author and the Authors of the *Vita Edwardi Regis*: Women's Literary Culture and Digital Humanities', *Interfaces* 8 (2021), 51.2 (2015), 160–213, https://riviste.unimi.it/interfaces/article/view/14204.
15. Mary Dockray-Miller, *The Books and the Life of Judith of Flanders* (Burlington, VT: Ashgate, 2015), introduction, 1–12.
16. Dockray-Miller, *Books and the Life*, ch. 3, 49–72.
17. Dockray-Miller, *Books and the Life*, ch. 2, 29–48.
18. Dockray-Miller, *Books and the Life*, ch. 4, 73–90.
19. Catherine Keene, *Saint Margaret, Queen of the Scots: A Life in Perspective* (New York: Palgrave Macmillan, 2013).
20. Keene, *Saint Margaret*, 184–5.
21. Keene, *Saint Margaret*, 210.
22. Richard Gameson, 'The Gospels of Margaret of Scotland and the Literacy of an Eleventh-Century Queen', in *Women and the Book: Assessing the Visual Evidence*, ed. Lesley M. Smith and Jane H. M. Taylor (Toronto: University of Toronto Press, 1997), 149–71 (165–6).
23. Rebecca Rushforth, *St Margaret's Gospel-Book: The Favourite Book of an Eleventh-Century Queen of Scots* (Oxford: Bodleian Library, 2007), 27 and 72.
24. Rushforth, *St Margaret's Gospel-Book*, 104–5.
25. Lois L. Huneycutt, *Matilda of Scotland: A Study in Medieval Queenship* (Rochester, NY: Boydell Press, 2003), 7.
26. Huneycutt, *Matilda of Scotland*, 143.
27. Matilda of Scotland, letters to and from various correspondents, in *Epistolae: Medieval Women's Latin Letters*, Columbia University, 2012–: epistolae.ctl.columbia.edu/woman/64.html.
28. Jude S. Mackley, *The Legend of St. Brendan: A Comparative Study of the Latin and Anglo-Norman Versions* (Leiden: Brill, 2008), ProQuest Ebook Central, 257, n. 1.
29. R. A. B. Mynors, R. M. Thomson, and M. Winterbottom (eds. and trans.), *William of Malmesbury Gesta Regum Anglorum: The History of the English Kings*, 2 vols. (Oxford: Clarendon Press, 1998), vol. 1, 5.
30. *William of Malmesbury*, vol. 1, 9.
31. *William of Malmesbury*, vol. 1, 7.
32. *William of Malmesbury*, vol. 2, 6–7.

33. Valerie Eads, personal email communication, 18 August 2020. Eads is preparing the first full English translation of Donizo of Canossa's text; the most current edition, with Italian translation, is P. Golinelli (ed. and trans.), *Vita di Matilde di Canossa* (Milan: Jaca, 2008).
34. Catherine Hanley, *Matilda: Empress, Queen, Warrior* (New Haven, CT: Yale University Press, 2019).
35. Kimberly A. LoPrete, *Adela of Blois: Countess and Lord (c. 1067–1137)* (Dublin: Four Courts Press, 2007).
36. Monika Otter (introduction and trans.), 'Baudri of Bourgueil: To Countess Adela', *Journal of Medieval Latin* 11 (2001), 60–141 (61).
37. Otter, 'Baudri of Bourgueil', 101.
38. Tyler, *England in Europe*, 288.
39. Tyler, *England in Europe*, 294.
40. Ralph V. Turner, *Eleanor of Aquitaine: Queen of France, Queen of England* (New Haven: Yale University Press, 2009).
41. Melrich Vonelm Rosenberg, *Eleanor of Aquitaine: Queen of the Troubadours and the Courts of Love* (Boston: Houghton Mifflin, 1937).
42. Jean Flori, *Eleanor of Aquitaine: Queen and Rebel*, trans. by Olive Classe (Edinburgh: Edinburgh University Press, 2007), https://doi.org/10.3366/edinburgh/9780748622955.001.0001, quotations from 283–4 and 293.
43. Lois Huneycutt, 'Tamar of Georgia (1184–1213) and the Language of Female Power', in *A Companion to Global Queenship*, ed. Elena Woodacre (Leeds: ARC Humanities Press, 2018), 27–38 (quotations from 31 and 29).
44. Shota Rustaveli, *The Knight in the Panther Skin*, trans. by Lyn Coffin (Tblisi: Poezia Press, 2015), quotation ll. 10–11.
45. Leonora Neville, 'Lamentation, History, and Female Authorship in Anna Komnene's *Alexiad*', *Greek, Roman & Byzantine Studies* 53.1 (2013), 192–218, 192.
46. Neville, 'Lamentation', 197.
47. Neville, 'Lamentation', 192 and 213.
48. Jitske Verfasser Jasperse, *Medieval Women, Material Culture, and Power: Matilda Plantagenet and Her Sisters* (Leeds: ARC Humanities Press, 2020).
49. Kathy Krause, 'From Mothers to Daughters: Literary Patronage as Political Work in Ponthieu', in *Medieval Elite Women and the Exercise of Power, 1100–1400: Moving Beyond the Exceptionalist Debate*, ed. Heather Tanner (New York: Palgrave Macmillan, 2019), 113–34.
50. Anne Rudloff Stanton, 'Isabella of France and Her Manuscripts: 1308–1358', in *Capetian Women*, ed. Kathleen Nolan (New York: Palgrave Macmillan, 2003), 225–52 (246).
51. Charity Scott-Stokes, *Women's Books of Hours in Medieval England* (Woodbridge: D. S. Brewer, 2006).
52. Jill C. Havens, 'A Gift, a Mirror, a Memorial: The Psalter-Hours of Mary de Bohun', in *Medieval Women and Their Objects*, ed. Jenny Adams and Nancy M. Bradbury (Ann Arbor: University of Michigan Press, 2017), 144–70 (147).
53. Jocelyn Wogan-Browne, 'Parchment and Pure Flesh: Elizabeth de Vere, Countess of the Twelfth Earl of Oxford, and Her Book' in *Medieval*

Women and Their Objects, ed. Jenny Adams and Nancy M. Bradbury (Ann Arbor: University of Michigan Press, 2017), 171–200.
54. Alexandra Barratt, 'Dame Eleanor Hull: The Translator at Work', *Medium Ævum* 72.2 (2003), 277–96.
55. Patricia Demers, '"God may open more than man maye vnderstande": Lady Margaret Beaufort's Translation of the *De Imitatione Christi*', *Renaissance and Reformation* 35.4 (2012), 45–61.
56. Ruby Lal, 'Historicizing the Harem: The Challenge of a Princess's Memoir', *Feminist Studies* 30.3 (2004), 590–616 (609).
57. Lal, 'Historicizing', 601.
58. Gulbadan Banu Begum, *The History of Humāyūn (Humāyūn-nāma)*, trans. by Annette Susannah Beveridge (London: Royal Asiatic Society, 1902), 102.
59. Lubaaba Al-Azami, 'Gulbudan Banu Begum: Princess and Pilgrim', *Medieval and Early Modern Orients*, 6 August 2020: memorients.com/articles/gulbudan-banu-begum-princess-and-pilgrim.
60. Lal, 'Historicizing', 592.
61. Ruby Lal, personal email communication, 13 August 2020. Lal's full analysis will appear in *Royal Vagabond: The Great Adventures of Gulbadan* (New Haven, CT: Yale University Press, 2024).
62. Tyler, *England in Europe*, 284.

Further Reading

Dockray-Miller, Mary (2015). *The Books and the Life of Judith of Flanders*, Burlington, VT: Ashgate.
Jasperse, Jitske Verfasser (2020). *Medieval Women, Material Culture, and Power: Matilda Plantagenet and Her Sisters*, Leeds: ARC Humanities Press.
Lal, Ruby (2024). *Royal Vagabond: The Great Adventures of Gulbadan*, New Haven, CT: Yale University Press.
Martin, Therese, ed. (2012). *Reassessing the Roles of Women as 'Makers' of Medieval Art and Architecture*, Leiden: Brill.
Scott-Stokes, Charity (2006). *Women's Books of Hours in Medieval England*, Library of Medieval Women, Woodbridge: D. S. Brewer.
Smith, Lesley M., and Jane H. M. Taylor, eds. (1997). *Women and the Book: Assessing the Visual Evidence*, Toronto: University of Toronto Press.
Tanner, Heather, ed. (2019). *Medieval Elite Women and the Exercise of Power, 1100–1400: Moving Beyond the Exceptionalist Debate*, New York: Palgrave.
Tyler, Elizabeth M. (2017). *England in Europe: English Royal Women and Literary Patronage, c.1000–c.1150*, Toronto: University of Toronto Press.
Woodacre, Elena, ed. (2018). *A Companion to Global Queenship*, Leeds: ARC Humanities Press.

CHAPTER 3

Woman-to-Woman Initiatives Between English Female Religious

Mary C. Erler

Vertical and Horizontal Learning

The connection between women and their male spiritual advisors has been the subject of much influential scholarship. The relationship has elements of the familial (father/daughter), the intellectual (teacher/student), and perhaps, what is more difficult to discern, the reciprocal (friend/friend). All of these aspects have provided ways of thinking about what was a central influence for both religious and lay women, surprisingly many of whom had 'ghostly fathers'.

Without question, this male–female bond, in its many easily visible forms, was vitally important to women's intellectual and spiritual lives. Linkages that have been more difficult to see, however, may call for attention. In what ways did women support each other intellectually or spiritually? How were women active – on behalf of other women – in the formation process at the centre of religious life? The most accessible instances are those which replicate the familiar male–female hierarchical relationship, though shared between two women. For example, we might examine the acquisition of books by abbesses and prioresses for the benefit of the community and, as well, the subsequent deployment of these books inside the community by superiors, via institutional reading at table and collation. In these examples of learning via traditional vertical interaction, a highly placed woman helps another with more limited resources, and such examples recall the act of reading, or the provision of books, by male spiritual directors to female clients.

Recent work on what has been called 'horizontal learning' opens another set of possibilities: of 'knowledge transmitted and acquired in a context of informal interactions'.[1] In this context, learning is firmly linked to the social and even physical environment in which it takes place; indeed it can involve adoption of a behavioural pattern and mindset, as well as factual knowledge, and its progress contributes to the formation of a collective identity.² Although this horizontal perspective has been used in both male and female religious formation, here we might ask whether there are particular ways of exploring female religious life that would illuminate this aspect of religious growth, with its strong emphasis on community.

Two examples from the English Birgittine abbey of Syon illustrate different ways of effecting personal change. Though the responsibilities of female heads of houses were richly diverse, at the centre was the religious formation of the nuns they ruled. Syon's abbess was reminded on every profession day that she had the responsibility of making her novices more holy. In a pontifical belonging to Archbishop of Canterbury Henry Chichele (1364–1443), a mid-fifteenth-century hand (before 1470) has written in the margins what the archbishop must say to the abbess at that ceremony:

> Doughter . . . I commende to þi kepyng þe sowles of þees spowses of god þe which yif be þi negligence þei falle our lord Ihu crist shal axe of hem of þe / kepe hem þerfore in such wyse þat at such tyme as þou shal answere for hem / þou maist yelde hem more holyer þan þou receyuest hem.³

Though this caution comes from the Birgittine Rule, accountability is similarly stressed in the widely used Benedictine Rule, where the second chapter warns the superior twice that she or he will answer for assigned souls on Judgment Day. The episcopal command to Syon's abbess, however, is slightly different: it focuses on the process of religious life and the gradual transformation that life is expected to produce. Although it deputises the abbess to be the instrument of that long change and hence takes a conventional vertical approach to formation, nonetheless its recognition of religious life as a process is implicit in the use of the comparative ('more holyer þan þou receyuest hem') to describe the slow acculturation particular to horizontal instruction.

A second illustration is narrower in its focus. A guide written for Syon novices, the *Dyetary of ghostly helthe* (STC 6833), recommends 'In your study and redynge of bokes . . . marke well all suche thynges as make to the exemple of good lyfe / bothe for to fele at your selfe / and to shewe it vnto other for the same intent' (sig.a vi). Here the traditional superior/inferior relationship between teacher and student is bypassed in favour of a change in perspective offered between peers. Moreover, the shared reading produces a shared emotional response ('fele at your selfe'). Thus, from the first days of the postulants' training in the Syon 'womanhouse', what might be called mutual formation becomes familiar as an aspect of community life.

Vertical Formation by the Superior

The Superior and the Rule

For nuns the Rule was a central teaching tool, but particularly for Syon, whose Rule stipulated that it be read aloud weekly. The two manuscripts of the Rule edited in facsimile by James Hogg do not show markings that would identify them as refectory reading.[4] However, describing some mid-fifteenth-century fragments of the Birgittine Rule discovered at Syon, Christopher de Hamel says that because 'medieval pauses and punctuation have been overwritten in red ink ... they are likely to be salvage from the Syon refectory at Isleworth'.[5] Acquisition of the Rule followed by a particular house might often be occasional rather than planned, in men's houses as well as women's. Writing about the development of monastic libraries, Richard Sharpe calls it 'for the most part accidental, by bequest or gift ... There is no evidence that librarians in ordinary circumstances had sufficient resources at their disposal to acquire books.'[6] Hence, the following examples in describing particular initiatives by female superiors enlarge our understanding of what was possible.

Two manuscripts of female formation can be connected with Syon (one certainly, the other probably), and in both cases with abbess Elizabeth Gibbs. Not formally belonging to any particular religious order, these instructions nonetheless resemble rules in their formal regulation of life. *The Manere of Good Lyvyng* is a translation of an early thirteenth-century tract written for a religious woman, *Liber de modo bene vivendi ad sororem*.[7] It was thought to have been composed by St Bernard and 'sent unto his own suster wherein is conteyned the Summe of every virtue necessary unto Cristis religion and holy conversation'.[8] A comprehensive overview of religious life, its principal source is Ps. Hugh of St Victor's commentary on the Augustinian Rule, according to its editor.[9] The *Manere's* Middle English translator is unknown; it survives in a single manuscript (Oxford, Bodleian Library, MS Laud Misc. 517) written by the Sheen Carthusian scribe William Darker.[10] Because in 1502 Darker produced another manuscript for Syon abbess Elizabeth Gibbs containing the first three books of the *Imitatio Christi* (Glasgow, Glasgow University Library, MS Hunter 136 (T.6.18)), it has been thought likely that the *Manere of Good Lyvyng* was also her commission – but more especially because its source, the *Liber de modo bene vivendi ad sororem*, was particularly favoured by St Birgitta. Its editor has observed that a Latin manuscript of the *Liber* in Sweden has this inscription: 'Our blessed mother St Birgitta continuously carried this book, which is entitled the doctrine of Bernard to his sister, in her lap and for this reason it must be kept among her relics.'[11] As the text has a somewhat rule-like quality suitable for training in the virtues of religious life, it constitutes a desirable acquisition for the superior of a female house.

The *Liber de modo bene vivendi* shares its comprehensive quality with a second thirteenth-century work on formation, David of Augsburg's (d. 1272) influential *Formula novitiorum*, and the two texts have been characterised as early and inclusive efforts at shaping religious life.[12] A Franciscan work, the *Formula* has been compared in importance with the *Meditationes vitae Christi* and the *Stimulus amoris*; the survival of its Latin manuscripts, like theirs, was widespread. Its author had been a novice-master in Regensburg and papal visitor to convents of women canons elsewhere in Germany. His work comprises three books; only the first is on the training of religious, while the second and third treat progress in the spiritual life more generally.[13] Michael Sargent has explored the relationships of the Middle English manuscripts of this text. The latest of these, Cambridge University Library, MS Dd.ii.33, was both copied and translated for the nuns by a brother of Syon, Thomas Prestius. The manuscript comes from the early sixteenth century; Abbess Gibbs ruled from 1497 to 1518, but because the year in which Prestius entered Syon is not known, whether the translation was a commission by the abbess is uncertain. The institutional focus on formation found in both these substantial, classic works – the *Liber de modo bene vivendi* and the *Formula novitiorum* – is, however, clear. The *Formula* was a keystone of the reading recommended in a 1510 treatise written for Dutch Franciscan tertiaries. Its editor says the convent, St Agnes in Amersfoort, 'did not belong to the sphere of influence of the Franciscans' but was 'one of the manifestations of the Modern Devotion'. Its confessor, Jan de Wael, addressed his *Manual for the Young Ones* to three groups of nuns and listed appropriate reading for each. Beginners (those in their first seven years, up to age thirty) were to read David of Augsburg's first book of the *Formula novitiorum*, 'which was used as a handbook for novices to get acquainted with their new life'. The more advanced groups were to read the following two books.[14] Syon's acquisition of these classics demonstrates its participation in the centuries-old mainstream of spiritual training for women.

Another example of a female superior's acquisition of the Rule shows a different set of circumstances. Prioress Margaret Stanburne of the Lincolnshire Benedictine house of Stamford owned one of the only two surviving copies of Bishop Richard Fox's 1517 edition of the *Rule of seynt Benet* (STC 1859).[15] The book bears three kinds of annotations. First, a reader has carefully copyedited the text: emending misspellings, supplying omissions, altering printed letters to conceal errors, and substituting correct readings for mistakes. The text's editor attributes this work to Prioress Stanburne 'and possibly other nuns',[16] as well as to a seventeenth-century hand, probably that of antiquarian Humphrey Dyson, whose signature appears on the title page. Second, the prioress has written her name six times in the book: near the beginning and the end, and four times elsewhere. The signatures correlate with the text – that is, they appear where the text speaks of the abbess. They are placed on the bottom margin of pages that discuss the responsibilities of the female head of house. The first signature, for example, accompanies chapter 2, on the qualities of the abbess. Third, someone has written 'Nota' marginally eleven times. The *Rule*'s editor assigns two of these occurrences to Prioress Stanburne, but does not observe that, like the signatures, the marginalia accompany passages about the duties of the abbess or prioress.

Examination of the first category, the editorial copyediting, shows high levels of attention and accuracy. Two passages raise the possibility that the prioress might not simply have been correcting the book from a critical reader's perspective but might have been using a Latin text of the Benedictine Rule. In the first instance the reviser changes the print's 'frutfull' to the correct 'ferefull' (sig. D iv v): 'understondynge the frutfull sentence of the apostle / saynge suche a woman is geuen to the deuyll', where the Latin reads 'terribilem'. This change is signalled by the use of a caret, which the text's editor associates with the sixteenth-century hand belonging to Dame Margaret. In a second substantial change the print's reading 'vnfrutfull' is altered to 'vnfaythfull' (sig. D v v): 'An vnfrutfull person / if she goo / let hir goo / lesse oon scabbyd shepe do infect … the hole flocke'. Here the Latin has 'infidelis'. Since this change is not signalled with a caret, whether it belongs to the prioress, and thus whether Margaret Stanburne was Latinate, remains unclear.

More information about the prioress became available with the publication of David Smith's catalogue of English heads of religious houses.[17] Smith notes that Margaret Stanburne came to Stamford from a larger Cistercian nunnery, Stixwould, in 1523, after the resignation of Alice Andrewe, Stamford's previous prioress, who was still receiving her pension in 1526. Stanburne was appointed by Bishop of Lincoln John Langland as compromissary, or compromise candidate. Her copious annotations in her copy of Fox's English rule, sometime between her appointment on 4 December 1523 and her death on 12 May 1529, seem to illustrate a strong desire, perhaps even an anxiety, to master her new position – or perhaps simply the wish to meet the obligations with which every religious Rule confronts its superior.

The Superior and Devotional Books

The manuscripts discussed so far, probably or certainly commissioned by a superior, have been related to the religious rule of life, yet we may wonder about the degree of access to the rule that many nuns had. In the fifteenth century, devotional texts may have represented a more accessible instrument of formation, available to both lay and religious women. An instance of an abbess using her personal resources to acquire a devotional book for her house, rather than a Rule or commentary, is provided by Elizabeth Horwode, the abbess of the London minoresses. She 'bow3th' a manuscript of three Walter Hilton texts, as an inscription in the manuscript says (London, British Library, MS Harley 2397), probably during the time she was superior between 1455/56 and 1481, since a later inscription says it belongs 'to the abbessry' [office of the abbess], 'hyt to Remayne to the vse off the Systeris of the sayde place'.[18] Whether this annotation was written by the abbess or by a later hand, the statement underlines the writer's understanding of the formative use of Hilton's writings.[19] A. I. Doyle discovered that the abbess was enabled to buy the book thanks to a monetary bequest from a friend of her father who was mentioned in the book's inscription.[20] Abbess Horwode's exercise of what might be called the initiative of office must stand in for other instances in which the superior's understanding of the duty of guidance was strengthened by monetary gifts from family and friends.

The difficulties a superior could encounter in the acquisition of books are illustrated by a Syon-initiated lawsuit filed by Abbess Agnes Jordan (The National Archives (hereafter TNA) C1/579/15). Vincent Gillespie has recorded the presence of London alderman and sheriff Richard Grey's name in the list of Syon's benefactors and special friends, together with a gift of forty pounds or more and the date of 1515. Because Grey's name appears in a six-volume bible printed in Basel, 1504, in Syon's library, it seems likely that the bequest was book-related.[21] Sometime between 1520 and 1529, however, Abbess Jordan sued Grey's estate (he had died suddenly on 20 October 1515), testifying that Grey had promised forty pounds to 'Elizabeth late abbess' (Elizabeth Gibbs, 1497–1518) and that ten pounds remained unpaid. Though the outcome is unknown, the lawsuit is a valuable record of Abbess Jordan's care for her responsibilities. The efforts of these women – Elizabeth Gibbs, Margaret Stanburne, Elizabeth

Horwode, and Agnes Jordan – enable us to see female attention to the realities of governance in various forms: obtaining the texts which would enlarge community understanding of a shared life, or presenting the requirements of that life, or reflecting on and studying a personal role in its development.

The Superior's Deployment of Books

In what ways did superiors ensure that the volumes they had acquired were profitably employed? We might imagine these books as used in private reading through the superior's agency, but more likely and more effective was the superior's selection of table reading for the entire house at meals. The sixteenth-century Vadstena abbess Anna Fickonis commissioned such refectory-collections for Syon's Swedish motherhouse, using similar earlier Vadstena table books as sources for the new ones. The first volume, the only one to survive, is dated 1502. It covers the calendar from 28 October to 1 January; the second book contained material from 1 January to Trinity Sunday, and the third began with that feast and ended with saints Simon and Jude. The books contain excerpts from Birgitta's revelations correlated with the liturgy of the day, Swedish translations of the *Legenda aurea*, the *Meditationes vitae Christi*, Mechthild's revelations, Suso's *Horologium divinae sapientiae*, and, of course, the Bible.[22] Interest in several of these works was shared by English nunneries: most popular was the *Legenda aurea*, mentioned in documents from six houses (Ankerwyke, Bruisyard, Kilburn, Kington St Michael, Holywell, Minster in Sheppey). Nicholas Love's translation of the *Meditationes vitae Christi*, the *Mirror of the Blessed Life of Christ*, appears four times (Barking, Nun Monkton, Sinningthwaite, Syon), while an English translation of Suso's *Horologium* was owned by Ankerwyke, Campsey, and Dartford.[23] The interest in saints' lives shown by the several copies of the *Legenda aurea* is visible in Campsey's fourteenth-century Anglo-Norman manuscript, which contains thirteen lives including St Elizabeth of Hungary and St Paul the Hermit and which has an inscription designating it for refectory reading.[24]

Another reading, chosen by the abbess, could occur at the weekly chapter (held at Syon on Thursday)[25] or late in the day at collation, the gathering after the evening meal and before compline. Isabelle Cochelin has given an attractive picture of twelfth-century male chapter activity during the abbacy of Peter the Venerable at Cluny (1122–56): 'Abbots were chosen there, novices were accepted, the unwell announced their departure to the infirmary and books, such as the Rule of St Benedict, spiritual treatises, and outside correspondence were read out loud.' She describes the chapter's 'didactic role as a sort of classroom and newsroom' where monks 'sometimes listened to sermons from visitors or senior monks and then discussed them'.[26] Separate chapters were held for women and men at Syon; the fifteenth-century *Additions for the Sisters* says that the chapter house was the place where deaths of brothers and sisters of the chapter (Syon-affiliated laypersons) were announced and the *De profundis* was said for them. Following this, 'And alle thynges tretyd than to be tretyd ... [that is, once the agenda had been completed] than / the legister schal rede what someuer the abbes assygneth'.[27] A. I. Doyle has noted one example of such reading: Longleat MS 14, a copy of Nicholas Love's *Mirror*, has 'an added list of chapters to be read at collation ... with an invocation of St Brigit of Sweden, suggesting Syon'.[28] Besides readings, the abbess's discretionary choice probably included speaking invitations. It is likely, for instance, that the first master of Jesus College Cambridge, William Chubbes, was known to the nuns of Syon through his preaching – perhaps in the chapter house. Chubbes had been a fellow of Pembroke College Cambridge at the same time as Syon's fifth Confessor, General Stephen Sandre, and he was a protégé of Margaret Beaufort.[29] A later fellow of Pembroke, Syon monk William Bonde, addressing the Syon nuns in his *Directory of Conscience* (STC 3275), recalls him fondly: 'that noble and deuoute clerke whom I suppose ye both knewe and loued for his singular vertew doctor chubbes' (sig. c iii). The chapter's 'newsroom' function noted by Cochelin at Cluny comes to mind in the account of the Bishop of London and the Confessor General's 1535 visit to the Syon nuns' chapter house, in an unsuccessful attempt to enlist the nuns' support for the king.[30] This female gathering place thus might seem a primary arena of activity for the abbess's efforts at formation.

Vertical and Horizontal Formation by the Community

In addition to these examples of vertical interaction, it may be that a horizontal instructive relation between religious was part of the formation process, either formally or informally. On Syon's profession day, the abbess gave a 'lytle exhortacion' to the sisters. It makes the role of horizontal learning explicit: 'do nothyng, but that the comen rewle commaundeth, or that the gode ensample of ȝour eldres enformeþ ȝowe. Lernyng of one [sister] mekenes, of anoþer pacience, of another deuocion, of another discrete abstinence, of another contynence, of another to kepe streyte sylence.'[31] Growth in the spiritual life of the community through imitation of others, as here, can be supplemented by reading, both when shared by peers with one another, as mentioned earlier, and when recommended by elders. The Dutch *Manual for the Young Ones* describes the role of elder sisters, specifying particular texts senior nuns should read 'as an aid for [them] to choose the right reading material for the young sister ... suitable for her stage of development'.[32]

The inscriptions left in women's books sometimes suggest a sponsoring relation and at other times can seem instead to witness a connection of friendship. Bell identifies several English houses where more than one owner's name is found in surviving books – Campsey, Dartford, the Aldgate minoresses and Syon – and behind these instances a variety of circumstances can be seen. At the death of a religious, her or his possessions were distributed as appropriate, and books went sometimes to the library, sometimes to individuals. At St Augustine's abbey, Canterbury, 'the customary specifically stated that in such circumstances it was the precentor's duty to take such books and to write the dead monk's name in them before bearing them off to the library'.[33] Some such procedure explains the presence of both Edyth Morepath's (d. 1536) and Kathryn Palmer's (d. 1576) names in a Syon copy of the 1493 edition of *The Chastysing of Goddes Chyldern* (STC 5065).[34] Kathryn Palmer appears in the boarding accounts for 1532–3,[35] presumably during her year of proof, hence she probably received Edyth Morepath's book at the elder nun's death, either from Morepath or more likely from the abbess. Sometimes these names reveal an in-house book exchange chain which includes both lay and religious women, as in a psalter which laywoman Betrice Carneburgh gave to London minoress Grace Centurio 'to have it to her for terme of her lyfe and aftir her discesse to remayne unto what syster of the Meneres that it shall please the same grace to gyf it'.[36]

Describing book exchange by Florentine nuns, Melissa Moreton says 'Passing of a book from one very devout female religious to another was a way for an experienced nun to foster the spiritual formation of a younger member of her community ... It was also a way for the donor ... to develop like-minded future leadership within the house.'[37] Evidence from Campsey in a formerly untraced copy of the 1493 *Chastysyng* now at the Morgan Library[38] shows that Elizabeth Wyllowby gave the book to Catherine Symonde; as with the minoresses's book, Catherine was to give it onward to 'one of the Sisters'. Bell noted that both women were present at visitations in 1514 and 1526, though in 1532 Elizabeth was absent. This suggestion of an age difference can be confirmed by evidence from a 1499 will which leaves five marks to Elizabeth Willughby [Wyllowby], nun of Campsey, demonstrating that Elizabeth's entrance to religious life was probably earlier than Catherine's.[39] As with the Morepath-Palmer volume, it seems the book was transmitted from an older to a younger nun. In addition, in 1532, after Elizabeth's disappearance Catherine held the office of subprioress, thus confirming Moreton's suggestion that book gifts were sometimes made by an elder sister as part of an informal process of education and training for leadership.

Besides such evidence of female guidance of other women, are there any witnesses to explicit female teaching? Two surviving books suggest two different modes. The first example was discovered three decades ago in a Syon manuscript when scholars were searching for signs of female scribal activity; it is now quite well known. Next to some prayers that she has transcribed in the book, the writer says 'Good Syster of yor charyte I you pray / remember the scrybeler when that ye may / with an aue maria or els thys swete word Ihesu.' The marginal monogram of Sister EW has been thought to belong to the eldest nun at the abbatial election in 1518, Sister Elizabeth Woodford, who might be either the writer or the owner of Lambeth Palace Library, MS 546.[40] Though the page does illustrate female scribal ability, in this context its value is rather its revelation of a shared culture – the writer's description of herself as a 'scrybeler' is intended to make her colleague smile – in which the assumption of superior/inferior roles in the shared work of prayer is playful rather than hierarchical.

The second example of female teaching, by contrast, is formally instructive rather than companionable. It presents a full-fledged, apparently original, spiritual regimen composed by one woman and directed to another ('religious sustir'); hence, it invokes the familiar relation of teacher and student. It too is likely to be from Syon, since one of its pages includes a cross made of five dots for the five wounds, a Birgittine emblem found in other books.[41] Written in 'a fine gothic formal liturgical bookhand' with coloured initials which have been dated 1430–50,[42] *The Festis and the Passion of Oure Lord Ihesu Crist* comprises a prayer sequence that meditates on the life of Christ. The sequence is preceded by a request to the recipient to pray that the Trinity 'make me a good woman'; it is followed by an epilogue.[43] The author of the most recent description of the manuscript says, 'Most likely the recipient was an enclosed religious woman. The author is learned and represents herself as a guide to others in the contemplative life.'[44] Alexandra Barratt points out that in the prayers the women who were part of Jesus's public life are prominently featured (the Samaritan woman, Mary Magdalen, the woman taken in adultery, the Canaanite woman).[45]

Though the form is instructive, the author nonetheless seeks to eliminate difference between the reader and herself and thus to transform this traditional vertical relationship of teacher and student into a horizontal one. She is deferential: 'I have set yow in this writing of lesse pris than I hope ye been in the syght of God', because of the importance of humility.[46] The author concludes the epilogue by recommending that the reader memorise the prayers: 'I wolde ye couden the sentence [meaning] withoutyn the book, for and ye so coude, ye schulden fele mochil more comforth and unyon in God to seye it so inforth, than forto seie it be scripture.' The tentative and provisional nature of this recommendation ('I wolde ye couden ... and [if] ye so coude'), framed as a suggestion, carefully avoids the language of authority in pursuing the gradual growth that religious life entails.

An attempt to create a community behaviour in which explicit signs of authority were lessened can be seen in the Syon instructions for the chantress. Since she was responsible for announcing in chapter the names of those who had committed faults in performance of divine service, she must be particularly careful to cultivate a manner which makes authority acceptable: to do nothing 'troblesly or commaundyngly', but in this exercise requiring submission from others, she must do everything 'quietly pesybly, religiously, and charitably, with goodly wordes or sygnes, and with maner of a mylde besechyng, that the sustres haue a ioy to do anythyng after her. For oftentymes, statly and vnreligious porte, causeþ murmur and grudgynge, to other, and excludeth grace from both partyes.'[47] This effort to minimise the hazards of an essentially authoritative system was deliberately framed to produce a culture of what might be called performative equality. This perspective recognises that harshness, or even excessive formality, 'excludeth grace from both partyes', both superior and inferior, and thus it attempts to devise an ethos that, once learned, would embody in social forms a commitment to monastic ideals of humility and love.

Syon's *Dyetary of ghostly helthe* (STC 6833), meditating on obedience, impels its novices even further towards this mode of behaviour: 'And it is specyally good to obey one to another / yf it letteth not the obedyence to the superyour. A true obedyencer is gladde to be seruyseable vnto euery one of his company / & sory to be chargeable or comberous to them. Louynge & gentyll to all / & deuoute vnto god' (sig. c. iv). Presented as an element in denial of self, this religious practice must also have been responsible for eliding many of the ordinary frictions of community life. At Syon, where this aspect of horizontal formation seems to have been most consciously developed, it may even have produced for community members a personal style especially mild and courteous, part of the gradual growth in holiness anticipated on profession day.

Notes

1. The phrase is from editors Micol Long, Tjamke Snijders, and Steven Vanderputten's 'Introduction' to *Horizontal Learning in the High Middle Ages: Peer-to-Peer Knowledge Transfer in Religious Communities* (Amsterdam: Amsterdam University Press, 2019), 9.
2. Tjamke Snijders, 'Communal Learning and Communal Identities in Medieval Study: Consensus, Conflict, and the Community of Practice', in *Horizontal Learning*, ed. Long et al., 17–46.
3. Martyn F. Wakelin, 'A New Vernacular Version of a Nun's Profession', *Notes & Queries* 229 (1984), 459–61. The manuscript is London, British Library, Additional MS 6157. Cambridge, Trinity College, MS B.XI.9 is also attributed to Chichele: see J. Brückmann, 'Latin Manuscript Pontificals and Benedictionals in England and Wales', *Traditio* 29 (1973), 391–458. The material written into Chichele's pontifical is part of a fuller description of the ceremonies of profession day, not found in the Syon *Additions for the Sisters* in London, British Library, Arundel MS 146, though the Arundel manuscript's chapter xvi is titled 'Of the Observaunce aboute, and in the day of profession'. The further material appears (in Latin) in British Library, Additional MS 5208, from which it was translated by George F. Aungier and inserted after chapter xvi in his edition of the *Additions for the Sisters* based on Arundel 146: *The History and Antiquities of Syon Monastery* ... (London: J. B. Nichols and Son, 1840), 312–16.
4. James Hogg (ed.), *The Rewyll of Seynt Sauioure ... edited from ... Cambridge University Library Ff.6.33 ... Analecta Cartusiana*, vol. 183 (Salzburg: Institüt für Anglistik und Amerikanistik, 2003).
5. Christopher de Hamel, *Syon Abbey: The Library of the Birgittine Nuns and Their Peregrinations after the Reformation* (Smith Settle: Oxley, Roxburghe Club, 1991), 71–2. The fragments are now at Exeter University. See also N. R. Ker and A. J. Piper (eds.), *Medieval Manuscripts in British Libraries IV* (Oxford: Oxford University Press, 1992), 348–9.
6. Richard Sharpe, 'The Medieval Librarian', in *The Cambridge History of Libraries in Britain and Ireland*, vol. 1: *to 1640*, ed. Elisabeth Leedham-Green and Teresa Webber (Cambridge: Cambridge University Press, 2006), 218–41 (219).
7. J. P. Migne (ed.), *Patrologia Latina* (Paris: Migne, 1844–65), 184: 1199–306.
8. Anne McGovern Mouron, '"Listen to me, daughter, listen to a faithful counsel": The *Liber de modo bene vivendi ad sororem*', in *Writing Religious Women: Female Spiritual and Textual Practices in Late Medieval England*, ed. Denis Renevey and Christiania Whitehead (Cardiff: University of Wales Press, 2000), 81–106.
9. Anne E. Mouron (ed.), *The Manere of Good Lyvyng: A Middle English Translation of Pseudo-Bernard's* Liber de modo bene vivendi ad sororem (Turnhout: Brepols, 2014), 3, 13.
10. A. I. Doyle, 'William Darker: The Work of an English Carthusian Scribe', in *Medieval Manuscripts, Their Makers and Users: A Special Issue of Viator in*

Honor of Richard and Mary Rouse, ed. Christopher Baswell (Turnhout: Brepols, 2011), 199–211.
11. Uppsala University Library, UUB, MS C 240.
12. Peter S. Jolliffe calls the *Formula novitiorum* 'one of the longest of its kind extant in Middle English' (273) and says 'perhaps of the tracts intended for Religious, that most comparable in size and treatment is the manere of good lyuynge in Bodleian MS Laud misc 517', 'Middle English Translations of *De Exterioris et Interioris Homines Compositione*', *Mediaeval Studies* 36 (1974), 259–77, n. 80.
13. Michael G. Sargent, 'David of Augsburg's *De Exterioris et Interioris Hominis Compositione* in Middle English', in *Satura: Studies in Medieval Literature in Honour of Robert R. Raymo*, ed. Nancy M. Real and Ruth E. Steinglanz (Donington: Shaun Tyas, 2001), 74–102. For more on this work, see Bert Roest, *Franciscan Literature of Religious Instruction before the Council of Trent* (Leiden: Brill, 2004), 209–14.
14. Sabrina Corbellini, '*The Manual for the Young Ones* by Jan de Wael (1510): Pastoral Care for Religious Women in the Low Countries', in *A Companion to Pastoral Care in the Late Middle Ages (1200–1500)*, ed. Ronald J. Stansbury (Leiden: Brill, 2010), 389–411.
15. Barry Collett (ed.), *Female Monastic Life in Early Tudor England with an Edition of Richard Fox's Translation of the Benedictine Rule for Women, 1517* (Aldershot: Ashgate, 2002).
16. Prioress Stanburne's editing of her print recalls the similar work of two Syon nuns, Margaret Windsor and Dorothy Codrington, whose correction of the prints of *The tree and xij frutes* from a Syon manuscript of the text, London, British Library, Additional MS 24192, has been described by J. J. Vaissier (ed.), *A deuout treatyse called the tree &.xii. frutes of the holy ghost* ... (Groningen: J. B. Wolters, 1960).
17. David M. Smith (ed.), *The Heads of Religious Houses: England and Wales, III.1377–1540* (Cambridge: Cambridge University Press, 2008), Stamford: III. 694; Stixwould: III.697.
18. N. R. Ker (ed.), *Medieval Libraries of Great Britain: A List of Surviving Books* (London: Royal Historical Society, 1964): mlgb3.bodleian.ox.ac.uk.
19. Michael Sargent has pointed out the textual relation of the Minoresses manuscript to other members of the London group of manuscripts of Hilton's *Scale of Perfection, Book II*, particularly to London, Lambeth Palace MS 472, one of the 'common profit' manuscripts intended to pass from hand to hand. That instead the abbess purchased the manuscript, according to its inscription, makes the circumstances of its acquisition puzzling. Michael G. Sargent (ed.), *Walter Hilton's The Scale of Perfection Book II*, Early English Text Society O.S. 348 (Oxford: Oxford University Press, 2017), xliii–xliv.
20. A. I. Doyle, *A Survey of the Origins and Circulation of Theological Writings in England in the 14th, 15th and early 16th Centuries* ... Unpublished PhD thesis, Cambridge University, 1953, vol. III, 213. In 1437 Robert Alkerton left twenty

shillings to Elizabeth and the same amount to the house. Doyle suggested that due to the similarity of their contents the manuscript was probably derived from Syon SS 2, M 26, an erased inscription in the Syon catalogue, and noted its membership in the London group.

21. Vincent Gillespie (ed.), *Syon Abbey with the Libraries of the Carthusians edited by A. I Doyle* (London: British Library and British Academy, 2001), 580–1.
22. Jonas Carlquist, 'Food for the Spirit: On the Table Reading of the Vadstena Sisters', *Birgittiana* 18 (2004), 125–33. The surviving volume is Stockholm, Kungl. Biblioteket, Cod. Holm. A.3.
23. David N. Bell, *What Nuns Read: Books and Libraries in Medieval English Nunneries* (Kalamazoo: Cistercian Publications, 1995), 225, 227.
24. London, British Library, MS Additional 70513; Bell, *What Nuns Read*, 124–5. The length ranges from two or three to sixty-seven leaves, so some readings must have extended for a week or longer. For other examples, see Mary C. Erler, 'Private Reading in the Fifteenth- and Sixteenth-Century English Nunnery', in *The Culture of Medieval English Monasticism*, ed. James G. Clark (Woodbridge: Boydell Press: 2007), 134–46.
25. '... the chapter holde as it is wonte yf it be Thursday'; James Hogg (ed.), *The Rewyll of Seynt Sauioure*, vol. 4, *The Syon Additions for the Sisters from the British Library MS Arundel* 146 (Salzburg: Institüt für Anglistik und Amerikanistik, 1980), 96.
26. Quoted in Marc Saurette, 'Making Space for Learning in the Miracle Stories of Peter the Venerable', in *Horizontal Learning*, ed. Long et al., 115.
27. *The Syon Additions for the Sisters*, 121.
28. A. I. Doyle, 'The Study of Nicholas Love's Mirror, Retrospect and Prospects' in *Nicholas Love at Waseda: proceedings of the international conference 20–22 July 1995*, ed. S. Oguro, R. Beadle, and M. G. Sargent (Cambridge: D. S. Brewer, 1997), 169–70.
29. For Chubbes, see A. B. Emden (ed.), *A Biographical Register of the University of Cambridge* (Cambridge, 1963), 136, and Malcolm G. Underwood, M. Chubbes [Jubbis], William (c. 1444–1505/6), college head. *Oxford Dictionary of National Biography*. Retrieved 24 Feb. 2023, from www-oxforddnb-com.avoserv2.library.fordham.edu/view/10.1093/ref:odnb/9780198614128.001.0001/odnb-9780198614128-e-5379. For Sandre, see Michael Tait, *A Fair Place: Syon Abbey 1415–1539* (np, 2013), 503–6.
30. Aungier, *History ... of Syon*, 88, from J. S. Brewer, et al. (eds.), *Letters and Papers, Foreign and Domestic, of the Reign of Henry VIII* (London: HMSO, 1862–1932), IX. 986.
31. *The Syon Additions for the Sisters*, 99.
32. Corbellini, *Manual*, 402.
33. Nigel Ramsay, 'The Cathedral Archives and Library', in *A History of Canterbury Cathedral*, ed. Patrick Collinson, Nigel Ramsay, and Margaret Sparks (Oxford: Oxford University Press, 1995), 341–407, 371.
34. Bell, *What Nuns Read*, 182–3.
35. TNA, SC6/Hen8/2238.

36. Bell, *What Nuns Read*, 150. The book is described in *Medieval and Renaissance Manuscripts in New Zealand Collections*, ed. M. M. Manion, V. R. Vines and C. F. R. de Hamel (Melbourne: Thames and Hudson, 1989), 119.
37. Melissa Moreton, 'Exchange and Alliance: The Exchange and Gifting of Books in Women's Houses in Late Medieval and Renaissance Florence', in *Nuns' Literacies in Medieval Europe: The Antwerp Dialogue*, ed. Virginia Blanton, Veronica O'Mara, and Patricia Stoop (Turnhout: Brepols, 2017), 383–410 (395).
38. Bell, *What Nuns Read*, 125, prints the inscription from the 1744 Harleian sale catalogue; the remains of the inscription, since washed, were in 2021 discovered in the Morgan Library copy; see the library's online catalogue, *Corsair*: http://corsair.morganlibrary.org. Wyllowby also gave Symonde a Walter Hilton manuscript: Cambridge, Corpus Christi College, MS 268 (Bell, 123).
39. The 1499 will belongs to Christopher Willoghby [Wyllowby], knight, lord of Willoughby and Eresby, Parham, Suffolk: TNA, PROB 11/11/278v–279. It also leaves ten marks to Jane Willoghby [Wyllowby], nun of Bruisyard, and asks for burial at Campsey, 'with my father'.
40. Veronica O'Mara, 'A Middle English Text Written by a Female Scribe', *Notes and Queries* 235 (December 1990), 396–8.
41. Vincent Gillespie, 'Walter Hilton at Syon Abbey' in *Stand Up to Godwards: Essays in Mystical and Monastic Theology in Honour of the Reverend John Clark on His Sixty-Fifth Birthday*, ed. James Hogg (Salzburg: Institüt für Anglistik und Amerikanistik, 2002), 9–61 (59). For other examples, see Mary C. Erler, *Women, Reading, and Piety in Late Medieval England* (Cambridge: Cambridge University Press, 2002), 44; for instance, the Lambeth Palace Library copy of *Mirroure of Our Lady* has this symbol written in ink on the binding of the lower cover (Lambeth 1530.3).
42. Oxford, Bodleian Library, MS Holkham misc. 41; see *Medieval Manuscripts in Oxford Libraries* (https://medieval.bodleian.ox.ac.uk) for 'draft description by Peter Kidd, late 1990s', 'not in *Summary Catalogue* (late accession)'. The text concludes with the Syon- and Sheen-associated verse beginning 'Syke and sorowe depely' (*IMEV* 3102) and is followed by an expanded English translation of the third recension of William Flete's *De remediis contra temptationes*.
43. William F. Pollard, 'Bodleian MS Holkham Misc. 41: A Fifteenth-century Bridgettine Manuscript and Prayer Cycle', *Birgittiana* 3 (1997), 43–53.
44. Jessica Lamothe, 'An edition of the Latin and four Middle English versions of William Flete's *De remediis contra temptationes*', PhD thesis, English, University of York, 2017, https:/etheses.whiterose.ac.uk.
45. Alexandra Barratt (ed.), *Women's Writing in Middle English* (New York: Longman, 1992), 205–18, prints the passages on New Testament women plus the epilogue.
46. Barratt (ed.), *Women's Writing*, 215.
47. Hogg, *Rewyll of Seynt Sauioure*, 150

Further Reading

Bell, David N. (1995). *What Nuns Read: Books and Libraries in Medieval English Nunneries*, Kalamazoo: Cistercian Publications.

Coakley, John (2006). *Women, Men, and Spiritual Power: Female Saints and Their Male Collaborators*, New York: Columbia University Press.

Corbellini, Sabrina (2010). 'The Manual for the Young Ones' by Jan de Wael (1519): Pastoral Care for Religious Women in the Low Countries. In Ronald J. Stansbury, ed., *A Companion to Pastoral Care in the Late Middle Ages (1200–1500)*. Leiden: Brill, 389–411.

Erler, Mary C. (2007). Private Reading in the Fifteenth- and Sixteenth-Century English Nunnery. In James G. Clark, ed., *The Culture of Medieval English Monasticism*. Woodbridge: Boydell Press, 134–46.

Hogg, James, ed. (1980). *The Rewyll of Seynt Sauioure*, vol. 4, *The Syon Additions for the Sisters from the British Library MS Arundel 146*, Salzburg: Institüt für Anglistik und Amerikanistik.

Long, Micol, Tjanke Snijders, and Steven Vanderputten, eds. (2019). *Horizontal Learning in the High Middle Ages: Peer-to-Peer Knowledge Transfer by Religious Communities*, Amsterdam: Amsterdam University Press.

Mouron, Anne E., ed. (2014). *The Manere of Good Lyvyng: A Middle English Translation of Pseudo-Bernard's Liber de modo bene vivendi ad sororem*, Turnhout: Brepols.

O'Mara, Veronica (1990). A Middle English Text Written by a Female Scribe. *Notes and Queries* 235.

II

Circles and Communities in England

CHAPTER 4

Ancrene Wisse, *the Katherine Group,* and the Wooing Group as Textual Communities, Medieval and Modern

Michelle M. Sauer

Ancrene Wisse, the thirteenth-century guidance text for anchoresses, is a central focus of the medieval English religious tradition, even if it took years for modern scholarship to acknowledge this, which makes it at once vitally important and complicated. Similarly, the anchoritic vocation was central to patristic and medieval Christianity even if many people have no idea what it comprises. Anchorites (or anchoresses) were men and women who lived lives of complete isolation in order to spend their days in contemplation and prayer. Many, although certainly not all, of these individuals lived in small cells attached to churches; many also resided in free-standing dwellings or naturally occurring spaces such as caves. The vocation can be traced back to the early Church, and more specifically to St Anthony of Egypt (251–356 CE). Seeking a way to better serve God and resist temptations of the flesh, Anthony sold all his possessions and fled into the desert. Though he lived alone in a cave, eschewing company, still his reputation for holiness drew followers. Eventually, he was persuaded to come out to teach and organise; thus, he is credited both with founding anchoritism and with beginning coenobitism. His life was devoted to prayer and contemplation and perfecting his resistance to temptation. He lived ascetically, without earthly comforts, and chastely, without sexual congress. Medieval anchorites generally followed this same path. Like Anthony, they were not required to profess any formal vows or to join a religious order. They also agreed to live simply and chastely, though *Ancrene Wisse* itself suggests only moderate asceticism. Before embarking upon this life, they petitioned their local bishop, who investigated their spiritual, financial, and emotional backgrounds. Only the strongest individuals who could withstand the rigours of solitude and the temptations of enclosure, as well as those who could support themselves and/or had pledged support, were accepted. Once enclosed, there was no release from the anchoritic life except through physical death. The enclosure rite itself was a type of 'living death' and consisted of a modified form of the requiem mass (Mass for the Dead). Though enclosed, anchorites were still active participants in their communities in numerous ways: they counselled parishioners, advised nobility, offered prayers for those in Purgatory, kept watch over the church, embroidered vestments and illuminated manuscripts, and even taught children.[1] Anchorites, both male and female, were also expected to be able to read, at least in the vernacular, and to consume edifying literature such as devotional treatises and hagiographies (saints' lives), and perhaps even Rules that addressed their vocation, such as *Ancrene Wisse*.

Ancrene Wisse, the Katherine Group, and the Wooing Group are thirteenth-century prose works that are connected to the anchoritic vocation, and even more specifically to the reclusive life for women, thus forming a literary community among the women who read them even though they were physically separated not only from each other but also from the world.[2] Together, these works comprise the *Ancrene Wisse* Group, which encompasses ten texts: *Ancrene Wisse* itself, the Wooing Group ('The Wooing of Our Lord', 'A Song of Praise Concerning Our Lord', 'The Song of Praise Concerning Our Lady', and 'An Exceedingly Good Orison to God Almighty', as well as two fragments, 'An Orison to Our Lord' and 'An Orison to Saint Mary'[3]), and the Katherine Group (three hagiographies – *St Katherine*, *St Margaret*, and *St Juliana* – along with *Sawles Warde* and *Hali Meidenhad*). While the manuscript versions of the Wooing Group are limited in number, both *Ancrene Wisse* and the various Katherine Group texts exist in multiple copies.

Ancrene Wisse is a guide for anchoresses, while the Wooing Group consists of a collection of prayers and prose treatises dedicated to the anchoresses' spiritual relationship with Jesus and/or Mary. The Katherine Group is comprised of several virgin martyr hagiographies that provide a model for spiritual marriage to Christ, as well as two treatises on earthly chastity (*Sawles Warde* and *Hali Meidenhad*). As a whole, these texts combine prayer, edifying reading, and rules with examples and explication as well as practical considerations for being enclosed. More specifically, *Ancrene Wisse*, also known as *Ancrene Riwle*, in its 'proto' form (if indeed there is such an entity) consists of eight sections. Parts One and Eight comprise the 'Outer Rule', which details everyday living, clothes, food, prayers, and dimensions of the cell, and covers regulations regarding activities, daily prayers, and so forth. Parts Two through Seven comprise the 'Inner Rule', that is, the inward contemplative and devotional life of the anchoress. Topics covered include the five senses as guardians and as gateways of temptation, the advantages of the reclusive life, the various temptations that must be resisted (including allegorical representations of the sins), an overview of confession and penance, and many passages devoted to the love of Christ, who is sometimes presented as a lover-knight in the courtly romance tradition. The hagiographies in the Katherine Group (Margaret, Juliana, and the eponymous Katherine) all follow a fairly standard hagiographic narrative. In each, a beautiful young woman is told she must marry a pagan. Each woman refuses because she has already married Christ. She is subsequently tortured – brutally, graphically, and publicly – in an attempt to change her mind and/or to punish her for resisting. She is saved through divine assistance until she is ready to die, whereupon she is beheaded, usually after converting many people. The torture scenes are akin to rape, as the saints are roughly stripped, their bodies are explicitly described, and leering crowds watch eagerly. *Sawles Warde* is an allegorical prose treatise that follows homily form. In it, the soul is represented as a castle where a married couple, Wit and Will, reside. Will is headstrong and does not keep close watch over the guardians of the household, the five senses, who are monitored by God's daughters: Vigilance, Strength, Moderation, and Righteousness. Despairing of the household's laxity, Vigilance sends Fear as a messenger to remind them to guard their senses lest they fall into hell. This sends everyone into sorrowful despair until Vigilance sends Love of Eternal Life to remind them of the bliss of heaven. And *Hali Meidenhad* is a prose treatise that reads like an anti-marriage tract but is supposedly a pro-virginity tract.[4] It is based on Hildebert of Lavardin's early twelfth-century Latin letter to the recluse Athalisa, as well as patristic writings including texts by Jerome and Ambrose.[5] It begins similarly to *Sawles Warde* by comparing the virgin to a tower, but it quickly turns into extremely vivid descriptions of the trials and tribulations of marriage. The author includes husbands who abuse their wives physically, emotionally, financially, sexually, and spiritually; children who are violent, ungrateful, or dead; and everyday life full of bitterness, drudgery, lechery, and filth. This is held in contrast to marriage to Christ, who is the ideal spouse in every way, and assures the virgin a blissful eternal life as well as a less troublesome earthly one. The Wooing Group texts are prayers in which the female speaker either woos Christ or reminds him why she has chosen him as her lover. The Wooing itself is the longest of these, and the most passionate. The speaker assures Christ that he is the most lovely, most kind, most compassionate, most generous spouse available, and that she will give up everyone and everything for him.

Although the anchoritic vocation is the most solitary of existences, its works appear to form a cohesive community. The name *Ancrene Wisse* Group was coined by Bella Millett as a collective way to discuss these texts since they seem to share an audience and premise. Moreover, although certainly similarities had been recognised prior to Millett's work, she was the first champion of a 'unified theory' of their origin, seeing all these prose texts as drawing from various English and Continental religious traditions, but contextualising them within the West Midlands tradition. In particular, she suggests they were part of the growing changes that preceded the Fourth Lateran Council. She especially sees these texts as a triumph of the vernacular and its intersection with both older and newer forms of preaching and pastoral care.[6] Still, she does caution that

> the linking of *AW*, KG, and WG as a larger group is also modern, and there is still no general agreement on whether we are dealing with a single, well-defined *oeuvre* or with a scattering of works by different authors and with ill-defined boundaries. Nevertheless, there are good reasons for treating these works at least provisionally as a single group with a common origin.[7]

Overall, the extant manuscript evidence and internal markers such as language and content, as well as the lingering influence on later texts, demonstrate the significance of this larger group to medieval English spirituality.

The manuscript connections are reasonably easy to trace since the Wooing Group does not have many extant copies. *Uriesun of God Almihti*, *Lofsong of ure Lefdi*, and *Lofsong of ure Laured* are all found in London, British Library, MS Nero A.xiv. Also in this manuscript is a version of *Ancrene Wisse*. The Wooing Group piece *Oriesun of Seinte Marie* is found in London, British Library, MS Royal 17 A.xxvii, as are *Seinte Katherine*, *Seinte Juliana*, and *Seinte Margaret*, as well as *Sawles Warde*. Finally, London, British Library, MS Titus D.xviii contains the only copy of *The Wooing of Our Lord*, along with *Seinte Katherine*, *Hali Meidenhad*, *Sawles Warde*, and a mostly complete but clearly adapted version of *Ancrene Wisse*. There are internal linguistic and thematic connections among the texts as well. For instance, in the introduction to her edition of *St Juliana*, Simonne R. T. O. d'Ardenne describes the *Wohunge* as 'the thoughts and prayers of Juliene written out at large'.[8] The Katherine Group is explicitly connected with *Ancrene Wisse* through textual tradition. *Sawles Warde*, which at first glance could seemingly apply to anyone, is really more suited for contemplatives than others. The description of heaven gives a detailed and vivid account of all the privileges virgins receive. Moreover, the treatise encourages moderation in discipline and in emotion, as does *Ancrene Wisse*.[9] Such themes, including the emotional and erotic connections between the women in the narratives and Jesus, suggest a larger literary community with a shared devotional approach and a mutual affect within religious expression. Other connections are more bare bones but just as useful in outlining a literary network, such as the direct reference to the text of *St Margaret* in Book Four of *Ancrene Wisse*, and the shared opening line among the hagiographies and most versions of *Ancrene Wisse*.

The number of extant manuscripts implies that some women were literate not only in the vernacular, but also at least somewhat in Latin and possibly French. The circulation of these manuscripts, not to mention pieces or passages from them, also demonstrates the importance of female-centred spirituality. We might conclude from this that the medieval English Christian tradition was so deeply concerned with regulating the female body that there was an abundance of texts produced, and, therefore, that more of these texts proportionately survive. Alternatively, and conversely, we might conclude that reclusive women claimed such an important space in the English religious tradition, and perhaps in society, that these texts proliferated – especially versions of *Ancrene Wisse* itself, which was preserved, adapted, circulated, included in miscellanies, and so forth, so that its value could be shared. A synthesis of these two premises is possible as well. Our conclusions depend in part on investigations of *Ancrene Wisse* more than the other texts as it is more widespread in different versions and carried through numerous adaptations. The Wooing texts, in contrast, are found only in one manuscript each. Although the hagiographies and treatises are found in a few manuscripts, the hagiographies have a longer textual history outside this particular context, whereas the treatises, especially *Sawles Warde*, lose favour outside of their era. While the principles of *Hali Meidenhad*, for example, remain popular and present, the central idea of virgins gaining hundredfold rewards, widows sixtyfold, and wives thirtyfold is drawn from Jerome originally, and the presentation of the argument, with its lurid depiction of the marital bed and brutal descriptions of domestic violence, is uniquely constructed to reflect thirteenth-century gentry concerns and the female perspective; the general premise relies on the *molestiae nuptiarum* (tribulations of marriage) tradition.[10] References specifically to Ælred of Rievaulx's *Rule for a Recluse* – an epistle written for his anchoress sister – mark this work as distinctly tied to the reclusive vocation as well. Overall, then, a discussion of the *Ancrene Wisse* Group means an extended discussion about *Ancrene*

Wisse itself, as it had the largest impact on medieval English Christianity. Millett concurs: '*Ancrene Wisse* is the longest, the most complex, and the most influential of an unexpectedly sophisticated group of religious prose works, produced in the West Midlands at a time when relatively little was being written in Middle English, and still less of any literary merit.'[11] During the rise of feminist scholarship in the 1980s, scholars began critically investigating *Ancrene Wisse* in terms of context, including a stronger focus on women's lives and networks as well as its importance to literary history in England. One of the two most impactful books on the study of anchoritism was Ann K. Warren's *Anchorites and their Patrons in Medieval England*, which clearly showed that although anchorites were 'solitaries', they certainly did not exist in a vacuum. Instead, they were vital members of the parish community. And, because they owned, wrote, bequeathed, read, and served as audience for numerous works, they were near the centre of many literary communities, and participants in a strong female literary movement. Other scholarship broadened the examination of gender and sexuality in the anchoritic vocation. This, in turn, led to an expanded definition of what constituted anchoritic works and how mystical texts interacted with more purely regulatory ones. Greater emphasis on how themes overlapped and interwove in various medieval literatures for (and by) women often found *Ancrene Wisse* at the heart of many texts.

Ancrene Wisse was adapted for a wide variety of devotional works in the later Middle Ages, many of which were meant for lay consumption. These adaptations also expanded the audience to include men and included linguistic shifts from the Middle English vernacular to Latin and French. Before we examine that broader literary community, however, we should first address the multiple communities found within *Ancrene Wisse* itself. Seventeen different manuscripts of the work survive today. These range from tiny fragments to complete versions. Clearly, then, *Ancrene Wisse* is not a static text with a single intended audience or even a definitive version. Instead, it is a dynamic literary creation that responds to the needs of adapter and audience. Yet, in modern scholarship, when we talk about *Ancrene Wisse* we often talk about it rather blithely, as if at least three things are true: first, that everyone is at least passingly familiar with the contents of the work; second, that the work falls broadly under the category of 'women's writing'; and third, that there is an agreed-upon version of this work. All three of these assumptions imply that *Ancrene Wisse* has reached at least the threshold of being a canonical work, and if inclusion in the *Norton Anthology of British Literature* is a marker, then it has achieved this status. Since the eighth edition of this anthology, which was first published in 2006, an excerpt from *Ancrene Wisse* has been included in it. It remains rather neglected, however, for a text that was both popular and informative in the Middle Ages – although considering the subject matter, this may not be surprising. For example, the *Prick of Conscience* survives in 130 manuscripts, and is rarely taught, anthologised, or even discussed. Similarly, *De doctrina cordis* (*The Doctrine of the Heart*), a 'relatively understudied text [that] was a devotional best-seller in the medieval period, with more than two hundred manuscripts', has been found in many major libraries and was translated into multiple vernaculars.[12] Despite the numerous adaptations of *Ancrene Wisse*, the general underlying assumption of most scholarship remains that it is a guide, a rulebook of sorts, for anchoresses. At its heart it is, but in many versions that fundamental anchoritic audience is expanded to include male monastics, laypeople, and even heretics. This brings us to the original female-oriented language and the fundamental female community-building sense. The idea that the original audience shaped how the text has been viewed should be acknowledged more directly. So, in considering the female literary communities that formed around and because of this important text, it is also important to investigate the development of the modern concept of *Ancrene Wisse*.

This chapter will now consider the history of scholarship on *Ancrene Wisse* in the late nineteenth and early twentieth centuries, and how this work continues to create a literary community today. Further, it will examine the construction of the female subject and reader both as woman and as anchoress. How does the vocation itself shape authorship and readership? In turn, how is this influence carried through in the various adaptations and versions of the text(s) found over time? How is it shaped by the source texts used, all of which were quite specifically male? Finally, the chapter will address the larger, expanded community created by the works and their influence. This will include a consideration of later works, such as *The Chastising of God's Children* or *The Abbey of the Holy Ghost*, and it will also consider the wider scope of the European community and connections to traditions such as the beguines and hermits. Again, this will result in an examination of women as readers and consumers and also as authors and influencers. Overall, what emerges is the idea of a woman-centred textual and linguistic community that supersedes standard boundaries of chronology and geography.

The first 'modern' edition of *Ancrene Wisse* was by James Morton, published in 1853, and was based on London, British Library, Cotton MS Nero A.xiv – the same manuscript that contains the three major pieces of the Wooing Group aside from 'The Wooing of our Lord'. Calling it

Ancrene Riwle (an unusual choice considering the Corpus manuscript bears the inscription 'Here begins the Ancrene Wisse'), Morton claimed the work was translated from a 'semi Saxon' manuscript of the thirteenth century and subtitled it *A Treatise on the Rules and Duties of Monastic Life*. In his preface, Morton made some erroneous claims that would plague anchoritic studies for more than a century. However, his preface also addresses some of the content beyond philology, unlike the majority of early Early English Text Society editions. He notes that four versions of the text are extant, instead of the seventeen we now know about. He addresses the two manuscripts 'lost' in the Cotton library fire of 1731: MS Vitellius E.vii in Latin, of which only scorched fragments remain, and MS Vitellius F.vii in French. (The latter manuscript was not actually lost, although it was heavily damaged, and an Early English Text Society edition of it was made in 1944.) Interestingly, Morton addresses the issue of trilingualism, and decides in favour of the vernacular. Previous discussants – namely, Thomas Smith, who catalogued the Cottonian collection in 1696; Humphrey Wanley, who catalogued ancient manuscripts in George Hickes' *Thesaurus Linguarum Septentrionalium* (1705); and Joseph Planta, who enlarged the Cottonian catalogue in 1802 – had all agreed (wrongly, as it would turn out) that the Latin text found in Oxford, Magdalen College, MS Latin 67 (*c*. 1400) was the original upon which all the Middle English (here called 'semi-Saxon') versions were based. But Morton is, on a number of points, incorrect, insisting, for example, that the anchoresses were a complete society unto themselves consisting of three women who, 'it is certain ... afterwards they were incorporated with the Cistertian [*sic*] order', and confidently asserting that *Ancrene Riwle* is the 'original and proper title of the work'.[13] He spends a good part of his introduction discussing the men who edited and catalogued the text, the men who supposedly authored the text or had a hand in its authoring (for example, Simon of Ghent and Richard Poor), and the history of the abbey at Tarrant Crawford and the Dissolution; he offers the odd speculation that *Ancrene Wisse* disputes the validity of transubstantiation and devotes multiple pages to exploring the 'Saxon' nature of the language he sees as barely different from that of Laʒamon. Morton's edition had a disproportionate impact on *Ancrene Wisse* studies, as Millett notes, since the Nero manuscript has retained 'a special position in *Ancrene Wisse* studies ... long after its defects had been pointed out'.[14] I would suggest that to this point we add the following: Morton's edition also unduly impacted *Ancrene Wisse* studies by asserting that the work's primary importance was philological and by contextualising it in terms of male-centred authorship rather than the devotional practices of women within the anchoritic vocation. In this way, anchoritic studies for years became about the peripherals involved and the men who made and enforced the rules (and the Rules), losing touch with the female community created during the Middle Ages through the adaptations and various versions of *Ancrene Wisse* and its associated works.

The Early English Text Society capitalised on this philological bent and determined that *Ancrene Wisse* would be the basis for a number of editions, with the possible goal of collating them all at a later point. This process began in 1944, with Herbert's edition of the French text from London, British Library, Cotton MS Vitellius F.vii, and continued through 2006, with the publication of Millett's edition of Cambridge, Corpus Christi College, MS 402, which not only improved and updated Tolkien's 1962 version but also included cross-references to textual variants. Along the way, there were also several translations produced, notably a facing-page edition and translation of the Introduction (sometimes called the Preface) and Part One by Robert W. Ackerman and Roger Dahood (1984), a translation of the complete *Ancrene Wisse* Group by Anne Savage and Nicholas Watson (1992), and Millett's corresponding translation of her edition (2009). The sheer number of modern versions produced – of a text with multiple medieval versions – demonstrates a continuing insistence on the significance of this work. And scholars seemingly agreed with this assessment of *Ancrene Wisse*'s importance as an individual text. However, the emphasis of these undertakings was almost exclusively philological in nature rather than social, let alone feminist. Introductions to Early English Text Society volumes until the twenty-first century contained only rare and brief mention of the contents but extensive commentary on word forms, letter forms, manuscript appearance, scribal hands, and so forth. Much of this is to be expected since these are editions based on individual manuscripts. However, it is still unusual that, for the most part, the editors chose not to even define what is meant by the term 'anchoress'. Anneke Mulder-Bakker has also commented on this frustrating scholarly trend, in particular noting that materials from the nineteenth century, such as encyclopaedias and religious handbooks, genericise the anchoritic experience, reducing it solely to deeply religious women who give up sex and motherhood to marry Christ metaphorically. As Mulder-Bakker notes, 'the scholars who wrote these books, themselves without exception men formed by the nineteenth-century Victorian ideal of the good housewife who longs for her husband or father in the seclusion of their home, could not imagine anything different'.[15] Implied but not articulated is that all these scholars were white, upper-class men. Indeed, it was not until the late twentieth century that scholars of colour and working-class scholars became prominent in the field.

Elizabeth Robertson has pointed out that 'the audience of the *Ancrene Wisse* will always be a fiction, both a historical fiction, one that is inevitably unstable, and a literary fiction found within the text itself'.[16] Yet it is clear that the original audience was female, despite the skittishness of early editions in discussing it. By concentrating on language exclusively and removing the essential 'female-ness' from the text, and by separating the women from their devotions, the various editors managed to situate one of the most explicitly female-centred texts in the early English corpus as one of the most valuable resources on early English even as they denied its feminist implications. Nicholas Watson calls E. K. Chambers and J. R. R. Tolkien 'early champions of *Ancrene Wisse*', based primarily upon Tolkien's (erroneous) assertion about the 'purity' of the so-called AB language in which *Ancrene Wisse* is written in two manuscripts.[17] This is a way to reassert male control over a textual tradition too uncomfortably female to acknowledge. As Watson indicates, 'Tolkien's and Chambers's interest in genealogy also involved casting the language and style of the *Ancrene Wisse* Group in masculine terms, as hallmarks of the "country gentleman" that English had, under the Normans, become'.[18] Morton's early edition kicked this tradition off with his introductory comments about *Ancrene Wisse* being appreciated by the 'class' of individuals who study and appreciate literary antiquities and language history – presumably wealthy white gentlemen. This directly goes against the medieval history of the manuscripts themselves, or at least one of the manuscripts. In Dobson's Early English Text Society edition of London, British Library, Cotton MS Cleopatra CVI, he discusses the provenance of the manuscript for several pages of his introduction. On the flyleaf, in handwriting of *c.* 1300, is an inscription indicating ownership by one 'M. de Clare', presumably Matilda de Clare, Countess of Gloucester and patroness of the Augustinian canonesses at Canonsleigh.[19] Though overlooked in Dobson's introduction, this inscription clearly demonstrates that women read, owned, and circulated books in the vernacular even in the Welsh Marches. Moreover, this was a book about women and for women owned by a woman and given to other women, a gift from a noble lady to a lady abbess. In fact, Matilda was responsible for refounding the house at Canonsleigh as a female monastery in 1284, when it had previously been occupied by monks, further demonstrating the power and influence wielded by an educated woman.

Another way to reassert male control over *Ancrene Wisse* and its associated works was the ever-present insistence on pinning down the (male) author. In this way, a man, presumably a male cleric, is placed as the architect of a way of life that will then be undertaken by women, decentring female spirituality from the heart of the vocation and perhaps nullifying any undue feminising influence on later versions of the work. Many men were suggested over the years, with the most frequent being the ones cited by Morton, namely Richard Poor and Simon of Ghent, but other names thrown into the ring include Gilbert of Sempringham, Robert Bacon, the hermit Godwine, and Brian of Lingen. The latter name was suggested by Dobson as the culmination of years of research encapsulated in his 1976 book *The Origins of Ancrene Wisse*. Dobson believed the author must be an Augustinian canon because of internal evidence, and Brian of Lingen was his choice based on proximity. Millett and more recent critics lean towards a Dominican friar as putative author, while not naming a specific person and also leaving room for the collaborative input of various authors as well as scribal contributions. This position allows for more nuanced readings of the various versions, while also embracing the idea of female authorship. Here, I do not only mean the feminist theory of collaborative feminist thought, but also the ability for the audience of a work to participate in shaping the work itself and its later reception, while also being formed by the work.

Further, more recent ideas about authorship and positionality suggest that medieval authors, scribes, and audiences were aware of the female origins involved and did not object. For example, one of the more interesting variants of *Ancrene Wisse* is Cambridge, Gonville and Caius, MS 234/120. It contains a redacted and rearranged text, including pieces of Parts Three, Four, Five, Six, and Seven, followed by the *Via patrum* (*Lives of the Desert Fathers*) in Latin. As John Scahill notes, 'Cambridge, Gonville and Caius 234/120 (hereafter G) is probably the fourth oldest manuscript of *Ancrene Wisse*, written in the third quarter of the 13th century'.[20] This version of *Ancrene Wisse* was most likely redesigned for use by a group of religious men. Scahill, again referencing Millett, lays out the argument: 'words such as ancre and ancrehuse are generally eliminated, and where other generalising manuscripts tend to add male terms to the female ones, G tends to delete female references entirely'.[21] As well, Scahill sees the radical cutting and readjustment of the order of sections as 'the product of the same operation as the masculinization', and 'in agreement with the clear tendency of the omissions to eliminate sections specifically relevant to anchoresses'.[22] This particular manuscript's scribe took pains to redesign the material to best fit the 'new' audience, the male monastic collective. However, the devotions, admonitions, and suggestions remained the same;

only the external parts of the rule – the ones specifically couched in terms of the female body, dress, and so forth – were removed. It was not, then, enactment of female-centred devotion that was feared by male monastics. The inclusion in this specific manuscript of the *Via patrum* after *Ancrene Wisse* mirrors the connection of *Ancrene Wisse* with the hagiographies found in the Katherine Group. The stories of desert fathers emphasise the same acts of piety encouraged within the anchoritic devotion: withdrawal from earthly concerns, bodily purity and chastity, contemplation and prayer, and asceticism in moderation. Overall, the manuscript demonstrates the influence that writing for women had on greater English religious society, and, in a way, can be seen as an extension of the female literary canon.

Similarly, the version of *Ancrene Wisse* found in London, British Library, Cotton MS Titus D.xviii, the same manuscript in which 'The Wooing of our Lord' is found, contains a modified version probably meant for a mixed male and female audience. Missing from this text are the Preface and most of Part One – again, the Outer Rule, and the portion very specific to female anchorites. Frances Mack, the (female) editor, comments that the scribe is sloppy with his emendations, resulting in 'carelessness in the use of personal pronouns ... particularly evident is the confusion between feminine and masculine that may occur when reference is made to the recluse'.[23] The slippage in pronouns continues throughout, as do both omissions and retentions of phrases such as '(my) dear sister(s)' and the like. Occasional sentences inserted as interpolations add a direction meant specifically for men. But, as Mack concludes in the final sentence of her introduction, 'the essential character of the *Ancrene Riwle* as a work written primarily for the instruction of women recluses has been only superficially disturbed in Titus'.[24] It is interesting that Mack, as the only female editor among the early Early English Text Society versions, is willing baldly to state the obvious. However, none of the implications are explored. Like her counterparts, Mack focused almost solely on linguistics in her opening. I see the fuzzy pronouns in Titus almost as representing a queerly prophetic moment: the later fourteenth-century work 'A Talkyng of the Loue of God' basically merges 'The Wooing of our Lord' with some material from Anselm; however, it is intended for a male monastic audience. To accomplish this switch, the scribe simply replaces female with male pronouns throughout the work, resulting in some luridly eroticised scenes between monks and Christ.[25]

The solely philological bent of *Ancrene Wisse* studies began changing in the 1980s, with the rise of feminist scholarship in the academy having wended its way through to medieval studies. Interestingly, the edition and translation by Robert Ackerman and Roger Dahood offers a judicious look at *Ancrene Wisse* and the life of an anchoress, centring much of the discussion on the vernacular nature of the prayers, the inclusion of 'popular' sources on sin and confession, and the other 'homey' touches found within the text, all of which lend themselves to a woman-centred devotional experience. This woman-centred focus seems to be more present in the translations more generally, in fact, although Sitwell's introduction to Salu's translation contextualises it within a broader male mystical tradition, related to the work of Richard Rolle, *The Cloud of Unknowing*, and Walter Hilton's *The Scale of Perfection*. In contrast, the later translation by Savage and Watson, which includes the entirety of the *Ancrene Wisse* Group, has an extensive introduction that covers the anchoritic vocation, the hagiographic and mystic traditions, and linguistics.

The multiple versions of *Ancrene Wisse*, the adaptations for different groups and different sexes, the relatively wide circulation – all of these demonstrate the history of women's literacy and education in the vernacular as well as the importance of female-centred spirituality. *Ancrene Wisse* is the best-preserved and best-circulated medieval English text for women. On one hand, as noted earlier, we could see this widespread manuscript preservation as a sign of the Middle Ages' deep concern with regulating the female body, signifying that there were so many texts of this kind in circulation that, proportionately, more would end up being saved. Alternatively, we could instead see this extensive preservation as gesturing towards the important space that women, and possibly recluses, claimed in medieval society and Christian devotional life – and the multiple adaptations and excerpts as further demonstrating the lack of fear of this feminine religious expression in later medieval devotional enactment. Though a definitive date for the composition of *Ancrene Wisse* has yet to be decided, it is generally agreed the work was composed in the thirteenth century, right at the cusp of the affective spirituality movement. The three main progenitors of this – Anselm of Canterbury, Bernard of Clairvaux, and Francis of Assisi – all lived in the twelfth century. Their ideas on spiritual affection were being reinterpreted by subsequent generations, a process that would continue as the Middle Ages progressed. We can see the beginnings of this in *Ancrene Wisse*, as the anchoress is certainly constructed as a Bride of Christ. Yet, the language is not as effusive as even that of the related works of the Wooing Group and the Katherine Group, which we can see as enactments of the principles explored in *Ancrene Wisse*.

For all the connections they made, however, scholars remained coolly silent about the Wooing Group and, to a lesser extent, the Katherine Group texts. Watson notes that Tolkien and Dobson, for example, 'had much less to say about the *Wohunge* and its colleagues' than any other members of the *Ancrene Wisse* Group and posited that the subject matter – an extended mystical relationship between Jesus as lover and the anchoress as Bride – made them uncomfortable.[26] He further notes that even early feminist scholarship denounced the Wooing Group as misogynist and overtly patriarchal in their depiction of female desire.[27] This is all the more fascinating because the editor of the Early English Text Society version of 'The Wooing' is a woman, W. Meredith Thompson. She acknowledges that there is no known author for any of these texts, and in a footnote lists the possibilities others have suggested. Her main approach, however, is indebted to Eugen Einenkel, who suggested in 1882 that one of the anchoresses wrote it. Thompson seized upon this and extended her musings to a heart-warming scene of one 'sister' passing the text along to another.[28] Some later critics have been excessively dismissive about this position, especially Dobson, but also some feminist scholars. Dobson was especially brutal in his dismissal of possible female authorship: 'it seems perverse to me to suppose that "my dear sister" is a form of address from a man to a woman in *Ancrene Wisse*, but from one woman to another in *Þe Wohunge of Ure Laured* ... the hypothesis is merely fanciful'.[29] The early anchoritic texts also stand in contrast to the late fourteenth-century anchoress Julian of Norwich, who was the first named female author of an English work.[30] Despite Dobson's fearful overreaction, however, Thompson's proposition is still a somewhat pervasive idea within anchoritic studies, thereby extending the women's literary community begun in the thirteenth century through to the present day. The Wooing Group in particular has gained traction as the feminist recovery of texts moved more towards the reinvestigation of works previously read in patriarchal perspective. In North America in the 1990s, for instance, three dissertations were written solely on the Wooing Group itself.

In the Middle Ages, *Ancrene Wisse* not only had an immediate impact, with its variations made for Lollards and male monastics, but also had a more diffuse effect. As an individual work, it was expanded, excerpted, folded into, and manipulated within a great many devotional works in the English Christian tradition, particularly in the later medieval period, the fourteenth and fifteenth centuries. These include: *The Form of Perfect Living* (1349) by Richard Rolle, *The Ladder [Scale] of Perfection* (14th c.) by Walter Hilton, *Speculum inclusorum* (*Mirror of Recluses*; 14th c.), *The*

Pore Caitif (14th c.), *The Cloud of Unknowing* (14th c.), *The Abbey of the Holy Ghost* (14th c.), *The Doctrine of the Heart* (14th c.), *Gratia Dei* (*Glory of God*; 14th c.), *The Tretyse of Loue* (1493), *The Ladder of Four Rungs* (15th c.), *The Chastising of God's Children* (15th c.), *The Seven Points of True Love and Everlasting Wisdom* (15th c.), *Speculum devotorum* (15th c.), *Disce mori* (*Learn to Die*; 15th c.), *Contemplations on the Dread and Love of God* (15th c.), *The Mirror of Our Lady* (15th c.), *Formula noviciorum* (15th c.), and *The Devout Treatise of the Tree and Twelve Fruits of the Holy Ghost* (15th c.). Some of these texts were meant solely for women, but many were meant for any devout person. Several were among the earliest works printed by Wynkyn de Worde. Further, Catherine Innes-Parker notes an additional kind of 'continuing influence' of *Ancrene Wisse*: 'texts such as Nicholas Love's *Mirror of the Blessed Life of Jesus Christ* [make] reference to *Ancrene Wisse* in a way that assumes the reader's familiarity with the text'.[31] We can even identify third-hand influence, as in Julian of Norwich who references *The Chastising of God's Children*, which in turn references *Ancrene Wisse*. *The Chastising*, a compilation text – meaning its creator took passages from other works, rearranged them, and wove them together into a complete narrative – dates from the fourteenth century and was written for religious women. It takes both its title and a great deal of its opening material straight from *Ancrene Wisse*, and was an especially popular text.[32] Nine complete manuscripts of it survive, along with printings (and reprintings) by Wynkyn de Worde and partial adaptations such as *Disce mori*. It was originally addressed to devout women, possibly nuns, but found widespread acclaim among male monastics (Carthusians primarily) and laywomen, with several copies having been willed by such women to female religious houses of varying professions or other women. The vowess Agnes Stapilton, for example, bequeathed a copy to the Cistercian nuns at Eastholt (near Leeds), while Mercy Ormesby left a copy to the Benedictine nuns at Easbourne Priory.[33] Innes-Parker calls such activities 'reading circles' within the 'legacy of *Ancrene Wisse*'.[34] Bound with eight copies of *The Chastising* is a prose treatise meant for aristocratic laywomen, *The Tretyse of Loue*, first printed in 1493. Much of its content comes from Part Seven of *Ancrene Wisse* and relies heavily on the imagery of Christ as the (courtly) lover-knight who writes love missives to the devout woman.[35] The author rearranges the material to follow the events of the Passion instead of keeping to *Ancrene Wisse*'s order. The opening of the text notes that the material is taken from the French version of *Ancrene Wisse* – which is itself a translation of the English version – and then translated, making *The Tretys of Loue* a rearranged translation of a translation. While *The*

Chastising and *The Tretys* take their material directly from *Ancrene Wisse*, other works draw inspiration from it by using evocative language and allusions instead. Nicole R. Rice examines the English version of *The Abbey of the Holy Ghost*, a fourteenth-century prose devotional treatise meant to advise laywomen how to live a contemplative life outside of a cloister, in this regard, noting that it instructs:

> 'ȝif ȝe wollen holden ow in gostlich religion, holdeth ow withinne and stekeþ or ȝates and so warliche kepeþ þe wardes of ȝor cloistre þat *non otter fondinges non innore* mowe haue eny entre to maken þi sylence to breken or sturen þe to synne' (7–8, emphasis added). With the reference to 'otter fondinges non innore', the *Abbey* alludes economically to several parts of *Ancrene Wisse*'s 'rule of the heart', which deal with the outer and inner senses, and temptation.[36]

Rice goes on to suggest that the *Abbey* does not trust its readers as much as *Ancrene Wisse* does, since the temptations are never explained; instead, the *Abbey* warns that they cannot be understood and suggests intervention from a confessor. In this case, the adapted text expects its readers to be familiar enough with *Ancrene Wisse* that, even as its principles are evoked and adapted, it need not be named nor even explicitly quoted. This passage is not found in the French versions of the *Abbey*, suggesting further that *Ancrene Wisse*'s influence was limited outside England but within the country was quite well-known. We can also see these various textual manipulations as an establishment of the female devotional perspective as the basis for all later medieval devotional expression, especially in England.

As mentioned, outside England *Ancrene Wisse* seemed to have had less direct influence, although certain literary traditions were shared between England and France in particular. *The Book of Vices and Virtues*, for example, was a fourteenth-century English translation of the *Somme le roi* of Lorens d'Orléans, but the tradition drew on the same sources as *Ancrene Wisse*. Other scholars suggest direct connections between *Ancrene Wisse* and different expressions of female religious interests: according to Cate Gunn, 'The text of *Ancrene Wisse* can be read as part of the fabric of the religious movement on the Continent in the twelfth and thirteenth centuries; in particular, its spiritual patterning bears comparison with the manifestations of female piety in the beguine movement of northern Europe.'[37] Beguines were laywomen who lived devout lives in situ without taking any formal vows. Many of them lived together in urban settings, working alone or together and pooling resources. They spent time in prayer, meditation, and contemplation, and a number became famed mystics and even authors themselves. To some extent, such a connection seems obvious since neither vocation requires professed vows. Further complicating matters, Gunn notes, were the structures of conventual life – not the discipline involved, but rather the aristocratic bias and the patriarchal power system. Non-noble women could not always devote themselves to charity and prayer in a manner they desired within the traditional nunneries. Moreover, beguines were urban, as were most anchorites, while hermits wandered the rural areas. Both vocations required investment personally, professionally, and monetarily. And while there is no beguine text that specifically incorporates *Ancrene Wisse* directly into its fabric, Gunn explains the relationship: 'James of Vitry and others preached sermons to beguines, and these sermons – as texts offering both spiritual advice and practical guidance – bear comparison with *Ancrene Wisse*. Such sermons ... often have the same moderate tone and emphasis on the endurance of suffering. As in *Ancrene Wisse*, the spirituality expressed is both penitential and contemplative.'[38] Even if *Ancrene Wisse* did not provide a direct and specific amount of text to any singular beguine work, the ideas about female devotional practice and internalisation of female spirituality closely match up.

Looking at the many ways *Ancrene Wisse* was written, rewritten, overwritten, and written into various texts demonstrates the universality of devotional material ostensibly constructed solely for women. It also shows us the ubiquitous nature of women's literacy, especially in the vernacular, but also in the major learned languages of the Middle Ages: Latin and French. The *Ancrene Wisse* Group stands at the forefront of a long, rich, and colourful devotional tradition for women and normalises the erotic discourse about Jesus as lover that will come to dominate later mystical works. It ushers in interior penance and bodily preparation against the backdrop of the Fourth Lateran Council requiring yearly confession. It urges women to think carefully about their bodies and how best to guard them while simultaneously offering them up to Christ. And it assumes women can, will, and should be able to read works referenced within, including texts from multiple genres and traditions.

Notes

1. There are now numerous sources on the anchoritic life, but the two classic texts, both authored by women, remain: Rotha Mary Clay, *The Hermits and Anchorites of England* (London: Methuen, 1914), and Ann K. Warren, *Anchorites and their Patrons in Medieval England* (Berkeley: University of California Press, 1985).

2. For a look at what I call 'synthetic sisterhood', whereby the anchoresses form a community of identity, see Michelle M. Sauer, '"Prei for me mi leue suster": The Paradox of the Anchoritic "Community" in Late Medieval England', *Prose Studies* 26.1–2 (2003), 153–75.
3. The Wooing Group (or Wohunge Group) is a term coined by W. Meredith Thompson to identify the common provenance of these texts in her Early English Text Society edition of the same name; see Thompson (ed.), *Þe Wohunge of Ure Laured* (also includes *On Uriesun of Ure Lourerde; On Wel Swuðe God Ureisun of God Almihti; On Lofsong of Ure Louerde; On Lofsong of Ure Lefdi; Þe Oreisun of Seinte Marie*) Early English Text Society O.S. 241 (London: Oxford University Press, 1958).
4. For more on this distinction, see Michelle M. Sauer, 'Enclosed Addresses: The Flexibility of Anchoritic Texts in the College Classroom', *SMART: Studies in Medieval & Renaissance Teaching.* 24.2 (2017), 59–70.
5. Bella Millett, '*Hali Meiðhad, Sawles Warde,* and the Continuity of English Prose', in *Five Hundred Years of Words and Sounds: A Festschrift for Eric Dobson,* ed. Eric G. Stanley and Douglas Gray (Cambridge: D. S. Brewer, 1983), 100–8.
6. Bella Millett, 'The *Ancrene Wisse* Group', in *A Companion to Middle English Prose,* ed. A. S. G. Edwards (Woodbridge: Boydell & Brewer, 2004), 1–17; and *Ancrene Wisse: A Corrected Edition of the Text in Cambridge, Corpus Christi College, MS 402 with Variants from Other Manuscripts,* trans. by Bella Millet (Oxford: Early English Text Society, 2006).
7. Bella Millett, George B. Jack, and Yoko Wada, *Annotated Bibliographies of Old and Middle English Literature,* vol. 2: *Ancrene Wisse, the Katherine Group, and the Wooing Group* (Cambridge: D. S. Brewer, 1996), 6.
8. Simonne R. T. O. d'Ardenne (ed.), *Þe Liflade ant te Passiun of Seinte Iuliene,* Early English Text Society O.S. 248 (London: Oxford University Press, 1961), xliii.
9. Anne Eggebroten, '*Sawles Warde*: A Retelling of *De Anima* for a Female Audience', *Mediaevalia* 10 (1984), 27–47. Eggebroten's work on the themes of *Sawles Warde* is still accepted as standard; however, her premise that it relies upon Hugh of St Victor's *De anima* is not. Most scholars now agree with Dobson, who has identified the Anselmian text *De custodia* as the main source, although it likely also served as the basis for *De anima*. See Eric J. Dobson, *The Origins of* Ancrene Wisse (Oxford: Clarendon Press, 1976), 146–54.
10. Jerome, for example, covers this topic in *Adversus Joviniamum,* and earlier treatises on virginity, such as *Speculum virginum,* do as well.
11. Millett, *Ancrene Wisse: A Corrected Edition,* ix.
12. Denis Renevey, 'Figuring Household Space in *Ancrene Wisse* and *The Doctrine of the Hert*', in *SPELL: Swiss Papers in English Language and Literature* 17, ed. David Spurr and Cornelia Tschichold (Tübingen: Gunter Narr, 2005), 69–84 (70).

13. James Morton (ed.), *The* Ancren Riwle*: A Treatise on the Rules and Duties of Monastic Life, Edited and Translated from a Semi-Saxon MS. of the Thirteenth Century* (London: Camden Society, 1853), xi and v.
14. Bella Millett, Ancrene Wisse, *The Katherine Group, and The Wooing Group*, Annotated Bibliographies of Old and Middle English Literature, 2, with the assistance of George B. Jack and Yoko Wada (Cambridge: D. S. Brewer, 1996), 52.
15. Anneke Mulder-Bakker, *Live of the Anchoresses: The Rise of the Urban Recluse in Medieval Europe*, trans. Myra Heerspink Scholz (Philadelphia: University of Pennsylvania Press, 2005), 3.
16. Elizabeth Robertson, '"This Living Hand": Thirteenth-Century Female Literacy, Materialist Immanence, and the Reader of the *Ancrene Wisse*', *Speculum* 78.1 (2003), 1–36 (3).
17. Nicholas Watson, 'Afterword: On *Eise*', in *'May your wounds heal the wounds of my soul': The Milieu and Context of the Wohunge Group*, ed. Susannah M. Chewning (Cardiff: University of Wales Press, 2009), 194–210 (196).
18. Watson, 'Afterword', 196.
19. See Dobson, The Origins of *Ancrene Wisse*, xxv–xxviii.
20. John Scahill, 'More Central than Deviant: The Gonville and Caius Manuscript of "Ancrene Wisse"', *Neuphilologische Mitteilungen* 110.1 (2009), 85–104 (85). In turn, he is basing his assertion, at least in part, on Millett, *Ancrene Wisse: A Corrected Edition*, xvi.
21. Scahill, 'More Central than Deviant', 89.
22. Scahill, 'More Central than Deviant', 89.
23. F. M. Mack (ed.), *The English Text of the Ancrene Riwle: Edited from Cotton MS. Titus D.xviii. and Bodleian MS. Eng. th.c.70*. Early English Text Society O.S. 252 (London: Oxford University Press, 1963), xiv.
24. Mack, *Ancrene Riwle*, xvii.
25. See, for instance, Michelle M. Sauer, 'Cross Dressing Souls: Same Sex Desire and the Mystic Tradition in *A Talkyng of the Loue of God*', in *Intersections of Sexuality and Religion in the Middle Ages: The Word Made Flesh*, ed. Susannah M. Chewning (Burlington, VT: Ashgate, 2005), 153–76.
26. Watson, 'Afterword', 196.
27. See Watson, 'Afterword', 197.
28. See Thompson, *Þe Wohunge of Ure Laured*, xxiii–xxiv.
29. Dobson, *The Origins of* Ancrene Wisse, 154, n. 2.
30. In his introduction to the Penguin edition of Julian of Norwich's *Revelations of Divine Love* (1998), A. C. Spearing begins by proudly proclaiming that 'Julian of Norwich is the first writer in England who can be *identified with certainty as a woman*' (vii, my emphasis). Spearing goes on to acknowledge that some of the numerous anonymous religious Middle English texts in existence may have been the product of women authors, although that premise is doubtful not primarily because of female illiteracy, since nuns were educated, but mostly because of their apparent complacence. It 'took some very unusual stimulus to impel a woman to write' (vii). While Spearing

probably intends for this to increase Julian's status as author, the statement effectively disqualifies women as writers because of their apathy.
31. Catherine Innes-Parker, 'The Legacy of *Ancrene Wisse*: Translations, Adaptations, Influences, and Readers', in *A Companion to* Ancrene Wisse, ed. Yoko Wada (Rochester, NY: D. S. Brewer, 2003), 145–73 (147).
32. See especially *The Chastising of God's Children and the Treatise of Perfection of the Sons of God*, ed. Joyce Bazire and Eric Colledge (Oxford: Blackwell, 1957); Hope Emily Allen, 'Further Borrowings from "Ancren Riwle"', *The Modern Language Review* 24.1 (1929), 1–15; and Hope Emily Allen, 'Some Fourteenth Century Borrowings from "Ancren Riwle"', *The Modern Language Review* 18.1 (1923), 1–8.
33. For more on the circulation of these texts in wills and estates, see Innes-Parker, 'Legacy', 165; Bazire and Colledge, *The Chastising of God's Children*, 37–41; and David N. Bell, *What Nuns Read: Books and Libraries in Medieval English Nunneries* (Kalamazoo: Cistercian Studies, 1995).
34. Innes-Parker, 'Legacy', 145ff.
35. For more on *The Tretyse of Loue*, see Carol M. Meale, '"Oft sithis with grete deuotion I thought what I might do pleysyng to God': The Early Ownership and Readership of Love's Mirror, with Special Reference to its Female Audience', in *Nicholas Love at Waseda: Proceedings of the International Conference, 20–22 July, 1995*, ed. Shōichi Oguro, Richard Beadle, and Michael G. Sargent (Cambridge: D. S. Brewer, 1997), 19–46.
36. Nicole R. Rice, *Lay Piety and Religious Discipline in Middle English Literature* (Cambridge: Cambridge University Press, 2008), 25.
37. Cate Gunn, Ancrene Wisse: *From Pastoral Literature to Vernacular Spirituality* (Cardiff: University of Wales Press, 2008), 36.
38. Gunn, *Pastoral Literature*, 44.

Further Reading

Ackerman, Robert W., and Roger Dahood, eds. (1984). Ancrene Riwle: *Introduction and Part I*, Binghamton, NY: Medieval & Renaissance Texts & Studies.
Dobson, Eric J. (1976). *The Origins of* Ancrene Wisse, Oxford: Clarendon Press.
Gunn, Cate (2008). Ancrene Wisse: *From Pastoral Literature to Vernacular Spirituality*, Cardiff: University of Wales Press.
Innes-Parker, Catherine (2003). The Legacy of *Ancrene Wisse*: Translations, Adaptations, Influences, and Readers. In *A Companion to* Ancrene Wisse, ed. Y. Wada. Rochester, NY: D. S. Brewer, 145–173.
Millett, Bella (2004). The *Ancrene Wisse* Group. In *A Companion to Middle English Prose*, ed. A. S. G. Edwards. Woodbridge: Boydell & Brewer, 1–17.
Millett, Bella, ed. and trans. (2006). Ancrene Wisse: *A Corrected Edition of the Text in Cambridge, Corpus Christi College, MS 402 with Variants from Other Manuscripts*, Oxford: Early English Text Society.

Millett, Bella, trans. (2009). Ancrene Wisse, *Guide for Anchoresses: A Translation*, Exeter: University of Exeter Press.
Robertson, Elizabeth (2003). 'This Living Hand': Thirteenth-Century Female Literacy, Materialist Immanence, and the Reader of the *Ancrene Wisse*. *Speculum* 78.1, 1–36.
Sauer, Michelle M. (2005). Cross-Dressing Souls: Same Sex Desire and the Mystic Tradition in *A Talkyng of the Loue of God*. In *Intersections of Sexuality and Religion in the Middle Ages: The Word Made Flesh*, ed. Susannah M. Chewning. Burlington, VT: Ashgate, 153–76.
Watson, Nicholas (2009). Afterword: On Eise. In *'May your wounds heal the wounds of my soul': The Milieu and Context of the Wohunge Group*, ed. Susannah Chewning. Cardiff: University of Wales Press, 194–210.

CHAPTER 5

Syon Abbey and the Birgittines
Laura Saetveit Miles

The importance of this volume's focus on women's literary culture rather than writing by women is well demonstrated by the topic of this chapter: Syon Abbey, the sole English house of the Order of St Saviour, a monastic order founded by the visionary St Birgitta of Sweden (1303–73), for up to sixty contemplative nuns supported by thirteen priest-brothers and four deacons. Syon Abbey fostered a strong textual community from the first professions in the 1420s through the members' scattering more than a hundred years later at the Dissolution. While the Birgittine brothers wrote for the sisters – prolifically – as did the neighbouring Carthusian monks at Sheen, what firm evidence do we have of these fairly literate women writing texts themselves, either composing or copying? So far, only a few folios copied by an anonymous nun and some later liturgical material copied by Sr Mary Nevel (d. 1557/8), as Veronica O'Mara's research has shown.[1] Such a significant lacuna highlights the challenges of understanding precisely what kind of women's literary culture developed at Syon, how it might have developed over time, or even whether as an institution Syon might be said to have a single overriding literary culture rather than a plurality of literary ecosystems. In many ways, the majority of surviving evidence presents a book environment powered by men for the benefit of a passive female reading audience who appear mostly silent in the written record. But there exist different ways of interpreting that evidence, and other evidence altogether, that suggest Syon functioned as a locus for women as active agents in the creation and transmission of texts – women both within and outside its walls. Just so is the legacy of Birgitta at Syon similarly nuanced. She was a prophet, an activist, an author, a political and theological reformer – a visionary in every sense of the word. These same aspects that made her such a charismatic saint also made her sainthood contentious, and we rarely see these sides of her promoted by English scribes for female readers at Syon. So what did Birgitta actually mean for them?

Syon Abbey and the Birgittines

This chapter will investigate the ways in which Birgitta, Syon Abbey as an institution, and a long series of men and women connected with the house shaped women's participation in literary culture in fifteenth- and early-sixteenth-century England. Birgitta might well be said to be the most influential female author in England for the 150 years leading up to the Reformation, though she never set foot in the country. By her forties, Birgitta had left behind Sweden and her aristocratic family life as the mother of eight children to lead a holy life in Rome. A series of male confessors helped document her near daily visions, achieve approval for a new double order dictated by revelation, support her campaign to bring the papacy back to St Peter's seat, and reform political and religious leadership across Europe. Foundational research by Roger Ellis, Ann M. Hutchison, and others has sketched out how Birgitta's massive account of more than 700 visions, the *Revelations*, as well as other related texts, were transmitted and utilised in England from the late fourteenth century on.[2] She was of interest politically because of her visions supporting the English side against the French in the Hundred Years' War, but her life and revelations also had a huge spiritual appeal in themselves for English readers.

Extensive attention has been given to Syon Abbey's development as a vital religious and textual community since its founding by Henry V in 1415.[3] The brothers built up an incredible library of more than 1,400 volumes, recorded in the library catalogue or *registrum*, edited by Vincent Gillespie, and including a range of theological, scholastic, and humanist works.[4] They likewise preached to both the sisters and the lay public, as is well documented by Susan Powell's work, and they distributed indulgences.[5] More books survive showing ownership by Syon nuns than from any other medieval English nunnery: at least sixty-five.[6] Their devotional reading was rich and diverse, as research has shown.[7] From rather early in the history of printing in England, Syon was investing in print books as well as actively engaging London printers to produce runs of compositions by the brothers, both for the house and for lay readers. Alexandra da Costa has detailed the political and religious activism expressed by Syon's printing activity in the lead-up to the Reformation, staunchly resisted by the Birgittines.[8] Syon's outreach was also devotionally directed: lay readers, especially prominent aristocratic women, had been involved with the textual community at the house long before the introduction of print. Beyond England's borders, Syon retained close communication with the Birgittine mother house in Vadstena, Sweden.[9] Syon and the Birgittines influenced, and were influenced by, both English and European textual traditions.

Here I build on the essential work of scholars such as Hutchison, C. Annette Grisé, Christopher de Hamel, Ellis, Gillespie, and others to take a broader view of the role of women in the literary culture at Syon. This chapter begins with what it meant that the legacy – or spectre – of a Continental visionary woman ended up being at the centre of arguably one of late medieval England's most prominent institutions in the intertwined literary and religious spheres. As suggested earlier, we must be careful not to assume that, as a woman, Birgitta's power automatically brought more power to other women or that her visionary vocation inspired visions. Indeed, there is evidence to the contrary on both counts, as will be discussed. Rather, the picture is complex and thus indicative of the landscape of women's literary culture: rarely a wide open plain, but more often one of convoluted paths and shadowy arbours, of different kinds of literary environments coexisting. Syon was a textual community with gendered and geographical contexts that made it simultaneously exceptional and yet still representative of the complexities of women's literary culture in the fifteenth and early sixteenth centuries. How, and to what extent, did Birgitta as a visionary and an author shape Syon's literary culture? How, and to what extent, did the sisters of Syon shape Syon's literary culture? How was Syon a regional, national, or even international centre for women's literary culture, and what was the tenor and influence of that culture in English society more broadly? While these are not necessarily new questions, this chapter brings them together for a fresh, if brief, assessment of the role played by Syon Abbey and the Birgittines in the history of women and medieval literary culture in the later Middle Ages.

Birgitta's visions provided an administrative, liturgical, and devotional foundation for all houses of the Birgittine order. The Latin *Revelations* themselves, preserved most notably in Syon's gargantuan volume British Library, MS Harley 612, was predictably a central text for the institution. It was translated into Middle English for the nuns, who seem to have always had much stronger vernacular literacy than Latinity (though some – for example, Joanna Sewell – seem to have managed quite challenging Latin). However, while two full independent translations of the *Revelations* survive (British Library, Cotton MS Julius F.ii and Cotton MS Claudius B.i), we do not know for sure if either originated at Syon or at other spiritual centres or religious institutions. If the nuns had read one of those two full translations, it would have mattered which one. Julius and Claudius each take their own approach to rendering the *Revelations* for vernacular readers: the Julius translation is not as stylistically elegant, though is generally more faithful to the text, while the Claudius translation systematically eliminates or moderates the Latin dozens of passages concerning affective piety or mystical ecstasy, exempla incorporating female images of God, and passages supporting women as figures of power.[10] For instance, as I have examined elsewhere, in the case of Birgitta's vision of the Visitation where Mary and Elizabeth meet and Mary utters the Magnificat, Julius offers a close translation of almost every word of the Latin.[11] Claudius, however, pares away much of the original that concerns Mary's ecstatic prophesying and minimises the women's voices by diluting their direct speech into indirect speech. Whoever translated Claudius succeeded in heteronormalising womens' queer touch, sterilising their unabashed affection, and suppressing a powerful demonstration of the special access to God that two holy women coming together could precipitate.[12] Which version or versions of the *Revelations* would the women at Syon have read? Did they know the effusive, progressive Virgin Mary of the Julius Visitation, or the reserved, terse Virgin Mary of Claudius, or yet another? We still have much to learn about the nuns' access to the *Revelations* and its representations of holy women like themselves.[13]

The *Rule of St Saviour*, regulating all aspects of the house and the basis for the more detailed *Additions to the Rule*, was likewise a revelation to Birgitta from Christ. The Birgittines consulted the *Rule* not only as a guide for their monastic life but also as a devotional text, as evidenced by its inclusion in the devotional miscellany Cambridge University Library, MS Ff.6.33. Birgitta's visionary voice governed the nuns' daily worship as well as their daily life: an angel spoke to Birgitta at the special matins readings for the nuns, the *Sermo Angelicus*, which transformed their performance of the Office of the Blessed Virgin into a unique celebration of women channelling the divine presence on earth.[14] According to Katherine Zieman, more than any other liturgy, 'the lessons of the *Sermo Angelicus* read daily at matins, went further to articulate a powerful Mariology that ... was meant to structure the Bridgittine community to reflect the exemplary authority it granted to the Virgin Mary'.[15] Nonetheless, the readings were repeated on a weekly and not a yearly basis, meaning that ultimately 'the complexities of learning available through it were not great if one compares it with the full monastic or cathedral hours of prayer', as Margot Fassler has pointed out.[16] In other words, the brothers following the Sarum rite were exposed to as extensive and diverse a set of readings as the sisters' were focused and feminist – for better or for worse.

While no sisters' views on their liturgy have been preserved, we do have one window into understanding the significance of the *Sermo Angelicus* for the women at Syon and how it might not necessarily have been as empowering as it first seems. Early on in the history of the house, a Birgittine brother set out to translate and explicate the Latin *Sermo* for his sisters, producing the long text titled *The Myroure of Oure Ladye*, which survives in a single manuscript copy (now split in two) and in early print.[17] It stands as one of the most remarkable documents illuminating the spiritual life of the women at Syon – indeed, illuminating late medieval devotional practice in general. More than a translation and commentary, it offers a 'complete ideology' of both their liturgy and extraliturgical devotional reading.[18] The brother-author emphasises throughout that these readings originated in Birgitta's authentic, sacred visions, and were documented through collaboration between the saint and one of her trusted confessors, Master Peter Olafson. The *Myroure* gives Birgitta the power of an *auctor* and empowers the nuns with 'a greater understanding of their Divine Office than had ever been made available to women religious in England, placing the nuns in a much more cleric-like relation to their liturgical texts'.[19] Despite this, Elizabeth Schirmer argues, 'he does not ever encourage them, nor indeed does he leave them any room, to *interpret* what they read'.[20] She rightly suggests that such a tension, inherent in an education that does not challenge but controls, seems to arise again and again in texts written by men (mainly Birgittine brothers and Carthusian monks) for the women of Syon. Whether or not this characteristic tension stemmed from a concern over Lollardy, as according to Schirmer,[21] or from a subtle and engrained misogyny is probably impossible to distinguish – it is most likely a blending of the two, as part of what could be deemed a typical late medieval English devotional and gendered conservatism.

Birgitta obviously loomed largest as a saintly figurehead for Syon. But she was only one of several Continental visionary women foundational to the literary culture at the house. The revelatory accounts of Catherine of Siena (1347–80), *Il Dialogo*, and Mechthild of Hackeborn (1240/1–98), *Liber specialis gratiae*, were read in their Latin originals and in vernacular translations: *The Orchard of Syon* and *The Book of Gostlye Grace*, respectively. Both were long, magisterial works, like Birgitta's *Revelations*, and all three books offer authorised and authoritative female voices for the house's women readers. Prepared specifically for the nuns at Syon, probably by a fellow brother or a monk from neighbouring Sheen, *Orchard* presents a Catherine carefully translated 'into a Bridgettine context ... from an Italian saint into an English mystic', Jennifer N. Brown explains.[22] The sisters encountered these visionary women through both their full books and through borrowings into Middle English devotional compilations, most notably *A Mirror to Devout People* (*Speculum devotorum*).[23] This meditational treatise was written by a monk of Sheen for the nuns of Syon and achieved circulation inside and outside the house. It is ostensibly a life of Christ based on the pseudo-Bonaventuran *Meditationes vitae Christi* but actually weaves together numerous other sources, including 'summe reuelacyonys of approuyd wymmen', as the author-compiler famously notes in the preface: Birgitta, Catherine, Mechthild, and Elizabeth of Hungary (or Töss or Naples).[24] He elevates their visionary insights into the gospel narrative, drawing attention to where their revelations provide reliable and fascinating extra-biblical details; in other places, he prioritises their female authority over male-authored alternatives, for example by citing Catherine for a discussion of the discernment of spirits.[25] Throughout, he emphasises the spiritual benefits of seeing through a female visionary's eyes, ensuring that 'the reader's aesthetic sense is fine-tuned to the frequency of the text and its female narrative voice', as I have argued elsewhere.[26] In other ways, however, the compiler is decisively conservative. Despite all his use of their visionary accounts, Birgitta, Catherine, and Mechthild are never explicitly identified as visionary models for imitation. Readers can meditate by means of these revelatory texts but should stop short of inviting revelatory experiences themselves. Likewise, he is not encouraging of readers' direct access to scripture and his treatise is meant as a replacement, not a supplement, for reading the Bible.[27]

Devotional texts like *A Mirror to Devout People* and *The Myroure of Oure Ladye* highlight the mixed legacy of Birgitta and other visionary women for the literary culture at Syon. Vincent Gillespie has recently argued that even though the Syon nuns read all these works by women visionaries, the men composing, translating, or otherwise mediating texts for the nuns never encouraged them to have visions or to emulate those female visionaries in their more transgressive prophetic habits: 'women's spiritual potential was dealt with by denial or disregard'.[28] Indeed, no proof of any visionary activity at Syon survives that we know of. In the nuns' strict enclosure they were to worship in common, read in private, pray, meditate, perhaps even contemplate – but not challenge the status quo, not dabble in advanced theology or mysticism, and certainly not prophesy.

Such an environment seems to stand in stark contrast to Birgitta and her life. She was never enclosed, travelling widely, going head-to-head with powerful leaders, lobbying for various causes, begging in the street, writing down her visions (or dictating them) without ceasing. Her outspokenness and radical prophecies also made her controversial: both her Order and her canonisation were challenged multiple times, with her legitimacy attacked by none other than the powerful French theologian and scholastic Jean Gerson, while she was also stalwartly defended by others, including Englishman Cardinal Adam Easton.[29] Syon preserved many of the texts that helped to uphold Birgitta's authority, such as Alphonse of Jaen's *Epistola solitarii ad reges*, which constructs the saint 'within the discourse of *discretio spirituum* as an exemplary visionary' because of her conformity to its restrictions, which ultimately empowered her.[30] Predictably, however, passages endorsing prophecy from the *Epistola* ended up being perverted in the Middle English treatise *The Chastising of God's Children*, a compilation written for a female audience before Syon's foundation but later read by its nuns. Here Alphonse's 'commendation of true visionaries' becomes rather 'a warning against the dangers of diabolic possession', as the text's editors put it, and Birgitta herself is not described as a politically powerful prophet, but only briefly mentioned as having 'lyuede euer vndir þe obedience and techyng of hooli clerkis and uertuouse and discreet elder men'.[31] This seems to be the majority view on Birgitta of the male clerics in late medieval England who had responsibility for women's pastoral care. While her visions were authentic, and important for the spirituality of Syon, it was Birgitta's obedience (to male clerics like themselves) that female readers should aspire to, not her disruptive channelling of the divine. (Though we will soon meet a reader taking exception to those wishes, in Elizabeth Barton.)

But perhaps it was Birgitta's active role in the actual documentation and dissemination of her visionary corpus that offered a more accessible inspiration for the women associated with the house. And perhaps her powers of textual production were not as threatening to Englishmen in power as her politics and prophecies. F. Thomas Luongo points out that in their revelatory texts, both 'Birgitta and Catherine were promoted as authors at the same time as they were promoted as saints. That Birgitta and Catherine were authors clearly mattered to the communities that participated in both the creation and the dissemination of their writings.'[32] He also analyses the fascinating Revelation 49 in Birgitta's *Revelaciones extravagantes*, which addresses the co-authorship between God, visionary, editors, and readers, and 'emphasizes that such mediation or collaboration does not diminish Birgitta's authority or authorship but puts her on a level with the evangelists and Doctors of the Church'.[33] While individual authorship seems to have remained out of reach for Syon's female inhabitants, there is ample evidence that they worked with men to have new texts composed and disseminated. The male authors of the two works discussed earlier – *The Myroure of Oure Ladye* and *A Mirror to Devout People* – declare they wrote their works for the 'daughters of Syon' (in the words of the *Myroure* author); those female readers could well have actively requested the texts – or, at least, their active involvement cannot be ruled out and thus should be considered, and perhaps even safely assumed.[34] I would argue that from its foundation Syon's nuns helped to enhance their access to texts through commissioning new works and new copies of existing works, as well as facilitating their printing. Two specific groups of women involved with Syon have the most explicitly demonstrable agency in energising textual production at Syon: aristocratic lay women, most notably Margaret Holland, Duchess of Clarence (d. 1439/40), along with her granddaughter Lady Margaret Beaufort (d. 1509), and abbesses, most notably Abbess Elizabeth Gibbs (d. 1518). These powerful figures exemplify how Syon functioned not just as a flourishing centre for literary culture, especially print culture, but one motivated, administered, funded, and promoted by women – in collaboration with men.

Since its earliest days, Syon had rich and studious lay women exerting their influence in its cloisters without being enclosed themselves. The house's founder was a king and the Order's founder was, after all, Swedish nobility, and Birgitta's exotic prestige attracted women from the highest classes. Margaret Holland was one of several official vowesses connected to Syon.[35] The women in this important category were usually widows, vowed to chastity, who retained their life in the world but were simultaneously allowed to live a spiritual life linked to Syon and with some degree of access to the monastery.[36] Of the seven books we know Holland gave to Syon, one of them preserves a marvellous illumination of Birgitta receiving the *Sermo Angelicus* from the angel.[37] Holland was the recipient of a vernacular *Life of St Jerome* from Birgittine brother Simon Wynter (d. 1448), who was her confessor.[38] In his preface, Winter relies on Holland's ability to have the text copied for herself and for others: 'I desire that hit sholde lyke youre ladyship first to rede hit and to do copye hit for yourself and syth to lete oþer rede hit and copye hit whoso wyll.'[39] She not only had the financial means to disseminate his text, but also was in the right reading circles to bring Syon's bespoke compositions out to a wider audience. Winter's appeal was more than mere flattery: it highlights the very real dependence Syon's brother-authors had on their female readers and patrons to help keep the house's literary reputation alive. Of the four surviving copies of Winter's *Life of St Jerome*, at least one is likely to be a Carthusian production intended for Holland's relatives or associates at court.[40]

Within a few decades of the death of the duchess of Clarence, Syon had become 'arguably the English religious institution with the greatest actual and virtual outreach'.[41] A matrix of activities contributed to the house's status. Lay visitors could come for the brothers' famous vernacular preaching and go home with alms, images, beads, rosaries, and indulgences. In 1434 Margery Kempe famously visited Syon 'for to purchasyn hir pardon thorw the mercy of owr Lord', and her characteristic 'plentivows teerys of compunccyon and of compassyon' in the monastery church were welcomed.[42] At the end of the fifteenth century, print brought exciting new opportunities for the house – opportunities made possible by powerful women. Older Syon classics began to be brought back into circulation with fresh print editions, the first of them Margaret Holland's *Life of St Jerome*, printed by Wynkyn de Worde in 1493.[43] It is possible de Worde's motivation behind that printing was his profitable working relationship with the duchess of Clarence's granddaughter and the mother of King Henry VII, Lady Margaret Beaufort.[44] Susan Powell has shown how, around this time, Lady Margaret Beaufort used her wealth and connections at Syon to print several texts with links to the house.[45] In 1491 she had de Worde's predecessor, William Caxton, print the devotional text known as *The Fifteen Oes*, which was often (wrongly) attributed to Birgitta and quite popular in England. In 1494, Beaufort instigated de Worde's printing of Walter Hilton's *Scale of Perfection*, a text transmitted by the Birgittines and Carthusians. Within the next decade Lady Margaret Beaufort's connections with Syon were strong enough to earn her status as 'an honored guest, with papal permission to eat with the Birgittines and with her own closet overlooking the church', as well as her own rooms.[46] Meanwhile, her patronage of London printers meant she could bring the textual culture of the house out to the lay world, and put more Birgittine books in more hands, both inside and outside their cloisters.

In this same period, the women within the house with the most agency to lead textual productions seem to have been the abbesses, as Mary Erler and Julia King's research shows (and see also Erler, Chapter 3 in this volume).[47] Abbess Elizabeth Gibbs, in charge of the monastery from 1497 until her death in 1518, launched a 'successful, continuous, programme of writing and publication' via London printers that helped make Syon the leading monastic printing powerhouse in England.[48] She commissioned a series of texts on spiritual formation from her fellow Birgittine brother Richard Whitford, starting with *A Dayly Exercyse and Experyence of Dethe* in c. 1513, and probably including at least three or four other texts by him.[49] Several of these are linked to Gibbs by the presence of her initials E. G. on the distinctive woodcuts of Birgitta marking Syon-sponsored print productions.[50] Erler also posits that Gibbs was behind the printing of *The Myroure of Oure Ladye*, which only survives in a 1530 edition but was likely to have been preceded by earlier editions dating from before Gibbs's death in 1518.[51] Agnes Jordan, the abbess after Gibbs, seems to have kept up her predecessor's momentum. In sum, the abbesses at Syon mobilised the wealth and literary resources of the house to guide not only the enclosed religious community, but also 'the literate laity who were part of Syon's cultural sphere of influence'.[52]

We see this especially in the way that Whitford and other Syon brothers responded to the sisters' needs or requests by composing texts that were printed in London and later reprinted for a wider readership, often still female and sometimes still enclosed. Whitford's *Pype or tun of Perfection* was requested by 'a good deuout religious doughter' and her 'systers', and circulated inside and outside the house.[53] Many of the printed works by Whitford survive in copies signed by Birgittine nuns such as Eleanor Fettyplace, but especially his later publications in the 1530s and 1540s also 'enjoyed significant popularity outside the cloister among lay readers eager for sophisticated spiritual exercises inspired by conventual practice'.[54] For example, *The Directory of Conscience* by Birgittine William Bonde, first published in 1527, states in the preface that it was written for 'one of the Systres of Syon', while a posthumous print edition in 1534 was directed towards a nun at the Benedictine house of Denny.[55] Syon's men wrote copiously not just for but also in collaboration with their conventual sisters and other religious women, while the commercial printing enterprises up the river gladly profited from the print runs.[56] It is undoubtedly true, as da Costa outlines, that 'Syon used its printed books for four, interrelated purposes: to augment inferior parochial instruction; to bolster orthodox faith and contradict evangelical argument; to resist Henry VIII's desire for ecclesiastical supremacy; and to defend the monastic way of life.'[57] I think it crucial that we should see not only the men of Syon as the sole driving force behind these motives, but also the women as rallying around these causes, initiating the composition of texts, helping administer their printing and dissemination, and, in general, collaborating with the men to achieve this multifaceted spiritual and political platform.

Abbess Gibbs, Lady Margaret Beaufort, and Margaret Holland, Duchess of Clarence, are somewhat exceptional in their visibility: their names emerge in patterns of women's literary agency (beyond reading) that are otherwise hard to discern in the history of Syon. All in all, the preponderance of hard evidence for the Syon nuns' participation in their house's literary culture comes down to us in the form of ownership inscriptions – forty, an impressive number – that hint at how these brief moments of writing allowed the nuns 'both to grow their community through individual devotion and to assert their individuality within communal life'.[58] Yet more inscriptions and wills reveal the networks of lay women readers passing reading material between each other and through the monastery's grate, ostensibly the nuns' only access to the outside world.[59] It is clear that Syon was an active, innovative centre of textual activity in many ways focused on women, and I suspect further research will illuminate more of the ways in which women actively steered the house's literary culture and were more than passive recipients of male monastic verbosity.

Nonetheless, Syon will never compare favourably to the output by female scribes and authors at similar-scale late medieval conventual institutions on the Continent, some of which the abbey was connected to through manuscript transmission networks.[60] Its motherhouse in Vadstena was a juggernaut for text and manuscript production by both men and women.[61] Around eighty manuscripts written by its nuns survive from after 1450. Swedish nuns came to England to help Syon get started, bringing important Birgittine texts along to copy, and also took back insular literature to Sweden. Sr Anna Karlsdottir even made her own copies of works by the English mystic hermit Richard Rolle.[62] Hutchison outlines the connections between Syon and Flemish Birgittines, with at least one Syon manuscript containing a woodcut design of Birgitta with Continental origins, probably from the house of Maria Troon, Dendermonde.[63] These few examples suggest how Syon was part of a matrix of Birgittine houses stretching across Europe, and with Sheen's help also connected to the prolific Carthusian scribal network. These networks brought many texts, especially copies of women's visionary accounts, across the Channel and into England, but never exported any such works by English women that we know of – and, as we have seen, Syon (nor indeed any English convent) was not cultivating new generations of Birgittas or Catherines. There was no Elsbet Stagel documenting her fellow nuns' revelations; no Hildegard of Bingen writing sophisticated theological and scientific tracts; no Helfta with Mechtild of Magdeburg, Gertrude the Great, and Mechthild of Hackeborn producing more than 1,200 pages of mystical writing between them. Margery Kempe and Julian of Norwich are the exceptions which highlight England's paucity.

However, Syon's last, and fateful, chapter did feature a female visionary. In 1525 a young servant woman, Elizabeth Barton, began to receive divine revelations, for which she soon developed a reputation, coming to be known as the 'Maid of Kent' or 'Nun of Kent' once she entered the religious life at the Benedictine priory of St Sepulchre, Canterbury, in 1527.[64] There, under the guidance of her confessor Edward Bocking, she learned about the lives and visions of Birgitta and Catherine of Siena; soon her own revelations took on a bolder political tone reminiscent of those Continental female predecessors (and new to the English tradition).[65] Syon began to show a cautious interest in Barton, especially in light of her prophecies critical of King Henry VIII and his plans for divorce from Katherine of Aragon, which they also opposed. Diane Watt has shown how 'just as St Bridget had turned bishops and monks away from their corrupt practices, so Barton attempted to manipulate the English churchmen who were facilitating the royal divorce', thus offering the Birgittine house perhaps its first opportunity to embrace a native female prophet in Birgitta's image whose politics could further their own.[66] When Abbess Agnes Jordan, General Confessor John Fewterer, and other nuns and brothers heard about Barton's revelations, they found them compelling enough to invite Thomas More to meet Barton at Syon in 1533. But their association with her was risky. Barton became more and more vocally critical of the king's divorce and reformist policies until she was arrested for treason in March 1534 and executed the next month. Syon Abbey would also soon feel the king's vengeance, being among the first of the large foundations to be suppressed, probably in retribution for their support of the Maid of Kent.[67]

Just after Barton's death, but before their own violent suppression, Syon printed both Richard Whitford's *A Daily Exercise of Death* and John Fewterer's *The Mirror or Glass of Christ's Passion*. Whitford tacks on an envoy that basically apologises for the house's association with Barton, whom he calls 'an vngraciouse woman & a diullysh' that deceived holy and devout men, while also explaining that they had 'ben moost glad to here that our lorde shulde so visyte and comforte hys people'.[68] In his work, Fewterer holds up as a female model of gifts of the Holy Spirit not Birgitta but the thirteenth-century beguine Marie d'Oignies. His odd choice to avoid the Order's foundress perhaps reflects 'the dangerous times in which writer and reader were living', where the Birgittine institution was in trouble with the Crown especially for its support of Barton.[69] Yet, at the same time, 'the text's support for female mysticism would implicitly challenge the government's denial of the Maid of Kent'.[70] Whitford and Fewterer's mixed messages capture some of the paradoxes of gender and religion at Syon. A house whose purpose, power, and reputation were all based on a woman's divine revelations; a house historically cautious about recognising women's more advanced spiritual potential; a house that finally dared to trust a living female prophet in their midst, who recanted those prophecies and hastened Syon's path to destruction (inevitable though it was). The

Dissolution and Reformation would see the martyrdom of a Birgittine brother, the ruin of Syon's magnificent buildings, and the scattering of its inmates, though not yet the formal closure of the house. Its remarkable textual legacy, fragmented by circumstance and time, survives as one of the most vibrant and fascinating testimonies to women's literary culture in late medieval England.

Notes

1. On the earlier anonymous scribe, see Veronica O'Mara, 'The Late Medieval English Nun and her Scribal Activity: A Complicated Quest' in *Nuns' Literacies in Medieval Europe: The Hull Dialogue*, ed. Virginia Blanton, Veronica O'Mara, and Patricia Stoop (Turnhout: Brepols, 2013), 78; on Mary Nevel, see O'Mara, 'A Syon Scribe Revealed by Her Signature: Mary Nevel and her Manuscripts' in *Continuity and Change: Papers from the Birgitta Conference at Dartington 2015*, ed. Claes Gejrot, Sara Risberg, and Mia Åkestam (Stockholm: Kungl. Vitterhets Historie och Antikvitets Akademien, 2017), 283–308.
2. Roger Ellis, '*Flores ad fabricandam ... coronam*: An Investigation into the Uses of the *Revelations* of St Bridget of Sweden in fifteenth-century England', *Medium Ævum* 51 (1982), 163–86; Roger Ellis, *Viderunt eam filie Syon: The Spirituality of the English House of a Medieval Contemplative Order from Its Beginnings to the Present Day* (Salzburg: Analecta Cartusiana, 1984); F. R. Johnston, 'The English Cult of St Bridget of Sweden', *Analecta Bollandiana: Revue critique d'hagiographie*, 103.1–2 (1985), 75–93; Ann M. Hutchison, 'Reflections on Aspects of the Spiritual Impact of St Birgitta, the *Revelations*, and the Birgittine Order in Late Medieval England', in *The Medieval Mystical Tradition in England: Exeter Symposium VII*, ed. E. A. Jones (Woodbridge: Boydell & Brewer, 1999), 69–82; Laura Saetveit Miles, 'St Bridget of Sweden', in *The History of British Women's Writing, 700–1500*, vol. 1, ed. Liz Herbert McAvoy and Diane Watt (London: Palgrave Macmillan, 2012), 207–15; Ann M. Hutchison, 'Birgitta and Late-Medieval English Spirituality', in *A Companion to Birgitta of Sweden and Her Legacy in the Later Middle Ages*, ed. Maria H. Oen (Leiden: Brill, 2019), 269–88. On circulating excerpts from the *Revelations*, see Domenico Pezzini, *The Translation of Religious Texts in the Middle Ages* (Bern: Peter Lang, 2008).
3. For an accessible and up-to-date history of the house, see E. A. Jones, *England's Last Medieval Monastery: Syon Abbey 1415–2015* (Leominster: Gracewing, 2015). Other important histories include John Rory Fletcher, *The Story of the English Bridgettines of Syon Abbey* (South Brent: Syon Abbey, 1933); Michael Beckwith Tait, *A Fair Place: Syon Abbey 1415–1539* (CreateSpace Independent Publishing Platform, 2013) and Christopher de Hamel, *Syon Abbey: The Library of the Bridgettine Nuns and the Peregrinations after the Reformation* (London: Roxburghe Club, 1991).
4. Vincent Gillespie, *Syon Abbey: with the Libraries of the Carthusians*, Corpus of British Medieval Library Catalogues 9 (London: British Library, 2002).

5. Susan Powell, *The Birgittines of Syon Abbey* (Turnhout: Brepols, 2017).
6. David N. Bell, *What Nuns Read: Books and Libraries in Medieval English Nunneries* (Kalamazoo: Cistercian Publications, 1995), 171–210, offers a core list, supplemented by Ann M. Hutchison, 'What the Nuns Read: Literary Evidence from the English Bridgettine House, Syon Abbey', *Mediaeval Studies* 57 (1995), 205–22, and Mary C. Erler, *Women, Reading, and Piety in Late Medieval England* (Cambridge: Cambridge University Press, 2002). For up-to-date coverage of inscriptions by the nuns, see Julia King, 'Inscriptions and Ways of Owning Books among the Sisters of Syon Abbey', *The Review of English Studies* 73.307 (2021), 836–59.
7. See especially Ann M. Hutchison, 'What the Nuns Read', 205–22; C. Annette Grisé, 'Women's Devotional Reading in Late Medieval England and the Gendered Reader', *Medium Ævum* 71.2 (2002), 209–25; and de Hamel, *Syon Abbey*.
8. Alexandra da Costa, *Reforming Printing: Syon Abbey's Defence of Orthodoxy 1525–1534* (Oxford: Oxford University Press, 2012).
9. The houses' correspondence from 1415–1510 is discussed and edited by Elin Andersson, *Responsiones Vadstenenses: Perspectives on the Birgittine Rule in Two Texts from Vadstena and Syon Abbey. A Critical Edition with Translation and Introduction* (Stockholm: Acta Universitatis Stockholmiensis, 2011).
10. Claudius is edited by Roger Ellis, *The Liber Celestis of St Bridget of Sweden*, Early English Text Society O.S. 291 (Oxford: Oxford University Press, 1988); Julius is in the process of being edited for the first time as part of my larger research project on Birgitta in medieval England, funded by the Research Council of Norway. Comparing the two versions in general, see Jane I. Hagan Gilroy, 'The Reception of Bridget of Sweden's *Revelations* in late medieval and early renaissance England', unpublished PhD thesis, Fordham University, NY (1999).
11. Laura Saetveit Miles, 'Queer Touch Between Holy Women: Julian of Norwich, Margery Kempe, Birgitta of Sweden, and the Visitation', in *Touching, Devotional Practices and Visionary Experience in the Late Middle Ages*, ed. David Carrillo-Rangel, Delfi I. Nieto-Isabel, and Pablo Acosta Garcia (Palgrave: New York, 2019), 203–35.
12. Miles, 'Queer Touch', 230.
13. Another relevant type of text here would be Birgitta's *vita* in its Latin and Middle English versions; see, most recently, Ann M. Hutchison and Veronica O'Mara, '*The Lyfe of Seynt Birgette*: An Edition of a Swedish Saint's Life for an English Audience', in *The Medieval Translator 14: Booldly Bot Meekly: Essays on the Theory and Practice of Translation in the Middle Ages in Honour of Roger Ellis*, ed. Catherine Batt and René Tixier (Turnhout: Brepols, 2018), 173–208.
14. A. Jefferies Collins (ed.), *The Bridgettine Breviary of Syon Abbey*, Publications of the Henry Bradshaw Society 96 (Worcester: Henry Bradshaw Society, 1969); John E. Halborg, *The Word of the Angel* (Toronto: Peregina, 1996).

15. Katherine Zieman, 'Playing *Doctor*: St. Birgitta, Ritual Reading, and Ecclesiastical Authority', in *Voices in Dialogue: Reading Women in the Middle Ages*, ed. Linda S. Olson and Kathryn Kerby-Fulton (Notre Dame, IN: University of Notre Dame Press, 2005), 330.
16. Margot Fassler, '"Voices Magnified": Response to Elizabeth Schirmer', in *Voices in Dialogue*, 338.
17. Aberdeen University Library, MS 138, and Oxford, Bodleian Library, MS Rawlinson C 941; Richard Fawkes, 1530, from which it is edited by John Henry Blunt, *The Myroure of Oure Ladye, containing a Devotional Treatise on Divine Service, with a Translation of the Offices and used by the Sisters of the Brigittine Monastery of Sion, at Isleworth, During the fifteenth and sixteenth centuries*, Early English Text Society E.S. 19 (London: Trübner, 1873). A composition date of between 1420–48 is offered in Ann M. Hutchison, 'Devotional Reading in the Monastery and in the Late Medieval Household' in *'De Cella in Seculum': Religious and Secular Life and Devotion in Late Medieval England*, ed. Michael G. Sargent (Woodbridge: Brewer, 1989), 215–27.
18. Michael Sargent, 'The Anxiety of Authority, the Fear of Translation: The Prologues to *The Myroure of oure Ladye*', in *Booldly Bot Meekly*, 231–44 (235). See also Ann M. Hutchison, '*The Myroure of Oure Ladye*: A Medieval Guide for Contemplatives', *Studies in St. Birgitta and the Birgittine Order* (1993), 214–27; and C. Annette Grisé, '"In the blessed vyneȝerd of oure holy saueour": female religious readers and textual reception in the *Myroure of oure ladye* and *The orchard of Syon*', in *The Medieval Mystical Tradition in England, Ireland and Wales: Exeter Symposium VI*, ed. Marion Glasscoe (Cambridge: D. S. Brewer, 1999), 193–212.
19. Elizabeth Schirmer, 'Reading Lessons at Syon Abbey: the Myroure of Oure Ladye and the Mandates of Vernacular Theology', in *Voices in Dialogue*, 345–76; 358.
20. Schirmer, 'Reading Lessons', 362.
21. Schirmer, 'Reading Lessons', 347.
22. Jennifer Brown, *Fruit of the Orchard: Reading Catherine of Siena in Late Medieval and Early Modern England* (Toronto: Toronto University Press, 2018), 123.
23. Edited by Paul J. Patterson, *A Mirror to Devout People (Speculum Devotorum)*, Early English Text Society O.S. 346 (Oxford: Oxford University Press, 2016). Examinations of the *Mirror* include C. Annette Grisé, '"In the blessed vyneȝerd of oure holy saueour"', 193–211; Vincent Gillespie, 'The Haunted Text: Reflections in *The Mirror to Devout People*', in *Medieval Texts in Context*, ed. Graham D. Caie and Denis Renevey (Abingdon: Routledge, 2008), 136–65; Paul J. Patterson, 'Translating Access and Authority at Syon Abbey', in *Devotional Culture in Late Medieval England and Europe: Diverse Imaginations of Christ's Life*, ed. Stephen Kelly and Ryan Perry (Turnhout: Brepols, 2014), 443–59; Paul J. Patterson, 'Female Readers and the Sources of the *Mirror to Devout People*', *The Journal of Medieval Religious Cultures* 42.2

(2016), 181–200. Several important essays on the *Mirror*'s manuscript tradition and readership can be found in *The Text in the Community: Essays on Medieval works, Manuscripts, Authors and Readers*, ed. Jill Mann and Maura Nolan (Notre Dame, IN: University of Notre Dame Press, 2006), including A. S. G. Edwards, 'The Contexts of Notre Dame 67', 107–28; Vincent Gillespie, 'The Haunted Text: Reflections in *A Mirror to Devout People*', 129–72; and Jessica Brantley, 'The Visual Environment of Carthusian Texts: Decoration and Illustration in Notre Dame 67', 217–37. On the contested identity of the visionary woman linked to a text known as *Revelations of Elizabeth of Hungary*, see Sarah McNamer, ed., *Meditations on the Life of Christ: The Short Italian Text* (Notre Dame, IN: University of Notre Dame Press, 2018), cxxxix–cxlvi.
24. *A Mirror to Devout People*, 6, l. 127; see also 'Introduction', xl–xliv.
25. Patterson, 'Female Readers', 195.
26. Laura Saetveit Miles, '"Syon gostly": Crafting Aesthetic Imaginaries and Stylistics of Existence in Medieval Devotional Culture', in *Emerging Aesthetic Imaginaries*, ed. Lene Johannessen and Mark Ledbetter (Lanham: Lexington Books, 2018), 79–91 (85).
27. Laura Saetveit Miles, *The Virgin Mary's Book at the Annunciation: Reading, Interpretation and Devotion in Medieval England* (Woodbridge: D. S. Brewer, 2020), 109–12.
28. Vincent Gillespie, 'Visionary Women and Their Books in the Library of the Brethren of Syon', in *Books and Bookmen in Early Modern Britain: Essays Presented to James P. Carley*, ed. James Willoughby and Jeremy Catto (Toronto: PIMS, 2019), 40–63 (45).
29. On Birgitta's canonisation process, see Bridget Morris, *St Birgitta of Sweden* (Cambridge: Boydell & Brewer, 1999), 143–59. On her defenders, see F. R. Johnston, 'English Defenders of St. Bridget', in *Studies in St Birgitta and the Birgittine Order*, vol. 2, ed. James Hogg, Analecta Cartusiana, 35.19 (1993), 125–50; and Roger Ellis, 'Text and Controversy: In Defence of St Birgitta of Sweden', in *Text and Controversy from Wyclif to Bale: Essays in Honour of Anne Hudson*, Medieval Church Studies 4, ed. Helen Barr and Ann M. Hutchison (Turnhout: Brepols, 2005), 303–21.
30. Rosalynn Voaden, *God's Words, Women's Voices: The Discernment of Spirits in the Writing of Late-Medieval Women Visionaries* (Woodbridge: D. S. Brewer, 1999), 79.
31. Joyce Bazire and Edmund Colledge (eds.), *The Chastising of God's Children and the Treatise of Perfection of the Sons of God* (Oxford: Blackwell, 1957), 64; quotation from their edition, 204, l. 17. See also the discussion in Marleen Cré, '"ȝe han desired to knowe in comfort of ȝoure soule": Female Agency in *The Chastising of God's Children*', *The Journal of Medieval Religious Cultures* 42.2 (2016), 164–80.
32. F. Thomas Luongo, 'God's Words, or Birgitta's? Birgitta of Sweden as Author', in *A Companion to Birgitta of Sweden and Her Legacy in the Later Middle Ages*, ed. Maria H. Oen (Leiden: Brill, 2019), 25–52 (29).

33. F. Thomas Luongo, 'Birgitta and Catherine and Their Textual Communities' in *Sanctity and Female Authorship: Birgitta of Sweden and Catherine of Siena*, ed. Maria H. Oen and Unn Falkeid (New York: Routledge, 2020), 14–34; and, in the same volume, Unn Falkeid, 'Constructing Female Authority', 54–73 (23).
34. John Henry Blunt, *The Myroure of Oure Ladye, containing a Devotional Treatise on Divine Service, with a Translation of the Offices and Used by the Sisters of the Brigittine Monastery of Sion, at Isleworth, During the fifteenth and sixteenth centuries*, Early English Text Society E.S. 19 (London: Trübner, 1873), 1.
35. Another notable woman reader devoted to Birgitta/Syon was Cicely Neville; see C. A. J. Armstrong, 'The Piety of Cicely, Duchess of York: A Study in Late Medieval Culture', in *For Hilaire Belloc: Essays in Honour of His 72nd Birthday*, ed. Douglas Woodruff (London: Sheed & Ward, 1942), 73–94.
36. Mary C. Erler, 'English Vowed Women at the End of the Middle Ages', *Mediaeval Studies* 57 (1995), 155–203; Mary C. Erler, 'Syon's "special benefactors and friends": Some Vowed Women', *Birgittiana* 2 (1996), 209–22. See also Erler, *Women, Reading, and Piety*, ch. 4 'Orthodoxy: The Fettyplace Sisters at Syon', 85–99 (86–7 on the vowess tradition).
37. The manuscript is now Karlsruhe, Germany, Badische Landesbibliothek Skt Georgen in Villingen cod. 12. See Ann M. Hutchison, 'Birgitta and Late-Medieval English Spirituality', in *A Companion to Birgitta of Sweden and Her Legacy in the Later Middle Ages*, ed. Maria H. Oen (Leiden: Brill, 2019), 269–88 (277).
38. Edited in Claire M. Waters, *Virgins and Scholars: A Fifteenth-Century Compilation of the Lives of John the Baptist, John the Evangelist, Jerome, and Katherine of Alexandria* (Turnhout: Brepols, 2008); discussed in Laura Saetveit Miles, 'Beinecke MS 317 and Its New Witness to the Latin Door Verses from London Charterhouse: A Story of Carthusian and Birgittine Literary Exchange', in *Manuscript Culture and Medieval Devotional Traditions: Essays in Honour of Michael G. Sargent*, ed. Jennifer Brown and Nicole R. Rice (Woodbridge: York Medieval Press/Boydell & Brewer, 2021), 3–24; George R. Keiser, 'Patronage and Piety in Fifteenth-Century England: Margaret, Duchess of Clarence, Symon Wynter, and Yale University MS 317', *Yale University Library Gazette* 60 (1985), 32–46.
39. New Haven, Beinecke Rare Book and Manuscript Library, MS 317, fol. 5r.
40. As suggested by Keiser, 'Patronage and Piety', 41–2.
41. Powell, *The Birgittines*, 226.
42. *The Book of Margery Kempe*, ed. Barry Windeatt (Cambridge: D. S. Brewer, 2004), Bk II, ch. 10, 384–428 (418–19).
43. Keiser, 'Patronage and Piety', 44.
44. Keiser, 'Patronage and Piety', 43–4.
45. On Beaufort and printing, see Powell, *The Birgittines*, 'Chapter 6: Lady Margaret Beaufort: Books, Printers, and Syon Abbey,' 153–214, as well as

136–7. See also Alexandra Barratt and Susan Powell (eds.), *The Fifteen Oes and Other Prayers* (Heidelberg: Universitätsverag Winter, 2021).
46. Powell, *The Birgittines*, 227.
47. Erler, *Reading, Writing, and Piety*; Erler, 'The Early Sixteenth Century at Syon: Richard Whitford and Elizabeth Gibbs', in *Manuscript Culture and Medieval Devotional Traditions*, 310–26; King, 'Caput et domina: Abbesses and Women' Leadership at Syon Abbey, 1415–1539' (work in progress).
48. Erler, 'The Early Sixteenth Century at Syon', 326.
49. See Erler, 'The Early Sixteenth Century at Syon', table, 326; and description, 310.
50. Erler, 'The Early Sixteenth Century at Syon' and Powell, *The Birgittines*, 125–50. Also Martha W. Driver, 'Nuns as Patrons, Artists, Readers: Bridgettine Woodcuts in Printed Books Produced for the English Market', in *Art into Life: Collected Papers from the Kresge Art Museum Symposia*, ed. Carol Garett Fisher and Kathleen L. Scott (East Lansing: Michigan State University Press, 1995), 236–67; Gillespie, *Syon Abbey*, li–lvi.
51. Erler, 'The Early Sixteenth Century at Syon', 320.
52. King, 'Caput et Domina'.
53. James Hogg (ed.), *Richard Whytford's The Pipe or Tonne of the Life of Perfection* (Salzburg: University of Salzburg, 1979), 23.
54. Brandon Alakas (ed.), *Richard Whitford's Dyuers Holy Instrucyons and Teachynges Very Necessary for the Helth of Mannes Soule* (Liverpool: Liverpool University Press, 2020), 7.
55. Erler, *Women, Reading and Piety*, 109.
56. For more on brother-authors, see Jan Rhodes, 'Syon Abbey and its Religious Publications in the Sixteenth Century', *Journal of Ecclesiastical History* 44 (1993), 11–15; Ann M. Hutchison, 'Reflections on Aspects of the Spiritual Impact of St. Birgitta, the *Revelations* and the Bridgettine Order', 69–82; and C. Annette Grisé, '"Moche profitable unto religious persones, gathered by a brother of Syon": Syon Abbey and English Books', in *Syon Abbey and its Books*, 129–54.
57. Da Costa, *Reforming Printing*.
58. King, 'Inscriptions', 4.
59. See Erler, *Women, Reading, and Piety*.
60. See the *Nuns' Literacies* volumes for many examples.
61. On Vadstena's nuns, see the important research by Ingela Hedström, 'Vadstena Abbey and Female Literacy in Late Medieval Sweden', in *Nuns' Literacies in Medieval Europe: The Hull Dialogue*, ed. Virginia Blanton, Veronica O'Mara, and Patricia Stoop (Turnhout: Brepols, 2013), 253–72; and *Medeltidens svenska bönböcker: kvinnligt skriftbruk i Vadstena kloster* (Oslo: Unipub, 2009).
62. Virginia R. Bainbridge, 'Syon Abbey: Women and Learning *c.* 1415–1600' in *Syon Abbey and Its Books: Reading, Writing and Religion, c. 1400–1700*, ed. Edward Alexander Jones and Alexandra Walsham (Woodbridge: Boydell & Brewer, 2010), 84; on Karlsdottir's prayerbook, see Clæs Gejrot, 'Anna

Karlsdotters bönbok. En tvåspråkig handskrift från 1400-talet', in *Medeltida skrift- och språkkultur*, ed. Inger Lindell (Stockholm: Sällskapet Runica et Mediævalia, 1994), 13–60.
63. Erler, 'The Early Sixteenth Century at Syon', 319.
64. Diane Watt, 'Barton, Elizabeth (*c.* 1506–1534)', *Oxford Dictionary of National Biography*, Oxford University Press, Sept. 2004; online ed., Jan 2008: www.oxforddnb.com/view/article/1598; Diane Watt, *Secretaries of God: Women Prophets in Late Medieval and Early Modern England* (Woodbridge: D. S. Brewer, 1997), ch. 3: 'Of the Seed of Abraham: Elizabeth Barton, the "Holy Maid of Kent"', 51–80.
65. Watt, *Secretaries of God*, 55.
66. Watt, *Secretaries of God*, 67. See also Watt, 'The Prophet at Home: Elizabeth Barton and the Influence of St Bridget of Sweden and Catherine of Siena', in *Prophets Abroad: The Reception of Continental Holy Women in Late-Medieval England*, ed. Rosalynn Voaden (Cambridge: Cambridge University Press, 1996), 161–76.
67. George James Aungier, *The History and Antiquities of Syon Monastery, the Parish of Isleworth, and the Chapelry of Hounslow* (London: J. B. Nichols and Son, 1840), 84–5; da Costa, *Reforming Printing*, 116.
68. Da Costa, *Reforming Printing*, 117.
69. Roger Ellis, 'Further Thoughts on the Spirituality of Syon Abbey', in *Mysticism and Spirituality in Medieval England*, ed. William F. Pollard and Robert Boenig (Woodbridge: D. S. Brewer, 1997), 238.
70. Da Costa, *Reforming Printing*, 138.

Further Reading

Bell, David N. (1995). *What Nuns Read: Books and Libraries in Medieval English Nunneries*, Kalamazoo: Cistercian Publications.
da Costa, Alexandra (2012). *Reforming Printing: Syon Abbey's Defence of Orthodoxy 1525–1534*, Oxford: Oxford University Press.
de Hamel, Christopher (1991). *Syon Abbey: The Library of the Bridgettine Nuns and the Peregrinations after the Reformation*, London: Roxburghe Club.
Ellis, Roger (1984). *Viderunt eam filie Syon: The Spirituality of the English House of a Medieval Contemplative Order from Its Beginnings to the Present Day*, Salzburg: Analecta Cartusiana.
Erler, Mary C. (2002). *Women, Reading, and Piety in Late Medieval England*, Cambridge: Cambridge University Press.
Gerjot, Claes, Sara Risberg, and Mia Åkestam, eds. (2010). *Saint Birgitta, Syon and Vadstena. Papers from a Symposium in Stockholm 4–6 October 2007*, Stockholm: Kungliga Vitterhets Historie och Antikvitets Akademien.
Gillespie, Vincent (2002). *Syon Abbey: with the Libraries of the Carthusians*, Corpus of British Medieval Library Catalogues 9, London: British Library.
Grisé, C. Annette (2002). The Textual Community of Syon Abbey. *Florilegium* 19, 149–62.

Hutchison, Ann M. (1995). What the Nuns Read: Literary Evidence from The English Bridgettine House, Syon Abbey. *Mediaeval Studies* 57, 205–22.
Jones, E. A., and Alexandra Walsham, eds. (2010). *Syon Abbey and Its Books: Reading, Writing, and Religion, c. 1400–1700*, Cambridge: Boydell & Brewer.
Powell, Susan (2017). *The Birgittines of Syon Abbey: Preaching and Print*, Turnhout: Brepols.
Warren, Nancy Bradley (2001). *Spiritual Economies: Female Monasticism in Later Medieval England*. Philadelphia: University of Pennsylvania Press.

CHAPTER 6

What the Paston Women Read

Diane Watt

The fifteenth-century Paston correspondence provides unique insights into the lives and book ownership of a late medieval gentry family, and also includes a large number of letters written by women.[1] Yet the most prolific of the correspondents, Margaret Mautby Paston, was almost certainly unable to write and probably unable to read, and she called upon her sons, servants, and chaplain to act as her scribes. However, having limited or no literacy skills did not necessarily prevent access to literary culture. Indeed, as I have argued previously, there is evidence within the Paston correspondence of women inheriting, bequeathing, lending, and borrowing books, which were quite frequently exchanged within extended familial and friendship networks.[2] In this chapter, I build on this previous research, looking at three of the women in the family – Agnes Berry Paston, her daughter-in-law Margaret Mautby Paston, and Margaret's daughter Elizabeth Paston (Yelverton) – and at books either in their possession or that they may have read, in order to speculate about their interest in these works and how they might have influenced them.

Agnes Berry Paston and the *Prick of Conscience*

Agnes Paston is mentioned, alongside her husband and eldest son, in the will of Robert Cupper, dated 20 November 1434 (the will was proved four years later, on 4 October 1438).[3] Cupper was a merchant of Great Yarmouth who had served as a bailiff, Member of Parliament, and Justice of the Peace for the town.[4] Cupper's will specifies that his son, also called Robert, is to inherit his Psalter and his 'best Primer' alongside 'a certain book called Stimulus Consciencie, and which book is now in the custody of Agnes, wife of William Paston of Paston, until the said Robert comes to years of discretion'. This work, which Agnes evidently had on an extended loan, was almost certainly a copy of the Middle English *Prick of Conscience*.[5]

At the time the will was written, Agnes would still have been a relatively young woman of around twenty-nine years of age. She had married William Paston I, who was some twenty-seven years her senior, when she was only around fifteen years old, and by 1434 she had three surviving children: her eldest son John, another son Edmund, and her daughter Elizabeth. Agnes's husband enjoyed a distinguished legal career, which included serving as a Justice of the Peace for Norfolk, and in 1429 he had been appointed Justice of Common Pleas. William accumulated considerable capital and property in the course of his career, and when Agnes's father, Sir Edmund Berry, died in 1433 (only a year before Cupper's will) she inherited his estates, having previously been gifted the manor of Oxnead by her husband. She thus became a very wealthy woman in her own right. The Paston family must have been close acquaintances, or indeed friends, of Robert Cupper and his wife (also Agnes), as the bequests in Cupper's will indicate. William was to inherit Cupper's 'beads of "Hawmber" [amber chaplet] marked for twelve', and John his '"baslard" [dagger] with girdle to the same belonging'. The (temporary) gift of the book to Agnes, alongside the parallel bequest of the chaplet to her husband, is reflective of the important role devotional objects played in establishing and maintaining social relationships among the moneyed mercantile, legal, and political elite of fifteenth-century East Anglia. However, that this valued book was in Agnes's possession and that she was clearly meant to keep hold of it for some years is also revealing about Agnes's reading practices and about her engagement with literary culture more broadly.

In the archive of Paston family correspondence some thirteen letters sent from Agnes to her husband and sons survive, alongside a handful of other documents, including drafts and extracts from her will. Robert Cupper's will pre-dates her first surviving letter by more than five years. Only four letters addressed to Agnes exist, and these are also from later in her lifetime. Critical debates about Agnes's level of literacy have centred on the question of whether or not one of her letters, the earliest that we have, which was sent by Agnes to her husband in around 1440, was written in her own hand.[6] But this is something of a distraction from the real issues at stake, because even if Agnes were, like Margaret Mautby Paston, unable to read or write herself, she clearly had family members, friends, neighbours, and employees whom she could and did call upon to act as her secretaries and scribes.

If we make the reasonable assumption that Cupper left the *Prick of Conscience* in Agnes's care because he knew she would make good use of it, then what can we deduce from this bequest about Agnes's tastes and interests? The *Prick of Conscience* was a mid-fourteenth-century spiritual guide written in narrative verse that proved to be hugely popular in late medieval England. The text, which has a Northern English provenance, survives in more than 130 manuscripts and circulated throughout the country, including in London.[7] Encyclopaedic in scope, the treatise offers catechetical instruction to the lay reader, placing great emphasis on self-examination and penance. A highly didactic work, the *Prick of Conscience* explicitly promises that it will teach its audience to internalise the habits of religious discipline:

> For if a man it rede and understande wele
> And the materes tharin til hert wil take
> It may his conscience tendre make
> And til right way of rewel bryng it bilyfe
> And his hert til drede and mekenes dryfe
> And til luf and yhernyng of heven blis,
> And to amende alle that he has done mys[8]

From her reading of this text (with its emphasis on following the 'right way of rewe' in order to instil 'bilyfe' or faith), whether privately or within her family, Agnes would gain a thorough knowledge of her responsibilities as a Christian woman. She would understand the importance of remorse, and she would thus be able to prepare herself for a good death and for the afterlife. Despite its notable and harrowing emphasis on Judgement, purgatory, and hell, Agnes would surely take from this reassurance about her own position within the world, and indeed within the cosmos, and about her relationship with God.

Agnes's surviving letters provide fascinating narrative insights into the experiences of a determined woman who was unwilling to see her authority questioned either by members of her own family or by members of the community in which she lived. One letter in particular stands out, written in around 1465 (when Agnes, by now long widowed, was about sixty years old) after her relationship with her eldest son, John, had broken down over disputes over her husband's will and John's treatment of his younger brothers. In this letter Agnes advised him to be less materialistic and to focus instead of the state of his soul:

> Be my counseyle, dyspose ȝoure-selfe as myche as ȝe may to haue lesse to do in þe worlde, 'ȝure fadyr sayde, 'In lityl bysynes lyeth myche reste'. Þis worlde is but a þorugh-fare and ful of woo, and whan we departe þer-fro, riȝth nouȝght bere wyth vs but oure good dedys and ylle. And þer knoweth no man how soon God woll clepe hym, and þer-for it is good for euery creature to be redy. Qhom God vysyteth, him he louyth.[9]

The letter has justifiably received some critical attention, not least because the aphorism 'þis worlde is but a þorugh-fare and ful of woo' resonates with Egeus's speech on life as a pilgrimage in 'The Knight's Tale'.[10] However, rather than being an allusion to Chaucer, the line may be simply proverbial, as is the phrase that introduces it in Agnes's letter: 'In lityl bysynes lyeth myche reste.' Indeed, as we can see from the quoted passage, the letter also strings together a series of Biblical paraphrases, from the conclusion 'and whan we departe þer-fro, riȝth nouȝght bere wyth vs but oure good dedys and ylle" (c.f. 1 Timothy 6:7) to the assertion 'And þer knoweth no man how soon God woll clepe hym, and þer-for it is good for euery creature to be redy. Qhom God vysyteth, him he louyth' (Matthew 24:44 and Hebrews 12:6).

In fact, the letter's emphasis on the importance of suffering and preparation for the afterlife is perfectly in keeping with the message of the *Prick of Conscience*, as is its mode of gathering together proverbial and Biblical material in order to drive home its didactic message. Perhaps, when Agnes was dictating the letter to her unidentified scribe, she had at the back of her mind the fifth part of the *Prick of Conscience* ('of the day of doom / And of the toknes that byfore shul coom'), which contains a passage describing the sites associated with Christ's life and crucifixion in Jerusalem and the Holy Land. This section is indebted to medieval pilgrimage accounts and itineraries, with the surprising exception that here it is Christ himself who directs the reader's gaze to the various loci. The section ends with a warning that Agnes would certainly want her eldest son to heed:

> Criste ful austerne then shal bee
> To synful men that hym shul se;
> Dredeful and hydous seyth the boke
> To here syght when they on hym loke[11]

The emphasis here is on Christ's judgement of the wicked rather than the righteous, but earlier in the same part the *Prick of Conscience* also draws on one of the same New Testament passages as Agnes, namely Matthew 24:44, when it warns that 'There shal no mon yitte certeyn be / What tyme Criste shal come to dome / So sodeynly he shal doune come.'[12] Of course, a common Biblical citation does not prove that Agnes's letter was directly influenced by her reading of the *Prick of Conscience* any more than a shared maxim proves that she was familiar with Chaucer's 'Knight's Tale'. Nevertheless, taken together with our knowledge that some thirty years' earlier she had had in her possession a copy *Prick of Conscience*, this letter seems to support the suggestion that Agnes had a real very interest in, and was influenced by, devotional reading and moralistic writing.

Margaret Mautby Paston and *The Abbey of the Holy Ghost*

Margaret Paston may have been the most prolific of the correspondents in the family, if the number of surviving letters in the Paston collection is anything to go by, but, according to Colin Richmond, 'for all her letter-writing, [she] was not a reader'.[13] Richmond continues: 'there is, to my knowledge, no mention of books in connection with Margaret, save "a booke wyth chardeqweyns", which she asked [her husband] John to send her from London in 1452 or thereabouts'.[14] Richmond interprets this as 'a recipe-book of spicy jams, which she would consume at breakfast as an antidote to the unhealthy air of Norwich', and he concludes '[a] cook-book does not a library make'. However, Richmond appears to be wrong to attribute even this 'cook-book' to Margaret because, according to the *Middle English Dictionary*, in this context, a 'booke' refers to a container.[15] Essentially, Margaret was requesting that John purchase her a measure of quince preserve for medicinal purposes.[16]

Yet, if Richmond is mistaken, on the basis of this passage, in accrediting Margaret with the possession of a recipe book, he is also wrong to assert that she neither expressed an interest in nor indeed owned any other books. In a copy of Margaret's will dated 1482, she requests that her executors should 'purveye a compleet legende in oon book and an antiphoner in another book'.[17] By this it seems she meant that they should obtain or purchase a collection of saints' lives and a book containing antiphons or liturgical chants; the will goes on to specify that these should be kept permanently at the parish church at Mautby, where she is to be buried. Margaret's will also states that, among a number of other bequests, her daughter, Anne Paston Yelverton, is to be given her 'premer' or prayer book, while her daughter-in-law, Margery Brews Paston, is to receive her 'massebook'. From this it is evident that, even if Margaret was indeed 'not a reader', as Richmond believes, she nevertheless recognised the importance of devotional works and liturgical texts for church services and private observances. Furthermore, she clearly valued her own religious books so much that she wanted to pass them on to the closest surviving female members of her family. Joel T. Rosenthal in *Margaret Paston's Piety* goes so far as to suggest that the evidence of her letters, which are typically dated according to the feasts of the saints, indicates that she may also have owned 'a book of hours and perhaps even a copy of *The Golden Legend*, Jacob of Voragine's popular and expansive collection of saints' lives.[18] In defiance of Richmond, he asserts that Margaret 'leaves us free – if we choose to follow this route – to speculate about other books and more books'. But what other books might Margaret have read, or had read to her?

Among the surviving Paston papers and correspondence is a fragmentary document written by Margaret Paston's son, John Paston II, in which he lists the 'Englysshe bokis' in his possession.[19] Tantalisingly, one of the texts mentioned here is *The Abbey of the Holy Ghost*, a late-fourteenth-century translation of a French work, *L'Abbaye du Saint Esprit* (c. 1300), which survives in more than twenty-five manuscripts.[20] The poem takes the form of an allegorical meditation which invites its readers to undertake a structured programme of spiritual improvement by imagining themselves as a community of nuns building their own monastic house. However, whereas the original French text was addressed to a female aristocratic readership, the Middle English translation is adapted with a wider audience in mind, as its opening reveals:

> Mi deore breþren and sustren, I seo wel þat monie wolde ben in religion but þei mowe not for pouert or for age or for drede of heore kin or for bond of mariage. And, þerfore, I make her a book of religion of herte þat is of þe abbeye of þe Holi Gost, þat alle þo þat mouwe not ben in bodi religion, þei mowe ben in gostly.[21]

As Christiania Whitehead points out, the author here 'addresses an audience of pious laymen and women, offering them a "religeon of the herte" which can be used alongside the church offices to enrich their private devotions'.[22] Nicole R. Rice argues that, in addition to adapting the work 'to a socially broader, mixed-gender English readership', the translator took a more conservative approach, allowing less lay independence and emphasising instead the role of clerical confessors as mediators between the individual and God.[23]

Even in this revised form, the text has a strong feminine bent and the gender of the allegorical personae remains the same.[24] The community is represented as a house of women, ruled by an abbess called Charity, with Wisdom as prioress, Meekness as subprioress, Discretion as treasurer, Orison as chantress, and so forth. The abbey finds itself assailed by the four daughters of the Devil but, with divine assistance, it is able to overcome them. With its emphasis on penitence, self-regulation, and meditation, the presence of this book in John Paston II's library seems somewhat at odds with what we think we know about him as a courtier and soldier, embroiled in disputes over property and inheritance. This apparent misalignment between text and reader has led Jennifer Bryan to ponder whether John II 'considered himself spiritually isolated from the political and personal turmoil around him'.[25] However, other explanations are possible, including that the work was intended for wider household consumption or that John II obtained it specifically for the use of another family member; if so, then John II's mother, Margaret Paston, is as likely a candidate as any.

Certainly, it is not hard to see why a text like *The Abbey of the Holy Ghost*, with its emphasis of self-control, would appeal to someone like Margaret Paston. For example, early on in the account of the foundation of the monastery, the text stresses the value of poverty, and of rejecting 'al þat is of eorþliche þinges and worldliche þouhtes, þat þei þat haue erþliche goodes, with loue, þei faste not heore hertes þeron'.[26] Like Agnes before her (and possibly echoing Agnes's own allusion to Hebrews 12:6), Margaret found reason to write to her own son to remind him of the importance of prioritising his spiritual health and of avoiding covetousness:

> And fore Goddys loue, remembyreyt rythe welle and takeyt pacyentely, and thanke God of hys vystitacyon; and yf any thyng haue be a mysse any othere wyse þan yt howte to haue ben be-fore thys, owthere in pryde ore in laues expencys ore in any othere thyng þat haue offendyd God, amend yt and pray hym of hys grace and helpe, and entend welle to God and to ȝowr neybors.[27]

For a woman like Margaret, *The Abbey of the Holy Ghost* would provide affirmative representations of her many roles in running the household, such as educating the young, obtaining necessary supplies, and caring for the sick.[28] One particularly striking letter from Margaret, written just a few years later, seems to be addressed to her chief confidant following the death of her husband, the priest James Gloys. Within it she talks about her concerns about the company her youngest son, Walter, is keeping, and offers medicinal recommendations and herbal remedies for a sick relative.[29] And, of course, Margaret, who literally found herself threatened and besieged when defending Paston properties from attack (famously writing to her husband requesting crossbows and other weapons),[30] may well have taken consolation from reading an allegory about an assault that proved ultimately to be unsuccessful.

In John II's list, the copy of *The Abbey* in his possession appeared, not untypically, as part of an anthology: 'A reed booke þat Percyvall Robsart gaff m(...) off the Medis off þe Masse, þe Lamentacion (...) off Chylde Ypotis, A Preyer to þe Vernycle (...) callyd The Abbeye off þe Holy Gooste.'[31] Julia Boffey's research has revealed that there is reason to think that women readers played an important role in the circulation of the English version of *The Abbey of the Holy Ghost* and were 'influential in shaping some of the anthologies' in which it is found, a number of which include lives of women saints and/or Marion treatises.[32] The 'reed boke' in

John II's list came second-hand into Paston possession, but, nevertheless, it may still have reflected Margery Paston's 'particular tastes and needs' (as Boffey puts it).[33] G. A. Lester suggests that the subject of 'þe Lamentacion' could have been Mary Magdalene or the Virgin Mary,[34] which would conform to the pattern identified by Boffey. According to Richmond, the 'Preyer to þe Vernycle' may simply have been a single-leaf woodcut,[35] but, alternatively, it could have been a version of 'O Vernicle' describing the *arma Christi* or the instruments of the Passion, a prayer poem that is often but not exclusively found in prayer rolls.[36] However, there also seems to be an instructive rather than simply devotional theme to the collection. Richmond tentatively identifies 'the Medis off þe Masse' as the Middle English verse 'Treatise of the Manner and Mede of the Masse', which David Jasper and Jeremy Smith regard as 'essentially a teaching poem' for the laity.[37] 'Chylde Ypotis', a Middle-English poetic dialogue between a three-year-old philosopher Ypotis and the Emperor Hadrian, has been described by its editor as 'catechism for younger audiences, providing an education in some of the basic elements of the faith'.[38] These works therefore cohere with the more didactic aspects of *The Abbey of the Holy Ghost*, and would form appropriate reading for a woman responsible for overseeing the moral welfare of her household. So, while a recipe book does not a library make, it could be argued that an anthology does. At the very least, the presence of this collection in the household may indicate a wider interest in books on the part of Margaret Paston than has been acknowledged previously.

Anne Paston (Yelverton) and John Lydgate's *The Siege of Thebes*

If there is no evidence to tie directly the 'reed booke' containing *The Abbey of the Holy Ghost* to Margaret Paston, a more concrete example of female book ownership is that of her daughter, Anne. One of her brothers notes that his sister possesses a copy of Lydgate's *The Siege of Thebes*, which she had lent to an illustrious family connection, the Earl of Arran: 'He hath a book of my syster Annys of þe Sege of Thebes. When he hathe doon wyth it he promysyd to delyuer it yow.'[39] This work can be identified as John Lydgate's poem of that title, written between 1421 and 1422, which describes the power struggle between Oedipus's sons Eteocles and Polynices and the Theban civil war.[40] It is no particular surprise to find it mentioned in the Paston correspondence. Other poetry by Lydgate, as well as some by Chaucer (*Troilus and Criseyde*, *Legend of Good Women*, and *Parliament of Fowls*), is included alongside *The Abbey of the Holy Ghost* and a wide range of other texts in John Paston II's library inventory.[41] Still more work by Lydate is found in London, British Library, MS Lansdowne 285, often referred to as 'Sir John Paston's Grete Boke', which John II had commissioned in the 1460s, and which focuses on chivalry and good governance.[42]

Unfortunately, no letters from Anne survive and so the information we have about her, and her tastes, comes to us second hand. What we do know is this. Anne was the younger of Margaret Paston's two daughters. Her elder sister, Margery, caused a family scandal when, in 1469, she secretly married the family bailiff, Richard Calle, and refused to give up on the relationship despite pressure from her mother and grandmother.[43] For a while it seemed to her kin that Anne might prove to be equally unruly. Having been placed in the household of Sir William Calthorp to complete her education in service, she was abruptly sent home, ostensibly because Sir William felt it was time for her to marry, though her mother suspected that it was actually due to misbehaviour of some sort.[44] As further evidence of her perceived misconduct, we know that Anne followed her sister's example and became involved with another servant of the Pastons, John Pamping. Urgent intervention was necessary. By 1472, the same year it was mentioned that Anne had loaned out her copy of *The Siege of Thebes*, and only a couple of years after she left the Calthorps, her family was busy negotiating her marriage to William Yelverton, the son of a Norfolk judge and an ally (and sometime opponent) of her father.[45] The following year, however, when the match stalled for financial reasons, Anne's eldest brother warned the family to 'be ware þat þe olde love off Pampyng renewe natt'.[46] In order to prevent this from happening he dismissed Pamping from his employment. On this occasion the family succeeded in blocking the socially unacceptable relationship and, four years later, Anne and Yelverton finally married, with the approval of her family.

Given her tumultuous and frustrated courtship, we would be justified in assuming that Anne was interested in the romantic content of Lydgate's poem. Indeed, we might be tempted to draw a parallel with the episode in Chaucer's *Troilus and Criseyde* in which Pandarus first sought out Criseyde and found her with two female companions listening to another maiden 'reden hem the geste / Of the siege of Thebes'.[47] There is certainly evidence to support the view that some of the women associated with the Paston family were interested in medieval romance and its close cousin, hagiography. Rebecca Krug suggests that at around the time that Margery Brews was composing (with the assistance of her scribe) her famous Valentine letters to John Paston III in February 1477, she and her mother, Dame

Elizabeth Brews, were actually in the process of reading Chaucer's *Parliament of Fowls*.[48] Juliana Dresvina goes even further and argues that Margery Brews' Valentine verses, addressed to her prospective husband, rework some lines of Lydgate's 'Life of St Margaret'.[49] Certainly, romances and saints lives had a wide audience that included many women, and *The Siege of Thebes* was itself a popular work, with thirty-one surviving manuscripts. What is more, Lydgate represents it as the last of *The Canterbury Tales*, related on the return journey back to Southwark. He also explicitly connects it to the 'Knight's Tale', which picks up the narrative at the point *The Siege of Thebes* draws to an end, when 'Theseus the noble worthy knyght, / Duk of Athenys, with his chyvalry / Repeyred hom out of Femynye'.[50] However, just as Criseyde has to correct Pandarus when he asks if the subject of the book she is listening to is 'love',[51] so it is probably a mistake to make similar stereotypical assumptions about Anne's taste, not least because *The Siege of Thebes* is critical of amorous relations and is, in fact, as Derek Pearsall notes, a deeply political work.[52]

Anne's loan of her copy of *The Siege of Thebes* to the Earl of Arran is fairly indicative of what we know of the work's reception in the fifteenth century. Initially, the poem's readership seems to have been limited to the courtly elite. For example, one manuscript, British Library, MS Arundel 119, bears the coat of arms of William de la Pole (1396–1450), 1st Duke of Suffolk.[53] William de la Pole was married to Geoffrey Chaucer's granddaughter, Alice, and Carole M. Meale argues that it was Alice herself who commissioned its production.[54] However, as the century progressed, it reached a wider audience that included members of the gentry class. Cambridge, Trinity College, MS O.5.2, for example, was owned by two Norfolk families: the Knevets and the Thwaites.[55] But the poem also seems to have appealed to members of the monastic orders. Two manuscripts that were owned by nuns are Oxford, Bodleian Library, MS Laud Misc. 416, which was in the library of the Birgittines at Syon, and British Library, Additional MS 18632, which belonged to the Benedictine house at Amesbury in Wiltshire. Nancy Bradley Warren offers an insightful analysis of its reception by these female religious. She points out, for example, that the Syon manuscript was a compilation with a strong emphasis on the common profit.[56] The Amesbury manuscript also stressed the importance of good governance: here *The Siege of Thebes* is found alongside Thomas Hoccleve's *Regiment of Princes*.[57]

What of the Earl of Arran, to whom Anne leant her copy of Lydgate's poem? Thomas Boyd (d. before 1474) was married to Princess Mary, daughter of James II of Scotland and sister of James III.[58] In 1469, while he was abroad, he was attainted for treason in Scotland. He returned to England in 1471 and remained there until his death a few years later. He was evidently highly regarded by the Pastons. In the same letter of 1472 in which he mentions the loan of his sister's book, John Paston III described the Earl as 'þe most corteys, gentylest, wysest, kyndest, most compenabyll, freest, largeest and most bowntefous knyght'.[59] As Rachel E. Moss points out, 'Despite their [Anne Paston's and Thomas Boyle's] differences in age, gender and rank, they could evidently find some common interest in this moralising verse history.'[60] Perhaps Anne also shared her eldest brother's interest in books about war and statecraft.

Conclusion

Reading books that the Paston women owned, or may have owned, alongside their letters and those of their family and wider circle offers us a deeper understanding of *how* as well as *what* women of the gentry classes in the fifteenth century read. In some respects, there are few surprises here. Agnes Berry Paston, the often stern and fierce family matriarch, was drawn to the *Prick of Conscience*, a moralistic penitential treatise. Margaret Mautby Paston may well have found in a didactic text like *The Abbey of the Holy Ghost* a model of devotion entirely suitable for a woman who often found herself managing the household and estates in her husband's absence, even having to brave physical attacks on her person. Anne Paston (Yelverton), in contrast, seems to have had rather different tastes. She had in her possession *The Siege of Thebes*, a secular romance rather than a religious poem. However, despite the turmoil in her personal life at the time, it seems less likely that it was the topic of love that drew her to this work. Rather, the poem's focus on chivalry and good governance may have been what interested her, and also what lay behind her loan of the book to one of her brothers' aristocratic friends. It is clear that, despite their apparent limited literacy, women of the Paston family did nevertheless have access to both devotional and secular books, and were able to choose for their own enjoyment works that reflected their interests and perspectives.

Notes

1. Norman Davis (ed., vols. 1 and 2) and Richard Beadle and Colin Richmond (eds., vol. 3), *Paston Letters and Papers of the Fifteenth Century*, 3 vols., Early English Text Society S.S. 20–2 (Oxford: Oxford University Press, 2004–5). All letters are cited by volume and letter number.

2. See Diane Watt, 'The Paston Women and Chaucer: Reading Women and Canon Formation in the Fifteenth Century', *Studies in the Age of Chaucer* 42 (2020), 337–50.
3. An extract of the will of Robert Cupper, burgess of Great Yarmouth in Norfolk Records Office, Norwich Consistory Court Will register, Doke, f. 65 is printed in *Norfolk Archaeologia* 4 (1855), 326–7.
4. 'CUPPER, Robert (d. *c.* 1434), of Great Yarmouth, Norf.' in *The History of Parliament* (online): www.historyofparliamentonline.org/volume/1386-1421/member/cupper-robert-1434.
5. James H. Morey (ed.), *Prik of Conscience*, TEAMS Middle English Texts Series (Kalamazoo, MI: Medieval Institute Publications, 2012), available online at: d.lib.rochester.edu/teams/publication/morey-prik-of-conscience.
6. Davis (ed.), *Paston Letters*, vol. 1, no. 13. On Agnes's literacy, see Diane Watt, *Medieval Women's Writing: Works by and for Women in England, 1100–1500* (Cambridge: Polity Press, 2007), 145; Jane Clayton, 'Could Agnes Paston Write? The Problem of Letter 13', *Women's Literary Culture and the Medieval Canon* (blog), 16 January 2017: blogs.surrey.ac.uk/medievalwomen/2017/01/16/could-agnes-paston-write-the-problem-of-letter-13.
7. Morey (ed.), *Prik of Conscience*, introduction, n.1; Ralph Hanna and Sarah Wood (eds.), *Richard Morris's Prick of Conscience: A Corrected and Amplified Reading Text*, Early English Text Society, O.S. 342 (Oxford: Oxford University Press, 2013), xiii–xiv.
8. Morey (ed.), *Prik of Conscience*, part 7, ll. 1873–9.
9. Davis (ed.), *Paston Letters*, vol. 1, no. 30.
10. Geoffrey Chaucer, 'The Knight's Tale', 1(A).2847–8, in *The Riverside Chaucer*, ed. Larry D. Benson, 3rd ed. (Oxford: Oxford University Press, 1988). All quotations from the works of Chaucer are taken from this edition.
11. Morey (ed.), *Prik of Conscience*, part 5, ll. 1185–8.
12. Morey (ed.), *Prik of Conscience*, part 5, ll. 808–10. I am grateful to James Morey for corresponding with me concerning these resonances.
13. Colin Richmond, *The Paston Family in the Fifteenth Century: Endings* (Manchester: Manchester University Press, 2000), 116.
14. Davis (ed.), *Paston Letters*, vol. 1, no. 144.
15. *Middle English Dictionary* s.v. 'bouk' n. 3b, https://quod.lib.umich.edu/m/middle-english-dictionary/dictionary/MED5704/track?counter=1&search_id=22353676.
16. *Middle English Dictionary* s.v. 'char' n. 3 1b, https://quod.lib.umich.edu/m/middle-english-dictionary/dictionary/MED7245/track?counter=3&search_id=22353690.
17. Davis (ed.), *Paston Letters*, vol. 1, no. 230.
18. Joel T. Rosenthal, *Margaret Paston's Piety* (New York: Palgrave Macmillan, 2010), 10. Jacobus de Voragine, *The Golden Legend: Readings on the Saints*, trans. William Granger Ryan, intro. Eamon Duffy (Princeton, NJ: Princeton University Press, 2012).
19. Davis (ed.), *Paston Letters*, vol. 1, no. 316.

20. D. Peter Consacro (ed.), *A Critical Edition of the Abbey of the Holy Ghost* (Fordham University PhD thesis, 1971), available online at: fordham.bepress.com/dissertations/AAI7126960.
21. Consacro (ed.), *Abbey of the Holy Ghost*, 1.
22. Christiania Whitehead, *Castles of the Mind: A Study of Medieval Architectural Allegory* (Cardiff: University of Wales Press, 2003), 76.
23. Nicole R. Rice, *Lay Piety and Religious Discipline in Middle English Literature* (Cambridge: Cambridge University Press, 2008), 22–3 (22).
24. For a discussion of the decision to gender the monastic house female, see Nancy Bradley Warren, *Spiritual Economies: Female Monasticism in Later Medieval England* (Philadelphia: University of Pennsylvania Press, 2001), 79.
25. Jennifer Bryan, *Looking Inward: Devotional Reading and the Private Self in Late Medieval England* (Philadelphia: University of Pennsylvania Press, 2007), 23.
26. Consacro (ed.), *Abbey of the Holy Ghost*, 3.
27. Davis (ed.), *Paston Letters*, vol. 1, no. 205.
28. Consacro (ed.), *Abbey of the Holy Ghost*, 22–4.
29. Davis (ed.), *Paston Letters*, vol. 1, no. 220.
30. Davis (ed.), *Paston Letters*, vol. 1, no. 130.
31. Davis (ed.), *Paston Letters*, vol. 1, no. 316.
32. Julia Boffey, 'The Charter of the Abbey of the Holy Ghost' and Its Role in Manuscript Anthologies', *The Yearbook of English Studies* 33 (2003), 120–30 (130).
33. Boffey, 'Charter', 130.
34. G. A. Lester, 'The Books of a Fifteenth-Century English Gentleman: Sir John Paston', *Neuphilologische Mitteilungen* 88 (1987), 200–17 (205).
35. Richmond, *Endings*, 63–4, n. 19.
36. Lisa H. Cooper and Andrea Denny-Brown (eds.), *The Arma Christi in Medieval and Early Modern Material Culture, With a Critical Edition of 'O Vernicle'* (Farnham: Ashgate, 2014).
37. Richmond, *Endings*, 63, n. 19; *The Lay Folks Mass Book; or, The Manner of Hearing Mass, with Rubrics and Devotions for the People, in Four Texts, and Office in English According to the Use of York, from Manuscripts of the Xth to the XVth Century*, ed. Thomas Frederick Simmons, Early English Text Society, O.S. 71 (London: N. Trübner, 1879); David Jasper and Jeremy Smith, '"The Lay Folks' Mass Book" and Thomas Frederick Simmons: Medievalism and the Tractarians', *Journal of Ecclesiastical History* 70 (2019), 785–804 (796).
38. 'Item 27, Ypotis: Introduction' in *Codex Ashmole 61: A Compilation of Popular Middle English Verse*, ed. George Shuffelton, TEAMS Middle English Texts Series (Kalamazoo, MI: Medieval Institute Publications, 2008), available online at: d.lib.rochester.edu/teams/text/shuffelton-codex-ashmole-61-ypotis-introduction.
39. Davis (ed.), *Paston Letters*, vol. 1, no. 352.

40. John Lydgate, *The Siege of Thebes*, ed. Robert R. Edwards, TEAMS Middle English Texts Series (Kalamazoo, MI: Medieval Institute Publications, 2001), available online at: d.lib.rochester.edu/teams/publication/edwards-lydgate-the-siege-of-thebes.
41. Davis (ed.), *Paston Letters*, vol. 1, no. 316.
42. British Library, Catalogue of Illuminated Manuscripts, 'Detailed Record for Lansdown 285', available online at: www.bl.uk/catalogues/illuminatedmanuscripts/record.asp?MSID=5248.
43. Davis (ed.), *Paston Letters*, vol. 1, no. 203.
44. Davis (ed.), *Paston Letters*, vol. 1, no. 206.
45. Davis (ed.), *Paston Letters*, vol. 1, nos. 216 and 352.
46. Davis (ed.), *Paston Letters*, vol. 1, no. 282.
47. *Troilus and Criseyde*, II.82–3.
48. Rebecca Krug, *Reading Families: Women's Literate Practice in Late Medieval England* (Ithaca, NY: Cornell, University Press, 2002), 42, n. 63.
49. Juliana Dresvina, *A Maid with a Dragon: The Cult of St Margaret of Antioch in Medieval England* (London: British Academy/Oxford University Press, 2016), 113. Lydgate's 'The Lyfe of Seynt Margarete' is edited in *Middle English Legends of Women Saints*, ed. Sherry L. Reames, TEAMS Middle English Texts Series (Kalamazoo, MI: Medieval Institute Publications, 2003), available online at: d.lib.rochester.edu/teams/text/reames-middle-english-legends-of-women-saints-lydgate-lyfe-of-seynt-margarete.
50. *The Siege of Thebes*, III.4506–8.
51. *Troilus and Criseyde*, II.97.
52. Derek Pearsall, 'Lydgate as Innovator', *Modern Language Quarterly* 53.1 (1992), 5–22 (15).
53. British Library, Catalogue of Illuminated Manuscripts, 'Detailed Record for Arundel 119', available online at: www.bl.uk/catalogues/illuminatedmanuscripts/record.asp?MSID=1707&CollID=20&NStart=119.
54. Carole M. Meale, 'Reading Women's Culture in Fifteenth-Century England: The Case of Alice Chaucer,' in *Mediaevalitas: Reading the Middle Ages*, ed. Piero Boitani and Anna Torti (Woodbridge: D. S. Brewer, 1996), 81–101 (92–3).
55. Trinity College Cambridge, The James Catalogue of Western Manuscripts, 'O.5.2', available online at: https://mss-cat.trin.cam.ac.uk/Manuscript/O.5.2.
56. Nancy Bradley Warren, 'Chaucer, the Chaucer Tradition, and Female Monastic Readers', *The Chaucer Review* 51 (2016), 88–106 (91).
57. Warren, 'Chaucer, the Chaucer Tradition, and Female Monastic Readers', 91.
58. Roland J. Tanner, 'Boyd family (per. *c.* 1300–*c.* 1480), landowners and administrators.' *Oxford Dictionary of National Biography* (23 September 2004), available online at: www.oxforddnb.com/view/10.1093/ref:odnb/9780198614128.001.0001/odnb-9780198614128-e-54141.
59. Davis (ed.), *Paston Letters*, vol. 1, no. 352.
60. Rachel E. Moss, *Fatherhood and Its Representations in Middle English Texts* (Cambridge: D. S. Brewer, 2013), 32.

Further Reading

Bryan, Jennifer (2007). *Looking Inward: Devotional Reading and the Private Self in Late Medieval England*, Philadelphia: University of Pennsylvania Press.

Davis, Norman, ed., vols. 1 & 2, and Richard Beadle, and Colin Richmond, eds., vol. 3. (2004–5). *Paston Letters and Papers of the Fifteenth Century*, 3 vols., Early English Text Society S.S. 20–2, Oxford: Oxford University Press.

Krug, Rebecca (2002). *Reading Families: Women's Literate Practice in Late Medieval England*, Ithaca, NY: Cornell University Press.

Moss, Rachel M. (2013). *Fatherhood and Its Representations in Middle English Texts*, Cambridge: D. S. Brewer.

Richmond, Colin (2000). *The Paston Family in the Fifteenth Century: Endings*, Manchester: Manchester University Press.

Rosenthal, Joel T. (2010). *Margaret Paston's Piety*, New York: Palgrave.

Warren, Nancy Bradley (2001). *Spiritual Economies: Female Monasticism in Later Medieval England*, Philadelphia: University of Pennsylvania Press.

Watt, Diane (2007). *Medieval Women's Writing: Works by and for Women in England, 1100–1500*, Cambridge: Polity Press.

Watt, Diane (2020). The Paston Women and Chaucer: Reading Women and Canon Formation in the Fifteenth Century, *Studies in the Age of Chaucer* 42, 337–50.

Whitehead, Christiania (2003). *Castles of the Mind: A Study of Medieval Architectural Allegory*, Cardiff: University of Wales Press.

III

Health, Conduct, and Knowledge

CHAPTER 7

Embracing the Body and the Soul
Women in the Literary Culture of Medieval Medicine

Naoë Kukita Yoshikawa

Women's contribution to medieval sciences is diverse. Even if their activities are not fully documented, extant textual and iconographical sources evince their engagement in a variety of fields. Medieval medicine is just such an area, but there are still gaps in perceptions of how women are represented as authors, readers, or subjects in a medical context within literary culture. Monica Green's 2008 study has shown that only forty-four female owners of medical books can be documented from the twelfth through to the beginning of the sixteenth centuries. These medical texts are often regimens, herbals, and simple recipe collections,[1] suggesting that even gynaecological or obstetrical texts were less closely tied to female readers/owners – further evidence for paradigms about the masculinisation of women's medicine in the later Middle Ages.[2] Although the theory and practice of medicine was predicated upon the cultural construction of womanhood, which was deeply inflected by contemporary gendered ideologies, women do emerge as potent agents of the health of the body and the soul within Christian culture. This chapter explores the literary culture of women's medicine, considering the topics of women's bodies and gendered literacy. It focuses on the texts written by and ascribed to Trotula (or Trota), allegedly a woman healer (*medica*) in eleventh- or twelfth-century Salerno, and also considers medical texts by Hildegard of Bingen (1098–1179), to discuss how medical, religious discourses are integrated into the culture of women's medicine.[3]

Women, Their Bodies, and Gendered Literacy: The Cultural Contexts of Medieval Medicine

As many recent studies have shown, the medieval response to the female body was highly ambivalent.[4] On one hand, the healing powers of the Virgin and saints encapsulated those of women as nurses and nourishers.

On the other, the Church not only stereotyped women as daughters of Eve but also emphasised their weakness by means of Hippocratic (Galenic) medical theories. Arguing that women's damp and fleshly bodies corresponded with the phlegmatic temperament, one of the four temperaments based on the four humours of the Greek medicine, theologians supported misogynistic stereotypes of female inferiority. Nevertheless, since women were valued for begetting offspring, their health was a serious concern both for family and society, and therefore the therapeutics related to fertility remained a vital part of medieval medicine.

Because of this emphasis on reproductive function, medieval women were often conceived, in synecdoche, in terms of the uterus. According to the Hippocratic tradition, the uterus was capable of moving through the body. As Green explains, 'such movement was thought to be caused by retention of the menses, excessive fatigue, lack of food, lack of (hetero) sexual activity, and dryness or lightness of the womb (particularly in older women)'.[5] The wandering uterus induced a typical female disease known as uterine suffocation, and the curse of menstruation was also linked to women's disease. Although menstrual blood was thought to nourish the embryo during pregnancy and to be turned to milk after childbirth, medieval medicine explained that menstruation was designed to get rid of harmful humours in the body and defined menstrual blood as poisonous.[6]

In this cultural milieu a compendium on women's medicine emerged from the medical school at Salerno, where medieval medicine advanced owing to the rediscovery of ancient medical texts and the translation of such treatises as Avicenna's *Canon of Medicine* and Aristotle's natural science into Latin. Originally written by several individuals and circulated independently, the compendium was entitled 'Trotula' (meaning 'little Trota'), which was believed to be the name of its author. Trota is thought to have written the second text, *De curis mulierum* (*On Treatments for Women*),[7] while the first text, *Liber de sinthomatibus mulierum* (*Book on the Conditions of Women*), and the third text, *De ornatu mulierum* (*On Women's Cosmetics*), were written by male physicians. A prologue to the first text recasts the creation story of Genesis into Galenic physiological terms: it explains 'how woman's subjugation to man allows reproduction to take place, which in turn is the chief cause of illness in the female body',[8] foregrounding women's bodies and their reproduction function.[9]

Like Trota, women practised medicine in eleventh- and twelfth-century Salerno,[10] although they were largely excluded from the opportunities of learning the new body of medical knowledge and principles of reasoning founded on a liberal arts education. The world of academic medicine was therefore primarily monopolised by male university-trained physicians whilst female practitioners remained outside of learned medicine. Obviously, midwives played a prominent role in women's medicine, with plenty of iconography of childbirth supported by a midwife and a group of women attesting to this. But 'the valorization of book learning'[11] meant that there were no midwives studying ancient theoretical medicine in Latin or any other language to recreate a vision of their profession, or to constitute a textual community of literate medical practitioners, either.[12] The midwives' task remained the hands-on practice of (normal) childbirth, and its procedures were transmitted as oral lore rather than written texts.[13]

More generally, women engaged in care and cure elsewhere,[14] supervising the health and welfare of their families, at the very least, and playing notable parts in medical treatment; this usually began at home, in the kitchen, where food was prescribed in accordance with humoral therapy. Women in the upper echelons of society also took advantage of their privileged literacy. In their bourgeois households in fifteenth-century Norfolk, the Paston women emulated men in employing their literate skills and collected the best remedies for the welfare of their family while men were away from home.[15] In connection to this, textual communities where wealthy women read or heard vernacular devotional texts and exchanged books could have worked as a space where women benefitted from the exchange of knowledge of medicine. As Green argues, 'once assembled in a common bond of reading, it was possible that such gatherings could have contributed to the dissemination of medical lore'.[16]

Nuns in late medieval monastic communities did not generally have the literate medical knowledge that their male counterparts had: 'hardly any medical texts have been found in female monastic libraries and few of these rise above the level of recipe collections'.[17] However, a dearth of extant manuscripts or catalogues does not rule out the possibility of nuns' access to medical writing. Hildegard of Bingen compiled medical advice in her *Causes and Cures*, consulting a variety of medical texts.[18] At the late-thirteenth-century German convent of Helfta, nuns probably read works on phlebotomy, regularly practised on members of the convent to restore humoral balance.[19] The visionary experience of Mechthild of Hackeborn (1241–98), recounted in her *Liber specialis gratiae*, suggests that she had a basic grasp of the anatomy of the venous system, and even deployed her medical knowledge in conveying her mystical experiences.[20] In Mechthild's description of union with Christ, for example, he presses her against his heart in a sweet embrace and fills her so plenteously with his grace that 'it felt as if her whole body were flowing like a river into all the saints, suffusing them with new and special joy'.[21] Given that medieval medicine explained that the veins functioned in the same way as a network of rivers or canals,[22] the rivers in Mechthild's vision might be identified with the veins of her body through which nutritious blood was carried to the bodies of others. Mechthild thus envisions her body as a vehicle for distributing Christ's redemptive blood originating in his heart, and, in so doing, merges medical and religious discourses.

Such symbiotic relationships between the body and the soul became widespread towards the end of the Middle Ages, when women's medicine also converged with popular devotion to the Virgin and the female saints who were enlisted for intercession, protection, and miraculous cure. It was often pregnant women who sought out holy women to intercede on their behalf, and they frequently made use of birthing girdles upon which were written charms and prayers.[23] Popular devotion is reflected in the proliferation of the images of holy women in childbed, though these images were not used to educate women about medicine but protectively, to enhance reproductive success and to teach women the importance of fertility and lineage.[24]

Within this cultural milieu, we see a growing interest in generation among both male physicians and the laymen. As early as the thirteenth century, the scientific, medical codices by Bernard Gordon (*fl.* 1270–1330) and Gilbertus Anglicus (*c.* 1180–*c.* 1250) included a few chapters on women's diseases and childbirth, and concern regarding reproduction continued tenaciously in the next centuries until such knowledge was received as 'one of the highest achievements of medical science'.[25] The interest in generation precipitated the creation of a distinct natural-philosophical tradition of women's medicine, represented by the *Secreta mulierum* (*Secrets of Women*) composed in late thirteenth-century Germany. Often falsely attributed to the Dominican theologian Albertus Magnus (d. 1280), this treatise endeavours to theorise generation, with an obsessive focus on menstruation, which scholastic authorities regarded as poisonous and dangerous, based on a Plinian account of the noxious properties of the menses.[26] The misogynistic treatise circulated both in Latin and vernacular translations among intellectuals, predominantly in German- and Dutch-speaking areas, but also in France, where Christine de Pizan criticised the pejorative discourse and dismissed it as a 'traittié tout de mençonges' (a treatise composed of lies).[27]

Although the theoretical emphasis of the *Secreta mulierum* sharply contrasts with the *Trotula*'s purpose of providing therapeutic medicine for women, by the fourteenth century their common focus on the issues of generation caused them to move towards each other, becoming 'virtually interchangeable, sometimes being paired with one another, sometimes circulating in identical codicological contexts'.[28] The 'Trotula' ensemble was appropriated by this tradition of and fascination with 'women's secrets', drastically narrowed down to the secrets of fecundity. Through this process, *Trotula* (as title or as author's name) assumed an authority relating to women's secrets, reaching beyond the scope of the original texts.[29] *Secreta mulierum* was less well known in England, but its misogynous discourse is embedded in the authority of Trotula, as in the Prologue to the 'Wife of Bath's Tale', which recounts that Jankyn, the Wife's fifth husband and a clerk, took pleasure in reading a book night and day, '[i]n which book eek ther was Tertulan, / Crisippus, Trotula, and Helowys'.[30] When Chaucer included Trotula in Jankyn's 'Book of wicked wives', a compendium of misogynistic lore, and called her an authority on 'women's secrets', Trotula's image was transformed negatively, separated from her original function of aiding women.

Women's Medicine: The Textual Traditions of Gynaecology and Obstetrics

Ancient and Late Antique Texts of Gynaecology and Obstetrics

Prior to the late eleventh century, there were two ancient traditions of women's medicine: the Hippocratic tradition and the Soranic tradition, based on the gynaecological writings of the Greek physician, Soranus of Ephesus (d. *c.* 129), who applied to women's diseases the theories of 'the Method'.[31] In the late antique period, Soranus's *Gynaecia* was rendered into Latin with some modifications by Muscio, and continued to circulate in the high and late Middle Ages. Muscio's *Gynaecology* is accompanied by an image of the uterus and a sequence of foetus-in-utero figures to show both normal and abnormal presentations to his contemporary midwives, who formed a professionalised corps to practise obstetrics, respected for their skill and literacy.

Muscio's text was adapted into two different works in the late eleventh or early twelfth century: *De passionibus mulierum B* (*On the Illnesses of Women, Version B*) and the *Non omnes quidem*; the latter was incorporated into the English translation, *The Knowing of Woman's Kind*, addressed to female readers.[32] Muscian images were co-opted (predominantly, though not exclusively) for professional male practitioners.[33] A fifteenth-century medical compilation that contains Albucasis and other surgical writings includes the foetus images adorned with the image of two female attendants assisting a woman in labour.[34] These may suggest that women were not envisaged as literate readers but aural and visual medical readers who would be shown the images by a physician or a surgeon, revealing that images serve as pedagogic supplements to texts 'read *to* women by men'.[35]

Hildegard's Medical Texts

As a medical thinker, Hildegard of Bingen also participated in the literary culture of medicine, producing her *Physica* (or *The Book of Simple Medicine*) and *The Causes and Cures*. Though rooted in monastic medicine, her medical work was influenced by a new medical corpus introduced in the twelfth century. Her borrowings from the *Pantegni* of Constantinus Africanus (d. ante 1098/99) evince 'the intellectual possibilities open to literate monastics'.[36]

The *Physica*, a pharmacopoeia, summarises the natural science of Hildegard's age in a logical encyclopaedic format.[37] *The Causes and Cures* is a medical treatise unified by a vision of the universe and a history of salvation. It is predicated upon the idea that disease entered the world as a consequence of the Fall but humanity was also granted medical knowledge and practice to cure the diseases.[38] This convergence of medical and theological discourses is articulated in Hildegard's vision in *The Book of Divine Works*, which culminates in a cosmic image of a God-given schematic order with the human at its centre, visualising the interconnectedness of the universe with God.[39]

The themes of gender differences, human sexuality, and reproduction also recur in *The Causes and Cures*. Hildegard had a healthy idea of the reproductive contributions of women and men. Following Galenic tradition, she considered that both men and women possessed generative seed and argued that gender complementarity began from the moment of conception.[40] She wrote emphatically on complexional differences, conception, pregnancy, and childbirth, and gave menstruation and its disorders a prominent place in her treatment.[41] While she followed a general view of gynaecology, she also had positive ideas concerning God's position on human sexuality, marriage, procreation, and women's physiology – ideas which permeate her *Scivias*. Notably, as Liz Herbert McAvoy argues, in her presentation of the menstruating woman, Hildegard 'offers a visionary response that displaces orthodox reactions of shame, disgust and contempt in favour of a deep compassion – and a compassion, moreover, commanded by God':[42]

> At this time the woman is in pain and in prison, suffering a small portion of the pain of childbirth. I do not remit this time of pain for women, because I gave it to Eve when she conceived sin in the taste of the fruit; but therefore the woman should be cherished in this time with a great and healing tenderness. Let her contain herself in hidden knowledge.[43]

This redeemed aspect of women's reproductive physiology is further developed through the tree/flower metaphor in Hildegard's *Causes and Cures*, where menstruation is called a 'flower': 'The stream of the menstrual period in woman is her generative greenness and floridity, which sprouts offspring... the female extrudes flowers from the viridity of the streams of menstrual blood and produces branches in the fruit of her womb.'[44] This natural imaginary epitomises Hildegard's medico-religious hermeneutics, where the female is the potent agent of flourishing, redeemed reproduction.

The Trotula *Ensemble*

The *Trotula*, as indicated earlier, consists of the *Liber de sinthomatibus mulierum* (*LSM*), *De curis mulierum*, and *De ornatu mulierum* – texts influenced by the new theories and practices of Galenic, Arabic medicine and the local Salernitan tradition. Written in the early twelfth century, the *LSM*, in particular, absorbed the speculative, philosophical ideas of Arabic medicine. Originating in the chapters on women's diseases from the *Viaticum* of Constantinus Africanus, this text replaced Soranic, Methodist theories with Hippocratic and Galenic principles of the four elements and four humours, and is concerned with gynaecological conditions, ranging from menstrual problems to control of fertility and aid for childbirth. Long sections are devoted to menstruation and the menses (commonly called 'the flowers'), with the implication of bearing fruit, resonant of Hildegard's deployment of the tree/flower metaphor for menstruation.[45] It thus contrasts with the misogynistic attitudes represented in the pseudo-Albertan text *Secreta mulierum* mentioned earlier.

De curis mulierum deals with gynaecology, obstetrics, and cosmetics, with an emphasis on the promotion of fertility, while *De ornatu mulierum* focuses on cosmetics and the hygienic needs of women. The female-authored *De curis mulierum* is distinct from the male-authored *LSM*, which centred on 'hands-off' gynaecology and emphasised diet and drugs. It is a treatise on 'hands-on' therapeutics that reflects a practical and largely oral tradition. Notably, the prologue of the *LSM* includes the shame topos – one element of a group of rhetorical topoi that figure the sentiments of 'shame' and 'embarrassment' as inherent to gynaecological practice and texts since antiquity, primarily to justify women's medical practice.[46] But this sentiment also reveals that 'the cultural obsession with female sexual purity rendered problematic any public discussion ... of diseases of the female genitalia'.[47]

The *Trotula* ensemble was disseminated as a single compendium and also independently, both in Latin and vernaculars, exerting a variety of influences on the literary culture of women's medicine. Though primarily addressed to female audiences in their earliest Latin versions, the *Trotula* was owned by 'literate' men, both privately and communally in monasteries and universities, and also incorporated into the handbooks used by learned medical practitioners. As mentioned, the *Trotula* was also excerpted, rearranged, or appropriated into medical texts, such as Gilbertus Anglicus's *Compendium medicinae* (c. 1240), which includes materials selected from *De curis mulierum*.[48] Thus, women did not remain the target audience, although there are a few exceptions, such as a small manuscript (Glasgow, Glasgow University Library, MS Hunter 341) that contains the *Trotula*, the size of which resembles the Books of Hours owned predominantly by women, suggesting its female readership.[49]

Vernacular Translations

The *Trotula* was translated into many vernaculars, with twenty-one known versions.[50] Several vernacular translations were meant for women, but most of the translations were owned by professional male readers, such as surgeons, barbers, and apothecaries, as well as wealthy laymen keen to have knowledge on the science of generation.

One of the earliest vernacular gynaecological texts is the thirteenth-century Anglo-Norman *Les Secrés dé femmes*, a verse text consisting of 165 octosyllabic and alexandrine lines.[51] It is based on a rough draft of the *LSM*, called *Tractatus de egritudinibus mulierum* (*Treatise on the Diseases of Women*). The *Secrés* lacks the prologue of the *LSM*, and goes directly to the chapters on infertility, starting with the phrase: 'Ypocras dit et [nous] enseigne / Les raisons de femme baraigne' ('Hippocrates says and teaches us / The reasons why women are barren').[52] But the text recognises both sexes as equal contributors to the problem of infertility. Identifying male homosexuality as the first reason, it gives moralising advice about the sexual debt of marriage and the need for harmony between husband and wife.[53] Here, the *Trotula* is shaped into a sermon-like text on the 'ideals and expectations of motherhood and fertility',[54] for the purpose of which three recipes for aiding conception are also addressed to women.

The novel title, *Les Secrés dé femmes*, antedates the pseudo-Albertan text and marks 'the introduction of the concept of "secrecy" into gynaecological discourse' that began in the thirteenth century.[55] It also reflects an increasing interest in the processes of generation on the part of natural philosophers and physicians, as a result of which gynaecological literature began to be called 'Secrets of Women', and such texts to excise practical, therapeutic treatments of female conditions in favour of a narrower focus on fertility and sexuality.[56]

There is, however, a more female-oriented French translation of the *LSM*. An early-thirteenth-century prose translation, entitled *Quant Dex nostre Seignor* (*When God our Lord*), envisaged a female audience that would share the gynaecological and obstetrical information among themselves. This translation exploits the shame topos to claim the choice of the vernacular: 'And because women are more ashamed to speak about their diseases to men than to women, I am composing for them this book in a language they understand.'[57] But every copy of this text is embedded within collections of medical treatises, often in Latin, suggesting that it strayed away from women's hands. We may assume that *Quant Dex nostre Seignor* originally circulated independently in small pamphlets among midwives and laywomen, or that the text was intended to be read by male practitioners or other literates to an audience of women.[58]

Quant Dex nostre Seignor was also rendered into Anglo-Norman verse around the mid-thirteenth century, to be called *Bien sachies femmes* (*Good Midwives*). At the start, it addresses women in general, but soon women are referred to as 'they', while second-person addresses are reserved for professional male readers. In this text, the shame topos also disappears, suggesting that the *Trotula* has been redacted to an exemplar of male medical practice. Thus, as Green argues, 'the French tradition of vernacularization of the *Trotula* presents a see-sawing pattern: some translations lay claim to a female audience, while others ... seem in fact to be putting the texts into the hands of professional male practitioners'.[59]

German gynaecological writing and translation were directed predominantly at professional male readers, and, to date, we know of only two translations of the *Trotula*, while the pseudo-Albertan *Secreta mulierum* was widely disseminated. There are three redactions of a fifteenth-century

Dutch translation, one of which envisages women as its audience, although some surgical, scientific materials added to one of the copies suggest that it was reoriented to male readers.[60]

Vernacular Tradition in England

During the twelfth and thirteenth centuries, a number of Latin medical texts arrived in England from southern Italy, as common Norman rule facilitated the quick transfer of medical texts and ideas.[61] The circulation of the *Trotula* in England was rapid and widespread, and its vernacular translations appeared from the thirteenth century onwards. There are six known English translations of the *Trotula*,[62] three of which were read by female audiences: the Anglo-Norman *Secrés*; *The Knowing of Woman's Kind in Childing* (*The Knowing*), the earliest of the English *Trotulas*, to which I return shortly; and the fifteenth-century *The Book called 'Trotela'*, which contains extensive obstetrical instructions for men and women who cope with childbirth in a domestic setting.[63]

i. The Knowing of Woman's Kind in Childing

Referred to by its name in London, British Library, MS Additional 12195,[64] *The Knowing of Woman's Kind in Childing* is a fusion of an Old French translation with two late antique Latin texts, selected by the translator with discrimination.[65] Its large sections come from *Quant Dex nostre Seignor*. Other sources include *Non omnes quidem*, an epitome of Muscio's *Gynaecia* and the *Genicia Cleopatrae ad Theodotam*, attributed to Cleopatra. The addition from *Non omnes quidem* of material on how to handle normal and malpresented births reflects the immediate need for such works for women and the medical role that women played for women.[66] The translator also added from an unidentified fourth source some new material on male/female differences, the possession of a womb, the physiology of menstruation, and uterine suffocation. As such, it is 'a novel fusing of several different texts and theoretical traditions into a single work'.[67]

The prologue claims that the author translated the text for women so that it would 'helpe hem & conceyle hem in here maledyes with-owtyn schevynge here dysese to man'.[68] Although the translator omits the reference to shame present in the French and Latin *Trotula*, he seeks to protect women from the potential shame of exposure to men by balancing women's linguistic disadvantage with the vernacular literacy.

The translator is also aware of the gendered struggle within the culture of women's medicine. Admitting that men may read this text, he cautions any male readers against misusing gynaecological texts and advises them to respect the 'preuytees' of women, since there are no more evils about a woman's body than there are evils in those women who are now 'seyntys in hevyn':

> And yf hit fall any man to rede hit, O pray hym & scharge hym in ovre Lady be-halue þat he rede hit not in no dyspyte ne sclavndure of no woman ne for no cause but for þe hele & helpe of hem, dredynge þat vengavns myht fall to hym as hit hath do to oþer þat have schevyd here preuytees in sclavndyr of hem, vndyrstondynge in certeyne þat þey have no oþer euylys þat nov be a-lyue than thoo women hade þat nov be seyntys in hevyn.[69]

The Knowing thus betrays uneasiness concerning masculine uses (and misuses) of gynaecological knowledge and 'voice[s] this concern about intrusive or prurient readings'.[70] But the reference to 'ovre Lady' and these women now in heaven gives, in the words of Mary Flannery, 'an aura of sanctity to women in general, incorporating them into a community defined by female saintliness', elevating 'their suffering, their illness, and even their shamefastness, which are here imbued with holiness-by-association'.[71] It is such emotional solidarity with female saints that materialises in the charms and prayers which midwives are advised (in this text) to write on birthing girdles to aid childbirth.[72]

Codicologically, *The Knowing* originally appears as an independent fascicle, and the codices are small enough to be conveniently consulted by midwives and laywomen.[73] The small format of three copies of the text is again 'reminiscent of the Books of Hours and prayerbooks'.[74] *The Knowing* was most probably ruminated upon privately, discussed in groups, and consulted in chambers of childbirth.

ii. The Sickness of Women
The Sickness of Women, the most widely circulated vernacular text of women's medicine in fifteenth-century England, contains gynaecological and obstetrical chapters excerpted from Gilbertus Anglicus's *Compendium medicinae*.[75] *The Sickness of Women* is extant in two versions. The first redaction (*Sickness 1*) translated fifteen chapters on women's diseases from book seven of the *Compendium medicinae*.[76] Its focus on the womb itself is implied in the title used in New Haven, Yale Medical Library, MS 47, and

London, Wellcome Library, MS 5650: the womb itself ('the moder id est matrix') is 'the sekenesse of wymmen'.[77]

The mid-fifteenth-century version (*Sickness 2*) includes all the material in the first version, but it has been rearranged and expanded with additional materials.[78] The prologue is added to *Sickness 2*, addressed to a female audience so that 'oo womman may help another in hir sikenes',[79] while *Sickness 1* opens with 'Sirs', addressed probably to surgeons or general practitioners. Also added to this version are new sections on childbirth from Muscio's *Gynaecia* and his foetus-in-utero figures, with instructions on how to extract malpresented foetuses, probably with the intention to provide midwives and birth attendants with medical knowledge. The writer of *Sickness 2* is concerned both with women's shamefastness concerning their ailments and with inappropriate male behaviour:

> as I saide, hem shamen for drede of resprevyng in tymes comyng and of discuryng of vncurteys men that loven wymmen but for their lustis and for their foul likyng; and if wymmen bien in disease, suche men han hem in dispite and thynken nat how moche disease wymmen han or than thei han brought hem furth into this world.[80]

The four extant manuscripts that contain *Sickness 2* suggest that this text could have reached female audiences through two different media: namely, through small pamphlets in which *Sickness 2* is the main text (London, British Library, MS Sloane 249, and London, Royal College of Surgeons, MS 129); and through collections of medical tracts (London, British Library, MS Sloane 2463, and Cambridge, Trinity College, MS R.14.52).[81] Notably, in MS Sloane 249, *Sickness 2* is preceded by a brief spiritual regimen that recommends one to say a series of Masses for one week, to be delivered from perils of life.[82] Among them is the death in 'geysyne' (childbirth), and the woman is advised to say the devotion in remembrance of St Susanna, imploring a safe delivery through her grace, as Susanna was understood as a model of deliverance from suffering through the power of prayer (Daniel 13). The Mass regimen with supplication to Susanna enhances the gender-specific focus of this pamphlet, produced for a woman preparing for the difficult task of childbirth.

Cambridge, Trinity College, MS R.14.52, a medical compendium, was commissioned by the London merchant Thomas Cook, and later owned by John de Vale, his secretary. The incorporation of the *Sickness 2* into this manuscript reflects the interest of the head of a bourgeois household in generation and measures to ensure his heirs.[83] But women in such a wealthy household might also have accessed the gynaecological texts in this manuscript, just as the gynaecological materials in the codex, Aberystwyth, National Library of Wales, MS Brogynton II.1, are likely to have been used by women of the house.[84] The vernacularisation of women's medicine thus increased women's access to texts, but it also expanded male readership, ranging from clerics and professional practitioners to lay elite, whose concern was to make the female body reproductively successful.[85] The subtle, rhetorical policing embedded in *The Knowing of Women's Kind* and *Sickness 2* illuminates efforts on the part of translators/editors to defend the gynaecological texts against inappropriate use by men.

Conclusion

The late medieval literary culture of women's medicine was inflected by male concerns regarding patrimony, and often shaped by a misogynistic, if not voyeuristic, perspective. Moreover, in a society where theoretical learning was conceived as intrinsically more valuable than hands-on knowledge, midwives and female healers could never enjoy the same authority as male practitioners. The gradual obscuring of the historical Trota and the original *Trotula* ensemble testifies to the marginalisation of women in women's medicine, undermining its traditional function as a therapeutic art addressed to alleviating women's ailments. In the context of this social and cultural transformation, the only field over which women had a monopoly was normal childbirth. Nevertheless, women were partakers in the literary culture of medicine, although the circulation of the texts available to them traced a narrow orbit. Further illumination concerning women's engagement with medical texts and the literature-medicine nexus that operated within this culture may be gained by interrogating a variety of dialogues between the medical, the religious, and gender in terms of women and their roles as healers in the later Middle Ages.[86]

Notes

1. Monica H. Green, *Making Women's Medicine Masculine: The Rise of Male Authority in Pre-Modern Gynaecology* (Oxford: Oxford University Press, 2008), 141.
2. See Green, *Making Women's Medicine Masculine*.
3. On the convergence of medicine and religion, see Naoë Kukita Yoshikawa (ed.), *Medicine, Religion and Gender* (Cambridge: D. S. Brewer, 2015),

'Introduction'; Virginia Langum, *Medicine and the Seven Deadly Sins in Late Medieval Literature and Culture* (New York: Palgrave Macmillan, 2016).
4. Joan Cadden, *Meanings of Sex Difference in the Middle Ages: Medicine, Science and Culture* (Cambridge: Cambridge University Press, 1993); Nancy Caciola, *Discerning Spirits: Divine and Demonic Possession in the Middle Ages* (Ithaca, NY: Cornell University Press, 2003), ch. 3, 129–75.
5. Monica Green (ed. and trans.), *The Trotula: An English Translation of the Medieval Compendium of Women's Medicine* (Philadelphia: University of Pennsylvania Press, 2001), 'Introduction', 22–5 (22).
6. For a medieval view of menstruation, see Bettina Bildhauer, 'The Secrets of Women: A Medieval Perspective on Menstruation', in *Menstruation: History and Culture from Antiquity to Modernity*, ed. Andrew Shail (Basingstoke: Palgrave Macmillan, 2005), 65–75.
7. See Monica H. Green, *Women's Healthcare in the Medieval West* (New York: Routledge, 2000) and her numerous works in Monica Green, *Bibliography on Medieval Women, Gender, and Medicine, 1980–2009*: www.sciencia.cat/biblio teca/documents/Green_CumulativeBib_Feb2010.pdf.
8. Green (ed. and trans.), *Trotula*, 'Introduction', 36.
9. For this compendium, see further below.
10. Green (ed. and trans.), *Trotula*, 'Introduction', 48.
11. Green, *Making Women's Medicine Masculine*, xiii.
12. Green, *Making Women's Medicine Masculine*, 138, 160–1.
13. Monica Green, 'The Sources of Eucharius Rösslin's "Rosegarden for Pregnant Women and Midwives" (1513)', *Medical History* 53 (2009), 167–92 (172). Literate midwives reappear only in the latter half of the fifteenth century.
14. See Montserrat Cabré, 'Women or Healers? Household Practices and the Categories of Health Care in Late Medieval Iberia', *Bulletin of the History of Medicine* 82.1 (2008), 18–51, where the fluidity of women's roles is discussed.
15. Green, *Making Women's Medicine Masculine*, 309; Rebecca Krug, *Reading Families: Women's Literate Practice in Late Medieval England* (Ithaca, NY: Cornell University Press, 2002); Diane Watt, 'Mary the Physician: Women, Religion and Medicine in the Middle Ages', in *Medicine, Religion and Gender in Medieval Culture*, ed. Naoë Kukita Yoshikawa (Cambridge: D. S. Brewer, 2015), 27–44.
16. Green, *Making Women's Medicine Masculine*, 161. For Brian Stock's concept of 'textual communities', see *The Implications of Literacy: Written Language and Models of Interpretation in the Eleventh and Twelfth Centuries* (Princeton: Princeton University Press, 1983), 522. For female ownership, sharing, and circulation of manuscripts containing gynaecological texts, excerpts, or recipes, see Theresa Lorraine Tyers, 'Family, Feud, and Fertility in Late Medieval Artois and Flanders', *Dynamis* 38.2 (2018), 389–406.
17. Green, *Making Women's Medicine Masculine*, 130.
18. Florence Eliza Glaze, 'Medical Writer: "Behold the Human Creature"', in *Voice of the Living Light: Hildegard of Bingen and Her World*, ed. Barbara Newman (Berkeley, CA: University of California Press, 1998), 125–48.

19. A number of books in their library were lost when the monastery was attacked in 1284. See Ulrike Wiethaus, 'Collaborative Literacy and the Spiritual Education of Nuns at Helfta', in *Nuns' Literacies in Medieval Europe: The Kansas City Dialogue*, ed. Virginia Blanton, Veronica O'Mara, and Patricia Stoop (Turnhout: Brepols, 2015), 27–46 (29).
20. Mechthild could also have has first-hand or similar experience.
21. Barbara Newman (trans.), *Mechthild of Hackeborn and the Nuns of Helfta: The Book of Special Grace* (New York: Paulist Press, 2017), 129. See *Liber specialis gratiae*, II.17, in *Revelationes Gertrudianae ac Mechtildianae*, 2 vols., ed. Dom Ludwig Paquelin (Paris, 1875–7), II, 151. For its Middle English translation, see *The Boke of Gostely Grace: The Middle English Translation, A Critical Edition from Oxford*, MS Bodley 220, ed. Naoë Kukita Yoshikawa and Anne Mouron, with the assistance of Mark Atherton (Liverpool: Liverpool University Press, 2022).
22. Carole Rawcliffe, *Leprosy in Medieval England* (Woodbridge: Boydell, 2006), 67.
23. See London, Wellcome Library, MS 632: blog.wellcomelibrary.org/2015/10/wellcome-ms-632-heavenly-protection-during-childbirth-in-late-medieval-england.
24. Elizabeth L'Estrange, *Holy Motherhood: Gender, Dynasty, and Visual Culture in the Later Middle Ages* (Manchester: Manchester University Press, 2008); Katherine Park, *Secrets of Women: Gender, Generation, and the Origins of Human Dissection* (New York: Zone Books, 2006).
25. Green, *Making Women's Medicine Masculine*, 91.
26. Green, *Making Women's Medicine Masculine*, 218. Monica Green, '"Traittié tout de mençonges", The *Secrés des dames*, "Trotula," and Attitudes toward Women's Medicine in Fourteenth- and Early-Fifteenth-Century France', in *Christine de Pizan and the Categories of Difference*, ed. Marilynn Desmond (Minneapolis: University of Minnesota Press, 1998), 146–78 (150–58); Helen Rodnite Lemay (trans.), *Women's Secrets: A Translation of Pseudo-Albertus Magnus' De Secretis Mulierum with Commentaries* (Albany: State University of New York Press, 1992), 'Introduction'. Aristotelian views of women as deformed males and his ideas concerning menstrual blood and female semen (in, e.g., Generation of Animals, II and IV) were also embedded in clerical misogyny.
27. See further Green, 'Traittié tout de mençonges'.
28. Green, *Making Women's Medicine Masculine*, 205; Green, 'Traittié tout de mençonges', 148.
29. Green, *Making Women's Medicine Masculine*, 220–1.
30. The Wife of Bath's Prologue, 669–70; 676–7, in Geoffrey Chaucer, *The Canterbury Tales*, in *The Riverside Chaucer*, ed. Larry D. Benson, 3rd edn (Boston: Houghton Mifflin, 1987). See further Green, *Making Women's Medicine Masculine*, 225–37.
31. The theories of 'the Method' posit that there are three basic states of human body: the lax, the constricted, and the combination of the two. See further Green (ed. and trans.), *Trotula*, 'Introduction', 15–16.

32. *De passionibus mulierum* B is a fusion of Latin Metrodora and Muscio, composed in southern Italy in the eleventh century. See Ron Barkai, *A History of Jewish Gynaecological Texts in the Middle Ages* (Leiden: Brill, 1998), 57. For *The Knowing of Women's Kind*, see later in chapter.
33. Green, *Making Women's Medicine Masculine*, 151–9. Only two illustrated texts (a Dutch translation of *Trotula* and *Sickness of Women* 2) were directed at a female audience.
34. Oxford, Bodleian Library, MS Laud misc. 724, fol. 97r.
35. Green, *Making Women's Medicine Masculine*, 150.
36. Glaze, 'Medical Writer', 140.
37. *Hildegard von Bingen's Physica: The Complete English Translation of Her Classic Work on Health and Healing*, trans. Priscilla Throop (Rochester, VT: Healing Arts Press, 1998).
38. Hildegard of Bingen, *On Natural Philosophy and Medicine: Selections from 'Cause et cure'*, trans. Margret Berger (Cambridge: D. S. Brewer, 1999), 12; Glaze, 'Medical Writer', 135–7. See also Debra L. Stoudt, 'The Medical, the Magical, and the Miraculous in the Healing Arts of Hildegard of Bingen', in *A Companion to Hildegard of Bingen*, ed. Debra L. Stoudt, George Ferzoco, and Beverly Kienzle (Leiden: Brill, 2013), 249–72 (272).
39. Hildegard of Bingen, *Liber divinorum operum*, ed. Albert Derolez and Peter Dronke, CCCM 92 (Turnhout: Brepols, 1996), I.2, 59–113.
40. Joan Cadden, 'It Takes All Kinds: Sexuality and Gender Differences in Hildegard of Bingen's "Book of Compound Medicine"', *Traditio* 40 (1984), 149–74 (153–6).
41. Cadden, 'It Takes All Kinds', 172. Hildegard also sees menstruation 'as an aspect of the general ebb and flow of blood, caused in both men and women by the waxing and waning moon' (173).
42. Liz Herbert McAvoy, *The Enclosed Garden and the Medieval Religious Imaginary* (Cambridge: D. S. Brewer, 2021).
43. Hildegard of Bingen, *Scivias*, trans. Columba Hart and Jane Bishop (New York: Paulist Pres, 1990), I.2.20, 83.
44. Hildegard of Bingen, *Causae et curae*, ed. Paul Kaiser (Leipzig: 1903, repr. Basel: Basler Hildegard-Gesellschaft, 1980), Bk. 2, 105, quoted in *Trotula*, ed. and trans. Green, 21. If the woman lacks the viridity of her flowering, she is called infertile. For the concept of *viriditas* (greenness) as a substance that circulates in the blood, see Victoria Sweet, *Rooted in the Earth, Rooted in the Sky: Hildegard of Bingen and Premodern Medicine* (New York: Routledge, 2006).
45. Green (ed. and trans.), *Trotula*, 'Introduction', 21–2.
46. See Green (ed. and trans.), *Trotula*, 65.
47. Green, *Making Women's Medicine Masculine*, 199.
48. Monica H. Green and Linne R. Mooney (eds.), 'The Sickness of Women', in *Sex, Aging, and Death in a Medieval Medical Compendium: Trinity College Cambridge MS R.14.52, Its Texts, Language, and Scribe*, ed. M. Teresa Tavormina, Medieval

and Renaissance Texts and Studies 292, 2 vols. (Tempe: Arizona Center for Medieval and Renaissance Studies, 2006), vol. 2, 455–568 (557–8, 567).
49. Green, *Making Women's Medicine Masculine*, 143.
50. Green, *Making Women's Medicine Masculine*, 165.
51. Monica H. Green, 'Making Motherhood in Medieval England: The Evidence from Medicine', in *Motherhood, Religion, and Society in Medieval Europe, 400–1400: Essays Presented to Henrietta Leyser*, ed. Conrad Leyser and Lesley Smith (London: Routledge, 2016), 173–203 (182–90).
52. Green, 'Making Motherhood in Medieval England', 184.
53. Green, 'Making Motherhood in Medieval England', 186–7. Hildegard of Bingen explains how emotional friction between a couple can adversely affect reproduction. Tony Hunt's edition of this text from Cambridge, Trinity College, MS I.1.20, 21rb–23rb is presented in his 'Obstacles to Motherhood', in *Motherhood, Religion, and Society in Medieval Europe*, ed. Leyser and Smith, 205–12.
54. Green, 'Making Motherhood in Medieval England', 176.
55. Monica H. Green, 'From "Diseases of Women" to "Secrets of Women": The Transformation of Gynecological Literature in the Later Middle Ages', *Journal of Medieval and Early Modern Studies* 30.1 (2000), 5–39 (12).
56. Green, *Making Women's Medicine Masculine*, chs. 2, 4, 70–117, 163–203, respectively.
57. Green, *Making Women's Medicine Masculine*, 169, based on London, British Library, MS Sloane 3525, fol. 246v.
58. Green, *Making Women's Medicine Masculine*, 170; Monica H. Green, 'Obstetrical and Gynaecological Texts', *Studies in the Age of Chauce* 14 (1992), 53–88 (58–9).
59. Green, *Making Women's Medicine Masculine*, 176.
60. See further Green, *Making Women's Medicine Masculine*, 178–83.
61. Green, 'Making Motherhood in Medieval England', 174; Monica H. Green, 'Salerno on the Thames: The Genesis of Anglo-Norman Medical Literature', in *Language and Culture in Medieval Britain: the French of England, c. 1100–c. 1500*, ed. Jocelyn Wogan-Browne, Carolyn Collette, Maryanne Kowaleski et al. (Woodbridge: York Medieval Press, 2009), 220–31.
62. Monica H. Green, 'A Handlist of the Latin and Vernacular Manuscripts of the So Called Trotula Texts: Part II: The Vernacular Texts and Latin Re-Writings', *Scriptorium* 51 (1997), 80–104 (84–9); Elizabeth Dearnley, *Translators and Their Prologues in Medieval England* (Cambridge: D. S. Brewer, 2016), 202 and n. 59.
63. *The Book Made [by] a Woman Named Rota*, the last medieval English translation, made probably as late as the turn of the sixteenth century, is not directly addressed to women, but one copy was 'clearly intended for the use of the patient who will be treating herself or for the use of her female attendant' (Green, *Making Women's Medicine Masculine*, 190).
64. Alexandra Barratt (ed.), *The Knowing of Woman's Kind in Childing: A Middle English Version of Material Derived from the Trotula and Other Sources*, Medieval Women: Texts and Contexts 4 (Turnhout: Brepols, 2001). There

are five extant English manuscripts. Barratt's edition is based on Oxford, Bodleian Library, MS Douce 37, and Cambridge, University Library, MS Ii.6.33. Green, 'Obstetrical and Gynaecological Texts', 64–8.
65. Barratt (ed.), *The Knowing of Woman's Kind in Childing*, 9.
66. Green, *Making Women's Medicine Masculine*, 185.
67. Green, 'Obstetrical and Gynaecological Texts', 64.
68. Barratt (ed.), *The Knowing of Woman's Kind in Childing*, 42, ll. 37, 20–1 (MS Douce).
69. Barratt (ed.), *The Knowing of Woman's Kind in Childing*, 42, ll. 37, 24–31 (MS Douce).
70. Dearnley, *Translators and Their Prologues*, 206.
71. Mary C. Flannery, 'Emotion and the Ideal Reader in Middle English Gynaecological Texts', in *Literature, Science and Medicine in the Medieval and Early Modern Periods*, ed. Rachel Falconer and Denis Renevey (Tübingen: Narr, 2013), 103–15 (111).
72. See Barratt (ed.), *The Knowing of Woman's Kind in Childing*, 64, ll. 369–71, and 66, ll. 372–6 (MS Douce).
73. See Barratt (ed.), *The Knowing of Woman's Kind in Childing*, 12, 14–16; Green, 'Obstetrical and Gynaecological Texts', 59.
74. See Green, *Making Women's Medicine Masculine*, 185.
75. For the extant manuscripts, see Green, 'Obstetrical and Gynaecological Texts', 72–4. Cf. n. 48.
76. Green and Mooney (eds.), 'The Sickness of Women', 457–58.
77. Green, 'Obstetrical and Gynaecological Texts', 74.
78. For four extant manuscripts, see Green and Mooney (eds.), 'The Sickness of Women', 459.
79. Green and Mooney (eds.), 'The Sickness of Women', 485.
80. Green and Mooney (eds.), 'The Sickness of Women', 485. See also Dearnley, *Translators and Their Prologue*, 206–7.
81. Green and Mooney (eds.), 'The Sickness of Women', 473–8.
82. Monica H. Green, 'Masses in Remembrance of "Seynt Susanne": A Fifteenth-Century Spiritual Regimen', *Notes & Queries* 50.4 (2003), 380–84. London, Royal College of Surgeons, MS 129 accompanies a recipe for aqua vitae: see Green and Mooney (eds.), 'The Sickness of Women', 474.
83. Green and Mooney (eds.), 'The Sickness of Women', 478.
84. Green, *Making Women's Medicine Masculine*, 193, n. 88, 192–3. More generally, women were readers of the 'household books' which included practical information on health: see Julia Boffey, 'Bodleian Library, MS Arch. Selden. B.24 and Definitions of the "Household Book"', in *The English Medieval Book: Studies in Memory of Jeremy Griffiths*, ed. A. S. G. Edwards, Vincent Gillespie, and Ralph Hanna (London: British Library, 2000), 125–34 (125).
85. Green, *Making Women's Medicine Masculine*, 194–5.
86. An excellent recent study is Laura Kalas, *Spiritual Medicine: Suffering, Transformation and the Life Course* (Cambridge: D. S. Brewer, 2020).

Further Reading

Blumenfeld-Kosinski, Renate (1990). *Not of Woman Born: Representations of Caesarean Birth in Medieval and Renaissance Culture*, Ithaca, NY: Cornell University Press.

Fissell, Mary E. (2008). Introduction: Women, Health, and Healing in Early Modern Europe. *Bulletin of the History of Medicine*, Special Issue: Women, Health, and Healing in Early Modern Europe, 81.2, 1–17.

Green, Monica H. (2005). Gynaecology and Midwifery. In *Medieval Science, Technology and Medicine: An Encyclopedia*, ed. Thomas F. Glick, Steven J. Livesey, and Faith Wallis. New York: Routledge, 214–16.

Green, Monica H. (2005). Bodies, Gender, Health, Disease: Recent Work on Medieval Women's Medicine. *Studies in Medieval and Renaissance History*, 3rd series 2, 1–46.

Green, Monica H. (2020). 'Who/What Is "Trotula"?', at: www.academia.edu/41537366/WHO_WHAT_IS_TROTULA_2020.

McCracken, Peggy (2003). *The Curse of Eve, the Wound of the Hero: Blood, Gender and Medieval Literature*, Philadelphia: University of Pennsylvania Press.

Rawcliffe, Carole (1995). *Medicine and Society in Later Medieval England*, Stroud: Alan Sutton.

Ritchey, Sara, and Sharon Strocchia, eds. (2020). *Gender, Health, and Healing, 1250–1550*, Amsterdam: Amsterdam University Press.

Robertson, Elizabeth (1993). Medieval Medical Views of Women and Female Spirituality in the *Ancrene Wisse* and Julian of Norwich's *Showings*. In *Feminist Approaches to the Body in Medieval Literature*, ed. Linda Lomperis and Sarah Stanbury. Philadelphia: University of Pennsylvania Press, 142–67.

CHAPTER 8

Gender and Class in the Circulation of Conduct Books
Kathleen Ashley

Guides to conduct form a substantial part of the immense body of didactic writing produced throughout the Middle Ages, which itself drew on classical, biblical, and medieval moral, sapiential, and political sources.[1] Medieval texts instructing lay wives on desired behaviour may be the most notorious examples of the popular genre known as 'conduct books'; however, the range of medieval works prescribing conduct was wide and diverse, making a single definition difficult. They were written throughout the Middle Ages by fathers and mothers to their male and female children, by husbands to their wives, and by authority figures both clerical and lay. Some addressed expectations among the highest aristocracy, while others depicted lifestyles of the gentry, bourgeoisie, or lower classes. Many – perhaps most – were intended as public texts with a readership beyond their specific addressee and context.

The messages conveyed by conduct books also varied but could include religious instruction in spiritual principles and devotional behaviours, lessons for the young, guidance in negotiating social hierarchies, hints for maintaining good relationships with kin and friends, marital counsel, and practical advice for everyday living in a household (courtly or bourgeois). The conduct book provided a model for its reader's life, including occasionally guidance on the art of dying. A corollary implication was that good behaviour in this life would earn a heavenly reward.

Conduct literature might appear to offer sharp gender distinctions; however, closer analysis of the production, contents, and reception of texts reveals the surprising gender complexity of medieval literary culture. The context in which a medieval work was produced and received cannot be reduced to one gendered aspect – whether that of the author, the dedicatee, the text's subject, the internal addressee, or its eventual ownership.[2]

Likewise, class and cultural boundaries were fluid, especially in the later Middle Ages. Conduct books that appeared first in an aristocratic milieu were often appropriated by bourgeois readers. French writing of the period was easily accessible by the English upper classes, given their fluency in the French language, and a flourishing translation business responded to public taste with English versions of such conduct books as those by Christine de Pizan and the Chevalier de la Tour Landry.

Aristocratic Conduct

Books of advice for those in the ruling class – the 'mirrors for princes' – formed an influential genre from the ancient world to Renaissance Europe. Although almost all early medieval examples were authored by and addressed to men, a theologically learned and moving text is the guide to right conduct written by Dhuoda, a ninth-century Frankish noblewoman. In the prologue to her *Liber manualis* (known in English as the *Handbook for William*), Dhuoda identifies herself as a mother writing out of concern for her teenaged son, from whom she has been separated. She intends the text to be a 'mirror' in which he can regard both his social and spiritual health: 'What is essential, my son William, is that you show yourself to be such a man on both levels that you are both effective in this world and pleasing to God in every way.'[3]

Carolingian ideology gave noble mothers a prominent role as moral educators of their children, and as a noblewoman Dhuoda also exercised broad administrative duties on behalf of her absent husband, Bernard, the count of Septimania. Dhuoda's *Handbook* (written between 841 and 843 in Uzès) has an emotional intensity reflecting the political insecurity of post-Carolingian warfare between the three heirs of Louis the Pious who were fighting each other over the territory of Francia.[4] Bernard was forced to offer fealty to Charles the Bald, with his teenage son William taken as hostage to the king. A newborn second son had also been removed to an unknown site. Separated from her children, Dhuoda sees her book as offering a mother's guidance to William, and she expresses the hope that he will eventually share her writing with his little brother. Dhuoda counsels William to maintain the proper attitude of 'reverence' to his 'lord and father, Bernard', to whom he owes obedience and loyalty above all other powerful men in their society.[5] Next, William is to demonstrate steadfast loyalty to his secular lord, Charles, so that in adulthood he will be wise enough to join the council of magnates. William should revere priests and bishops for their intercessory powers, but Dhuoda tells him to choose only virtuous models. He should follow 'good men seeking after worthy goals' who can 'offer counsel in the most useful of ways, in their true subjection to the wishes of their lords', as a result of which they will be rewarded 'both from God and in the secular world'.[6]

As a guide to her son's behaviour within elite socio-political networks, Dhuoda's *Handbook* supports patriarchal structures but ultimately places moral responsibility on William's own decision-making. She points out that there are rich and successful people who hide their evil intentions under the pretence of good will. She offers spiritual remedies against sins such as pride, lust, anger, and greed, and she acknowledges life's many difficulties (temptation, persecution, deprivation, and illness) while advising him how to handle those difficulties in the right spirit. She uses an authoritative voice based on her parental role to educate her son for an honourable life.[7]

The spiritual and moral guidance Dhuoda offers her son shows her familiarity with Benedictine practices of prayer and Psalm recitation as well as the writings of contemporary Christian intellectuals such as Alcuin and earlier Church fathers such as Augustine. Above all, she finds pertinent examples of exemplary and cautionary behaviours in the Old Testament, especially the dramatic story of King David. These intellectual sources for the *Handbook* mark her as a member of the lay nobility who had an education in the biblical and moral texts that formed the curriculum of the Carolingian palace schools.[8] Thomas Noble describes the aim of this education as creating 'secular sanctity' for the lay nobility, a 'Christian ideal of public service'.[9] Janet Nelson also argues that we should see Dhuoda's *Handbook* not just as an expression of maternal authority but as the product of a public intellectual who believed in 'a life of Christian mindfulness'.[10] Unlike male-authored 'mirrors' of the early Middle Ages that were well known and widely circulated among contemporaries, Dhuoda's *Liber manualis* survived in only two problematic manuscripts.[11] Nevertheless, it has become an important source for our understanding of ninth-century culture, and especially for the agency of aristocratic women.

Noble parents in later centuries also wrote conduct guides for their children who would occupy elevated positions in society. The thirteenth-century French king Louis IX left his *Enseignemenz* (*Teachings*) in the form of public letters to his son and to his daughter.[12] Unlike Dhuoda's *Liber manualis*, which has survived by chance, Louis' two letters were well preserved in official copies and, unlike Dhuoda, Louis was writing to adult children: Philippe was heir to the throne, while Isabelle was queen of Navarre. Dhuoda herself is known only through her unique conduct text, but 'Saint' Louis was one of the most prominent rulers of the French

Middle Ages, recognised by contemporaries as a model of Christian kingship. When he died in 1270 on crusade in North Africa, the royal confessors and chroniclers began to assemble documents to make the case for his canonisation. By the time he was canonised in 1297, the documentation included innumerable copies of the letter to Philippe.

The background to the *Enseignemenz* is given in a biography of Louis IX by Geoffrey de Beaulieu, the king's confessor. According to Beaulieu, Louis was a devoted father who gave his children moral guidance and made sure all – girls as well as boys – were educated in French and Latin. Beaulieu translated Louis' letter to Philippe from French into Latin and included it in his official biography of the king, but the parallel letter to Isabelle was not included. Uncounted copies of Philippe's letter circulated in both a short and a long version in documentation by the royal scriptorium at Saint Denis. To Isabelle, Louis says he wrote in his own hand because he believed she would 'retain things more willingly from me, out of love for me, than you would from various others'.[13] This letter survived in just two biographies of the king: one by William of Saint-Pathus, the confessor to Louis' wife Queen Marguerite, and another by Jean de Joinville that the Queen also commissioned. Circulation of Louis IX's *Enseignmenz* thus reveals a gender divide in the reception of the two letters, with Isabelle's only reproduced (it seems) at the instigation of her mother.

Although differing in reception, a comparison of the contents of the letters shows that Louis wrote similar moral advice to both daughter and son. Identical passages urge love of God as the fundamental value, with avoidance of mortal sin. As he says to both, you should 'let all your limbs be cut off and your life taken by cruel martyrdom rather than sin knowingly'.[14] Persecution or illness should be borne patiently as it has been sent by God for one's good, while gifts of prosperity or bodily health should be humbly and thankfully received. Both son and daughter are urged to confess often, choosing well-educated and holy confessors who can teach and reprimand, and they should attend church services often, without 'dawdling' or 'speaking idle words' (especially during the taking of the sacraments).[15]

The two texts diverge where Louis addresses his son as a future king who will be worthy of the position; the advice for Isabelle is briefer, mostly urging compassion and modesty. She is to respond to the unfortunate with comfort and alms, avoiding ostentatious almsgiving and dress. She should obey her husband, father, and mother – but only in things that are godly: 'Against God's wishes you should not obey anyone', he tells Isabelle.[16] It is a caution against unthinking obedience also found in subsequent female conduct texts, as we shall see.

The context for aristocratic women's conduct literature had changed dramatically by the end of the Middle Ages. In place of Dhuoda's lonely voice addressing her far away son with wise counsel that appears to have had few readers, late medieval royal women writers offering advice for their daughters drew on well-known texts by their predecessors – confident that their views would circulate in aristocratic circles and even among a broader set of literate lay readers. Anne de France, Duchess of Bourbon, who wrote a conduct book for her unmarried daughter Suzanne de Bourbon (*c.* 1500), is part of a royal network of female bibliophiles. Anne, the daughter of King Louis XI and sister to King Charles VIII, inherited a large library from her mother, Charlotte de Savoie.[17] In the *Enseignements* (*Lessons*) she wrote for Suzanne, Anne recommends a reading list of moral 'teachings' that includes 'the small book of the noble Saint Louis', which Sharon Jansen suggests may be the king's *Enseignemenz*.[18]

Anne's *Lessons* offer traditional advice to a female of high status who should be aware of her position in society: 'Noblewomen are, and should be, a mirror, a pattern, and an example for others in all things.'[19] As in other aristocratic mirrors, moral precepts underpin the responsibilities of those with God-given social status. Anne begins her *Lessons* with reference to the theologians Augustine, Bernard of Clairvaux, Thomas Aquinas, Boethius, and Ambrose on the transitory nature of this life and the imminence of death and Judgement.[20] Every decision in one's life should be made with awareness of vulnerability to temptation and sin. A noblewoman must avoid prideful behaviours and understand that nobility is found only in 'a humble, benign, and courteous heart, and every other perfection you might have – like beauty, youth, wealth, or power – is vile without the aforesaid virtues'.[21] The trope of 'true nobility' based on virtue rather than blood is ubiquitous in aristocratic conduct books and was well-received by non-aristocratic readers.

Evidently a formidable and shrewd woman, Anne was made guardian for her underage brother and de facto regent of the kingdom from 1483–91 by her father before he died. Her administrative skills were also recognised by subsequent rulers, and her conduct guide for her daughter Suzanne reflects that worldly experience of the ways a princess can maintain her honourable reputation in a corrupting political environment. The *Lessons* portray a courtly setting rife with hypocrisy, envy, and greed: flattering servants who mock behind one's back, foolish and self-indulgent nobles who will not listen to good advice, and men who attempt to deceive well-born women. The importance of relying on loyal friends with good judgement, while avoiding the untrustworthy, is emphasised in all aristocratic conduct books. The noblewoman must carefully manage the behaviour of those attending her while remaining aware of her public image. One of the main themes of the *Lessons* is self-control: how to use humility, patience, courtesy, and circumspect behaviour to avoid sin and earn a reputation for true nobility.

Among the recurrent concerns in the text are proper use of speech and appropriate dress, both nuanced to fit the lifestyle of the noblewoman. While loose or arrogant talk is always unwise, the *Lessons* describe in some detail the proper use of conversation tailored to the listener and their interests: with the devout, speak about morality and spirituality; with the wise, about honourable things; for the young and high-spirited, arrange for entertaining stories to be told; to the householder, speak about household management; to the foreigner, about customs, laws, and noble people of their land; to the 'lesser folk', offer sympathy in their circumstances. The well-bred aristocrat will obviously have flexible conversational and diplomatic skills. Likewise, clothing must be chosen with considerable care to be weather-appropriate as well as calibrated to the wearer's social status. For example, the mistress demonstrates her position above her attending women through her demeanour as well as through her richer headdress and robes.[22]

Looking forward to Suzanne's eventual marriage and motherhood, Anne again emphasises the necessity to avoid pride if married to a man of high estate: 'guard yourself well from becoming too proud or arrogant because you should always maintain your humility'.[23] Her husband is owed (after God) 'perfect love and complete obedience', and his relatives should be honoured. However, she is not to forget that 'whatever great alliance you achieve, you must never out of some foolish pride fail to value highly your own ancestors, those from whom *you* are descended'![24] If she has children, her main responsibility will be to cultivate virtue in them, for there is 'no greater joy in the world to a father and mother than to have wise and well-taught children'.[25]

Anne's daughter Suzanne – no doubt well-taught by her mother – made arrangements in 1521 with a Lyon printer to produce the *Lessons* in print, guaranteeing a much wider readership than the manuscript copy permitted. Cynthia Brown suggests that the 'sharing, consumption and exchange of female culture among middle-class bookmakers and readers that the print industry facilitated may explain why Suzanne sought to venture outside of royal circles to propagate her mother's work'.[26] A text designed for aristocratic readership could thus be appropriated by non-noble readers.

Circulation of Conduct Literature

Suzanne de Bourbon's decision to share her mother's conduct book with a wider public in the early sixteenth century exemplifies the movement of conduct literature across class and cultural boundaries, a process that is evident from the thirteenth century on. Fascination with the etiquette and behaviour of nobles encouraged social mobility by the middle classes; less commented on is the interest in bourgeois conduct books by readers of higher rank. Likewise, advice on conduct may be addressed separately to males and females, but we have evidence that the texts were owned – and presumably read – by members of both sexes. Charlotte de Savoie's library, for example, included most of the late medieval male 'mirrors for princes', as well as the best-known women's conduct books written by non-aristocrats during the period.[27]

The expanded readership for fourteenth- and fifteenth-century conduct literature benefitted not just from the invention of print but also from translation of texts from one language to another, especially French into English. Most later medieval conduct texts were written initially in the vernacular but some, such as the *Speculum dominarum*, began as Latin texts. The Franciscan confessor Durand of Champagne composed it in Latin for Jeanne de Navarre, who then ordered it translated into French (*c.* 1300). As the *Miroir des dames*, the work circulated in many vernacular manuscripts throughout the fourteenth and fifteenth centuries at royal courts, with the explicit aim of shaping the godly conduct of women in the governing class.[28]

No one demonstrates the flourishing and fluid late medieval context for production and reception of conduct books better than its pre-eminent public intellectual, Christine de Pizan, who lived from 1365 to *c.* 1430 (see also Nancy Bradley Warren, Chapter 21 in this volume). It is tempting to celebrate her for her uniqueness as the only successful professional lay woman writer of her time, and she certainly occupies a well-deserved pedestal in women's literary history. However, here I will focus on her conduct writing in its specific cultural setting of royal patronage.

Christine came from a scholarly Italian family that provided her with an education she would later draw on. Her father, Thomas of Pizzano, who held degrees in medicine and astrology from the University of Bologna, took a position at the court of Charles V of France, where Christine grew up. At age fifteen she married another well-educated civil servant, Etienne du Castel, who died after ten years of marriage, leaving her with three children and other relatives to support. The misfortunes of her widowhood that led her to become a writer are described in *L'Avision Christine*.[29]

Despite her personal tragedies, Christine's upbringing at court provided her with the resources and royal support a writer of her time required, and virtually all of her work was therefore commissioned by those patrons and shaped by their interests and concerns. Christine had started her writing career with poetry in a courtly mode but soon expanded her repertoire to allegories with social implications as well as political history and commentary. She was well positioned to assess the problems of the polity and offer advice to rulers.

Although Christine de Pizan's reputation now rests on writings explicitly addressed to women, during her career she wrote works on supposedly 'male' topics that we cannot assume were only intended to be read by men. For example, *L'Epistre d'Othéa la déesse à Hector* is a book of advice to a young knight that was immensely popular with both male and female readers in both France and England. One manuscript of *Othéa* was produced for Queen Isabeau, wife of king Charles VI. Nancy Regalado argues persuasively that 'Christine shapes it in three ways to appeal to her women readers: by authorising her woman speaker; by assertive rewriting and interpretation of the stories she cites; and by subtle adjustments in the illustrations of the Queen's manuscript'.[30] Christine's synthesis of classical and medieval writings on military strategy (*Le Livre des faits d'armes et de chevalerie*) was translated and printed by Caxton in 1489–90 for an English readership which may well have included women. We know that a handsome manuscript (British Museum, Royal 15 E.vi) that included this work of warfare was made by John Talbot, Earl of Shrewsbury, as a gift for Margaret of Anjou, who married Henry VI in 1445.[31] Our contemporary tendency to categorise every aspect of a work by a fixed 'gender' identity is far too reductive to accommodate the surprising fluidity in gender possibilities of most medieval and early modern writing.

Christine wrote conduct advice to both males and females. There are *Enseignemens moraux* (moral and practical advice in quatrains) for her son Jean and, with a commission from the Duke of Burgundy in 1404, she wrote a biography of the esteemed king Charles V, *Le Livre des faits et bonnes moeurs du sage Roy Charles V*. As we might gather from the term 'bonnes moeurs', the biography was intended as a 'mirror for princes' that would instruct the inexperienced heir to the French throne, Louis de Guyenne. In 1405, Christine wrote a woman's 'mirror of honour', *Le Livre des trois vertus*, that she dedicated to Marguerite de Nevers, the young wife of Louis de Guyenne.[32] Numerous manuscripts of the *Livre des trois vertus* circulated among aristocratic women readers, and print versions in French and Portuguese were owned by Queen Anne of

Brittany and Queen Leonor of Portugal. Less beautifully produced copies on paper testify to a non-aristocratic readership as well.[33]

Christine expects her primary readership for the *Livre des trois vertus* to be noble women, from whom her teachings will trickle down to lower-class readers. As she explains,

> Our first students must be those whose royal or noble blood raises them above others in this world. Inevitably, the women, as well as the men, whom God establishes in the high seats of power and domination must be better educated than others. Their reputations will lead to great worthiness in themselves and in others. They are the mirror and example of virtue for their subjects and companions.[34]

The proportion of her conduct book devoted to the princess and her companions clearly supports her statement of intention: more than two-thirds of the text focuses on advice relevant to female behaviours in a court setting.

Christine is a perceptive sociologist, so her analysis of non-aristocratic women's lives – discussed in the final third of her conduct book – has been of keen interest to modern readers for its portrait of gendered work in medieval society. Nevertheless, the advice offered to this latter third of her addressees is very succinct compared to that for courtly ladies. Christine's main concern appears to be correcting the conduct of the ruling class, whose chief obligation is to embody worthiness for the realm.

Consistent with the tropes of noble femininity, the princess is warned against pride in her status; rather, she must always be seen to exhibit humility, charity, and good judgement – a 'politics of visibility' is the term Rosalind Brown-Grant uses.[35] Christine is surprisingly explicit compared to other writers of aristocratic conduct books about the ethic of 'dissembling' that underlies the performance of worthiness at court. Since the noble wife's duty is to care for the health of her husband's body and soul, if he behaves reprehensibly the prudent wife makes no public acknowledgement of his errors but behaves kindly towards him, adhering to forms of social interaction that will mask his unworthy deeds and reinforce her honour and good repute.[36] Even when people around her act with envy or ill will, she should pretend she wants their advice.[37] 'Discreet dissimulation', according to Christine, is not 'vicious but rather a great virtue when employed for the common good, to maintain peace, or to avoid detriment or greater harm'.[38] 'Justifiable hypocrisy' will thus encourage goodwill among the lady's subjects.[39]

In addition to maintaining her own public image, the princess is responsible for fostering proper conduct among her female companions at court. Christine offers extensive counsel to these women, who should always defend and promote their mistress's good name; however, in a case involving sin or vice '[n]o one is obliged to obey another and thereby to disobey God'.[40] The very young princess, who may be tempted by 'boisterous amusements' and immoderate behaviours, is another concern in Christine's conduct book. The young noblewoman requires guidance to avoid the dangers of compromising her reputation, especially with 'illicit love'.

To illustrate mature reasoned advice on such a love, Christine adapts a letter taken from her earlier work of courtly romance, *The Book of the Duke of True Lovers*. There, the wise governess wrote to her young mistress with multiple arguments about why entering into an adulterous love affair would dishonour her. The original letter came as a culmination to the long and tortured affair of the Duke and his married lover dramatised in the *Book*'s letters and poetry. Christine had accepted the commission from a 'Duke' to write about his romance, but it seems evident that she disapproved of the tale she had agreed to tell and therefore inserted a powerful rebuke in the form of a letter from Sebile de Monthault, Dame de la Tour.[41] In appropriating this cautionary text from a fictionalised romance and placing it in her didactic conduct book, Christine adopts a technique common in sermons and conduct books during the later Middle Ages: use of lively exempla to illustrate moral teachings.

Stories of Good and Bad Wives

As the foregoing discussion has shown, advice on marriage is not a substantial topic in conduct literature intended for royalty or the uppermost ranks of the aristocracy. There may be conventional acknowledgement that the wife should obey and honour her husband, but the real heart of the instruction is how rulers or future rulers can avoid dishonour and model virtuous behaviours for their companions and their subjects. Since many of the aristocratic conduct books are addressed to children by their parents, we might assume that marital relationships would not be a subject of in-depth consideration. However, *Le Livre du Chevalier de la Tour* (translated as *The Book of the Knight of the Tower*), written in 1371/2 by Geoffrey de la Tour Landry for his three daughters, invites us to reconsider that assumption; its sustained focus is on the behaviours that will mark the daughters as good rather than bad women – and especially on the rules for a virtuous marriage.[42] The Prologue of Caxton's English translation describes the contents as 'doctryne & techyng by which al yong gentyl wymen specially may lerne to bihave them self virtuously / as wel in their vyrgynyte as in their wedlok & wedowhede'.[43] The reward for their learning to 'governe them vertuously in this present lyf' will be 'worship and good renommee'.[44] Although modern critics have emphasised the Knight's 'noble' status in their interpretations, I would place his text in another category of late medieval conduct books where gendered marital advice is central. These books address young women who must learn to 'govern' themselves virtuously *not* in order to govern the country but to fulfil their obligations within the family, to which the wife's honourable reputation is crucial.

Geoffrey IV de la Tour Landry, as a member of an Angevin military family,[45] insists on his noble status – for example, pointing out that non-noble men (Fr. 'roturiers') may hit their wives but noble husbands respect their elite wives too much to chastise them physically![46] Despite these references to nobility, the knight's instructions for his daughters differ fundamentally from those given in the royal 'mirrors for princesses'. In his conduct book, discussion of his daughters' future public lives is absent; their social roles will be as respectable wives. His book draws on a dizzying mélange of exemplary sources to inculcate virtuous female behaviours, to which are added numerous personal anecdotes as well as an unusual, staged debate with his wife over courtly love (Fr. 'fin amor'), usually understood to be adulterous.

The stories that the knight includes come primarily from the Bible and clerical writing, but he also claims historical sources that turn out to be fictive references.[47] He does not identify the source of two-thirds of the exemplary stories of good and bad women he uses; these were in fact taken from the *Miroir des bonnes femmes* (*Mirror of Good Women*), a collection of moralised narratives of good and bad women composed by a Franciscan *c.* 1300.[48] The Chevalier's adoption and reshaping of the *Miroir* source exempla (in chapters XXXVII–CX) has attracted critical attention, with some scholars arguing that his revisions intensify the presentation of both commendable and reprehensible female behaviours.[49]

One of the unique aspects of the Chevalier's conduct book is that the father-narrator, who presents himself as the authoritative teacher of his daughters, gives up that moral authority to his wife towards the end of the narrative (chapters CXXII–CXXXIII). Their debate interrogates the courtly concept of 'fin amor', only to reject it in favour of marital fidelity. The book opens with the narrator in an April garden, nostalgically

Gender and Class in the Circulation of Conduct Books   171

remembering his youthful experiences as well as his companions who (less romantically) boasted of seducing 'damoyselles'. He makes the argument that taking 'peramours' is 'gay and Joly' and in so doing the man is encouraged to demonstrate his valour in arms and become a better knight.[50] His wife, however, condemns adulterous love in no uncertain terms. She tells her daughters not to listen to their father but to her! Attending to seductive talk, she says, draws a woman's heart from God and inhibits pious behaviour, as well as opening women to public mockery and scorn. The knight protests that not all men have bad intentions and the daughters should be able to enjoy their company, but his wife lays out strong reasons why marriage is a sacrament and why love affairs detract from the woman's commitment to it.[51] She says her responsibility is to keep her daughters out of danger; accordingly, they may be convivial but cannot indulge in 'the amerous loke', which leads to 'kyssynge' and worse![52] The wife has the last word in the debate, illustrating Glenn Burger's claim that the *Livre* dramatises a transformation of 'noble desire' from the 'Garden of Love to the Married Household'.[53]

The foregrounding of marriage and the family unit we see in the Chevalier's *Livre* marks late medieval conduct literature that had a special appeal to non-noble readers. Emma Lipton describes this depiction of 'marriage as a partnership between husband and wife' as a 'horizontal vision' that helped disrupt the hierarchy of the three estates.[54] The 'vices and virtues of women' motif emphasises that women have crucial moral choices to make that affect their reputations and those of their households.

All these newly prominent elements in conduct books indicate an ideological shift towards what Felicity Riddy calls a 'bourgeois ethic'.[55] Riddy sees the urban household as the 'locus of production and trade', with members who are kin but also apprentices and servants. In late medieval conduct books, the household therefore represents a set of values important to the middle classes: thrift, industry, bodily self-discipline, piety, and moderation. Although the male head of household, the 'goodman', may have exercised economic dominance, the 'goodwife' became 'the repository and maintainer of bourgeois values', Riddy proposes.[56] Whereas most so-called 'courtesy books' in an earlier aristocratic context concerned young males at court, a conduct poem such as 'What the Goodwife Taught Her Daughter', popular at the end of the Middle Ages, focuses on proper female behaviours that will foster a respectable marriage and a well-managed home.[57]

The avid appropriation of conduct and courtesy literature originally written for aristocrats expressed not just a desire for mobility into an upper class with its attractive lifestyle but, more fundamentally, acceptance of the idea that 'true nobility' is based on social behaviours rather than rank at birth. Conduct books persuade their bourgeois consumers that self-governance will lead to social advancement, material success, and spiritual reward.[58]

Household Books

The epitome of an affluent bourgeois focus on the economy and significance of the household is the late fourteenth-century conduct book, *Le Ménagier de Paris* (*The Goodman of Paris*).[59] It is a compendium of immense scope: instructions on daily religious rituals to be practised by the housewife and detailed advice on how to treat one's husband, how to manage the household operations (including servants), and how to care for a garden and plan meals. It culminates in a treatise on hunting and an enormous recipe collection. The text purports to be written by a sixty-year-old Parisian citizen who has just married a fifteen-year-old wife and realises she needs guidance in running a household. Given its length and the range of topics covered in this one conduct book, no brief recapitulation is possible. Roberta Krueger has insightfully analysed the male householder's 'micro-management of domestic details' and concluded that his book 'attests to the enormous attention, labor, and perseverance involved in constructing and maintaining bourgeois status in the late Middle Ages – a process described here and in other books of the period as "*tenir son estat*" (upholding one's estate)'.[60] Above all, the *Ménagier* makes clear the wife's central role in the bourgeois project.

More than any of the conduct books discussed in this chapter, the *Ménagier* illustrates the development of 'household anthologies' that can include conduct texts among their diverse contents. Fascinating as the details of daily life spelled out in this book may be, the *Ménagier* is also important in showing how texts first created for 'literary' contexts might function as exemplary guides for practical living in an anthology. The *Ménagier* includes the well-known story of Griselda the obedient wife that appeared in works by Boccaccio, Petrarch, Philippe de Mézières, Christine de Pizan, and Chaucer. The book also retells the allegory of the wise wife Prudence and her impulsive husband Melibee found in Italian, French and English literature, and it includes the 2,500-line allegorical poem *Chemin de Pauvrete et de Richesse* by Jacques Bruyant.[61] Anthologies, Myra Seaman argues, appeal to a female readership for whom social honour, virtuous behaviour, and economic reward coalesce into one goal.[62] Conduct texts addressed to women were thus absorbed into diverse compilations aimed at a broad readership, with reception often based in the household.

Readers of medieval conduct books will doubtless first notice the foregrounding of strong gender and class messages that structure these texts. Advice is offered to people defined unambiguously as male or female and clearly assigned a place in the social hierarchy of the period. On a literal reading, there seems no reason to question that the authors' firm counsel about appropriate gender and status behaviours is directed to the designated recipient according to established medieval norms.

However, attention to the historical circulation of conduct texts should destabilise this initial assumption. Gender and class may provide avenues of entry to this genre of writing, but the reception by actual readers and book owners can challenge both literal readings and normative assumptions. 'True nobility' came to be interpreted metaphorically as a moral condition rather than literally as an inheritance of blood, making aristocratic conduct literature more widely accessible to non-nobles. Instructions about the proper behaviour of bourgeois wives were a matter of concern to the whole household, the honour of which the women symbolised. Many conduct books, too, were repositories of interesting stories to be enjoyed in their own right, not necessarily taken as direct admonitions. Attention to the circulation – the historical reception – of conduct literature reveals the breadth and depth of its appeal for many centuries in multiple countries.

Notes

1. For a survey of the didactic literature of which conduct books were a significant part, see Roberta L. Krueger, 'Introduction: Teach your Children Well: Medieval Conduct Guides for Youths', in *Medieval Conduct Literature: An Anthology of Vernacular Guides to Behaviour for Youths, with English Translations*, ed. Mark D. Johnston (Toronto: University of Toronto Press, 2009), ix–xxxiii.
2. For theoretical discussion of conduct books, see Kathleen Ashley and Robert L. A. Clark, 'Introduction. Medieval Conduct: Texts, Theories, Practices', in *Medieval Conduct*, ed. Ashley and Clark (Minneapolis: University of Minnesota Press, 2001), ix–xx.
3. Dhuoda, *Handbook for William: A Carolingian Woman's Counsel for Her Son. Translated and with introduction and afterward by Carol Neel* (Washington, DC: The Catholic University of America Press, 1999; orig. publ. 1991), 5.
4. Peter Dronke gives a perceptive reading of Dhuoda's work, 'Dhuoda' in *Women Writers of the Middle Ages: A Critical Study of Texts from Perpetua (d. 203) to Marguerite Porete (d. 1310)* (Cambridge: Cambridge University Press, 1984), 36–54.

5. Dhuoda, *Handbook*, 21.
6. Dhuoda, *Handbook*, 31.
7. M. A. Clausen argues this is a model of spiritual parenting that provides an alternative to secular patriarchy in 'Fathers of Power and Mothers of Authority: Dhuoda and the *Liber manualis*', *French Historical Studies* 19 (1996), 785–809. Julia M. H. Smith posits a Carolingian intersection around the subject of wives of 'ideas about gender and about moral or political ideology', with women setting the moral standards for men: 'Gender and Ideology in the Early Middle Ages', in *Gender and Christian Religion*, ed. R. N. Swanson, Studies in Church History 34 (Woodbridge: Boydell and Brewer, 1998), 53.
8. Dhuoda, *Handbook*, xix.
9. Thomas F. X. Noble, 'Secular Sanctity: Forging an Ethos for the Carolingian Nobility', in *Lay Intellectuals in the Carolingian World*, ed. Patrick Wormald and Janet L. Nelson (Cambridge: Cambridge University Press, 2007), 36.
10. Janet L. Nelson, 'Dhuoda', in *Lay Intellectuals in the Carolingian World*, 112.
11. Pierre Riché (ed.), *Dhuoda. Manuel pour mon fils*, trans. Bernard de Vrégille and Claude Mondésert, Sources chrétiennes 225 (Paris: Editions du Cerf, 1975).
12. See my introduction and translation of the two letters: 'The French Enseignemenz a Phelippe and Enseignement a Ysabel of Saint Louis', in *Medieval Conduct Literature*, 3–22.
13. Ashley, *Enseignemenz*, 17.
14. Ashley, *Enseignemenz*, 7, 18.
15. Ashley, *Enseignemenz*, 8, 19.
16. Ashley, *Enseignemenz*, 20–1.
17. Anne-Marie Legaré, 'Charlotte de Savoie's Library and Illuminators', *Journal of the Early Book Society* 4 (2001), 32–87; see 69–79 for the list of books later owned by her daughter Anne.
18. Sharon L. Jansen (ed.), *Anne of France: Lessons for my Daughter. Translated from the French with Introduction, Notes and Interpretive Essay* (Cambridge: D.S. Brewer, 2004), 14–16.
19. Jansen, *Lessons*, 49.
20. Jansen, *Lessons*, 25–7. Works by all these theologians are listed in inventories of the Bourbon library at Aigueperse or in her library at Moulins, according to Jansen, *Lessons*, 10–11.
21. Jansen, *Lessons*, 65.
22. Jansen, *Lessons*, 50, 57.
23. Jansen, *Lessons*, 43.
24. Jansen, *Lessons*, 44.
25. Jansen, *Lessons*, 60.
26. Cynthia J. Brown, 'Anne de Bretagne and Anne de France: French Female Networks at the Dawn of the Renaissance', in *Founding Feminisms in Medieval Studies: Essays in Honor of E. Jane Burns*, ed. Laine E. Doggett and Daniel E. O'Sullivan (Cambridge: D. S. Brewer, 2016), 181.

27. Legaré, 'Charlotte de Savoie's Library', 42; Jansen, *Lessons*, 12–14.
28. Constant J. Mews, 'The *Speculum dominarum* (*Miroir des dames*) and Transformations of the Literature of Instruction for Women in the Early Fourteenth Century', in *Virtue Ethics for Women, 1250–1500*, ed. Karen Green and Constant J. Mews (Heidelberg: Springer, 2011), 13–30. Mews lists the French translations of the text, 22–3.
29. For a reading of *L'Avision* as a 'mirror for princes', see Rosalind Brown-Grant, '*L'Avision-Christine*: Autobiographical Narrative or Mirror for the Prince?', in *Politics, Gender and Genre: The Political Thought of Christine de Pizan*, ed. Margaret Brabant (Boulder, CO: Westview Press, 1992), 95–112.
30. Nancy Freeman Regalado, 'Page Layout and Reading Practices in Christine de Pizan's Epistre Othéa: Reading with the Ladies in London, BL, MS Harley 4431', in *Founding Feminisms in Medieval Studies*, 222–3. *Othéa* was very popular; it survives in more than forty French manuscripts and also in print versions. It was translated three times for its many English readers; see Curt F. Bühler (ed.), *Stephen Scrope. The Epistle of Othea*, Early English Text Society 264 (London: Oxford University Press, 1970), xii–xiii; also Douglas Gray, '"A Fulle Wyse Gentyl-Woman of Fraunce": *The Epistle of Othea* and Later Medieval English Literary Culture', in *Medieval Women: Texts and Contexts in Late Medieval Britain. Essays for Felicity Riddy*, ed. Jocelyn Wogan-Browne et al. (Turnhout: Brepols, 2000), 237, 246–7. The history of appropriations of Christine's writing in England by Jennifer Summit shows that when Christine's works were adapted to the English context they were often designed for 'not literate women, but gentlemen': *Lost Property: The Woman Writer and English Literary History, 1380–1589* (Chicago: University of Chicago Press, 2000), 68. Shifts in gender of reader were effected by changes in titles, prefaces, patron dedicatees, and so forth.
31. *The Book of Fayttes of Armes and of Chyvalrye. Translated and printed by William Caxton*, ed. A. T. P. Byles, Early English Text Society O.S. 189 (London: Oxford University Press, 1932; Kraus Reprint, 1988), xvi. See xiv–xxvi for a list of the many manuscripts of this work in both French and English. On this manuscript, see Michel-André Bossy, 'Arms and the Bride: Christine de Pizan's Military Treatise as a Wedding Gift for Margaret of Anjou', in *Christine de Pizan and the Categories of Difference*, ed. Marilynn Desmond (Minneapolis: University of Minnesota Press, 1998), 236–56. Also Charity Cannon Willard, 'Christine de Pizan on the Art of Warfare', in *Categories of Difference*, ed. Desmond, 3–15.
32. Both these conduct works are discussed by Charity Cannon Willard in *A Medieval Woman's Mirror of Honor: The Treasury of the City of Ladies*, trans. and introduction by Willard and ed. and introduction by Madeleine Pelner Cosman (New York: Bard Hall Press/Persea Books, 1989), 38–43. On the *Enseignemens* and the *Livre des Trois Vertus*, see Roberta Krueger, 'Christine's Anxious Lessons: Gender, Morality, and the Social Order from the Enseignemens to the Avision', in *Categories of Difference*, ed. Desmond, 19, 31–4.

33. Willard, *Medieval Woman's Mirror of Honor*, 43–5.
34. Willard, *Medieval Woman's Mirror of Honor*, 70.
35. Rosalind Brown-Grant, *Christine de Pizan and the Moral Defense of Women: Reading Beyond Gender* (Cambridge: Cambridge University Press, 1999), 200–01.
36. Willard, *Medieval Woman's Mirror of Honor*, 98–101.
37. Willard, *Medieval Woman's Mirror of Honor*, 106.
38. Willard, *Medieval Woman's Mirror of Honor*, 106–7.
39. Willard, *Medieval Woman's Mirror of Honor*, 109–11.
40. Willard, *Medieval Woman's Mirror of Honor*, 154.
41. Willard, *Medieval Woman's Mirror of Honor*, 139–47. For the letter in *The Book of the Duke of True Lovers. Translated, with an introduction by Thelma S. Fenster. With lyric poetry translated by Nadia Margolis* (New York: Persea Books, 1991), 110–20.
42. The *Livre* was tremendously popular in the fifteenth century throughout Europe. It survives in more than twenty French manuscripts; Caxton translated it into English for a 1484 printing, and a German translation was printed in Basle in 1493, then reprinted often in the sixteenth century and thereafter. On the work's European circulation, see Marguerite Y. Offord (ed.), *William Caxton, The Book of the Knight of the Tower*, Early English Text Society S.S. 2 (London: Oxford University Press, 1971), xviii–xxvi. Geoffrey the Knight of the Tower claims to have also written a conduct text for his sons, but it has not survived.
43. Offord, *Book of the Knight*, 3.
44. Offord, *Book of the Knight*, 3.
45. Anne Marie De Gendt, *L'Art d'éduquer les nobles damoiselles: Le Livre du Chevalier de la Tour Landry* (Paris: Champion, 2003), 21–35, connects Geoffrey de la Tour Landry's interpretation of his clerical sources to his aristocratic rank, although she points out that the knight says little about the political and economic responsibilities of noble women (237–8), focusing instead on a woman's obligations towards her husband (213–34).
46. Offord, *Book of the Knight*, 37: 'moyen peple chastysen theyr wyves by buffettys and strokes / but gentyl wymmen ought to be chastysed by fayre semblaunt and by curtosye'. Both the *Miroir* source and the *Book of the Knight* emphasise that no matter how reprehensible her husband may be, a good woman will not obey him rather than stay in God's service (133).
47. De Gendt, *L'Art d'éduquer*, 37–9.
48. The discovery that the *Miroir des bonnes femmes* was the source of the *Livre*'s exempla was made by John L. Grigsby; see his three articles: 'Miroir des bonnes femmes', *Romania* LXXXII (1961), 458–81 and LXXXIII (1962), 30–51, and 'A New Source of the Livre du Chevalier de la Tour Landry', *Romania* LXXXIV (1963), 171–208. A text of the *Miroir* now in Dijon is combined with two other moral treatises in a manuscript dated 1406 that was owned by four generations of the Beaumont and Thésut families in Chalon-sur-Saône, Burgundy; marginal notes on the manuscript identify both men

and women as its owners. See Kathleen Ashley, 'The Miroir des bonnes femmes, Not for Women Only?', in *Medieval Conduct*, 86–105.
49. In addition to Grigsby's detailed analyses, see De Gendt, *L'Art d'éduquer*, 39–48, 79–98, 147–79.
50. Offord, *Book of the Knight*, 163.
51. Offord, *Book of the Knight*, 170–2. Emma Lipton sees sacramental marriage as a model that in the later Middle Ages created a value system for members of the emergent middle classes of society, 'helping them to construct an identity for themselves and understand themselves as a social group': *Affections of the Mind: The Politics of Sacramental Marriage in Late Medieval English Literature* (Notre Dame, IN: University of Notre Dame Press, 2007), 2.
52. Offord, *Book of the Knight*, 175.
53. Glenn D. Burger, *Conduct Becoming: Good Wives and Husbands in the Later Middle Ages* (Philadelphia: University of Pennsylvania Press, 2018), 88–104.
54. Lipton, *Affections of the Mind*, 9.
55. Felicity Riddy, 'Mother Knows Best: Reading Social Change in a Courtesy Text', *Speculum* 71 (1996), 66–86.
56. Riddy, 'Mother Knows Best', 67, 68.
57. On bourgeois conduct poems, see Claire Sponsler, *Drama and Resistance: Bodies, Goods, and Theatricality in Late Medieval England* (Minneapolis: University of Minnesota Press, 1997), 50–74.
58. On the role of courtesy books 'at the border of gentility, the nobility and the urban elite', see Mark Addison Amos, '"For Manners Make Man": Bourdieu, de Certeau, and the Common Appropriation of Noble Manners in The Book of Courtesy', in *Medieval Conduct*, 25.
59. The modern French edition is *Le Mesnagier de Paris. Texte édité par Georgina E. Brereton et Janet M. Ferrier. Traduction et notes par Karin Ueltschi*. Lettres Gothiques (Paris: Librairie Générale Française, 1994).
60. Roberta L. Krueger, 'Identity Begins at Home: Female Conduct and the Failure of Counsel in *Le Menagier de Paris*', *Essays in Medieval Studies* 22 (2005), 25.
61. Krueger discusses all these exempla in 'Identity Begins at Home', 28–34.
62. Myra J. Seaman, 'Late-Medieval Conduct literature' in *The History of British Women's Writing, 700–1500*, vol. 1, ed. Liz Herbert McAvoy and Diane Watt (Houndmills, Basingstoke: Palgrave Macmillan, 2012), 124–9.

Further Reading

Amsler, Mark (2012). *Affective Literacies: Writing and Multilingualism in the Later Middle Ages*, Turnhout: Brepols.
Armstrong, Nancy, and Leonard Tennenhouse, eds. (1987). *The Ideology of Conduct: Essays on Literature and the History of Sexuality*, New York: Methuen.
Ashley, Kathleen, and Robert L. A. Clark, eds. (2001). *Medieval Conduct*, Minneapolis: University of Minnesota Press.

Burger, Glenn D. (2018). *Conduct Becoming: Good Wives and Husbands in the Later Middle Ages*, Philadelphia: University of Pennsylvania Press.
Ferster, Judith (1996). *Fictions of Advice: The Literature and Politics of Counsel in Late Medieval England*, Philadelphia: University of Pennsylvania Press.
Green, Karen, and Constant J. Mews, eds. (2011). *Virtue Ethics for Medieval Women, 1250–1500*, Heidelberg: Springer.
Hentsch, Alice (1975). *De la littérature didactique s'adressant spécialement aux femmes*, Cahors, 1903; repr. Geneva: Slatkine.
Johnston, Mark D., ed. (2009). *Medieval Conduct Literature: An Anthology of Vernacular Guides to Behaviour for Youths, with English Translations*, Toronto: University of Toronto Press.
Lipton, Emma (2007). *Affections of the Mind: The Politics of Sacramental Marriage in Late Medieval English Literature*, Notre Dame, IN: University of Notre Dame Press.
Sponsler, Claire (1997). *Drama and Resistance: Bodies, Goods, and Theatricality in Late Medieval England*, Minneapolis: University of Minnesota Press.

CHAPTER 9

Women's Learning and Lore
Magic, Recipes, and Folk Belief

Martha W. Driver

'Lore', derived from the Old English strong feminine noun *lár*, traditionally refers to instruction, education, and the teaching of moral principles and religious doctrine, along with advice and counsel, and, more recently (since 1766), to 'the body of traditional facts, anecdotes, or beliefs ... [such] as animal lore, bird lore, fairy lore, plant lore'.[1] Beginning with Old English charms, this chapter will look at texts in manuscript codices and rolls and in printed books that illustrate this latter sense of 'lore', with its particular emphasis on folk belief and its ties to both the natural and the supernatural worlds. Among these texts are amulet rolls thought to have healing or protective powers, particularly in childbirth. Edible charms for successful childbirth, also described in English manuscripts, were inscribed on butter or cheese; other charms were intended to be placed on a woman's body for healing or to manipulate a situation. Herbal lore appears in recipes of various kinds. There is also the rather sophisticated advice given by Dame Juliana Berners (or Barnes) to her children, or 'dere sonnys', in her *Book of Hawking, Hunting, and Blasing of Arms*, composed in the fifteenth century and intended for socially mobile readers on the rise, while the folksy prose and poetry in *The Kalender of Shepherds* addresses both men and women, purportedly derived from the knowledge of shepherds. Judging from its print history, *The Kalender* was a very popular book, in print in the fifteenth and sixteenth centuries.

In *How the Good Wiif Taughte Hir Doughtir*, a versified instruction manual circulating from about 1350 to 1500, the mother says: 'Betere were a child unbore / Than untaught of wijs lore'.[2] Her instructive monologue promotes conventional, bourgeois religious teachings for girls. Her motherly advice, 'Kepe thee from synne, fro vilonye, and fro blame', and 'Borowe not to besely', or do not borrow money too frequently, might still be given to children today.[3] But there were other kinds of more arcane lore that medieval women knew, may have encountered, or even possibly may have written, which are the subject of this chapter.

Charms and Amulets

Magical incantations and formulae date back to before the classical era. It is not always clear whether the earliest Old English survivals were intended for men, women, or both. One of the most famous examples is a delightful charm to remove a wen, or skin blemish, that works through the power of diminution, or reducing it, at least verbally, from the very first line: 'Wenne, wenne, wenchichenne' [Wen, wen, little wen]. The charm then makes the wen smaller and smaller, line by line, so that it finally becomes nothing at all: 'alswā litel þū gewurþe þet þū nāwiht gewurþe' (just as you become little you become nothing).[4] Many surviving Old English charms have to do with blessing the fields with fertility, restoring lost cattle, or the restoration of health, and there are some recipes or charms that pertain to women. Their mixture of Christian and pagan reference has been noticed by many scholars. As Karen Jolly remarks, 'authors of literate records were not just using popular folklore as part of some propaganda for the church, but they lived in the folk culture just as much as the popular participants did because folkways were part of a shared culture'.[5]

The charms survive in the *Leechbook* (London, British Library, MS Royal 12 D.xvii, *c.* 950) and the *Lacnunga* (Harley 585, *c.* 1050), 'both made up of recipes collected from a wide variety of sources that reveal the complex mixture of religious, medical, and folkloric ideas current in late Saxon England'.[6] While conventional wisdom and certainly later texts suggest that women were the healers of families and extended families (as, for example, in the book of instruction written by the Ménagier of Paris, in works by Christine de Pizan, and in medieval romances),[7] it is difficult to know whether women were healers in this early period, but there is no reason to think otherwise. Richard Kieckhefer notes that even in the fourth century, John Chrysostom preached against women's using magic to heal sick children.[8] In describing the *Lacnunga* and *Leechbook*, Corinne Saunders observes that the former, an early medieval version of an herbal attributed to Apuleius, contains 'a rather various set of remedies, prayers, and charms, and includ[es] more "magical" material'.[9] She comments further that 'traditions of medical and protective magic appear to have endured from the Anglo-Saxon period without much change', as did the use of amulets or talismans, 'overlapping with the use of protective religious objects'.[10] Many of these were used for women and by women for other women.

One popular charm is the magic square, 'the sator-arepo formula' (Illustration 9.1), a mysterious text that reads the same way when read from top to bottom, left to right, bottom to top, and backwards right to left:

SATOR
AREPO
TENET
OPERA
ROTAS

The earliest example dates from a first-century Christian house in Pompeii, but the formula was also used as a birthing charm.[11] This magic formula is recommended in the *Trotula*, a well-known women's health handbook originating in twelfth-century Salerno which, as Naoë Kukita Yoshikawa notes in Chapter 7 in this volume, incorporates medical knowledge from Graeco-Roman and Arabic sources.[12] According to Don Skemer, the *Trotula* advised the midwife to write 'a charm including the SATOR AREPO formula on a piece of cheese or butter for the woman to eat'.[13] Kieckhefer says the sator-arepo inscription is found on cloths used on a pregnant mother's belly, a form of birth girdle.[14] Magical and religious texts associated with easing childbirth are often found inscribed in medieval scrolls, which may also have been used as birth girdles, often literalised

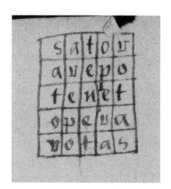

Illustration 9.1 'Sator Arepo' Magic Square. Written upside down in the margin. Old Library F.3.21: Nicolai de Lyra, *Tabula in Libros Veteris Ac Novi Testamenti*. Cologne: Johann Koelhoff, the Elder, not before 1480, sig. t8 r. By permission of the Master & Fellows of Magdalene College, Cambridge.

as belts placed on the expectant mother's stomach to promote an easy birth or to aid in a difficult one.

There is debate about which manuscripts literally functioned as birth girdles and which probably did not. Morgan Glazier 39, for example, made between 1484 and 1500 at the Premonstratensian Abbey of the Blessed Virgin Mary in Coverham, in the North Riding of Yorkshire, is a roll almost twenty feet long, written in English and Latin, which seems to have had several uses. While Curt Bühler describes it as an 'amulet based on the measurement of the length of the body of our Lord' which can 'be found from Iceland to the Balkans', Mary Morse has specifically called it a birth girdle.[15] Other scholars, among them Jeanne Krochalis and Don Skemer, have suggested that protection in childbirth was one of the roll's several uses, which is, in fact, borne out by its images and texts invoking saints for various kinds of healing.[16] In the text, there is a drawing of a tau cross surrounded by a religio-magical formula in Middle English (Illustration 9.2) which explains that those observing this cross, which is one-fifteenth of the height of Christ ('XV tymes is þe trew lenth of our Lorde Ihesu Criste'), or wearing it will be protected against evil spirits in battle, from plague, and during childbirth. As is the case with many talismans, the scroll is as much charm as orthodox document, a place where religion and superstition meet.

The roll ends with a poem that identifies its author as a Canon Percival, who says of himself 'þis schrowyll I dyd wryte' (this scroll I did write), which, according to Bühler, is one of the earliest appearances of the word 'scroll' in English.[17] Percival thus identifies himself with the text, in this case as its maker, compiler, scribe, and possibly artist. The roll may have been used by the monks in Coverham, though both Morse and Skemer indicate that it likely travelled out after it was copied and, in Skemer's words, may 'have been used devotionally and amuletically for the benefit of family and household'.[18] In other words, this roll functions as a multipurpose amulet that is simultaneously magical and religious, used by both women and men.

While there are several extant rolls made as talismans that have a variety of applications to employ in various situations (warfare, childbirth, plague, other illness, including mental instability), only two rolls, Wellcome MS 632 and Takamiya MS 56 (Illustration 9.3), 'are persuasive examples of birth girdles' because they contain 'instructions [that] specify that the woman should gird herself with the manuscript'.[19] There are, however, codices that also mention the scroll formula for scrolls intended as ephemera. Examples of these are found in *The Knowing of Woman's Kind in*

Illustration 9.2 Tau cross. Multipurpose Prayer Roll. New York, The Morgan Library & Museum, MS Glazier 39, fol. 7 r (Yorkshire, England, made *c.* 1484–1500). Gift of the Trustees of the William S. Glazier Collection, 1984. By permission of the Morgan Library & Museum.

Illustration 9.3 Birth girdle. New Haven, Beinecke Rare Book and Manuscript Library, Takamiya MS 56 (possibly Tewkesbury, c. 1435–50). By permission of the Beinecke Library, Yale University, New Haven.

Childing, a fifteenth-century Middle English work also discussed by Yoshikawa (Chapter 7, this volume) that 'has considerable significance as a medical text written on the subject of women made for a female audience'.[20] Extant in five manuscripts, both the prologue and the text are directed to women readers, though the author or compiler is not known. In one manuscript of this text, there is this charm for easing labour: 'tak a lytyll scrowe & wryt þys with-in: + In nominee Patris et Filijj & Spiritus Sancti Amen + Sancta Maria + Sancta Margareta + ogor + sugor + nogo + and kyt þat scrov in-to small þecys & ȝiffe here to drynk.'[21] As was sometimes the case with the sator-arepo palindrome and other childbirth charms written on butter or cheese and eaten, this scroll was intended to be written, torn into pieces, then drunk, presumably in wine, by the woman in labour. For another remedy for cases of difficult labour, the midwife is advised to 'write in a skrowe all the psalme of Magnificat and gerde hit a-bowte here', or belt it about her.[22] A variant text says to 'wrytt in a long scrow all þe psalme of Magnificat anima mea & gyrde hit a-boute here'.[23] The Magnificat (Luke 1:46–55) spoken by Mary at the time of the Visitation when the pregnant Virgin visits her pregnant cousin Elizabeth is appropriate here as a form of invocation to the Virgin. In this familiar text, Mary describes herself as God's handmaiden, extolling the power of God and his exaltation of the lowly and humble, and moves through a series of reversals ('He has filled the hungry with good things / but has sent the rich away empty') which might serve to console a woman in the throes of childbirth.

Another fifteenth-century Middle English remedy book cites a charm that again uses the sator-arepo formula in a birthing girdle: 'For a woman that is in travelyng of chyle bynde to her wombe thes words.'[24] And, like the examples from *The Knowing of Woman's Kind in Childing*, a childbirth charm in this volume invokes the Virgin Mary and instructs the midwife to 'sey this charme thrice and she shall sone have childe if it be her tyme'.[25] There is a similar caveat in the charms in *The Knowing of Woman's Kind*. Charms or prayers should only be used in preparation for the birth but will not themselves bring on the birth: 'wit wel that this nor non othir helpith a woman at comenabill (suitable, appropriate) tyme of deliuerance and therfore let euery mydwyf helpe with her besynesse'.[26] The notion here seems to be that use of the charm in tandem with nature will effectively bring on the birth.

If a scroll has its practical purposes, whether it is to be read aloud or even to be eaten as a religio-magical conveyance, one place one might not think to look for magical formulae is in Books of Hours, the popular bestselling prayer books of the Middle Ages, which were often owned by women. Later additions to the Beaufort Hours (London, British Library, MS Royal 2 A.xviii), made in part for Margaret Beauchamp (b. 1405/6, d. 1482) before 1443, for example, include remedies for migraine and for 'healthy body, clear wits, memory, and prolongation of life'.[27] Skemer notes some examples which have 'rubrics instructing the reader to wear or place the text on one's body'.[28] In the Burnet Psalter Hours (University of Aberdeen Library, MS 25), produced on the Continent for the English market in the fifteenth century, there are charms on 'at least a half dozen folios ... which promise general protection to the supplicant (famulum N) or whoever carried or placed the apotropaic text on their bodies, or whoever read them aloud or looked at them each day'.[29] These sorts of texts are also found in other fifteenth-century Hours – for example, those that were 'made for Princess Katherine of France around 1405 (Oxford, Bodleian Library, MS Lat. Liturg. F9)', as well as in Princeton MS 138.44, fragments removed from what may have been a Book of Hours 'for use in a birthing kit'.[30]

There is also a curious example to be found in Morgan Glazier 9 (Illustration 9.4): a Sarum Hours of the Virgin, probably made in England between 1450 and 1460, with borders supplied by English painters and illuminations by Continental artists.[31] This stunningly beautiful manuscript has many annotations by readers, including obituaries of the Smithson family of Horsham, Sussex, and later of London. There is also a recipe or charm carefully written in a fifteenth-century hand on the last leaf of the volume that opens: 'take vyyolettes, daundelion, southestell, borage, borell & hysopp', which are to be boiled with leaves of anise and fennel seed, along with licorice, 'and let hit be dronk warme'.[32] Some of these herbs – for example, borage, anise, and fennel – are also found in recipes for abortifacients or to bring on the menses, another aspect of women's lore that was known from an early date.

Hildegard of Bingen (1098–1117) includes seven plants in her *De simplices medicinae*, or *Physica*, that could be used either to stimulate menstrual bleeding or as abortifacients. The *Trotula*, too, advises on this, saying that drinking artemisia in wine before taking a bath or taking artemisia with other herbs, including pennyroyal, a well-known poison from the classical period, would abort a foetus.[33] *The Knowing of Woman's Kind in Childing* cites a 'medycyn that a lady Salerne vsid' (which may be an indirect reference to the *Trotula*, a main source but unnamed in the text) as an emmenagogue.[34] Although these are recipes, sometimes quite poisonous ones, not magical charms, the church frowned on them from early

Women's Learning and Lore 187

Illustration 9.4 Annunciation, Flemish artist. Sarum Book of Hours. MS Glazier 9, fol. 11 v (England, made c. 1440–1450). New York, The Morgan Library & Museum. Gift of the Trustees of the William S. Glazier Collection, 1984. By permission of the Morgan Library & Museum.

on; St Jerome, for example, was opposed to 'sterility drinks', comparing their use to homicide.[35] However, magical formulae for contraceptives appear more frequently than one might expect. Kieckhefer describes the case of Matteuccia Francisci, tried for magic in the early fifteenth century for advising the mistress of a priest to 'take the ashes from the burnt hoof of female mule, mix them with wine, and drink them',[36] in effect taking on the sterility of the animal.

Even more idiosyncratic charms used by women are the 'fern' or 'farn', recommended by Hildegard and identified by John M. Riddle as asplenon (or asplenium) as an amulet in childbirth. If 'placed near the birth canal the farn would be the first thing that a newly born infant would smell. This odor would prevent the Devil from having the first opportunity to capture the newborn.'[37] Beatrice de Planisolles, a Cathar noblewoman of the late thirteenth and early fourteenth centuries, kept her grandsons' umbilical cords to help her win lawsuits and linens with her daughter's first menstrual blood to be used in a potion that would be drunk by her daughter's husband to retain his love.[38] And in 1446, Anna of Württemberg, Countess of Katzenelnbogen, admitted to having used a spell to make her husband love her. Her charm involved a nutshell inside of which was a live spider. She believed that 'if she kissed anyone with it in her mouth, he would be bound to love her unconditionally'.[39] A slightly less eccentric formula, this time to increase fertility, is described by Le Ménagier of Paris in his manual for his young wife. Of mandrake roots (Illustration 9.5), he says that according to the *Catholicon*, 'the fruit can help barren women conceive, unless they are too old'.[40] In this case, as in the birthing charms mentioned earlier which describe birth as taking place when it is time, the magic of the mandrake may be invoked, but nature also plays a part.

These examples suggest that there were more dimensions to what medieval women knew than the Good Wiif teaches (or, if she was aware of the close interplay of magic and religion, she does not mention this to her daughter). Instead, the Good Wiif advises what one might expect: regular church attendance, proper behaviour in church, considerate treatment of husbands, avoidance of taverns and gambling venues, and competently overseeing children and household. Another subject on which the Good Wiif remains silent is hunting, usually seen as an aristocratic or wealthy middle-class pastime, to which I shall now turn.

Proper Subjects for Women

Understanding all the points of the hunt might not be within the modern purview of medieval women's learning, but the range of expertise of medieval women sometimes surprises us. Subjects were not necessarily gendered, or were not gendered in the way we might think now. A case in point is Christine de Pizan's *Le Livre des fais d'armes et de chevalerie*, an adaptation of Vegetius's *De re militari*, a classical work on warfare, written about 1410. It was later translated into English by William Caxton as the *Fayt of Armes and of Chyualrye* and published on 14 July 1489.[41] In this work, Caxton makes a point of citing Christine as the author in chapter 1 and alludes to her throughout, retaining her instructive voice. As Cynthia Brown points out, Caxton's edition 'not

Illustration 9.5 Mandragora (Mandrake). Matthaeus Platearius, *Compendium Salernitanum*. MS M.873, fol. 61 v (N. Italy, possibly Venice, 1350–75). New York, The Morgan Library & Museum. By permission of the Morgan Library & Museum.

only provided a literal translation of Christine's original title, but also carefully promoted her authorship, her Italian heritage, and relationship to her sources'.[42] A woman's authorship of a work on warfare was no issue at all in fifteenth-century England, apparently, though in later printed editions Christine disappears as the author of this work, and, later still, some scholars doubted she had written it.[43]

A similar case is *The Book of Hawking, Hunting and Blasing of Arms*, also known as *The Book of St Albans*, ascribed from its first printing to one Dame Juliana (or Julian) Berners by the so-called Schoolmaster Printer at St Albans in 1486.[44] Her authorship of even the one tract in this volume which contains her name has often been doubted, and certainly her full role or connection to the entire work remains unclear. Did she write all of it? Part of it? Or did she compile it? Her gender has even been called into question.[45] Whatever her role in its making, whether as author, compiler, or both, Dame Juliana continues to be associated with the book's authorship in subsequent printed editions through to 1614; she is named in one fifteenth-century manuscript (Magdalene College Cambridge, Pepys Library, MS 1047), which was probably copied from a printed edition, and cited by the initials 'JB' in British Library, MS Harley 2340.[46]

We find Dame Juliana's name at the end of the second treatise in the collection, verses on 'the manere of huntynge for all manere of bestys'. Part of this takes the form of an instructive verse monologue from a mother to her sons, which she says is based on the lore known to 'Tristram', the hero of the Tristan and Isolt story who was well known for his hunting prowess; this knowledge should be known to all 'gentill personys'.[47] In the first verse of the text, she opens with these commanding words: 'Lystyn to yowre dame and she shall yow lere' (sig. e1 r) – clearly the voice of authority. She then lists the various wild beasts to be hunted (the buck, doe, fox, and hare, among others) and how to hunt them. Another section of this treatise is instruction from a master to his man; the mother then returns to speak to her children about the correct way to hunt the wild boar and to butcher a deer, explicit detail reminiscent of that found in *Sir Gawain and the Green Knight*.[48] The text concludes: 'Explicit Dam Julyans / Barnes in her boke of huntyng' (sig. f4 r).

An early owner of *The Book of St Albans* named William Burton identified Juliana as the 'Lady Prioresse of Sopwell Abbey', though there is no mention of her in the fragmentary records of that institution.[49] Alexandra Barratt points out, however, that there was Dame Alyanore Hulle, or Eleanor Hull, living at Sopwell Abbey at about the same time, a widow who translated two works from French into Middle English: a collection of prayers and meditations for the seven days of the week, and a lengthy, detailed, and theologically sophisticated commentary on the Seven Penitential Psalms. Of the latter, Barratt comments, 'if so unlikely a text turns out to have been the work of a woman, we should be wary of automatically excluding the possibility of a woman's authoring any medieval text on *a priori* grounds'.[50]

Like Alyanore Hulle, Dame Juliana was using French sources for her work on hunting: the section of advice from a mother to her children derives from *L'art de venerie* (*Art of Hunting*) by Guillaume Twici or Twiti, huntsman to Edward II; the second section, a dialogue between a master and his man,

Women's Learning and Lore

Illustration 9.6 Hunting rabbit. Gaston III Phébus, Count of Foix, *Livre de la Chasse*. MS M. 1044, fol. 79 v (Paris, c. 1406–1407). New York, The Morgan Library & Museum. Bequest of Clara S. Peck, 1983. By permission of the Morgan Library & Museum.

comes from the *Livre de la chasse* (*Book of the Hunt*, Illustration 9.6), composed between 1387 and 1389 by Gaston III (1331–91), Count of Foix and Viscount of Béarn, also called Phébus for his blond hair.[51] The latter work was translated into English between 1406 and 1413 as *The Master of the Game* by Edward, Duke of York, younger son of Edward III, and is the oldest English-language book on hunting. These are both grand and noble antecedents for the modest *Book of Hunting*, which aspires simply to teach sons to be gentlemen through learning the art of venery. Barratt observes that this work (and perhaps those accompanying it):

> might appropriately be compiled by someone engaged in the elementary education of upper-class children, as the subjects covered included what one might now call natural history, domestic science, and etiquette as well as the sport [of hunting] itself. Nor did the fifteenth-century printer of *The Book of St Albans* find it inherently implausible that a woman should have written this poem; he no doubt knew that medieval women took part in hunts, particularly in hare coursing and rabbiting.[52]

Hunting and hawking seem to have been readily accepted as pastimes for medieval women; women are depicted hunting in medieval poetry (*Sir Orfeo*, for example) and on medieval tapestries. But Dame Juliana's text is very technical, describing, in addition to how to hunt the hart, roe, wild boar, and rabbit, the appropriate reward for hunting dogs, for example, again reminiscent of *Sir Gawain and the Green Knight*: 'The hunter shall rewarde hem then with the hede / With the shulderis and the sides and with the bowellis all', a passage found in *The Book of St Albans* at signature e3 v (like many medieval manuscripts, this printed book is unpaginated but retains signatures for its gatherings).[53] Advice for the treatment and training of hunting dogs runs over several chapters, and there is much description of how to ascertain the health of animals.

In his manual for his wife, the Ménagier of Paris expresses similar concerns in his instructions for maintaining a healthy falcon or hawk. He writes that he has included this treatise 'so that in the hunting season you can divert yourself with this pursuit if you so choose'.[54] As in *The Book of St Albans*, the Ménagier's text includes a list of which animals to hunt in season and instruction on choosing and training hunting dogs, along with how to raise sparrow hawks and train them to hunt, and how to care for hawks, including checking droppings to be sure a hawk is healthy and how to heal sick hunting birds by various means.[55]

Writing in 1967, Rachel Hands suggested that Dame Juliana may not have authored the hunting treatise; her more likely role was as compiler of the whole *Book of St Albans* for the printer: 'The heterogeneous material of the manuscripts seems much more likely to have been assembled by a woman.'[56] The other treatises included with the *Book of Hunting* certainly contain some fascinating (and memorable) material. The first treatise, *The Book of Hawking*, has, for example, a list of birds ranked by class (evocative of Geoffrey Chaucer's *Parliament of Fowls*). The eagle is among the birds appropriate for an emperor, while a prince should own 'a Tercell gentil'.

Ladies hunt with merlins, yeomen with goshawks; even a priest should have a 'Spare hawke', or sparrow hawk (sigs. d2 v–d3 r).⁵⁷ After the explicit citing of 'Dame Julyans' (sig. f4 r), there follow items like 'The propretees of a good hors', which compares the aforesaid horse to properties seen in man, woman ('Off a woman fayre brestid faire of here & esy to lip [leap] vppon'), fox, hare, and ass, ending with a remark perhaps worthy of the Good Wiif, who also advises her daughter to stay at home: 'Well trauelid women ner well trauelid hors wer neu͟er goode' (sig. f5 r). Then quickly there follows advice more in line with that given by the Wiif to her daughter:

> Arise erly, serue god deuouteli . and the worlde besily doo
> thy werke wiseli ... Go to thi mete appetideli.
> Sit ther at discretely. Of thi tonge be not to liberally
> .... Goo to thi soper soborly And to thy
> bedde merely. Be in thyn Inne Jocu͟ndely Please thy love du
> ly. And slepe surely. (sig. f5 r)

On the verso is a version of the proverb verses known from the 'Wife of Bath's Prologue':

> Who that byldys his hous all of salowes.
> And prickyth a blynde hors ouer the falowys.
> And suffrith hys wyfe to seche mony halowys.
> God sende hym the blysse of euerlastyng galowis. (sig. f5 v)⁵⁸

Also memorable in this section is a list of collective terms for 'beestys and fowlys' which is still well known.⁵⁹ The hart, hind, buck, and doe roam in herds, as do swans; ladies travel in a bevy, as do quails; one might also have a 'Congregation of peple', 'an Exaltyng of Larkis', 'an hoost of men', 'a flight of Doues', 'a Route of knyghtis', 'a Scole of Clerkis', and even 'a Worship of Writeris' (sigs f6–f 7 r). The next and last treatise in *The Book of St Albans* concerns heraldry, or 'the linage of coot armis' (sig. A1 r), in which all nobility, as in the 'Wife of Bath's Tale', is said to come from God: 'all gentilnes cummys of god of heuyn' (sig. A1 r).

Without further documentary evidence, the role Dame Juliana played in the production of *The Book of St Albans* remains unknown, but this hardly matters. Her name is associated with both manuscript and printed editions of the text, and the book was unquestioningly ascribed to her in printed editions through the early seventeenth century. The subjects Dame Juliana teaches are not expected, or conventional, but show 'the medieval woman writer as a transmitter of traditional wisdom, a compiler and adapter of the ideas of others',⁶⁰ as well as the range and versatility of what medieval women knew.

Shepherds' Lore: Advice for Women

The Kalender of Shepherds, a huge compendium purporting to contain the wisdom and lore of shepherds, often makes a point of addressing its texts to both men and women as concerning subjects people should generally know, though some texts are directed to, describe, or characterise women more specifically. Judging from its reprint history, the *Kalender* was extremely popular, with eight printings in Paris and Geneva between 1493 and 1500. The first English edition appeared in 1503.[61] According to the Revised Short-Title Catalogue, following this edition *The Kalender of Shepherds* remained in print in England in a variety of versions until 1631, going through some nineteen editions.[62] A miscellany of shepherd's lore, tables for finding the dates of moveable feasts, descriptions of the torments of purgatory, and explications of the Ten Commandments, Lord's Prayer, and Apostles' Creed, along with medical and other practical information, the Shepherd's *Kalender* was heavily illustrated; the pictures in the English editions are derived from woodcut models in the French editions, printed first by Guy Marchant and then published by Antoine Vérard. Copies were owned in France and England by aristocratic and middle-class readers. The English versions are not, however, direct translations from the French editions, which are themselves variable. There are even marked differences between the *editio princeps* brought out by Guy Marchant in 1493 and his subsequent editions of 1496 and 1500.[63] Rather, the English texts are adapted or re-presented from the French. The discrete texts that comprise *The Kalender of Shepherds* also move, like the images illustrating them, between various editions: 'the *Kalender* was altered and added to at each appearance'.[64]

The work is:

> a compilation, the single parts of which have been ransacked from various sources. It contains nothing which was not known with regard to the subjects in question at the end of the fifteenth century, and its chief advantage, and probably the cause of its success, was the fact that it united the different subjects of interest into one printed volume.[65]

The *Kalender* includes basic religious material (the Ten Commandments, the Lord's Prayer) along with numerous texts 'derived from various sources, such as treatises on health, anatomy, and phlebotomy'; it is, in effect, a whole home encyclopaedia.[66] The first English version of the *Kalender* published by Vérard, for example, contains astrological charts and calendar pages with lists and woodcuts of saints.[67] There is an account of Lazarus's visions of hell (which emphasise hell's inclusivity, with the chapters mentioning the torments of proud men and women, envious men and women, covetous men and women, and so on), prayers, and an exposition of the Apostles Creed. Also included is a 'balad of the shepherde' (which begins 'I knowe that god hathe formed me', sig. g1 r–g1 v). The speaker is interestingly unrepentant: though he knows he faces death, 'And yet my lyfe amend nat I', a refrain repeated three times.[68]

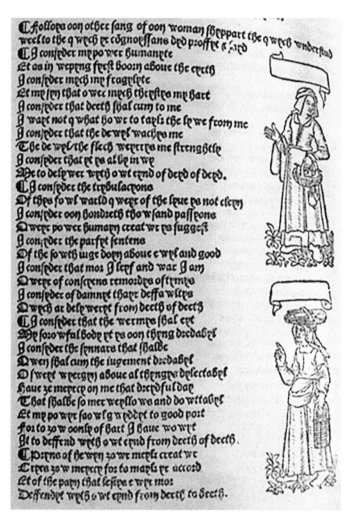

Illustration 9.7 Songe of a woman shepherde. *Kalender of Shepherds*. Paris: Antoine Vérard, 1503, sig. g1 v. From the facsimile by H. Oskar Sommer (London: Kegan Paul, Trench, Trübner, 1892). Photography by author.

The mood of the companion poem, 'the songe of a woman shepherde that vnderstone well', is more humble, sombre, and pious (Illustration 9.7). The shepherdess considers the sorrows of this world and her own mortality ('I consydre my fragilete'). She knows death will come, 'but the houre wote nat I', and describes herself as a sinner; the world and flesh are her enemies, and she fears Judgement. The speaker seems also to have seen a written source, 'I consydre for synne some dampned as the boke setth', though this may simply be a reference to the Bible. She says further, 'I consydre that wormes shall ete me', perhaps a biblical reference to the fate of Herod (Acts 12:23). She concludes with a verse prayer to the Virgin, asking Mary to 'Haue mercy of me' on the 'dredeful daye' of death and to intercede for her with Mary's son, the 'Prynce of heuen'. She then vows 'neuer to synne more' and asks Mary to save her 'without ende fro dethe to dethe'.[69] This is less shepherd's lore than a penitential prayer as poem that instructs the reader to lead a virtuous, humble life.

There are also verses on the estates, which in the Wynkyn de Worde edition of 1508 [1516] were probably added by the printer/translator Robert Copland.[70] One of these is an eight-line verse that echoes the same sentiments as the Wiif's instruction to her daughter. Women must not be disobedient to husbands or wish to rule them ('Desyre not aboue them to haue the souerante'), a desire here compared to Lucifer's wish to overthrow God. For women, the text further recommends 'Shamfastnes / drede / clenes and chastyte'.[71]

There is much here in many editions on health (from Vérard, 'Syngys [Signs] by the qwych shyppars wnderstondys to be hoyl and weeldysposyt [well disposed] in thayr body', sig. h3 v). We are told that healthy people have a good and regular appetite and should not eat greedily, 'wyth owt that they mayk exces'. They 'reioy[ce] them wyth them qwych ar ioyous' (rejoice with those who are joyous) and should seek their company. Then follow health regimes appropriate to the season: for example, in 'the prym tym mars / awryl / & may', one should dress lightly in linsey-woolsey and have one's blood let. Diet should include 'lyght meyt wych refreshys as chekyns kyddys with wertws' (cabbages) and other vegetables (sigs h4 v–h5 r). Autumn, 'september / october /nouember', is 'the saysson of the year that ys moost dangerows of seyknes / in the qwych perylows seyknes happynnes' (sig. h5 r–h5 v). In this season, when threatened by potential illness, one should avoid fruit but consume capons and rabbits and 'drynk good wyn'. Readers are cautioned not to drink cold water nor to bathe in it in autumn but to use it simply to wash 'thayr hondys'. People should sensibly 'keep thayr heyd from coold in the nyght and in the mornyng' (sig. h5 v).

After this section (which is rather like a list of seasonal activities in an Ayurvedic manual), the Vérard edition includes a section on the astrology and cosmography known to shepherds. Remarkable here is the comment (which seems to occur in all English editions) that 'the world ys rownd y soon appel', this statement some eighty years before Galileo. This is then elaborated: 'Et after the wys shyppars yt ys not possybyl to sayd thing artyfycyal mor reond than the world' (sig. h7 r); nothing can be rounder than the world.

In the 'physonomy of the shyppars' (sig. k6), there are descriptions of how physical features are indicators of character. Among these, one finds that a 'great plente of heer betokenythe in wymmen bowstyousnes and couetous' and 'a great voyce in a woman is an euyll syne. a swete voyce betokeneth a parson fulle of enuy and susspeccion and full of lesynges'.[72] Though we learn today (ideally) to look beyond appearances, thick, full hair or loud or sweet voices in women were taken as signs of innately flawed character. In the section on astrology, there are profiles of personalities of both men and women by sign. For example, the Scorpio woman is 'amyabyl & fayr. Et shal not be long wyth [h]yr fyrst howsband bot after sho shal reioy[ce] wyth oon other be [h]ys good and faythful serwys sho shal haue honnowr & wyctor [victory] of hyr ennemys' (sig. m4 r). Her lucky days are Tuesday and Saturday, worthy of a newspaper horoscope.

A mock-battle poem that is introduced near the end of de Worde's *Kalender* edition describes the war between a woman, armed men, and a snail, entitled 'Of an assaute agaynst a Snayle'.[73] The French editions earlier published by Guy Marchant illustrate this text with a woodcut of a large snail seated on a pedestal who does battle with its horns against a woman and two armed knights (Illustration 9.8, sig. n1 v).[74] This illustration was copied in the later English editions of de Worde and Julian Notary.[75] The poem opens with this stage direction: 'The woman speketh with an hardy courage.' She then berates the snail for consuming tree buds and blooms and threatens him with her distaff: 'Oute of this place / or I shall the sore bete / With my dystaffe / bytwene thy hornes twayne' (sig. T8 r). Then there is a second caption: 'The men of armes wt theyr spers countenaunce'; the knights command the snail to 'lyghtly thy hornes downe lay' and threaten him with their 'sharpe wepons'. They say further: 'We shall the flee [flay] / out of thy soule skyn / And in a dysshe / with onyons and peper / We shall the dresse / and with stronge vyneyger.' The snail then has his own speech ('The Snayle spycketh'): he says he is 'a beest / of ryght greate meruayle', for he carries his house on his back, and that all armed men fear him ('yf that these armed men / approche me nere / I shall them soone / vaynquysshe euerychone / But they dare not / for fere of me alone'). The playlet concludes: 'Thus fynyssheth this geste / composed onely to passe the tyme there with.'

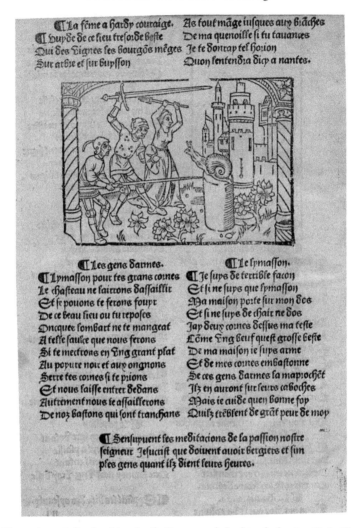

Illustration 9.8 Battle with a Snail. *Compost et kalendrier des bergiers*. Paris: Guy Marchant, 1496, sig. n1 v. Florence, Biblioteca Nazionale Centrale di Firenze. Available at https://archive.org/details/ita-bnc-in2-00001137-001.

This is a comedy sketch, a little 'gest' that appears between a comparison of the months and the ages of man (in December, when a man is seventy-two years old, 'he leuer haue a warme fyre / than a fayre lady')[76] and meditations on the passion of Christ, 'that Shepeherdes and simple people oughte to haue in herynge', quick shifts in register and subject that are indicative of the character of the whole book. Presented under the rubric 'Kalender', the text is partially an almanac with descriptions of days, weeks, and seasons, as the title implies, but it is also a rich source for folk remedies and folk belief directed at both women and men.

Conclusion

This chapter has explored esoteric lore that medieval women knew and presumably practised, some of which might be surprising even to modern readers. Their range of expertise was wide, far wider than conventional advice texts like *How the Good Wiif Taughte Hir Doughtir* might suggest. In fact, many of the works considered here contain just what a good wife might not necessarily want her daughter to know! Women's knowledge ranged from charms deriving from folk belief that were used in healing and childbirth to the clandestine use of emmenagogues and abortifacients. Judging from *The Book of St Albans* and the Ménagier's manual, women also knew how to maintain the health of hawks and hounds and which animals to hunt in season, and, as we have seen, Dame Juliana also furnishes very precise instructions for butchering game. An encyclopaedic miscellany such as *The Kalender of Shepherds* contains a wide range of materials women might apply to almost any occasion, whether consulting their horoscopes, moon phases, or phlebotomy charts, praying to the Virgin, or even enjoying an amusing skit like the comic poem of woman versus snail. Recovering medieval lore is, of course, imprecise, as much was based on oral tradition passed from woman to woman, but the evidence suggests more than a few ways women were empowered in a broad range of situations, as well as providing a partial record of words to consult, prayers to say, or talismans to conjure with.

Notes

1. 'Lore', Oxford English Dictionary, n. 1 and 5a: www.oed.com/view/Entry/110 333?rskey=Jz9vBW&result=1#eid.
2. Claire Sponsler, 'The English *How the Good Wiif Taughte Hir Doughtir* and *How the Wise Man Taught His Sonne*', in *Medieval Conduct Literature: An Anthology of Vernacular Guides to Behaviour for Youths, with English Translations*, ed. Mark D. Johnston (Toronto: University of Toronto Press, 2009), 285–304(297, ll. 207–8).
3. Sponsler, 'The English *How the Good Wiif*', 290 (296).
4. 'Metrical charm 12: Against a wen', Internet Sacred Text Archive: sacred-texts.com/neu/ascp/a43_12.htm.

5. Karen L. Jolly, *Popular Religion in Late Saxon England: Elf Charms in Context* (Chapel Hill, NC: University of North Carolina Press, 1996), 23.
6. Jolly, *Popular Religion*, 107.
7. See also Naoë Kukita Yoshikawa, Chapter 7 in this volume.
8. Richard Kieckhefer, *Magic in the Middle Ages*, Cambridge Medieval Textbooks (Cambridge: Cambridge University Press, 1990), 39.
9. Corinne Saunders, *Magic and the Supernatural in Medieval English Romance* (Cambridge: D. S. Brewer, 2010), 91.
10. Saunders, *Magic and the Supernatural*, 93.
11. Kieckhefer, *Magic in the Middle Ages*, 78.
12. See Monica H. Green, *The Trotula: A Medieval Compendium of Women's Medicine* (Philadelphia: University of Pennsylvania Press, 2001), esp. the introduction, 1–67.
13. Don C. Skemer, *Binding Words: Textual Amulets in the Middle Ages* (University Park: Pennsylvania State University Press, 2006), 238. He cites Green, *Trotula*, 100, no. 98.
14. Kieckhefer, *Magic in the Middle Ages*, 78.
15. Curt F. Bühler, 'Prayers and Charms in Certain Middle English Scrolls', *Speculum* 39 (1964), 270–8 (273); Mary Morse, 'Alongside St Margaret: The Childbirth Cult of Saints Quiricus and Julitta in Late Medieval English Manuscripts', in *Manuscripts and Printed Books in Europe, 1350–1550: Packing, Presentation and Consumption*, ed. Emma Cayley and Susan Powell (Liverpool: Liverpool University Press, 2013), 187–206 (194, 195, 198, 201–2); Mary Morse, '"Girde hry wythe thys mesure": Birth Girdles, the Church, and Lollards', in *Pregnancy and Childbirth in the Premodern World: European and Middle Eastern Cultures, from Late Antiquity to the Renaissance*, ed. Costanza G. Dopfel, Alessandra Foscati, and Charles Burnett (Turnhout, Belgium: Brepols, 2019), 135–70 (151, 154–6, 159).
16. Jeanne E. Krochalis, 'God and Mammon: Prayers and Rents in Princeton MS 126', *Princeton University Library Chronicle*, 44 (1983), 209–21, 211 n. 7; Skemer, *Binding Words*, 262–3. For a description of G. 39, see Martha W. Driver and Michael T. Orr, *An Index of Images in English Manuscripts from Chaucer to Henry VIII: US Libraries, New York City: Columbia University–Union Theological* (London and Turnhout, Belgium: Brepols, 2007), 38(n. 24), 168 (fig. 9).
17. Bühler, 'Prayers and Charms', 278, n. 52.
18. Skemer, *Binding Words*, 263.
19. Recent scientific analysis of Wellcome MS 632 has found 'human proteins that are specific to cervico-vaginal fluid, suggesting the birth girdle was used during labour itself' (*AMARC Newsletter*, issue 76, April 2021, 8–9). Katherine S. Hindley, '"Yf a woman travell wyth chylde gyrdes thys mesure abowte hyr wombe": Reconsidering the English birth girdle tradition', in *Continuous Page: Scrolls and Scrolling from Papyrus to Hypertext*, ed. Jack Hartnell (London: Courtauld Books Online, 2020), 159–73. Continuous Page is available at: courtauld.ac.uk/research/courtauld-books-online/continuouspage.

20. Alexandra Barratt (ed.), *The Knowing of Woman's Kind in Childing: A Middle English Version of Material Derived from the Trotula and Other Sources*, Medieval Women: Texts and Contexts (Turnhout: Brepols, 2001), 1.
21. Barratt (ed.), *Knowing of Woman's Kind*, 27, 64–6.
22. Barratt's edition is a facing-page transcription of two manuscripts, Oxford Bodley MS Douce 37 and Cambridge University Library MS Ii.6.33. Example in Barratt (ed.), *Knowing of Woman's Kind*, 65.
23. Barratt (ed.), *Knowing of Woman's Kind*, 66.
24. Louise M. Bishop, *Words, Stones, Herbs: The Healing Word in Medieval and Early Modern England* (New York: Syracuse University Press, 2007), 162, has found the sator arepo formula on folio 97 recto of Oxford, Bodley 591.
25. Bishop, *Words, Stones, Herbs*, 162.
26. Barratt (ed.), *Knowing of Woman's Kind*, 65–7.
27. Charity Scott-Stokes, *Women's Books of Hours in Medieval England. Selected Texts Translated from Latin, Anglo-Norman French and Middle English* (Cambridge: D. S. Brewer, 2006), 147–8.
28. Skemer, *Binding Words*, 269.
29. Skemer, *Binding Words*, 271.
30. Skemer, *Binding Words*, 271.
31. See Driver and Orr, *Index of Images*, 37 (no. 23); John Plummer with Gregory T. Clark, *The Last Flowering: French Painting in Manuscripts, 1420–1530* (New York: Pierpont Morgan Library, 1982), 16 (item 23); John Plummer, *The Glazier Collection of Illuminated Manuscripts* (New York: Pierpont Morgan Library, 1968), 36 (item 47); J. J. G. Alexander, 'A Lost Leaf from a Bodleian Book of Hours', *Bodleian Library Record*, 8.5 (1971), 248–51 (251); Kathleen L. Scott, 'A Mid-Fifteenth-Century English Illuminating Shop and its Customers', *Journal of the Warburg and Courtauld Institutes*, 31 (1968), 170–96 (193 n. 130); Kathleen L. Scott, *A Survey of Manuscripts Illuminated in the British Isles*, vol. 2, *Later Gothic Manuscripts, 1390–1490* (London: Harvey Miller, 1996), 296–9 (item 108).
32. Morgan Library & Museum, MS G.9, folio 176v. The Morgan Library's internal file contains this anonymous comment: 'The recipe written in English on the last leaf is interesting but bears too close a resemblance to a witch's broth to be recommended.'
33. John M. Riddle, *Contraception and Abortion from the Ancient World to the Renaissance* (Cambridge: Harvard University Press, 1992), 116.
34. Barratt (ed.), *Knowing of Woman's Kind*, 87.
35. Riddle, *Contraception and Abortion*, 111. Riddle further notes that in the early Middle Ages, 'the principle of the early church fathers that abortion was homicide was not accepted in secular law' (109), and outlines the variations in laws governing early and late pregnancy (109–12).
36. Kieckhefer, *Magic in the Middle Ages*, 59.
37. Riddle, *Contraception and Abortion*, 116.

38. Emmanuel Le Roy Ladurie, *Montaillou: The Promised Land of Error*, trans. B. Bray (New York: G. Braziller, 1978), 32.
39. Edith Ennen, *Medieval Woman*, trans. Edmund Jephcott (Oxford: Blackwell, 1989), 244.
40. *The Good Wife's Guide (Le Ménagier de Paris), A Medieval Household Book*, trans. Gina L. Greco and Christine M. Rose (Ithaca, NY: Cornell University Press), 100.
41. English printed books are cited by their entry number in the notes in *A Short-Title Catalogue of Books Printed in England, Scotland, and Ireland and of English Books Printed Abroad, 1475–1640*, first compiled by A. W. Pollard and G. R. Redgrave, 2nd ed. begun by W. A. Jackson and F. S. Ferguson, completed by Katharine F. Pantzer, 3 vols. (London: Bibliographical Society, 1976–91), hereafter abbreviated as STC. STC 7269.
42. Cynthia Brown, 'The Reconstruction of the Author in Print: Christine de Pizan in the Fifteenth and Sixteenth Centuries', in *Christine de Pizan and the Categories of Difference*, ed. Marilynn Desmond (Minneapolis: University of Minnesota Press, 1998), 215–35 (216).
43. Charity Cannon Willard (ed.), *The Book of Deeds of Arms and of Chivalry*, trans. Sumner Willard (University Park: Penn State University Press, 1999), 1–9. Brown, 'Reconstruction of the Author', 216–19. See also Nancy Bradley Warren, Chapter 21 in this volume.
44. STC 3308.
45. Julia Boffey notes that '"Dam Julyans" is perhaps a corruption of "Daun Julyan"', in 'Berners [Bernes, Barnes], Juliana (fl. 1460)', *Dictionary of National Biography*, 23 September 2004: www.oxforddnb.com/view/10.1093/ref:odnb/9780198614128.001.0001/odnb-9780198614128-e-2255?rskey=mwNV62&result=1>.
46. See William Blades, *The Book of Saint Albans by Dame Juliana Berners Containing Treatises on Hawking, Hunting and Cote Armour* (London: Elliot Stock, 1899), 22–3; Rachel Hands, 'Juliana Berners and The Boke of St. Albans', *Review of English Studies* 18.72 (1967), 373–86 (377–9); Rachel Hands, *English Hawking and Hunting in The Boke of St. Albans* (Oxford: Oxford University Press, 1975), xvii–xxii; Sylvia Tomasch, 'Berners, Juliana', in *Women in the Middle Ages*, vol. 1, ed. Katharina M. Wilson and Nadia Margolis (Westport, CT: Greenwood Press, 2004), 88–9.
47. Sig. e1r. Tristram's skill in hunting and knowledge of butchering animals is described in several of the legends. See Joseph Bédier, *The Romance of Tristan & Iseut*, trans. Hilaire Belloc (New York: Vintage, 1994), 5, 7–9.
48. Sigs. f2v–f4r. Compare the butchering scene in *Sir Gawain and the Green Knight, Pearl, Sir Orfeo*, ed. J. R. R. Tolkien (New York: Ballantine Books, 1975), parts 53–4, 74–5.
49. Alexandra Barratt (ed.), *Women's Writing in Middle English* (New York: Longman, 1992), 232.

50. Alexandra Barratt, 'Dame Eleanor Hull: A Fifteenth-Century Translator', in *The Medieval Translator: The Theory and Practice of Translation in the Middle Ages*, ed. Roger Ellis (Cambridge: Boydell & Brewer, 1989), 87–101 (101).
51. Hands, *English Hawking and Hunting*, xxiii–xxx (xxxii–xliv).
52. Barratt (ed.), *Women's Writing*, 232.
53. Compare Tolkien (ed.), *Gawain*, 'they fed their hounds then / on the liver and the lights and the leather of the paunches with bread bathed in blood blended amongst them' (75).
54. Greco and Rose, *Good Wife's Guide*, 233.
55. Greco and Rose, *Good Wife's Guide*, 239, 252.
56. Hands, 'Juliana Berners and *The Boke of St. Albans*', 382.
57. Sigs. d2v to d3r. One recalls the three tercel eagles vying for the hand (claw?) of the formel eagle in Chaucer's *Parliament of Fowls* and the interfering sparrow hawk: see *The Riverside Chaucer*, ed. by Larry D. Benson, 3rd ed. (Oxford: Oxford University Press, 1988), ll. 415–665.
58. Compare the lines from the Wife of Bath's Prologue (ll. 655–57): 'Whoso that buyldeth his hous al of salwes, / And priketh his blynde hors over the falwes, / And suffreth his wyf to go seken halwes, / Is worthy to been hanged on the galwes!'. For two further manuscript witnesses, see DIMEV, www.dimev.net /record.php?recID=6567; these are Cambridge, St John's College, MS L.1 (235), f. 82 and London, British Library, Lansdowne 762, f. 16v.
59. One can still today purchase a collective-noun tea towel that features some of these groupings. See www.acornonline.com/UM4066.html.
60. Barratt (ed.), *Women's Writing*, 233.
61. Bibliographical background on *The Kalender of Shepherds* is supplied in H. O. Sommer, *The Kalender of Shepherdes, The Edition of Paris 1503 in Photographic Facsimile: A Faithful Reprint of R. Pynson's Edition of London 1506*, 3 vols. in 1 (London: Kegan Paul, Trench, Trübner, 1892) I: Prolegomena, 11–57. On the editions produced by Guy Marchant, see Sandra L. Hindman, 'The Career of Guy Marchant (1483–1504): High Culture and Low Culture in Paris', in *Printing the Written Word: The Social History of Books, c. 1450–1520*, ed. Sandra L. Hindman (Ithaca, NY: Cornell University Press, 1991), 68–100. See also Martha Driver, 'When is a Miscellany not Miscellaneous? Making Sense of the *Kalendar of Shepherds*', *Yearbook of English Studies* 33 (2003), 199–214.
62. According to the STC, following the edition printed by Vérard in a Northern English dialect by a non-native speaker in 1503, *The Kalender of Shepherds* remained in print through 1631 (Pollard and Redgrave, *A Short-Title*, II, 329). STC numbers for the editions follow: 22407 *The kalendayr of the shyppars* [xylographic], trans. from 'Le Compost et Kalendrier des Bergiers', fo. (Paris: for A. Vérard, 1503); 20480 Claudius Ptolemy, *Here begynneth the Compost of Ptholomeus, trans. oute of Frenche* (R. Wyer, [1530?]), consists of extracts from 22407; for further editions all by Wyer, see STC 20480a [1540?], 20481 [1550?], 20481.3 [1552?], 20481.7 (pr. T. Colwell [1562?]); 20482 (M. Parsons for

H. Gosson, sold by E. Wright [638?]); 22408 [another ed., rev. into English] *Here begynneth the Kalender of shepherdes*, fo. (R. Pynson, 1506); 22409 [another ed., rev. by R. Copland] *The kalender of shepeherdes* (W. de Worde, 8 December 1508 [1516]); 22409.3 [another ed. of 22408] fo. (R. Pynson, 1517?); 22410 [another ed.] *Here begynneth the kalender of shepardes*, fo. [J. Notary, 15 8?]; 22411 [another ed.] *The kalender of shepeherdes* (W. de Worde, 24 January 1528); 22412 [another ed.] (W. Powell, 1556); 22413 [another ed.] (W. Powell for J. Walley, 1559); 22415 (T. Este for J. Wally [1570?]); 22416 (J. Charlewood for Jhon Wally [c. 1580]); 22416.5 (J. Charlewood and G. Robinson for John Wally [c. 1585]); 22417=22418; 22418 (V. S[immes], assigned by T. Adams [1595?]; ass'd to R. Walley, 7 March 1591; to T. Adams, 12 October 1591); 22419, fo. [V. Simmes for T. Adams? 1600?]; 22420 (G. Elde for T. Adams, 1604); 22421 (for T. Adams, 1611 I); 22422 (for T. Adams, 1618); 22423 (Eliot's Court Press for J. Wright, 1630; ass'd to A. Hebb, 6 May 1625). Joseph Gwara has pointed to bibliographic errors in the study of a de Worde edition of the text: 'Wynkyn de Worde, Richard Pynson, and *The Kalender of Shepeherdes*: A Case Study in Cast-Off Copy and Textual Transmission', *Papers of the Bibliographical Society of America*, 112.3 (September 2018), 293–356.

63. Hindman, 'Career of Guy Marchant', 95, items 40, 42, 46.
64. Robert Copland, *Robert Copland, Poems*, ed. Mary C. Erler (Toronto: University of Toronto Press, 1993), 54.
65. Sommer, *Kalender of Shepherdes*, 87.
66. Sommer, *Kalender of Shepherdes*, 93.
67. Reproduced in facsimile in Sommer, *Kalender of Shepherdes*, are the 1503 edition of Vérard and a transcription of Pynson's edition of London 1506.
68. Sommer, *Kalender of Shepherdes*, sigs. g1r–g1v; compare transcription, 86.
69. Sommer, *Kalender of Shepherdes*, sigs. g1v–g2v; compare Pynson transcription, 86–7.
70. STC 22409, with the comment 'the cuts and device ... are in a state *c.* 1516.' Erler (ed.), *Robert Copland*, 49–51.
71. Erler, *Robert Copland*, 50.
72. Sommer, *Kalender of Shepherdes*, 146–7; compare Sommer facsimile, sigs. K7v–8r.
73. STC 22411, sig. T7v.
74. Guy Marchant, *Compost et kalendrier des bergiers* (1496), sig. n1v. See Hindman, 'Career of Guy Marchant', 8, notes 1, 2.
75. STC 2241, STC 2270, STC 22410; see also Edward Hodnett, *English Woodcuts 1480–1535* (Oxford: Oxford University Press, repr. 1973 (1935)), fig. 210.
76. On the enduring popularity of depictions of man's warfare against the snail, see Lilian M. C. Randall, 'The Snail in Gothic Marginal Warfare', *Speculum* 37.3 (1962), 358–67, which appears first near the end of the thirteenth century and recurs in the fifteenth century. The snail fight in the *Kalendar of Shepherds*, Randall suggests, was written 'to ridicule the recently established peasant militia', 359–60. For the ages of man, see Elizabeth Sears, *The Ages of*

Man: *Medieval Interpretations of the Life Cycle* (Princeton, NJ: Princeton University Press, 1986), who discusses this popular text more fully, 116–18.

Further Reading

Barratt, Alexandra, ed. (2001). *The Knowing of Woman's Kind in Childing: A Middle English Version of Material Derived from the Trotula and Other Sources*, Medieval Women: Texts and Contexts, Turnhout: Brepols.

Bishop, Louise M. (2007). *Words, Stones, Herbs: The Healing Word in Medieval and Early Modern England*, Syracuse, NY: Syracuse University Press.

Bühler, Curt F. (1964). Prayers and Charms in Certain Middle English Scrolls. *Speculum* 39, 270–8.

Christine de Pizan (1999). *The Book of Deeds of Arms and of Chivalry*, ed. Charity Cannon Willard, trans. Sumner Willard, University Park: Penn State University Press.

Driver, Martha (2003). When Is a Miscellany Not Miscellaneous? Making Sense of the *Kalendar of Shepherds*. *Yearbook of English Studies* 33, 199–214.

Erler, Mary C., ed. (1993). *Robert Copland, Poems*, Toronto: University of Toronto Press.

Green, Monica H. (2001). *The Trotula: A Medieval Compendium of Women's Medicine*, Philadelphia: University of Pennsylvania Press.

Jolly, Karen L. (1996). *Popular Religion in Late Saxon England: Elf Charms in Context*, Chapel Hill: University of North Carolina Press.

Kieckhefer, Richard (1990). *Magic in the Middle Ages*, Cambridge Medieval Textbooks, Cambridge: Cambridge University Press.

Riddle, John M. (1992). *Contraception and Abortion from the Ancient World to the Renaissance*, Cambridge, MA: Harvard University Press.

Saunders, Corinne (2010). *Magic and the Supernatural in Medieval English Romance*. Cambridge: D. S. Brewer.

Skemer, Don C. (2006). *Binding Words: Textual Amulets in the Middle Ages*. University Park: Pennsylvania State University Press.

Sommer, H. O. (1892). *The Kalender of Shepherdes, The Edition of Paris 1503 in Photographic Facsimile: A Faithful Reprint of R. Pynson's Edition of London 1506*, 3 vols. in 1, London: Kegan Paul, Trench, Trübner.

Sponsler, Claire (2009). *The English* How the Good Wiif Taughte Hir Doughtir and How the Wise Man Taught His Sonne. In Mark D. Johnston, ed., *Medieval Conduct Literature: An Anthology of Vernacular Guides to Behaviour for Youths, with English Translations*. Toronto: University of Toronto Press.

CHAPTER 10

Women and Devotional Compilations
Denis Renevey

Compilatory activity has been recognised as a significant medieval literary undertaking since Malcom Parkes' influential article, 'The Influence of the Concepts of *Ordinatio* and *Compilatio*'.[1] It consists in creating a new text by thoughtfully arranging extracts of texts or whole texts into a new whole, for a different readership than that of the source texts. Compilation may take place simultaneously with translation activity; it may also involve abbreviating extracts and providing new parts, either brief linking passages from one extract to another, or extensive ones to fill in what the compiler would consider major gaps in his or her material. Compilatory activity produced an extensive set of late medieval devotional texts. The collection of essays *Late Medieval Devotional Compilations in England* and Denissen's monograph *Middle English Devotional Compilations* have recently extensively explored this flourishing late medieval genre.[2] The dynamics of devotional compilations, concepts of manuscript transmission, compilations as prescriptive treatises for devotional practice, including mystical texts for the most ambitious ones, as well as the translation of emotion via texts and images, are among some of the themes discussed in *Late Medieval Devotional Compilations*. Denissen's *Middle English Devotional Compilations* adds to these discussions by approaching compiling as a literary activity, with emphasis on agency and creativity, rather than simply technically unravelling the ways in which compilers deal with their source texts.

Despite the wide range of topics covered by these recent publications, a critical gap remains to be filled with regard to the parts played by women in the processes of compilatory activity.[3] Although their roles as models, patrons, recipients, and active readers have been highlighted in relation to the processes of composition in the investigation of specific devotional compilations, the overall contribution of women to the genre of devotional compilation has, rather surprisingly, not yet been well assessed.[4] This chapter aims to pave the way for further investigations by highlighting some of the areas that most urgently need appraisal. It begins by addressing the question of female subjectivity as a model for both male and female devout readers, using evidence from *Þe Lyfe of Soule* and *Pore Caitif*, with a brief reference to *Þe Pater Noster of Richard Ermyte*.[5]

If female personae seem to be used as exemplary Christian readers in need of education, some compilations are more specific in their addresses to aristocratic women. This part of the chapter looks at the transformation of anchoritic material for late medieval women by, first, using evidence from *A Tretyse of Loue* and, second, studying images linked to a wealthy household and pointing to a well-to-do vowess as the initial recipient of *Disce mori*.[6] As argued recently, *A Talkyng of the Loue of God* may also have appealed to a female readership made up of nuns with well-to-do backgrounds.[7]

The construction of interpersonal male/female relationships within some compilations is based on Rollean models, as exemplified by some of Richard Rolle's Middle English writings. *Disce mori*, *A Little Treatise Against Fleshly Affections*, and *A Good Remedie Aȝens Spirituel Temptacions* invent such a dialogic space based on the example of the Rollean one.[8] *Book to a Mother* is markedly dialogic in its creation of a son/mother exchange that has an historic reality.[9] However, that model, constructed on an intimate relationship, also allows the compiler to create a text that mediates biblical information for his female reader. *A Myrror to Devout People* is used alongside *Book to a Mother* here in order to assess how modes and levels of instruction differ depending on whether the compilation targets lay or religious women.[10]

The final part of this chapter looks first at compilations in which material by approved women plays a significant role. *A Myrror to Devout People* (*Speculum devotorum*) includes extracts from Mechthild of Hackeborn, Elizabeth of Töss, Catherine of Siena, and Birgitta of Sweden, whom it qualifies as 'approuyd wymmen'. *The Westminster Compilation*, Westminster Cathedral Treasury, MS 4, presents a significant extract from Julian of Norwich's *Revelation of Love* as one of its four fragments.[11] The use of women's writings in the creation of compilations testifies to the growing authority of spiritual texts by women in the late medieval period. But women are also to be found at the heart of the dynamics of compilatory activity. Despite difficulty with identifying the many Anglo-Norman sources that Eleanor Hull used for the composition of her own texts, there is sufficient evidence to show that her translations are the result of very considered choices in selection, deletion, and abbreviation, which show her to be actively engaged in a dual process of translation and compilation.[12]

Female Personae, Model Christians

A variety of counter-discourses present the female persona as a kind of model Christian engaged in a process of perfectibility that can be appropriated by male and female, lay and religious readers.[13] Half of the content of *Þe Lyfe of Soule* is made up of quotations of the Bible in Middle English. This late fourteenth-century compilation, extant in three manuscripts, offers basic catechetical knowledge using dialogic exchange that could possibly be rendered by means of performance. The treatise rehearses basic instruction that Archbishops Peckham in 1281 and Thoresby in 1357 distributed in English for the edification of the laity and the secular clergy. Information about the seven virtues, the seven deadly sins, the commandments, the works of mercy, and other basic aspects of the faith is rendered more attractive by the dialogic exchange which begins the treatise, but which fades out halfway through. Each extant manuscript depicts different characters engaging in this dialogic exchange: Oxford, Bodleian Library, MS Laud Misc. 210 sets the scene with a 'Sire' asking questions to a 'frend'; San Marino, Huntington Library, MS HM. 502 shows a son and a father; while London, British Library, MS Arundel 286 has a sister receiving advice from a brother.[14] Each manuscript seems therefore to have been custom made for a specific readership, with the latter manuscript most likely implying a monastic setting in which a nun may receive instruction from a brother, even if a blood relationship cannot be excluded. Whatever the case may be, *Þe Lyfe of Soule* shows, first, that there was a demand for catechetical instruction from a female readership and, second, that a female persona could stand for any Christian reader.

Apart from the fact that *Pore Caitif* shares with *Þe Lyfe of Soule* some of its content on the ten commandments, it initially offers basic catechetical information, organised in fourteen distinct chapters, but progressively moving to a more ambitious spiritual programme that points to the contemplative life.[15] The prologue to the *Pore Caitif* names precisely the audience it has in mind: the phrase 'eueri cristen man and womman' is all-encompassing, thus including, as well as a lay reading public, a cloistered audience for whom the material would also be available in Latin. The treatise continues by stating the method of construction ('compilid') and hence the genre of the treatise as a compilation, the status of the compiler ('pore caitif'), and the humble disposition of the target audience ('symple men and wommen of good wille').[16] Whether or not the accidents of compilation contribute to the rather lax reference to the target audience in the various tracts, one is left with the impression that the compiler wishes to point out at strategic moments of his compilation his awareness of a female persona as a potential model Christian. The tract called 'Active and Contemplative Life', which derives in part from chapter 12 of Rolle's *Form of Living*, contains an epilogue that surely suggests it was considered at some point to conclude *Pore Caitif*.[17] By claiming to 'schewe to my pore briþeren and sistren what grace and loue þat oure Lord Ihesu haþ schewid to soulis in þis liif', it reopens the possibility of a monastic audience, even if this specificity disappears in the following tract, which addresses 'ech man'.[18]

'The Mirrour of Chastite', the fourteenth and final tract of *Pore Caitif*, begins with a substantial prologue and corroborates further its rather loose link with the rest of *Pore Caitif*, which must have been designed at some point to end with the discussion of the active and contemplative lives. The compiler, far from posturing as a 'pore caitif', as in the general prologue, or as a 'caitif and wrecche', as in the epilogue to the preceding tract, confidently introduces himself and this tract on chastity by presenting it as a fight between David and Goliath.[19] Preserving chastity by combating the stirring of the flesh inflamed by the five senses requires strong motivation and equally stirring imagery. Like *Ancrene Wisse* and its accompanying texts, the 'Mirrour' invites its audience to perceive the inner senses as the guardians of the spiritual castle of the soul. This combative virile imagery soon makes way in the treatise itself for a multiplicity of female personae who function as exemplary chaste characters, with the Virgin Mary as the ultimate model.

Maidens, widows, and wives represent various statuses offered to the reader to reflect on his or her own spiritual trajectory. The life of the soul is perceived as that of a chaste spouse wedded to Jesus: unlike Dinah, who loses her maidenhood (Genesis 34) as a result of her imprudent look, the reader is asked to be watchful, following the example of the five wise virgins (Matthew 25:1–13). The prologue casts further light on its use of female personae for a mixed readership: 'Seynt Poul seiþ þat a widowe lyuynge in delicis is deed; whi not so a maide eþer oþer bi þe same resoun, siþin we alle schulden be widowe, sones and douʒtris?'[20] The 'myrrour of maidens' proper presents first the Virgin Mary's maidenhood from the perspective of Joseph, hence opening up the attraction of maidenhood for both male and female, with the Virgin Mary as the second best model (after Jesus) for all: 'mayden tofore hir childinge, maiden in hir childinge, and mayden aftir hir childyng'.[21] The compiler readjusts traditional medieval misogynistic values by showing that an undisciplined soul in manly flesh is feminine, whereas a woman showing spiritual virtues is manly and can be counted among the saints. Although misogyny remains, the labels 'female' and 'male', when applied to the figurative life of soul, have a different valence. The female label clearly stands for 'weakness' ('neschenes') and is applicable to anyone undisciplined and easily giving in to lust:

> And þouȝ he be in bodi a man, in soule he is vndirstonde a womman, and þerfor he is not noumbrid wiþ seyntis. A womman forsoþe, if sche haþ hir manlynes in goostli vertues, and þouȝ in bodi sche be a womman, in soule naþelees sche is a man and is noumbrid wiþ seyntis. Þerfore it was in figure þat wommanli flesch was repellid eþer put out.[22]

This figurative approach to gender allows the compiler to display a multiplicity of female personae as part of his argumentation in support of chastity.[23]

Since to be womanly is to be weak, it may be best for the readership to be provided with examples of female personae that prove that a disciplined soul in a female body can achieve chastity to be in closer proximity to the divine. Probably using the Sarum Breviary as his source, the compiler, after offering a summary of the chaste lives of Agnes, Lucy, Agatha, Cecilia, and Katherine, invites the Christian man or woman to make a garland of these fair red roses, with Christ, the brightest of roses, capping it.[24]

This part of *Pore Caitif* echoes some of the concerns expressed in virginity treatises such as *Hali Meiþhad*, for example. Although written for men and women, possibly both lay and religious, it draws its imagery and concepts from antecedent texts associated with the ideals of the anchoritic life, thus offering an idealised female persona as the most powerful model for late medieval Christians to emulate. It seems that by the late fourteenth and early fifteenth centuries, the putative female religious reader becomes the hallmark of a large number of devotional treatises, with *Þe Pater Noster of Richard Ermyte* a good case in point. Although not a compilation in the strict sense of the term,[25] this treatise shows that the notion of female religious readers as exemplary models becomes the norm, whether or not the female readers of these texts can be identified with historical characters.[26]

Reconfiguring the Anchoritic Tradition

While this female persona, sometimes described as a female solitary, has become a literary topos with no obvious historical existence in several devotional compilations, in others she appears with specific attributes that give more credibility to a specific female target audience. In this respect, *The*

Tretyse of Loue offers an interesting contrast to the impersonal female devout subject represented in *Pore Caitif*. The *Tretyse*, translated from French into English, was printed in 1493 by Wynkyn de Worde.[27] As expected, it assembles fragments of various texts to make a new and coherent devotional treatise. Significant borrowings from *Ancrene Wisse* demonstrate the desire to transfer the anchoritic ideal to a new readership.[28] In the case of this compilation, the new time period, more than two centuries after the composition of *Ancrene Wisse*, and the distance from the social status of the initial recipient, imply a translation of the material into a new socio-cultural context. The compilation addresses a well-to-do female devout reader of whom the compiler seems to have direct knowledge. If the noble status of his recipient is not unlike that of the three anchoresses for whom *Ancrene Wisse* was initially written, nonetheless the task of the compiler is not to ask her to forget her well-to-do background, as with the three blood sisters, but to offer her the spiritual essentials of the anchoritic life within her household. As noted by Denissen, the compiler adapts the material to suit her own background: although the substitution of the needle and scissors for the axe, plough, and spade may seem trifling, it denotes a refined assessment of the new context in which anchoritic ideology has to be deployed.[29] Further on in the treatise, the opulent social setting of the female lay reader is highlighted both by a description of her stylish bed and a social occasion similar to a banquet: 'Ye sytte at þe tabyll so rychely arayd & *serued*, & goodly Ientylmen abowte yow so well araid & wel *seruinge*, þat *serue* yow so nobely wyth cuppys of gold & syluyr vessel, wyth so many & dyuerse & good metys, wyth delycyous sawses & pleysaunt wynes.'[30] However significant the luxury of the utensils and the sophistication of their contents are, as well as the company of gentlemen, the social standing of the wealthy lady, displayed by the number of servants attending to her needs, may be an impediment to her spiritual progress. The compiler does not ask for a transformation of her material conditions, but nevertheless contrasts her situation with that of Christ: 'He cam not in erthe to be serude but to serue', which translates Matthew 20:28. The compilation continues with the description of an episode recounted by St Peter to St Clement describing the way Jesus served his disciples on an occasion where the disciples were suffering from hunger and cold. Finding shelter in an old ramshackle house, Jesus physically protects them from the cold by placing himself in front of the opening to stop the draft, as well as covering them with his own clothes. The demonstration of Jesus's selfless service culminates with an account of the Passion. In order to satisfy the needs of the new audience, *The Tretyse* distances itself from the strategies of *Ancrene Wisse* by asking the well-to-do laywoman to contrast her excellent material conditions with those of Christ, while *Ancrene Wisse* instead draws analogies between the life of Christ and the spartan material conditions of the anchoresses.

This technique of contrast is further elaborated in the descriptions of the comfortable bed of the wealthy lady and the narrow, hard, and poorly dressed bed of the Virgin Mary, which offers very little comfort. These images of material comfort are based on a reality that the compiler knows to be that of his primary recipient. Whether this is also the case for the recipient of *Disce mori* is more difficult to say. As proposed by the editor of the part of the compilation called the '*Exhortacion*', its recipient, Dame Alice, was most probably a vowess who embarked on a religious vocation and who had a relationship with Syon Abbey.[31] Whether she had a previous lay life as a wealthy woman is impossible to ascertain from internal evidence. However, the use of the image of a luxurious bed in the text, functioning as a mnemonic tool at the centre of the chamber, assumes literal or representational knowledge of this kind of sophisticated material object by Dame Alice.[32] Around thirty items are described in relation to this piece of furniture, which was the only item in the household to belong to women.[33] Litter, canvas, mattress, blankets, top and bottom sheet, coverlet, pillows, traversin, head drapery, and several other items make a luxurious bed a perfect mnemonic tool:

> Þe ii pelowes vndre þe hede shal be pitie and pacience – þat is, þat þou haue euere pitie on þin owne soule, and on þe pouere, and þat þou be pacient in alle aduersitees. Þe bolster þat þees pilowes shal lye vpone shal be besynesse and wakyng in alle goode werkes, lest heuynesse wolde make þe to falle into dispaire, or to slepe or rest longe in synne. Þe testour at þe hede shal be *liberum arbitrium* þat is yeuen by God to man, he to chese noþing ayenst his comandementes or þe helth of his soule.[34]

The passage, borrowed from the treatise *An Honest Bede*, draws on the long tradition of commentaries and glosses on the verse *lectulus noster floridus* ('our bed is flourishing') (Canticum Canticorum 1:15). But the luxury bed of *Disce mori* as well as the brief reference to the comfortable bed of the aristocratic lady of *The Tretyse* point to the ways in which this image is adapted to suit the tastes and habits of a lay female audience familiar with the furniture of a wealthy household.

Thirteenth-century anchoresses were familiar with the nuptial mysticism that developed out of the commentary tradition of the Song of Songs. The compiler of *The Tretyse* contributes to its spread by adapting it for a late medieval female readership. Similarly, *A Talkyng of þe Love of God*, a compilation made up of Anselmian and anchoritic meditations from the

Wooing group, also undertakes the substantial redeployment of these for a late medieval readership.[35] The only complete version of the *Talkyng*, found in the Vernon manuscript, is grouped with *Ancrene Wisse*, thus showing the compiler's awareness of the anchoritic origin of his source texts and the desire to offer them as such to the audience of the Vernon anthology.[36] The latter is strongly linked to the Cistercian monastery of Bordesley Abbey and may have been conceived for a community of religious women.[37] Compilatory activity generates a layering of multiple voices within the new text, blending the voices from the source text with that of the compiler(s). This broad-minded display of voices invites multiple readers to add their own in their performative reading. It is with this end in mind that the compiler refrains from organising his composition as if expressing a single subject perspective. The following two passages, which develop further the loving relationship between Jesus and the 'I-voice', encourage the reader to enact a female subject position:

> Bote mony mon for strengþe. and mony for his hardischupe. is ofte muchel i leten of; and loued and honoured. And is eny so hardi.so bold.and so douhti.as þou art my leue lyf founden in a say;

> Noble men and gentil.and gentil of heiȝ kuynde; mony wimmen leeten menske forte loue.A.swete Ihesu Merci.on what herre mon; mai I.sette my loue.ȝif þat I.þe lete;[38]

Elsewhere, the bestowing of love upon Jesus is depicted as an affair between him and the soul, which can be given manly or womanly attributes. Equally malleable is the representation of Christ, who is both mother and the ultimate male embodiment of strength and courage.[39]

The adaptation of anchoritic material for the attention of a late medieval readership follows different pathways. In the case of *The Tretyse*, evidence points to its subtle adaptation for an aristocratic devout woman; the multifaceted use of voices in *A Talkyng* and the lack of strong evidence for a primary readership nevertheless show the degree to which source material initially addressed to female anchoritic readers plays an important function in incentivising devout behaviour in late medieval compilations intended for both men and women.

Rollean Models: Male Writers, Female Readers

Richard Rolle's reputation as an experienced contemplative led his writings to become guides for the spiritual life of nuns and anchoresses.[40] In his Middle English epistles *Ego dormio*, *The Commandment*, and *The Form of*

Living, his relationship with the female recipients is represented as playing a fundamental role in triggering a devout predisposition on their parts. In *Ego dormio*, Rolle situates himself as the messenger who will bring the epistle's recipient, a nun of Yedingham, to the Lord's bed. The importance of his role as a spiritual guide and his mediation of spiritually empowering texts for his female recipient is unequivocal: 'Til þe I write specialy, for I hope mare godenes in þe þan in another.'[41] Rolle's indispensable presence as a messenger implies an active engagement on the part of the recipient in this indirect dialogic exchange with Rolle. The latter provides his female reader with a way of measuring her spiritual progress by comparing it to three different degrees of love, which represent states of consciousness.[42] The end of *Ego dormio* encourages the nun to appropriate the voice of the final lyric, the *Cantus amoris*. Rolle's persona has receded into the background by this point, letting the nun discover on her own terms, by the means of the *Cantus*, the benefits of the spiritual life. While *Ego dormio* quickly moves from the general to the particular, *The Commandment*, written for a nun of Hampole, does not posit a particular relationship between Rolle and his recipient with the same level of immediacy and confidence. However, once he has moved from introductory considerations, Rolle uses the second-person singular pronoun as his preferred mode of address throughout the remaining part of the epistle. The degree of intimacy between Rolle and his recipient is attenuated in contrast to *Ego dormio*, either because the epistle represents a relationship that was not as intense in reality, or because it fulfils an altogether different function, more in line with the rational approach to the spiritual life of his *Emendatio vitae*. There is more than one Rollean male writer/female reader model, as is disclosed further in *The Form of Living*, written to a young female recluse, identified as Margaret, or Dame Merget Kyrkby. *The Form of Living*'s success, attested by the large number of extant manuscripts and its integration within devotional compilations such as *Pore Caitif*, is the result of a very subtle arrangement of significant spiritual instruction, presented in affectionate and personal terms by Rolle to his primary recipient.

Disce mori was composed in the London area and may have originated within a Syon context. One of the most convincing pieces of evidence for a Syon connection is the fact that a manuscript of *The Chastising of God's Children* from the Syon and Sheen Charterhouse milieu is closer than any other extant manuscript to the one used by the *Disce mori* compiler. In addition to this, Oxford, Jesus College, MS 39 (J), one of the two extant manuscripts of *Disce mori*, dated to the period 1453–64, was in Syon in the sixteenth century.[43] The most credible hypothesis about the genesis of

Disce mori is that it was commissioned from a brother of Sheen or Syon by a vowess as a guide to her new vocation. She received the archetype, while the compiler kept a copy, probably J, which he used as the basis for another compilation, *Ignorancia sacerdotum*.[44]

The final and most ambitious part of *Disce mori*, the '*Exhortacion*', begins with a direct address to his readership as 'Suster'. As discussed, this may still refer to 'my best-beloued sustre Dame Alice' of the envoy, a vowess with a close link to Syon Abbey. But by shortening it to 'suster', it opens itself to a wider readership, enabling the compiler to present his material using the Rollean model. Considering the explicit reference to Richard Rolle and the abundant use of his material within the treatise, both the heading of the '*Exhortacion*', called 'A lessone of perfit lyuyng', and the inclusion in the first paragraph of 'a litel fourme hou ye shal lyue' are not coincidental.[45] In fact, the compiler not only uses fragments from Rolle's writings as part of his compilation, but also openly confirms his imitation of the dynamics of Rolle's model in the development of his own relationship with his putative female recipient: 'As to kepyng of abstinence, þe hooly heremite Richard Hampole wrote ful descretely in his dayes to suche a woman as yee be, in wise as foloweth.'[46] The affectionate tone, combined with a sense of authority on the part of the compiler towards his female recipient, ventriloquises the Rolle of the Middle English epistles. For instance, 'I wolle þat þou be euermore clymbyng vpward to Ihesu, and wenyng & willyng þi loue and seruice towardes him – and not as fooles doon, for þei begynne in þe highest degree, and come downe into þe lowest' combines the authority and confidence of Rolle's voice in his own epistle.[47] Further, the compiler makes direct reference to Richard Hampole when quoting his words on the Name, when reporting the well-known episode of his temptation by the Devil in the form of fair woman, and when using a long fragment from *Emendatio vitae* in his discussion of the three degrees of love.[48]

Like other compilations, the '*Exhortacion*' part of *Disce mori* plays with multivocality, at times integrating compiler and reader together as God's children in the practice of chastity, as in the parable of the wise and foolish virgins (Matthew 25:1–13).[49] By initially embracing the Rollean male writer/female reader model in the first folios of the '*Exhortacion*', the compiler creates a context which allows him to have recourse to spiritual concepts deeply dependent on female-based experiences or settings. Predictably, chastity is discussed with reference to the wise and foolish virgins, the Virgin Mary is evoked as a model of linguistic restraint and humility, and conduct in the household, with an allegorical description of the bed, as well as the duties of married women towards their husbands, is offered with a female subject in mind.[50] Equally, as discussed elsewhere, the way in which the compiler undoes the artifices of external feminine beauty in order to gain insight into the inner self forces the readership to assume a female subject position that has been consolidated by the use of the Rollean model.[51]

The *Little Treatise Against Fleshly Affections*, possibly a Syon Abbey production as well, exhibits the potential dangers associated with a Rollean model based upon a real physical relationship between a male spiritual guide and his female religious disciple.[52] This compilation has a female audience in mind ('women allonly') in the first place, but almost immediately opens up to a larger audience that is made of 'euery man havyng discrecion'.[53] On the basis of internal evidence, Parreiras Reis hypothesises that male spiritual advisors to Syon nuns and female novices or vowesses informally attached to the monastery would benefit from the *Little Treatise*, since carnal relationships between advisor and disciple could easily develop out of spiritual exchanges.[54] The warning against falling into fleshly 'affection' also targets priests and religious people:

> moch more a preste or a religious person, the which by their profession ar bounden to greter perfeccion and hyer degre of loue of God, ar but paynted and not beynge as þei appere, if þei fall in eny such dotage and blynde affeccion whereof folowith all thes inconuenientis and gret hurte of conscience.[55]

Little Treatise shows the limits of the Rollean model when its textual representation is strongly anchored in physical reality. Mediating the word of God and offering spiritual instruction within these gendered parameters could be fraught with ambiguity and deviant behaviour, as may possibly have been the case between the Carthusian monk James Greenhalgh and the Syon novice Joanna Sewell, whose mutual friendship was considered to be suspect by their superiors.[56]

Book to a Mother negotiates the ambiguities linked to male/female spiritual instruction by representing a filial relationship between a priest and his mother, a widow at the time of writing.[57] Autobiographical details support the hypothesis that, as in the case discussed earlier, the representation of this relationship is based on a lived reality. The priest persona reminds his mother about her support in trying to help him enter a convent of canons in exchange for 'twenti marc': unable to gather this sum, the son does not join the order and remains a member of the secular clergy.[58] However, he invites his 'leue dere modir' to construct an imaginary cloister in her mind, made up from four walls of justice, fortitude, wisdom, and temperance, with Christ as her abbot.⁵⁹ As highlighted by its editor, *Book to a Mother* focuses mainly on a female audience and provides a form of spirituality that would speak more directly to a woman. Although ultimately the compilation provides instruction that would benefit every Christian ('wite ȝe wel þat is desire euerych man and woman and child to be my moder'), the fact that it is based on a genuine filial relationship enables the use of intimate, affectionate, but unambiguous vocabulary.⁶⁰

It is the filial relationship, rather than the priestly function, that the compiler highlights when instructing his female recipient. As with the maiden instructing her father in the famous late fourteenth-century alliterative poem *Pearl*, the traditional parent/child pattern is reversed. However, affectionate and personal modes of address are absent from the extensive scriptural section that makes up about a fifth of the compilation. This section adopts a more sober and impersonal tone, with the compiler's function limited to the translation of well-chosen biblical fragments provided entirely in English.⁶¹ The male/female Rollean model dressed as a son/mother relationship offers the compiler an unequivocal model for disseminating significant biblical knowledge.

The *Myrror to Devout People (Speculum devotorum)* assumes a male/female relationship for the dissemination of devotional instruction within a monastic context that preserves it from the ambiguities discussed by *A Little Treatise*.⁶² Written for the attention of a female religious, most likely a Syon nun, the compilation addresses its reader as 'gostly sister' or 'relygyus sister' throughout. The compiler, a Sheen Carthusian monk, and the religious sister share a personal relationship ('whenne we spake laste togyderys') that may have been conducted mainly in writing, with the possibility of a few rare meetings on the occasions of his visits to the well-furnished Syon library to stock up on the source texts used to compile *A Mirror*.⁶³ Although, as in the case of *Disce mori* and *Book to a Mother*, the compiler personally knows his initial recipient, the tone and form of address lack the familiarity of the preceding compilations. The official monastic context within which this exchange takes place influences the affective restraint displayed in the text, so much so that the phrase 'relygyus syster, I haue sumwhat tolde yow' and its many variations become literary formulae that can easily be appropriated or dispensed with by a broader public. In fact, one of the two manuscripts in which *A Mirror* is extant, Notre Dame, Indiana, University of Notre Dame, MS 67, was made available for a pious laywoman, Elizabeth Chaworth/Scrope, who took the veil as a vowess and was one of the many well-do-do vowesses associated with Syon.⁶⁴ However, unsurprisingly, readership of *A Mirror* is not limited to a female religious audience: the work also invites engagement from lay female readers and male religious contemplatives and preachers, which points, as noted by Gillespie, to the Syon brothers.[65]

The Birgittine milieu of Syon, with its complex network involving the neighbouring Carthusian monastery of Sheen, the Syon brothers and nuns, as well as the lay women informally attached to the abbey, seems to have been the ideal locus for the emergence of compilations using variations on the Rollean male/female model in order to disseminate devotional instruction to a broad lay public.[66]

Women Compiled, Women Compiling

There seems to be a correlation between the need for devotional texts by devout religious and lay women from the Syon milieu and the use of female religious as exemplary models and/or literary authorities. Alongside specific references to Rolle (four times) and Hilton (two times) and several other male *auctores*, the '*Exhortacion*' part of *Disce mori* includes a precise reference to book 1, chapter 7, of 'Seint Maude's Reuelacions'.[67] Saint Maude, as Mechthild of Hackeborn was known, appears again in *A Mirror* as part of a group of 'approuyd wymmen', together with Birgitta of Sweden, Catherine of Siena, and Elizabeth of Töss, whose texts were available in the Syon brothers' library and were possibly translated into Middle English by the brothers.[68] Although they are not referenced as generously as other male authors, their presence within *A Mirror* attests to the influence of female continental mystics on an English public of lay and religious women within the Syon milieu.[69] In this respect, the extensive references to Birgitta and the use of her writings as source material is not surprising. The compiler acknowledges the *Reuelacyon* of Birgitta as the main material for his chapter on the life of Christ from the age of twelve to his baptism.[70] Chapter 22 describes the crucifixion of Christ according to Birgitta's own account: 'Thys ys the maner how oure Lorde was crucyfyed aftyr the *Reuelacyon* of Seynt Brygytte.'[71] That manner, according to Birgitta, is conveyed in order to trigger strong devotional feelings from the reader of *A Mirour*, who possibly also had access to the *Reuelacyon* as supplementary reading. By inserting four 'approuyd wymmen' as part of its sources, *A Mirror* ushers these four continental female authors into an approved post-Arundelian group that also includes Rolle and Hilton, as part of its ongoing reflections on the authority of translated sources.[72]

The extensive extract from Julian of Norwich's *A Revelation of Divine Love* found in London, Westminster Cathedral Treasury, MS 4, along with an exposition of Psalm 90 (*Qui habitat*), an exposition of Psalm 91 (*Bonum est*), and Walter Hilton's *Scale of Perfection*, deserves special mention.[73] Unlike the four named 'approuyd wymmen' of *A Mirror*, Julian's authorship is not acknowledged in this compilation. Although the transition from Hilton's *Scale* to Julian's *Revelation*, with a shift from a third-person perspective to the 'I-voice' of the Julian fragment, is linguistically precarious, the topic of the clean soul is carried over from one fragment to another, showcasing the compiler's strategy and sense of unity at this juncture.[74] The compiler's silent use of the Julian fragment is consistent with his overall strategy, and it does not diminish the importance of her text as an authoritative account of a revelation judiciously written down and interpreted for the profit of all Christians. This silent approval of the theological content of a text written by a woman, and its integration into a new whole, does not reflect a desire to hide the female authorship of text or its use of female imagery. Although it would not be impossible for the reader of the compilation to assume that a male author was responsible for this fragment, the overwhelming importance given to the notion of motherhood points strongly to female authorship: 'The moder may suffer her childe to perishe, but oure heuenly moder Ihesu Criste may neuer suffer vs þat be his chyldryn to peryshe, for he is almyghty, all wysedomm and all loue, and so is noon but he.'[75] Unlike most of the other compilations discussed so far, the Westminster Compilation addresses a hypothetical 'wyse man' who finds in the last fragment from Julian's *Revelation* the spiritually most ambitious moment of the compilation.

Examples of female compilatory activity are scarce, but it is not impossible to conjecture from the large corpus of anonymous compilations that some were compiled by women. The *Meditations Upon the Seven Days of the Week* by Eleanor Hull are as much the product of compilatory as translation activity. While, in the absence of a large bulk of her Anglo-Norman source material, little firm evidence can be offered in support of this claim, translation and compilation activities derive from a very similar set of principles, and the act of translation very often implies compilation as well.[76] In the case of Eleanor Hull, the abbreviation of elements of her source text in order to create a new whole is visible in the following instance. The incipit of the *Meditations upon the Seven Days of the Week* in Cambridge University Library, MS Kk 1.6, reads:

> Thes orysons and thes meditacions þat folowen here ben in party takyn of Seynt Austyn, party of Seynt Ancelm, party of Seynt Barnard, and party of oþer wrytingis for to enflawme the hert and the corage of hem þat redyn it in the love of God and for-to make a man to know hymself.[77]

As Alexandra Barratt points out, it bears a very close resemblance to an Anglo-Norman sequence of meditations in British Library, Cotton MS Vitellius F.vii with the following incipit: 'Ces orisons et ces meditations qe ici s'ensuient sunt prises partie de seint Augustin, partie de seint Anselm, partie de seint Bernard, partie de seintes scriptures' (The following orisons and meditations are borrowed in part from St Augustine, from St Anselm, from St Bernard, and from Holy Scripture).[78] Probably working with the Anglo-Norman version found in Cotton Vitellius, or a copy of it, Hull shapes her compilation of meditations from an existing Anglo-Norman one. One important decision that she makes with regard to her source text, for instance, is to omit a meditation on the name of John, in order to present the meditations to the Names of Jesus and Mary in close proximity, as a kind of diptych. Several other decisions are reached by Hull in an effort to prepare a sequence of meditations for her own consumption and that of her household. The fact that she works from a text in Anglo-Norman which is itself a compilation adds to the complexity of understanding her own activity within compilatory parameters.[79] Further work needs to be done in order to understand better her contribution, and possibly that of other female authors, to the genre of the devotional compilation.

Devotional Compilations: A Gendered Genre?

Devotional compilations are characterised by multivocality, open-endedness (the gift that keeps on giving), mouvance, moderation, humility, and multiplication (of books and words).[80] Even if this chapter is only a first foray into women's agency in the composition, production, and dissemination of devotional compilations, nonetheless it points to a more significant involvement than recognised so far. In particular, the fact that a large number of compilations suggest the female subject position as the most effective posture for their appraisal points to a late medieval devotional culture that is ideologically highly feminine.

Notes

1. Malcolm Parkes, 'The Influence of the Concepts of *Ordinatio* and *Compilatio* on the Development of the Book', in *Medieval Learning and Literature: Essays Presented to Richard William Hunt*, ed. J. J. G. Alexander and M. T. Gibson (Oxford: Clarendon Press, 1976), 115–41.

2. Marleen Cré, Diana Denissen and Denis Renevey (eds.), *Late Medieval Devotional Compilations in England*, Medieval Church Series 41 (Turnhout: Brepols, 2020); Diana Denissen, *Middle English Devotional Compilations: Composing Imaginative Variations in Late Medieval England*, Religion and Culture in the Middle Ages (Cardiff: University of Wales, 2019). Together, these volumes offer the most up-to-date reflections about devotional compilations.
3. I have begun to explore this theme in '"Olde feble wymmen with perseuerance ouercome many longe pilgrimages": Mapping the Feminine in *Disce mori*', *Studies in the Age of Chaucer* 42 (2020), 351–64.
4. See, for instance, E. A. Jones's work on *Disce mori* and related texts; *The 'Exhortacion' from 'Disce Mori': Edited from Oxford, Jesus College, MS 39*, ed. E. A. Jones, Middle English Texts 36 (Heidelberg: Universitätsverlag Winter, 2006).
5. Paul Schaffner (ed.), *Life of Soul: An Edition from MS Laud Misc. 210*, available at quod.lib.umich.edu/c/cme/lifesoul/1:1?rgn=div1;view=toc; a partial edition is also available in Anne Clark Bartlett's and Thomas H. Bestul's edition *Cultures of Piety: Medieval English Devotional Literature in Translation* (Ithaca, NY: Cornell University Press, 1999), 217–31; see also Helen H. Moon (ed.), *'Þe Lyfe of Soule': An Edition with Commentary*, Elizabethan and Renaissance Studies, 75 (Salzburg: Universität Salzburg, 1978); Karine Moreau-Guibert (ed.), *Pore Caitif: A Middle English Manual of Religion and Devotion* (Turnhout: Brepols, 2019); Teresa Brady, 'The Pore Caitif: Edited from MS. Harley 2336, with Introduction and Notes', unpublished PhD thesis, University of Fordham (1954); Florent G. A. M. Aarts (ed.), *Þe Pater Noster of Richard Ermyte: A Late Middle English Exposition of the Lord's Prayer* (Nijmegen: Jansen, 1967).
6. John H. Fisher (ed.), *The Tretyse of Loue*, Early English Text Society O.S. 223, new edn (Oxford: Oxford University Press, 1970).
7. Wolfgang Riehle, *The Secret Within: Hermits, Recluses, and Spiritual Outsiders in Medieval England*, trans. Charity Scott-Stokes (Ithaca, NY/London: Cornell University Press, 2014), 59–69; for a more cautious approach, see Denissen, *Middle English*, 88.
8. Ana Rita Parreiras Reis (ed.), 'A Little Treatise Against Fleshly Affections: Edited from London, British Library, MS Royal 17 C XVIII', *Journal of Medieval Religious Cultures* 48.2 (2022), 113–46; F. N. M. Diekstra, 'A Good Remedie Aȝens Spirituel Temptacions: A Conflated Middle English Version of William Flete's "De Remediis contra Temptationes" and Pseudo-Hugh of St Victor's "De Pusillaninitate" in London BL MS Royal 18.A.X', *English Studies* 4 (1995), 307–54.
9. Adrian James McCarthy (ed.), *Book to a Mother: An Edition with Commentary*, Salzburg Studies in English Literature (Salzburg: Institut für Anglistik und Amerikanistik, 1981).

10. Paul J. Patterson (ed.), *A Mirror to Devout People (Speculum Devotorum)*, Early English Texts Society O.S. 346 (Oxford: Oxford University Press, 2016).
11. Marleen Cré, 'London, Westminster Cathedral Treasury, MS 4: An Edition of the Westminster Compilation', *The Journal of Medieval Religious Cultures* 1 (2011), 1–59.
12. Sheila H. Conard, 'Dame Eleanor Hull's *Meditacyons Vpon the VII Dayes of the Woke*: First Edition of the Middle English Translation in Cambridge University Library MS. Kk.i.6, unpublished DPhil thesis, University of Cincinnati (1995) (hereafter Hull, *Meditacyons*, ed. Conard); Alexandra Barratt (ed.), *The Seven Psalms: A Commentary on the Penitential Psalms translated from French into English by Dame Eleanor Hull*, Early English Text Society 307 (Oxford: Oxford University Press, 1995); Alexandra Barratt (ed.), *Women's Writing in Middle English*, Longman Annotated Texts (London: Longman, 1992), 219–31; Mireille Sarrasin, 'An Introduction to the *Meditations Upon the Seven Days of the Week*: Translated by Eleanor Hull', unpublished MA thesis, University of Lausanne (1998); Camille Marshall 'The *Meditations Upon the Seven Days of the Week Translated by Dame Eleanor Hull: Edition of the Meditations for Monday, Tuesday, Thursday and Sunday*', unpublished SPEC MA thesis, University of Lausanne (2012).
13. Ann Clark Bartlett's book *Male Authors, Female Readers: Representation and Subjectivity in Middle English Devotional Literature* (Ithaca, NY: Cornell University Press, 1995) covers aspects linked to this issue.
14. See Schaffner (ed.), *Life*, 119.
15. For a discussion of *Pore Caitif* as compilation, see Denissen, *Middle English*, 21–54.
16. Moreau-Guibert (ed.), *Pore Caitif*, 110.
17. Brady (ed.), *Pore Caitif*, 242.
18. Moreau-Guibert (ed.), *Pore Caitif*, 203.
19. Moreau-Guibert (ed.), *Pore Caitif*, 203; this change of tone does beg the question of a possibly different compiler for the 'Mirrour of Chastite'.
20. Moreau-Guibert (ed.), *Pore Caitif*, 204.
21. Moreau-Guibert (ed.), *Pore Caitif*, 205.
22. Moreau-Guibert (ed.), *Pore Caitif*, 209.
23. Moreau-Guibert (ed.), *Pore Caitif*, 210–11.
24. Moreau-Guibert (ed.), *Pore Caitif*, 216; for the Sarum Breviary borrowings, see *Pore Caitif*, ed. Brady, 247.
25. Middle English devotional compilations are derivative and incorporate fragments from existing texts that, in many cases, have been translated from a Latin original to form a new whole; see *Late Medieval*, ed. Cré et al., 1, for a more extensive definition. *Þe Pater Noster* borrows from a large number of sources, some of them yet unidentified, but they do not occur as rearranged fragments.
26. See Kathryn Vulić, '*Þe Pater Noster of Richard Ermyte* and the Topos of the Female Audience', *Mystics Quarterly* 34 (2008), 1–43.

27. For a thorough investigation of *The Tretyse*, with a discussion of its initial female aristocratic recipient, see Denissen, *Middle English*, 55–77.
28. For a detail of the borrowings, see Denissen, *Middle English*, table 3.1, 56–7.
29. Denissen, *Middle English*, 62. The daily regimen of the Duchess of York specified doing needlework while listening to Hilton's *Scale of Perfection*; see Mary C. Erler, *Women, Reading, and Piety in Late Medieval England*, Cambridge Studies in Medieval Literature (Cambridge: Cambridge Univerity Press, 2002), 5.
30. Fisher (ed.), *The Tretyse*, 26 (italics are mine).
31. Jones (ed.), *The 'Exhortacion'*, xiii.
32. For the use of the household as allegorical representation of the spiritual life, see Christiania Whitehead, *Castles of the Mind: A Study of Medieval Architectural Allegory*, Religion and Culture in the Middle Ages (Cardiff: University of Wales Press, 2003), 117–41. It seems that the use of this material object as representation of the spiritual life occurs at the same time as demands for devotional books by the laity became most acute. For instance, the treatise *An Honest Bede*, which is the source of the bed passage in *Disce mori*, was written in the middle of the fifteenth century; see A. I. Doyle, '"Lectulus noster floridus": An Allegory of the Penitent Soul', in *Literature and Religion in the Later Middle Ages: Philological Studies in Honor of Siegfried Wenzel*, ed. Richard G. Newhauser, Siegfried Wenzel, and John A. Alford, Medieval and Renaissance Texts and Studies, 118 (New York: Binghamton, 1995), 179–90.
33. Denissen, *Middle English*, 66; for a recent study on this topic, see Hollie L. S. Morgan, *Beds and Chambers in Late Medieval England: Readings, Representations and Realities* (Woodbridge: York Medieval Press/Boydell & Brewer, 2017).
34. Jones (ed.), *The 'Exhortacion'*, 16.
35. See Catherine Innes-Parker (ed.), *The Wooing of our Lord and the Wooing Group of Prayers* (Peterborough: Broadview Editions, 2015); see also W. Meredith Thompson (ed.), *Þe Wohunge of Ure Lauerd*, Early English Text Society 241, new edn (Oxford: Oxford University Press, 1970).
36. The Vernon manuscript shelfmark is Oxford, Bodleian Library, MS Bodleian Eng. Poet. a.1; for a discussion of *A Talkyng of the Love of God*, see Denissen, *Middle English*, 79–103.
37. See Daniel McCann, 'Charming Words: A Possible Source for the Opening Section of *A Talkyng of the Love of God*', *Notes and Queries* 68 (2021), 158–60.
38. Salvina M. Westra (ed.), *A Talkyng of the Love of God* (The Hague: M. Nijhoff, 1950), 34–5.
39. For Christ compared to a loving mother, see Westra (ed.), *A Talkyng*, 6.
40. For a discussion of the three Middle English epistles, see Claire Elizabeth McIlroy, *English Prose Treatises of Richard Rolle* (Cambridge: D. S. Brewer, 2004).
41. Hope Emily Allen (ed.), *English Writings of Richard Rolle, Hermit of Hampole* (Oxford: Oxford University Press, 1988), 62.

42. For a discussion of the degrees of love in the English epistles, see Denis Renevey, *Language, Self and Love: Hermeneutics in the Writings of Richard Rolle and the Commentaries on the Song of Songs* (Cardiff: University of Wales Press, 2001), 122–50.
43. Jones (ed.), *The 'Exhortacion'*, xxviii.
44. I am summarising Jones (ed.), *The 'Exhortacion'*, xxx.
45. Jones (ed.), *The 'Exhortacion'*, 3.
46. Jones (ed.), *The 'Exhortacion'*, 9.
47. Jones (ed.), *The 'Exhortacion'*, 9–10.
48. Jones (ed.), *The 'Exhortacion'*, 32–4, 55.
49. Jones (ed.), *The 'Exhortacion'*, 3–4, 7.
50. Louise Campion, *Cushions, Kitchens and Christ: Mapping the Domestic in Late Medieval Religious Writing*, Religion and Culture in the Middle Ages (Cardiff: University of Wales Press, 2022) offers illuminating information about beds, bed chambers and their ornaments in lated medieval English culture.
51. See Renevey, 'Mapping', 361.
52. For a summary about the origin of the compilation and its audience, see Parreiras Reis (ed.), *Little Treatise*, 7–12.
53. Parreiras Reis (ed.), *Little Treatise*, 129.
54. Parreiras Reis (ed.), *Little Treatise*, 118–20.
55. Parreiras Reis (ed.), *Little Treatise*, 136.
56. Parreiras Reis (ed.), *Little Treatise*, 10–11, discusses this episode in further details.
57. For discussion of the structure of *Book to a Mother* and the book imagery, see Elisabeth Dutton, *Julian of Norwich: The Influence of Late-Medieval Devotional Compilations* (Woodbridge: D. S. Brewer, 2008), 123–60; for a discussion of its reformist tendencies, see Nicholas Watson, 'Fashioning the Puritan Gentry – Woman: Devotion and Dissent in *Book to a Mother*', in *Medieval Women: Texts and Contexts in Late Medieval Britain*, ed. Jocelyn Wogan-Browne, Rosalynn Voaden, Arlyn Diamond, et al. (Turnhout: Brepols, 2000), 169–84.
58. McCarthy (ed.), *Book*, 122.
59. McCarthy (ed.), *Book*, 122–5; see Christiania Whitehead, 'Making a Cloister of the Soul in Medieval Religious Treatises', *Medium Ævum* 67 (1998), 1–29, esp. 21–3.
60. McCarthy (ed.), *Book*, 1; for further autobiographical details, see xxvii–xxviii.
61. For details of the scriptural fragments, see McCarthy (ed.), *Book*, xxiii.
62. For a thorough investigation of *A Mirror*, Vincent Gillespie, 'The Haunted Text: Reflections, in *The Mirror to Deuout People*', in *Medieval Texts in Context*, ed. Graham D. Caie and Denis Renevey (London: Routlege, 2008), 136–66.
63. Patterson (ed.), *Mirror*, 3; see Gillespie, 'Haunted', 155, who offers a much more nuanced perspective on this possibility.
64. Gillespie, 'Haunted', 136 and 146; Patterson (ed.), *Mirror*, 23–24.
65. Gillespie, 'Haunted', 147.

66. The Syon library owned several treatises by Rolle; *The Form of Living* was in the brothers' library in what is now MS 118; see Jones (ed.), *The 'Exhortacion'*, 75.
67. Jones (ed.), *The 'Exhortacion'*, 9, 32, 49, 55; for the reference to Mechthild of Hackeborn's *Revelations*, see 63; see also Naoë Kukita Yoshikawa, 'The *Liber specialis gratiae* in a Devotional Anthology: London, British Library, MS Harley 494', in *Late Medieval*, ed. Cré et al., 341–60.
68. Patterson (ed.), *Mirror*, 40–44. On this subject, see also Liz Herbert McAvoy's chapter in this volume.
69. Patterson (ed.), *Mirror*, 41.
70. Patterson (ed.), *Mirror*, 57–9.
71. Patterson (ed.), *Mirror*, 118.
72. Paul J. Patterson, 'Translating Access and Authority at Syon Abbey', in *Devotional Culture in Late Medieval England and Europe*, ed. Stephen Kelly and Ryan Perry (Turnhout: Brepols, 2014), 443–59.
73. Cré, 'London', 1.
74. I agree with Cré with regard to the compiler's careful selection of fragments for the making of his compilation; Cré, 'London', 2.
75. Cré, 'London', 47.
76. Denis Renevey, 'The Choices of the Compiler: Vernacular Hermeneutics in *A Talkyng of the Loue of God*', in *The Medieval Translator* 6, ed. Roger Ellis, René Tixier, and Bernd Weitemeier (Turnhout: Brepols, 1998), 232–53.
77. Hull, *Meditacyons*, ed. Conard, 1; University of Illinois, MS 80 (Hull, *Meditacyons*, ed. Conard, 212), offers a very similar version.
78. Alexandra Barratt, 'Dame Eleanor Hull: The Translator at Work', *Medium Ævum* 72 (2003), 277–96 (278–9).
79. See Ralph Hanna, 'Compilation: The Gift that Keeps on Giving', *Late Medieval*, ed. Cré et al., 63–81.
80. See Hanna, 'Compilation', 63; *Disce mori* uses the expression 'without multiplicacioun of wordes' when mentioning the Virgin's response to Gabriel, while *Pore Caitif* aims to offer instruction in the faith 'wiþout multiplicacioun of manye bookis'; see Jones (ed.), *The 'Exhortacion'*, 8; see Moreau-Guibert (ed.), *Pore Caitif*, 110.

Further Reading

Bell, David (1995). *What Nuns Read: Books and Libraries in Medieval English Nunneries*, Kalamazoo: Cistercian Publications.

Bryan, Jennifer (2008). *Looking Inward: Devotional Reading and the Private Self in Late Medieval England*, Philadelphia: University of Pennsylvania Press.

Cré, Marleen, Diana Denissen, and Denis Renevey, eds. (2020). *Late Medieval Devotional Compilations in England*, Medieval Church Series 41, Turnhout: Brepols.

Denissen, Diana (2019). *Middle English Devotional Compilations: Composing Imaginative Variations in Late Medieval England*, Religion and Culture in the Middle Ages, Cardiff: University of Wales.
Dutton, Elisabeth (2008). *Julian of Norwich: The Influence of Late-Medieval Devotional Compilations*, Woodbridge: D. S. Brewer.
Erler, Mary C. (2002). *Women, Reading, and Piety in Late Medieval England*, Cambridge: Cambridge University Press.
Gillespie, Vincent (2011). *Looking in Holy Books: Essays on Late Medieval Religious Writing in England*, Turnhout: Brepols.
Miles, Laura Saetveit (2020). *The Virgin Mary's Book at the Annunciation*, Cambridge: D. S. Brewer.
Minnis, Alastair (2010). *Medieval Theory of Authorship: Scholastic Literary Attitudes in the Later Middle Ages*, 2nd ed., Philadelphia: University of Pennsylvania Press.
Olsen, Linda and Kathryn Kerby-Fulton, eds. (2005). *Voices in Dialogue: Reading Women in the Middle Ages*, Notre Dame, IN: University of Notre Dame Press.
Parkes, Malcolm (1976). The Influence of the Concepts of *Ordinatio* and *Compilatio* on the Development of the Book. In J. J. G. Alexander and M. T. Gibson, eds., *Medieval Learning and Literature: Essays Presented to Richard William Hunt*. Oxford: Clarendon Press, 115–41.

IV
Genre and Gender

CHAPTER 11

Lyrics
Meditations, Prayers and Praises; Songs and Carols
David Fuller

Sacred lyrics: meditations, prayers, praises. After poems addressed to Christ, the largest group of these is addressed to a woman, the central purely human figure of Christian history: Mary, the Blessed Virgin. This Mary of the medieval church, a comprehensive figure from human suffering mother (*mater dolorosa*) to quasi-divine Queen of Heaven (*regina caeli*), is not the Mary of the New Testament (in which she appears very little), because in early Christianity non-canonical writings (in which Mary appears frequently) were treated as authoritative; because Mary's role was elaborated by the Church to incorporate what were understood as theological implications of the canonical narratives; and because Mary was understood as present in various Old and New Testament texts interpreted symbolically or typologically. All of this meant that by the late medieval period Mary was celebrated by the Church in a cycle of annual feast days, and in liturgical texts and practices, well-known hymns, and special devotions. This is the great period of the English lyric, in which Mary is a central figure.[1]

Every aspect of Mary's earthly and heavenly existence is celebrated in lyrics, often in terms of 'joys' and 'sorrows' which show her presence in all major aspects of the divine scheme of salvation. The joys were by convention five: the Annunciation, the Nativity, the Resurrection, the Ascension, and the Assumption (Mary's bodily ascent to Paradise, which included her coronation as Queen of Heaven).[2] The complementary sorrows are mostly aspects of the Crucifixion, particularly her role as *mater dolorosa* at the foot of the Cross. The heroic humility and willing co-operation with the divine plan for salvation shown in the Annunciation are models for all, male and female. At the foot of the cross Mary is the archetypal suffering mother, with special appeal to the experience of women in a culture of common child mortality, but also as a vehicle for identification by men and women seeking to intensify their response to the sufferings of Christ. As Queen of Heaven Mary is mediatrix between the penitent sinner and the divine judge, a compassionate female complement to the otherwise more rigid and potentially terrifying scheme of eternal justice presided over by the Son. More generally, praises of and prayers to Mary were an aid to both men and women in leading the earthly life required for salvation.

Mary was not only 'alone of all her sex': she was unique – the only person in Christian history conceived free from Original Sin, the sinful nature entailed on all his posterity by the primal sin of Adam. While as a doctrine this idea – the 'Immaculate Conception' – is a nineteenth-century formulation, the idea itself was current in early Christian theology and was especially promoted during the later medieval period by Franciscans, also an important source of lyric poetry. Unique among human beings in being able to resist and control the powers of the Devil, Mary was not only Queen of Heaven but also Empress of Hell, a female figure of tremendous power.

From a feminist point of view it is possible to see more than a little ambiguity in aspects of the presentation of Mary in lyrics: given a humanity (motherhood) that is unlike that of actual women (ever virgin); sometimes presented in learned and complex Latinate diction and thing-like metaphors that tend to distance, objectify, and dehumanise the qualities evoked; and empowered in a context compromised by the relative powerlessness of actual women.[3] But it is possible to see all this in other terms. In central aspects of Mary's motherhood – her tenderness at the Nativity, her sufferings at the Crucifixion – her virginity plays little or no part; and in the real world celibacy was an ideal for men as for women. The Latinity that comes to the fore in fifteenth-century Marian lyrics is not much present in earlier poems, and even when present is often complemented by simplicity. As for the clash between literary presentation and social context, that can be seen as problematising the real as well as the ideal, particularly given that some actual women did exercise power in the period.[4] And, more generally, contemporary reappropriations of Mary from feminist viewpoints work with qualities that – though they might now be differently understood or inflected – were always present and therefore available to be in some sense recognised.[5] Marian lyric poetry, like Marian visual art – presentations of a human figure held to be greater than any other and specifically unique (free from sin) in a context of quasi-divine veneration – is likely to have meant more to those who read it in the context of Mary's position within the medieval Church than the orthodox theology within which it was circumscribed suggests. Whether this rendered her co-redemptrix with her Son, a being more than human, partaking of the divine, was open to interpretation. The view was proposed by some early theologians and developed throughout the Middle Ages as an extrapolation from Mary's powers and place in the divine scheme of salvation and judgement.[6] How far such a conception might be inferred from Mary's presentation in lyric poetry, particularly by readers not sharply aware of learned parameters of theological orthodoxy but very well aware of the copious elaboration with which Mary was celebrated by the Church, is open to judgement.

Some evidence of medieval sensitivity to the possibility of heretical implications may be elicited from variant texts of the lyric 'Stond wel, moder, under rod', a Crucifixion dialogue between Mary and her Son.[7] The aims of the poem are intellectual and affective: Christ conveys the theology of the Crucifixion, as the tragic prelude to the Resurrection; in identifying fully with the pains of Christ ('I deye ... of thine wounden'), Mary models for the reader (male and female) an experience of full participation in his sufferings. That the poem is found in six extant manuscripts and in a variety of dialects indicates its wide circulation. The beginning is a free adaptation of the Latin sequence 'Stabat iuxta Christi crucem', and in two of the manuscripts it has accompanying music, which may indicate that the poem was performed liturgically. In the earliest manuscript of the poem (Bodleian Library, MS Digby 86, c. 1275), it has nine stanzas. In this form it ends with Mary as she began, unable to comprehend the paradox of Christ's assertions that his agony is ultimately to be understood as her joy. In three other manuscripts the poem has eleven stanzas and incorporates a post-Resurrection resolution: Mary's sorrow is transformed into the joy adumbrated in the dialogue.[8] There is also a significant difference between the eleven-stanza versions in the poem's final prayer for salvation. In British Library, MS Harley 2253 uniquely the final address turns from Mary to Christ:

> Blessed be thou [Mary], ful of blysse;
> Let us never hevene misse
>   Thourh thi suete sones myht.
> Louerd [Lord], for that ilke blod
> That thou sheddest on the rod,
>   Thou bring us into hevene lyht! Amen.[9]

Harley 2253 is one of the most famous manuscripts of medieval lyrics, and its texts are usually reliable, but with this poem it contains a major error, displacing what in other manuscripts is stanza six to stanza three, where it disturbs the sequence of development. (This displacement does not occur in the otherwise similar version in Trinity College Dublin, MS 301.) On the basis of a variety of differences between all the manuscripts, the great early editor of medieval lyrics, Carleton Brown, judged that British Library, MS Royal 12 E I offers 'the most authentic text of this poem'.[10] Its final lines read:

> Blisced be thou, quen of heuene,
> bring us out of helle levene [lightning, flames]
>   thurth thi dere sunes mith.
> Moder, for that hithe blode
> that he sadde [shed] vpon the rode,
>   led us in-to heuene lith. AmeN.

Here, as in the Latin sequence on which it is based, the poem stays with and affirms the salvific power of Mary. It is Mary, as Queen of Heaven, who can both save the sinner from hell's flames and lead the supplicant into heaven's light. It is impossible, of course, to be sure how this difference came about, but it seems probable that so distinct a change as the address to Christ in Harley 2253 implies unease with the power attributed to Mary in the scheme of salvation in the text of the poem as recorded in Royal 12 E I.[11] This version too offers a glimpse of Mary as co-redemptrix that can be seen as implied by so much of the Church's exaltation of 'Our Lady'. The Royal manuscript version shows Mary as a figure of greater power than orthodox theology permitted.[12]

As befits Mary's gamut from *mater dolorosa* to *regina caeli*, lyrics reflecting her centrality to the Christian scheme of salvation range from simple poems to be heard by a non-literate audience to poems to be read by an educated clerisy. In the simpler style, 'I syng of a myden that is makeles' is one of the most famous (Brown, *XV*, 119). Its imagery from nature – 'as dew in aprille' – can be understood entirely in natural terms, though for the educated reader there are other resonances: the dew of the Advent prose, 'Rorati caeli de super' (drop down ye heavens from above); the dew on the fleece of Gideon (Judges, 6:36–40), understood as typologically prefiguring Christ's conception by the operation of the Holy Spirit. 'Makeles' is 'matchless' (alluding to the Virgin's power) and 'without a mate' (alluding to her uniqueness as virgin-mother). This is conventional, but at a crucial moment in the divine plan often construed in terms of the gendered virtue of obedience (Luke, 1:38, 'be it unto me according to thy word'), in the lyric Mary is not a passive instrument but an active agent: 'che ches' (she chose).

In the more learned style, though Mary's overt presence in the Bible is limited, she can be understood as present from Genesis to Revelation through the method of symbolic and typological exegesis implied by Christ when he reveals to the disciples his presence in the law, the psalms, and the prophets (Luke, 24:44–45). As the angel's greeting at the Annunciation is taken to imply (Ave), Mary reverses the sin of Eve (Eva), in this – again with possible implications of co-redemption – directly parallel to Christ, who reverses the sin of Adam (1 Corinthians, 15:22). She is the woman clothed with the sun whose child will rule the nations (Revelation, 12:1–6). Similarly, the Bride of the Song of Songs, the Wisdom of Ecclesiasticus, the salvific women of Old Testament and deutero-canonical Jewish history, Esther and Judith – all these are understood as adumbrations of Mary.[13] 'Marye, mayde mylde and fre' builds from these and other central and peripheral types and symbols of Mary:[14] the dove of Noah (which brings peace); the burning bush of Moses (which contains God); the rod of Aaron (which God causes to blossom miraculously); the mountain of Nebuchadnezzar's dream (which initiates a kingdom that will never be destroyed). She has transformed the history of the world ('yryght that was amys, / Ywonne that was ylore') and the relations of divine and human ('Ine thee hys [God's] wreche [vengeance] bycome myld [merciful]'). She spans a gamut from transcendent grandeur adumbrated throughout sacred history to compassionate attention to the plea of the individual penitent.

Some poems leave their intentions as secular or sacred ambiguous, making Mary also a figure congruent with the heroine of romance. Brown gives a lyric beginning 'Goe, lytyll byll' the title 'A Love Message to My Lady', though he acknowledges an analogue in a lyric in which secular language is clearly given a sacred application (Brown, *XV*, 75, 308). The poem's imagery of the lily and the rose offers flowers of romance which are also especially associated with the Virgin. Stretching a point, a contemporary manuscript annotation justifies 'feyrest paramour' as the language of the Song of Songs (though it is not quite: 'pulcherrima mulierum' [fairest among women]); and though 'dalyaunce' invokes the language of courtly rather than sacred love, the lady as 'medyatryce' (mediatrix, intercessor) tips the finely poised balance in favour of a sacred reading. Even more open to alternative readings is this:

>At a sprynge-wel under a thorne,
>Ther was bote of bale
>A lytel here aforn;
>Ther bysyde stant a mayde,
>Fulle of lofe ybounde.
>Hoso wol seche trwe love,
>Yn hyr hyt schal be founde.[15]

Douglas Gray reports the interpretation of the homily in which the poem is preserved: the 'sprynge-wel' is the spear wound in the side of the crucified Christ. Peter Dronke interprets the imagery as related to the Annunciation (citing apocryphal accounts which include a fountain and thorn bush).[16] On both views the maiden is Mary. But the mysterious poem is written in terms of a romance setting: a loving young woman beside a spring or fountain; and 'bote of bale' (remedy for sorrow) and a bond of love are equally familiar in secular and sacred contexts. The homily shows that a religious contemporary could understand this as a poem about the Virgin, but that a homilist could see a pious significance does not mean that is the only possibility. A reader of romances might as readily see an encounter with the fairy otherworld.

Many poems clearly addressed to the Virgin combine sacred love with the language of erotic feeling and the conventions of romance.[17] This language and these conventions are not in themselves simply gendered. Lyrics addressed to Christ invoke the Song of Songs in which he is interpreted as the Bridegroom; they also present him as a knight who jousts for mankind, as a lover rejected by the beloved, mankind, even as a mother.[18] Nevertheless, in poems to the Virgin erotic language and romance convention often imply a male speaker and addressee, as in 'In a tabernacle of a toure' (Brown, *XIV*, 234–7). The poem is a vision of Mary appealing to mankind to ask for forgiveness, to understand that the purpose of her existence is the redemption of sinners: as earthly mother, making possible the Incarnation; as heavenly queen, urging penitence on the wrong-doer, mercy on the judge. Each stanza ends with a refrain from the Song of Songs, 'quia amore langueo' (because I languish for love), where the words are spoken by the Bride (2:5, 5:8), understood in one kind of symbolic reading as the Virgin. Like the Song of Songs, the poem mixes the language of religious and secular love. The Virgin is mother and sister, but also wife; the human soul is child and brother, but also beloved. As Mary is the archetype of motherhood all human beings are in some sense her children; all members of the human family are brothers and sisters. The use of language more familiar in secular poetry ('grete longynge', 'languys-shyng') is an extrapolation from symbolic readings of the Song of Songs, in which the beloved is also both sister and bride (4:9–12, 5:1; Vulgate, *soror, sponsa*), and which is actually more erotic in its physicality. Spiritual desire is seen as engaging the whole person: the spiritual is not divorced from the physical. The Virgin's appeal to the sinful soul is an impassioned love song.

At the extreme of sacred–secular ambiguity, one of the most celebrated of medieval lyrics, 'Maiden in the mor lay', has at its centre a mysterious female figure set in an enigmatic symbolic context.[19] Its imagery has been interpreted in religious terms: its night signifying before the birth of Christ; its moor, the wilderness of the Old Law; its well-spring, the water of God's grace; its roses charity and its lilies purity. The maiden in the moor, the wilderness of this world, is Mary (D. W. Robertson).[20] A similar kind of reading, which also claims to be historically informed about the poem's symbols, reads them differently: the maiden is any Christian, male or female (R. J. Schoeck). This whole method of reading has been criticised ('this-sense-or-no-sense allegory') as substituting the learning of the reader for the art of the poet (E. Talbot Donaldson). Holy meanings have also been undermined by scholarship. The episcopal register of a fourteenth-century Irish bishop contains a Latin poem on the Virgin, written (it was argued) to displace pollution by this too-popular secular lyric, which was understood by an informed contemporary as precisely not about Mary. In this reading the maiden is under a spell, or is weaving a spell for somebody else (Richard Leighton Greene). Or, in a reference to the lyric in a sermon of *c.* 1360, the poem is called a carol, meaning it was a secular song that was danced as well as sung. Its maiden is a figure of popular belief, a woodland spirit, water-sprite, or fairy, presented as exemplifying humankind in the innocence of the Ovidian Golden Age (Siegfried Wenzel). But displaced holy meanings have been reinstated. The Irish bishop's register, it has been argued, shows only that the secular poem and its holy replacement had matching tunes, and the tune of the secular lyric could be used for its holy replacement. In this reading the lyric is related to ballads of the penance and conversion of St Mary Magdalene. The Marian foreground is supported by a background of a congruent transformation: from sin to penance, analogous to the movement from law to freedom to which the Virgin is key. The maiden is both the Virgin and the Magdalene.[21] Yet another context has been suggested of children's singing games that confront the mystery and sorrow of death. In its attempt to come to terms with mortality the poem is still religious, but located in the uncomprehending imagination of a child (Ronald Waldron).

Even a great poem can be over-read, the imagination disabled by awareness of multiple interpretive possibilities which, far from taking the reader more deeply into a text, paralyse direct engagement with it. Some element of imaginatively provocative enigma is a usual feature of medieval lyric that in some accounts is a property of all great poetry. Goethe speaks for a fundamental view:

> A work of art, especially a poem, that leaves nothing to conjecture, is not a true work of art. Its highest function must always be to stimulate

reflection, and it can only really commend itself to the reader when it compels him to interpret it in his own way, and to complete it, so to speak, by creative re-enactment.[22]

For 'Maiden in the mor lay', such evidence about context as there is cannot be conclusive. The reader cannot avoid the Goethean virtue of imaginative conjecture. A sense of awe, perhaps a sacred sense, can be adduced from the poem's structure and rhythms, but whether that awe should be Christian or pagan – whether the maiden's flowers and her well-spring should be understood naturalistically or according to Christian conventions – is for the reader to decide. Are primroses and violets congruent (beautiful in their natural delicacy) or opposite (fleshly/pure)? Are roses and lilies a gamut (intense colour/complete absence of colour) or a unity (both symbols of the Virgin)? Whether or not Marian, whether or not the poem's structural music and its images are 'translated' into anything more precise than a sense of the magical and mysterious, the poem attributes a semi-mystical value to a central female figure.[23]

While Mary is clearly the dominant female figure of sacred lyrics, in secular lyrics – songs and carols – women appear as subjects through a great variety of perspectives, from frankly physical desire to idealised love, the conventions of so-called 'courtly love' or 'fin'amor' and impersonal formulae of 'beauty'. Women are often conceived in terms that can be related to traditional (male) conceptions of love, but some women speakers offer what has been understood as a critique of these traditions, or a voice not of convention but of experience, that has been taken in some cases to imply that the author is a woman.

As in other medieval writings, in lyrics misogynistic views of women are common. As in *fabliaux* and anti-feminist satire, women appear as untrustworthy, vain, avaricious, and sexually licentious. Women are often presented in their own voices as sexually forward, though perhaps with a moral emphasising vulnerability ('alas, I go with chylde') and a focus on wit and pleasure that is often also positive. One of the most frequently printed of such lyrics, 'As I went on Yol Day' (Robbins, *XIV/XV*, 21–2), is a lively and humorous account in a woman's voice of the seductive charisma of a priest: his reading, his singing, his performance of the mass, his attractively tight-fitting outfit, and his flirtatious insinuations. A pun on the mass's petition for divine mercy and the speaker's name (eleison/Alison) sets up an irreverent-cum-sacrilegious mixing of liturgical and sexual which a pious reader–listener might have found disconcerting but which can also be seen as boldly witty. To see this presentation as misogynistic would be to moralise as the poem does not: the primary impression is of the speaker's exuberance and energy. And the situation can be reversed, as in 'My deth y love, my lyf ich hate' (Brown, *XIII*, 112–14), a dialogue in which a lively young woman rejects with colloquial vigour the high-flown rhetoric of an ardent young cleric. Though eventually she decides the pleasure to be had in accepting the young man outweighs the force of parental opposition, the main effect is not of sexual licence but the vigorous independence with which she expresses both her choices.[24]

Fabliau-type women in lyrics are complemented by romance types, women as the embodiment of ideals of love, beauty, and honour, who prompt a kind of obsessive but distanced 'love' that may seem remote from modern experience. It is a mode of feeling which depends on an unbridgeable gap between the lover and the love-object – a situation such as might have been common in modern times in pre-reform homosexual experience, but which changes in sexual behaviour and gender expectations have otherwise rendered largely alien. It can, however, be the basis of very beautiful poems of unfulfillable longing. 'Litel wot it any man / How derne [secret] love may stonde' exemplifies the mode, especially striking because it is paired in its manuscript source with a parody which implies the quasi-religious nature of the love-experience: the woman is replaced by Christ (Brown, *XIII*, 161–3). The speaker in poems of this kind is invariably a man, the woman present only as the unattainable focus of the man's desire. But since it is in the nature of things that love cannot always be mutual, while the specific presentation is gendered, the fundamental feelings can resonate beyond the gender of presentation: 'Euer & oo [always], for my leof icham in grete thohte; / y thenche on hire that y ne seo nout ofte' – but 'y thenche on him' could be supplied as necessary by the reader. 'The man that I loued al ther best' (*DIMEV*, 5386) in its contemporary manuscript has feminine pronouns written above the masculine, changing the speaker from a woman to a man. Here, evidently, a medieval reader felt that the same mode of feeling in love might apply indifferently to either sex.[25]

To catch the tone and gender implications of a rather different poem of secret love, 'A wayle whyte as whales bon', one needs to imagine performance, sung or declaimed, which is written into the manuscript with a minstrel's or performer's opening call to the audience ('do lystne me'). With poems of this kind it is also important to grasp the effect of a refrain (rarely actually repeated in printed versions), here containing sexual puns (bird names ending in 'cock' imagined as in the woman's underwear), which in performance would attract a crescendo of emphasis in the repetitions.[26] The ideals of female beauty which in a courtly context might seem conventional (skin whale-bone white, eyebrows curved, eyes 'grey'; beauty like a jewel set in gold), in a minstrel-bourgeois context ('in tounes') take on a different colouration: the extravagance of these displaced refinements becomes a source of comedy. The sexual innuendo of the comic chorus is matched by the freedom with which the supposedly painful 'derne love' is in effect celebrated; and the woman celebrated, far from being a passive object, is presented as emphatically making her own choices. The artificial terms of women's beauty are not incompatible with natural warmth of feeling.

Satire of women was also a popular subject for lyrics. 'In euery place ye may well see, / that women be trew as tirtyll on tree' (Robbins, *XIV/XV*, 35–6), praises women in terms of ironic inversions of negative stereotypes (they can always keep a secret, never gossip, and so on), and in case the ironic intention is missed a chorus emphasises it in the 'secret code' of a Latin refrain ('of all Creatures women be best: / Cuius contrarium verum est' [of which the contrary is true]). Robbins provides a by no means exhaustive list of a dozen similar poems (*XIV/XV*, 239), making clear that this was a conventional mode of comedy in popular and sophisticated contexts. The best he prints, 'O Wicket wemen, wilfull, and variable' (*XIV/XV*, 225–6), is vigorous alliterative abuse somewhat in the manner of the Scots flyting, though without the usual dialogue-debate. On the more sophisticated end of this not very wide spectrum is 'Weping haueth myn wonges wet' (Brown, *XIII*, 141–43) – penitent weeping about the poet's own anti-feminist writings, but in ambiguous terms. He was misled into misogyny by considering the turpitude of Eve, but now sees that Mary has more than compensated for this. Since she gave birth to the Saviour no women have sinned: all women are now as gracious as a hawk in a hall. But how gracious is that? Multiple ambiguities and possible double meanings indicate that the poem's extravagant professions of penitence and hyperbolic affirmations about women are not to be taken straight.

More downright misogyny is found in Bodleian MS Digby 86, a collection that has been likened to the book of wicked women of the Wife of Bath's fifth husband, Jankyn, which prompts the Wife's great question about perspective and gender, 'who painted the lion?'.[27] The collection's best lyrics are religious, and none illustrate the grossly misogynistic disposition evident in the manuscript elsewhere. Even its debate-lyric of the thrush and the nightingale offers the compiler's Jankynesque disposition only limited satisfaction. The standard terms of debate about the supposed good and bad qualities of women are rehearsed, but the thrush's misogynistic point of view is decisively countered by the nightingale's invocation of the Virgin. The debate about women epitomised by the thrush and the nightingale is echoed in separate lyrics from many sources presenting the antithetical views. 'Wymmen beth bothe goud and truwe: / Wytnesse on Marie' (Greene, *EEC*, §395a) is the refrain of a carol which matches contradictions of negative stereotypes with positive affirmations: all the good qualities of the Virgin are really found in actual women. A lyric with the refrain 'Of wimmen cometh this worldes welle' (Brown, *XIV*, 174–7) overtly tackles standard anti-feminist topoi: the betrayal of men by women (Eve, Delilah) has been exaggerated; men have been far worse betrayers (Judas). Christ's view is exemplary: he 'worshupped wimmen in his lyue, / And kept hem in his cumpaygnye'. Women have all the virtues: conventional misrepresentations ('monnes false song') are based not in reality but in the clichés of anti-feminist rhetoric.

But do women speak for themselves in medieval lyrics? In the extant manuscripts only three poems are attributed to women: a poem in praise of Venus by 'Queen Elizabeth'; a poem on the five joys of Mary attributed to 'a holy anchoress of Mansfield'; and a hymn to the Virgin by Eleanor Percy, Duchess of Buckingham (d. 1530).[28] This last is a translation (a free version of a well-known Latin poem, 'Gaude virgo, mater Christi') which shows more sincerity of holiness than skill with rhythm or rhyme. The poem attributed to an anchoress in Bodleian MS Ashmole 59 exists in two other sources, in one of which (London, British Library, Additional 29729) it is attributed to Lydgate. It is fine rhetorical praise, loosely structured around the five joys. If it is not by Lydgate it is an excellent imitation of his manner.[29] The hymn to Venus attributed to 'Queen Elizabeth' (an attribution not in the hand of the poem's scribe) is the most considerable of these lyrics.[30] In form it is a variation of the sestina: each stanza after the first begins with the next line of the first stanza, with that line repeated at the stanza's end. It is a demanding structure handled with skill and expressivity to construct circling repetitions of two central ideas: the enjoyment of pleasure in love ('to Venus'); the hope for its long continuance.

That two of these are accomplished poems in complex forms may indicate the difficulty of the default assumption of assigning anonymous work to male authors – but that these same two also present problems of attribution hardly supports any polemical view on this. In this context, the 'Findern' manuscript (Cambridge, Cambridge University Library, MS Ff. i.6) has attracted particular attention because it may contain some of the earliest poems written in English by women whose names are known. Compiled in the fifteenth and early sixteenth centuries by a group of gentry-class families in Derbyshire, it is mainly made up of poems by Chaucer, Gower, Hoccleve, and Lydgate, and the romance, *Sir Degrevant*. The texts included are miscellaneous, but there appears to be a guiding issue to the selection focused on the roles, eloquence, and agency of women. Scattered throughout the manuscript are some twenty-four lyrics, all but four unique to this source, which makes it one of the main lyric collections of its period.[31] Some of the lyrics contain corrections which, it has been argued, suggest the scribe may have been the author (changes which may be second thoughts rather than the correction of errors). The manuscript includes work by about forty different scribes, most of whom appear to be amateurs. It contains the names of five women, some of which may be signatures, two of which, however, are in the hand of the second *Sir Degrevant* scribe, who may have been an itinerant professional. None of the possible signatures are in the same hand as any of the lyrics. The possibility that some of the named women may have been not only compilers and scribes but also authors of some of the lyrics has made this one of the most studied of late medieval manuscripts, and the postulate of women's authorship one of the more controversial issues of recent lyric scholarship.[32] Also at issue is how far the collection implies a readership knowing and sophisticated in its interpretations, aware of possible ironies and multiple perspectives on its female voices (quasi-courtly), or a readership straightforward, even naïve, in its literalism (provincial).[33]

Though the possibility that some of the lyrics were composed by women was suggested in the earliest modern study of the manuscript,[34] the possibility became more controversial with later studies which argued that most of the lyrics were by women. There were two views. Elizabeth Hanson-Smith argued that the lyrics are about secret and illicit love affairs, and overall can be read as giving a woman's point of view, usually unvoiced, of the conventions of 'courtly love'.[35] While accepting the idea of a critique of 'courtly love', Sarah McNamer read the poems not as about adultery but as in the voices of – and written by – women separated from their husbands, 'sincere expressions of authentic female emotional experience'.[36] As such, she argues, the poems constitute a distinctive new genre of Middle English lyric: the woman's lament which is non-parodic, non-dramatic, an 'I' of felt experience. In assigning authorship to women McNamer relied partly on arguments about how situations implied by the lyrics relate to those reflected in women's correspondence of the period (in the Paston, Stonor, and Cely letters), partly on echoes of the language of contemporary marriage vows as taken by women, and partly on how the 'authenticity' of a voice of female experience might be judged: by expressions of personal feeling felt to be sincere, a sense of the immediate and personal, a mode not overtly dramatised and amenable to alternative perspectives – tones supposedly associated with male authors.[37] These 'authenticity' tests have themselves been tested by a critique which found them exemplified similarly by 'Come home, dere herte, from tarieng', a Findern lyric identified by McNamer as by a woman on grounds of its content and emotional stance, and another poem in the manuscript, 'The Complaint of Venus', a translation and reworking by Chaucer of poems by Oton de Grandson originally written in a male voice.[38] More generally, can it be supposed that the tones of authentic experience are created in a poem without the exercise of art, and that any test can tell whether that art is exercised on a basis of experience or imagination? Fundamentally, is there any necessary connection between the creation of a convincing gendered persona, male or female, and an assumption about authorial gender? Though McNamer quotes Rosemary Woolf – 'it is a fallacy to equate an impression of sincerity conveyed by style with personal revelation' – she does so only to assert that, with the Findern manuscript, that impression is the reality. Finally, McNamer's claims about authorial gender are not demonstrable: whether the Findern lyrics describe actual or imagined experiences cannot be known.[39] Whether the claims may be felt intuitively probable each reader must decide. Nevertheless, the human circumstances McNamer invokes to read the poems open up possibilities of interpretation which make them more interesting regardless of authorial gender.[40]

Women's authorship of some of the Findern lyrics has also been proposed on the basis of codicological and palaeographic evidence, but this too has proved inconclusive. Arguments here draw on the manuscript as a whole and its complex make-up,[41] particularly the text of *Sir Degrevant*, the problematic construction of which (divided between two quires and two scribes) can be variously construed, with consequent different accounts of the women's names written at its conclusion (one as the second scribe's signature; or both as scribal acknowledgement of the commission or the provision of copy; or as evidence about authorship).[42] Wider issues affecting judgement about women's authorship in the manuscript as a whole are also relevant: about non-clerical women's literacy in the period; about gentry-class views of scribal work (as for servants?); and about the variety of ways in which names in a manuscript might signify. Given that the cultural, codicological, and palaeographic issues involved are multiple, and all interpretable, their complexities – like those about author and persona – seem often to be resolved in ways congruent with a commentator's preferences.[43]

There has been no general acceptance of the predominantly female authorship of the Findern lyrics postulated by McNamer, and only a limited consensus about which lyrics in the manuscript best represent the work most likely to have been written by women. Anthologies that discuss the issue present different selections.[44] Among the poems most regularly favoured, 'What-so men seyn' arraigns the deceit of men in love and proposes that they be paid in kind. Its short lines linked by rhyme (aaab/aaab) are a technical tour de force of great musical beauty, with an overall movement of argument congruent with this technical control. That the form is also found in medieval Latin lyrics, and is a variation of the French *virelai*, suggests that the writer was well educated and widely read (beyond the level of literacy taught to gentry girls in nunnery schools, however good).[45] Other lyrics in the manuscript show a similar technical skill in the handling of metre, rhyme and stanza pattern: 'My woofull hert' uses an even more demanding pattern, with only two rhymes in the whole poem; 'Continvance / Of remembrance' transmutes the pain of lovers' parting into sound effects which show an ear for the singing line. Others show rather the reverse: unease with patterns of rhyme and metrical structure. In 'Where Y haue chosyn, steadfast woll Y be', one of the poems McNamer identifies as using the language of women's marriage vows, the hobbling metre may contribute to what she hears as the authentic (because unpolished) voice of experience. 'Yit wulde I nat the causer faryd amysse' plunges in vigorously with the tone of the speaking voice, and is striking in its unconventional forgiveness of betrayal. Though it does not sustain the energy of its opening, again weakness may be felt as a kind of strength, a lack of sustained art conveying the voice of true feeling. The most interesting poem is the most ambitious: 'Come home, dere herte, from tarieng', a sequence of stanza groups (five lines, three lines, five lines, rhyming aabba / aab / aabba), with each group taking up a rhyme sound from the group preceding it – an intricate pattern impressively executed.[46] There is, however, a puzzle: the final group is a line short (4-3-5). Robbins assumes a simple lacuna.[47] Barratt postulates a coded message: in place of the fifty-two lines of the complete form (5-3-5 x 4), she suggests that fifty-one lines signify the actual weeks of absence – a secret meaning which would make sense only on McNamer's supposition of an underlying real situation.[48] Are some of these lyrics, then, by women? There is really no way of telling.[49]

Women found themselves reflected in medieval lyrics as subjects, in poems sacred and secular, as readers, collectors, compilers, and scribes, and perhaps as authors. In all these areas poems offered models that went beyond standard forms. With the Virgin, though unique, she was also in aspects of her being a model equally for men and women, an epitome of their best qualities, a model of aspiration, and a figure representing compassion in an otherwise inflexible scheme of divine justice. For women particularly she also sacralised the experience of motherhood, in the example of her sufferings perhaps made more tolerable the common experience of child mortality, and offered a model of power which, while unusual, was not without congruent forms in the real world. The language of love and conventions of romance also made this unique and otherwise potentially remote figure more approachable, and in ways that, as comparable treatments of Christ indicate, did not imply the gendered reader that might otherwise be supposed. It was a shift of mode that could be extended to female figures through which the sacred might be freshly experienced free from terms too familiar or the limitations imposed by doctrine. As in other forms of medieval writing, women found themselves satirised and denigrated in terms of misogynistic stereotypes. But lyrics also offer answers to stereotypes: language and ideas that push back against these or which simply escape them – in love, from pleasure in rehumanising standard tropes to energetic and witty delight in the popularly sanctioned illicit; in reading, by gathering together texts that bore variously on the experience of women, and finding or perhaps creating in lyric voices in which, as other forms of medieval writing indicate, they spoke, or appeared to speak, from experience.

Notes

1. The term 'lyric' is anachronistic for medieval writings (it enters English in the late sixteenth century) and may mislead in grouping together short poems of different kinds. For an examination of critical fundamentals, see Jonathan Culler, *Theory of the Lyric* (Cambridge, MA: Harvard University Press, 2015). For the argument that medieval lyric as it is found in modern editions is the creation of print culture and post-Romantic critical practices, see Ardis Butterfield, 'Why Medieval Lyric', *English Literary History* 82.2 (2015), 319–43. Butterfield's edition of medieval English lyrics based on these views is forthcoming in Norton Critical Editions.
2. See Karen Saupe (ed.), *Middle English Marian Lyrics* (Kalamazoo, MI: Medieval Institute Publications, 1998). Mary's earthly joys might also number seven, including Epiphany and Pentecost. These were later complemented by seven heavenly joys: see Carleton Brown (ed.), *Religious Lyrics of the XVth*

Century (Oxford: Clarendon Press, 1939), 59–65 (Brown, *XV*); also Rosemary Woolf, *The English Religious Lyric in the Middle Ages* (Oxford: Clarendon Press, 1968), chs IV, VIII, 114–58, 274–308.
3. For this view, see Helen Phillips, '"Almighty and al merciable Queene": Marian Titles and Marian Lyrics', in *Medieval Women: Texts and Contexts in Late Medieval Britain*, ed. Jocelyn Wogan-Browne, Rosalynn Voaden, Arlyn Diamond, et al. (Turnhout: Brepols, 2000), 83–99.
4. See Mary Erler and Maryanne Kowaleski (eds.), *Gendering the Master Narrative: Women and Power in the Middle Ages* (Ithaca, NY: Cornell University Press, 2003), and the same editors' *Women and Power in the Middle Ages* (Athens, GA: University of Georgia Press, 1988). On the range of positions from which gender issues could be represented, see Susan L. Smith, *The Power of Women: A Topos in Medieval Art and Literature* (Philadelphia: University of Pennsylvania Press, 1995). On women in European contexts as writers, correspondents, readers and patrons, see Joan M. Ferrante, *To the Glory of her Sex: Women's Roles in the Composition of Medieval Texts* (Bloomington: Indiana University Press, 1997).
5. For a range of perspectives, learned and popular, see Marina Warner, *'Alone of all her Sex': The Myth and the Cult of the Virgin Mary* (London: Weidenfeld, 1976; 2nd ed., Oxford: Oxford University Press, 2013). On feminist theology, Luce Irigaray, and Mary, see Tina Beattie, *God's Mother / Eve's Advocate: A Marian Narrative of Women's Salvation* (New York: Continuum, 2002); and for a variety of perspectives, see Amy-Jill Levine, with Maria Mayo Robbins (eds.), *A Feminist Companion to Mariology* (London: T&T Clark, 2005).
6. See Matthew Levering and Robert Fastiggi in *The Oxford Handbook of Mary*, ed. Chris Maunder (Oxford: Oxford University Press, 2019). They discuss Biblical texts and theological commentaries which imply co-redemption, including developments from Alcuin (d. 804) to the fifteenth century.
7. Carleton Brown (ed.), *Religious Lyrics of the XIIIth Century* (Oxford: Clarendon Press, 1932), 87–91 (Brown, *XIII*); Linne R. Mooney, Daniel W. Mosser, Elizabeth Solopova et al. (eds.), *The Digital Index of Middle English Verse*, 5030 (*DIMEV*): www.dimev.net.
8. British Library, MS Royal E 12 I; Trinity College Dublin, MS 301 (both early fourteenth century); and British Library, MS Harley 2253 (*c*. 1330–40).
9. Susanna Fein (ed.), *The Complete Harley 2253 Manuscript*, trans. Susanna Fein, David Raybin and Jan Ziolkowski (Kalamazoo, MI: Medieval Institute Publications, 2014), 3 vols, 2.266. Trinity College Dublin, MS 301 follows Harley 2253 at this point, but it is not an independent witness: see E. J. Dobson and F. Ll. Harrison, *Medieval English Songs* (London: Faber, 1979), 152–60 (which provides a collation of variants).
10. Brown, *XIII*, 205. Brown's conclusion is supported by Dobson (*Medieval English Songs*), who argues that the East Midlands of the Royal manuscript version is the dialect in which the poem was written.

11. For a study of variants between the six manuscripts, see Christiania Whitehead, 'Musical and Poetic Form in "Stond wel, moder, under rod"', in *Middle English Lyrics: New Readings of Short Poems*, ed. Julia Boffey and Christiania Whitehead (Cambridge: Brewer, 2018), 227–39.
12. For a differently transgressive reading, see Sarah Stanbury, 'The Virgin's Gaze: Spectacle and Transgression in Middle English Lyrics of the Passion', *PMLA* 106 (1991), 1083–93 (1087–9). This applies the theory of the male gaze and its consequences for women who violate its norms (here, Mary looking on the crucified Christ) and interprets the conventional paradoxes by which the Virgin's Son is also her father, brother, and spouse as a 'rhetoric of incest', to see Mary as a figure of 'sanctified transgression'. Whether this reading is elicited in light of a changed cultural context that allows it to become visible, or imposed in ways that diminish the otherness of reading in historical context, is the fundamental issue raised by any application of modern theory to premodern texts.
13. For a list of types and titles under which Mary appears in lyrics, see R. T. Davies, *Medieval English Lyrics: a Critical Anthology* (London: Faber, 1963), appendix.
14. Carleton Brown (ed.), *Religious Lyrics of the XIVth Century* (1924), 2nd ed., rev. G. V. Smithers (Oxford: Clarendon Press, 1957), 46–49 (Brown, *XIV*).
15. Douglas Gray (ed.), *A Selection of Religious Lyrics* (Oxford: Clarendon Press, 1975), 57 and note, 131–2. Brown (*XIV*, 286) compares an Epiphany carol from the commonplace book of Richard Hill (*DIMEV*, 5566), but though this contains a blossom sprung from a thorn (the Rod of Jesse) and a well sprung from Mary (Christ) the symbolism is explicit, not suggestive.
16. Peter Dronke, *The Medieval Lyric* (London: Hutchinson, 1968; 2nd ed., 1978), 69–70.
17. For a selection see Saupe (ed.), *Marian Lyrics*, 147–57.
18. See 'In the vaile of restles mynd', a lyric addressed to Christ using the language and conventions of secular love, also echoing the Song of Songs, and also with the refrain 'Quia amore langueo'. For a study that prints the versions of both extant manuscripts see Susanna Greer Fein, *Moral Love Songs and Laments* (Kalamazoo, MI.: Medieval Institute Publications, 1998), 57–86.
19. Rossell Hope Robbins (ed.), *Secular Lyrics of the XIVth and XVth Centuries* (Oxford: Clarendon Press, 1952; 2nd ed. 1955), 12–13 (Robbins, *XIV/XV*). The unique manuscript is fragmentary and the poem can be realised in different ways. See Ardis Butterfield, 'Poems without Form? "Maiden in the mor lay" Revisited', in *Readings in Medieval Textuality: Essays in Honour of A. C. Spearing*, ed. Cristina Maria Cervone and D. Vance Smith (Cambridge: Cambridge University Press, 2016), 169–94.
20. References for sources of the readings by Robertson, Schoeck, Donaldson, Greene, Wenzel, and Waldron are given in Saupe (ed.), *Marian Lyrics*, 267–8.
21. Joseph Harris, '"Maiden in the moor" and the Medieval Magdalene Tradition', *Journal of Medieval and Renaissance Studies* 1 (1971), 59–87.

22. Flodoard von Biedermann (ed.), *Goethes Gespräche* (Leipzig: Biedermann, 1909–11), 5 vols., 4.477 (my translation).
23. For a similarly enigmatic lyric with a central female figure poised between romance and Christianity, see the Corpus Christi carol: Richard L. Greene (ed.), *The Early English Carols* (Oxford: Clarendon Press, 1935; 2nd ed. 1977), §322D (Greene, *EEC*). Greene discusses a range of interpretations (423–7).
24. For other clerical seducers whose activities are narrated through female personae, see *DIMEV* 393, 3044, 3971, 5369, and 5679.
25. For a similar flexibility with the gendering of sin, cf. 'Lullay, lullay, litel child' (Greene (ed.), *EEC*, §157a), in which the non-gendered speaker becomes Eve as archetypal sinner ('An appel I tok of a tre') but is de-gendered again ('us') to include all who have chosen disobedience to God.
26. The poem is sometimes printed without its chorus and double sexual puns, as in Thomas G. Duncan, *Middle English Lyrics and Carols* (Cambridge: Brewer, 2013), 55–6. For a text with puns and chorus, see Fein (ed.), *The Complete Harley 2253 Manuscript*, 2.150–7.
27. See Susanna Fein (ed.), *Interpreting MS Digby 86: A Trilingual Book from Thirteenth-Century Worcestershire* (Woodbridge: Boydell & Brewer, 2019), 'Introduction', 4. On gender conflict and misogyny in this manuscript, see the essays in the same book by Neil Cartlidge and Marilyn Corrie.
28. *DIMEV* 3506, 1713, and 1496. All three are printed in Alexandra Barratt (ed.), *Women's Writing in Middle English* (London: Routledge, 1992; 2nd ed., 2010), 294–9.
29. Barratt prints the version attributed to an anchoress which has a line missing in the second stanza and other inferior readings, including 'descended' for 'ascended' in the stanza on the Ascension. For an alternative version see Brown, *XV*, 53–4.
30. 'Queen Elizabeth' is perhaps Elizabeth Woodville, wife of Edward IV, or perhaps their daughter, Elizabeth of York, wife of Henry VII. On the choice, see Julia Boffey, *Manuscripts of English Courtly Love Lyrics in the later Middle Ages* (Woodbridge: Brewer, 1985), 84.
31. One other manuscript collection containing a number of female-voiced lyrics (poems 7, 19, 44, 45, 54, and 59), but also some misogynistic satire, is Bodleian Library Rawlinson C.813. For a modern edition see Sharon L. Jansen and Kathleen H. Jordan (eds.), *The Welles Anthology: MS. Rawlinson C.813. A Critical Edition* (Binghamton, NY: SUNY, 1991). Three poems from this manuscript are printed in Barratt (ed.), *Women's Writing in Middle English*, 284–8, but ignoring the modern edition. According to Jansen and Jordan, Barratt's first poem from the manuscript is the last part of a longer poem (§49), ll. 1–3 and 32 of which indicate the speaker is male, ll. 41–4 of which indicate the speaker is female. They postulate diverse sources carelessly revised. The problem is echoed in *DIMEV* 1201 and 3608.
32. For a full bibliography of studies to 2018, see *Oxford Bibliographies – Medieval Studies*, Cynthia Rogers, 'The Findern manuscript (CUL Ff.i.6)': doi: 10.1093/obo/9780195396584-0248.

33. For the first view see Ashby Kinch, '"To thenke what was in hir wille": A Female Reading Context for the Findern Anthology,' *Neophilologus*, 91.4 (2007), 729–44; for the second Carol M. Meale, 'The Tale and the Book: Readings of Chaucer's *Legend of Good Women* in the Fifteenth Century,' in *Chaucer in Perspective: Middle English Essays in Honour of Norman Blake*, ed. Geoffrey Lester (Sheffield: Sheffield Academic Press, 1999), 118–38; for further details see Rogers (n. 32, this chapter), 'Scholarship on Findern's longer texts'.
34. Rossell Hope Robbins, 'The Findern Anthology', *PMLA* 69 (1954), 610–42.
35. Elizabeth Hanson-Smith, 'A Woman's View of Courtly Love: the Findern Anthology', *Journal of Women's Studies in Literature* 1 (1979), 179–94; for further details, see Rogers (n. 32, this chapter), 'Hypothesized Female Production of the Findern Manuscript'.
36. Sarah McNamer, 'Female Authors, Provincial Setting: The Re-Versing of Courtly Love in the Findern Manuscript', *Viator* 22 (1991), 279–310 (280): for further details see Rogers (n. 32, this chapter), 'Hypothesized Female Production'. McNamer acknowledges that the idea of 'courtly love' is controversial, but accepts the account of John Stevens, *Music and Poetry in the Early Tudor Court* (London: Methuen, 1961). More fully cognisant of the pan-European nature of the subject and the controversies surrounding it is Bernard O'Donoghue, *The Courtly Love Tradition* (Manchester: Manchester University Press, 1982). McNamer reprises her views in 'Lyrics and Romances', in *The Cambridge Companion to Medieval Women's Writing*, ed. Carolyn Dinshaw and David Wallace (Cambridge: Cambridge University Press, 2003), 195–209 (197–201).
37. On the issue of implied distance between female speaker and poet in male-authored lyrics, McNamer cites John Plummer, 'The Woman's Song in Middle English and its European Backgrounds', in John Plummer (ed.), *Vox Femina: Studies in Medieval Women's Songs* (Kalamazoo: Medieval Institute Publications, 1981), 135–54.
38. Jay Ruud, 'Female Personae and Women Writers: Chaucer and the Findern Manuscript', *Medieval Perspectives* 20 (2005), 112–32; for further details, see Rogers (n. 32, this chapter), 'Hypothesized Female Production'.
39. The test for the authorial gender of lyrics in Barratt (ed.), *Women's Writing in Middle English*, is a less exigent version of McNamer's: 'speaking voices represented as female without irony or detachment and not overtly dramatized may well be identical with those of the writers of the poems' (2010, 282) – may well be, and equally well may not be.
40. For an additional lyric (*DIMEV* 1237) apparently related to a real situation such as McNamer postulates for the Findern lyrics, see Linne R. Mooney, '"A Woman's Reply to her Lover" and four other new courtly love lyrics in Cambridge, Trinity College MS, R.3.19', *Medium Ævum* 67.2 (1998), 235–56.
41. See Kate Harris, 'Origins and Make-up of Cambridge University Library MS Ff.1.6', *Transactions of the Cambridge Bibliographical Society* 8 (1983), 299–333, complemented by Ralph Hanna III, 'The Production of Cambridge University Library Manuscript MS Ff.1.6', *Studies in Bibliography* 40 (1987),

62–70; for further details, see Rogers (n. 32, this chapter), 'Scribes' (Harris) and 'Construction of the Manuscript' (Hanna).

42. For the assumption that the second name is a signature, see Linda Olson, 'Romance in the Provinces: The Findern Manuscript', in *Opening up Middle English Manuscripts: Literary and Visual Approaches*, ed. Kathryn Kerby-Fulton, Linda Olson, and Maidie Hilmo (Ithaca, NY: Cornell University Press, 2012), 142. For a contrary view, see the review of this by Richard Beadle, *JEGP* 113 (2014), 227–30. For speculation on the possible female authorship of *Sir Degrevant* see McNamer, 'Lyrics and Romances', 206–7.

43. On fundamental issues about women and authorship in the period, see Julia Boffey, 'Women Authors and Women's Literacy in Fourteenth- and Fifteenth-Century England', in *Women and Literature in Britain, 1150–1500*, ed. Carol M. Meale, 2nd ed., (Cambridge: Cambridge University Press, 1996), 159–82; for further details, see Rogers (n. 32, this chapter), 'Hypothesized Female Production'.

44. Barratt (ed.), *Women's Writing in Middle English*, prints four poems: *DIMEV* 6255, 3668, 1044, and 6863. Of these, Davies (ed.), *Medieval English Lyrics*, prints *DIMEV* 6255 and 6863, and also *DIMEV* 1074. This is also printed, with *DIMEV* 6255, by John C. Hirsh, *Medieval Lyric: Middle English Lyrics, Ballads, and Carols* (Oxford: Blackwell, 2005), who prints two other poems as by women, *DIMEV* 6492 and 261. Of Barratt's selection, Duncan (ed.), *Medieval English Lyrics and Carols*, prints only *DIMEV* 6255. Derek Pearsall (ed.), *Chaucer to Spenser: An Anthology of Writings in English 1375–1575* (Oxford: Blackwell, 1999), prints as '(by Women?)' five poems: *DIMEV* 6255, 3668, and 1044 (all in Barratt), and *DIMEV* 1074 (in Davies and Hirsh) and 643.

45. Eileen Power, *Medieval English Nunneries, c. 1275 to 1535* (Cambridge: Cambridge University Press, 1922), ch. VI, 'Education', 237–84.

46. In the manuscript, the pattern of a rhyme taken over from one group to the next indicates that the last 5-3-5 group should be written first, a mistranscription which makes it improbable that the scribe was the author or that the author was a member of the Findern circle. McNamer (1991, 305–6) ignores the problem and prints the poem in the manuscript arrangement.

47. Robbins, 'The Findern Anthology', 634.

48. Barratt (ed.), *Women's Writing in Middle English*, 290.

49. For a just post-medieval manuscript undoubtedly including poems by women, see the Devonshire manuscript (British Library Additional 17492; 1530s), which includes poetry by Lady Mary Douglas, Mary Fitzroy, and Mary Shelton (all associated with the court of Henry VIII): www.bl.uk/manuscripts/FullDisplay.aspx?ref=Add_MS_17492. Elizabeth Heale (ed.), *The Devonshire Manuscript: A Women's Book of Courtly Poetry* (Toronto: Toronto University Press, 2012). For a European perspective on women in lyrics, see Anne L. Klinck (ed.), *An Anthology of Ancient and Medieval Woman's Song* (New York: Palgrave Macmillan, 2004).

Further Reading

Primary Texts

The classic collections of medieval lyrics are those published by the Clarendon Press, edited by Carleton Brown (1924, rev. by G. V. Smithers, 1952; 1932; and 1939), Rossell Hope Robbins (1952; 2nd ed., 1955), and Richard Leighton Greene (1935; 2nd ed., 1977). More recent selections include those edited by R. T. Davies (1964), Douglas Gray (1975), Karen Saupe (1991), Thomas G. Duncan (2013), John C. Hirsh (2016), and Anne L. Klinck (2019). More specialised editions include those of Bodleian Library Rawlinson manuscript C.813, ed. Sharon Jansen and Kathleen Jordan (1991), and British Library Harley manuscript 2253, ed. Susanna Fein (2014–15), which supersedes the edition of the lyrics only by G. L. Brook (1948; 4th ed., 1968). Details of these selections and editions are given in the notes. An important resource for textual issues (with some information about scholarship and criticism) is Linne R. Mooney, Daniel W. Mosser, Elizabeth Solopova, et al. (eds.), *The Digital Index of Middle English Verse*: www.dimev.net.

Scholarship and Criticism

Barratt, Alexandra, ed. (2010). *Women's Writing in Middle English*, 2nd ed., London: Routledge.

Boffey, Julia, and Christiania Whitehead, eds. (2018). *Middle English Lyrics: New Readings of Short Poems*, Cambridge: Brewer.

Butterfield, Ardis (2009). Lyric. In Larry Scanlon, ed., *The Cambridge Companion to Medieval English Literature 1100–1500*, Cambridge: Cambridge University Press, 95–109.

Dronke, Peter (1978). *The Medieval Lyric*, 2nd ed., London: Hutchinson.

Duncan, Thomas G. (2005). *A Companion to the Middle English Lyric*, Cambridge: Brewer.

McNamer, Sarah (2003). Lyrics and Romances. In *The Cambridge Companion to Medieval Women's Writing*, ed. Carolyn Dinshaw and David Wallace. Cambridge: Cambridge University Press, 195–209.

Woolf, Rosemary (1968). *The English Religious Lyric in the Middle Ages*, Oxford: Clarendon Press.

CHAPTER 12

'It satte me wel bet ay in a cave / To bidde and rede on holy seyntes lyves'
Women and Hagiography

Christiania Whitehead

Early in Chaucer's *Troilus and Criseyde*, faced with Pandarus' insinuations about a new suitor, Criseyde declares it would be more in keeping with her widowhood to pray and read about saints' lives 'in a cave'.[1] Clearly, she sees hagiography as a *women's* genre, applicable to the circumstances of pious lay life. Situating her hypothetical reading in a cave, she also acknowledges its links with enclosure and the ascetic life of the early Church. We may even fancy that she is conversant with the overlap between hagiography and romance, lightly pondering in which direction to nuance her own life narrative. Criseyde's rational decision in favour of a romance narrative closes down the discourse of hagiography, for this poem at least. However, the associations she gives to the genre, not least its connection with women, surface at several other points in Chaucer's œuvre.[2]

What Criseyde does *not* foreground (and it is hard to see how she could, given her widowed status) are the genre's valorisation of a mythic virginity perfected in death and its interest in monastic foundation and governance, often set within a regional or national frame. With reference to the first: virgin martyr narratives promote an early Christian chronotope centred on Rome and the near East, recording the persecution of the nascent church via its effects upon the female body. These stories retain a pre-eminent position in English hagiographic culture from the pre-Conquest era until the end of the Middle Ages. And with reference to the second: the lives of the Early English founder-abbesses, shining a spotlight on more local geographies and histories, also prove remarkably resilient. This chapter will track the evolution of these two narrative models and use them to structure its discussion of women as subjects, writers, and readers of hagiography within the trilingual circumstances of medieval English literary culture over the *longue durée*.

Early English Abbesses and the Mission to Germany

The fourth book of Bede's *Historia ecclesiastica gentis anglorum* (c. 730) is largely dedicated to commemorating three seventh-century abbesses whose exemplary lives play a seminal part in his larger project of extolling the triumph of Christianity in England. Their lives, however, are given distinctly different emphases. Æthelburga, first Abbess of Barking, presides over a convent where virtue, in a time of plague, manifests itself principally through miracles giving meaning to the suffering and deaths of the nuns.[3] Æthelthryth, the next to be described, is lauded for her chaste marriages to two husbands prior to founding a convent at Ely, where she devotes herself to ascetic disciplines. When she dies after suffering from a neck tumour, her body miraculously fits the contours of a white marble sarcophagus from the time of the Roman occupation, indicating that her sanctity conforms to specifically Roman models of Christian exemplarity. Bede's Romanising agenda becomes yet more explicit in the hymn which follows his account of her life. Here, he names Æthelthryth as the most recent in a long list of Roman virgin martyrs, arrogating a Mediterranean trope to English soil, and lauds this sisterhood for their heroic participation in a new spiritual epic surpassing the worldly themes of Virgil's *Aeneid*.[4] While Æthelthryth is developed as a type of Roman virginity, the third abbess, Hilda of Whitby, is principally commended for the *national reach* of her monastic virtue and good governance. Initially identified symbolically as a jewel in her mother's womb whose radiance illuminates all of Britain, Hilda is constructed by Bede as the spiritual mother and mentor of a generation of bishops who minister to different parts of England, and of Caedmon, the 'father' of English poetry. People flock from the four corners of the country to seek Hilda's counsel and, when she dies, nuns from the daughterhouses within her federation are made miraculously aware of her apotheosis, indicating her spiritual influence upon a widespread ecclesial network.[5] It is not surprising that Bede would wish to present Northumbria as a point of origin for an English episcopate and for vernacular sacred verse; his partiality for his homeland is not a secret. But perhaps not enough has been made of the fact that Bede also locates this point of origin in a saintly abbess.[6]

Bede's accounts of these abbesses, woven into the broader history of the Anglo-Saxon kingdoms, appear to constitute the earliest *vitae* of English women saints. In addition, the enduring textual authority of the *Historia* means that they remain prototypical of female monastic sanctity for centuries to come. However, there are some things that Bede is unable to achieve with these portraits. While we read of Hilda's discernment and learning, we never see it first hand, and while we are left in no doubt of these women's good governance, it is painted in solely static terms. All the Christian mobilities of the *Historia* – fighting for the faith, exercising mission and ministry – remain male prerogatives.

But Bede's *Historia* is not the whole story. And, when we turn from it to an alternative set of texts linked with the eighth-century English mission to the German-speaking lands, some much more active images of female sanctity and authorial agency come into relief.[7] St Boniface's mission to Germany from his abbacy at Nursling in 716 led to a series of invitations to English nuns to join him in the mission field. One of these, Leoba (d. 782), became the subject of a sizeable *vita* composed by Rudolf of Fulda in the 830s to celebrate the second translation of her relics, while another, Hugeburc, authored two *vitae*, of Willibald, Bishop of Eichstätt, and of his brother Winnebald, in the late 770s. Both these women significantly shift the perimeters of our thinking about pre-Conquest female sanctity.

In addition to forming the subject of Rudolf's *vita*, Leoba briefly comes into visibility as an author in her own right. In the 730s, while still in Wessex, at Wimborne Abbey, she corresponds with Boniface, requesting his protection and sending him a religious praise poem in Latin for correction.[8] While this letter may well have influenced Boniface's decision to invite Leoba to Germany, where she was subsequently appointed as Abbess of Bischofsheim, her poetic skill goes unmentioned in Rudolf's *vita*.[9] He does, however, present her as a figure of remarkable learning, widely read in the works of the church fathers, conciliar decrees, and canon law, whose absorption in holy scripture miraculously seems to continue even when she is asleep.[10] Like Hilda, she is pre-ordained for sanctity from the womb. Her mother dreams of her as a ringing church bell, and later Leoba dreams of an infinite purple thread issuing from her bowels through her mouth and coiling up into a ball, symbolising her Christian teaching and counsel. Unlike the dream of Hilda's mother, however, these dreams ignore the vocabulary of adornment, dwelling instead on the strength and amplitude of Leoba's public voice. Interestingly, it is elderly women – a nurse and a nun – who offer enlightened interpretations of them rather than more conventional clerical exegetes. To an unprecedented degree, Rudolf renders authority female in this *vita*, locating Leoba's sanctity within a female spiritual lineage headed by Abbess Tetta of Wimborne (who receives a potted saint's life of her own at the beginning of the narrative), foregrounding her friendship with Charlemagne's queen, a spiritual soulmate, and emphasising her mastery of the hostile elements.

In one particularly dramatic episode in Bischofsheim, Leoba casts off her cloak and confronts a diabolic storm with the sign of the cross at her church door, while the terrified villagers take shelter inside. Rudolf's account of Boniface's attitude towards Leoba seems, on the face of it, equally reverential; on his departure for Frisia, he leaves her his monastic cowl (a gesture of transferred authority) and instructs his monks to enshrine their bodies together. However, Rudolf's record of post-mortem miracles at the Fulda shrine restores more conservative hierarchies, detailing supplicants who report visions of a young nun presenting their afflictions to the bishop for healing. Assured and independent during her lifetime, after death Leoba's spiritual power recedes to become a subsidiary of Boniface's archiepiscopal sanctity.

While Leoba's first-person voice is confined to a single letter, her contemporary, Hugeburc (*fl.* 760–80), an English nun at the double monastery at Heidenheim, leaves a much more extensive hagiographical record. In the preface to her *vita* of Willibald, the saintly brother of her abbess, Walburg, Hugeburc depicts herself as a 'little ignorant creature', hampered by the 'womanly frail foolishness of my sex', who contents herself with faithfully recording the words which drop from Willibald's lips.[11] However, the sophisticated rhetoric with which she conveys these sentiments, taken in tandem with her literary skill in interpreting the events of Willibald's life, substantially contradict this self-depreciation, pointing instead towards an educated writer with a well-formed authorial purpose who consciously employs a topos of humility.

The *Vita Willibaldi*, more commonly titled *Hodoeporican* (itinerary), is in fact a most unusual hagiography, with the greater part of its narrative spent relaying Willibald's travels to the Holy Land prior to his mission to Bavaria.[12] Nonetheless, Hugeburc never loses sight of her objective of describing sanctity. In her account, Willibald encounters a Europe mapped solely in relation to its saints' shrines and relics: the body of Agatha in Sicily, the body of Ananias in Damascus. In the Holy Land itself, these encounters intensify into biblical re-enactments: falling ill, Willibald descends to the pool of Bethesda to be eased; visiting Gaza, he loses his sight and remains blind for two months. Offering far more than simple reportage, Hugeburc moulds Willibald's journey to sanctity by ushering him between established saints and then slipping him through a range of biblical models. There is arguably even a little glint of Virgilian heroism in his curiosity to experience a glimpse of hell at Mount Etna in Sicily on his way home, and his awe in the face of its fearful sound and fire.[13] Back in Bavaria, Hugeburc describes Willibald putting to good use all he has seen and learned by consecrating a multitude of churches and populating them with saints' relics. People from many countries now flock to him. Effectively, Willibald's centrifugal movement out into Europe has been replaced by a centripetal impulse in which he draws the sanctity of the Christian Mediterranean back into his own local sphere. None of this is artless or ignorant; on the contrary, it demonstrates a sophisticated level of literary crafting.

The author of the *Hodoeporican* overtly identifies herself only as an 'unworthy Saxon woman' ('indigna Saxonica'). However, in 1931, an encrypted passage of text situated between the two *vitae* in the earliest manuscript was successfully deciphered, uncovering a much more individualised statement of authorship: 'I, a Saxon nun named Hugeburc, wrote this' ('Ego, una Saxonica nomine Hugeburc ordinando hec scribebam').[14] The names of female authors of hagiography will remain few and far between during the time period of this study, but here, right at the start, we encounter one of their clearest signatures. Furthermore, Hugeburc is not entirely alone in naming herself thus. The abbeys of the German-speaking lands seem to have proved favourable environments for female hagiographical composition, and in the mid-tenth century we find another woman religious: Hrotsvitha of Gandersheim (*c*. 935–73), an Augustinian canoness, who writes an even more extensive repertoire of metrical saints' legends (*Carmina*), many of them couched as dramas.[15] Like Hugeburc, Hrotsvitha signs her name in her prefaces, additionally qualifying herself as 'the strong voice of Gandersheim'.[16] Yet, even more than Hugeburc, she also refers repeatedly to her intellectual inadequacies as a woman, lavishly decrying her slow intelligence and limited female mind in a preface to learned male patrons. The disingenuousness of Hrotsvitha's protestations becomes clear as soon as we open her playscripts. Explicitly couched as rebuttals to Terence's depictions of licentious women in his Roman comedies (a posture that is itself a display of learnedness), Hrotsvitha presents her readers instead with a series of early Christian women of extraordinary moral strength, who unhesitatingly submit to martyrdom to preserve their virginity and faith. While we will encounter hagiographies of the early Christian virgin martyrs many times in this chapter, Hrotsvitha's versions stand out on several fronts. First, they include some unusually authoritative female characters: for instance, Sapientia bests the Emperor Hadrian by subjecting him to a lecture on mathematics that he finds incomprehensible (*Sapientia*). Second, they present the virgin martyrs as members of *communities* of women, frequently sisters, rather than individuals. And third, and most audacious, they include episodes of unexpected humour directed against the men who attempt to oppress the virgins. In *Ducitius*, incensed by the beauty of the virgins he holds captive, the governor of Thessalonica visits their prison to rape them, but gets confused in the darkness and ends up fondling pots and pans in the kitchen and blackening himself with soot, to the derision of the girls watching through the keyhole: 'Now he presses the saucepans tenderly to his breast, now the kettles and frying pans! He is kissing them hard!'[17] It is not hard to imagine the Gandersheim canonesses finding this hilarious. No other account of virgin martyrdom from the remainder of the Middle Ages manages to debunk the threat of sexual violence at the heart of these saints' lives in such self-confident terms.

Regulated Communities of Writing and Reading in the Long Twelfth Century

The burgeoning of insular hagiographical composition in the 150 years following the Conquest, very largely a Norman project, is accompanied by its linguistic diversification into Anglo-Norman and Early Middle English, alongside Latin, and its reception by new reading audiences. New Latin lives of Early English saints are produced by many of the monastic institutions responsible for curating their shrines, and their spiritual patrons are reshaped to fit contemporary agendas. A number of Bede's saintly abbesses reappear in this contemporary guise – for example, in Goscelin of Saint-Bertin's *vitae* of Æthelthryth of Ely, Æthelburga, and Hildelith of Barking – while others with few pretensions to holiness in Bede's *Historia* (Æbbe of Coldingham and Bega) also acquire cults qualifying them to join this pantheon. Several Latin lives of women saints composed during this period exemplify a contemporary Benedictine interest in early Irish and Welsh sanctity (for example, the lives of Brigit of Ireland, Modwenna of Burton-on-Trent, and Wenefrid of Wales),[18] while others commemorate holy women from more recent times, notably Margaret, Queen of Scotland (1045–93), and Christina of Markyate (1098–1155).[19] Elaborating upon Bede's vignettes, a number of these women's lives now include episodes in which, early in their careers, their protagonists successfully evade the pursuit of rapacious suitors, fleeing to remote topographical sites and committing themselves to divine protection prior to founding abbeys (for example, Æthelthryth, Æbbe, Bega, Christina of Markyate, Frideswide of Oxford). Such episodes presumably show the influence of the early Christian virgin martyr legends which will also play such a prominent role within vernacular communities.

As noted earlier, all of these Latin lives are *monastic* productions designed for cloistered male reception. However, when we turn to Anglo-Norman saints' lives of women, more diverse reading communities come into relief, together with a trio of female hagiographers. Jocelyn Wogan-Browne has done groundbreaking research on the mixed audiences of Anglo-Norman hagiographies ('clerc u lai, muïne u dame'), emphasising the involvement of secular noblewomen who engaged with these texts as their patrons and recipients.[20] Although the work was later utilised in conventual circumstances, it is probable that such an audience was initially envisaged for the *Vie seinte Audrée* (Æthelthryth) of 'Marie' (c. 1180–1200), speculatively identified as either Marie de France or a nun of Chatteris Abbey, Cambridgeshire.[21] Marie retells the story of Æthelthryth in octosyllabic verse, drawing upon both Bede and the twelfth-century *Liber Eliensis* written by an anonymous monk from Ely. Like her sources, Marie pays extensive attention to Æthelthryth's royal kinship, so that her family narrative effectively retells the history of several of the Anglo-Saxon kingdoms. Reiterated in this way, at a cultural moment preoccupied with assimilating the ruptures of the Viking and Norman invasions, Æthelthryth's life seems designed to epitomise the sanctity of seventh-century England, presenting its readers with an Anglo-Saxon chronotope, so to speak.[22] Not only does the *Vie* offer a comment on the seventh-century Christian nation as perceived from the twelfth century, it also adds a regional inflection. Jane Sinnett-Smith notes how Marie's *Vie* makes more of Æthelthryth's connections with her Northumbrian female forebears, Sts Hilda and Æbbe (her maternal and spousal aunts), defining her sanctity as a northern inheritance now relocated south.[23]

Composed in the conversational, loosely digressive style characteristic of Anglo-Norman romance as well as hagiography, Marie's *Vie* includes a number of passages that suggest her expectation of a female readership. Writing about Æthelthryth's early life and two marriages, she provides a frank and intimate picture of the heroic self-restraint necessary to retain virginity within youthful marriage: 'Envis seroit onkes trovee / Pucele que fust mariee, / Ke ne fust vencue et surprise / Par icel charnel coveitise' (It would be difficult to find a young married woman who has not been compelled and overwhelmed by carnal desire, ll. 381–4), and paints an equally realistic picture of King Ecgfrith's dissatisfaction with her abstinence: 'Come le roy pur son delit / Ert cochiez en son real lit, / Si com Deu plesoit somellioit, / Et la roÿne se levoit .. en prïere / Ert' (Whenever the king lay in his royal bed awaiting his pleasure, it pleased God to have him fall asleep. The queen then would get up to pray, ll. 931–6).[24] The focus on Æthelthryth's virginity, publicly scrutinised and verified at every turn, as the ground of her spiritual martyrdom might suggest composition by a nun writing for other nuns, but, equally, the interest in the sexual difficulties and negotiations of her marriages, and the space allotted to Æthelthryth's spiritual exemplarity as a married woman and a queen, suggest a voice seeking to engage the marital experience of aristocratic women.

Allied with this focus on sanctity in secular life, Marie's *Vie* also contains moments of pragmatic comment that seem to indicate a first-hand familiarity with the feudal economy. Æthelthryth's spiritual friendship with Bishop Wilfrid of York is shown to include a transactional dimension in which his appointment of her as Abbess of Ely is repaid by the tax exemptions she is able to obtain for him from the king and other nobles (ll. 1655–68).[25] Later, as Æthelthryth lies on her deathbed, repenting the wealthy adornments that have led to the tumour on her neck, Marie notes sardonically 'Les riches pur lur seingnorie, / Les povres pur lur grant aïe / De ceo ke lur donoit suvent / Ses asmones mut largement' (Rich men are burdened and so are the poor: the rich because of their noble duties, the poor because of their heavy taxes, often imposed by the very one who gives them generous alms, ll. 1933–8), diverting interpretation of the saint's illness from the gendered discourse of adornment, to emphasise instead the injustices of feudal taxation.[26] All these examples combine to support the sense that Marie has constructed a saint fitted to reflect the domestic and economic spheres of management familiar to married Anglo-Norman noblewomen.

While the identities of Marie and her intended audience remain matters of hypothesis, we have a much more definite understanding of the institutional circumstances underpinning our other two twelfth-century female hagiographers. Both Clemence and the anonymous 'Nun' of Barking (who may be one and the same), are religious of Barking Benedictine Abbey, an affluent royal foundation situated east of London with a reputation for Latin learning.[27] This competent Latinity is borne out by the source texts of the two Anglo-Norman lives composed in the abbey: the 'Nun's' *Vie d'Edouard le confesseur* reworks the Latin life written by Ælred of Rievaulx in 1163 to promote the King's cult, while Clemence's *Vie s. Catherine* translates an eleventh-century version of Catherine of Alexandria's Latin Vulgate *vita*.[28] Between them, these lives exemplify the two main strands of insular hagiography structuring this chapter: veneration of the early Christian martyrs and the more localised 'Anglo-Saxon' tradition. Both seem to have had their place within Barking's devotional routine, and to have been composed with a mixed audience of nuns, clerics, and aristocratic guests in mind.

Although the two lives share common institutional circumstances of composition, they convey very different pictures of male authority and governance, and offer differing degrees of authorial self-confidence. Probably the earlier of the two, the 'Nun's' *Edouard* seems more in tune with the religio-political agendas of the Angevin regime: Edward's saintly 'English' kingship was widely held to have been revived by Henry II, suturing the wound of the Norman invasion. The 'Nun' links this revived concept of sacred kingship to Barking, inserting petitions for prayer for her community, and describing Edward miraculously healing nuns there from his shrine at Westminster, in effect positioning Barking as a secondary cult centre, closely aligned with royal spiritual power.[29] The 'Nun' empowers her institution but plays down her own intellectual agency, refusing to name herself individually in the same textual space as Edward, and decrying her defective command of language and scholarly knowledge.[30] Although much of this is conventional, it nonetheless implies a less secure authorial position than the one assumed by Clemence. Clemence chooses a female subject, Catherine, who vies against tyrannical and scholarly male authority by means of her intelligence, learning, and strong public voice, out-arguing the panel of philosophers summoned by the pagan governor Maxentius to quash her Christian allegiance. Several scholars have noted how Clemence's choice of female subject acts self-reflexively to authorise her own authorial voice and support her learning (in this instance, she signs her name).[31] In addition, some have interpreted Catherine's faith-driven stance against the tyrant Maxentius (who executes his wife and best friend for their conversion to Christianity) as a veiled criticism of Henry II, famously responsible for the political martyrdom of Thomas Becket, his erstwhile friend, in 1170.[32] Becket's sister, Mary, appointed abbess of Barking in 1173, is thought to have commissioned an Anglo-Norman hagiography of her brother from Guernes de Pont-Sainte-Maxence, and it is possible that Clemence's *Vie* may also be intended to refract this clash between religious and secular power, adroitly concealed behind an innocuous narration of the early Roman persecutions. If this is true, it shows Barking as a site of politically adept hagiography, which moves from an early endorsement of Henry's kingship via the saintly template of Edward the Confessor towards a more distanced and critical position.

Fascinatingly, all three of these hagiographies by women are copied, alongside seven other Anglo-Norman lives of principally British saints, into a late thirteenth-century manuscript, British Library, Additional MS 70513, which was possibly commissioned by Isabel de Warenne, Countess of

Arundel (1226–82), and is known to have been read aloud at mealtimes at the Augustinian nunnery of Campsey Ash, Suffolk, in the fourteenth century.[33] The journey of this collection reflects the easy transmission of saints' lives between aristocratic and cloistered women, and while its content demonstrates a predictable interest in female saints (Mary Magdalen, Osith, Fey, Modwenna, Æthelthryth, and Catherine), it is also possible to discern a more intriguing grouping of recent episcopal saints known for their contention against monarchs (Thomas Becket, Edmund of Canterbury [d. 1240] and Richard of Chichester [d. 1253]). Sts Edmund and Richard both came into conflict with Henry III, as indeed did Isabel de Warenne, the putative commissioner of this collection. Should we view this collection as a site of ecclesiastical resistance to secular authority, and interpret its inclusion of Clemence's Catherine from this additional political perspective?

While Barking Abbey and Campsey Ash Priory both provide examples of monastically regulated communities involved in the writing and reading of hagiography, a rather different form of female regulation can be glimpsed by turning to the thirteenth-century manuscripts of the Katherine Group, an early Middle English body of works intended for anchoritic readers.[34] Consisting of the Lives of Sts Catherine of Alexandria, Margaret of Antioch, and Juliana, *Hali Meiðhad* and *Sawles Warde*, and designed to be read alongside *Ancrene Wisse*, an anchoritic rule of life, the Katherine Group exemplifies the lives of the Roman virgin martyrs being used as components within a more *extensive* spiritual programme, oriented towards the valorisation and defence of virginity. This context, taken in tandem with the almost total physical confinement and invisibility of the target readers, arguably produces a set of different narrative emphases to the Barking *Catherine*. Living severely ascetic existences construed as living deaths, anchoresses are invited not simply to admire the virgin martyrs, but to *claim* them as their direct spiritual forebears. This means that when we read of Margaret doing battle with a dragon within her prison cell, watched through the window by the women who bring her food, or read of Catherine being miraculously nourished in her prison cell by a heavenly dove, it is easy to imagine these scenes being interpreted by their readers as directly applicable to their own trials and consolations within the anchorhold.[35]

There are, however, stark differences, and the public setting of the virgin martyrs' confrontations with imperial authority, the power and extent of their dissenting voices, and the exposure of their tortured naked bodies in front of large crowds all contrast notably with the silence imposed on anchoresses by the clerical author of the *Ancrene Wisse* and the reams of instructions exhorting them to shield their bodies from the worldly gaze.

Responding to these contradictions, one might read these narratives simply as compensations, providing the anchoresses with the opportunity to experience through fantasy the public acclaim they lack within their cells. Alternatively, it is possible to opt for a more complex hermeneutic melding public and private, and to view the narratives as statements of the public spiritual authority acquired *by* nurturing a hidden life of virginity in conditions of silence and concealment. Commenting on the meaning of the repeated spectacle of the saints' apparent impassibility to the tortures enacted on their bodies, Sarah Salih notes perceptively that it enables the deeply hidden fact of physical virginity to be brought to the surface, and performed upon the exterior of the body.[36] Impassivity to physical pain equals sexual integrity in this reading. One revised redaction of the *Ancrene Wisse* addresses an expanded community of anchoritic recipients with the spiritual potential to spread throughout the nation, referring to them collectively as the 'ancren of englond' (ll. 14–15).[37] What this means is that when the Katherine Group identifies Roman martyrdom with the privations of the anchorhold, a nationalist project is also in train, transferring Roman saintly capital to England via the virtue of its anchoresses, and consolidating this transfer by couching it in the native vernacular. Whereas in Bede's *Historia* the body of the Early English abbess Æthelthryth is fitted to a Roman sarcophagus, here the life of the Roman virgin martyr is reconvened in an English anchorhold: the vessel and its contents have swapped places.

Manuscript Collections of Female Saints in Late Medieval England

Although it is probable that women composed and translated hagiographies in late medieval England, despite the decline in Latin learning in convents, unfortunately we retain no firm textual evidence of this. Nonetheless, lives of female saints continued to be reproduced in increasing numbers in the fourteenth and fifteenth centuries, proving to be popular reading in lay households and nunneries, and were eventually grouped together on the basis of gender to form several coherent manuscript collections. Before turning to these collections, a few words are in order about gender balance in the major legendaries.

While most scholarly attention has been directed towards the vernacular legendaries circulating in England (*South English Legendary*, *Gilte Legende*, Abbotsford *Legenda aurea*), where female saints tend to be poorly represented and native female saints get equivalently short shrift,[38] a surprisingly different picture is created by turning to Latin legendaries of insular saints.

Here, in these largescale, principally Benedictine compilations, female saints play a much more prominent role. British Library, MS Lansdowne 436 (early s.xiv), owned by Benedictine nuns in the fifteenth century, includes sixteen women among its forty-three native lives; the *Sanctilogium* of John of Tynemouth (mid s.xiv), associated with St Albans Abbey, contains thirty-three female lives out of 167; and Bodleian Library, MS Bodley 240 (1377), designed for Benedictine male novices at Bury St Edmunds, contains seventeen female lives out of a total of forty. Contrary to expectations, it would seem that *wider* selections of female lives were digested within Latinate monastic circles, and that insular sanctity in particular was tilted towards a more even gender distribution.

A heavily selective response to the *Sanctilogium* underpins the first of our three vernacular collections of women saints' lives. Cambridge University Library, MS Add. 2604 (late s.xv) contains the lives of twelve Anglo-Saxon abbesses translated from the *Sanctilogium*, bookended by those of eight universal virgin martyrs, and a sprinkling of lives of virginal men.[39] Presumably intended to be read by nuns, this collection demonstrates the continued vitality of the Early English abbessial model as a source of female exemplarity in the fifteenth century. Cynthia Turner Camp has done important work on the way the structure of this collection flattens the temporal divisions between early Christian, Early English, and contemporary religious women, offering a static account of female sanctity which effectively fuses virgin martyrdom with abbessial good governance (hence incipits refer to Martha, sister of Mary, Domitilla, and Justina of Antioch as abbesses or nuns). However, the compiler of Add. 2604 does not simply draw out a representative selection of Early English abbesses from the *Sanctilogium*; rather, he inflects it to centralise Æthelthryth, her sisters, nieces, and more distant relatives, and orients his choices towards female saints venerated in East Anglia and Kent. Hilda, an outlier from Whitby, gets in by virtue of her status as Æthelthryth's aunt. Here, in the late fifteenth century, native female sanctity is still constructed with primary reference to regionality and kinship networks; northern saints are still made auxiliaries of southern cults. At some levels, nothing much seems to have changed since Marie's *Vie seinte Audrée*.

However, another manuscript collection, composed a little earlier in East Anglia in the 1440s, shows that there were alternative templates for creating a model of composite female sanctity. British Library, MS Arundel 327 contains thirteen lives of female saints, written by Osbern Bokenham, an Augustinian friar from Suffolk.[40] This collection, far better known than Add. 2604, turns back to the perennially popular virgin martyrs of early

Christianity, together with the Virgin's mother, Anne, Mary Magdalene, and the thirteenth-century widow, Elizabeth of Hungary. Bokenham revisits a long-familiar model of female sanctity; nonetheless, there are features of this collection which give it a peculiarly contemporary and pragmatic thrust. Self-consciously writing in the shadow of Chaucer's *Legend of Good Women* and the encyclopaedic female saints' lives of his East Anglian contemporaries, Capgrave and Lydgate,[41] Bokenham's awareness of these literary predecessors, and his status relative to them, are made a central part of the reading experience. That is, the author's anxieties about his place in male hagiographical tradition vie with the expression of female sanctity. Of course, female hagiographers express anxieties too, and we have surveyed a number of declarations of inadequate worth and ignorance linked to gender. Bokenham expresses incapacity on entirely different terms, repeatedly referring to his sense of having arrived in the literary sphere too late (Gower, Chaucer, and Lydgate have gathered all the best flowers of rhetoric), his old age, and his apprehension of impending death. Assertions of old age and deathliness need to be treated with care: post-Chaucerian poets persistently refer to themselves in these terms. Nonetheless, in a genre focused upon the apotheotic deaths of a succession of dazzling young women, they do mean that we are continually forced to measure these idealised martyrdoms against the author's sense of his own, fallible mortality.

Arundel 327 was commissioned for presentation to a Cambridge nunnery. However, the prologues to individual lives within the collection indicate that most were also initially commissioned by wealthy East Anglian women whose first names coincide with the female saints in question. So, the life of Elizabeth of Hungary is written for Elizabeth de Vere, Countess of Oxford, and so forth. It does not seem to me to be pushing things too far to suggest, as Sarah Salih does, that these lives operate as 'a very superior kind of consumer good', consolidating these women's spiritual refinement.[42] Whereas Add. 2604 obfuscates the temporal difference between virgin martyrs and founding abbesses and the fifteenth-century nuns who read about them, benefitting from the fact that they share literal virginity in common, Arundel 327 turns from the body to the word (the act of naming) to assert a similar connection between the Roman virgin martyrs and upper-class lay women. While the names of women who stage hagiography have often proved oblique, sometimes available to us only via encryption (Hugeburc), here the names of female patrons are anchored centrally within the text and within posterity by virtue of their lexical identity with the women whose lives they commission. The insecure signature of the female hagiographer at the margins of the text has been replaced by the emboldened signature of the female patron within its title.

Although in most of the Lives in Arundel 327 Bokenham is forced to invent rather unobvious parallels between third-century virgins and fifteenth-century married women, the case is made a little easier with the *Life of St Anne*. Here, Bokenham capitalises on the late medieval popularity of the mother of the Virgin to create a narrative celebrating the potential for holiness in human marriage.[43] Nor is this a perpetually unconsummated marriage, as in the case of Æthelthryth and her two husbands, but rather one where adequate fertility is the subject under scrutiny. Joachim's humiliation at his barrenness leads to his temporary estrangement from Anne, whose grief at her childlessness is compounded by her anxieties about her absent husband and the disrespectful heartlessness of her maid: "'Thow God thy wombe wyth bareynesse / Hath shet, and thyn husbonde takyn away, / Wenyst thou these myscheves I myht redresse? / Nay, nay!'" (ll. 413–16).[44] Shortly after, angelic announcements remedy the situation, leading to their joyful reunion and the subsequent birth and dedication of Mary. Not only does this *Life* lend itself to identification by married women and mothers, it also deals compassionately and frankly with the marital problems created by difficulties of conception. The *Life*'s valorisation of a saintly female lineage experiences something of a jolt in the epilogue, where it is revealed that John and Katherine Denton, the East Anglian landowners who commissioned the *Life* and who already have a daughter named Anne, are hoping to conceive a son and would value St Anne's prayers in that enterprise (ll. 692–9).[45] The *Life* valorises a holy female lineage; it is used instrumentally to facilitate male succession. Clearly, in the 'real world' of fifteenth-century gentry politics, a daughter is not enough!

While Early English abbesses and Roman virgin martyrs offer viable models of corporate female sanctity in the fifteenth century, newer saints and forms of sanctity are also making themselves felt. The vernacular reception of the lives of continental holy women such as Mechthild of Hackeborn, Catherine of Siena, and Bridget of Sweden, conveying new definitions of female sanctity as a visionary and prophetic vocation, receives attention elsewhere in this volume.[46] A final manuscript collection of female saints' lives offers us another new direction imported from the Continent. Bodleian Library, MS Douce 114 (*c.* 1420–50) contains fifteenth-century Middle English translations of the lives of three early-thirteenth-century holy women from Brabant-Liège – Elizabeth of Spalbeek, Christina Mirabilis, and Marie d'Oignies – originally composed in Latin by French and Flemish clerics.[47] We know that these Latin *vitae* were in circulation in England in the late Middle Ages, read by Carthusian and Benedictine monks. Indeed, Bodley 240, referred to earlier, collates the lives of

Anglo-Saxon abbesses with the Low Country lives of Elizabeth, Christina, and Lutgard, constructing a British/Flemish nexus of female sanctity (perhaps corresponding to trading links), and seemingly detecting continuities between their modes of piety.[48]

On the face of it, these continuities are not very apparent. The three lives in Douce 114 offer extraordinary pictures of female devotional practice centred on bodily performance and pain. Elizabeth of Spalbeek bears Christ's wounds on her body and re-enacts the stages of his Passion on a daily basis at the times of the seven monastic hours, hitting her cheeks and beating her head on the ground in accordance with the blows inflicted by the soldiers, jerking from side to side as though being pulled against her will, and balancing her body cruciform on one foot in imitation of the crucifixion. In between these dramatic episodes she lapses into unconsciousness, apparently exhausted by her exertions. Unlike the lives we have surveyed elsewhere in this chapter, no details of her life story or familial circumstances are given. Elizabeth comes into visibility as she enacts Christ. To a degree, the spectacle of bodily pain that Elizabeth presents bears comparison with the trials of the virgin martyrs, although it should be noted that it is self-inflicted and eerily silent. Rather than watch this dumbshow, we would be relieved to hear the assertive voice of a Margaret or a Catherine, scorning their oppressor. There is also more emphasis on the *moving* body. At Matins, Philip of Clairvaux, Elizabeth's Cistercian hagiographer, describes the way she 'sche bowith her arme and strekith oute hire fynger nexte the thumbe, drawynge the tothere fyngers togedir into hir hande' (ll. 98–9), prior to attempting to gouge out her eye. At Tierce, she joins her arms in front of her breast and interlinks her fingers under the elbows to signify her binding to the pillar (ll. 225–35).[49] This is not a naked female body hung out lasciviously before crowds but a modestly clothed one, recorded without any overt reference to virginity, rehearsing minutely observed movements within a domestic space. Nonetheless, like the virgin martyrs, this is a body which works like a text, communicating *through* its pain and performances. Philip describes these performances not simply as figures, but as *expositions* of Christ crucified. Through Elizabeth's body he learns new things about Christ's body (ll. 521–2).[50]

Elizabeth's life rewrites the virgin-martyr narrative. It also engages with the monastic saint narrative, attaching her performances to the seven Hours and interpreting them as a kind of substitute liturgy: 'in steed of salmes . . . [she] settith her flesche for an harpe and hir chekys for a tymber (drum) . . . [enacting] a newe maner of syngynge' (ll.115–18).[51] Probably we see the hand of Philip here, trying to make sense of Elizabeth's confounding piety by linking it with his own monastic regime of devotion. It is telling that Margery Kempe, attempting to construct herself as a saint through amanuenses in the 1430s, but conscious that she did not quite fit any template, should also have turned to the lives of the Liège holy women for inspiration (Marie d'Oignies, in this instance).[52]

Conclusion

Margery Kempe is a good endpoint for this chapter. Based in East Anglia, such a fertile ground for authors and manuscripts of female saints in the fifteenth century, she assimilates nearly all of the hagiographical models covered here, providing an invaluable picture of middle-class lay reception. With many of her visions experienced in the church of St Margaret of Antioch in Lynn, her spiritual identity is deeply founded on the lives of the virgin martyrs, while the content of her visions shows her engagement with biblical holy women: Mary, Elizabeth, and Anne. In rendering her devotion through tears and cries, Margery draws upon the dramatic piety of the Low Country *mulieres religiosae*, while the potential for sanctity in her marriage and motherhood is validated by reference to Bridget of Sweden (see Anthony Bale, Chapter 20 in this volume). It is only native pre-Conquest saints who fail to find a foothold in Margery's female pantheon. She tours English minsters and cathedrals, but we hear little of the saints enshrined there, still less of local patrons such as Æthelthryth of Ely. While interest in the Anglo-Saxon abbesses remains solid within regulated communities in the fifteenth century, responsive to the mix of virginity and nationalism they represent, it would appear that aspiring laywomen have their sights set on more cosmopolitan spiritual models, drawing energy jointly from the *auctoritas* and prestige of the Roman virgin martyrs, and the visions, prophecies, and experimental modes of expression pioneered by continental holy women.

Notes

1. Geoffrey Chaucer, *Troilus and Criseyde*, in *The Riverside Chaucer*, ed. Larry Benson, 3rd ed. (Oxford: Oxford University Press, 1988), II.117–18
2. Two out of Chaucer's three women pilgrims in *The Canterbury Tales* opt to tell saints' lives (a Miracle of the Virgin and a virgin martyr *passio*), demonstrating the genre's associations with female orality as well as reception. His *Legend of Good Women* is a classicising variant upon a legendary of female saints' lives.
3. Bede, *Ecclesiastical History of the English People*, ed. Bertram Colgrave and R. A. B. Mynors (Oxford: Clarendon, 1969), IV.6–9.
4. Bede, *Ecclesiastical History*, IV.19–20.
5. Bede, *Ecclesiastical History*, IV.23–4.

6. See further, Clare Lees and Gillian Overing, 'Birthing Bishops and Fathering Poets: Bede, Hild, and the Relations of Cultural Production', *Exemplaria* 6 (1994), 35–65; Diane Watt, 'The Earliest Women's Writing? Anglo-Saxon Literary Cultures and Communities', *Women's Writing* 20 (2013), 537–54.
7. See C. H. Talbot (ed. and trans.), *The Anglo-Saxon Missionaries in Germany* (London: Sheed and Ward, 1954); Diane Watt, *Women, Writing and Religion in England and Beyond, 650–1100* (London: Bloomsbury, 2019).
8. Munich, Bayerische Staatsbibliothek, Clm 8112, fols 106r–v.
9. Talbot (ed. and trans.), *Anglo-Saxon Missionaries*, 205–26.
10. Both Leoba's letter to Boniface and Rudolf's comment suggest that she gained an excellent Latin education at Wimborne.
11. Translated in Peter Dronke, *Women Writers of the Middle Ages* (Cambridge: Cambridge University Press, 1984), 34.
12. Talbot (ed. and trans.), *Anglo-Saxon Missionaries*, 153–77.
13. Virgil, *Aeneid*, III.570–87.
14. Thijs Porck, 'Anglo-Saxon Cryptography: Secret Writing in Early Medieval England', blogpost, May 15, 2017: thijsporck.com/tag/latin/.
15. *Hrotsvit: opera omnia*, ed. Walter Berschin (Leipzig: Teubner, 2001). See also Sue Niebrzydowski, Chapter 14 in this volume.
16. 'Preface to the Plays of Hrotswitha', in *The Plays of Roswitha*, trans. Christopher St. John (London: Chatto & Windus, 1923), xxvi.
17. *Dulcitius*, in *Plays of Roswitha*, trans. St. John, 39.
18. Composed respectively by Lawrence of Durham (1130s); Geoffrey of Burton (1114–51); Robert of Shrewsbury (1138), and anon. (probably a Cistercian of Basingwerk). See Robert Bartlett, 'Cults of Irish, Scottish and Welsh Saints in Twelfth-Century England', in *Britain and Ireland, 900–1300: Insular Responses to Medieval European Change*, ed. Brendan Smith (Cambridge: Cambridge University Press, 1999), 67–86.
19. Composed respectively by Turgot of Durham (1100–7), and a monk of St Albans.
20. Jocelyn Wogan-Browne, '"Clerc u lai, muïne u dame": Women and Anglo-Norman Hagiography in the Twelfth and Thirteenth Centuries', in *Women and Literature in Britain, 1150–1500*, ed. Carol M. Meale (Cambridge: Cambridge University Press, 1993), 61–85.
21. June McCash and Judith Barban (ed. and trans.), *The Life of Saint Audrey: A Text by Marie de France* (Jefferson: McFarland, 2006). See Emma Campbell, Chapter 18 in this volume.
22. Cynthia Turner Camp utilises Bakhtin's concept of chronotopes extensively in *Anglo-Saxon Saints' Lives as History Writing in Late Medieval England* (Cambridge: Brewer, 2015), esp. 17–21.
23. Jane Sinnett-Smith, 'Ætheldreda in the North: Tracing Northern Networks in the *Liber Eliensis* and the *Vie de seinte Audree*', in *Late Medieval Devotion to Saints from the North of England*, ed. Christiania Whitehead, Hazel J. Hunter Blair, and Denis Renevey (Turnhout: Brepols, 2022), 285–304.
24. McCash and Barban (ed. and trans.), *Life of Audrey*, 44–5, 70–1.
25. McCash and Barban (ed. and trans.), *Life of Audrey*, 105–6.

26. McCash and Barban (ed. and trans.), *Life of Audrey*, 116–17.
27. Delbert Russell, '"Sun num n'i vult dire a ore": Identity Matters at Barking Abbey', in *Barking Abbey and Medieval Literary Culture*, ed. Jennifer Brown and Donna Bussell (Woodbridge: York Medieval Press, 2012), 117–34.
28. Clemence of Barking, *The Life of St Catherine*, ed. William MacBain, ANTS 18 (Oxford: Blackwell, 1964); Östen Södergård (ed.), *La Vie d'Edouard le confesseur: poème anglo-normand du XIIe siècle* (Uppsala: Almqvist, 1948).
29. Jennifer Brown, 'Body, Gender and Nation in the Lives of Edward the Confessor', in *Barking Abbey*, ed. Brown and Bussell, 145–63 (159–63).
30. Jocelyn Wogan-Browne, Thelma Fenster, and Delbert Russell (eds. and trans.), *Vernacular Literary Theory from the French of Medieval England* (Cambridge: Brewer, 2016), 19–25.
31. Tara Foster, 'Clemence of Barking: Reshaping the Legend of St Catherine of Alexandria', *Women's Writing* 12 (2005), 13–27.
32. Diane Auslander, 'Clemence and Catherine: *The Life of St Catherine* in its Norman and Anglo-Norman Context', in *Barking Abbey*, ed. Brown and Bussell, 164–82 (178–82).
33. Electronic Campsey Project: margot/uwaterloo.ca. Sara Gorman, 'Anglo-Norman Hagiography as Institutional Historiography: Saints' Lives in Late Medieval Campsey Ash Priory', *Journal of Medieval Religious Cultures* 37 (2011), 110–28. This codex was later bound together with an early fourteenth-century codex comprising three additional lives.
34. Emily Huber and Elizabeth Robertson (eds.), *The Katherine Group MS Bodley 34: Religious Writings for Women in Medieval England* (Kalamazoo, MI: Medieval Institute Publications, 2016). See Michelle M. Sauer, Chapter 4 in this volume.
35. *The Liflade ant te Passiun of Seinte Margarete*, 31.1–2; *The Martyrdom of Sancte Katerine*, 40.1, in *Katherine Group*, ed. Huber and Robertson.
36. Sarah Salih, *Versions of Virginity in Late Medieval England* (Cambridge: D. S. Brewer, 2001), 74–98.
37. J. R. R. Tolkien (ed.), *Ancrene Wisse, Edited from MS. Corpus Christi College, Cambridge 402*, Early English Text Society 249 (1962), 130.
38. The ratio of male to female lives in the *South English Legendary* is approximately 6:1; in the *Gilte Legende* it is between 7:1 and 8:1. The *SEL* includes six native women: Frideswith, Mildrith, Eadburh, Æthelthryth, Helen, and Wenefrid, while the *GiL* 'supplementary lives' include Frideswith, Bridget, and Wenefrid.
39. For a full list of contents see Camp, *Anglo-Saxon Saints' Lives*, 94–5.
40. Mary Serjeantson (ed.), *Osbern Bokenham, Legendys of Hooly Wummen*, Early English Text Society O.S. 206 (1938). Nine of these lives also appear in the recently discovered Abbotsford *Legenda aurea* of Bokenham, reorganised back into kalendrical order, and in some cases devoid of their personalising prologues.
41. John Capgrave, *The Life of Saint Katherine*, ed. Karen Winstead (Kalamazoo, MI: Medieval Institute Publications, 1999); John Lydgate, *A Critical Edition of John Lydgate's Life of Our Lady*, ed. Joseph Lauritis (Pittsburgh: Duquesne University, 1961); John Lydgate, 'The Life of St Margaret', in *John Lydgate: The Minor Poems*, vol. 1: *Religious Poems*, Early English Text Society E.S. 107, ed. Henry N. MacCracken (1911, repr. 1961), 173–92.

42. Sarah Salih, 'Introduction', in *A Companion to Middle English Hagiography*, ed. Sarah Salih (Cambridge: D. S. Brewer, 2006), 1–23 (12).
43. Sherry Reames (ed.), *Middle English Legends of Women Saints* (Kalamazoo, MI: Medieval Institute Publications, 2003), 249–53.
44. Bokenham, 'The Life of St Anne', in *Women Saints*, ed. Reames, 287–8.
45. Bokenham, 'The Life of St Anne', in *Women Saints*, ed. Reames, 296.
46. See the contributions by Mary C. Erler, Laura Saetveit Miles, Liz Herbert McAvoy, Anthony Bale, and Nancy Bradley Warren, in this volume (Chs. 3, 5, 13, 20, and 21, respectively).
47. Jennifer Brown (ed.), *Three Women of Liège* (Turnhout: Brepols, 2008).
48. See my forthcoming article on the Low Country female saints lives in Bodleian Library, MS Bodley 240, in *Festschrift for Professor Naoë Kukita Yoshikawa* edited by Marleen Cré, Mami Kanno and Anne Mouron (Turnhout: Brepols, 2024).
49. 'The Middle English Life of Elizabeth of Spalbeek', 32, 38, in *Three Women*, ed. Brown.
50. 'Elizabeth of Spalbeek', 50, in *Three Women*, ed. Brown.
51. 'Elizabeth of Spalbeek', 32, in *Three Women*, ed. Brown.
52. Lynn Staley (ed.), *The Book of Margery Kempe* (Kalamazoo, MI: Medieval Institute Publications, 1996), 149. Margery's access to Marie probably came via aural reception of her Latin *vita*: *Three Women*, ed. Brown, 21–2.

Further Reading

Blanton, Virginia (2007). *Signs of Devotion: The Cult of St Aethelthryth in Medieval England, 695–1615*, University Park: Pennsylvania State University Press.
Brown, Jennifer, ed. (2008). *Three Women of Liège*, Turnhout: Brepols.
Brown, Jennifer, and Donna Bussell, eds. (2012). *Barking Abbey and Medieval Literary Culture*, Woodbridge: York Medieval Press.
Camp, Cynthia Turner (2015). *Anglo-Saxon Saints' Lives as History Writing in Late Medieval England*, Cambridge: D. S. Brewer.
Campbell, Emma (2008). *Medieval Saints' Lives: The Gift, Kinship and Community in Old French Hagiography*, Cambridge: D. S. Brewer.
Salih, Sarah (2001). *Versions of Virginity in Late Medieval England*, Cambridge: D. S. Brewer.
Salih, Sarah, ed. (2006). *A Companion to Middle English Hagiography*, Cambridge: D. S. Brewer.
Sanok, Catherine (2007). *Her Life Historical: Exemplarity and Female Saints' Lives in Late Medieval England*, Philadelphia: University of Pennsylvania Press.
Szarmach, Paul, ed. (2013). *Writing Women Saints in Anglo-Saxon England*, Toronto: University of Toronto Press.
Watt, Diane (2019). *Women, Writing and Religion in England and Beyond, 650–1100*, London: Bloomsbury.
Wogan-Browne, Jocelyn (2001). *Saints' Lives and Women's Literary Culture, c. 1150–1300: Virginity and Its Authorizations*, Oxford: Oxford University Press.

CHAPTER 13

Tears, Mediation, and Literary Entanglement
The Writings of Medieval Visionary Women

Liz Herbert McAvoy

Any discussion of the physical interaction of Margery Kempe (d. *c.* 1438) with other holy women has largely been restricted to her now famous meeting with the local visionary and anchoress, Julian of Norwich (d. after 1416). In this meeting, it is frequently pointed out, Julian is warm and supportive, warning Margery against the pitfalls of visionary experience, yet encouraging her to believe that she, like her experienced interlocutor, is also subject to inspiration of the Holy Spirit.[1] Such interaction is conceptualised by Kempe as 'holy spechys and dalyawns', and again, later, as 'holy dalyawns',[2] reflecting close, private, conversational, and ultimately female-coded connection that incorporates important topics of concern to holy women: *discretio spirituum*; God as divine love; affective bodily response to holy matters; tears and weeping; divine union with the human soul; the Devil's intrinsic failure to be ultimately meaningful; and how to endure the obstructive 'langage of the world'.[3] All these topics, moreover, are to be found in Julian's own texts, where they are anatomised and resolved via a complex and intensely intellectual theology and hermeneutic style. These provide echoes that offer this conversational episode a high level of veracity as esoteric communication between women who recognise synergies between and within one another. There is, of course, no evidence that Julian's writings ever circulated widely – or even at all – during her lifetime, and it is therefore unlikely that Kempe ever had access to them. However, this conversation over the 'many days that thei were togedyr'[4] has a long-lasting effect upon Margery's spirituality and, like many subsequent episodes in the *Book*, points towards the type of orality and the community-producing discourse constructed through such 'dalyawns' that was intrinsic to the literary lives and endeavours of medieval visionary women. This chapter's focus on such visionary women, therefore, deploys the *Book* as a type of literary 'hub' in order to offer a glimpse of the type of communications and entanglements that led to women's visionary writing becoming one of the most insistent of genres during the later Middle Ages – one whose importance, moreover, has been largely been overlooked in service of a medieval canon-construction that has been relentlessly conceptualised as an unbroken paternal line drawn from the *Beowulf*-poet to Chaucer to Shakespeare and beyond.

While this encounter with Julian may be the only synchronic physical 'interaction' between Margery and another verifiable holy woman documented in the *Book*, nevertheless we should read the text in terms of its construction out of a plethora of such interactions – or, more specifically, what I prefer to term *intra-actions* – in ways that subtly reveal the types of communities, both synchronic and diachronic, that characterised the lives of visionary holy women from the twelfth to the fifteenth centuries. Here, I make a crucial differentiation between the commonly used term 'interaction' and the neologism 'intra-action', the latter coined by Karen Barad in the context of her call for a feminist approach to quantum physics. In her work, Barad examines the agency of matter not as inherent to differentiated *individual* bodies able to exercise it ('interaction'), but as a dynamism of forces within which there is constant exchange, intermingling, and diffraction working between all matter. Thus, the term operates effectively as an articulation of the type of entangled 'dalyawns' between holy women and their writings that is of such concern to this present chapter – an intra-action, moreover, that was both synchronic and diachronic.

These literary intra-actions served additionally as crucial and dynamic identity-forming mechanisms, whether these holy women lived among other women or alone.[5] For example, some seven years after meeting Julian, Kempe's *Book* relates how in 1320 Margery was subjected to a protracted period of persecution in her home town of Bishop's Lynn by a visiting friar, possibly the renowned William Melton.[6] Here, the *Book* records how Margery's trusted confessor (and second scribe), Robert Springold, was quick to abandon her in response to a particularly vicious sermon directed at Margery and her affective devotional practices of loud weeping and physical collapse.[7] Similarly, their fellow parishioners, long accustomed to and tolerant of Margery's diverse affective responses during Mass and at other times, also turned against her in deference to the aggressive mendicant preacher who, she tells us, smote 'hys hand on the pulpit' as he castigated the congregation for its historical acceptance of her behaviour. As a result, Springold purposed 'nevyr to a levyd hir felyngys aftyr'[8] – that is, until he so happened upon a copy of the *vita* of a much earlier visionary holy woman from the Low Countries, Marie d'Oignies (d. 1213), who offered an authoritative exemplar for Margery's embodied affect.[9] Marie, like

Margery, had been a married laywoman but had ultimately relinquished her marriage to take up the life of an anchoress in a cell near the church at Oignies. Also like Margery, Marie's particular devotional activities had centred on ecstasies that featured uncontrollable weeping ('the plenty-vows teerys that sche wept ... made hir so febyl and so seyke that sche myth not endur to beheldyn the crosse') and collapse.[10] Such a closely correlating 'dalyawns' between the two women, in spite of geographical and temporal separation, is so striking for Springold that he even inserts into Margery's book citations from the chapters of Marie's *vita* that affected him most of all, particularly one recounting Marie's own priestly persecution: '[H]e tretyth specyaly in the boke befor wretyn the xviij *capitulo* that begynnyth, *Bonus es, domine, sperantibus in te*, and also in the xix *capitulo* wher he tellyth how sche, at the request of a preyste that he schulde not be turbelyd ne distrawt in hys messe wyth hir wepyng and hir sobbyng.'[11] The identification of Marie as an exemplar for the equally lacrimose Margery constitutes an intra-action further intensified by Springold's own identification, here and elsewhere, with Marie's abusive priest, who, having expelled Marie from his church for disrupting the Mass, is immediately overcome with the same affective weeping, so much so that 'he wett hys vestiment and ornamentys of the awter ... ne he myth not restryn it'.[12] Here, via a series of literary and affective intra-actions, Springold acknowledges the type of superior spiritual insights made available via female-coded practices of weeping and bodily dissolution.[13] Concomitantly, he also recognises the need for both Marie's priest and himself to find a way to feel and speak 'woman' – certainly if he is to continue his textual collaboration with Kempe. In arguing for this I draw on Luce Irigaray's conception of medieval mystical discourse as inherently feminine or female-coded, requiring men (and socially conditioned women) to learn to 'speak woman' if they are to engage with and comprehend its discourses. This position is supported by the more recent work of Sarah McNamer, who, in positing the femininity of affective meditational practices in the later Middle Ages, demonstrates the ways in which religious empathy and the compassion on which affective devotional practices were predicated were fundamentally expressions of cultural femininity.[14] As Springold admits, his intra-actions with Margery, Marie, the priest, and the text cause him to read 'mech more seryowslech'; reappraise Margery, to whom 'he drow ageyn and inclined mor sadly'; and, more to the point, focus on writing down her book, which previously 'he wrote lesse therof' because 'he had not ryth cler mende of the sayd mater whan he wrot this tretys'.[15]

The appearance of these precisely referenced episodes from Marie's *vita* in the *Book* thus works with the Julian episode to form part of a systematic citational practice devised by Kempe together with her scribe to embed representation of the visionary, Margery, deep within a culture of female visionary and literary authority – one that had previously found its comfort zone within wider European contexts during the twelfth and thirteenth centuries, particularly at the Saxon nunnery of Helfta, and had surfaced again with some dynamism and persistence within the Syon Abbey-dominated environment of female spirituality in fifteenth-century England. Such citational practice, moreover, enhances a much more subtle citational hermeneutic, one that fits neatly with what Nicholas Royle has identified as the tantalising presence of 'textual phantoms' in all writing – that is to say, traces and echoes of other written works which 'do not necessarily have the solidity or objectivity of a quotation', but which hover restlessly at the margins and between the lines. As such, they provide a swirling entanglement of allusion and resonance of con-texts and pre-texts that never necessarily 'come to rest anywhere', instead haunting the later text – and often each other too – with their heard and almost-heard echoes of other writings.[16] Such is the case not only with Kempe's *Book* but also with a good many other writings circulating in England in the late fourteenth and fifteenth centuries, within which resonances of women's visionary experiences restlessly pace the text. Within this context, therefore, Kempe's *Book*, as mentioned earlier, constitutes a type of 'hub' for such holy-woman textual hauntings – fitting with what Allen memorably refers to as the 'flotsam and jetsam of popular devotion' based on an insistent orality as its primary vehicle.[17]

Another of the other influential texts cited by Kempe's scribe in the same chapter is the 'tretys' of Elizabeth of Hungary – a set of visionary revelations that were for centuries misattributed to the Elizabeth (d. 1231) who was a popular married saint and daughter of the thirteenth-century King Andreas II of Hungary (d. 1336). Recent scholarship, however, has posited the *Revelations* as having been authored in the fourteenth century by Elizabeth's great niece – a visionary nun, also an Elizabeth, but this time of Töss in Switzerland – who died in 1336.[18] Still others suggest that 'Elizabeth of Hungary' was actually the 'Elizabeth of Naples' (d. 1322), who was a Dominican nun in that city.[19] Whatever its authorship, this text, probably written down in Middle High German by a sister nun soon after Elizabeth's death, survives both in Latin and in a range of European vernaculars, Middle English included, and was certainly circulating in Norfolk in that form during Kempe's lifetime.[20] Like the *Book*, therefore, it is complicated in terms of scribal mediation and, like many other female-authored visionary writings, it prefers to use the third-person perspective as a means of authorial distancing. Whether Kempe or her scribe was familiar with, or discussed, the Latin version of this text or its Middle English translation is unclear, but there is no doubt that the *vita* of Marie d'Oignies, Elizabeth's *Revelations*, and *The Book of Margery Kempe* share many aspects of a holy woman's construction of a visionary self. Indeed, even a cursory reading of these precursors shows that they found their way into Kempe's *Book* in a number of different manifestations beyond their mere name-check in chapter 62.[21]

Like his reference to Marie's *vita*, Kempe's scribe's single overt citation of Elizabeth's *Revelations* is used to support and vindicate Margery's more dramatic responses to the Passion and place them within a wholly precedented and orthodox tradition: Elizabeth, too, is described as having a similar predilection for holy tears accompanied by a 'lowde voys, as is wretyn in hir tretys'.[22] However, there are many more episodes in the *Book* where Elizabeth's affective activities are more subtly at play, haunting the text beyond its margins. For example, Elizabeth's treatise begins with a depiction of her as the Virgin's 'handmaydyn' by invitation, in which role she will acquire the necessary teaching and reshaping to be worthy of Christ as his spouse; so, too, the *Book* goes to some length to display Margery protractedly as the Virgin's handmaiden and her eventual apotheosis as spouse to the Godhead. Here, the *Book* echoes exactly the type of 'homely spech' and intimate interactions with the Virgin-as-mother-in-law that dominate Elizabeth's *Revelations*: as the Virgin tells Elizabeth, 'qwanne þou art suffysently tawt . . . of me, I schal brynge þe to my Sone'.[23]

Other entanglements within and between the two texts become pronounced where, in both cases and on careful reading, we begin to detect similar hauntings by other female-authored visionary texts: the bestselling *Liber specialis gratiae* attributed to the thirteenth-century Saxon nun, Mechthild of Hackeborn (d. 1298), for example. Mechthild was part of a widespread collaborative visionary culture at the Saxon nunnery of Helfta that also included the writers Gertrude the Great (d. 1301) and, in her later years, the former beguine, Mechtild of Magdeburg (d. *c.* 1394). As Anna Harrison has established, the visionary writings emerging from this well-educated intensely intellectual milieu – works that, beside the *Liber*, included the *Legatus divinae pietatis*, attributed to Gertrude and the second book of Mechtild of Magdeburg's *Das fließende Licht der Gottheit* – were ultimately collaborative projects, the result of widespread reading, conversation, and other intellectual interactions that formed what

Harrison perceptively terms 'a tangle of talk' within this all-female and ultimately independent monastic setting.[24] As I have argued elsewhere, however, this 'tangle of talk' operated not only in the local setting of Helfta but was also part of a far more widespread communicative entanglement, one that in Mechthild's own day saw 'many straungers (religiouse and seculers) which com from fer [who] seyd þat þay founde never so moch conforte of man ne woman as þey did of her,'[25] but which also, like Margery Kempe's 'dalyawns', operated diachronically as Mechthild-attributed writings were quickly disseminated in various formats throughout Europe during the fourteenth century. In the process, her book soon became a popular 'best seller'. Indeed, as Naoë Kukita Yoshikawa and I have recently argued, the influence of Mechthild's writing, whether in its original Latin redaction or Middle English translation, is paramount to *The Book of Margery Kempe* and probably featured as one of the unnamed texts read to her between 1413 and 1421 by a supportive priest and buried within the 'swech other' works supplementing a reading and discussion regimen the *Book* does name.[26] Thus, when the *Book* describes Margery's physical reaction to representations or thoughts of the Passion in terms of physical change and uncontrollability ('sche kept it in as long as sche mygth ... til sche wex as blo as any leed ... And whan the bodyt myth ne lengar enduryn the gostly labowr ... than fel sche down and cryed wondyr lowde'),[27] we are not only caught up with a diachronic 'tangle of talk' between Margery and Marie d'Oignies, for whom similar attempts to control her weeping led to feeling 'wel nyghe strangelyd',[28] but also Mechthild, whose book reports a mystical 'swouning' characterised by 'spredyng abrode her hondes' and a dramatic change of complexion.[29] Likewise, Elizabeth recounts being 'takyn fro myself' and feeling 'grouelyngys in my face as ded'.[30]

Moving beyond these intra-active responses to the Passion, a plethora of other visionary experiences in these and other writings are described in startlingly similar terms, thus providing another snapshot of a complex and intra-active 'tangle of talk' within which a conglomeration of 'homely' holy women are caught up, along with their scribes, confessors, confidants, and readers, both synchronically and diachronically. Moreover, this entangled discourse community and the 'conversational theology' it promotes is, like Margery's 'dalyawns' with Julian or Marie's with her own recalcitrant priest, encoded as female, extending from Saxony to Switzerland, to the Low Countries and Norfolk, sustained from the early thirteenth century to the mid-fifteenth century.[31] Indeed, it also constitutes the foundation and substance of the type of visionary and 'affective' turn that McNamer has written about so convincingly as important to all genders, identities, and communities in the later Middle Ages.[32] Such an 'affective turn', moreover, insinuates its way into a dazzling array of late medieval male-authored texts that have rarely been examined in terms of an intra-action with affirming female-coded discourses (as opposed to their also prevalent oppositional and misogynistic femininities). Indeed, Barbara Newman has recently taken up an old suggestion and argued convincingly for Mechthild's book, for example, as having been a primary influence upon Dante's *Commedia* (especially the *Purgatorio*).[33] We also know that Boccaccio was familiar with Mechthild's writing, as he mentions her and her prayers in the *Decameron*; and, as I also argue elsewhere, there are clear echoes of Mechthild's *Liber* in the works of the *Pearl*-poet, especially *Pearl* itself.[34] Nor was Chaucer immune to the perspectives on culture, religion, and human intra-action provided by the female-coded 'tangles of talk' of visionary holy women and their associates that permeated his cultural milieux.[35] When we take all this into account, the arbitrariness of women's traditional exclusion from the canon is laid starkly bare: its presence and influence have, in effect, been hiding there in plain sight.

Mechthild and the other women of Helfta were not writing in a vacuum, however. More than a century previously, other nunneries bore witness to equally extraordinary learning and visionary activity. Both Herrad of Hohenburg (d. 1195) and Hildegard of Bingen (d. 1179) oversaw communities of nuns engaged in all kinds of literary activities and book production, with Hildegard, of course, becoming one of the most renowned holy women of her day.[36] While Herrad's book, the *Hortus Deliciarum*, is not a mystical text and remained uncirculated and unknown until the eighteenth century, Hildegard's many writings, including her visionary work, *Scivias*, were widely disseminated during her lifetime, although the latter, unlike Mechthild's writing, seems never to have been translated into Middle English. What her writing shares with the Helfta texts, however, is a close reliance on a hermeneutics of the natural world, particularly pertaining to enclosed gardens, as a means of articulating a holy woman's special relationship with a nurturing God. Most famous, of course, is Hildegard's theology of *viriditas* – that is to say, the 'greening' of all creation by means of close intra-action with a God who is both nourishing and maternalistic. As Hildegard explains: 'spiratio Spiritus sancti velut pluvia ipsum irrigat, et sic eum discretio velut bona temperies aeris ad perfectionem bonorum fructuum ducit' (the breath of the Holy Spirit, like the rain, will water [the Christian], and so discernment, like the tempering of the air, will lead him to the perfection of good fruits).[37] For Hildegard,

God *is* the greening of the natural world to which we as humans are integral; he flows through and by N/nature into our holistic selves, 'greening' us and facilitating the production of the 'fruits' of good works that can turn each one of us into a regained Eden. Hildegard's Eden is thus a place of *process* where abundance is the result of the action that is *intra*-action – and which is, by implication, immanent, ubiquitous, cyclical, and perpetual: it blooms; it gives; it supplies; it oozes splendid aromas; it imbues the occupant with joy:

> Sed paradisus est locus amoenitatis, qui floret, in viriditate florum, et herbarum, et deliciis omnium aromatum, repletus optimus odoribus, dotatusque in gaudio beatarum animarum, dans fertillissimam fecunditatem aridae terrae, qui fortissimam vim terrae tribuit, velut anoma omen vires praebet.
>
> (But Paradise the place of delight, which blooms with the freshness of flowers and grass and the charms of spices, full of fine odors and dowered with the joy of blessed souls, giving invigorating moisture to the dry ground; it supplies strong force to the earth, as the soul gives strength to the body).[38]

The intra-action inherent to Hildegard's primary hermeneutic manifests also in the writings emerging from Helfta more than a century after Hildegard's death. There is some internal evidence to suggest that both Gertrude and Mechthild of Hackeborn had been exposed in some way to Hildegard's writings, perhaps even through the conversational theology that formed part of the Helfta mystical praxis. For example, both writers, like Hildegard, envision union with God in terms of an intra-action in which all boundaries, subjectivities, and matter dissolve and flow into, from, between, and within the ineffable, greening presence of God, just as the sunlight and rain bring about the nurturing, growth, and (re)productivity within the natural world. Subsumed into this horticultural intra-action, too, is the fruitful and dynamic exchange of human sexuality, but one that relinquishes a traditional heteronormative paradigm based on the lovers of the Song of Songs in favour of one where Christ and his spouse take on, exchange, and relinquish sex and gender roles, continually penetrating and flowing into one another in another hermeneutic expression of an immanence and unity that is simultaneously all-gendered and de-gendered. Indeed, in one extraordinary encounter between Christ and Mechthild, he proceeds to morph continuously between a range of nurturing personae, including male and female lovers both penetrating and penetrated. During this encounter, Mechthild enjoys 'delycyouse and swete drykes' from Christ's open wound, nibbling off a 'herde fruyte' growing on the divine heart therein. This moment is accompanied by a type of erotic 'pillow-talk' as she and Christ work towards consummation. In response to Christ's instructions on how to best achieve union, Mechthild enquires 'O myn only lover, how may y do þat', receiving the reply 'My love shall performe þat in þe'. The result of this eroticised intra-active encounter is a moment of complete dissolution, of *jouissance*, a 'passyng joying' that causes Mechthild's mystical register to slip as she voices her ecstasy at this moment of utter entanglement when being becomes non-being: 'A, a, love, love'.[39] What begins as a conversational 'dalyawns', then, intensifies as an intra-action, where agency is absorbed and refracted at the very moment it establishes itself. Soon, however, Christ's identity is re-established – but now in the form of divine love, who is also a nursing mother. As he memorably announces:

> þou shalt nempne thy moder oonly in me and my love shall be þy moder. And as childryn souke her moders, so shalt þou souke of love as of þyne moder an inward comforte and softnesse which may nouȝt be shewyd in speech. And þat moder shall ȝeve þe mete and drynke, and she shall cloth the, and in all þy nedys love shall procur for þe.[40]

Any idea we may harbour of Julian of Norwich as originator of the developed and extended hermeneutic of God-as-Mother that makes such a presence felt in her own writings a hundred years later is here dispelled. Indeed, while a whole variety of possible sources have been posited for Julian's treatment – Bernard of Clairvaux, *Ancrene Wisse*, William Flete's *Remedies*, to name but a few[41] – it is possible that, given Julian's East Anglian location and its proximity to the Low Countries, it is Mechthild's influence that surfaces in Julian's primary *Revelation of Love* hermeneutic. As Julian writes:

> The moder may geve her childe sucke her milke. But oure precious moder Jhesu, he may fede us with himself, and doth full curtesly and full tenderly with the blessed sacrament that is precious fode of very life ...
>
> And that shewde he ... in this swet worde where he seyth, 'Lo, how I loved thee', beholding into his blissed side, enjoyeng.[42]

Here, we not only witness an entanglement of Eucharistic theologies, but synergies and resonances on the level of imagery, lexis, and even the use of direct speech for amorous mystical pronouncement – another example of how the diachronic 'tangle of talk' permeates all these writings and their intra-active receptions.

Besides the lover/mother hermeneutic, other rather more prosaic image sets weave their way through women's visionary writings. For example, startling resonances resound between Book V of Mechthild's text and the 1422 *A Revelation of Purgatory*, written by a Syon-connected anchoress of Winchester. Here, the text adheres closely to Mechthild's account of close connections and friendships with other women religious and visitations from Purgatory from nuns and others she once knew.[43] Similarly, both texts contain passages depicting otherwise unique hybrid, animal purgatorial tormentors that include dogs, cats, and the worm of conscience (in Mechthild's case combined into one strange body that takes up occupancy within the hearts of human souls-in-waiting).[44] Both texts, too, echo the same Virgin-as-mother-in-law trope as mentioned earlier in the case of Elizabeth's *Revelations* and Kempe's *Book*, with both Mechthild and the unnamed anchoress's friend, Margaret, being led to Christ-the-Bridegroom by his mother, Mary.[45]

Elsewhere, another vivid episode from Mechthild's text infiltrates a range of later writings: that of the soul as a king's house needing to be swept clean of sin as an analogy for the imperative of confession. In Book II, for example, Christ tells her 'þe house ys made clene þat noþing may be sene ther þat shuld desplece hys sy3t.' If, however, there is no time to clean it, then the remaining 'fylth' should be placed in a 'herne' and cast out at a later date.[46] This same analogy resurfaces in the fourteenth-century *Liber Celestis* of Birgitta of Sweden (d. 1373), a work known to Margery Kempe and which shows familiarity with Mechthild's writing. The *Liber*, also translated into Middle English in the fifteenth century, records a conversation between Christ and the Virgin about a departed soul's need for grace: 'For ... ife he ordainde his house, 3it he swepid it no3t besili with reuerens, ne he strewed it no3t with floures of vertuse'.[47] Although Birgitta does not mention the conceit's origins by name, Mechthild does receive an explicit name-check in the allusion to this same passage included in another Middle English work: a 'rationale' of the Birgittine office known as *The Myroure of oure Ladye*, written for the nuns of Syon Abbey probably between 1420 and 1428 and attributed to the sometime anchorite and first Confessor General of Syon, Thomas Fishbourne (d. 1428). Here, the exemplum receives a direct citation to confirm its provenance: 'And hereof ye haue a notable example in saynt Maudes reuelacions'.[48]

By the fifteenth century, such reproductions, echoes, and entanglements were clearly moving beyond women's mystical literature and finding their place within other devotional contexts, as well as spilling over into more secular spheres, as suggested earlier. Additionally, manuscript patronage, ownership, and preservation demonstrate similarly entangled connections between texts, families, and the religious orders. We know that the sole surviving manuscript of *The Book of Margery Kempe* was initially used and preserved by Carthusians at the Yorkshire house of Mount Grace.[49] Carthusian patronage was also implicated in the preservation and dissemination of Mechthild's work, as well as the other texts produced at Helfta. The printed edition of Elizabeth's *Revelations* may also owe a debt to the Sheen Charterhouse across the Thames from Syon; two Oxford, St John's College manuscripts (182 and Douce 114) of the Middle English *Life* of Marie d'Oignies were also eventually housed at the Charterhouses of Witham and Beauvale, respectively. Even more significantly, the only extant copy of Julian of Norwich's first text, *A Vision Shewed be the Goodenes of God to a Devoute Woman*, in London, British Library, MS Additional 37790 (the Amherst Manuscript) was preserved by the Carthusians, also ending up at the Sheen Charterhouse at some stage in its early history, and its scribe was also responsible for copying the Middle English version of Mechthild's book found in London, British Library, MS 2006.[50]

Alongside Julian's text in Additional 37790 appears another visionary text, also preserved by the Carthusians and intimating another set of complex entanglements. The deeply esoteric *The Mirror of Simple Souls* was written in the early fourteenth century by the French beguine, Marguerite Porete (d. 1310), surviving in only two copies in England: one in Latin, the other in its Middle English translation preserved alongside *A Vision*. Like those other texts discussed here, the *Mirror* is intensely dialogic, 'homely' and conversational, reflecting exactly the type of entanglements I have been discussing, whilst at the same time engaging in further entanglement of its own. Such an entanglement proved more sinister, however, and involved Marguerite's arraignment for producing an heretical work and her eventual execution in Paris. Indeed, this fate reflects what remained the greatest worldly anxiety of both Julian and Kempe in their early reluctance to write or to be seen in any way as 'teacher' within the dangerously anti-heretical climate of fifteenth-century England. Margery was, on a number of occasions, directly accused and examined for heresy, narrowly escaping a burning on more than one occasion. Julian, too, expresses overt anxieties in *A Vision* when she appeals to her reader not to see her as teacher but to recognise her as 'a woman, lewed, febille, and freylle'. As she famously adds for safe measure: 'Bot in alle thinge I lyeve as haly kyrke techis.'[51] Almost all the women visionaries discussed here were alert to such dangers and, without exception, address their fears of only having at their disposal the 'langage of the world' to articulate what ultimately lies beyond language. Marguerite would therefore have been well apprised of such sentiments. Nevertheless, she developed an unique mystical theology that was predicated not on regular passing union but on the complete 'annihilation' of the individual soul and its permanent intra-active deification with and *as* God. Condemned in 1310, Marguerite was taken to the Place de Grève in Paris and burned as a relapsed 'heretic' alongside her book.

Via a reappraisal of such synergetic resonances within and between medieval women's visionary writings, then, with their multiple layers of conversation, tangles of talk, and affective articulations, we are able to add depth and complexity to the role played by such women and their texts within the arena of medieval literary culture, and to add considerable nuance to the assessment of Ulrike Wiethaus, who was among the first to identify that medieval holy-women's women's friendship groups (although she is largely envisaging synchronic interaction here) were able to achieve common goals 'by reciprocal support, high emotional rapport, and generosity in the sharing of resources'. In turn, for such women (and, sometimes, those men who were accepted into the circle of these friendships), intra-action of this kind 'represented an antidote to patriarchal structures and functioned as an alternative model to social relations that were subject to ... domination and submission.'[52] Tracing the shared voices and reflected imaginaries of these women over time and across geographical locations therefore offers us a clearer idea of how the alternative perspectives on this world and the next which they created, shared, and disseminated became a lasting challenge to patriarchal domination of the literary canon, both in their own day and in ours, as they trod – and taught others to tread – the unstable pathway between the orthodox and heterodox.

Notes

1. Margery Kempe, *The Book of Margery Kempe*, ed. Barry Windeatt (Cambridge: D. S. Brewer, 2000, repr. 2004), cited as *BMK*, chapter and page number (here at 18.119–23). For discussion of this episode as a re-enactment of the Visitation, see Laura Saetveit Miles, 'Queer Touch Between Holy Women: Julian of Norwich, Margery Kempe, Birgitta of Sweden, and the Visitation', in *Touching, Devotional Practices, and Visionary Experience in the Late Middle Ages*, ed. David Carillo-Rangel, Delfi I. Nieto-Isabel, and Pablo Acosta-Gardia (London and New York: Palgrave Macmillan, 2019), 203–35.
2. *BMK*, 18.120 and 123.
3. *BMK*, 18.122. On *discretio spirituum*, see Rosalynn Voaden, *God's Words, Women's Voices: The Discernment of Spirits in the Writing of Late Medieval Holy Women Visionaries* (University of York: York Medieval Press, 1999).

4. *BMK*, 18.123.
5. See Karen Barad, *Meeting the Universe Halfway: Quantum Physics and the Entanglement of Matter and Meaning* (Durham, NC: Duke University Press, 2007).
6. *BMK*, note to line 4979, 286.
7. *BMK*, 62.292. On the identity and input of the second scribe, see Nicholas Watson, 'The Making of *The Book of Margery Kempe*', in *Voices in Dialogue: Reading Women in the Middle Ages*, ed. Linda Olson and Kathryn Kerby-Fulton (Notre Dame, IN: Notre Dame University Press, 2005), 395–434.
8. *BMK*, 62.292.
9. Written in Latin by Jacques de Vitry (d. 1244), Marie's *vita* was translated into Middle English in the fifteenth century, for an edition of which (Oxford, Bodleian Library MS Douce 114), see *Three Women of Liège: A Critical Edition of and Commentary on the Middle English Lives of Elizabeth of Spalbeek, Christina Mirabilis, and Marie d'Oignies*, ed. Jennifer N. Brown (Turnhout: Brepols, 2008), 85–190 (hereafter cited as *Life*).
10. *BMK*, 62.292-3.
11. *BMK*, 62.293.
12. *BMK*, 62.294. See also Springold's account of his own uncontrollable weeping as he continues writing Margery's words (*BMK*, 89.382).
13. On the history of 'holy tears', see Kimberley Christine Paton and John Stratton Hawley (eds.), *Holy Tears: Weeping in the Religious Imagination* (New Jersey: Princeton University Press, 2005). On women's tears as redemptive agents, see Barbara Newman, *From Virile Woman to WomanChrist* (Philadelphia: University of Pennsylvania Press, 1995), 108–36.
14. Luce Irigaray, 'La Mystérique', in *Speculum of the Other Woman*, trans. Gillian C. Gill (Ithaca: Cornell University Press, 1985), 191–202; Sarah McNamer, *Affective Meditation and the Invention of Medieval Compassion* (Philadelphia: University of Pennsylvania Press, 2009).
15. *BMK*, 62.294.
16. Nicholas Royle, *The Uncanny* (Manchester: Manchester University Press, 2003), 280.
17. Hope Emily Allen, 'Prefatory Note', in Margery Kempe, *The Book of Margery Kempe*, ed. Sandford Brown Meech and Hope Emily Allen, Early English Texts Society O.S. 212 (London: Oxford University Press, 1997), lix.
18. For full discussion of the debate, see the introduction to Sarah McNamer's *Two Middle English Translations of the Revelations of St Elizabeth of Hungary* (Heidelberg: Universitätsverlag C. Winter, 1996), 9–53. All references will be to this edition, cited by chapter and page number.
19. See, for example, Laura Saetveit Miles, *The Virgin Mary's Book at the Annunciation* (Cambridge: D. S. Brewer, 2020), esp. 116.
20. *Revelations*, Introduction, 15.
21. *Revelations*, Introduction, 9, 46.
22. *BMK*, 62.

23. *Revelations*, I.58. See also V.68. *BMK*, 6.75–8; 7.78–80; 79.340–5.
24. Anna Harrison, '"Oh! What Treasure is in This Book?" Writing, Reading, and Community at the Monastery of Helfta,' *Viator* 35.1 (2008), 75–106 (94).
25. Mechthild of Hackeborn, *The Boke of Gostely Grace*, ed. Anne Mouron and Naoë Kukita Yoshikawa (Liverpool: Liverpool University Press, 2022). All references are to this edition, cited by book, chapter and folio number (here at V.22, fol. 99r). I am grateful to the editors for sharing their pre-publication manuscript with me.
26. *BMK*, 58.278–80. The literature on Margery's bodily affect is extensive. However, for a recent study casting it through a medico-spiritual lens, see Laura Kalas, *Margery Kempe's Spiritual Medicine: Suffering, Transformation and the Life Cycle* (Cambridge: Boydell and Brewer, 2020). For further discussion of the implications of the supportive priest episode and links between Kempe's *Book* and Mechthild's *Liber*, see Liz Herbert McAvoy and Naoë Kukita Yoshikawa, 'Mechthild of Hackeborn and Margery Kempe: An Intertextual Conversation', *Spicilegium* 5 (2021), 3–20.
27. *BMK*, 28.165–6.
28. *Life*, 93.
29. *Boke*, V.22, fol. 99v.
30. *Revelations*, V.74.
31. I borrow the term 'conversational theology' from Laura Grimes' work on the influence of Augustine's writings on the Helfta nunnery in her 'Theology as Conversation: Gertrude of Helfta and her Sisters as Readers of Augustine', unpublished doctoral dissertation, University of Notre Dame (2004).
32. See n. 20. See also Caroline Walker Bynum, *Fragmentation and Redemption: Essays on Gender and the Human Body in Medieval Religion* (New York: Zone Books, 1991).
33. Barbara Newman, 'The Seven-Storey Mountain: Mechthild of Hackeborn and Dante's Matelda', *Dante Studies* 136 (2018), 62–92.
34. Giovanni Boccaccio, *Decameron*, ed. Jonathan Usher (Oxford: Oxford University Press, 1993), VII.1, 419; Liz Herbert McAvoy, *The Enclosed Garden and the Medieval Religious Imaginary* (Cambridge: D. S. Brewer, 2021), 195–259.
35. See Roberta Magnani and Liz Herbert McAvoy, 'What is a Woman: Enclosure and Female Piety in Chaucer's "The Knight's Tale"', *Studies in the Age of Chaucer* 20 (2020), 311–24.
36. On Hildegard, see Barbara Newman, *Sister of Wisdom: St Hildegard's Theology of the Feminine* (Berkeley and Los Angeles: University of California Press, 1987). On Herrad, see Fiona J. Griffiths, *The Garden of Delight: Reform and Renaissance for Women in the Twelfth Century* (Philadelphia: University of Pennsylvania Press, 2007).
37. Hildegard of Bingen, *Scivias in Sanctae Hildegardis abbatissae Opera Omnia*, ed. J.-P. Migne, *Patrologiae cursus completes, series Latina 197* (Paris: Oudin, 1855), 1.4.25, col. 428B. All translations are from *Hildegard of Bingen: Scivias*,

trans. Columba Hart and Jane Bishop (Mahwah: Paulist Press, 1990), here at 123–4.
38. *Scivias* 1.2.28, PL 197, cols 400A–B (trans. by Hart and Bishop, 86).
39. *Boke*, II.ix, fol. 61r.
40. *Boke*, II.ix, fol. 61r. On the God-as-Mother trope, see Caroline Walker Bynum, *Jesus as Mother: Studies in the Spirituality of the High Middle Ages* (Berkeley: University of California Press, 1984).
41. On Flete's influence, see Vincent Gillespie, '"[S]he do the police in different voices": Pastiche, Ventriloquism and Parody in Julian of Norwich', in *A Companion to Julian of Norwich*, ed. Liz Herbert McAvoy (Cambridge: D. S. Brewer, 2008), 192–207 (198–9); Liz Herbert McAvoy, 'Bathing in Blood: The Medicinal Cures of Anchoritic Devotion', in *Medicine, Religion and Gender in Medieval Culture*, ed. Naoë Kukita Yoshikawa (Cambridge: D. S. Brewer, 2015), 85–102.
42. Julian of Norwich, *A Revelation of Love*, in *The Writings of Julian of Norwich*, ed. Nicholas Watson and Jacqueline Jenkins (Turnhout: Brepols, 2006), 60.313. See also *BMK*, 5.74, where a weeping anchorite tells Margery, 'Dowter, ye sowkyn evyn on Crystys brest, and ye han an ernest-peny of hevyn.'
43. On this and what follows, see *A Revelation of Purgatory*, ed. and trans. Liz Herbert McAvoy (Cambridge: D. S. Brewer, 2017), especially the Introduction, 1–69.
44. *Revelation*, lines 168–9, 94; *Boke*, V.ix, fol. 95r.
45. *Boke*, V.xxj, fol. 98r, e.g., *Revelation*, ll. 702–9, 152.
46. *Boke*, II.xvj, fol. 60r.
47. Roger Ellis (ed.), *The Liber Celestis of St Bridget of Sweden*, 2 vols., Early English Text Society O.S. 291 (Oxford: Oxford University Press, 1987), here at II.2.118.
48. John Henry Blunt (ed.), *The Myroure of oure Ladye*, Early English Text Society E.S. 19 (London: N. Trübner, 1973), 38–9. For a discussion of this text in terms of the vernacular theology culture of Syon Abbey, see Elizabeth Schirmer, 'Reading Lessons at Syon Abbey: *The Myroure of Oure Ladye* and the Mandates of Vernacular Authority', in *Voices in Dialogue: Reading Women in the Middle Ages*, ed. Linda Olson and Kathryn Kirby-Fulton (Notre Dame, IN: University of Notre Dame Press, 2005), 345–76. Fishbourne was at the centre of a devotional circle that also included the patrons of the Winchester anchoress mentioned earlier.
49. A note on the verso of the binding leaf of the manuscript, London, British Library, Additional MS 61823, reads 'Liber Montis Gracie. This boke is of Mountegrace'.
50. Formerly the 'Amherst Manuscript', this version was copied sometime around 1435 from an exemplar dated 1413, for a study of which see Marleen Cré, *Vernacular Mysticism in the Charterhouse: A Study of London, British Library, MS Additional 37790* (Turnhout: Brepols, 2006). Interestingly, this is the same year as Margery Kempe made her documented visit to Julian.

51. Julian of Norwich, *A Vision*, ed. Nicholas Watson and Jacqueline Jenkins (Turnhout: Brepols, 2005), §6.75.
52. Ulrike Wiethaus (ed.), *Maps of Flesh and Light: The Religious Experience of Medieval Women Mystics* (Ithaca, NY: Syracuse University Press, 1993), Introduction, 5.

Further Reading

Cré, Marleen (2006). *Vernacular Mysticism in the Charterhouse: A Study of London, British Library, MS Additional 37790*, Turnhout: Brepols.

Gillespie, Vincent (2008). '[S]he do the police in different voices': Pastiche, Ventriloquism and Parody in Julian of Norwich'. In *A Companion to Julian of Norwich*, ed. Liz Herbert McAvoy. Cambridge: D. S. Brewer, 192–207.

Harrison, Anna (2008). 'Oh! What Treasure is in This Book?' Writing, Reading, and Community at the Monastery of Helfta. *Viator* 35.1, 75–106.

Magnani, Roberta, and Liz Herbert McAvoy (2020). What is a Woman: Enclosure and Female Piety in Chaucer's 'The Knight's Tale'. *Studies in the Age of Chaucer* 42, 311–24.

McAvoy, Liz Herbert (2021). *The Enclosed Garden and the Medieval Religious Imaginary*, Cambridge: D. S. Brewer.

McAvoy, Liz Herbert (2017). Introduction. In *A Revelation of Purgatory*, ed. and trans. Liz Herbert McAvoy. Cambridge: D. S. Brewer.

McAvoy, Liz Herbert, and Naoë Kukita Yoshikawa (2021). Mechthild of Hackeborn and Margery Kempe: An Intertextual Conversation. *Spicilegium* 5, 3–20.

Miles, Laura Saetveit (2019). Queer Touch Between Holy Women: Julian of Norwich, Margery Kempe, Birgitta of Sweden, and the Visitation. In *Touching, Devotional Practices, and Visionary Experience in the Late Middle Ages*, ed. David Carillo-Rangel, Delfi I. Nieto-Isabel, and Pablo Acosta-Gardia. London and New York: Palgrave Macmillan, 203–35.

Newman, Barbara (2018). The Seven-Storey Mountain: Mechthild of Hackeborn and Dante's Matelda. *Dante Studies* 136, 62–92.

Paton, Kimberley Christine and John Stratton Hawley, eds. (2005). *Holy Tears: Weeping in the Religious Imagination*, New Jersey: Princeton University Press.

Schirmer, Elizabeth (2005). Reading Lessons at Syon Abbey: *The Myroure of Oure Ladye* and the Mandates of Vernacular Authority. In *Voices in Dialogue: Reading Women in the Middle Ages*, ed. Linda Olson and Kathryn Kirby-Fulton. Notre Dame, IN: University of Notre Dame Press, 345–76.

Voaden, Rosalynn (1999). *God's Words, Women's Voices: The Discernment of Spirits in the Writing of Late Medieval Holy Women Visionaries*, University of York: York Medieval Press.

Wiethaus, Ulrike, ed. (1993). *Maps of Flesh and Light: The Religious Experience of Medieval Women Mystics*, Ithaca, NY: Syracuse University Press.

CHAPTER 14

Convent and City
Medieval Women and Drama

Sue Niebrzydowski

In the fifteenth-century *Processional of the Priory of the Blessed Virgin Mary*, Chester, its Benedictine nuns are instructed on 'Sher Thuresdai' or Maundy Thursday to wash the altars, and 'Goo to seynt Mary auter w[ith; singing] thys antym of the assumpcion', which is identified as 'Ascendit christus'(Christ ascended above the Heavens).[1] The *Processional*, the gift of one of the nuns at the Priory, Dame Margery Byrkenhed, whose name suggests a woman brought up in the locality to the north of the city, records song and movement accompanying the devotional activity on Maundy Thursday of stripping the altars of their hangings, after which the altars are washed with water and wine, and then swept with a broom of sharp twigs. The ritual performance is interpreted by Eamon Duffy as an allegorised ceremony in which the altar represents the body of Christ, the water and wine the water and blood from Christ's body, and the broom of twigs both the scourges and the Crown of Thorns.[2]

The Cestrian 'Sher Thuresdai' can be categorised as drama by virtue of its constituent elements: performers, song, gesture, movement, and props. Jody Enders has noted how the terms employed by critics (including spectacle, performance, ritual, pageant, parade, procession, dance, song, allegory, and dialogue) reveal how perplexing medieval theatre is to identify, and the reluctance to acknowledge the ubiquity of theatrical and proto-theatrical forms in this period has skewed what can be considered as part of this broad genre: ritual, liturgical performance, interludes, morality plays, Corpus Christi plays, saints' lives, processions, and dramatised performances of texts.[3]

If the identification of medieval drama is perplexing, that of the role played by nuns and their secular sisters therein is even more so. We are indebted to *Records of Early English Drama* (REED) for locating and editing the written traces of original dramatic productions, whence a clearer picture of women's association with secular drama continues to emerge and upon which this chapter draws extensively. Putting women centre stage in any discussion of medieval drama requires that we adopt, as this chapter does, a broad definition of 'stage' or playing place, of 'performance', and of the nature of women's engagement with this diverse genre. In this chapter the nomenclature of 'costume' and 'actor' associated with modern drama is avoided, as Philip Butterworth advises, since these 'run the risk of imposing modern theatrical consciousness on medieval conditions'.[4] Following in the footsteps of Elisabeth Dutton and Liv Robinson, this chapter employs the terms 'performer' and 'participant' rather than 'actor'.[5]

Included in what follows is an examination of women's participation in the drama performed in convents, parish churches, cathedrals, and that which was played out in the streets of medieval cities. Women did perform publicly. As they participated in the services associated with Holy Week, congregants might see nuns taking key roles in drama associated with the liturgy. Beyond the convent walls, spectators at celebrations welcoming royal visitors watched their female relatives embody, in the sense of bringing to life through representation, cardinal virtues and female saints. We have evidence of women's involvement in the drama performed in their parish churches. In the annual, midsummer Corpus Christi plays of York and Chester, women undertook responsibility for funding and producing an entire pageant. Women's performance in the Corpus Christi plays of the British Isles remains speculative; while scholars continue to seek the evidence to establish without question that this was the case, we should continue to heed Katie Normington's advice: 'Though medieval women are silent within the production of the cycles, they are not absent.'[6]

Evidence of women's association with drama (the umbrella term that this chapter employs to cover the many varieties of dramatic performance of the Middle Ages), fragmentary and tantalising as it is, suggests that women's relationship to the genre is both complex and deserving of inclusion in a volume devoted to women and medieval literary culture. What follows is an examination of the many ways in which women engaged with medieval drama in its many forms, and a *dramatis personae* of the women by whom our understanding of medieval drama is indebted and enriched.

Performance Opportunities for *Sponsae Christi*

The nuns of Chester's Priory of the Blessed Virgin Mary were not alone in their dramatic performance. Liturgical drama (drama associated with the ritual forms of worship of the Church) and stand-alone productions were fostered within convents and were as much a part of the theatrical experience of those living outside of the cloister as those living within.

In the British Isles, the sine qua non of women's liturgical drama is the *Visitatio Sepulchri* from another Benedictine house: that of Barking Abbey of the Blessed Virgin Mary and St Æthelburga, in Essex. Abbess Katherine of Sutton (elected 1358–d. 1376) saw drama as the means to invigorate the devotion of her nuns and congregation, as is recorded in the Barking Abbey *Ordinale*. Katherine may have commissioned or composed three liturgical dramas for Holy Week: the *Depositio* or Removal from the Cross and Entombment of Christ, the *Decensus/Elevatio* or Descent of Christ into hell (the Harrowing of Hell) and his raising from the tomb, and the *Visitatio Sepulchri* or Visitation at the Tomb.[7]

The dramas evince that nuns were authors, performers – playing both male and female roles – manufacturers of costume, and providers of playing spaces within their Abbey. The most recent editors of Barking's dramas note that seven chants in the *Visitatio* appear to be unique to the Barking manuscript and suggest that they represent compositions by the nuns.[8] The sisters appeared alongside priests, joining in with the singing of antiphons and undertaking mimetic roles. In the *Decensus/Elevatio*, the sisters played the part of patriarchs. In the *Visitatio Sepulchri*, women are central to the action. Selected sisters represented Mary Magdalene, Mary the mother of James, and Mary Salome – women who were revered for their role in Christian history and who were the first witnesses to the Resurrection.

The *Visitatio Sepulchri* required costumes, and the *Ordinale* records that particular performance techniques were utilised. The Magdalene Chapel served as a 'dressing room', and here the nuns playing the Marys replaced their black habits with 'dazzling [white] surplices' and the abbess placed white veils over their heads.[9] The nuns may have manufactured the surplices and veils, as well as the cloth required for the Easter sepulchre. Women certainly furnished fabric for the Easter Sepulchre in their local parish church. In 1373 Agnes Pikerell, widow of William, a saddler whose business Agnes ran after his death, bequeathed material for covering the Easter sepulchre to the Church of St Vedast, Cheapside, London, in which she and her husband were buried. Agnes leaves a number of expensive fabrics for this purpose: 'A cloth of sarzinet [silk]', which she has in her house, and another to match, which she directs her executors to buy and which are to be embroidered, after Agnes and her late husband, with the letters 'W' and 'A', plus her 'coverlit smalchekerd [small checkered bedspread]' and 'best sheet of cloth of Reynes [linen from Rennes]'.[10]

The purchase of the additional cloth is to be funded by the sale of Agnes' 'ladies' saddles, brouded and unbrouded [ornamented and plain]' – the portion of the family saddlery that she did not gift to her son, Robert.[11] Agnes's bequest suggests that she had every hope of her and William's future resurrection being remembered during the Easter celebrations by her friends and neighbours in the church that was home to the Guild of Saddlers to which the couple had belonged.

As with any performance, a range of gesture and vocal inflection was required to convey the emotional import of the antiphons and responses, responsibility for the creative interpretation of which may have lain with the *cantrix* whose role was that of performance director, possibly in collaboration with Abbess Katherine. The *Ordinale* records how verses required delivery in a 'tearful and subdued voice', or 'plaintively', and that Mary Magdalene 'sighs' as the three women sing 'To you I sigh'.[12] On seeing the risen Christ, Mary Magdalene must sing her next verse in a way that 'should communicate her delight to her companions in a joyful voice'.[13] The drama is brought to a close with Mary Magdalene pointing to the empty tomb and displaying the head shroud to the priests, clerics, and nuns playing Christ's disciples who, in turn, kiss the shroud.[14] Having removed their attire and donned their habits, the three nuns pray before the empty tomb before resuming their place among their sisters.

At each successive performance of the *Visitatio Sepulchri*, the Resurrection of Christ is witnessed by the women whom the Gospels identify as present at his tomb and who are, for the duration of the performance, also three representatives of Barking's own female community. An effect of inhabiting the roles of the three Marys was that of a powerful memorial for the nuns performing these roles, as observed by Liv Robinson and Elisabeth Dutton: 'the imposition of white veils, the feel of white surplices and the touch of the Abbess's hands might "cue" sisters to take a mental step backwards in time towards the moment of their own profession, touch functioning as the medium by which this event is brought into the present'.[15] A further mnemonic function was served by the nuns inhabiting the roles of Christ's close female followers. For those watching, the chosen nuns' performance created a visual and verbal link between Christ's first female followers and successive generations of Barking's sisters who had also chosen a life dedicated to God. The Mary Magdalene chapel at Barking was the burial location of three of its abbesses – Æthelburga (d. after 686), Hildelith (d. *c.* 725), and Wulfhilda (*c.* 940–*c.* 996) – and two former nuns – Tortith and Edith. Katherine of Sutton's decision to promote drama ensured that the liturgical spectacle celebrating the Magdalene served to remind the Abbey priests, the local community, and the nuns of Barking Abbey, annually, at the most holy time of the Church year, that women had been the first to witness Christ's Resurrection, and, as importantly, continued to play an important role in disseminating this narrative.

Liturgical drama was not the only theatre that took place within convents. Looking to Europe provides examples of female-authored, dramatised saints' lives and moral allegories produced within the cloister, the like of which may well have existed in the British Isles but evidence of which has been lost. Stephanie Hollis advises that we look outwards towards Europe to fill this lacuna.[16] The drama of Hrotsvit (*c.* 935–*c.* 975) and Hildegard of Bingen (1098–1179) reveals that nuns composed original drama, some of which employed music, that saints' and morality plays were considered appropriate subject matter for those who had taken the veil, and that conventual drama might take the form of fully staged performances requiring the apparatus and physical embodiment traditionally associated with theatre.

Hrotsvit, the self-styled 'strong voice of Gandersheim' Abbey, composed six Latin plays in rhymed prose, 'to glorify, within the limits of my poor talent, the laudable chastity of Christian virgins in that self-same form of composition which has been used to describe the shameless acts of licentious women'.[17] Written with the support of her abbess, Gerberga II, *Gallicanus*, *Dulcitius*, *Calimachus*, *Abraham*, *Paphnutius*, and *Sapientia* are dramatised *vitae* or saints' lives set in the period of Roman persecution of the early Christians. The plays champion female chastity by repurposing the stereotypical female characterisation of Terentian comedy (the *meretrix*/deceitful 'courtesan', the *ancilla* or loyal and clever 'slavewoman', the *mulier* or shrewd wife, and the *virgo*/maiden) that may have been performed at Gandersheim but of whose performance history has left no trace.[18]

Hrotsvit's plays are capable of performance as closet drama, read aloud by her fellow nuns and canonesses and accompanied by gesture and movement, and also as fully staged performances. Each play requires a small cast and props, and scene changes prefaced by dialogue help signpost the audience to the new 'how', 'when', and 'where' of the action taking place. The way in which the plays were performed may have been influenced by the occasion and audience for their staging: a private performance by the nuns for their own entertainment and instruction, or a public performance before guests to the Abbey.

Teaching lessons in morality, chastity, patience, faith, and loyalty to Christ, Hrotsvit's drama replicates the narrative pattern of the saint's life: a refusal to marry, repeated torture of the heroine (each incidence of which is more outlandish than the preceding punishment), the disaffection of the torturers, and the final triumphant death and spiritual reward of the heroine who refuses to recant her faith. Her plays provide exciting narratives, exotic locations, pain, torture, demons, temptation, and salvation. Hrotsvit's characterisation is deft. There are men at whom we laugh, such as Dulcitius, as he embraces pots and pans believing them to be Agape, Chionia, and Irena after whom he lusts (*Dulcitius*, scene X). There are other men at whom we recoil in horror, such as Callimachus, who desires to enact necrophilic desires on Drusiana's corpse (*Calimachus*, scene VII). We grieve with the women helping Sapientia prepare her daughters for burial (*Sapientia*, scene VIII). Gesture and facial expression animate the dialogue and prayers. The action is dynamic, requiring entrances and exits, disguises, costumes, and props, such as a vat of boiling pitch into which Faith and Hope are thrown in *Sapientia*.

Hrotsvit provided the nuns of Gandersheim with opportunities to perform in praise of the life of a *sponsa Christi*. A century later Hildegard of Bingen, the Abbess of Rupertsberg, presented the sisters at Rupertsberg with the chance to enact Christian virtues. Hildegard composed the *Ordo Virtutum* (*Play of the Virtues, c.* 1155), a neumed or plainsong drama. The play has much in common with later morality plays in that it is allegorical and its *dramatis personae* comprises characters who are abstractions (Death and the Soul) and personified Christian virtues. The play dramatises a psychomachia or battle waged between the Devil and the Virtues led by their Queen, Humility, for Anima (the soul), who strays from the path of virtue when tempted by the flesh. The outcome is never in doubt, as Anima returns, repentant, but this is not before the Devil attacks Anima, at which point the Virtues capture and bind him. The play closes with the Virtues singing of the power of Christ's crucifixion to save souls from Satan and instructing audience participation as they genuflect before God.

The *Ordo* was staged, possibly originally for the dedication of the new convent in Rupertsburg. Richard Axton suggests how this performance might have taken place:

> [T]he Virtues and their queen, Humility, are on a raised throne reached by steps. On the lower level is the Devil, who never reaches beyond the foot of the steps in his struggle to constrain the soul within the carnal world inhabited by the audience. After his defeat by the Virtues, he is bound with his own chains while Anima is led aloft, aided by the condescending Virtues.[19]

Binding the Devil, dancing, and Anima's migration between the approach to heaven (the altar steps) and Earth (the space at their foot) exemplify the investment in the physical demanded of staged performance. Peter Dronke advises that we look to Hildegard's visionary work, *Scivias* (*Know the Ways of the Lord*, c. 1151/52), for details of how the Virtues may have been costumed: 'Caritas has a dress the colour of the heavens, with a golden stole reaching to her feet; Fides, a scarlet dress, a token of martyrdom; Obedientia wears a hyacinth colour, and has silver fetters at her throat, hands and feet.'[20] The *Ordo Virtutum* dramatises – for the nuns and distinguished visitors alike – the sin about which all Christians should be vigilant and the daily struggle against this in which all Christians should be engaged.

Women and Drama Beyond the Convent Walls

While conventual drama presented performance opportunities for nuns, the evidence of that for secular women is at best sketchy and reliant on a few, much-cited examples. Locating definitive evidence of premodern women acting outside of the cloister remains elusive. Scholars have conjectured that women might have performed in the Corpus Christi plays in which cities showed off not only their piety but also their prestige. James Stokes hypothesises a pre-existing, medieval tradition of women on the stage, but does so from a range of examples that are predominantly seventeenth century.[21] Citing a lost Chester Assumption pageant (discussed later in this chapter), Jeremy P. Goldberg also suggests a preexisting tradition in which wives or widows of guild members performed alongside men 'in truly amateur guild productions that ... were more normal in the later fourteenth or earlier fifteenth centuries', but acknowledges that the existence of such informal groups predating the later formalised guilds is speculative.[22] Matthew Sergi proposes the likelihood of 'ongoing participation of women in the Chester plays' and that Noah's wife and her Gossips 'seem likely to be women', but provides no archival detail to support his assertion 'that the Wives are active in procession or performance'.[23]

Many reasons have been given in explanation of why women did not perform in the Corpus Christi plays: that most craft guild members and the characters in the York cycle were men, that male choristers and clergy were responsible for singing the treble parts, and that women's voices could not be heard in open-air spaces have all been cited as reasons for women's absence from Corpus Christi plays.[24]

While the possibility of women performing remains conjectural, the list of Guilds for 1499–1500 and Chester's Pre-Reformation or early Banns (1539–40) record a lost Chester pageant of 'our Lady thassumpcion' that was once part of the city's Corpus Christi play, and which definitively associates the city's wives and widows with civic, public, theatrical performance:

> The wurshipfull wyffys of this towne
> ffynd of our Lady thassumpcion
> It to bryng forth they be bowne
> And meytene with all theyre might.[25]

By the Reformation the Chester Cycle had been moved to Whitsuntide, and all mention of 'our Lady thassumpcion', along with its text, had disappeared. The 'wurshipfull wyffys' were most probably the spouses and widows of the small group of merchant families who held the main civic offices in Chester throughout the later fourteenth and earlier fifteenth centuries. Capable of taking on what would have been a significant financial obligation, these prominent women would have paid for commissioning the script and the pageant's associated expenses: the acquisition and maintenance of props and costume, and payment of musicians and actors.

Also important in assessing the significance of women's association with Chester's 'Assumption' is its performance history. The 'Assumption' was performed at High Cross in 1489/90 before Sir George Stanley, ninth Baron Strange of Knockin, Shropshire (1460–1503), stepbrother of Henry VII, and a decade later at the gates of St Werberg's Abbey in North Street in honour of the royal visit to the city by Henry VII's heir, the fourteen-year-old Prince Arthur, who had been made Earl of Chester in 1489.[26] The 'Assumption' was deliberately selected due to its possessing 'some spectacular dramatic effect'.[27] Its place of performance was also significant. Viewing the 'Assumption' at High Cross offered Sir George Stanley a clear overview of this Marcher city's juridical and economic centres (the Pentice and the Rows). Performance of the 'Assumption' in honour of Prince Arthur at the Abbey gate offered the prince drama played out before a backdrop of the Assumption that was itself 'the subject of the entire West Front of St Werburgh [sic]'.[28] Housing the shrine and relics of Chester's patron saint, herself the daughter of royalty, and as the burial location of the Anglo-Norman earls of Chester, the Abbey of St Werberg demonstrated to Chester's young earl the power and status of the Church within this walled city.

Further brief, tantalising, and invaluable references to secular women's association with liturgical, civic, and hagiographical drama survive in a variety of records demonstrating that Chester's wives were not alone in their dramatic endeavours. In York, women in the Drapers' Guild (responsible for the pageant of 'The Death of the Virgin') contributed to the pageant expenses.[29] The Records of the Chester Innkeepers, the guild responsible for 'The Harrowing of Hell', note payment in 1585/6 to 'the Wydowe Ellis fro iii yerdes of fringe the some of xvj d' for a banner that was then sewn by the unnamed wife of Thomas Poole.[30] Women were particularly resourceful – and necessary – in providing costumes for the female leads in performances.

In the Coventry Cycle, a woman was responsible for attiring Pilate's wife. In 1487, the Smiths' accounts for their now lost 'Passion of Christ' record payment to 'Maisturres Grymesby' of xiid 'for lendyng off her geir is ffor pylatts wife'.[31] The Smiths' Guild included not only blacksmiths but also goldsmiths, so we might conjecture that Mistress Grimsby was the wife of a goldsmith and that her 'geir', a dress or robe, would have been of suitable quality for Procula, wife of the prefect of Judea; as much is suggested by the insurance of 12d that its owner is paid for the loan of the gown. A communar's or administrator's account of 1470/1 from Wells Cathedral records payment of seven pence to Christine Handon for 'tinctura & factura dictorum indumentorum' (tinctures and robes) that Handon appears to have sourced for the 'Three Marys play'.[32] The reference to 'tinctures' suggests a dyeing agent or pigment, used here most probably for fabric for costumes. In 1504 Agnes Burton, wife of Richard, of Taunton, bequeathed 'vnto the said Sépulcre service there [of St Mary Magdalene Church, Taunton] my rede damaske mantell & my mantell lined with silke that I was professed yn to thentent [for the purpose] of Mary Magdaleyn play'.[33] Her will describes the gift of two cloaks, one of which Agnes wore when she took a vow of celibacy, that, after her death, were be worn by two of the Marys in the 'Mary Magdaleyn play'.

The examples from Wells and Taunton may have been to liturgical drama associated with the Easter week services as at Barking, but what is referred to might equally be drama distinct from liturgical celebration: a saint's play, such as that presenting the life of Mary Magdalene which has survived from late fifteenth-century East Anglia. The Digby *Mary Magdalene* (Oxford, Bodleian Library, MS Digby 133) dramatises the life of Mary Magdalene, the daughter of a well-to-do family who forgoes the life of concupiscence into which she has been tempted to become a desert contemplative.[34] Having atoned for her former sin, on her death Mary

Magdalene joins the company of heavenly virgins. Theresa Coletti notes the demands required to stage this play:

> The play is remarkably spectacular. It provides for frequent journeying of human and divine messengers, sudden appearances and disappearances of Jesus on earth and in heaven, a cloud that descends from on high to set a pagan temple on fire, and seven devils that 'devoyde' (l. 691, s.d.) from Mary during the feast at the home of Simon the Pharisee. A floating ship crosses the playing space with saintly and regal cargo; Jesus orders visionary appearances of Mary and attendant angels; the saint is elevated into the clouds for daily feedings with heavenly manna.[35]

The Digby *Magdalene* is no minor theatrical endeavour, requiring a cast of more than sixty in which women are central. Mary Magdalene, her sister, Martha, the Queen of Marseilles, Mary Jacobe, and Mary Salome (in the *Visitatio Sepulchri* tradition), and the allegorical Lechery (of the Seven Deadly sins), frequently personified as female, and described in the Digby *Mary Magdalene* as 'flowyr fayrest of femynyté' (l. 423), all play significant roles and dominate the playing space. Coletti advises that 'we should not entirely rule out the possibility of women performing on the Digby *Magdalene*'s stage'.[36] Persuasive as this suggestion is, it remains conjectural.

Confirmation exists of women taking significant parts in the static *tableaux vivantes* of pageantry, 'as honorands, as makers and as performers' in royal entries such as that given in honour of Margaret of Anjou's entry into Coventry in 1456.[37] The event celebrated Margaret's roles as wife of King Henry VI and mother of Prince Edward with a pageant of the cardinal virtues and another devoted to St Margaret slaying the dragon. As in the drama that Hildegard of Bingen created for her sisters, in welcoming Margaret of Anjou to their city women took the parts of the cardinal virtues (prudence, temperance, fortitude, and justice) and, on this royal occasion, Queen Margaret's own namesake, the dragon-dispatching, patron saint of childbirth, St Margaret.

Prudence welcomes Margaret as a queen and mother of an heir who will restore peace to England (at this point Henry VI was a prisoner of the Yorkists, having been captured at the first Battle of St Albans):

> Welcum you dame margarete queen crowned of this lande
> The blessyd babe þat ye haue born Prynce Edward is he
> Thurrowe whom pece & tranquilite shall take þis reme on hand
> We shall endowe both you & hym clerely to vnderstonde
> We shall preserue you personally & neuer fro you disseuer
> doute not princes most excellent we iiij shall do oure deuer.[38]

Prudence promises to preserve Margaret's wellbeing and that of her three-year old son, Edward of Westminster, heir to Henry VI. Margaret of Anjou witnessed the pageant of St Margaret slaying the dragon, with the saint surrounded by an assembly of young girls ('[she] was arayed right well with as mony Virgyns as myght be þervppon') as she addressed the Queen:

> Most notabull princes of Wymen erthle
> Dame margaret þe chefe myrth of þis empyre
> ye be hertely welcum to þis cyte
> To the plesur of your highnes I wyll sette my desyre
> Bothe nature & gentilnes doth me require
> Seth we be both of one name to shewe you kyndnes
> Wherfore by my power ye shall 'haue' no distresse.[39]

St Margaret promises to intercede for Margaret's protection and offers personal protection to the queen. Such intercession was timely since in 1456 Henry VI was mentally incapacitated, imprisoned, and rumoured not to be the prince's father, at the moment when Richard Plantagenet, Duke of York, made a competing claim to the throne.

Women indubitably made a significant contribution to the production of medieval drama in its broadest sense. Under the protection of its Abbess and with her support, ironically, convent walls may have offered its inmates greater freedom to compose drama and to perform liturgical celebrations, saints' plays, and allegorical drama. As Matthew Cheung-Salisbury, Liv Robinson, and Elisabeth Dutton suggest, 'While convent plays share their Scriptural sources with civic drama, they differ in giving a greater role to women when translating the masculine-dominated stories of the Latin Vulgate', because convents exist outside 'the influence of civic authorities for whom public playing was an opportunity for the display of power and prestige'.[40]

The spectacle of a motionless woman embodying and voicing one of the virtues in a *tableau vivant* appears to have caused little concern. In such *tableaux* women's bodies and voices present controlled and scripted allegories of virtue, not the outspoken, unpredictable, somatically leaky, and vice-prone creatures that medieval misogyny considered women at their worst to be, many of whom feature in the Corpus Christi plays. One need only recall Mrs Noah, Gyl in the Wakefield 'Second Shepherds' Pageant', and the *mulier* who is a brewer and tapster condemned to hell for cheating her customers in Chester's 'Harrowing of Hell', for examples of these 'unruly' women. The containment of the female form and voice in the *tableaux vivantes* might well have played a part in the acceptance of this kind of female performance.

Absence of evidence is not necessarily evidence of absence, however, and the possibility remains that women may have performed in the Corpus Christi plays that portrayed a broad spectrum of womanhood in terms of virtue, vice, social class, age, and sexuality.

Medieval drama brought to life the history of human salvation, dramatised the lives of saints, celebrated the entry of monarchs into their cities, and provided valuable lessons in how to live virtuously in this life in preparation for the next. The evidence that survives of this ephemeral medium, frustratingly fragmentary as it is, suggests, nonetheless, that the medieval stage – in its various forms – was not the sole preserve of men. As composers, commissioners, sponsors, wardrobe mistresses, and performers, women featured among the *dramatis personae* of medieval drama and made a significant contribution to performances that entertained, inspired devotion, and instructed in how to obtain salvation during the premodern period.

Notes

1. J. Wickham Legg (ed.), *The Processional of the Nuns of Chester*, Henry Bradshaw Society (London: Harrison, 1899), 7.
2. Eamon Duffy, *The Stripping of the Altars: Traditional Religion in England 1400–1580* (New Haven, CT: Yale University Press, 1992), 28.
3. Jody Enders, 'Critical Stages edited by Mike Sell', *Theatre Survey* 50.2 (2009), 317–25 (319).
4. Phillip Butterworth, *Staging Convention in Medieval English Theatre* (Cambridge: Cambridge University Press, 2014), 1.
5. Olivia (Liv) Robinson and Elisabeth Dutton, 'Drama, performance and touch in the medieval convent and beyond', in *Touching, Devotional Practice and Visionary Experience in the Late Middle Ages*, ed. David Carrillo-Rangel, Delfi Isabel Nieto, and Pablo Acosta Garcia (London: Palgrave Macmillan, 2020), 43–68 (47, n. 9).
6. Katie Normington, *Gender and Medieval Drama* (Cambridge: D. S. Brewer, 2004), 5.
7. Anne Bagnall Yardley and Jesse D. Mann (ed. and trans.), *The Liturgical Dramas for Holy Week at Barking Abbey*, Medieval Feminist Forum, Subsidia Series, vol. 3 (2014), 4.
8. Yardley and Mann, *Liturgical Dramas*, 4.
9. Yardley and Mann, *Liturgical Dramas*, col. 25.
10. R. R. Sharpe (ed.), *Calendar of Wills Proved and Enrolled in the Court of Husting, London: Part 2, 1358–1688* (London: Her Majesty's Stationery Office, 1890), 155.
11. Sharpe (ed.), *Calendar of Wills*, 155.
12. Yardley and Mann, *Liturgical Dramas*, cols. 24 and 26.

13. Yardley and Mann, *Liturgical Dramas*, col. 29.
14. Yardley and Mann, *Liturgical Dramas*, col. 29.
15. Robinson and Dutton, 'Drama, Performance and Touch', 63.
16. Stephanie Hollis, 'The Literary Culture of the Anglo-Saxon Royal Nunneries: Romsey and London, British Library, MS Lansdowne 436', in *Nuns' Literacies in Medieval Europe: The Hull Dialogue*, ed. Virginia Blanton, Veronica O'Mara, and Patricia Stoop (Turnhout: Brepols, 2013), 169–84.
17. Christopher Marie St John (ed.), *The Plays of Roswitha* (London: Chatto & Windus, 1923), xxix. See also Christiania Whitehead, Chapter 12 in this volume.
18. Albrecht Classen, 'Sex on the Stage (and in the Library) of an Early Medieval Convent: Hrotsvit of Gandersheim, a Tenth-Century Convent Playwright's Successful Competition Against the Roman Poet Terence,' *Orbis Litterarum* 65.3 (2010), 167–200 (169).
19. Richard Axton, *European Drama of the Early Middle Ages* (London: Hutchinson University Library, 1974), 95.
20. Peter Dronke, *Poetic Individuality in the Middle Ages: New Departures in Poetry 1100–1150* (Oxford: Oxford University Press, 1970), 170.
21. James Stokes, 'Women and Mimesis in Medieval and Renaissance Somerset (and Beyond)', *Comparative Drama*, 27.2 (1993), 176–96.
22. P. J. P. Goldberg, *Women in England c. 1275–1525* (Manchester: Manchester University Press, 1995), 45, n. 84.
23. Matthew Sergi, *Practical Cues and Social Spectacle in the Chester Plays* (Chicago: University of Chicago Press, 2020), 150–1.
24. See Glynne Wickham, *The Medieval Theatre* (Cambridge: Cambridge University Press, 1987), 93–4.
25. Lawrence M. Clopper (ed.), *Records of Early Drama: Chester* (Toronto: University of Toronto Press, 1979), 85.
26. Clopper (ed.), *Records of Early English Drama*, xlviii.
27. Clopper (ed.), *Records of Early English Drama: Chester*, xlvii.
28. Theodore Lerud, *Memory, Images and the English Corpus Christi Drama* (New York: Palgrave Macmillan, 2008), 135.
29. Alexandra F. Johnson and Margaret Rogerson (eds.), *Records of Early English Drama: York*, vol. 1 (Toronto: University of Toronto Press, 1979), 231.
30. Lawrence M. Clopper (ed.), *Records of Early English Drama: Chester*, 209.
31. R. W. Ingram, *Records of Early English Drama: Coventry* (Toronto: University of Toronto Press, 1981), 69.
32. James Stokes (ed.), *Records of Early English Drama: Somerset* (Toronto: University of Toronto Press, 1996), 495.
33. Stokes (ed.), *Records of Early English Drama: Somerset*, 495.
34. Theresa Coletti (ed.), *The Digby Mary Magdalene Play* (Kalamazoo, MI: Medieval Institute Publications, 2018), 'Introduction': d.lib.rochester.edu/te ams/text/coletti-the-digby-mary-magdalene-introduction.
35. Coletti (ed.), *The Digby Mary*, 'Introduction'. Published online at https://d.lib .rochester.edu/teams/text/coletti-the-digby-mary-magdalene-introduction.

36. Coletti (ed.), *The Digby Mary*, 'Introduction'. Published online at https://d.lib.rochester.edu/teams/text/coletti-the-digby-mary-magdalene-play.
37. Nicola Coldstream, 'The Roles of Women in Late Medieval Civic Pageantry in England', in *Reassessing the Roles of Women as 'Makers' of Medieval Art and Architecture*, ed. Therese Martin (Leiden: Brill, 2012), 175–96 (175).
38. Mary Dormer Harris (ed.), *The Coventry Leet Book*, Part 1 (London: Kegan Paul, Trench, Trubner, 1907), 288–9.
39. Harris (ed.), *The Coventry Leet Book*, 292.
40. Matthew Cheung-Salisbury, Elisabeth Dutton, and Olivia (Liv) Robinson, 'Medieval Convent Drama: Translating Scripture and Transforming the Liturgy', in *A Companion to Medieval Translation*, ed. Janet Beer (Leeds: Arc Humanities Press, 2019), 63–74 (63).

Further Reading

Bagnall Yardley, Anne, and Jesse D. Mann (2014). *The Liturgical Dramas for Holy Week at Barking Abbey*, Medieval Feminist Forum, Subsidia Series, vol. 3, Medieval Texts in Translation 1, pp. 1–41, available online at https://scholarworks.wmich.edu/cgi/viewcontent.cgi?article=1985&context=mff.

Classen, Albrecht (2010). 'Sex on the Stage (and in the Library) of an Early Medieval Convent: Hrotsvit of Gandersheim, a Tenth-Century Convent Playwright's Successful Competition Against the Roman Poet Terence'. *Orbis Litterarum* 65.3, 167–200.

Clopper, Lawrence M., ed. (1979). *Records of Early English Drama: Chester*, Toronto: University of Toronto Press.

Coldstream, Nicola (2012). 'The Roles of Women in Late Medieval Civic Pageantry in England'. In *Reassessing the Roles of Women as 'Makers' of Medieval Art and Architecture*, ed. Therese Martin. Leiden: Brill, 175–96.

Coletti, Theresa, ed. (2018). *The Digby Mary Magdalene Play*, Kalamazoo: Medieval Institute Publications.

Johnson, Alexandra F., and Margaret Rogerson, eds. (1979). *Records of Early English Drama: York*, vol. 1, Toronto: University of Toronto Press.

Normington, Katie (2004). *Gender and Medieval Drama*, Cambridge: D. S. Brewer.

Robinson, Olivia (Liv), and Elisabeth Dutton (2020). 'Drama, performance and touch in the medieval convent and beyond'. In *Touching, Devotional Practice and Visionary Experience in the Late Middle Ages*, ed. David Carrillo-Rangel, Delfi Isabel Nieto, and Pablo Acosta Garcia. London: Palgrave Macmillan, 43–68.

Sergi, Matthew (2020). *Practical Cues and Social Spectacle in the Chester Plays*, Chicago: University of Chicago Press.

St John, Christopher Marie, ed. (1923). *The Plays of Roswitha*, London: Chatto & Windus.

CHAPTER 15

Women and Romance

Corinne Saunders

Romance has frequently been perceived as a 'woman's genre', female-centred, gendered feminine. Yet such perceptions are simplistic, indicative in part of reductive and post-medieval notions of romances as clichéd love stories.[1] Romance's connections with women in the medieval period are intimate but complex, reflecting the variety and fluidity of the genre itself. The French writers of the twelfth century were not consciously developing a genre, but rather rendering familiar story matter in their vernacular language, *romanz*, in the light of new cultural interests in chivalry, courtliness, and the individual. To classical and historical subjects, they added the 'matter of Britain' – in particular, legends of King Arthur and the Round Table – and to an emphasis on military exploits, a focus on emotional experience and the inner life. By the late thirteenth century, when romance began to be written in English, the genre had become familiar, its conventions readily recognisable. English romance answered to the demand for imaginative literature from non-courtly audiences who did not read French, the country gentry and the new merchant class, and hence may be seen as more 'popular' in its concerns, though, despite frequent references to minstrels, audiences, and music, suggesting orality, English romance writers are most often adapting French and Anglo-Norman written texts.[2] Romances are most obviously linked by the motifs or, as Helen Cooper has recently termed them, 'memes' that form their backbone: exile and return; love, quest, and adventure; family, name, and identity; pagan and Christian.[3]

While recent scholarship has primarily adopted a mimetic approach to romance, it may also be seen in terms of its deep structures and transhistorical themes: growing up, separation from and return to the family, the journey, testing and adventure, romantic love, and identity. Northrop Frye in *The Secular Scripture* identified powerful recurrent patterns characteristic of literary works from the *Odyssey* onwards: the development of the hero and the winning of the heroine, the great cycles of life and death, the ideal, and the ascent or descent to 'otherworlds'.[4] In the seasonal cycle within which Frye conceives of the relation of fundamental literary modes (autumn/tragedy, winter/irony and satire, spring/comedy), romance, as the mythos of summer, leads from order through darkness, winter, and death, to rebirth, new order, and maturity. Adventure is central, as is the quest, the movement through conflict and struggle to self-realisation. Romance also, however, engages acutely with the pressing social concerns of its writers and readers. Erich Auerbach interprets the archetypal pattern of medieval romance, the movement from court to forest, 'setting forth' in search of adventure, in socio-cultural terms, as engaging with and shaping the values of the new, chivalric class of twelfth-century France.[5] Susan Crane persuasively places English medieval romance as growing out of and reflecting the conservative social concerns of the baronial classes.[6] Romances provide entertainment but also offer serious moral and ethical messages and speak to individual fears and desires, sometimes in radically experimental ways.

What was the social relation of women readers to romance? Women were patrons, owners, occasional writers, and, most of all, readers of books.[7] As well as the close and productive connection between women and devotional writing,[8] as a number of essays in this volume show, it is clear that there was an intimate connection between women and secular literature in medieval England and on the Continent. It is not coincidental that of the two twelfth-century writers whose names survive and who were largely responsible for shaping the genre of courtly romance, one was a woman, Marie de France (see Emma Campbell, Chapter 18 in this volume). Denis Piramus' description of the pleasure taken by women in her *lais*, 'De joie les oient e de gré, / Qu'il sunt sulum lir volenté' (They listen to them joyfully and willingly, / For they are just what they desire), provides one perspective.[9] That Marie probably wrote for the English court of Henry II (1154–89) may reflect the taste of Henry's queen, Eleanor of Aquitaine, a celebrated patron of the arts, 'at [whose] court the move from history-writing to the composition of romances was first made'.[10] Chrétien de Troyes' *Le Chevalier de la Charrete*, the first work to narrate the love of Lancelot and Guinevere, is presented as written in direct response to the request of Eleanor of Aquitaine's daughter, Marie de Champagne. Three centuries later, Caxton, in his prologue to *Blanchardyn and Eglantine*, states that he has translated it at the 'commandement' of Margaret Beaufort, who was most associated with religious books.[11] The prologue, as Amy Vines suggests, indicates 'the function romance should serve in the life of the reader', aligning it with rather than setting it in opposition to didactic works.[12]

Evidence concerning the part played by romances in medieval women's literary culture, however, is not clear cut. Carol Meale observes that romances, particularly French Arthurian romances, 'form the second largest generic grouping amongst women's books in the Middle Ages as a whole'.[13] Meale offers a series of instances of fourteenth- and fifteenth-century English women known to have owned the romances of Lancelot and Tristan, from Isabel, Duchess of York, who left to her son her 'launcelot', to Elizabeth Darcy, whose husband bequeathed her his 'Launselake' in 1411, to Elizabeth of York, whose signature occurs on a manuscript of the Prose *Tristan*.[14] Chaucer's 'Nun's Priest's Tale' gestures more ironically to the phenomenon, in his reference to 'the book of Launcelot de Lake, / That wommen holde in ful greet reverence'.[15] Internal evidence implies that romances were read aloud in courtly circles and aristocratic households to mixed audiences, as well as by individual male and female readers. As Sarah McNamer notes, English romances are repeatedly addressed to male audiences, 'Lordingis', 'werthy men', but also to mixed audiences.[16] The depiction in Chaucer's *Troilus* of Criseyde and her women listening to a maiden read the tale of the siege of Thebes offers a tantalising image of a group of female readers (II.80–109). While aristocratic women were clearly engaged with French romance, there is considerably less evidence of women readers of English romance, perhaps reflecting its more 'popular' quality, and the interests of less aristocratic audiences in prowess and adventure rather than courtship and love. Romances known to have been owned by women represent only a 'small fraction' of the total, though, as we shall see, later romances are strongly engaged both with married women as models of active, virtuous suffering and with the figure of the enchantress.[17] McNamer, drawing on the work of Meale, identifies three manuscripts containing Middle English romances believed to have been compiled for women.[18] Intriguingly, a female context has also been suggested for the Auchinleck manuscript.[19] Were women authors of romances in this period? McNamer draws attention to the signatures by two women at the end of *Sir Degrevant*, contained in the Findern manuscript, celebrated for its connections with and perhaps compiled for women readers (see David Fuller, Chapter 11 in this volume). The names may suggest that the women copied the romance, or, even more tantalisingly, that they were themselves authors of a work that presents its three central women with animation and empathy, as lovers, intermediaries, and peace-weavers: 'at the very least, the presence of this text in the Findern manuscript testifies to the capacity of women to procure the kind of romance in which they could see their gender celebrated – even, in an era of romance's masculinization, against the odds'.[20] Yet, as Melissa Furrow suggests, the picture is complicated: 'romances were in the minority of what was read by men or women', and the manuscripts that contain them typically include other, in particular, pious works.[21]

The question of how women read is more complex still. D. H. Green's suggestive analysis of ways of reading distinguishes different kinds of 'literal reading': to the self or others, aloud or silently, in different languages, as a writer; but also different kinds of 'figurative reading': reading 'with the mind's eye in the absence of any material written text', reading pictures, memorised reading.[22] Reading is a creative act, in which the imagination plays a key role. This is especially true of reading and listening to literary works: reading provides ways of interpreting the world outside the text, and opens onto imaginative worlds. As Furrow emphasises, it is impossible to define a characteristic female reading of romance, for the stances of women readers, like those of men, are likely to have been as various as those of the works they read.[23] After Marie de France, there is no English equivalent to Christine de Pisan, whose works clearly respond to and challenge preconceptions of the genre.[24] Stories of adultery such as those of Lancelot and Guinevere and Tristan and Isolde, for example, must surely have attracted very different responses, from empathy to condemnation, as in almost any cultural context. The very material that thrilled some audiences may well have shocked others. Responses will have been shaped by social and intellectual contexts, individual experience, moral perspectives, and imaginative engagement. Nor is the question of what subjects and stories women engaged with straightforward: it would be reductive in the extreme, for instance, to assume they were interested only in narratives of empowered women or romantic love, or in situations that mirrored or positively rewrote their own. Women may have been at least as much interested in reading about men, and men about women. Men owned and bequeathed Arthurian romances; women including Anne Paston and Margaret Beaufort owned Lydgate's *Siege of Thebes* and *Troy Book*, for example.[25] If we cannot access the lived experience of medieval readers, we can consider the tapestries romances weave about women: their roles as subjects and objects, protagonists and antagonists; their social relations and predicaments; their agency, voices, and ethical concerns; their desires and fears; their thoughts and feelings – which, in turn, may suggest some of the affective qualities of romance reading for women. There is no single romance woman: romance is as multifarious as its readers will have been. At the same time, romances represent imaginative spaces to which women are central and in which the feminine plays critical roles. As Amy Vines suggests, romance is far from being simply 'escapist and wish-fulfilling': 'Of medieval genres, none provided more narrative possibility and agency for female characters, and, in turn, their female readers.'[26] This chapter explores three thematic emphases around which romance treatments of women weave: love and consent, virtuous suffering, and magic and enchantment. Examples are drawn from a range of Middle English romances, and from the grand tapestry of Malory's *Morte Darthur*.

Love and Consent

With some notable exceptions – in particular, the works of Chaucer (treated in this volume by Venetia Bridges; see Chapter 17) and *Sir Gawain and the Green Knight* – Middle English romance is less engaged than French romance with the probing of individual psychology. Nevertheless, the powerful agency of romance women continues to be demonstrated, though not always positively, through their roles as lovers, heroines, and enchantresses, while romance also continues to engage with the constraints on women. English narratives, like their French and Anglo-Norman predecessors, image both wishes and fears surrounding the female body. As the *lais* of Marie de France demonstrate, Anglo-Norman romance repeatedly presents women as actively wooing lovers, an emphasis sustained in Middle English romances.[27] The English *King Horn* (*c*. 1225) exemplifies this in the passion of the princess Rimenhild for Horn: 'Heo lovede so Horn child / That negh heo gan wexe wild'; she is startlingly direct, inviting him into her bedchamber and proposing marriage to him.[28] This work also explores the predicament of enforced marriage with immediacy.[29] Rimenhild's distress and resistance to her prospective wedding to King Modi of Reynes are vividly described:

> Ne mighte heo adrighe [forbear]
> That heo ne weop with ighe.
> Heo sede that heo nolde
> Ben ispused with golde ...   (ll. 1037–40)

She responds by concealing a knife in order to kill both Modi and herself. The narrative defends the woman's desire to choose her husband, but makes clear that winning her lands or the consent of her parents equates to the right to her person: Rimenhild's only recourse is to violence, and she is eventually saved by her true 'husebonde' (l. 1041), Horn. This problematisation of consent recurs in *Havelok the Dane* (*c*. 1300), often paired with *Horn*, though deploying considerably more material detail. Here, the wicked earl Godrich attempts to gain rule of all England by giving King Athelwold's daughter Goldborw to Havelok, apparently a peasant and cook's knave. Her fear and grief at the enforced marriage are acutely rendered:

> Sho was adrad for he [Godrich] so thrette,
> And durste nought the spusing lette;
> But they hire likede swithe ille,
> Sho thoughte it was Godes wille:
> God, that makes to growen the corn,
> Formede hire wimman to be born.³⁰ (ll. 1163–8)

The difference of class heightens the shame of the marriage. Arranged marriage is presented as an inevitable and tragic aspect of the female existence, a realistic possibility. In this romance, the punishment of rape is specified in the depiction of King Athelwold's 'gode lawes' (l. 28, ll. 83–6), which contrast starkly with Godrich's lawlessness, but Goldborw's resignation makes clear that such prohibitions are not directed to arranged marriage. Only providence may intervene, in this instance through the miraculous kinglight that proves Havelok's noble identity.

The later, dynastic romance of *Sir Beves of Hamtoun*, popular across Europe and well into the age of print, takes up this theme at more length. The narrative of Beves' exile and regaining of his rightful lands is interwoven with his adventures in the Middle East where Josian, the daughter of the king of Armenia, falls in love with him. She is startlingly forthcoming: 'Ichauede þe leuer to me lemman, / Þe bodi in þe scherte naked, / Þan al þe gold, þat Crist haþ maked'.³¹ Her offer to convert to Christianity, in the context of this Crusading narrative, proves the depth of her desire. Josian not only woos her chosen beloved, but also defends her chastity through a sequence of threats of enforced marriage, most remarkably when, in a narrative sequence recalling the story of Judith and Holofernes, she encourages the revelry of her new husband, Earl Miles, and then strangles and hangs him (in the Anglo-Norman and later English versions, by means of a slip-ring in her own girdle, emblem of her chastity).

Josian is distinguished by her learning, especially her sophisticated medical knowledge: 'While ȝhe was in Ermonie, / Boþe fysik and sirgirie / ȝhe hadde lerned of meisters grete' (ll. 3671–3). She is imagined as having access to an ancient, especially Arabic tradition of learned medicine, and as taught by practitioners from the great centres of medical learning, Bologna and Toledo. Though rare, the female physician is not a romance invention: records survive of female medical practitioners across Europe, and the medical school at Salerno was associated with the semi-legendary female healer Trota, said to have practised there in the twelfth century.[32] Josian's medical skills allow her to heal Beves' wounds with 'an oyniment' (l. 715) and 'riche baþes' (l. 732) that soon make him 'boþe hol and sonde' (l. 734), and later to act as her own midwife at the birth of her twins. Seized by a giant, she knows which herb to pick to transform her appearance to that of a leper, dramatically repelling the enemy king who pursues her. She also possesses a magic ring that preserves her chastity when she is married against her will. While Josian is extraordinary – an active lover, learned, skilled in the arts of medicine and natural magic – she is not entirely unique in romance.[33] The lady Felice in *Guy of Warwick*, for example, has been taught the seven arts by the monks of Toulouse, and her learning too is empowering: she repeatedly refuses Guy her hand in marriage until he shows his worth in a sequence of battles, and she eventually participates in his holy life.

As all these works suggest, however, romance is also deeply engaged with the lady's need for a defender and lord, if only to save her from other would-be defenders. Chrétien de Troyes' *Yvain* and its early fourteenth-century English rewriting, *Ywain and Gawain*, dramatise this problem in Laudine/Alundyne's decision to marry the killer of her husband. Her handmaiden Lunete offers a pragmatic choice:

> 'If twa knyghtes be in the felde
> On twa stedes, with spere and shelde,
> And the tane the tother may sla:
> Whether es the better of tha?'
> Sho said, 'He that has the bataile.'[34]

Alundyne's consideration of her predicament focuses not on feeling but on practical need, for a 'knyght, / Forto seke hir land thorghout, / To kepe Arthur and hys rowt' (ll. 1022–4). While Lunete manipulates Alundyne's fears to further Yvain's love, the narrative intimates the impossibility of independent female existence within the chivalric society depicted in romance: women cannot defend themselves, and there is no recourse against the man who wins the woman's person in battle.

Repeatedly, romance treats such situations in wish-fulfilment terms, where the defender is or becomes the lady's beloved. How did these imagined scenarios connect to lived experience? Consent was a complex issue. Women were governed by fathers and husbands. There was little private space and women enjoyed little public freedom, making modern notions of 'getting to know each other' unrealistic. The Church insisted on consensual marriage, taking up the Roman idea of the contract and the Christian notion of 'a spiritual bond between spouses'; clandestine marriages depended on the legal authority afforded to a consenting bond between spouses.[35] Yet, as Dyan Elliott emphasises, 'what constituted free consent would remain a problem throughout the Middle Ages'. There is no doubt that for aristocratic women marriages were political and economic, connecting family lands and fortunes. 'Consent' in marriage more generally may have been very much shaped by family wishes, which children were expected to obey: the case of Elizabeth Paston, confined to her room and beaten daily for opposing marriage to a widower thirty years older, offers a celebrated example of successful but perhaps rare resistance.[36] Cases of *raptus* (abduction) could be with the consent of the women, equating to elopements.[37] By contrast, while women may not usually have been in need of knightly protectors, as the Paston letters show, their lands could be under threat. For women readers, then, romance situations may have raised complex questions concerning consent, freedom to love, protection, and guardianship, as well as wishes and desires relating to romantic love.

Suffering Virtue

Romances also take up the patterns of hagiography in their portrayal of female models of active, suffering virtue, often in the secular contexts of married love and motherhood.[38] McNamer notes the shift in fourteenth-century English romances away from the emphasis on the wooing woman characteristic of earlier romances to an interest in this type of 'family' romance.[39] Particularly popular were tales of the calumniated queen or virtuous lady wrongly accused, as exemplified by the Constance story, versions of which are told by both Chaucer and Gower. Women model innocent suffering, their virtue put to the test by ill-wishing enemies, from would-be lovers to jealous husbands to malign mothers-in-law. *Sir Tryamowre* offers an archetypal example: its queen, Margaret of Aragon, is falsely accused of adultery by the steward whose advances she rejects, and banished although she is pregnant. Set against the dissembling of the steward is her natural and virtuous feeling, her swoon evoking pity both in the court and in the reader or listener. The death of her aged companion, Sir Roger, as he defends her from villainous attack, his faithful dog's guarding of his body, and her giving birth in the woods as she flees heighten the depiction of extreme suffering. Yet the emphasis is not on the queen's overwhelming grief but on her actions in comforting her child, her beauty and courtly virtues which make her beloved of the household of the knight who rescues her, and her instruction of her son, 'And [she] taght hum evyr newe'.[40] While the righting of wrongs is brought about by her son, she retains a powerful voice, giving him leave to depart and offering her blessing. When she and the king are brought to her son's court, her comment to the king is acute: 'Syr, ... / Sometyme was ye cowde me kenne, / And ye were well bethogt' (ll. 1645–7). The failure of visual perception highlighted by the queen recalls the earlier failure of moral perception in the king, in contrast to her own spiritual insight, reflected in her physical beauty.

Saintly figures, then, can be far from ciphers. *The Erle of Tolous* (c. 1400) offers an especially striking example of this story type. Here, great delicacy is required to protect the lady Beulybon, wife of the Emperor, and the Earl from the suspicion of illicit desire. The Emperor's misjudgements, exemplified in his battle against the Earl, are set against the Empress's clear moral judgements: 'Ye have the wronge and he the ryght'.[41] Similarly, corrupt and innocent love are set against each other: in contrast to the excessive love-sickness of the two knights who betray her, feeling is understated and honourable between the Earl and the Empress, blazoned in the account of her appearance in the chapel at his request: her jewelled, rich attire, beauty and angelic aspect, and the gift of the ring 'so free', given 'Yn ese of hym, and for no synne' (ll. 1023, 1025). The 'pyte' of the Earl (l. 915), by contrast to the Emperor's belief in the accusations, leads to his defence of her. The placing of feeling is careful: no affective detail is given regarding their eventual reunion and marriage once the Emperor has died, sustaining the focus on innocence, virtue in suffering, and pity, rather than illicit desire.

The closest analogue to the Constance story, *Emaré*, has at its heart the haunting image of Emaré on the sea, exiled by her father when she refuses his incestuous advances and then by her wicked mother-in-law. This work introduces a supernatural element in the exotic mantle that turns Emaré into a 'glysteryng thyng', 'non erdly thyng', a creature of faery.[42] The robe seems to make material the effects of desire, rendering Emaré what she seems in the eyes of the desirer. Emaré, like Queen Margaret in *Sir Tryamowre*, combines her 'karefull herte' and 'sykyng sore' (l. 676) with her 'meke and mylde' (l. 640) demeanour, praying and singing a lullaby to her child. And like the queen too, Emaré not only nurtures her infant but teaches him 'nortowre' (courtly behaviour, 731) as he grows older, just as she teaches fine needlework to Sir Kador's household. The cloth that renders her faery, which depicts and incites desire, is also the product of feminine skill and connected with courtly order: 'its shimmer', as A. C. Spearing suggests, is 'an expression of unresolved tensions within the patriarchal culture from which it emerged', including the disordering force of incestuous desire resisted by Emaré at the start.[43]

Like Shakespeare's romances later, these works chart the workings of traumatic actions and events on the virtuous women around whom they revolve and who are distinguished both by affect and action, figures of pathos and power, whose voices and images resonate across their narratives. They uphold Christian virtues and offer their readers powerful ethical models that complement the lives of the saints, in particular the *vitae* of the virgins and martyrs, with life-enhancing models, inhabiting more familiar, secular spheres, lived out in the context of those they love, husbands and children. The testing of the heroine proves Christian providence, but also offers paradigms of active, virtuous life in the context of adversity. Affect is extreme, yet interwoven with a sense of agency and with the shaping influence these women have on those around them.

Magic and Enchantment

The spheres of magic and enchantment have special associations with the feminine, in both positive and negative ways. Magic can afford women power of different kinds, both licit and illicit, but they can also be victims of its forces or of mysterious otherworldly powers, as in a series of Breton *lais*.[44] *Sir Degaré* recounts an otherworldly rape which is benignly rewritten as love in the reunion of Degaré's mother with her faery rapist. *Sir Gowther* deals with the frightening possibility that a rash word might summon the Devil, and with the possibility of demonic conception. *Sir Orfeo* reworks the Orpheus and Eurydice myth in its narrative of Heurodis' taking by the King of Faery. Her summons as she lies sleeping beneath an 'ympe-tre' is deeply sinister in its depiction of the invasion of the psyche by otherworldly forces.[45] She wakes to reveal that she has been bidden to accompany the King of Faery to his world: 'thou shalt with us go / And live with us evermo' (ll. 143–4). The violence of this command is marked by Heurodis' act of mutilation of her own body on awakening:

> She crid and lothly bere gan make;
> She froted hir honden and hir feet,
> And crached hir visage – it bled wete.
> Hir riche robe hie al to-rett
> And was reveysed out of hir wit. (ll. 54–8)

Despite the guard of Orfeo and a thousand armed knights, Heurodis is 'taken', spirited away. The violence of the act, although not sexual as in *Sir Degaré* and *Sir Gowther*, is made explicit in her own response.[46] That the King of Faery's actions are left unexplained compounds the eeriness of the narrative, as does the later depiction of the figures who inhabit the otherworld of faery, all seized in different forms of violent death or, like Heurodis, taken suddenly. In this work, gender relations are played out in the absolute power of the faery king over the human queen, and though Heurodis is ultimately won back by Orfeo, she is also written out of the story, which ends with the endorsement of the loyalty of Orfeo's steward and their reunion. This narrative of the taken, female body is unique in its play on nightmarish fears: its depiction of something akin to a psychotic break, its engagement with the sudden, violent horror of death and disappearance, and its evocation of the uncanny.

By contrast, *Sir Launfal*, which reworks and extends Marie de France's *Lanval*, depicts a powerful otherworldly woman in Tryamour, the daughter of the King of Faery, who seeks Launfal from afar and asserts her power over the human world, including Guinevere. The opulent material wealth and erotic love Tryamour offers make this a wish-fulfilment romance, but she is also a demanding mistress, in both her response to Launfal's breaking of the taboo and her punishment of Guinevere through blinding.[47] Her actions expose the failures of the ideal in Arthur's court, evident in the betrayal of the structures of largesse and in Guinevere's lechery. It is fitting that she resolves the great trial at the end of the tale, and that Launfal returns from her world once a year to challenge the best knights: she figures as the arbiter of the chivalric ideal. The violence and power of Tryamour also, however, signal the more ambiguous sides of the enchantress. In *Melusine*, for example, Melusine's love, generosity, and motherhood are set against the monstrous shape to which she is condemned when her husband breaks the taboo and sees her in dragon form, while the narrative remains troubled by the disfigurements and excesses of her children. The figure of the *lamia* – half woman, half serpent – may reflect male fears of female sexuality, but also suggests the complex blend of power and weakness, assertion and subjugation, that can distinguish female magic. This is more evident when the practitioners of magic are human.

The romance of *Partonope of Blois*, extant in two fifteenth-century versions, both finding their origins in versions of the late twelfth-century French *Partonopeus de Blois*, exemplifies this ambiguity: it is not coincidental that the French romance is likely to have been composed for Eleanor of Aquitaine's daughter, Alix of France, at a time when the Blois dynasty had close connections with the English court, or that it is one of the romances known to have been owned by an English woman, Isabel Lyston of Norwich.[48] As Vines notes, the lady Melior is strikingly learned, employing the arts of 'nygromansy' to bring her beloved Partonope via a magical ship to what seems an enchanted country where she joins him in bed, 'for alle here delyte / And alle here plesaunce was hym to haue / To here husbande'.[49] Her pursuit is combined with reticence, but her shame and distress at Partonope's consummation of their love are rapidly reversed when she is revealed to be Queen of Byzantium, who has used her arts to ensnare him. Her magic is learned: her father, the Emperor of Constantinople, has had her schooled in the seven arts, medicine, divinity, and magic: 'Then to Nygromancy sette I was, / Then I lerned Enchawntementes / To knowe þe crafte of experimentes' (ll. 5933–5). Though the narrator emphasises Melior's Christianity, Partonope's mother fears her arts are demonic and uses her own magic to enable Partonope to break the taboo and see Melior's face. Eventually, after a long series of tests, the lovers are reunited, but we hear no more of Melior's magical abilities: she is drawn back into the more traditional stereotype of the woman as an object to be desired and possessed, celebrated for her beauty. Occult arts both empower and render vulnerable their possessors, and their potential for harm is strongly realised.

The fourteenth-century alliterative romance *William of Palerne*, said to have been commissioned by Sir Humphrey de Bohun, and derived from the French *Guillaume de Palerne* (*c*. 1200), offers a much more negative view of enchantment in its depiction of the destructive magical arts of Alphonse's stepmother, set against the limited and benign love-magic of the maidservant Alisandrine (an opposition not found in the French original).[50] Braunde employs forbidden learning to transform Alphonse into a wolf: 'For al þe werk of wicchecraft wel ynou3 che cou3þe; / nede nadde 3he namore of nigramauncy to lere' (ll. 118–19). This work perhaps reflects unease concerning female learning and the occult sciences more generally, while offering intriguing details of specialised rituals, including concoction of a magical ointment. Her 'healing' of the werewolf accords with the rituals set out in magical handbooks: a ring containing a stone of power is bound about the wolf's neck and a spell is read from a 'fair bok' kept safely in a casket (l. 4432). Braunde also, however, recognises the limits of human magic: 'ich forschop þe þanne / in þise wise to a werwolf and wend þe to spille; / but God wold nou3t þat þou were lorne' (ll. 4394–6). Magic offers powers of transformation and shape-shifting that to some extent align human practitioners of magic with otherworldly figures, but these arts are also treated with suspicion, their dangers evident and their extent limited. Magic is not exclusively the sphere of women in romance: clerics are most associated with these arts, as in Chaucer's 'Franklin's Tale', but they are certainly available to women, in relation to whom some of the same questions arise concerning the dangers of opposing providence.[51]

Sir Gawain and the Green Knight makes explicit the two faces of the otherworldly lady and the ambiguity of human practitioners of magic in its presentation of the beautiful Lady Bertilak and the loathly old woman, later revealed to be Morgan le Fay. As in *Partonope*, the lady who seems to invite courtly pursuit turns out to be firmly in control. The paradox is pointed up by the Lady's apparent invitation to rape: 'Me behouez of fyne force / Your seruaunt be, and schale'; 'ȝe ar stif innoghe to constrayne wyth strenkþe, ȝif yow lykez'.[52] The peculiar menace of her attempts to seduce Gawain, by contrast, is heightened by the interwoven narrative of Bertilak's hunt, which echoes the violence of the beheading at the start through the detailed images of chase, capture, and death in the successive hunts of deer, boar, and fox, and particularly in the graphic description of the dismemberment of the deer. The repeated metaphors of imprisonment, capture, and binding used by the Lady reiterate the theme of the hunt. The bedchamber scenes conceal a chase by the enchantress for her prey of a more threatening kind than in *Partonope*, setting Hautdesert, with its rival court presided over by Morgan le Fay, against Arthur's court at Camelot and pressing the chivalric code to its limits.

The conclusion, that all was effected by Morgan le Fay to frighten Guinevere, seems unsatisfying in its reductiveness. The poem's enigmatic power rests in part on the difficulty of categorising the supernatural, which seems at once divine, demonic, marvellous, and magical, and is focused in the ambiguous figure of the Green Knight. Yet this ambiguity is ultimately heightened by the image of the veiled, older lady in the shadows whose spells manipulate the whole and who, as 'Morgne þe goddes' (2452), also schooled in clerical arts by Merlin, is herself both otherworldly and human. The poem's actions are defined by the women who entangle Gawain in their net of seduction, their power invested in the feminine gift of the girdle, which is set against the masculine object of the Pentangle. Through them, the Christian virtues of chivalry are tested and found wanting against the human desire to preserve life.

Malory's *Morte Darthur*

Written on the cusp of the early modern period and printed by William Caxton in 1485, Malory's *Morte Darthur* (1469/70) offers a retrospective and summation of Arthurian romance, but is also, as Caxton's preface makes clear, embedded in the cultural concerns and values of its time. For Caxton, its message was ethical and educative: it is directed to 'al noble lordes and ladyes wyth al other estates, of what estate or degree they been of ... that they take the good and honest actes in their remembraunce, and to folowe the same'.[53] Malory's direct address to his audience also explicitly includes women: 'I praye you all jentylmen and jentylwymmen that redeth this book of Arthur and his knyghtes from the begynnyng to the endynge, praye for me' (XXI, explicit, 1260). Caxton's conclusion, directing the book 'unto alle noble pryncees, lordes, and ladyes, gentylmen or gentylwymmen', like Malory's phrasing, reiterates both the gender and range of his readership, reaching beyond the aristocracy to the gentry and merchant classes. The *Morte* is a 'book of arms', concerned with the practical living out of the bonds and conflicts between knights.[54] Its celebration of homosociality repeatedly casts women as dangerous, and it is desire for them that most threatens the stability of Arthur's realm, through the love affairs of Launcelot and Guinevere, Tristram and Isode, Lamorak and Morgause. It also, however, depicts women with complexity, empathy, and pathos. Their actions, positive and negative, exhibit power and agency even within a world of strongly patriarchal structures, and their voices resonate through the book. Queens, lovers, mothers, sisters, daughters – all have crucial roles to play, as does the mysterious network of enchantresses who inhabit the world beyond the court.

The book opens with Uther's begetting of Arthur on Igrayne, wife of Gorlois, Duke of Tintagel, through Merlin's shape-shifting. While the extraordinary is recounted with a matter-of-fact pragmatism, Malory also signals Igrayne's confusion and distress: 'But whan the lady herd telle of the duke her husband, and by all record he was dede or ever kynge Uther came to her, thenne she mervellied who that myghte be that laye with her in lykenes of her lord. So she mourned pryvely and held hir pees' (I.2, 9). Female emotions are silenced within the male chivalric world, and the emphasis is on public honour rather than on personal violation. Later, accused of causing 'mortall warrys' by concealing Arthur's identity (I.21, 45), Igrayne makes explicit her disempowerment: 'I saw the childe never aftir, nothir wote nat what ys hys name; for I knew hym never yette' (I.21, 45-6). Her role is that of onlooker – yet her voice is immediate.[55]

The defence of women plays a crucial role in the code of chivalry established by Arthur. The chivalric oath sworn by all the knights at Pentecost each year, one of Malory's most striking additions to his sources, presents the protection of women as a central tenet: 'allwayes to do ladyes, damesels, and jantilwomen and wydowes [socour:] strengthe hem in hir ryghtes, and never to enforce them, uppon payne of dethe' (I.15, 120). Throughout the rest of the *Morte*, the protection of women from violence functions as a leitmotif, epitomised early on in Arthur's defeat of the giant of Mont-Saint-Michel, whose crimes include the rape and murder of the Duchess of Brittany. The other side of the equation, however, is the custom of Logres: that a knight who wins a lady through battle has the right to her person.[56] Episodes recur in which women figure as objects who are to be fought over and won by the male brotherhood, causes for male rivalry. Within a world where might is firmly equated with right, the new mode of courtesy and protection is repeatedly set against an ethic based on force. The focus of the story of Gareth, probably Malory's invention, becomes the possibility of marriage based on active mutual consent. Here the Red Knight enlists the power of military victory to claim Lyonesse: 'she is my lady, and for hir I have done many stronge batayles' (VII.16, 321). For Gareth, by contrast, these battles indicate precisely that she is not the Red Knight's lady: 'For and I undirstoode that she were nat ryght glad of my commynge I wolde be avysed or I dud batayle for hir; but I undirstonde by the segynge of this castell she may forbere thy felyshyp' (I.16, 322). Lyonesse herself articulates the need for active consent and love: 'he attendyth unto nothyng but to murther, and that is the cause I can nat prayse hym nother love hym' (VII.14, 318). Despite Gareth's claims that he has won Lyonesse's love lawfully in defeating her attacker, Lyonesse sends him away so that she may assure herself of his identity and general worthiness, while her sister Lynette intervenes through magical illusion to stop the couple from sleeping together before their marriage.

If this episode advocates the moderation of 'hoote lustis' (VII.22, 333) and their absorption within the social structures of consensual marriage, much of the rest of the *Morte* is structured by uncontrolled sexual desire. In the central Tristram section, adulterous love forms a counterpoint to the chivalric quest. The love of Tristram and La Beale Isode, like that of Launcelot and Guinevere, is treated empathetically by Malory: it is natural, enhanced by but not caused by the potion, and it precedes King Mark's command to Tristram to win Isode for him. Malory carefully realises the movement of affect in Isode: 'And there Tramtryste lerned hir to harpe and she began to have a grete fantasy unto hym' (VIII.9, 385). While much in these books is devoted to the adventures and battles of Tristram and the other great Arthurian knights, the responses of ladies, both in word and in feeling, provide a counterpoint and commentary. A letter from Isode to Tristram memorably implies a sense of courtly community: 'there be within this londe but foure lovers, and that is sir Launcelot and dame Gwenyver, and sir Trystrames and quene Isode' (VIII.31, 425). Yet adultery creates a menacing undercurrent throughout: Tristram is pursued and threatened by King Mark, and the books circle around his repeated battles with his dark counterpart, Palomides, the Saracen knight also in love with Isode. Ultimately, Tristram's death will occur when he is treacherously killed by Mark's knights as he sits harping in front of Isode. In the same way, his frequent companion and equal in chivalric greatness, Lamorak, is pursued by Gawain and his brothers and killed treacherously for his affair with their mother, Queen Morgause of the Orkneys. Adultery is not condemned, but its dangers are acutely evident.

Within the male structures of the chivalric world, the arts of enchantment offer a crucial means of female empowerment, and the work suggests a female network of both benign and malign practitioners of magic who inhabit the Arthurian world beyond the court, their arts complementing and sometimes interweaving with the disruptions of desire.[57] The arts of the Lady of the Lake span natural magic and more ambiguous enchantments, including the marvel of the sword held by a mysterious 'arme clothed in whyght samyte' (I.25, 52). At the first appearance of Nenyve, 'one of the damesels of the Lady of the Laake' (IV.1, 125), sometimes herself termed the Lady of the Lake, we are reminded that she is the same lady who 'put Merlyon undir the stone' (IV.9, 142, original to Malory). Yet Nenyve and her damsels appear at crucial moments across the narrative, usually to endorse Arthur's rule and defend right: 'ever she ded grete goodnes unto kynge Arthure and to all hys knyghtes thorow her sorsery and enchauntementes' (XVIII.8, 1059, Malory's addition). Her inverse is Morgan le Fay, 'the false sorseres and wycche moste that is now lyvyng' (VIII.34, 430).[58] Malory emphasises Morgan's learned arts rather than her otherworldly nature: she 'was put to scole in a nonnery, and ther she lerned so moche that she was a grete clerke of nygromancye' (I.2, 10), a term that in the *Morte* signals harmful magic. As Arthur's half-sister, she has her own rival court and is established as his great opponent: he is 'the man in the worlde that she hatyth moste, because he is moste of worship and of prouesse of ony of hir bloode' (IV.11, 145). As well as attempting to destroy Arthur, for example by the theft of Excalibur, and set up her own lover, Accolon, against him, Morgan employs her arts of shape-shifting, illusion, and enchantment; and her ability to cause illness and cure are deployed against female rivals and other Arthurian knights, in particular Launcelot, as when 'quenys sorserers foure' (VI.18, 287) discover him sleeping:

'I shall put an inchauntement uppon hym that he shall nat awake of all this seven owres, and than I woll lede hym away unto my castell. And whan he is surely within my holde, I shall take the inchauntement frome hym, and than lette hym chose whych of us he woll have unto paramour.' (VI.3, 256)

Enchantment affords power over bodies and presents a means of inflicting physical harm, aligning its practitioners with figures such as Sir Tarquin, who imprisons knights, and Sir Perys de Forest Sauvage, who rapes ladies. The most sinister threat to the body is presented by 'Hallewes the Sorseres, lady of the castell Nygurmous' (VI.15, 281), a figure not found in the French prose *Lancelot*, perhaps with her origins in the thirteenth-century French *Perlesvaus*.[59] In Hellawes' dark arts, sex and death are equated in a highly threatening way as her wish for revenge on the Round Table merges with the desire to possess Launcelot's body dead if she cannot have it alive: 'Than wolde I have bawmed hit and sered hit, and so to have kepte hit my lyve dayes; and dayly I sholde have clypped the and kyssed the, dispyte of quene Gwenyvere' (VI.15, 281). Enchantment replaces physical force, and traditional gender roles are reversed. Despite her magical powers, however, the woman becomes the victim: Hallewes dies of unrequited love within a fortnight. The dubious arts of the enchantress are rewritten in the Quest of the Sankgreall, in which the Grail Knights encounter a series of demonic temptresses, against whom is set Sir Perceval's virginal, nun-like sister, who sacrifices her life to save that of another lady in emulation of Christ's sacrifice for sinful man. The ambiguity with which occult arts practised by women are treated in romance, then, is sustained and heightened by Malory, perhaps reflecting increasing fears of witchcraft in the period. Yet, as in *Sir Gawain and the Green Knight*, enchantment also offers agency in a patriarchal world, complicating assumptions concerning the equation of might and right and weaving a network of power that can manipulate and threaten the ethical structures of Logres.

The love of Launcelot and Guinevere is central to the downward spiral of destiny by which the last books are structured. Increasingly problematic, it is also treated by Malory in notably more positive terms than in his French sources. The existential questions raised by love are memorably focused in the narrative of the tragic love of Elaine of Astolat for Launcelot. Malory emphasises the virtue and eligibility of Elaine, and the misfortune that Launcelot cannot love her, while Elaine, overcome by her passion, is as frank a wooing lover as Rimenhild or Josian: 'have mercy uppon me, and suffir me nat to dye for youre love' (XVIII.19, 1089). Launcelot's material offer of an immense dowry is opposed by the affect of Elaine's physical response, her shrill shrieks and swoons. Her defence of her right to love Launcelot, however, is extraordinary in its rational power and animation: 'Why sholde I leve such thoughtes? Am I nat an erthely woman? And all the whyle the brethe ys in my body I may complayne me, for my belyve ys that I do none offence, though I love an erthely man, unto God; for he fourmed me thereto, and all maner of good love comyth of God' (XVIII.19, 1093). Malory, like Tennyson after him, makes the most of the pictorial drama of Elaine's corpse, dressed in rich clothes and floating down the Thames in a barge covered with black samite: 'And she lay as she had smyled' (XVIII.20, 1096). The episode portrays love as a natural, virtuous, and inevitable emotion – but also as deeply destructive. Launcelot articulates to Guinevere the impossibility of manipulating love, which 'muste only aryse of the harte selff, and nat by none constraynte' (XVIII.20, 1097). At the end of Book XVIII, Malory takes up these themes of freedom and stability to make his strongest defence of the love of Launcelot and Guinevere. In the context of the month of May, he contrasts true and 'unstable love', destroyed with 'a lytyll blaste of wyntres rasure' (XVIII.25, 1119). Guinevere is the exemplar of steadfast love: 'whyle she lyved she was a trew lover, and therefor she had a good ende' (XVIII.25, 1120). Marriage in the *Morte* is not necessarily equated to love: it is political, economic, and public rather than coinciding with individual desire. The potential tension between love and marriage must have resonated with at least some of the book's female readers. For Malory, it is not sinfulness but the unhappy configuration of tensions surrounding the love of Arthur and Guinevere and the making public of what should remain private that eventually causes the destruction of the Arthurian world.

Passion is shadowed by violence and tragedy throughout the last books, as Launcelot's defences of Guinevere become more and more problematic. Guinevere, most often portrayed as a demanding figure, becomes an object, fought over, rescued from death by burning, restored to Arthur at the command of the Pope, threatened by Mordred with enforced marriage. Yet her response is forceful: she flees to the Tower, and, after the last battle, she steals away to the abbey of Amesbury to live in penance, 'a nunne in whyght clothys and blak', her role as queen replaced by that of 'abbas and rular, as reson wolde' (XXI.7, 1249). It is Guinevere's active choice to adopt a holy life that triggers Launcelot's penance. Her words, articulating both responsibility and grief, are as remarkable as Elaine's in their agency and immediacy:

'Thorow thys same man and me hath all thys warre be wrought, and the deth of the most nobelest knyghtes of the worlde; for thorow oure love that we have loved togydir ys my moste noble lorde slayne. Therefore, sir Launcelot, wyte thou well I am sette in suche a plyght to gete my soule hele.' (XXI.9, 1252)

Characteristically, she questions Launcelot's promise to follow her: 'I may never beleve you ... but that ye woll turne to the worlde agayne' (XXI.9, 1252). In what is perhaps Malory's most important alteration to his French source, the book ends not with a sense of their flawed natures but with an emphasis on their 'good ends'. The death of Guinevere is not recounted in the Stanzaic *Morte Darthur*, which mentions only her funeral, while the *Mort Artu* briefly remarks that Launcelot hears of Guinevere's death on the day of the battle of Winchester. In Malory's narrative, her death is rendered profoundly holy by the fact that she foresees it two days before, and knows that it will be conveyed in divine vision to Launcelot. Her example has laid the foundations for Launcelot's saintly death, lying 'as he had smyled, and the swettest savour aboute hym that ever they felte' (XXI.12, 1258). The grand obsequies orchestrated by Launcelot, his devotions and swoon of grief, as he buries Guinevere next to Arthur, and his commemoration of Arthur and Guinevere, 'of hir beaulté and of hir noblesse, that was bothe wyth hyr kyng and wyth hyr' (XXI.11, 1256), are crucial to the interweaving of tragedy and redemption at the end of Malory's book. The image of the four queens, Morgan le Fay and others, who weep and shriek as they carry Arthur to Avalon by boat (XXI.5, 1241), then, is symbolic of the shaping role of women in the work.

While women were patrons, owners, readers, and sometimes authors of romance, romance as a genre may also be seen as a conversation, perhaps a debate, about women. Women are lovers and desired objects, virtuous wives and mothers, practitioners of magic and enchantresses. Female bodies are catalysts within the narrative structures of romance, the objects of human and sometimes otherworldly desire. Women in romance experience and pursue their own desires, for love, power, and knowledge. Their arts can be learned, with the potential to heal, transform, and threaten bodies. As protagonists, they pursue and further love; exemplify and teach Christian virtue; voice love and loss; and promote ethical action. They also, however, represent powerful antagonists whose actions can oppose social order, destroy relationships, and ruthlessly promote desire. In widely differing ways, which reflect but also challenge cultural assumptions, they profoundly influence those they encounter and the worlds around them, their minds, hearts, and bodies central to the workings of narrative. In this sense too, romance and women are inextricably connected.

Notes

1. For a transhistorical exploration of romance, see *A Companion to Romance: From Classical to Contemporary*, ed. Corinne Saunders (Oxford: Blackwell, 2004).
2. Further on popular romance, see *The Spirit of Medieval English Popular Romance*, ed. Ad Putter and Jane Gilbert (Harlow: Pearson, 2000) and *A Companion to Medieval Popular Romance*, ed. Raluca L. Radulescu and Cory James Rushton (Cambridge: D. S. Brewer, 2009).
3. Helen Cooper, *The English Romance in Time: Transforming Motifs from Geoffrey of Monmouth to the Death of Shakespeare* (Oxford: Oxford University Press, 2004), 3.
4. Northrop Frye, *The Secular Scripture: A Study of the Structure of Romance* (Cambridge, MA: Harvard University Press, 1976), 55.
5. Erich Auerbach, *Mimesis: The Representation of Reality in Western Literature*, trans. Willard R. Trask, intro. Edward W. Said, revised ed. (Princeton, NJ: Princeton University Press, 2003; first published in German, 1946), 'The Knight Sets Forth', 123–42.
6. Susan Crane, *Insular Romance: Politics, Faith and Culture in Anglo-Norman and Middle English Literature* (Berkeley: University of California Press, 1986).
7. See further Jennifer Ward, *Women in Medieval Europe, 1200–1500* (London: Pearson, 2002), ch. 8, 'Laywomen and the Arts', 209–19; *The History of British Women's Writing*, vol. 1: *700–1500*, ed. Liz Herbert McAvoy and Diane Watt (Basingstoke: Palgrave Macmillan, 2012), in particular part 3, 'Literacies and Literary Cultures', 133–86; and Dennis H. Green, *Women Readers in the Middle Ages* (Cambridge: Cambridge University Press, 2007).
8. See further Jessica Brantley, *Reading in the Wilderness: Private Devotion and Public Performance in Late Medieval England* (Chicago: University of Chicago Press, 2007); Jennifer Bryan, *Looking Inward: Devotional Reading and the Private Self in Late Medieval England* (Philadelphia: University of Pennsylvania Press, 2008); and Mary Erler, *Women, Reading, and Piety in Late Medieval England* (Cambridge: Cambridge University Press, 2002).
9. *La Vie Seint Edmund le Rei: poème anglonormand du xiie siècle*, ed. Hilding Kjellman (Göteborg: Elanders, 1935), vv. 46–8; translation from *The Lais of Marie de France*, trans. Glyn Burgess and Keith Busby, 2nd ed. (Harmondsworth: Penguin, 1999), Introduction, 11.

10. Green, *Women Readers in the Middle Ages*, 213. For a discussion of the works associated with the courts of Henry II and Eleanor of Aquitaine and Marie de Champagne, see 213–15.
11. Green, *Women Readers in the Middle Ages*, 199.
12. Amy N. Vines, *Women's Power in Late Medieval Romance* (Cambridge: D. S. Brewer, 2011), 5. Vines's focus is on women 'as holders of power via intellectual, material and cultural expertise', in particular, through 'acts of patronage', 10–11.
13. Carol M. Meale, '" ... alle the bokes that I haue of latyn, englisch, and frensch": Laywomen and Their Books in Late Medieval England' in *Women and Literature in Britain, 1150–1500*, ed. Meale (Cambridge: Cambridge University Press, 1993), 128–58 (139); see also Julia Boffey, 'Women Authors and Women's Literacy in Fourteenth- and Fifteenth-Century England', in *Women and Literature in Britain*, ed. Meale, 159–82.
14. Meale, '" ... alle the bokes"', 140–1.
15. Geoffrey Chaucer, *The Canterbury Tales*, in *The Riverside Chaucer*, ed. Larry D. Benson, 3rd ed. (1987; Oxford: Oxford University Press 1988), VII.3212–13. Subsequent references to Chaucer's works are to this edition, cited by title and line number.
16. Sarah McNamer, 'Lyrics and Romances', in *The Cambridge Companion to Medieval Women's Writing*, ed. Carolyn Dinshaw and David Wallace (Cambridge: Cambridge University Press, 2003), 195–209 (203).
17. McNamer, 'Lyrics and Romances', 203; and see Meale, '... alle the bokes', for details of ownership of individual romances, 140–2.
18. Cambridge University Library, MS Gg.iv.27 (*King Horn* and *Floris and Blancheflour*); Oxford, Bodleian Library, MS Digby 181 (*King Ponthus and the Fair Sidone*); Oxford, Bodleian Library, MS eng.poet.a.1, the Vernon Manuscript (*Robert of Sicily*, *The King of Tars*, *Joseph of Arimathea*); see McNamer, 'Lyrics and Romances', 203.
19. See Carol M. Meale, '"gode men / Wiues maydnes and alle men": Romance and its Audiences', in *Readings in Medieval English Romance*, ed. Meale (Cambridge: D. S. Brewer, 1994), 209–25, citing an unpublished paper by Felicity Riddy, 'The Auchinleck Manuscript: A Woman's Book', 212; Meale also posits a female recipient for Bodleian Library, MS Ashmole 45, a sixteenth-century copy of *The Erle of Toulous*, which includes a presentation miniature of a woman, fol. 2r, 222.
20. McNamer, 'Lyrics and Romances', 207.
21. Melissa Furrow, *Expectations of Romance: The Reception of a Genre in Medieval England* (Cambridge: D. S. Brewer, 2009), 229, and see her detailed discussion of manuscripts, 230–1.
22. See Green, *Women Readers in the Middle Ages*, 3–77.
23. See Furrow, *Expectations of Romance*, 5–6 and 225–31.
24. See further Roberta Krueger, *Women Readers and the Ideology of Gender in Old French Verse Romance* (Cambridge: Cambridge University Press, 1993). The connection between genre and gender has been problematised, in particular,

in relation to French romance: the misogyny of romance and its masculine focus is taken up by Simon Gaunt in *Gender and Genre in Medieval French Literature* (Cambridge: Cambridge University Press, 1995), while Sarah Kay critiques portrayals of female agency in French romance in *The Chansons de Geste in the Age of Romance: Political Fictions* (Oxford: Oxford University Press, 1995), 25–48.

25. Meale, 'Laywomen and Their Books', 139, 141–2.
26. Vines, *Women's Power in Late Medieval Romance*, 1.
27. See Judith Weiss, 'The Wooing Woman in Anglo-Norman Romance', in *Romance in Medieval England*, ed. Maldwyn Mills, Jennifer Fellows and Carol M. Meale (Cambridge: D. S. Brewer, 1991), 149–61. On desiring women in romance, see Cooper, *The English Romance in Time*, ch. 5, 'Desirable Desire', 218–60.
28. *King Horn*, in *Of Love and Chivalry: An Anthology of Middle English Romance*, ed. Jennifer Fellows (London: Dent, 1993), 1–41, ll. 251–2. All subsequent references to *King Horn* are to this edition and cited by line number.
29. On enforced marriage in Middle English romance, see Corinne Saunders, *Rape and Ravishment in the Literature of Medieval England* (Cambridge: D. S. Brewer, 2001), 187–233.
30. *Havelok the Dane*, in *Middle English Verse Romances*, ed. Donald B. Sands (1966; Exeter: Exeter University Press, 1986), 158–9, ll. 1163–8. All references to *Havelok the Dane* are to this edition, cited by line number.
31. *The Romance of Sir Beues of Hamtoun*, ed. Eugen Kölbing, Early English Text Society, E.S. 46, 48, 65 (London: Kegan Paul, Trench, Trübner, 1885, 1886, 1894), ll. 1106–8 (Auchinleck MS). Subsequent references are to this edition, cited by line number.
32. See further *The Trotula: An English Translation of the Medieval Compendium of Women's Medicine*, ed. Monica H. Green and Ruth Mazo Karras (Philadelphia: University of Pennsylvania Press, 2002): the introduction offers an extensive discussion of the milieu of Salerno, the Salernitan texts on women's medicine known as the *Trotula*, their connections with and the evidence for the female author 'Trota' (47–51), and their circulation (1–64). See also Naoë Kukita Yoshikawa, Chapter 7 in this volume.
33. On magic and enchantment, see Corinne Saunders, *Magic and the Supernatural in Medieval English Romance* (Cambridge: D. S. Brewer, 2010); on Josian's arts, see 121–4.
34. *Ywain and Gawain*, in *Ywain and Gawain, Sir Percyvell of Gales, the Anturs of Arther*, ed. Maldwyn Mills (London: J. M. Dent, 1992) 1–102, ll. 999–1003. Subsequent references are to this edition, cited by line number.
35. Dyan Elliott, 'Marriage', in *Companion to Medieval Women's Writing*, ed. Dinshaw and Wallace, 40–57 (41).
36. The case is widely cited; see, for example, Elliott, 'Marriage', 43. See further *The Paston Letters and Papers of the Fifteenth Century*, 2 vols, ed. Norman Davis (Oxford: Clarendon Press, 1971–6), no. 446, 2: 32.
37. On *raptus*, see Saunders, *Rape and Ravishment*, 33–75.

38. See further Cooper, *The English Romance in Time*, ch. 6, 'Women on Trial', 269–314.
39. McNamer, 'Lyrics and Romances', 205.
40. *Sir Tryamowre*, in *Of Love and Chivalry*, ed. Fellows, 147–98, l. 465. Subsequent references are to this edition, cited by line number.
41. *The Erle of Tolous*, in *Of Love and Chivalry*, ed. Fellows, 231–65, l. 154. Subsequent references are to this edition, cited by line number.
42. *Emaré*, in *Six Middle English Romances: The Sege of Melayne, Emaré, Octavian, Sir Isumbras, Sir Gowther, Sir Amadace*, ed. Maldwyn Mills (London: Dent, 1973), 46–74, ll. 350, 396. Subsequent references are to this edition, cited by line number.
43. A. C. Spearing, '*Emaré*: The Story and its Telling', in *Medieval Romance, Arthurian Literature*, ed. A. S. G. Edwards (Cambridge: D. S. Brewer, 2021), 61–76 (76).
44. On the role of force in constructions of heterosexual desire, see Louise Sylvester, *Medieval Romance and the Construction of Heterosexuality* (New York: Palgrave Macmillan, 2008), in particular, ch. 2, 'Romance and Rape', 43–65, which focuses on *Sir Degaré* and *Sir Gowther*. On the Breton *lais*, see also Saunders, *Rape and Ravishment*, 224–33.
45. *Sir Orfeo*, in *Middle English Verse Romances*, ed. Sands, 185–200, l. 46. All references to *Sir Orfeo* are to this edition, cited by line number.
46. For an interesting positive reading focused on the ethical and political importance of Heurodis' survival of ravishment, see Suzanne M. Edwards, *The Afterlives of Rape in Medieval English Literature* (New York: Palgrave Macmillan, 2016), 118–30.
47. On *Sir Launfal* and female patronage see Vines, *Women's Power in Late Medieval Romance*, 115–39.
48. See Meale, '"gode men / Wiues maydnes and alle men"', 223–5 and Vines, *Women's Power in Late Medieval Romance*, 90–1.
49. *The Middle-English Versions of 'Partonope of Blois'*, ed. A. Trampe Bödtker, Early English Text Society, E.S. 109 (London: Kegan Paul, Trench, Trübner and Oxford University Press, 1912 for 1911), ll. 876, 1221–3. References are to this edition, British Museum, MS Add. 35, 288, cited by line number. On the relation between French and English texts, see further *Partonopeus in Europe: An Old French Romance and Its Adaptations*, ed. Catherine Hanley, Mario Longtin, and Penny Eley, *Mediaevalia* 25 2, special issue (2004). On Melior's 'craft', see further Vines, *Women's Power in Late Medieval Romance*, 85–114.
50. See *William of Palerne: An Alliterative Romance*, ed. G. H. V. Bunt (Groningen: Bouma's Boekhuis, 1885), Introduction, 33–4. All subsequent references are to this edition, cited by line number.
51. See further Megan G. Leitch, 'From Sorceresses to Scholars: Universities and the Disenchantment of Romance', in *Medieval Romance, Arthurian Literature*, ed. Edwards, 16–33.
52. *Sir Gawain and the Green Knight*, in *The Poems of the Pearl Manuscript: Pearl, Cleanness, Patience, Sir Gawain and the Green Knight*, ed. Malcolm Andrew

and Ronald Waldron, 5th ed. (Exeter: Exeter University Press, 2007), 207–300, ll. 1239–40, 1496. Subsequent references are to this edition, cited by line number.
53. *The Works of Sir Thomas Malory*, ed. Eugène Vinaver, rev. P. J. C. Field, 3rd ed., 3 vols. (Oxford: Clarendon Press, 1990), Caxton's Preface, cxlv. All subsequent references are to this edition, cited by Caxton's book and chapter numbers, and page number.
54. See further Andrew Lynch, *Malory's Book of Arms: The Narrative of Combat in 'Le Morte Darthur'* (Cambridge: D. S. Brewer, 1997).
55. Rosemary Morris demonstrates that Igrayne plays a more authoritative role in the *Morte* than she does in the work's analogues, and argues that she becomes 'a self-sufficient lady who, like the great dames of the Wars of the Roses, can survive in a world of power politics – though, unlike many of those ladies, she retains her virtue unsullied'; see 'Uther and Igerne: A Study in Uncourtly Love', in *Arthurian Literature IV*, ed. Richard Barber (Woodbridge: D. S. Brewer, 1985), 70–92 (88).
56. Donald Maddox, *The Arthurian Romance of Chrétien de Troyes: Once and Future Fictions* (Cambridge: Cambridge University Press, 1991), 42. Maddox argues that the conditions attached to this and the Custom of Gorre (seen in Meleagaunt's practice of imprisonment) structures the entire narrative, 36–48.
57. See further Elizabeth Edwards, 'The Place of Women in Malory's *Morte Darthur*', in *A Companion to Malory*, ed. Elizabeth Archibald and A. S. G. Edwards (Cambridge: D. S. Brewer, 1996), 37–54.
58. See further Carolyne Larrington, *King Arthur's Enchantresses: Morgan and her Sisters in Arthurian Tradition* (London: I. B. Tauris, 2006).
59. See *The High Book of the Grail: A Translation of the Thirteenth-Century Romance of 'Perlesvaus'*, trans. Nigel Bryant (Cambridge: D. S. Brewer, 1978), Branch X, 220–5.

Further Reading

Cooper, Helen (2004). *The English Romance in Time: Transforming Motifs from Geoffrey of Monmouth to the Death of Shakespeare*, Oxford: Oxford University Press.

Dinshaw, Carolyn, and David Wallace, eds. (2003). *The Cambridge Companion to Medieval Women's Writing*. Cambridge: Cambridge University Press.

Furrow, Melissa (2009). *Expectations of Romance: The Reception of a Genre in Medieval England*, Cambridge: D. S. Brewer.

Meale, Carol M., ed. (1994). *Readings in Medieval English Romance*, Cambridge: D. S. Brewer.

Meale, Carol M., ed. (1993). *Women and Literature in Britain, 1150–1500*, Cambridge: Cambridge University Press.

Putter, Ad, and Jane Gilbert, eds. (2000). *The Spirit of Medieval English Popular Romance*, Harlow: Pearson.

Radulescu, Raluca L., and Cory James Rushton (2009). *A Companion to Medieval Popular Romance*, Cambridge: D. S. Brewer.
Saunders, Corinne (2010). *Magic and the Supernatural in Medieval English Romance*, Cambridge: D. S. Brewer.
Saunders, Corinne, ed. (2004). *A Companion to Romance: From Classical to Contemporary*, Oxford: Blackwell.
Vines, Amy N. (2011). *Women's Power in Late Medieval Romance*, Cambridge: D. S. Brewer.

CHAPTER 16

Trouble and Strife in the Old French Fabliaux
Neil Cartlidge

Tall Tales and Wee Stories

Tall Tales and Wee Stories is the title of a recent book by the veteran Scottish comedian Billy Connolly, which gathers together a selection of the material used in his stand-up comedy performances over the years;[1] as it happens, this phrase would also serve rather nicely as a thumbnail-definition of the Old French *fabliaux* (and of the texts that imitate or resemble them in other languages).[2] The *fabliaux* are typically 'tall tales' in the sense that they tend to depict situations that are deeply improbable, preposterous, and/or extreme. This is a quality that the *fabliaux* themselves actively promote, for they often pose as tales of the extraordinary, or even as outright 'marvels'.[3] They also tend to insist rather loudly on their own truthfulness, as if tacitly admitting just how unlikely it seems that they could actually be true.[4] At the same time, the *fabliaux* are typically 'wee stories' – at least in the sense that the very word *fabliau* originated as a diminutive of the Latin word for 'fable' (*fabula*), so that *fabliaux* are quite literally '*little* fables'.[5] Compared with other types of medieval narrative, such texts are always relatively short, rarely more than a few hundred lines long.[6] This too is a quality that they sometimes specifically promote. So, for example, one author promises a *fabliau* which he characterises as both 'brief and little' ('brieve et petite');[7] he introduces another of his works as a '*fabliau* that is courtly and small' ('.i. flablel courtois e petit').[8] Sometimes it is suggested that such tales are so short that it can hardly do any harm to listen to them,[9] and sometimes their very brevity is presented as a selling-point.[10]

Yet there is another important sense in which the *fabliaux* might be said to be diminutive, and that is morally. These are texts that apparently pride themselves on the very reductiveness of their view of human nature. This might be seen as a consequence of their efficiency – the ruthless economy of their humour translating, perhaps inevitably, into a certain brutality of spirit. Yet their brutality goes far beyond what can be explained simply as a side effect of their concision. It is not just that the *fabliaux* tend to be little: they also tend to *be*little. For example, they frequently rely on that particular short cut to comedy that lies in laughing *at* people, rather than with them. If humour always depends on a 'momentary anaesthesia of the heart', as Henri Bergson once suggested, then the anaesthesia demanded by the *fabliaux* might be said to be both chronic and acute.[11] Rarely are the inhabitants of such texts even remotely attractive, let alone admirable, and most of them seem to be motivated entirely by appetite, greed, jealousy, rivalry and/or revenge – to the extent that the *fabliaux* might be said to engage their audiences in a kind of conspiracy of low expectations.[12] Being even momentarily optimistic about the goodness of other people, to trust in anybody's 'better nature', is in this context interpreted as a form of squeamishness – and, in the *fabliaux*, squeamishness of any kind is almost always self-defeating.[13]

By contrast, such texts generally make a virtue of 'plain-speaking', even if this means frankly embracing obscenity.[14] Their underlying assumption, apparently, is that euphemism of any kind (whether represented by the language of honour, decorum, or politeness, or by deference to other people's dignities) is inevitably a form of snobbery, a fantasy, or a scam.[15] For those characters in the *fabliaux* who allow themselves to be seduced by such delusions, the consequences can be remarkably severe. They generally end up being humbled in elaborately spectacular ways; indeed, the *fabliaux* appear to take a vindictive delight in exposing and then ritualistically punishing folly or weakness – to the extent that humiliation can be seen not just as a recurrent theme, but as a characteristic fetish.[16] The lack of human sympathy in the *fabliaux* is obvious, and obviously cultivated, to the extent that bemoaning it seems redundant. It would be like objecting to knock-knock jokes on the grounds that they contain too much percussion.

All of these qualities would seem to stand in the way of any attempt at reading them as plausible witnesses to the treatment of women in medieval society, or to medieval attitudes towards gender in general. It would certainly be a mistake to expect them to provide anything like a Middlemarchian attention to the 'social lot of women' in the Middle Ages.[17] The portrayal of gender and gender relations offered by the *fabliaux* is in most cases so unapologetically ugly and unjust that it is perhaps best regarded as a form of caricature. Yet caricature can still be revealing, especially if it is understood that its very excesses are a way of emphasising particular interpretative models. As Stephanie Ross argued, 'caricature transforms exaggeration, distortion, and falsification into vehicles for succinct comment and easy identification' – to the extent (she suggests) that it might be said to take on some of the expressive privileges of metaphor.[18] Take, for example, the way that the *fabliaux* choose to represent parish priests: these men are almost universally cast as libertines who blatantly breach the obligation to celibacy (which was a condition of priestly status) – either by keeping a concubine, by using prostitutes, or by simply preying ruthlessly on their own flocks. Even if it is unlikely that the medieval priesthood was ever *universally* corrupt, the *fabliaux* choose to depict priests *as if* it were, and the effect of this is to reflect or highlight anxieties that were clearly very widespread: for example, that priests might use the resources of the church to support illicit (non-marital) relationships, or that the very exclusion of priests from marriage might make them more of a temptation or threat to women.[19]

However, the authors of fabliaux never openly admit to offering an account of medieval society that it is anything but realistic. Even if their picture of medieval society is in some ways obviously exaggerated or distorted, they often pose as thoughtful analysts of the human condition, and of the categories by which it is fundamentally defined, such as gender. This is perhaps why the *fabliaux* often seem so strangely amenable to the tropes and approaches characteristic of recent literary theory.[20] For example, they sometimes lay claim to an interest in semiotics (that is, in the creation and interpretation of signs and symbols);[21] sometimes they concern themselves with verbal hygiene, linguistic decorum, and the use or abuse of language;[22] and sometimes they pretend to address questions of identity, including the nature of the relationship between embodiment and gender.[23] In practice, though, the treatment of such themes in the *fabliaux* tends to be so extravagant or strange as to approach burlesque, with the result that any attempt at enlisting them into a serious debate about gender inevitably risks looking critically naïve – or even inadvertently Crewsian (Frederick Crews being the literary critic who notoriously subjected A. A. Milne's stories about Winnie-the-Pooh to a series of tongue-in-cheek 'applications' of different literary-theoretical approaches).[24]

It also seems as if the *fabliaux* go out of their way to accommodate arguments that are conspicuously circular or reversible. So, for example, several of them explicitly suggest that all women are by nature sexually voracious.[25] On the one hand, this is a blatant libel, a generalisation that is both 'tall' (in the sense of being preposterously exaggerated), and also 'small' (in the sense of being obviously malicious and mean-spirited). On the other hand, it suggests an equally libellous corollary, which is that men are, in comparison, not voracious enough, and therefore that, compared with women, they are sexually 'inadequate' by definition. Similarly, several *fabliaux* assert that women are particularly adept at deceit;[26] but this too has an obvious corollary, which is that men are all too easily deceived: that is, that men are innately gullible. Some *fabliaux* allege that women are more garrulous and/or verbally ingenious than men,[27] but this is once again a readily reversible argument: in this case it is implicitly contradicted, for example, by the very nature of the *fabliaux* themselves, whose (generally male) authors often use language in ways that are conspicuously excessive.[28] Interpretative short circuits of this kind emerge so regularly in the *fabliaux* that they seem to be (as it were) permanently 'wired in'. This, in turn, perhaps suggests that their authors were ultimately much more interested in the dramatic effects created by the polarisation of viewpoints, rather than in advocating any particular viewpoint(s) themselves. One consequence of this is that, even though it is always relatively easy to pick out moments in the *fabliaux* that seem frankly misogynistic, it is generally unsafe to cite them as evidence for the widespread acceptance of misogynistic attitudes in medieval society. One of the guiding assumptions in such texts seems to be that antagonism between the genders is not just self-perpetuating, but largely self-defeating. The very reversibility of many of the 'libels' committed by the *fabliaux* means that on the whole nobody emerges from them with any credit. When mud is thrown in such texts (as it often is), it generally sticks to everybody involved, the detractors as much as the detracted, and the aggressors as much as the aggressees.

Berengar Longbottom

One of the stranger effects of the fabliau known as 'Berengier au long cul' (or 'Berengar Longbottom', to offer one possible Anglicisation of this title) is to turn the representation of sexual identity upside down.[29] Not only does it literally oblige the reader to imagine looking at a woman rather closely from underneath, it also invites a reconsideration of traditional gender roles 'from the bottom up'. How it does this is by telling a story about a knight from Lombardy, who happens to be a coward (as Lombards were often reputed to be),[30] and who attempts to conceal his cowardliness from his wife by repeatedly pretending to go off on chivalric adventures. In fact, what he does on each of these occasions is to find a secluded place in the wilderness, where he deliberately dents his shield and armour in such a way as to give the impression, when he returns, that he has been in battle. However, this fraudulent strategy does not deceive his wife, who sets about countering it by borrowing a horse and equipment, riding out to meet him, and then boldly challenging him to fight her. Unexpectedly faced with this mysterious opponent, and not recognising his wife, the cowardly knight immediately surrenders, whereupon she tells him that the price of mercy is that 'vos me vaudroiz o cul baissier / tres o mileu o par delez' ('[you] will kiss my ass / right on the hole or close beside it').[31] In other words, she forces him to perform a gesture that is implicitly an extreme form of humiliation: namely, to kiss her arse.

As has long been recognised, this story is clearly intended to serve as 'a satire upon a sort of knight-errantry',[32] and indeed it parodies some of the canonical texts in the medieval romance-tradition quite directly.[33] Yet what makes it most remarkable is surely the curious use to which it puts the motif of the 'shameful kiss'. Here, the 'baise honteuse' functions not just as a means and a measure of the knight's abjection, but also as an opportunity for him to discover that the person who has just humiliated him is in fact a woman. As it turns out, the Lombard knight is apparently so naïve or inept that he fails to recognise the sex of his assailant even when her genitals are staring him in the face.

There is no question that, on the tale's own terms, it is the knight who is punished most severely. He is emphatically the victim of his own cowardice, and his wife's insistence that he kiss her arse is clearly an example of the kind of ritualisation of humiliation which I have suggested is characteristic of the *fabliaux*'s tendency to cruelty. In this case, the fact that the author of the knight's downfall is a woman (rather than another man) certainly intensifies his humiliation, if only because of the way it draws attention to his failure to live up to the expectations of his own gender. If knightliness is a prerogative of masculinity (as chivalric culture generally defined it),[34] then his failure as a knight is all the greater for the fact that he is defeated by someone whose non-masculinity is (as it turns out) presented to him with such dramatic directness. In that sense, the loser of this particular battle of the sexes is clearly the husband rather than the wife; indeed, one of the obvious implications of the tale is a challenge to the very idea that knighthood is necessarily or naturally a prerogative of masculinity. It clearly makes the point that it is bravery that defines chivalric competence, not masculinity as such, so a woman who is demonstrably brave will naturally make a much better job of being a knight than a man who is demonstrably a coward. On the face of it, this seems like a manifestly 'feminist' perspective. The woman in the story shows that she is more qualified to do this particular job than her husband is, despite the expectation (on which the Lombard knight himself relies) that it is, by definition, 'man's work'. From this point of view, 'Berengar Longbottom' apparently demands to be read as the tale of one woman's (literally) fundamental victory in the fight against inequality: in practice, however, this is not a reading that the text ultimately makes at all comfortable.

To begin with, it could be argued that the effect of the tale is at least as demeaning to the knight's wife as it is to the knight himself. After all, it is her genitals, not his, that are put so disconcertingly on display, and indeed subjected to a degree of scrutiny that certainly seems more than a little disrespectful. It is only through the eyes of the cowardly knight that we are invited to undertake this close inspection of some of his wife's anatomy, and he is clearly no reliable interpreter of what he sees:

> do cul & del con: ce li sanble
> que trestot se tienent ensanble.
> A lui meïsmes panse & dit
> onques mais si grant cul ne vit ... (D19, ll. 243–6)
>
> (Asshole and cunt so close do lie,
> they seem like one hole to his eye.
> He thinks and mutters in between
> his teeth, 'The biggest hole I've seen'!)

In other words, he is unable to distinguish her vulva from her anus, and so imagines that what he is looking at is a single big arsehole ('si grant cul').[35] This reading of the female body is not just ridiculously distorted, it also suggests distaste – a distaste that seems intrinsically misogynistic. If the wife's anus is implicitly so disgusting that kissing it is deeply shameful, then the knight's reading of her vulva as a kind of continuation of her anus implicitly extends that disgust to the vulva as well. In other words, interpretation of these lines seems to invite one of those interpretative 'short circuits' I described earlier: the spectre of the 'grant cul' is paradoxically both a symbol of the wife's triumph and, at the same time, an image that implicitly demeans her. Even in the very moment when the text seems to celebrate a feminine victory, in other words, it also seems to admit a pungent waft of misogyny. Misogynistic aggression is perhaps implicit in the *fabliau*'s insistence on speaking so 'plainly' about parts of the female anatomy that women generally prefer to keep private. Even if it is the wife who chooses to expose her 'private parts' to her husband, the *fabliau*'s retailing of his view of her 'grant cul' – in such a way as to share this image, implicitly, with a much wider public – still seems like an invasion of her privacy.

At the same time, the *fabliau* might also be read as an invitation to think about the relationship between gender and biological sex. On the one hand, it suggests that the knight's wife ought to be able 'prove' that she is a woman simply by exposing her 'con'. On the other, the cowardly knight's failure to recognise the wife's 'con' for what it is might just be a symptom of his stupidity, but it might also be read as a suggestion that this exposure is perhaps not such a self-sufficient 'proof' of femininity (or of a lack of masculinity) after all. The cowardly knight himself is perhaps particularly conditioned to read his wife's vaginal opening as part of a 'grant cul' by his expectation of seeing a penis instead, but the matter-of-fact way in which he accepts the absence of a penis here perhaps also suggests a recognition on his part that there might be some 'men' whose genital equipment is different. In other words, even if 'Berengar Longbottom' is a fictional personality, the possibility that not all knights would be able to display a 'normal' penis is one that the Lombard knight, at least, is prepared to consider.[36] Medieval people were certainly aware of the existence of bodies that fall outside male/female binaries, and of the possibility of genital difference due to injury (or to some particular physical condition), but the question of the extent to which male/female genitals are a 'proof' of gender-identity or not is one to which they might well have been quite receptive anyway, because of the way it seems to reflect the characteristically medieval preoccupation with the philosophical relationship between categories and signs.[37]

More generally, the invitation to contemplate the wife's 'long bottom' might be read as a deliberate attempt at poetic 'defamiliarisation': that is, even if the 'long arsehole' is merely a figment of the cowardly knight's own foolish imagination, it nevertheless serves to remind us of just how arbitrary are the meanings that we generally invest in bodies – how strange it is that we see them in particular ways and that we endow them with particular significances. Yet even this argument only seems to create another critical short-circuit: if the knight's reading of the female body is a product of his own remarkable foolishness, then surely it could be argued that taking it seriously (even for a moment) means participating in (or even implicitly endorsing) the knight's foolishness? Even to discuss this scene is closely as I have possibly risks falling into a kind of vicious circle of absurdity, for if the knight's idea of the 'long cul' is implicitly silly, then debating its significance must (logically) be just as silly – if not more so. In the end, the knight's wife effectively cuts through all of these possible complexities by boldly adopting 'Longbottom' as her chivalric *nom de guerre*. When the knight asks her identity, she calls herself Berengar Longbottom ('j'é non Berangiers au lonc cul') – who, she adds, has a reputation for putting cowards to shame ('qui a toz les coarz fait honte').³⁸ In this way, she effectively conjures up the idea of an aristocratic affinity to which all women naturally belong, and through which all of them can implicitly share in this particular wife's victory over masculine vanity and incompetence – as fellow-members of the Longbottom clan.

The several different interpretations of this tale that I have just suggested might seem bewilderingly various, and in several cases mutually contradictory, but this is precisely what I want to illustrate here – the extent to which the tale seems to encourage a multiplicity of competing and/or incompatible readings. The one interpretation of 'Berengar Longbottom' that does *not* seem particularly compelling is the one that is explicitly offered by the narrator himself. In the concluding line of his text, he suggests that its moral is that husbands ought to keep a close watch on their wives – although he actually puts this point somewhat more pungently: 'A mol pastor chie los laine', he says (literally, when the shepherd is weak, the wolf shits wool, because it has eaten so many sheep at the shepherd's expense).³⁹ The cowardly knight could certainly be seen as a bad shepherd, but the tale as a whole hardly insists on the competence of husbands as 'shepherds', and it hardly precludes sympathy for his wife in her unwillingness to play the part of an obedient 'sheep'.

Fabliaux in British Library, MS Harley 2253

The evidence that French-language *fabliaux* circulated in England is extensive, although often patchy or indirect.⁴⁰ The most substantial collection of *fabliaux* to be found in any English manuscript occurs in London, British Library, MS Harley 2253, which contains four such texts, although they are not gathered together in such a way as to suggest that the compiler saw them as a distinct group.⁴¹ Indeed, out of the 116 separate items in three different languages (French, English, and Latin), these four do not necessarily loom very large in the collection as a whole. Traditionally, it is the Middle English lyrics in this manuscript that have tended to shape critical accounts of its contents, which accordingly tend to dwell on the lyrics' characteristic interest in the theme of love, their celebration of the reawakening of nature in spring-time, and their general air of optimism or light-heartedness.⁴² Yet even the relatively limited presence of the *fabliaux* here suggests the possibility of a very different story, one in which the apparent innocence and 'freshness' of the Middle English lyrics is counterweighed by the *fabliaux*'s characteristic preference for cruelty, cynicism, and discord. The four *fabliaux* that survive in Harley 2253 do not seem to me to be very different in kind or quality from those that survive only in continental manuscripts.[43] Indeed, as a group, they might even be seen as a conveniently representative selection of the genre as a whole. I briefly characterise three of them here.

Like 'Berengar Longbottom', the *fabliau* known as 'The Wager' ('La gageure') deliberately takes a reductively bottom-up view of human sexuality.[44] It tells the story of a lady who, snobbishly believing that she has been disparaged by her marriage, attempts to take revenge on her husband's kin by playing a trick on his younger brother. The lady learns that this young man has taken a fancy to her young cousin. She is apparently aware that her cousin is somewhat ignorant about sex, so she attempts to turn this to her own purposes by suggesting that she should ask the young man to prove his devotion by (quite literally) kissing her (that is, the cousin's) arse. The purpose of this manœuvre is apparently to embarrass the husband via his brother: to force the young man to perform a gesture which (as in 'Berengar') is understood to be a humiliation of the deepest kind. The lady is so confident that the amorous young man will be happy to kiss her cousin's arse that she invites her husband to come with her to spy on the two young people at their rendezvous. The husband, however, cannot believe that his brother would debase himself in this way, and he is so confident of this that he wagers a cask of wine: a wager which the lady willingly accepts. The husband and wife then watch as the young woman lifts her skirts so that the young man can give the shameful kiss – however, the latter suddenly decides to take advantage of the situation instead, and to do so in a particularly ruthless way:

> Pus pensout, 'Si a bon mester!'
> L'esquier, a soun voler,
> De son affere ne vodra failler.
> Yl sake avaunt bon bordoun,
> Si l'a donné enmy le coun. (ll. 75–8)
>
> (Then he thought, 'Here's a good office!'
> The squire, following his will,
> Didn't want to fail in his business.
> He draws out the sturdy staff
> And gives it to her in the centre of the cunt.)

This is clearly a depiction of rape. Yet the lady's reaction suggests that she thinks her cousin is by no means quite so unhappy about it as she thinks she ought to be, for she accuses her both of treachery and of acting like a whore ('puteyne'). The husband clearly approves of the young man's behaviour, loudly cheering him on, and then later arranging for the young couple to be married. In the *fabliau*'s own terms, it is certainly the men who come out 'on top' here:[45] the squire does *not* kiss the maid's arse, and, as a result, it is the husband who wins the wager. There is even a suggestion that the wife 'learns her lesson', according to the misogynist logic of the tale. Yet, what this means in practice is that the *fabliau* supplants one very negative assessment of masculine (hetero-)sexuality with another assessment that is, if anything, even more damning. The lady's estimation of men is initially so low that she thinks the squire will be willing to kiss the maid's arse in order to win her love, and yet what the tale itself eventually suggests is that, whenever any man is faced directly with a woman's 'con' or 'cul', his default response is naturally an attempt at rape. In a sense, then, the snobbish lady succeeds in her purposes rather too completely: if her intention was to show that men are deeply and inescapably enslaved to their basest instincts, then the young man's behaviour completely vindicates her point – but only at the immediate cost of making the lady herself effectively complicit in his sexual assault on her cousin. At the same time, this fabliau seems to suggest (like 'Berengar Longbottom') that the 'con' and the 'cul' are so closely collocated as to be in some ways interchangeable. Rather than accepting the young woman's 'cul' as a means of his own humiliation, the young man's appropriation of her 'con' instead suggests that the 'con' offers a convenient opportunity for *him* instead to humiliate *her*. In other words, not only does this text depict a rape, it also suggests that for a woman to be penetrated by a man is *always* and inherently degrading for her. This is (to put it mildly) a provocatively pessimistic assessment of the social and psychological dynamics of heterosexual sex.

In 'The Three Ladies who found a Penis' ('Les trois dames qui troverent un vit'),[46] the text begins, implicitly, with a castration. The three ladies of the title are travelling on pilgrimage to Mont-Saint-Michel when one of them discovers a penis lying in the road:

> Si trova un vit, gros e plener,
> Envolupé en un drapel.
> N'i out descovert qe le musel.   (ll. 13–16)

> ([She] found a prick, thick and swollen,
> Wrapped in a piece of cloth.
> Only the tip was uncovered.)

Throughout the story this object is referred to as a penis ('vit') – never as a dildo, or as a model or facsimile of some kind – which means that (logically speaking) there ought to be a man attached to it. However, if such a castration has occurred, it seems that it was the man who was removed from the penis, rather than the other way around. In other words, what the tale's presentation of this object suggests is not so much a dismemberment as a dispersonment. Indeed, it is striking that no (whole) man ever appears in the action of the tale – only this (relatively) small part of one. The three ladies are so delighted with their find that they immediately fall to quarrelling over which of them should take ownership of it. Their dispute proves so intractable that they eventually decide to seek arbitration at a local convent (where the nuns, we are told, view the 'vit' with similar delight), but the abbess refuses to grant it to any of the three ladies, instead declaring that it is in fact the bolt from the front gate of the convent, which (she says) went missing a few days previously.

This interpretation of the object is not quite so arbitrary as it might seem. Implicit here, I think, is that the bolt is not a slide-bolt (like most modern door-bolts), but part of a mechanism in which the bolt is pushed forwards through a hole in the latch in such a way as to stop the latch being lifted. This arrangement would rather lend itself to being seen as a re-enactment (in ironmongery) of the act of sexual penetration. At the same time, the abbess's story would seem, on the face of it, to suggest that the object was really just a door-bolt all along (and so simply misidentified as a penis), but in fact the text continues to refer to it as penis ('vit') even after the abbess has laid claim to it, which would seem to suggest that it is indeed a penis, and that the nuns are using it as a bolt only because it happens to be so rigidly erect. Indeed, it is consistently suggested throughout this narrative that the disputed object is a particularly superlative example of a penis, remarkable not just for its size and girth ('gros e plener'), but also for its equally remarkable (and apparently perpetual) state of hardness. On the one hand, the *fabliau*'s insistence on the fascinating effect of this object on all the women in the tale (even women on pilgrimage or living in religious communities) might be read as the expression of a complacently masculine belief in the universal irresistibility of phallic objects to women. The text even goes so far as to suggest that the 'vit' was treated as a relic ('come relyke') and universally honoured by women everywhere ('de totes dames honoree'). On the other hand, the very excellence of this particular penis is perhaps a reproach to more ordinary examples of its kind – and so, by extension, to all the men who possess them, while the complete excision of any masculine character from the story otherwise would seem to suggest that – from the point of view of the women in the story at least – men themselves are largely disposable.[47]

In 'The Knight who made Vaginas Talk' ('Le chevalier qui fist les cons parler'),[48] body parts seem to take on a similarly disconcerting independence, although in this case the body parts in question belong to women. This *fabliau* tells the story of a knight who is lucky enough to meet three fairies in the wilderness, who grant him magical powers, including the power to compel both the 'cul e coun' (the arsehole and the cunt) not just to talk, but to tell the truth about what they know. The text describes the knight's enjoyment of each of these privileges. For example, he meets a priest who is keeping a mistress and using his parish's alms-money to do so, and he finds this out because the vulva of the priest's horse ('le coun al jumente') snitches on her owner. However, the culmination of the action is the knight's triumph over a lady who, in an attempt to prevent her vulva from blabbing, stuffs it full of cotton – not knowing that he can simply call on the advice of her anus instead. All of this produces what Barbara Nolan calls 'a stunningly ungenteel focus on the countess'[s] nether parts, [which are] presented as at once enormous and vocal'.[49] Again like 'Berengar', this *fabliau* seems to suggest that vulva and anus are to some extent interchangeable, in this case because both are complicit in the lady's misdeeds and both are magically enabled to confess them. It also resembles 'Berengar' in the way it uses a display of female anatomy to stage a kind of ritualised humiliation, but in this case the object of the humiliation is a woman (not an inadequate man), and the point of her humiliation seems to be to prove that women *always* have something to hide. From this perspective, the 'Knight' barely hides the misogyny of many of its assumptions, but it is at the same time so energetically absurd as to make these assumptions seem inherently laughable. Indeed, I have argued elsewhere that its real point lies in the fact that it is a deliberate parody of the masculine wish-fulfilment fantasies implicit in courtly *lais* such as 'Lanval' or 'Graelent'.[50] From this point of view, it is men, and specifically the conceits of men as they are written into medieval literature, that the tale ultimately ridicules. Yet the tale itself seems to celebrate the indignities of the knight's role, implicitly allowing him to take ownership of the tale's obscenity in much the same way as the knight's wife does in 'Berengier au long cul'. Just as she became 'Berengar Longbottom', so he becomes 'the Cunt-Knight' ('Chevaler de Coun'), and his squire 'Little Arsehole-Hugh' ('Huet de Culet').

Conclusion

Fabliaux often seem to be deeply invested in the idea that mutual antagonism between the genders is necessary and eternal, and to take a generally pessimistic view of the possibilities for happy relations between them. Yet their willingness to contemplate such perspectives is perhaps best seen as both tactical and provisional – as a means to an end. That is, what they testify to, ultimately, is so not so much a belief in such a bleak view of the human condition as a fear that it might actually be justified; at the same time, they also attempt to offer a mechanism for dealing with this fear – which is to translate it into shared laughter, the shared laughter of audiences/readers specifically imagined as *communities*. Much of the unhappiness depicted in the *fabliaux* is located within the experience of married life, and it is perhaps implicit that their intended reception is primarily among people who already know something about the stresses and strains of daily cohabitation.[51] In other words, the communities that such texts implicitly imagine largely (or typically) consist of people who identify themselves either as husbands or as wives. The *fabliaux* endorse 'plain-speaking' about bodies because they are implicitly addressing married couples who are likely to be very conscious of having 'seen it all' already; they foreground sexual discontents and discomforts because they recognise that such discontents/discomforts are an inevitable corollary of the sexual obligations and/or expectations written into marriage;[52] and they constantly recur to depictions of betrayal and deceit because marriages are social and economic partnerships to which trust is (even more than in most relationships) particularly essential. Thus, when the *fabliaux* characterise women as a source of 'trouble and strife', it is perhaps not so much because they are women as because they are *wives* – a line of thought which is, of course, implicit in the traditional significance of this very collocation in rhyming-slang.[53] Conversely, the bad behaviour of men in the *fabliaux* is almost always bad behaviour of a kind that marks them as bad *husbands* (as much as, or more than, bad men). In other words, the gender antagonisms expressed in the *fabliaux* are not so much pathological as pragmatic. These texts deliberately provoke competing and mutually contradictory responses because they implicitly address people whose everyday lives are closely and inescapably shaped by experiences of gender that are likewise competing and mutually contradictory – if only because some of them are husbands, and some of them are wives.[54] Just as stand-up comedians like Billy Connolly often tell stories that invite contrasting and sometimes explicitly partisan responses from within a single audience, so too the *fabliaux* paradoxically attempt to unite their imagined audiences in an amusingly exaggerated dramatisation of their differences.[55]

Notes

1. Billy Connolly, *Tall Tales and Wee Stories* (London: Two Roads, 2019).
2. The extent of the corpus of Old French *fabliaux* is in practice defined by collections such as those of Anatole de Montaiglon and Gaston Raynaud (*Recueil général et complet des fabliaux des XIIIe et XIVe siècles imprimés ou inédits, publiés avec notes et variantes d'après les manuscrits*, 6 vols. (Paris, Librairie des bibliophiles, 1872–90) and Willem Noomen and Nico van den Boogaard (*Nouveau recueil complet des fabliaux*, 10 vols. (Assen: Van Gorcum, 1983–8) [henceforth *NCRF*]). For convenience, *fabliau*-texts are generally cited here from the anthology of texts with facing-page translations by Nathaniel E. Dubin (*The Fabliaux* (New York: Norton, 2013)), which I abbreviate to D, citing the number of the tale in this collection, then the line numbers.
3. See, for example, D4.1 (p. 16), D22.2 (260), and D45.1 (530), where the tale is in each case presented as '*une merveille*'. Cf. also D14.15 (144) and D38.2 (467).
4. See, for example, D21.2–5 (244), D34.23–4 (406), D56.3 (818), and D67.1–6 (930–2).
5. See *OED*, s.v. 'fabliau', n.
6. The longest of the *fabliaux* in *NCRF*, 'Trubert' (no. 124) runs to 2,978 lines, but this is exceptional.
7. D39.8, 482. On the author of this *fabliau* (a certain 'Garin'), see *Dictionnaire des lettres françaises: le Moyen Âge*, ed. Geneviève Hasenohr and Michel Zink (Paris: Fayard, 1992), 582 (s.v. 'Guérin ou Garin').
8. D40.3, 490.
9. For example, D65.1–2, 919; D53.1–2, 696.
10. D16.4–5 (180); D.32.1–6, 372–4.
11. Henri Bergson, *Laughter: An Essay on the Meaning of the Comic*, trans. Cloudesley Brereton and Fred Rothwell (New York: Macmillan, 1911; repr. 1914) (first published in French in 1900, as *Le Rire: Essai sur la signification du comique*), 5.
12. Cf. Dubin, Fabliaux, 816: 'The *fabliaux* do not present a flattering view of the human condition.'
13. See, for example, D.60.201–6 (870–2).
14. See, for example, D57.131 (846).
15. See, for example, D61.2–9 (872); D60.201–5 (870–2).
16. See, for example, D5.19–22 (22); D6.416–37 (46); D7.69–92 (52). Cf. Howard Bloch, *The Scandal of the Fabliaux* (Chicago: Chicago University Press, 1986), 63, 120–1.
17. George Eliot, *Middlemarch: A Study of Provincial Life* (1871–2, repr. Oxford: Oxford World's Classics, 1997), 4. Dubin claims that 'no medieval genre provides a more exhaustive overview of the society of its times than the *fabliaux*'. However, he also admits that 'these are not serious sociological studies', 2.

18. Stephanie Ross, 'Caricature', *The Monist* 58.2 (1974), 285–93, 285. As she puts it, 'caricature is to realistic art as metaphor is to literal expression', 293. The idea that *fabliaux* might be seen as a form of caricature goes back at least to Thomas Wright, *A History of Caricature and Grotesque in Literature and Art* (London: Virtue Bros., 1865): see, for example, 112–17.
19. For example, D2.45–9 (10); D14.276–81 (158). See further Daron Burrows, *The Stereotype of the Priest in the Old French Fabliaux: Anticlerical Satire and Lay Identity* (Bern: Lang, 2005).
20. Cf. Cary Howie's assertion that 'the erotic phenomenology of the *fabliaux* is rude theory' (in 'Rude Theory: The Rough Trade of the Fabliaux', in *Comic Provocations: Exposing the Corpus of Old French Fabliaux*, ed. Holly Crocker (New York: Palgrave Macmillan, 2006), 163–74, 165.
21. For example, D34, esp. 247–355 (420–6); D60 (862–72); D61, esp. 128–210 (878–84). Cf. Bloch, *Scandal*, 67–90; and also Lesley Johnson's remark that in *fabliaux* 'those who take the most irreverent view of language and conventional sign/referent relationships often hold the key to success' (in 'Women on Top: Antifeminism in the *Fabliaux*?', *Modern Language Review* 78 (1983) 298–307, 299.
22. For example, D4 (16–20); D61, 872–84.
23. For example, D1 (4–8); D64 (908–16). Cf. Holly Crocker's claim that 'the fabliaux work to define the body's limits and its deeper meanings' (in her 'Foreward' to *Comic Provocations: Exposing the Corpus of Old French Fabliaux*, ed. Crocker (New York: Palgrave Macmillan, 2006), vii–viii, vii).
24. Frederick C. Crews, *The Pooh Perplex: A Freshman Casebook* (New York: Dutton, 1963).
25. See, for example, in D40.57–60, 494.
26. See, for example, D24.9–15 (314); D47.94–105 (588); D49.117–18 (626); D56.151–3 (826); D63.218–24 (904–6).
27. See, for example, D1.66–7; D24.9–14.
28. See, for example, D62.103–20 and 143–56 (890–2).
29. This *fabliau* (D19) survives in three manuscripts, one of which attributes it to a certain 'Guérin', who may or may not be identifiable with the 'Garin' mentioned in n. 7. Dubin calls it 'Long Butthole Berengier'.
30. The poet says that Lombardy is a land 'o la gent n'est gaires hardie' (D19.12). On the proverbial association between Lombards and cowardice, see, for example, Lilian M. C. Randall, 'The Snail in Gothic Marginal Warfare', *Speculum* 37 (1962) 358–67, 362–6.
31. D19.226–7.
32. Wright, *History of Caricature*, 116.
33. See Roy J. Pearcy, 'An Instance of Heroic Parody in the *Fabliaux*', *Romania* 98 (1977) 105–8; Keith Busby, '*Fabliau et roman breton: le cas de Berengier au lonc cul*', *Épopée animale, fable, fabliau*, ed. Gabriel Bianciotto and Michel Salvat (Paris: Presses Universitaires de France, 1984), 121–32.

Old French Fabliaux 339

34. For an exception (but one that perhaps proves the rule), see the romance of *Silence*, ed. and trans. Sarah Roche-Mahdi (East Lansing: Michigan State University Press, 1992; repr. 2007).
35. Cf. the Old French poem known as '*Le Débat du Con et du Cul*' ('The Debate of the Cunt and the Arsehole', ed. Anatole de Montaiglon and Gaston Raynaud, *Recueil général*, 2: 133–6), which survives only in Paris, BNF MS f. fr. 837. Here the Cunt observes that the distance between it and the Arsehole is less than the thickness of 'a piece of wet parchment' ('uns parchemins qui est moillié'). E. Jane Burns argues that such readings of the female body reflect an inability to see female bodies as anything other than faulty versions of male ones: such 'medieval construction[s] of femininity', she suggests, mask 'the specificity of female genitalia by replacing the vagina with a roughly analogous male orifice' (*Bodytalk: When Women Speak in Old French Literature* (Philadelphia: University of Pennsylvania Press, 1993), 34).
36. Bloch suggests that the knight's failure to recognise his wife's body 'implies that he too has no testicles' (*Scandal*, 104), so that, in effect, this text offers 'a staging of castration' (121).
37. In the terms of medieval philosophy, does biological sex define gender in the way a 'realist' would say that words define ideas? Or is the relationship more analogous to a kind of 'nominalism', by which sex is merely a conventional signifier of gender, just as words are only conventional signifiers of ideas?
38. D19.258–9.
39. D19.295.
40. See, for example, Neil Cartlidge, 'An Intruder at the Feast? Anxiety and Debate in the Letters of Peter of Blois', in *Writers of the Reign of Henry II*, ed. Ruth Kennedy and Simon Meecham-Jones (New York: Palgrave Macmillan, 2006), 79–108 (93–4); Nico van den Boogaard, 'Le fabliau anglo-normand,' in *Third International Beast Epic, Fable and Fabliau Colloquium, Münster 1979: Proceedings*, ed. Jan Goossens and Timothy Sodmann (Cologne: Böhlau, 1981), 66–77; John Hines, *The Fabliau in English* (London: Longman, 1993), 37–44.
41. They are conveniently translated together by Carter Revard, in 'Four *fabliaux* from London, British Library MS Harley 2253, translated into English Verse,' *Chaucer Review* 40 (2005) 111–40; and can also be found in *The Complete Harley 2253 Manuscript*, ed. Susanna Fein, et al., 3 vols. (Kalamazoo, MI: TEAMS, 2014–15), items 75a, 82, 84, and 87. Only one of them (D14, 'The Knight who made the Cunts Talk' = Fein, item 87) appears in Dubin, so they are all cited here from Fein. For discussion of these texts and their contexts, see Barbara Nolan, 'Anthologizing Ribaldry: Five Anglo-Norman *Fabliaux*,' in *Studies in the Harley Manuscript: The Scribes, Contents and Social Contexts of British Library MS Harley* 253 (Kalamazoo, MI: TEAMS, 2000), ed. Susanna Fein, 289–327; Keith Busby, '*Esprit gaulois* for the English: The Humor of the Anglo-Norman Fabliau', in *The Old French Fabliaux: Essays on Comedy and Context*, ed. Kristin L. Burr, John F. Moran, and Norris J. Lacy (Jefferson NC: McFarland, 2008), 160–73 (166–71). Both Nolan and Busby also count a fifth Harley text (item 75, 'The Jongleur of Ely') as a *fabliau*.

42. See, for example, G. L. Brook (ed.), *The Harley Lyrics: The Middle English Lyrics of MS. Harley 2253* (Manchester: Manchester University Press, 1948), 20–2; and cf. Nolan, 'Anthologizing', 289.
43. Cf. Busby's view that 'The humour of the Anglo-Norman fabliaux is not essentially different from much of that found in the larger corpus of continental texts' ('Esprit gaulois', in *The Old French Fabliaux: Essays on Comedy and Context*, *The Old French Fabliaux*, ed. Kristin L. Burr, John F. Moran, and Norris J. Lacy (Jefferson, NC: McFarland, 2008), 160–73 (161)).
44. Fein (ed.), *Complete Harley 2253*, 3: 170–75. It is preserved only in British Library, MS Harley 2253.
45. I borrow this phrase (and its provocativeness in this context) from Johnson's essay: see n. 21.
46. Fein (ed.), *Complete Harley 2253*, 3: 110–14. Harley's copy is one of the two extant.
47. Nolan ('Anthologizing', 309) points out that saints' relics often consisted of excised body parts, which, as she says, may 'obliquely raise taboo questions about the pervasive devotion to saints' preserved body-parts as relics in the late Middle Ages'.
48. Fein (ed.), *Complete Harley 2253*, 3, 204–19. This text is attributed to 'Garin' (or some variant of that name) in all seven the extant manuscripts: see n. 7.
49. Nolan, 'Anthologizing', 324.
50. Cartlidge, 'The Fairies in the Fountain: Promiscuous Liaisons?', in *The Exploitations of Medieval Romance*, ed. Laura Ashe, Judith Weiss, and Ivana Djordjevic (Cambridge: D. S. Brewer, 2010), 15–27.
51. Happy marriages are very rare in the *fabliaux*, and even when they do occur it is implicit that their happiness is fragile (see, for example, D59. 49–51).
52. D47 triples the picture of marital discontent in such a way as to suggest that it is universal. Such discontent is not always illustrated by reference to sex: for example, some *fabliaux* foreground marital tensions prompted by food, as in D56, or by work, as in D62.32–43 (886).
53. *OED*, s.v. 'trouble', n., sense 1g. (b.).
54. For further discussion and illustration of this point, see my essay, ' Gender Trouble? *Fabliau* and Debate in Oxford, Bodleian Library MS Digby 86', in *Manuscript Digby 86: Devotion, Science, and Literary Diversions for a Worcestershire Household, c. 1280*, ed. Susanna Fein (Cambridge: D. S. Brewer, 2019), 130–61 (143–4, 159–61).
55. The resemblances between *fabliaux* and modern modes of comedy are often suggestive: see John F. Moran, '"So This Vilain Walks into a Bar: The Fabliau as Stand-up Comedy', in *The Old French Fabliaux*, ed. Burr et al., 30–41; Logan E. Whalen, 'Modern Dirty Jokes and the Old French Fabliaux', in *The Old French Fabliaux*, ed. Burr et al., 147–59). However, there are also important differences: for example, unlike contemporary stand-up, the *fabliaux* were composed and performed in verse.

Further Reading

Bloch, Howard (1986). *The Scandal of the Fabliaux*, Chicago: Chicago University Press.

Burns, E. Jane (1993). *Bodytalk: When Women Speak in Old French Literature*, Philadelphia: University of Pennsylvania Press.

Burr, Kristin L., John F. Moran, and Norris J. Lacy, eds. (2008). *The Old French Fabliaux: Essays on Comedy and Context*, Jefferson, NC: McFarland.

Crocker, Holly, ed. (2006). *Comic Provocations: Exposing the Corpus of Old French Fabliaux*, New York: Palgrave.

Fein, Susanna, ed. (2000). *Studies in the Harley Manuscript: The Scribes, Contents and Social Contexts of British Library MS Harley 2253*, Kalamazoo, MI: TEAMS.

Hines, John (1993). *The Fabliau in English*, London: Longman.

Muñoz, Nathalie (2014). *Disabusing Women in the Old French Fabliaux*, New York: Peter Lang.

CHAPTER 17

Chaucer and Gower

Venetia Bridges

In this chapter, the wide-ranging topic of women's literary culture is addressed via the following question: what does the representation of femininity enable in the works of Chaucer and Gower, or, to put it slightly differently, what and how do women 'mean' in these literary contexts? Considering this question involves thinking about the nature of the cultures that both poets inhabit, as well as their own individual poetics. The textual culture of the late fourteenth century in England is one in which gender portrayal is intimately bound up with modes of interpretation inherited from long-established texts and traditions, both in terms of Chaucer's and Gower's own specific influences and the textual cultures that transmitted them. It is also a culture that emphasises *translatio studii* or 'transfer of learning': the conceptual and practical process that constructs these traditions.[1] Such a hermeneutic emphasis demonstrates the need for a transnational rather than solely an insular approach, since these texts and traditions are pan-European.[2] It also necessitates a multilingual approach, as many of them are composed in Latin and French or in the more localised but 'literary' vernacular of Italian, all languages to be heard in fourteenth-century London.[3] Women's literary culture, therefore, considered here in terms of feminine representations and meanings in Chaucer's and Gower's writings, is formed through wider transnational, transhistorical, and multilingual networks. This conceptualisation is at the heart of the chapter that follows, which reviews Chaucer's key poetic works and genres (*The Canterbury Tales, Troilus and Criseyde*, and the three major dream visions) and Gower's major works (the *Confessio amantis, Vox clamantis, Mirour de l'Omme*, and *Cinkante Balades*), and concludes with a comparative analysis of major female figures that both Chaucer and Gower portray (Dido, Medea, Constance, the 'loathly lady', and Alcyone). The study is informed by feminist and gender theory in general, and Chaucer scholarship in these areas in particular, taking the approach that attitudes to gender both in literature and in society are cultural constructs influenced by a wide range of factors.[4]

The wider literary culture constructed by the multilingual and transnational networks on which both poets draw is itself not gender neutral. As is demonstrated most famously by the Wife of Bath – 'it is an impossible / That any clerk wol speke good of wyves / But if it be of hooly seintes lyves' – it is inherently masculinist and anti-feminist, in that it predominantly focuses upon the requirements of its male-majority audience.[5] The interpretative approaches constructed by and used in this culture inevitably give rise to a further gendering of literary discourse, since 'medieval hermeneutics ... genders reading, writing, and interpretation as masculine activities enacted upon a text gendered as feminine'.[6] Both in terms of its assumptions and its interpretative approaches, then, this complex literary discourse depicts women and femininity as subordinated to masculine hermeneutic needs.

These hermeneutic needs construct women's meanings in ethical terms. This is not necessarily a gendered point in itself, as the traditional justification for reading and writing non-religious literature was that it contributed to moral development in general: such texts were categorised as 'ethice supponitur', 'pertaining to ethics'.[7] However, this moral hermeneutic results in femininity primarily being used to signify vice and/or virtue, as demonstrated in well-known pro- and anti-feminist texts that appear to have circulated widely, and as seen in the Wife of Bath's assumption that clerks' views of women are ethically binary.[8] This connection of women with ethics has several important ramifications. First, it creates a hermeneutic assumption that women's primary function is to illustrate moral, frequently sexual, behaviour, which relates femininity strongly to the concept of erotic love (as seen, for example, in the highly influential *Roman de la rose*).[9] Second, femininity is seen in binary terms as 'good'/ 'bad', limiting its interpretative range. Third, the portrayal of femininity is fundamentally allegorical, since it creates meaning that is other than (or displaced from) itself; women's narratives and needs are interpreted for others' purposes rather than signifying in their own terms. Finally, therefore, gender is strongly correlated with questions about how language itself, and literary discourse in particular, is able to construct meaning.[10]

In short, Chaucer's and Gower's engagement with women's literary culture (in terms of their own poetic portrayals) is likely to be framed by inherited hermeneutic ideas that see gender, and in particular femininity, as ethically valent. This context is especially notable for Gower, famously called 'moral' by Chaucer at the end of *Troilus and Criseyde*. Yet it is also important for Chaucer, whose interest in the art of interpretation, as well as in the portrayal of women and gender, is a constant presence across his oeuvre. The representation of women and their literary cultures is thus a theme that pierces to the heart of Chaucer's and Gower's poetic identities, transcending their differences of language, style, and content.

Chaucer

Narrating Women in The Canterbury Tales: *The Wife of Bath and the Prioress*

The question of women as agents of meaning is at the core of *The Canterbury Tales*, whether those tales be romance, hagiography, *exemplum*, or *fabliau*, and whether they involve women as narrators or as subjects.[11] The *Tales* have long been identified by readers as especially concerned with issues of feminine representation: for example, the concept of the 'Marriage Group' highlights a persistent thematic focus on issues of female sovereignty in marriage.[12] Beyond this debated grouping,[13] the roles, capacities, and expectations of women feature in many of the other tales, including the 'Tale of Melibee', 'The Second Nun's Tale', 'The Physician's Tale', 'The Man of Law's Tale', 'The Knight's Tale', and 'The Miller's Tale'; in fact, it is difficult to identify one of the collection's stories that does not engage with these issues.

The Wife of Bath is an extraordinary creation. Wealthy, independent, garrulous, much-married, well dressed, and well travelled, she has been described as 'embod[ying] almost all the faults traditionally imputed to women' in anti-feminist discourse,[14] yet her Prologue complicates this presentation. Her argument in favour of marriage is a textually explicit one, relying upon biblical texts for its justification, and its dramatic climax occurs because of the lengthy list of 'wikked wives' drawn from patristic and classical texts. It stages a debate over women's agency within marriage via 'auctoritee' (despite the apparent preference for 'experience' at the start), and it does so not just by textual citation but by the violent damaging of a physical text, Jankyn's book. Much has been written about the Wife's (ab)use of texts in her arguments, but it is worth pointing out that her technique of textual citation and elaboration is highly orthodox; despite what appears to be her pro-feminist argument in favour of marriage, in terms of process she could be considered 'masculinist', since she uses the gendered tools of intellectual tradition. In short, her portrayal and argument complicate the pro-/anti-feminist binary that the text appears to set up, and does so by invoking differently gendered textual discourses. The Wife of Bath is thus both heavily gendered as female (mostly in a negative sense, if read alongside inherited stereotypes), but also in textual terms as male. She is therefore more complex when the gendered nature of textual discourse is brought into play, an observation that sets the scene for her Tale (discussed in the 'Shared Subjects' section).

The Prioress is not so enthusiastically textual, although her portrayal in the General Prologue owes much to the conventions of romance as well as to ideals of religious women's demeanour. In her beautiful appearance and courtly behaviour (despite her provincial French), her religious depiction is intertwined with that of a romance heroine, the two united in her brooch inscribed with the Virgilian phrase 'Amor vincit omnia'.[15] These two roles are not mutually exclusive, especially for women, given the potentially elite status of senior nuns and the generic interactions of romance and hagiography, but they are in playful tension in the General Prologue; Madame Eglentyne seems more interested in her courtly demeanour than her religious vocation. Importantly, her portrayal draws on accepted feminine attributes in both contexts.

'The Prioress's Tale' also displays what may be termed 'femininity' in some of its aspects, although it may not originally have been written for the Prioress specifically.[16] In composing his version of a well-known miracle of the Virgin, Chaucer emphasises its pathos and the innocence of the murdered 'little clergeon' (l. 503) repeatedly, describing the latter as 'litel child', 'yong and tendre', 'innocent' (ll. 516, 552, 596; 524; 566). These attributes are explicitly related to the Prioress when she refers to herself in the tale's Prologue as 'a child of twelf month oold', with the requisite 'wayk ... konnyng' (ll. 484, 481). These connections between limited understanding, innocence, and youth are therefore overtly gendered before the beginning of the tale proper. Yet it has long been noted that the tale's narrator also focuses on – perhaps even revels in – details of violence and degradation.[17] Such details form a strong contrast to the Prioress's desire to identify herself with childish innocence. Whilst dwelling on these details is perhaps inevitable in a devotional tale, with its need for stark binaries of good and evil, the juxtaposition of innocent purity and violence also questions the Prioress's feminised and childlike self-characterisation. It is telling that at a moment of such juxtaposition, when the narrating teller's voice jumps from describing the 'blood' and 'cursed dede' of the murder straight to a portrayal of 'the white Lamb celestial' (ll. 578, 581), the narration briefly steps outside the tale proper by inserting 'quod she' at the end of the same line to highlight that it is a female voice narrating not just innocence and pathos but also violence and degradation. Childishness and purity are not the only characteristics of femininity on display here. It could perhaps be argued that the gendered nature of the tale is troubled if violence is thought of as a typically masculine concept; certainly, the treatment of such violence raises questions about the Prioress's femininity.

Whilst the Prioress is not as engaged in explicitly textual gendering as the Wife of Bath, Chaucer plays with generic and gendered expectations in her tale to depict a stereotypically feminised woman whose choice of narrative is both apt and disturbing, echoing the tensions seen in her portrait. It is important not to over-read the Prioress's shadow side, given that the miracle genre requires binaries in order to function and that attitudes to religious difference have altered significantly since the fourteenth century; however, it is undoubtedly the case that Chaucer plays with generic expectations of femininity to complicate her portrayal.

Women as Subjects: Alysoun, May, Emelye, Griselda, Dorigen, Cecilia, Virginia, the 'loathly lady'

Women feature as subjects across the different genres of *The Canterbury Tales*' narratives, filtered through the narrating voice of each tale's teller and also that of Chaucer the pilgrim. These additional layers of narration complicate what may appear to be simplistic or straightforward presentations of women: it is salutary to remember that both the garrulous Wife of Bath and the quiet and passive Emelye in 'The Knight's Tale' are ventriloquised by male narrating voices. Crucially, women as narrators and subjects throughout the *Tales* are used to highlight wider ethical questions, meaning that Chaucer's playful deconstruction of literary traditions and discourses is based upon a fundamentally moral conception of femininity.

Many of Chaucer's female subjects are wives (hence the idea of the 'Marriage Group'). Alysoun and May, the young wives of the Miller's and Merchant's *fabliaux* respectively, are depicted in terms that emphasise their youth and beauty but that also parody the descriptions of romance heroines such as Emelye.[18] This generic interplay, which is particularly strong between the Knight's and Miller's tales given their explicit textual relationship, is a reminder that what may appear to be clear-cut portrayals of femininity within a particular tale can be nuanced by broader cross-tale comparison.[19] For example, Alysoun's frank sexual desire in 'The Miller's Tale' contrasts with Emelye's plea in 'The Knight's Tale' to remain unmarried, a comparison that is highlighted via the romance conventions used to describe both women; this cross-genre comparison brings to the fore the interconnected ethical issues of sexual desire and female agency that both tales consider. Such a deliberate thematic consciousness connects both tales to others that are not explicitly related to them, such as the 'Wife of Bath's Prologue' and 'Tale'. Chaucer's interest in exploring concepts of agency and desire is even more overt in 'The Franklin's Tale', with its intimate analysis of an apparently equal marriage that turns out to be constrained by desire for public honour and that ultimately demonstrates a lack of feminine liberty in the figure of Dorigen, the romance heroine.[20] The question of 'sovereigntee' is of course the object of the knight's quest in 'The Wife of Bath's Tale', another tale whose explicitly stated theme is explored in the context of female agency; an even more extreme example is Griselda in 'The Clerk's Tale'. 'The Physician's Tale' depicts a woman, Virginia, who has no agency at all but is simply an *exemplum* of virtue over which two men fight; arguably, the tale is more akin to a hagiography, although she is not the central focus as would be expected in that genre, and the setting is pre-Christian Rome.[21] The figure of Prudence in the 'Tale of Melibee' is more a personified virtue, comparable to Lady Philosophy in *Boece*, than a gendered subject.

Yet Chaucer also complicates the idea of an overarching gendered theme connecting different tales. 'The Franklin's Tale' ends with its narrator asking which of the male characters is the most 'fre' (noble and generous: l. 1622), suggesting that the interpretative framework through which he views the tale in retrospect is focused upon male ideas of behaviour rather than directly concerned with female agency.[22] More complex is the case of 'The Clerk's Tale', which appears to present Griselda as an *exemplum* of feminine obedience in a mode highly reminiscent of hagiography but whose narrator comments disapprovingly upon her treatment at points throughout and at the end explicitly forbids wives from reading it as didactic.[23] So, whilst *The Canterbury Tales* is evidently highly interested in the question of female agency within marriage, exploring both its apparent presence and absence in ways that often do not provide resolution, it also deconstructs the idea of a consistent thematic narrative by foregrounding problems of hermeneutics, both specifically with reference to women's agency and more widely throughout the text.

The other important feminine role in *The Canterbury Tales* is that of the saint. As mentioned earlier, both 'The Clerk's Tale' and 'The Physician's Tale' contain hagiographical features in their presentation of women as secular saints, emblematic of beauty, virtue, and obedience, but the only tale that has a female saint at its centre is that of the Second Nun, who tells the story of St Cecilia. Although this double gendering (both narrator and subject) might suggest that the construction of femininity is an important theme for the story, this is deceptive, since the tale may not be connected to its teller.[24] The tale itself gives Cecilia persuasive spiritual power in conventional hagiographical mode, making her an active tool of God but without personal agency. More interesting is the start of the Prologue, which discourses on the evils of idleness and recommends the story as a remedy; this unexpected preamble provides an ethical interpretative framework for the tale that sits somewhat oddly with its hagiographical content, reminiscent of the more explicitly disruptive tensions seen between tale and hermeneutic frame elsewhere. Here again gender provides the means for wider questions of interpretation.

In *The Canterbury Tales*, the representation of femininity is revealed to be intimately and intricately bound up with the act of reading and interpretation, demonstrating Chaucer's ongoing preoccupation with the opportunities women as subjects provide for exploring the instabilities of textual discourse. Importantly, many of these opportunities involve individual women being interpreted via an ethical lens to provide a wider meaning. The Wife of Bath's ethically negative portrayal as a 'bad' woman complicates her arguments about feminine agency; Dorigen's dilemma about fidelity is the catalyst for the tale's question concerning the most generous male character; the Prioress's religious virtue produces an ethically polarised saint's *vita*; and so on. Chaucer uses these morally valent women to deconstruct accepted literary discourses and, in so doing, inevitably problematises the ethical hermeneutic that labels femininity as 'good' or 'bad'. Fundamentally, however, this binary moral interpretation of women remains at the core of his poetics in *The Canterbury Tales*.

Troilus and Criseyde

Of all Chaucer's works, *Troilus and Criseyde* (1382–5) has probably generated the largest corpus of modern commentary in terms of gender representation, focusing naturally on Criseyde but more recently upon Troilus as well.[25] This intense textual activity is not confined to contemporary criticism focusing solely on Chaucer's work, however, since Criseyde has been written and written about from the classical era onwards; her portrayal in his Troy romance joins the representations of Dares' and Dictys' late antique accounts, Benoît de Sainte-Maure's twelfth-century *Roman de Troie*, Boccaccio's *Il Filostrato*, and Henryson's later *Testament of Cressid*. In this sense, Chaucer's Criseyde is potentially the most written, and hence gendered, of all his female creations.

And she knows it. 'O, rolled shal I ben on many a tonge!' she cries as she betrays Troilus, showing a foresighted awareness of her own future textual interpretation.[26] At her first appearance, too, she is engaged in reading herself, as Dinshaw observes: the 'romance of Thebes' in which she is engrossed as Pandarus appears to tell her of Troilus' love narrates her second lover Diomedes' family history, meaning that Criseyde's reading is an act of future self-fashioning.[27] It is also a gendered act, since her 'romaunce' is associated with femininity (in Dinshaw's terms, open-endedness[28]), in contrast to Pandarus' reference to the Latin *Thebaid*, a part of the masculinist intellectual tradition. His dismissive response to her comments on the Thebes romance explicitly constructs a linguistic and generic hierarchy in which the Latin epic is superior to the French romance, the male reader to the female one.[29] This hierarchy of course also applies to the interwoven texts upon which *Troilus and Criseyde* as a whole draws; even allowing for the stark nature of Pandarus' binary generic categorisation, the Latin, French, and Italian source material is preoccupied with narrating masculine experiences, of love as well as of war, and beyond that act of narration is itself part of the gendered medieval intellectual tradition. Criseyde's attempt to construct herself via literary texts is thus already gendered even before Pandarus' intervention, and their conversation simply makes this gendering explicit.

Chaucer's Criseyde is inevitably defined by the ethical view of women as either 'good' or 'bad' that is fundamental to medieval literary culture. She has been read in these terms for centuries, from *Troie*'s anti-feminist diatribe that uses her behaviour to condemn the whole sex to modern feminist studies that see her in more positive terms (or, at least, in less negative ones).[30] For Criseyde, this binary categorisation is ironic given her 'slydying' and ambiguous presentation. Perhaps her most-referenced characteristic – her changeable, multifaceted persona – means that she cannot be defined consistently in relation to feminine standards of behaviour. This results in the questioning of these gendered norms: Criseyde becomes 'a female figure who resists, and ultimately proves inadequate, the categories usually employed in literary analysis of character'.[31] So, the need to read Chaucer's Criseyde ethically, in the binary terms encouraged by intellectual history but also on occasion by the text itself (as in her lament about her future reputation), is ironically strongly correlated with, perhaps even produced by, her complexities and inconsistencies.

These complexities and inconsistencies are related to the highly, and often explicitly, intertextual nature of the poem. Chaucer frequently reworks his inherited material to complicate Criseyde, as happens in her contemplation of Troilus's love in Book II.[32] Her complex thought process unites the practical concerns seen in the Italian text with extended consideration of more philosophical concepts (for example, feminine 'libertee', l. 773) added by Chaucer, drawing on ideas that implicitly indicate her debts to wider intellectual traditions of thought.[33] What is particularly interesting about this brief moment of expansive *translatio* is how it invokes ideas of gender and ethics. Without becoming essentialist, Criseyde's thinking, described as 'plited ... in many folde' (l. 697), could be read as characteristically feminine in its mutability, but it is striking how her analysis of the 'matere' draws on scholastic habits of thought in its weighing of both sides of the question, considering both practicalities and more philosophical and moral concerns such as freedom and honour; it could be described, therefore, as more masculine in its approach. The *translatio* here evokes gendered ideas about intellectual capabilities, complicating Criseyde's feminised presentation, since she is characterised using differently gendered attributes. Importantly, since Criseyde's variously gendered thinking draws heavily upon concepts such as 'mesure', 'honour', and 'shame', it is clearly formed by an ethical approach, which reveals once again that gendered discourse is inevitably rooted in ethical assumptions about femininity and masculinity.[34] *Translatio* is therefore an act bound up with ethical expectations of femininity and masculinity in the poem. However, Chaucer troubles the idea of gendered (and ethical) binaries by depicting Criseyde not as a masculinist interpreter of a feminised text, nor solely as a feminised object of such interpretation, but as a more complex reader characterised by habits identified with both genders. This troubling of gender and ethical binaries is perhaps one reason why Criseyde's presentation and behaviour has provoked such divergent interpretations.

Dream Visions

Chaucer's dream visions – *The Book of the Duchess*, *The House of Fame*, and *The Parliament of Fowls*, in probable order of composition – are among his most complex poems in terms of textual discourse and structure. All are deeply interested in the interpretative possibilities offered by inherited texts, whether the Ovidian tale of Ceyx and Alcyone (*The Book of the Duchess*), the Troy narrative as told in the *Aeneid* (*The House of Fame*), or the *Somnium Scipionis* (*The Parliament of Fowls*), to name only the clearest examples. The gendered nature of medieval intellectual traditions means that such overt intertextual discourse brings issues of femininity very much to the fore before thematic considerations are borne in mind; this is particularly evident in the tale of

Ceyx and Alcyone in *The Book of the Duchess* and the Troy *Aeneid* narrative in *The House of Fame*, both of which explicitly engage with the roles and fates of women. All three works also reflect upon gendered concerns, such as the loss of the perfect lover (*The Book of the Duchess*), the role of women in the construction of fame (*The House of Fame*), and the question of natural authority and choice in marriage (*The Parliament of Fowls*). Structurally, thematically, in terms of textual discourse and sometimes in their potential occasionality (*The Book of the Duchess* and John of Gaunt, *The Parliament of Fowls* and Richard II's marriage), these three poems are therefore strongly implicated in questions of femininity and its ethical signifying possibilities.

Femininity in *The Book of the Duchess* is constructed in a context of love and loss. Alcyone is the perfect 'noble wyf' (86) and Lady White is a paragon of female beauty and virtue; both perform a similar and very recognisable erotic role as love object. The lengthy, lyrical exposition of the Black Knight's love in all her conventional perfection that forms the major part of *The Book of the Duchess* is experienced after reading the story of Ceyx and Alcyone, suggesting that the two episodes are thematically connected; both of course describe the tragic loss of a true love to death, Ceyx and then Lady White. Yet it is notable that both tales focus upon the emotional impact of that love upon the bereaved lover, rather than upon the love itself (and lost lover) that is the ostensible subject of the narratives. Alcyone's loss is marked both by her sleepless anxiety and then her sudden death, and the Black Knight's introduction is characterised at length by his sorrowful affect. In the latter case in particular, the emphasis throughout is upon his own emotional responses. When he is describing his love's beauty, for example, he consistently returns to its impact upon his own thoughts and feelings.[35] Love here is portrayed through its affects upon individuals, which emphasises the issue of interpretation; emotion's meaning is not self-evident but must be read through its outward signs. The dreamer-narrator also brings this hermeneutic issue to the fore, first by comically reading Alcyone's tragedy as primarily a remedy for his sleep deprivation, and then by failing to interpret the Black Knight's narrative correctly, as his many questions indicate. He is a literal reader who finds it difficult to interpret the signs that he sees, whether textual or physical.[36]

Both these tales involving women are therefore perhaps less about the representation of femininity as it loves (Alcyone) and is loved (Lady White) than they are about the hermeneutics of emotion, and specifically this emotion as interpreted by men. Both the Black Knight and the dreamer-narrator are focused on the narratives' impact upon themselves, on their own readings of them and their effects, rather than upon any wider interpretation. The use of these narratives apparently focused upon women as in fact a means of revealing male emotional self-centredness is a clear example of how gendered medieval hermeneutics might be, especially in the hands of a poet such as Chaucer.

The House of Fame's exploration of femininity is rooted in classical material and related intellectual traditions, and as a result engages with gendered characteristics in more explicitly ethical terms than does *The Book of the Duchess*. The narrative anticipates its description of the House itself with a depiction of the Temple of Venus that features a long retelling of the *Aeneid*'s version of the Troy story with influence from Ovid's *Heroides*.[37] In this, Dido explicitly rebukes 'wikke Fame' (l. 249) for her lost reputation (ll. 346, 348), reminiscent of Criseyde's similar textual awareness in *Troilus and Criseyde*, and the narrator develops this with a long excursus on the 'untrouthe' (l. 384) of men towards women.[38] This excursus is sympathetic to its subjects, but it is somewhat ironic that the narrator here is spreading their 'wikke fame' in just the way that Dido has recently bewailed. The return to Aeneas' story immediately after this passage reinforces this sense of an imposed hermeneutic fate, since the apparently sympathetic list of abandoned women is bracketed by the inevitable onward movement of the imperialist, masculinist narrative that has caused their sorrow. All these women are victims not just of male abandonment but also of the textual traditions that depict them as sufferers at the hands of men; that gender's ability to write its own story, to depict Aeneas as not primarily a false lover but as an empire-founder, is distinct from women's fixed portrayal as victims in a textual tradition that focuses on male deeds.

Geffrey's visit to the House of Fame itself reinforces this textual tradition in its portrayal of canonical authors honoured on pillars, including 'Stace', 'the gret Omer', 'Dares and Tytus', 'Guydo ... de Columpnis, / and Englyssh Gaufride', all described in terms of the Troy narrative.[39] Yet this weighty, seemingly monolithic tale has hermeneutic cracks; before the narrator moves on to other related narratives' poets (Virgil, Ovid, Lucan, and Claudian), he highlights 'a litil envye' between the Troy authors over Homer's veracity, demonstrating that its interpretation is not a fixed matter despite the potency of traditional narratives.[40] Chaucer, in a characteristically double move, upholds the Troy narrative tradition's canonical nature whilst suggesting that it is not hermeneutically static, despite the seemingly fixed fate of the women entrapped within it in the Temple of Venus. This mixture of permanence and fluidity is of course thematically apt for the appearance of Fame herself, 'a femynyne creature' (l. 1365) in line with literary tradition,[41] who constantly changes in size and whose decisions about fame or its absence appear to be arbitrary. This connection of fickleness with femininity in the depiction of Fame is not new to Chaucer (she is personified similarly in the *Aeneid*), but in its *House of Fame* context it adds another layer to the interactions of gender, ethics, and textual tradition, since it shows a particularly chaotic force, gendered feminine, controlling the fates of canonical authors. In this sense, Fame's random autonomy is a counterbalance to the static fate of the women trapped by textual tradition in Venus' temple. *The House of Fame*, therefore, plays with gender as a concept through which to explore the ways canonical narratives and their interpretations alter as well as how they remain constant. This playful deconstruction is enabled by the fundamentally ethical basis of traditional hermeneutics. Such a basis portrays women in binary terms, either as virtuous if foolish victims of masculinist narratives or more negatively as powerful yet chaotic beings making irrational decisions; it is this ethical binary that fuels Chaucer's exploration (and exploitation) of his inherited narratives' possibilities.

The Parliament of Fowls reflects upon questions of autonomy and authority that are also addressed via a gendered approach. The interplay of liberty and limitation seen in the formel (female) eagle's request to delay her choice of one of her three suitors for a year has been much discussed, but especially pertinent here is the depiction of this interplay in terms of feminine agency.[42] This is central to *The Parliament of Fowls*' narrative, given the parliament's explicit purpose, but it is also highlighted in the Temple of Venus that the dreamer-narrator describes before the parliament proper begins. The temple portrays different aspects of erotic love, both pleasurable and painful, but the sorrow of abandoned women is the main mode by which the latter is conveyed. As in *The House of Fame*, the dreamer-narrator lists women who were victims of love, framing this as a female narrative despite the presence of some men.[43] This connection of erotic tragedy with femininity as well as erotic pleasure is the backdrop for the parliament that follows, and is a reminder that the comedic politics of the birds' wrangling is not the only discourse of love in the poem; although the lower orders go away content after Nature's intervention, the formel's reluctance to marry relates thematically to the deceived and forced women listed in Venus' temple. Once again, femininity's wider meanings, here relating to autonomy and authority, are rooted in an ethical understanding of women as inferior to men, and hence as the latter's victims; meaning is constructed through an ethical conception of gender. This gendered ethics is highlighted further at the end of the text, since free erotic choice for women turns out to be constrained by necessity (social, political, philosophical), despite the ideal that each female 'agre to his [her suitor's] eleccioun' (l. 409). Even Nature, 'the vicaire of the almighty Lord' (l. 379), has limitations upon her authority, since she cannot, or chooses not to, make the formel decide on a mate, and the poem is left hermeneutically open as the latter considers her options and the dreamer-narrator returns to his books for enlightenment – 'and thus to rede I nyl nat spare' (l. 699).

In all three poems, love's gendered ethics are used to explore questions of authority, whether those concern loss and consolation, textual traditions, or liberty and choice.

Chaucer the Ethical Poet?

This analysis of Chaucer's key works has shown not only how frequently that textually sensitive poet exploits the nexus of gender and ethics in composing his work, but also how his much-discussed irony and disruption of literary discourse is rooted in traditional hermeneutics that see femininity as primarily an ethical signifier. In other words, Chaucer's poetic innovation, so appropriate to modern readers, is based upon playful manipulation of existing traditions rather than wholly novel approaches. His depictions of women may be read (with historicist caveats) as proto-feminist in their focus on women's agency, but this focus is constructed via traditional hermeneutics that rely on femininity having a subordinate political, social, and ethical status.

Gower

The observation that Chaucer is a more ethically engaged poet than is frequently allowed may nuance our view of 'moral' Gower. In one sense, this term is an accurate description of the ethical issues so prominent across Gower's oeuvre, whether these be political (as in *Vox clamantis*), more theologically and philosophically inflected (the *Mirour de l'Omme*), or the complex interplay of different aspects of virtue and vice – 'lust' and 'lore' (Prologue, l. 19) – seen in *Confessio amantis*. Yet it also suggests that Gower's ethical focus is more important than his poetry, which fails to allow for the complexities of his works.[44] In fact, the epithet highlights Gower's concern for, and probing of, a moral hermeneutics, the idea that he explores 'the limitations of the ethical structures available to him' and the multiplicity of readings that this suggests.[45] This is particularly apparent in the *Confessio*, given the explicit interpretative framing built into its structure, the ideas of sin and virtue taken from traditional Christian doctrine that ostensibly provide the means by which Amans moves from being driven by desire to following reason.[46] Whilst this framing is not present in *Vox clamantis*, the poem's use of the dream vision form also foregrounds a moral hermeneutics related to the approach of the *Confessio*, and the two works are further thematically linked by the *Confessio*'s concern for the current state of affairs seen in its Prologue.[47] This study will consider Gower's representation of women and femininity by using the idea of a moral hermeneutics that comes under various pressures.

Describing both Chaucer and Gower in ethical terms may seem to be aligning the two poets rather more closely than is habitual. One significant difference between them is that for Gower the representation of women and femininity, except in *Confessio amantis*, is often less of an overt subject than it is for Chaucer. However, the former frequently uses these concepts even when they are not the direct subject of his poetry as signifiers of other concerns; the anti-feminist passage in chapter 6 of Book v of *Vox clamantis* occurs in the context of a discourse upon correct knighthood, for example. The *Mirour de l'Omme* is also heavily invested in the possibilities of women as ethical signifiers, since its theological and moral approach is constructed through female personifications of vice and virtue.[48] Given this, it is important to consider all Gower's works from this perspective, despite the relatively limited representation of women and gender beyond the *Confessio*.

Confessio amantis

The *Confessio*'s collection of exemplary stories is given an explicitly ethical and religious framework, as the poem is organised into sections based on the seven deadly sins that in turn are connected by the overall confession narrative of Amans to Genius, priest of Venus. Yet there are tensions between this framework and the narrative. The Christian theology of the deadly sins at times sits uneasily with a conceptualisation of love that may be both religious and erotic in nature, creating a sense of hermeneutic distortion that is exacerbated by the odd fit between some of the individual tales and their apparent ethical interpretation as illustrations of particular sins.[49] Whilst the interpretation of Acis and Galatea's tale as an *exemplum* of the negative effects of envy is apposite (II.104–200), and the story of Phoebus and Daphne (III.1685–720) is plausibly read as a warning against 'folhaste' in love (l. 1742), the narrative of Iphis and Ianthe (IV.451–505) is awkwardly moralised as an indication of the need for persistence rather than sloth in love. In this last example, the tension between narrative and interpretation is caused by the overarching ethical hermeneutic (sloth). Whether deliberately or not, the effect here is to highlight the interpretative problems that may arise when the analysis of erotic narrative is constrained by ethical considerations.

This hermeneutic problem also affects the presentation of femininity, female subjects, and subjects assigned female at birth. It is noticeable that the examples referred to earlier require the reworking of the *Confessio*'s source material (primarily Ovid's *Metamorphoses*) to diminish their voices and agency; Galatea's role in changing Acis into a river god, Daphne's desire never to marry, and Iphis's grief at being born female (all prominent features of the Latin text) are omitted from the *Confessio*.[50] The need for these figures to be ethical *exempla* results in the reduction of their agency, a clear indication of the gendered power of hermeneutics discussed earlier. This might indicate that the epithet 'moral' is highly apt for the *Confessio* poet. However, the overt tension this interpretative need creates between tale and moral also suggests that, to some extent, this ethical approach deconstructs itself, since the visible strain it requires questions its efficacy. The point made earlier about a moral hermeneutics that is both highly present and also under pressure from its literary context is salient here.

Vox clamantis

Gower's Latin poem lamenting the ills of the traditional three estates does not feature women as subjects as frequently as does the *Confessio*, but Book v contains several chapters that focus on the dangers that women pose to true knighthood. Femininity is bound up with erotic power and fear: 'quid honoris victor habebit, / si mulieris amor vincere possit eum?' ('what honour shall a conqueror have, if a woman's love is able to conquer him'? ll. 19–20). As powerful agents of Venus, women entrap men (specifically knights here) with their 'fatuo . . . amore' ('foolish love', l. 30), but they are also depicted as weak and in thrall to erotic desires themselves.[51] The *Vox* repudiates the idea that love for women may encourage noble chivalric deeds, seeking to define knighthood in spiritual terms.[52]

This paradox of erotic weakness combined with power is hardly new to Gower, since it is a staple of Latin literature.[53] The text rejoices in the rhetorical possibilities of this paradox, describing love in a *tour de force* of contradictory phrases that begins 'amor est egra salus, vexata quies, pius error' ('love is sickly health, troubled rest, pious sin', 2.53).[54] Whilst this dazzling display of love's unnatural power is not explicitly gendered here, it is connected to that concept in the previous chapter ('women's love', l. 20) and even more clearly related to women in the chapter following, much of which is devoted to describing female beauty (chapter 3). Love's contradictions are read in a context that implicitly aligns them with women, a gendered connection made all the stronger by well-known traditions of anti-feminist writing on which they clearly draw.

In this section of the *Vox*, then, Gower depicts love in negative terms through its strong connection with femininity, uniting the two concepts in a highly morally charged context that inevitably means that women are used to exemplify evil. Yet this ethical relationship also undermines the ostensible subject of this part of the *Vox*: correct knighthood. It is notable that knighthood frequently disappears underneath the sheer weight of anti-feminist rhetoric, so that love feels somewhat disconnected from the concept it is seemingly illustrating and critiquing; the subject has in effect become the erotic power of women, which is ironically celebrated in the dazzling rhetoric used to condemn it. The power of this negative moral association between femininity and love has overwhelmed the narrative.

Ballades

Representations of women are a more obvious topic in Gower's *Cinkante Balades*. Rare French examples of the form in late fourteenth- or early fifteenth-century England, these owe much to continental French poets such as Machaut, Deschamps, and Froissart, as well as to Anglo-Norman stylistic features.[55] The holistic nature of the collection of fifty poems is debated, but the overarching theme, the pains and pleasures of love, is clear. The *ballades* are mostly addressed to a lady (or ladies) by a male lover,[56] but nos. 41–4 and 46 are composed in the voice of a woman, so it is on these that the analysis will focus.

These five poems present different situations. Ballades 41–3 are spoken by female voices lamenting false male lovers, whereas 44 and 46 are part of a sequence of professions of faithful love expressed by male and female speakers (44–7). Gower's decision for women to experience and voice the pain of infidelity as victims contrasts with the presentation of femininity in *Vox clamantis*, where women are presented as faithless themselves. However, the role of women in both the Latin and French works is fundamentally to signify love's inevitable framing in terms of moral discourse. This ethical valency is emphasised clearly in the lexis of *ballades* 41 and 42, which is that of falsity and deceit, especially in 41's refrain 'Bon est qe bone dame bien s'avise' ('it is good that a good woman take good care').[57] Although it is true that the active female speaker has a certain agency in depicting her own plight, the framing of this plight ties her signifying potential to ethics, limiting personal, emotive reflections in preference for highlighting moral consequences.[58] The need to depict the experience as a general and generic one reduces the sense of personal connection with the speaker, and hence its emotional impact.

It is true that this impersonality contrasts with the more emotive approach seen briefly in Ballade 42 and particularly Ballade 43.[59] Here the female speakers present their experience primarily in affective terms, which might suggest a greater sense of personal engagement and, hence, agency. However, these laments are themselves highly stylised, drawing upon conventions of French lyric poetry,[60] so that reading them as more 'personal' in an individualising way is likely to be misleading; rather, in addition to an ethical mode, they are adopting another conventional form of discourse, that of affect, to define femininity.[61] Gower's depiction of women as signifiers of ethical issues in his other works, particularly *Vox*, is joined here by an affective focus that is equally habitual in lyric poetry.

The following two poems (44 and 46) that depict faithful love voiced by women frame it slightly differently. Here the lexis and literary background is that of romance and the values praised those of chivalry.[62] Although this is a discourse that does not deploy such explicitly ethical terms as poems 41 and 42 with their repetition of 'false', 'true', 'good', *etc.*, in context it is clear that this description of courtly *gentillesse* is similarly morally valent, depicting a male exemplar of faithful love and 'loialté' who should be responded to in kind. Ballades 45 and 47, with male narrating subjects, are in the same mode.[63] In these last four *ballades*, then, the modes of discourse vary, but the basic ethical focus remains the same.

Mirour de l'Omme

A long poem (probably around 34,000 lines) composed in Anglo-Norman French and extant in only one manuscript (Cambridge University Library, Additional MS 3035), the *Mirour* addresses the problem of human salvation through personifications of sin and virtue before describing corruption in contemporary life, and then turns to the importance of the Virgin Mary as the instigator of God's solution to the problem. Although it includes elements familiar from complaint, *psychomachia*, allegory, satire, and penitential discourses, it is '*sui generis* ... no medieval genre exists which embraces so many elements'.[64] The contents may seem removed from questions of what and how gendered discourse may signify, but R. F. Yeager points out that, like the *Confessio*, the *Mirour* is indebted to 'the courtly world initiated by the *Roman de la rose*', and that it reveals 'how central to Gower's poetic imagination were the language and rituals of love'.[65] This reliance on courtly, erotic discourse inevitably introduces gendered and ethical perspectives that are heightened by the allegorical discourse of marriage and procreation and by the framing of the text with Eve and the Virgin.[66] Both women are depicted in terms that relate to 'the language and rituals of love' (and hence ethical hermeneutics), as Eve behaves 'come fole amie' ('like a foolish lover', l. 149) and the descriptions of the Virgin are similar to those of love lyrics.[67] The poem also begins by casting its readership in erotic terms: 'Escoulte cea, chascun amant, / Qui tant perestes desirant / Du pecche, dont l'amour est fals ... Lors est il fols qui ses travauls / Met en amour si desloiauls, / Dont au final nuls est joyant' ('Listen to this, every lover who seems so desirous of Sin, whose love is false ... he is foolish who exerts himself in a love so treacherous that in the end no one rejoices in it' (ll. 1–2, 7–9). Combining the discourses of Christian salvation and eroticism is reminiscent of English romance of the period, itself seen as a 'feminised' genre owing to its interest in the capacities and roles of women.[68] This eroticised discourse in the *Mirour* thus evokes gendered ideas about love and salvation even though the sinning subject is 'any man' (l. 25). In addition, the personification of vices and virtues as female cements the connections between gender and ethics (here, Christian morals), reinforcing the idea that women signify primarily in ethical terms.

'Moral' Gower

'Moral' Gower is thus both an accurate description and an oversimplification of the poet's approach to feminine representation. Deeply invested in women as signifiers, and in ethical hermeneutics in general, his works nevertheless highlight some of the difficulties involved in combining the two, especially in relation to retelling antique tales (*Confessio amantis*). Like Chaucer, Gower represents women via traditional hermeneutics that rely on femininity having a subordinate political, social, and ethical status, but, in contrast to the former's playful engagement with such traditions, Gower's approach has a more serious, even anxious, tone; it is a moral poetics with a distinct sense of purpose.

Shared Subjects: Dido, Medea, Constance, the *Tale of Florent* and 'The Wife of Bath's Tale', Alcyone

The *Legend of Good Women* (c. 1386) and the *Confessio* are the works in which Chaucer and Gower's relationship, and thus their representations of femininity, are most direct and explicit, since the poems depict several of the same female figures.[69] However, this relationship is multifaceted, since it occurs within a mutual textual culture as well as between their own works. It is often triangulated via Ovid, 'a sort of broker ... between Chaucer and Gower', since his work is the ultimate (if not sole) source for much of the shared material in the *Legend* and *Confessio*.[70] The work of the Latin poet is not the only arena for Chaucer and Gower's poetics, since the classical women depicted in the *Legend* and *Confessio* do not stand in an unmediated relationship directly with their sources, but are part of the complex network of textual and hermeneutic inheritances mentioned in the introduction to this chapter.

The nature of the *Legend of Good Women*'s *translatio* is ostensibly ethical and recuperative.[71] However, Chaucer combines it with markedly religious lexis and hagiographical discourse to portray the women as martyrs to love, creating what has been described as a 'disjuncture between the poem's classical content and hagiographical form'.[72] Although this 'classical content' is filtered through a variety of medieval as well as classical texts and translations, meaning that any 'disjuncture' between such content and hagiography may be mediated by hermeneutic strategies, it is still notable that Chaucer chooses to contextualise his pagan 'goode women' through a medieval religious framework anachronistic to them. This choice puts questions of interpretation explicitly at the centre of the *Legend*'s poetics, since it provides its readers with competing (or, at least, not wholly overlapping) modes of reading and understanding these non-Christian martyrs to love. The poem's overall framing therefore demonstrates that *translatio* of classical tales may lead to plural, potentially disjunct, interpretations of women, highlighting again that a binary approach to gender in ethical terms is likely to be unhelpful.

Dido

The story of Dido is the third tale in the *Legend of Good Women* as it now stands, and appears in the *Confessio* as part of Book IV's discourse on the sin of sloth.[73] Although the story is broadly the same, Gower relies primarily upon Ovid's lament in the *Heroides* whereas Chaucer focuses on Virgil's imperial narrative, meaning that the medieval poets' works may be inflected via the classical authors' different emphases. Chaucer's interaction with Virgil is much more interrogative than is Gower's with Ovid, but there is more scope for such engaged *translatio* in Chaucer's full retelling of Dido's narrative than in its use by Gower as an *exemplum*. This difference, as well as that between the classical authors, may affect both works' representations of women.

Chaucer's reliance on Virgil is perhaps due to the Latin text's thematic emphasis on 'fame' (l. 1242), which is also apt for the medieval poet's focus on female reputation in the *Legend of Good Women*.[74] If anything, Chaucer increases the focus on reputation, as is demonstrated in his subtle changes to his inherited narrative.[75] This heightened emphasis on reputation is particularly clear concerning Dido, whom Chaucer seeks to exculpate from Virgil's implication of sexual incontinence and lack of concern for her 'fame' by making Aeneas the instigator of their relationship.[76] Chaucer here seeks to shift the blame from Dido to Aeneas, in line with his aim to write about 'goode women ... trewe in lovynge' (P.G.484–5, F.474–5), and he does so in a way that ameliorates her 'fame'. Yet this *translatio* diminishes her agency, since she is no longer the instigator of their love, as in the Latin. Dido has become one of Chaucer's 'sely wemen, ful of innocence' (l. 1254) rather than the strong-willed queen she is in the *Aeneid* as a result of his rewriting of her in more positive terms.[77] So, Chaucer's heightened emphasis on the Virgilian theme of 'fama' has a significant impact upon his representation of Dido, apparently positive in an ethical sense but more negative regarding her agency. The power of inherited hermeneutics that focus upon women's ethical status is strong even when, as here, that status is being rewritten in more positive terms.

Gower's version of Dido's story is more concise, in keeping with his overall exemplary focus. Dido herself is far less prominent as an individual, and her name does not appear until four lines after her role as 'qweene' is mentioned.[78] Her agency is also notable by its absence. Her love for Aeneas is characterised by doing 'al holi what he wolde' (l. 90), and although she commits the active step of suicide, she attributes this act to him (ll. 130–1). Although interestingly there is no moral judgement of Dido's love, or of her death, this is perhaps because a different hermeneutic (sloth) is to the fore. The question of active agency is key to this hermeneutic, and its absence may of course be an ironic comment on the vice's very nature, but it is clear that Aeneas and Dido are differently depicted in this sense, since he is active (leading his men from Troy, travelling to Italy, *etc.*) until his lethargy in returning is mentioned, in contrast to her consistent passivity. Here Gower's *translatio* is similar to Chaucer's in that he presents Dido as less morally culpable than in Virgil and as having less agency, but this is achieved differently; Chaucer actively seeks to rewrite Dido as an individual, whereas Gower is not interested in the queen save as an instrument for his wider didactic purpose. The same ethical drive is evident in both poems, with different results.

These two portrayals of Dido demonstrate the versatility of a fundamentally ethical *translatio studii*, since, despite these significant differences in emphasis, both poets are ultimately reading her narrative through such a gendered hermeneutic lens.

Medea

The story of Medea as told by both Gower and Chaucer has a more complex textual tradition than does that of Dido, since it is drawn from a mixture of medieval French and Latin texts as well as directly from Ovid's *Metamorphoses* and *Heroides*.[79] Medea's sources present her as more multifaceted than Dido as she is both a lover and a skilled enchantress, although these two important aspects are not presented with equal weight in the key texts.[80] The sources, therefore, provide Gower and Chaucer with a significant amount of material that differs in its emphases.

Chaucer juxtaposes Medea with Hypsipyle, both Jason's wives, and in so doing frames their mutual story via their relationships with him, 'sly devourerer and confusioun / Of gentil wemen' (ll. 1368–70). The same framing appears again at the start of Medea's story, where 'false Jason' is 'of love devourer and dragoun' (ll. 1585, 81), so that she, 'so wis and fayr' (l. 1599), is inevitably cast as his victim. This is apt given Chaucer's focus on virtuous and faithful women, but it is notable that, in contrast both to the *Historia destructionis Troiae* and also to Gower's account, the Medea of the *Legend of Good Women* is not depicted so explicitly as a witch, nor as the murderer of her children with Jason – probably a conscious omission.[81] Whilst these absences ameliorate Medea morally, since here she is neither a magician nor a murderer, they also remove significant aspects of her agency; her importance is solely as an abandoned lover. Chaucer here performs the same moral rewriting as in his tale of Dido but using a different form of *translatio*, omission, to more marked effect; like Dido, Medea becomes just another deserted woman. Crucially, this *translatio* is itself gendered, since although it removes what might be thought of as Medea's most 'feminine' attribute (her witchcraft), it also erases her violence, traditionally seen as 'male'. In addition, although witchcraft was predominantly associated with women, Medea's skills as depicted in the *Historia* are those of a 'clerk' as much as a witch, since she is an expert in what would now be called natural sciences.[82] In removing both her murderous behaviour and her magic, Chaucer not only reduces her agency but to some extent simplifies her gendered characterisation so that she becomes more conventionally feminine.

Gower's narrative of Medea, which is much longer and more involved than Chaucer's, occurs in Book v of the *Confessio*, which is devoted to the sin of avarice (often in the sense of covetousness). The Confessor interprets the narrative as a warning against perjury, which again places Jason and his actions as the interpretative key to the tale (he is condemned for breaking his promise of love to Medea).[83] Yet this reading, whilst appropriate in terms of its emphasis on Jason's abandonment, does not wholly fit the narrative as Gower tells it. He includes a long description of Medea's magical prowess in rejuvenating Jason's father Aeson, bringing together the narratives of the *Historia destructionis Troiae* and the *Metamorphoses*, and also refers to Medea's murder of her children.[84] This might indicate an ethically negative *translatio* of Medea as a witch and a killer, despite the interpretative emphasis on Jason's betrayal, but instead she is presented in more positive terms. Gower's Medea and Jason declare their love simultaneously, and Medea makes marriage an explicit condition of her help, in contrast to her unilateral declaration of love without conditions in the *Historia*.[85] Like Chaucer, Gower here seeks to ameliorate Medea in a moral sense, but unlike Chaucer he does so less by omission than by subtle re-ordering. However, Gower takes a different approach in the later passage in which Medea uses magic to return Aeson's youth. Here, Gower actively depicts Medea as bestial, even mad, and also temporarily removes her ability to speak as a human.[86] The effects of this animalistic *translatio* are in tension with one another ethically, since she is both dehumanised (negative) and yet also as powerful as a goddess (positive).[87] This complex presentation complicates Medea's status in terms of conventional femininity and its morals; a mixture of various roles associated with femininity (for example, witch, lover, young girl, abandoned wife), this involved and plural gendering makes her morally opaque. When combined with the Confessor's somewhat strained interpretation of the tale as concerning perjury, it becomes apparent that reading the tale in a single exemplary mode is not straightforward.

Gower's and Chaucer's versions construct their Medeas using different forms of *translatio* despite drawing on predominantly the same sources and adopting the same fundamentally ethical perspective. These forms of ethical *translatio* reveal their gendered nature in the roles and attitudes that they expect of women. In order for Medea to be made one of Chaucer's 'goode women', her magic and murders have to be removed, since the power and agency that they represent (not to mention the violence that they involve) do not correlate with contemporary medieval ideas of virtuous femininity. Gower's Medea is a more complex construction: depicted as less subject to erotic desire but animalistic in her magical power, her portrayal brings together ideas of femininity that ethically are in tension with one another but that are all recognisable feminine attributes, making her a confusing moral *exemplum* even before the hermeneutic of avarice, Book v's conceptual framework, is considered.

Constance

The tale of Constance differs from those of Dido and Medea in its apparent lack of classical origins, meaning that she is less subject to inherited interpretations. The travails of Constance, daughter of the Emperor of Rome, are told by both Chaucer and Gower, who take their material from Nicholas Trivet's Anglo-Norman *Chronicle*.[88] Chaucer's version of this story is narrated by the Man of Law and Gower's account forms part of Book II of *Confessio amantis*.[89] Since it is probable that Chaucer read Gower's version of the Constance tale in the *Confessio* before writing his narrative, his approach may be inflected by both Trivet's and Gower's accounts.[90]

The Introduction to 'The Man of Law's Tale' consciously provides an explicitly gendered framework for the story, since the Man of Law mentions some of Chaucer's tales of 'noble wyves and thise loveris' by name.[91] Yet immediately afterwards the Prologue introduces a tonal and hermeneutic shift, since it bewails the state of poverty (ll. 99–133), which seems unrelated to the previous lines' literary and gendered theme. This worldly approach also sits oddly with the developing tale, which is focused on Constance as an *exemplum* of spiritual virtue. The tension here between different themes and approaches creates a sense of uncertainty, which highlights the fact that the nature of the narrative to come is not hermeneutically determined at this point.

Constance, like Griselda in 'The Clerk's Tale', suffers extraordinary vicissitudes before her eventual reunion with her husband and father in Rome, but unlike Griselda Constance's troubles and triumphs are explicitly due to her Christian faith, making her tale generically akin to hagiography as well as to romance. This religious emphasis is also the dominant theme of Trivet's tale, but Chaucer does not simply reproduce his Anglo-Norman source's Christianity. Rather, the later poet seeks to link this theme more strongly to Constance's gender, as is seen explicitly in the well-known lines 'Women are born to thraldom and penance, / And to been under mannes governance' (ll. 287–8). In contrast to both Trivet's and Gower's accounts, where Constance's religious influence is brought to the Sultan's attention before her attractive appearance is described, in Chaucer's tale she is primarily a beautiful and desirable woman who happens also to be a faithful Christian.[92] This small but telling alteration causes femininity (here meaning appearance) to be more strongly correlated with religious belief, a form of *translatio* also seen at other points in 'The Man of Law's Tale', such as Constance's first exile on the sea.[93] Dramatic pathos at such moments further connects virtuous femininity with fervent religious belief, making gender and its affects a vital aspect of the tale's spiritual narrative.[94] Similarly, the Sultan's mother is characterised through the use of gendered and rhetorically dramatic religious discourse absent from Trivet's and Gower's texts, again intertwining gender, Christianity, and affect (this time in a negative sense).[95] In adapting the tale using this gendered approach, Chaucer makes it more complex, generically and conceptually.[96]

Gower's version of Constance's narrative is similar in length to Chaucer's, but is less rhetorically elaborate as there are no narratorial interventions and less direct speech. Book II's hermeneutic of envy, which is key to Gower's adaptation, is conveyed in gendered terms; the Sultan's mother's envy of Constance is rooted in the stereotype of feminine desire for wealth (l. 649: see also the Wife of Bath), and Alla's mother deceives her son through the female vices of 'bacbitinge' and 'treson of hir fals tunge' (ll. 1281, 1299). Even when the sin of envy is committed by a man, it is caused by a woman, as in the case of the knight who murders Hermyngeld through desire for Constance, maintaining the gendered nature of this hermeneutic approach. This might suggest that Gower is similar to Chaucer in choosing to intertwine characteristics that habitually define femininity with other features in order to highlight affect and meaning. However, it is notable that Constance's gendering is much less pronounced in Gower's tale. As in Trivet's text, she is introduced as 'ful of feith' (l. 598); her feminine characteristics of 'beaute and ... grace' are only mentioned in passing in a subclause (l. 622) and the feminised pathos seen in the rhetorical interjections of 'The Man of Law's Tale' is absent, as is much of the direct speech of Chaucer's text. The intersection and interaction of femininity and religion that are such a key framework of the tale do not feature in the *Confessio*. In this sense, Gower's account is less gendered than Chaucer's despite the former's insistent connection of envy and femininity. Both texts, however, construct Constance as an ethical and religious *exemplum* with noticeably less complexity than they do the well-known classical figures of Dido and Medea.

Tale of Florent

This story, which is likely to be the source for Chaucer's 'Wife of Bath's Tale', does not appear itself to be derived from a known text, but was possibly concocted from folk motifs and 'loathly lady' traditions by Gower himself.[97] It therefore draws upon different literary cultures from Dido's, Medea's, and Constance's narratives. The tale occurs in Book 1 of the *Confessio* as an *exemplum* of the need to be obedient to Love without complaint, as Florent the knight ultimately allows his wife to make her own decision about her state. Importantly, his predicament is framed as a plot hatched by a woman, the grandmother of the knight Florent has killed in a fair fight; this means that the tale's moral (obedience) is framed by the anti-feminist trope of the deceitful or scheming female. The knight's explicit description as a paragon of chivalry (ll. 1435–6) thus helps to create a gendered binary between virtuous masculinity and devious femininity. However, as the tale continues the depiction of women focuses on physical appearance more than ethical behaviour (although, of course, the two are interrelated). The loathly lady's ugliness is important primarily as a lens through which to demonstrate male ethical behaviour (Florent's noble behaviour and sacrifice in marrying her) rather than to illuminate her qualities as a woman. This focus on her unattractive appearance is strengthened as the tale builds to its climax with Florent's aesthetic choice. Whilst his honour as a knight is implicated in the idea that her beauty in public (that is, by day) reflects well on him, it is hard to avoid the sense that, of itself, feminine physical appearance does not signify any meaning beyond sexual attraction. Yet this literal reading of physicality is not the only hermeneutic at work. The tale closes by mirroring the wicked woman trope seen at the start, as the now-beautiful and young wife explains that her previous state was the result of her stepmother's 'hate' (l. 1844); despite the seeming lack of interest in exploring the ways in which female appearance may signify in ethical terms, this detail reinforces the point that a gendered perception of women as (im)moral agents drives the plot. Femininity in the *Tale of Florent* therefore both constructs its own literal meaning, in terms of female aesthetics, and is also used to illustrate male ethical status; it does not depict women themselves as moral signifiers.

Chaucer's 'Wife of Bath's Tale', by contrast, places feminine attributes and capacities at its centre when portraying its protagonists' behaviour. The tale complicates the moral binary (already inverted in comparison with Gower's version by the knight's sexual violence) in depicting the loathly lady as ethically dubious in her marriage request.[98] However, her later disquisition on 'gentillesse', in which she claims true nobility 'cometh fro God allone' (l. 1168) and that it is morally defined ('vileyns synful dedes make a cherl', l. 1164), proclaims her as a signifier of virtue. In 'The Wife of Bath's Tale', women's ethical meanings shift, and do so not necessarily in relation to their physical forms. This point is made explicit in the choice with which the lady presents the knight: he may have beauty with deceit or ugliness with faithfulness. This choice confuses any sense of a constant relationship between outward sign and inner reality, since beauty signifies its ethical opposite (and vice versa); it is not self-evident to decode. Feminine appearance can only be a problematic signifier of moral status here, but (in contrast to *Florent*) it is able to mean beyond itself. The tale's ending reinforces this point about femininity's shifting signification, since its interpretation is unclear: is it a pro-feminist display of 'maistrie', or does the reversion of the wife to a young, beautiful, and obedient woman indicate a parallel return to submissive femininity? And which view is the 'virtuous' one? This much-debated question reveals the extent to which Chaucer and the Wife rework *Florent*'s gendered binary and feminine lack of signification into a more complex tale in which ethical problems are bound up with gender and its accepted hermeneutics.

Ceyx and Alcyone

Both Gower's and Chaucer's retellings of the Ceyx and Alcyone story (based on Ovid's *Metamorphoses* xi.410–748) focus on the emotive power seen as inherent to women, but to different effect and via different frameworks. The *Confessio* situates the tale in the context of the truth-claims of dreams within the larger framing of Book iv's focus on sloth, drawing the apposite moral that some dreams are true (iv.3125–7). Chaucer's version in *The Book of the Duchess* is also focused on the importance of sleep and dreams, as the narrator illustrates with his response, but its wider narrative context makes this seem hermeneutically jarring, in contrast to Gower's interpretation. The most noticeable difference between the two medieval reworkings is the depiction of Alcyone. In Chaucer's and Ovid's versions, the queen's loss is marked by her anxious affect, both physically (fainting, weeping, sleeplessness) and rhetorically.[99] Chaucer's Alcyone expresses her anxiety and grief in direct speech, but in Gower's tale her unvoiced emotions are simply reported. This voicelessness is further emphasised by the non-verbal way in which her emotions and desires are recounted by the narrator. Alcyone's actual words are never spoken, even indirectly; her reaction to her dream of Ceyx is wordless grief (l. 3066) and her speech act in retelling this nightmare is glossed over briefly with a single phrase: 'Hir swevene hath told hem everydel' (l. 3073). The nearest the tale comes to reporting her speech occurs when she is praying to Juno (l. 2964–69), but even at this moment her actual words are concealed. A key effect of this voicelessness and lack of language is to diminish Alcyone's power as an emotional signifier in contrast to her presence in the *Book of the Duchess*, where her affective portrayal is an anticipatory parallel to the Black Knight's experience of love and loss. This less emotive version may well be due to the *Confessio*'s primary interest in sleep and the truth-claims of dreams rather than the pain of loss. Yet Alcyone does signify powerful emotion at Gower's tale's end. Her joy at Ceyx's transformation into a living bird is expressed vividly through her own new-found avian physicality, as she 'beclipte and keste [him] in such a wise / As sche was whilom wont to do' (ll. 3104–5). Animal transformation for Alcyone allows emotional communication in a way that her humanity denied. This portrayal of feminine physicality as paramount resembles the concern for aesthetics highlighted in Gower's *Tale of Florent*, since both depict women as signifying subjects primarily in terms of their bodies. Yet there is a difference in emphasis between these two examples. Whereas in *Florent* the loathly lady's body is important for its physicality rather than any ethical or emotional valency, in 'Ceyx and Alcyone' the feminine form is able to signify human emotion. However, this is only possible after Alcyone has been transformed into a bird, a paradox that in its contrast with her previous silence highlights her lack of signification when she was human and female. Both tales depict femininity as primarily important in physical terms, yet 'Ceyx and Alcyone' takes this a step further in allowing femininity to construct meaning only when it is no longer human. This is the significant hermeneutic difference between the two poets' retellings.

Shared Approaches

This analysis has shown that Chaucer habitually complicates his inherited narratives, whether classical or medieval, more so than does Gower. His willingness to do so also affects his interpretative approaches, which, although rooted in femininity as ethically valent, frequently play with the varied possibilities, even contradictions, that this enables, as is the case in 'The Wife of Bath's Tale'. Gower's tales also engage with these possibilities but rejoice in them less; it is telling that *Florent* seeks to close down women's signifying power by reducing it to a literal physicality when Chaucer's version does precisely the opposite.

Two Poets, Both Alike in Morality?

If Chaucer intended to imply a contrast between himself and Gower via the word 'moral', he succeeded for a long time. For much of the twentieth century, critics perceived the two poets in terms of their differences rather than their similarities, with Chaucer as the exciting innovator and Gower the more pedestrian moralist.[100] Yet this analysis of women's representation in their work has shown that, despite their notable differences (of language, tone, and subject matter), both poets earn the label 'moral', since both participate in and contribute to the ethical hermeneutic that pervades medieval literary culture; in this context, they are not so different as *Troilus and Criseyde*'s *envoi* would suggest. However, this moral focus is common to almost all medieval poets, so to say that both authors engage with what is a typical poetic attitude would be a somewhat flat conclusion; it is the subtle (and sometimes not so subtle) differences between Chaucer and Gower in terms of their depiction of women as ethical signifiers that are most revealing. Chaucer's portrayal of women and their meanings is more adaptive, suggesting enjoyment of deconstructing binaries and stereotypes (whether in rewriting inherited classical texts or taking inspiration from more contemporary sources) whilst remaining rooted in the interpretative framework that limited women's power to signify. His Criseyde is the most high-profile example of this approach, a woman torn between different interpretations of femininity who knowingly cannot escape her literary and ethical fate, yet the Wife of Bath and, above all, the women of the *Legend of Good Women* also fit this description, despite their different circumstances, sources, and genres. Gower makes more explicit use of a stated ethical framework throughout his *oeuvre*, with the *Confessio* and *Vox* perhaps the clearest examples of this tendency, but he is far from being a humourless moralist where women and their meanings are concerned. The tensions sometimes created between the hermeneutics he employs and the women's stories that he tells to illustrate them (for example, in his account of Medea) reveal that he is heavily invested in enabling femininity to represent meaning, even when the meanings that it suggests are multifaceted and escape from textual control (as with the anti-feminist rhetoric of the *Vox* that paradoxically celebrates women's erotic power). The difference between the two poets is perhaps most easily imagined in terms of enjoyment and anxiety. Whereas Chaucer appears to enjoy playing with the possibilities of feminine signification, for Gower this is an anxious business; even within the shared hermeneutic tradition of ethical interpretation, his women cannot represent meaning as freely as can Chaucer's, since his adaptive approach is less fluid. This distinction may seem unfairly to reaffirm the two poets' traditional critical *personae*; in fact, it is more accurate to say that they occupy different positions on an interpretative spectrum.[101] Chaucer's approach is characterised by playfulness, Gower's by a more evident sense of purpose, but both are balanced between 'ernest and game'.

Notes

1. For a brief overview of this concept and its history, see Venetia Bridges, *Medieval Narratives of Alexander the Great: Transnational Texts in England and France* (Cambridge: Brewer, 2018), 19–22.
2. The Troy story is the highest-profile example of this, moving from Greek to Latin to French and other vernaculars across Europe. On Troy narratives important in England, see, for example, Wolfram R. Keller, *Selves and Nations: The Troy Story from Sicily to England in the Middle Ages* (Heidelberg: Winter, 2008) and Sylvia Federico, *New Troy: Fantasies of Empire in the Late Middle Ages* (Minneapolis: University of Minnesota Press, 2003).
3. See Marion Turner, *Chaucer: A European Life* (Princeton, NJ: Princeton University Press, 2019), 17–19, on the cosmopolitanism and hence the multilingualism of London at the time of Chaucer's childhood.
4. Key theoretical perspectives include Judith Butler's idea of gender performativity. The large body of scholarship on Chaucer, women, and gender that has developed in the last half-century is too vast to delineate in detail, but key works include Carolyn Dinshaw, *Chaucer's Sexual Poetics* (Madison: University of Wisconsin Press, 1989), Elaine Tuttle Hansen, *Chaucer and the Fictions of Gender* (Berkeley: University of California Press, 1992), and Susan Crane, *Gender and Romance in Chaucer's Canterbury Tales* (Princeton, NJ: Princeton University Press, 1994). For a recent overview (which has caused controversy in its characterisation of Chaucer), see Samantha Katz Seal and Nicole Sidhu, 'New Feminist Approaches to Chaucer: Introduction', *Chaucer Review* 54.3 (2019), 224–9.
5. 'Wife of Bath's Prologue', ll. 688–90, in *The Riverside Chaucer*, ed. Larry D. Benson, 3rd ed. (Oxford: Oxford University Press, 1987). The Wife gives examples of such material, including the well-known anti-feminist text the *Dissuasio Valerii* and writings of St Jerome: see her Prologue, ll. 671–5. Unless otherwise noted, all further citations of Chaucer's works are from the *Riverside Chaucer* (*RC*).
6. Betsy McCormick, Leah Schwebel, and Lynn Shutters, 'Looking Forward, Looking Back on the *Legend of Good Women*: Introduction', *Chaucer Review* 52.1 (2017), 3–11 (4–5), describing Carolyn Dinshaw's approach in *Chaucer's Sexual Poetics*.
7. For examples of this attitude, see *Medieval Literary Theory and Criticism c. 1100–c. 1375: The Commentary Tradition*, ed. A. J. Minnis and A. B. Scott

with David Wallace, rev. ed. (Oxford: Clarendon Press, 1998), and for discussion J. B. Allen, *The Ethical Poetic of the Later Middle Ages* (Toronto: University of Toronto Press, 1982). My approach to ethics in this chapter is similar to that of J. Allen Mitchell, *Ethics and Exemplary Narrative in Chaucer and Gower* (Cambridge: D. S. Brewer, 2004).

8. See the collection of texts in *Woman Defamed and Woman Defended: An Anthology of Medieval Texts*, ed. and trans. Alcuin Blamires with Karen Pratt and C. W. Marx (Oxford: Oxford University Press, 1992), and 'Wife of Bath's Prologue', ll. 688–90.

9. On the importance of the *Rose* in the late fourteenth century, see Turner, *A European Life*, 73–5.

10. See, for example, Diane Watt, *Amoral Gower: Language, Sex, and Politics* (Minneapolis: University of Minnesota Press, 2003), xvi, who notes that 'the link between language, gender, and ethics was well established in the Middle Ages', highlighting Alan of Lille's influential *De planctu Naturae* and the connections it makes between these concepts.

11. Although the Second Nun also narrates a tale, she is not described in the 'General Prologue' and may have been a substitute narrator introduced at a later date; she is therefore not considered here. In taking this approach I follow, for example, Priscilla Martin, *Chaucer's Women: Nuns, Wives and Amazons*, 2nd ed. (Basingstoke: Palgrave Macmillan, 1996), with the caveat that, as Martin herself says in the introduction to the second edition, the concept of 'women' is not 'a very stable category' and is perhaps better framed as 'the problem of gender', as it is in this chapter ('Preface to the 1996 Reprint', xi).

12. On the misattribution of this coinage to George Lyman Kittredge instead of Eleanor Prescott Hammond, see Elizabeth Scala, 'The Women of Chaucer's Marriage Group', *Medieval Feminist Forum* 45.1 (2009), 50–6.

13. Kittredge popularised Hammond's idea in his article 'Chaucer's Discussion of Marriage', *Modern Philology* 9 (1912), 435–67. This led to a flood of critical discussions debating the theme and its extent, not all of which accepted the formulation (see, for example, N. F. Blake, 'The Wife of Bath and Her Tale', *Leeds Studies in English* 13 (1982), 42–55, who argues against the grouping on structural grounds).

14. *RC*, ed. Benson, 11.

15. 'General Prologue', *Canterbury Tales*, ll. 152–4, 139–40.

16. *RC*, ed. Benson, 913.

17. The descriptions in 'Prioress's Tale' of the Jews' 'wardrobe' and their deaths are relevant here: the 'wardrobe' into which the child's body is cast is highlighted as 'where as thise Jewes purgen hire entraille' (l. 573), and the Jews are killed indiscriminately 'with wilde hors' and hanging (ll. 633–4). See, for example, Merrall Llewellyn Price, 'Sadism and Sentimentality: Absorbing Antisemitism in Chaucer's Prioress', *Chaucer Review* 43.2 (2008), 197–214.

18. 'Knight's Tale', ll. 1035–55.

19. The complex structural situation of the *Tales* in terms of its unfinished nature and varied ordering in MSS makes this kind of reading more difficult, but Chaucer clearly intended the tales to interact and to rephrase one another given his habit of including reactions to many of them from the listening pilgrims.
20. See, for example, Alison Ganze, '"My Trouthe for to Holde – Allas, Allas!": Dorigen and Honor in the *Franklin's Tale*', *Chaucer Review* 42.3 (2008), 312–29.
21. She is described as a 'book' for 'maydens' to imitate ('Physician's Tale', ll. 107–98).
22. A similar interpretation, arguing against the idea of equality, is proffered by Angela Jane Weisl, *Conquering the Reign of Femeny: Gender and Genre in Chaucer's Romance* (Cambridge: D. S. Brewer, 1995), 106.
23. See 'Clerk's Tale', ll. 1142–4.
24. The reference to the narrator as 'sone of Eve' (l. 62) and the lengthy etymology of the saint's name in the Prologue (ll. 85–112) indicate that its original narrating voice was an educated male comparable to the Clerk.
25. Turner, *Chaucer*, 269, n. 9, and 169. Carolyn Dinshaw's seminal essay, 'Reading Like a Man: The Critics, the Narrator, Troilus, and Pandarus', in *Chaucer's Sexual Poetics*, 28–64, links gender and reading in a perpetually useful study. More recent work has focused on Criseyde's varying presentations (*New Perspectives on Criseyde*, ed. Cindy L. Vitto and Marcia Smith Marzec (Asheville, NC: Pegasus, 2004) and upon concepts of masculinity (*Men and Masculinities in Chaucer's Troilus and Criseyde*, ed. Tison Pugh and Marcia Smith Marzec (Cambridge: Brewer, 2008)).
26. *Troilus and Criseyde*, v.1061. Robert Henryson's *Testament of Cresseid* focuses solely on Criseyde's betrayal of Troilus and its negative consequences for her, for example.
27. Dinshaw, *Chaucer's Sexual Poetics*, 52.
28. 'Dilation, delay, incessant deferral', in Dinshaw, *Chaucer's Sexual Poetics*, 52.
29. *Troilus and Criseyde*, II.106 and 108.
30. For an excellent survey of the trajectory of twentieth-century Criseyde criticism to 2004, see Lorraine Kochanske Stock, '"Slydynge" Critics: Changing Critical Constructions of Chaucer's Criseyde in the Past Century', in *New Perspectives*, ed. Vitto and Smith Marzec, 11–36.
31. Kochanske Stock, '"Slydynge" Critics', 36.
32. *Troilus and Criseyde*, II.694–808.
33. See, the useful parallel Italian translation and Middle English texts of this passage printed in *Troilus and Criseyde*, ed. Stephen A. Barney (New York: Norton, 2006), 96–103.
34. *Troilus and Criseyde*, II.715, 762, 763.
35. See, for example, *The Book of the Duchess*, ll. 895–905.
36. The narrator's perceptiveness, or lack thereof, has been much debated: for a useful overview, see Arthur W. Bahr, 'The Rhetorical Construction of Narrator and Narrative in Chaucer's *Book of the Duchess*', *Chaucer Review* 35.1 (2000), 43–59 (48–9).

37. *House of Fame*, ll. 151–467.
38. *House of Fame*, ll. 388–426.
39. *House of Fame*, ll. 1460–80.
40. The issue of Homer's truthfulness was an important one throughout the Middle Ages: see, for example, Benoît de Sainte-Maure, *Le roman de Troie*, ll. 1–144, much of which is devoted to discussion of Homer and other sources (trans. Glyn S. Burgess and Douglas Kelly (Cambridge: Brewer, 2017), 43–4).
41. See the description of Fama in *Aeneid* IV.179–88.
42. See, for example, Kathryn L. Lynch, 'The *Parliament of Fowls* and Late Medieval Voluntarism: Part I', *Chaucer Review* 25.1 (1990), 1–16.
43. *Parliament of Fowls*, ll. 285–7.
44. As Diane Watt says, 'the epithet … has proved sufficient to dissuade many from exploring his poetry' (*Amoral Gower*, xi).
45. Watt, *Amoral Gower*, xii. My approach to Gower is indebted to Watt's connection of language, interpretation, and gender in this book.
46. James Simpson, *Sciences and the Self in Medieval Poetry: Alan of Lille's Anticlaudianus and John Gower's Confessio amantis* (Cambridge: Cambridge University Press, 1995), 252–71.
47. The *Confessio amantis* Prologue sums up the corruption the narrator sees in the world's turn from love to hate (ll. 126–32), and the text then describes this in the contexts of church and commons (ll. 193–584). John Gower, *Confessio amantis*, ed. Russell A. Peck and trans. Andrew Galloway, 3 vols. (Kalamazoo, MI: Medieval Institute Publications, 2006).
48. In taking this approach, Gower is following in a long line of medieval authors and texts, including the *Psychomachia* and Alan of Lille's *Anticlaudianus*.
49. Watt makes a similar point from a sexual perspective about the story of Lot and its interpretation: 'Gower himself is guilty here of interpretative violence insofar as he has to change his source to fit his moral' (*Amoral Gower*, 34).
50. *Metamorphoses* XIII.738–897, I.452–567, IX.666–797.
51. John Gower, *Vox clamantis*, V.3.218, in *The Complete Works of John Gower*, ed. G. C. Macaulay, 4 vols. (Oxford: Clarendon, 1899–1902), vol. 4, *The Latin Works* (1902).
52. Gower, *Vox clamantis*, 7.491–2.
53. See, for example, 'De coniuge non ducenda', translated in *Woman Defamed and Woman Defended*, ed. Blamires et al., 125–9.
54. This passage draws heavily on Alan of Lille's *De planctu Naturae*, Ch. 9.1–18, with some of the phrases almost identical: see Alan of Lille, *Literary Works*, ed. and trans. Winthrop Wetherbee, DOML, 22 (Harvard: Dumbarton Oaks, 2013), 114–15.
55. Peter Nicholson, 'Introduction', in John Gower, *Cinkante Balades*, ed. and trans. Peter Nicholson (John Gower Society, 2021), 7, 11–12, 18–19, 25: johngower.org/john-gowers-cinkante-balades. Christine de Pizan may also have been an influence.
56. For more on the role of gender in lyrics of the era, see David Fuller's 'Lyrics: Meditations, Prayers and Praises; Songs and Carols', Chapter 10, this volume.

57. Gower, *Cinkante Balades*, 231–44.
58. Gower, *Cinkante Balades*, 233. See also 41.8–10.
59. See Balade 42 stanza 2 and Balade 43's refrain.
60. R. F. Yeager describes them as *centos* drawing on Machaut, Deschamps, and Grandson: see 'John Gower's French', in *A Companion to Gower*, ed. Siân Echard (Cambridge: D. S. Brewer, 2004), 137–51 (147).
61. On this convention, see Yeager, 'John Gower's French', where Balade 43's refrain is described as 'a formulaic collocation . . . a lyric commonplace' (146).
62. See Balade 44.1–2, for example.
63. See 45.18–19 and 47.10 for examples.
64. Yeager, 'John Gower's French', 142.
65. Yeager, 'John Gower's French' 143.
66. Yeager, 'John Gower's French', 143.
67. Yeager states that the Virgin is 'presented as a *donna* in the manner of lyric', 'John Gower's French', 143.
68. See R. F. Yeager, 'Gower's French Audience: The *Mirour de L'Omme*', *Chaucer Review* 41.2 (2006), 111–37 (112–13). A classic work on the connections of genre and gender is Susan Crane, *Gender and Romance in Chaucer's Canterbury Tales* (Princeton, NJ: Princeton University Press, 1994).
69. On this debated relationship, see Andrew Cole, 'John Gower Copies Geoffrey Chaucer', *Chaucer Review* 52.1 (2017), 46–65, especially 47 and n. 4.
70. Richard Axton, 'Gower – Chaucer's Heir?', in *Chaucer Traditions: Studies in Honour of Derek Brewer*, ed. Ruth Morse and Barry Windeatt (Cambridge: Brewer, 1990), 21–38 (23–4).
71. *Legend of Good Women*, F.483–5, 479, and G.473–5, 469.
72. Regarding lexis, see, for example, G.250, 'devocyoun', 256, 'heresye', 296, 'holynesse', 299 and 309, 'hethene', *etc*. The incipits for each tale address the individual women as 'martiris', for example, 'Incipit Legenda Didonis martiris, Cartaginis Regine' (*RC*, ed. Benson, 608). The quotation is taken from McCormick, Schwebel, and Shutters, 'Introduction', 3–11 (6).
73. *Legend of Good Women*, ll. 924–1367; and *Confessio amantis* IV.77–137.
74. See for example *Aeneid* IV.173–97, where Rumour (*fama*) flies throughout Libya telling of Dido's relationship with Aeneas.
75. A good example is Aeneas' different reactions to the image of Troy's fall in Juno's Temple: compare *Legend of Good Women*, ll. 1030–1, with *Aeneid* I.461–3.
76. *Legend of Good Women*, ll. 1232–4; *cf. Aeneid* IV.170–2.
77. This observation is in line with critical views of *Legend of Good Women* as ironic: see McCormick, Schwebel, and Shutters, 'Introduction', 5.
78. *Confessio amantis* IV.84–7.
79. See Venetia Bridges, 'Beyond Nations: Translating Troy in the Middle Ages', in *England and Bohemia in the Age of Chaucer*, ed. Peter Brown and Jan Čermák (Woodbridge: Boydell and Brewer, forthcoming). Ovid narrates Medea's tale in *Metamorphoses* VII.1–424 and *Heroides* XII. A key source for both Chaucer and Gower is Guido de Columnis' *Historia destructionis Troiae*, which draws on both Latin texts.

80. See Bridges, 'Beyond Nations', forthcoming.
81. Chaucer refers explicitly to *Heroides* XII at the end of Medea's story (*Legend of Good Women*, ll. 1670–9. Medea's murders are hinted at in *Heroides* XII. 210–11.
82. See Guido de Columnis, *Historia destructionis Troiae*, ed. Nathaniel Edward Griffin (Cambridge, MA: The Mediaeval Academy of America, 1936), II. p. 15, l. 24–p. 17, l. 8.
83. *Confessio amantis* V.4223–4.
84. *Confessio amantis* V.3247–4242.
85. *Confessio amantis* V.3388–91; cf. *Historia destructionis Troiae*, ed. Griffin, II, p. 18, l. 3–p. 19, l. 2; and p. 21, ll. 8–12.
86. V.4083–4, 98. See also the analysis of this passage in terms of language and gender in Watt, *Amoral Gower*, 43–4.
87. *Confessio amantis* V.4105–7, 4109–110.
88. Both the French text and an English translation are printed as 'The Life of Constance', trans. Edmund Brock, in *Originals and Analogues of Some of Chaucer's* Canterbury Tales, I, ed. F. J. Furnivall, Edmund Brock, and W. A. Clouston (London: Trübner, 1872), 2–53.
89. 'The Man of Law's Introduction, Prologue and Tale'; *Confessio amantis* II.587–1613.
90. For a detailed comparison of the Constance narrative in all three versions, see Douglas J. Wurtele, 'Chaucer's Man of Law and Clerk as Rhetoricians', unpublished PhD thesis (McGill, 1968), 56–66; for a study of Chaucer and Gower's versions, see Elizabeth Allen, 'Chaucer Answers Gower: Constance and the Trouble with Reading', *English Literary History* 64.3 (1997), 627–55. Gower removed lines in praise of Chaucer from the end of the first recension of the *Confessio*, possibly after reading a passage in 'The Man of Law's Prologue' that apostrophises what may be Gower's version of Canacee and Apollonius.
91. 'Man of Law's Tale', ll. 53–76.
92. 'Man of Law's Tale', ll. 162, 164.
93. 'Man of Law's Tale', ll. 446–55.
94. A similar point about the relationship between religion and gender is made at greater length by Elizabeth Robertson, 'The "elvyssh" Power of Constance: Christian Feminism in Geoffrey Chaucer's *The Man of Law's Tale*', *Studies in the Age of Chaucer* 23 (2001), 143–80 (147–9).
95. 'Man of Law's Tale', ll. 358–70.
96. For a useful if brief overview of key critics' positions on Constance's agency in the twentieth century, see Robertson, 'Christian Feminism', 159–60.
97. Russell A. Peck, 'Folklore and Powerful Women in Gower's "Tale of Florent"', in *The English 'Loathly Lady' Tales: Boundaries, Traditions, Motifs*, ed. S. Elizabeth Passmore and Susan Carter (Kalamazoo MI: Medieval Institute Publications, 2007), 100–45.
98. She entraps the knight by failing to reveal her desire for marriage until after he has promised her his 'trouthe' and thus cannot refuse her.

99. *Book of the Duchess*, ll. 101–23.
100. On both poets' reputations, see John Fisher, *John Gower: Moral Philosopher and Friend of Chaucer* (New York: New York University Press, 1964), 1–37.
101. Such a reading builds on Elizabeth Allen's observation regarding the Constance story, but more widely applicable, that Gower is 'less ... an anchor for the "slydyng" Chaucer than ... a fellow muddier of moral waters' ('Chaucer Answers Gower', 629).

Further Reading

Axton, Richard (1990). Gower – Chaucer's Heir? In *Chaucer Traditions: Studies in Honour of Derek Brewer*, ed. Ruth Morse and Barry Windeatt. Cambridge: Brewer, 21–38.

Blamires, Alcuin, with Karen Pratt, and C. W. Marx, eds. (1992). *Woman Defamed and Woman Defended: An Anthology of Medieval Texts*, Oxford: Oxford University Press.

Dinshaw, Carolyn (1989). *Chaucer's Sexual Poetics*, Madison: University of Wisconsin Press.

Echard, Siân, ed. (2004). *A Companion to Gower*, Cambridge: D. S. Brewer.

McCormick, Betsy, Leah Schwebel, and Lynn Shutters, eds. (2017). Looking Forward, Looking Back on the *Legend of Good Women*. *Chaucer Review* 52.1, 3–11.

Mitchell, J. Allen (2004). *Ethics and Exemplary Narrative in Chaucer and Gower*, Cambridge: D. S. Brewer.

Pugh, Tison, and Marcia Smith Marzec, eds. (2008). *Men and Masculinities in Chaucer's Troilus and Criseyde*, Cambridge: Brewer.

Turner, Marion (2019). *Chaucer: A European Life*, Princeton: Princeton University Press.

Vitto, Cindy L., and Marcia Smith Marzec, eds. (2004). *New Perspectives on Criseyde*, Asheville, NC: Pegasus.

Watt, Diane (2003). *Amoral Gower: Language, Sex, and Politics*, Minneapolis: University of Minnesota Press.

V
Women as Authors

CHAPTER 18

Marie de France
Identity and Authorship in Translation
Emma Campbell

The twelfth-century writer today known as 'Marie de France' is one of the few medieval authors generally known by name within – sometimes beyond – academic circles. This authorial identifier is a sixteenth-century coinage based on Marie's self-presentation in a fable collection, where the francophone writer evidently working in England for an aristocratic patron claims to be 'from France' ('Marie ai nun, si sui de France', *Fables*, Epilogue, 4).[1] The Marie who signs this work appears to be a settler in Britain positioned between two francophone cultures: that of the English nobility and that of Continental France – most likely the Île-de-France. The writer we today refer to as 'Marie de France' has consequently been hot property in English as well as French literary studies. The extensive scholarly attention Marie has received has secured her place among the earliest named women authors working in French and established her significance for English and French literary histories. Questions of authorship and attribution have, understandably, been a major focal point in these endeavours. Such studies have sometimes attempted to connect Marie to particular religious orders or royal houses. Arguments have thus been made to the effect that Marie was the Abbess of Shaftesbury, half-sister to Henry II; that she can be identified as the Abbess of Reading; that she could have been Marie de Meulan or Marie de Boulogne; and that she might have been Mary Becket, sister to the martyred Archbishop Thomas of Canterbury.[2] Though tantalising, such claims about Marie's historical identity nonetheless remain speculative. All we really know about Marie is her name and that she may have written up to four works in French aimed at patrons and audiences in late twelfth-century England (*c.* 1160–90). The texts most frequently attributed to her range across the major medieval genres of courtly, didactic, and religious writing: the *Lais* (a collection of short stories on Celtic themes), *Ysopë* (a fable collection), and the *Espurgatoire Saint Patrice* (a text about Saint Patrick's discovery of purgatory). A case has also been made for Marie's authorship of a vernacular life of St Audrey, though this attribution currently commands less scholarly consensus.[3] The scarcity of evidence concerning Marie's identity means we cannot be certain the same author composed even the three works conventionally ascribed to this female writer. As attempts to identify her attest, 'Marie' was a common name for women in medieval Christendom. What is more, the linguistic distinctiveness of the texts that bear this authorial signature seems to point to their composition by four separate individuals.[4] The vibrancy of late twelfth-century Anglo-Norman literary culture, which included women as readers, patrons, and scribes, as well as writers, also means it is not inconceivable that there was more than one woman composing vernacular texts under the same moniker. In other words, we might be dealing with a single female writer, but this corpus could equally represent the work of up to four different Maries.

Celebrating a twelfth-century female author who can rival male contemporaries undoubtedly has its value. Nevertheless, the cult of authorship that has developed around Marie's name in scholarly work sometimes inadvertently overshadows aspects of this corpus relevant to a multilingual understanding of medieval women's literary culture. Until recently, scholarship on Marie as a 'French' writer working in Britain painted her as a uniquely talented author positioned within the francophone literary canon. These traditional accounts tend to emphasise the female author's connection to nationalising literary histories that downplay the polyglot nature of the culture that produced the works attributed to Marie, along with its reliance on translation.[5] This emphasis has shifted in more recent scholarship, even if modern disciplinary boundaries continue to determine – and to circumscribe – the critical reception of this corpus.[6] Although a comprehensive examination of the links between work attributed to Marie and its broader, multilingual context exceeds the scope of this chapter, I consider here what it might mean to see Marie (singular or plural) as a participant in a polyglot culture that valued translation and adaptation as much as individual authorship. This approach offers a means of demonstrating the embeddedness of Marie's writing in translation, as well as the relevance this has for questions of gender and language.

The work attributed to Marie encourages us to view her writing within textual networks. As scholars have often indicated, Marie is not an author in today's sense of the term. Medieval textual culture challenges modern assumptions about authorship as a form of inspired, autonomous creativity by embedding literary production in more collaborative practices, ranging from the commissioning of works to the translation, paraphrase, citation, and copying of texts in manuscript. Marie's presentation of her work accordingly connects textual composition to the commissioning, reading, and transmission of other works, as well as to translation and adaptation. The General Prologue to the most complete collection of Marie's *lais* in the Harley manuscript (British Library, Harley MS 978) dedicates the work to a 'noble king' (usually identified as Henry II of England) and suggests the project intentionally preserves Breton oral compositions that might otherwise vanish. Marie aligns this conservationist endeavour with the translation of antique sources into the vernacular already popular among contemporary writers at the Angevin court, while dismissing that option as already oversubscribed and therefore less appealing (*Lais*, Prologue, ll. 28–42).[7] When introducing her fable collection, Marie situates her commission within an illustrious didactic tradition that she traces back to the Roman emperor Romulus and to Aesop, who translated the fables from Greek into Latin for his imperial master (*Fables*, Prologue, ll. 12–40). The edifying text's production in this case explicitly includes both translation and a collaboration between noble patron and writer that equally belongs to the textual tradition that contextualises Marie's collection. Later, in the epilogue to the *Fables*, Marie's claim that she was working from a source by King Alfred further connects her work to a tradition of writing and translation in English still tangible after the Conquest (ll. 13–18). In the *Espurgatoire*, Marie similarly attributes her motivation for writing to a noble patron, while targeting her vernacular translation of a Latin text at simple folk who implicitly lack her literacy and education (*Espurgatoire*, ll. 1–48).[8] Marie's writing – like that of other medieval authors – is thus invested in interpersonal and interlinguistic processes of commissioning, adaptation, compilation, and translation. Her qualities as an author can only fully be understood within that collaborative, polyglot setting.

The works bearing Marie's name further locate the activity of composing and translating into French within a broader multilingual context especially relevant to Angevin Britain. The sources and influences for works identified with Marie situate this corpus at the confluence of French, Latin, Breton, Celtic, English, and Arabic cultures and languages. A striking feature of the three texts most commonly identified with Marie is the writer's explicit engagement with the vernacular multilingualism of their English context. Insular writers working in French frequently point to their use of Latin sources; the commentary we find in Marie's texts on the translation of material into French is therefore relatively conventional. More unusually, her work contains references to languages including

Breton and English vernaculars, as well as idioms more widely used for written texts during this period, such as Latin. Though, as far as we know, Marie composed only in French, the works attributed to her bear witness to knowledge of multiple languages. The *Lais* claim to derive from oral Breton sources and include what are presented as English as well as Breton terms; *Ysopë* evokes Aesop's Greek-to-Latin translations while also mentioning a (now lost) English version, which Marie claims is her source; finally, the *Espurgatoire*, which translates into French an identifiable Latin text by an English Cistercian monk, also evokes the need for linguistic interpreting that results from interactions between the Irish population and the clerical settlers of Ireland, including St Patrick himself. This multilingual frame of reference anchors this corpus in the linguistic environment of Angevin Britain, with its francophone court, socially mixed community of bilingual English and French speakers, mass population of anglophones, and Celtic-speaking minorities. It also reflects a geopolitical situation in which Angevin dominion reached beyond the English kingdom to Ireland and Brittany, as well as to duchies and counties on the Continent. The Anglo-Norman, Angevin culture in which these texts were written was profoundly multilingual and multicultural: it tapped into rich transnational resources, while also privileging the elaboration of insular histories and institutions. The details of this situation are not extensively discussed in Marie's writing; nonetheless, these texts deliberately contextualise the activity of composition in French within a network of languages relevant to Angevin Britain and the aspirations of its ruling classes.

How, then, do the languages of the culture in which Marie was working shape the French texts attributed to her? And what is the significance of this for thinking about the female writer's position within a literary culture in which women actively participated? The choice of French had a particular resonance for writers working in England, including women writers. Marie – if indeed there was only one of her – was by no means the only multilingual woman composing French texts in Britain in the twelfth century. Clemence of Barking's theologically and stylistically accomplished translation of the Latin life of St Catherine of Alexandria is testament to that, as is the anonymous nun of Barking's life of St Edward the Confessor (a woman who may be Clemence herself, though, as ever, concrete evidence is hard to come by).[9] The religious works attributed to Marie (the *Espurgatoire* and, possibly, the *Vie seinte Audrée*) are, from this perspective, more typical of contemporary women's vernacular writing in England. Though the writing portfolio attributed to Marie – which includes works from secular, courtly genres as well as religious ones – fits the profile of well-known male contemporaries, including Continental French writers such as Chrétien de Troyes, the stakes of writing French in England in this period are distinct from those associated with Continental uses of the language. As a preferred vernacular of England's elite, French had an additional prestige that may have appealed to writers such as Marie and Clemence – not to mention the female patrons and readers who supported the vibrant culture of French literary production in such circles.

If we look to the texts themselves, works attributed to Marie not only draw upon a networked, collaborative model of authorship that encompasses and passes through translation but also highlight her role as a woman who participates in – even guarantees the continued vitality of – that network. In all of these texts, the female writer locates herself within a broader tradition dominated by male authorities and, in doing so, subtly underscores the dependence of that tradition on her own efforts. These texts also thematise the work of textual production and translation in other ways, some of which explicitly include women or emphasise their contributions. In line with the different model of authorship that her writing represents, Marie does not necessarily make herself or other women points of origin for textual production; rather, women are part of collaborative networks that produce, translate, read, circulate, and modify narratives in textual and non-textual forms. Indeed, no single model of women's narrative agency emerges from this corpus. As we shall see, Marie's depiction of women's roles in textual-translational networks and her positioning as the francophone writer behind the vernacular text are calibrated differently in the various works traditionally ascribed to her.

Critics have often emphasised women's depiction in the *Lais* as readers, writers, composers, or storytellers.[10] This attention to women's involvement in the genesis of the *lai* is not restricted to those associated with Marie: it is also a feature of the genre more broadly.[11] In the most complete compendium of Marie's twelve *Lais* – conventionally known as the 'Harley' collection, after the manuscript that transmits these works – women occupy various roles in the networks that generate the composition we encounter in Marie's French text. These roles can have negative as well as positive outcomes. Women's speech acts are narrative catalysts in *Equitan*, where a lady in an adulterous relationship with a king plots to murder her husband, and in *Le Fresne*, where a woman's malicious gossip about how her female neighbour's twins were conceived rebounds on her when she herself gives birth to twin girls. In other cases, women initiate, construct, or transmit the tale that becomes the *lai* Marie recounts in her turn. In *Yonec*, an unhappily married woman prays for an adventure like those she has heard others recount and has her wish granted by the appearance of Muldumarec, a bird-knight with whom she has a son, Yonec. When Muldumarec is killed by her jealous husband, the lady keeps the adventure a secret with the aid of a magic ring until Yonec is grown; then, as Muldumarec predicted, she reveals the story to her son before his father's tomb, prompting Yonec to slay his stepfather. The simultaneous occupation, transmission, and elaboration of the story is also a family affair initiated by a female character in *Milun*. In this *lai*, a young noblewoman who begins a relationship with an outstanding knight called Milun becomes pregnant with his child and instructs him to take the baby to her sister in Northumberland, to be raised in secret. The lady asks Milun to pass on a ring and a letter she has written, which names him as the child's father and gives an account of her own adventure. These tokens are transmitted to the child when he reaches maturity. For twenty years the lovers continue secretly to correspond with one another through letters hidden among the feathers of a swan, while their son grows into a young knight determined to live up to his illustrious parentage. Milun eventually encounters his son in combat at a tournament and is, for the first time, unhorsed by his opponent. The young man's ring, along with the story of his parentage taken from his mother's letter, confirm his identity to his jubilant father. On returning from the tournament, Milun receives a final missive from his lady indicating her husband has recently died, enabling the pair to be reunited and married by their son. *Yonec* and *Milun* thus emphasise women's roles in the written as well as the oral transmission of the tale that eventually becomes the *lai*. In *Chaitivel*, a noblewoman is presented even more explicitly as the work's composer, though the *lai* once again represents the creative process that brings it into being as a shared enterprise. *Chaitivel* relates the story of a lady with four valiant lovers, three of whom die in a tournament. The fourth lover survives, albeit seriously injured, and is cared for by the lady. To commemorate her deep sadness, the lady announces she will make a *lai* that she proposes to call *Quatre Dols* (The Four Sorrows); her surviving lover nonetheless convinces her to alter the title to *Le Chaitivel* (The Wretched One), in recognition of the particular suffering he endures at being near his beloved but unable to act on his feelings for her. *Chaitivel*'s double title and narration of its own composition thus points to the open-ended, originless nature of poetic composition, which involves negotiation between male and female actors positioned differently within the story, as well as among writers and audiences who reshape and reinterpret the *lai* in their turn.[12] Depictions of literary production such as these draw attention to women's participation in compositional networks; they invite audiences to reflect on Marie's poetic practice and uses of language, as well as on their own involvement as readers in the collaborative production of the work.

Laüstic and *Chevrefoil* offer further examples of tales where women's involvement in the networks underpinning the French text intersect with Marie's multilingual framing of the *lai* and her interest in translation as a form of literary composition.[13] In both cases, Marie translates the Celtic title of the *lai* into one or more languages, including French. These interlinguistic translations are not principally aimed at providing French equivalents of terms unfamiliar to medieval contemporaries. Rather, Marie uses interlingual translation to draw attention to the porous boundaries between languages which her francophone audience would almost certainly have encountered by other means and, in turn, to relate this to the thematics of translation developed in the works themselves. Translation is, in other words, used self-consciously in these *lais* to underline and to comment on the text's composition – a process that includes female characters within the French text as well as the female writer who transmits it.

Laüstic foregrounds the relationship between the translation of bodies and stories on the one hand and its own poetic elaboration on the other. Similarly to the Harley *lais* already mentioned, it depicts a woman's collaborative involvement in those processes as part of the narrative Marie translates into written French. The crux of the story is a covert love affair: a lady and her neighbour are in the habit of meeting at night at the windows of their adjoining homes. When the lady's husband demands an explanation for her night-time wanderings, she tells him she gets up to listen to the nightingale. In response, her husband contrives to trap a nightingale, kills it before her, and throws its body at her, staining her dress with blood. Having lost her excuse for rising at night, the lady resolves to send the bird and an explanation of the adventure to her lover; she wraps the nightingale's body in an embroidered cloth and sends it to him with an orally delivered message. On receiving the gift and the tale, the knight places the wrapped bird in a specially made casket, which he keeps with him. The story, we are told, soon circulated and was made into a *lai*.

Laüstic has frequently been read as a story about the process of poetic composition behind the work itself.[14] It also highlights the interplay between preservation and loss that characterises translation as a mechanism of textual transmission. The nightingale that gives its name to the *lai* begins life as a fabrication to conceal an adulterous affair. When its real-life counterpart is discovered and killed, the body then undergoes a process of material and textual translation that eventually leads to the creation of the *lai* that Marie translates in her turn. The intimate connection between the nightingale and the accretion of narrative elements that makes up the *lai* means the significance of the bird can only be understood in relation to the story Marie tells. At the same time, the meaning of the nightingale shifts as it is translated. The bird that lends its name to the *lai* initially stands for a secret that cannot be openly disclosed; this meaning evolves as the bird the lady dreamt up as an excuse materialises as a living creature that is killed, then is subject to reinterpretation and misinterpretation by characters within the narrative. The woman's use of the bird as an excuse fails to convince her husband, who plays along with her story while intuiting its distortion of the truth. The lady's husband correctly interprets her lie; his response brutally commits her to it, by substituting a real bird for the lady's courtly fiction. If the husband understands the lady's tale in a way that is both true and false, her lover seems partially to misinterpret the significance of the nightingale she sends him. Whereas the lady's gift commemorates her adventure and continues her communication with her lover, the knight instead prefers to venerate the bird as the symbol of a dead rather than a living love affair, transforming the lady's gift into a relic. The *lai* thus highlights the process of displacement that underwrites poetic composition and transmission, connecting that process to the material and textual translations performed by male and female characters, which ultimately constitute the work Marie writes in French.

Marie's use of interlinguistic translation in presenting this text can be read in this light. The opening of the *lai* outlines in miniature the process within the story itself, whereby the lady's *aventure* is transformed through translation into a poetic composition that subjects the nightingale to different interpretations:

> Une aventure vus dirai
> Dunt li Bretun firent un lai;
> Laüstic ad nun, ceo m'est vis,
> Si l'apelent en lur païs;
> Ceo est russignol en franceis
> E nihtegale en dreit engleis. (*Laüstic*, ll. 1–6)

> (I will tell you an adventure, which the Bretons made into a *lai*. I believe it has the name 'Laüstic' and is so called in their country; that is 'Rossignol' in French and 'Nightingale' in correct English.)

Marie's glossing of the nightingale's name focuses on the process of translation while underscoring the partial untranslatability of the term

Marie provides as a title. Even though the Breton word is translated linguistically in these opening lines, 'laüstic' is used throughout Marie's French text to refer to both bird and *lai*. These usages underline the singularity of this word by making its meaning dependent on the context of the story itself: rather than speaking of 'the nightingale' in French (*russignol*), Marie refers to 'laüstic' as a foreign term that is comprehensible in context but requires an additional effort of interpretation. The non-translation of the title thus encapsulates an important feature of Marie's *lai*: the nightingale's meaning only becomes apparent in relation to the story Marie recounts, while also shifting as the fictional bird becomes a living creature, a dead body, a gift, a relic. By continuing to use the Breton term, Marie presents her audience with a word that advertises its own linguistic and conceptual distinctiveness. The meaning of 'laüstic' becomes progressively apparent not only through the linguistic translation offered in the introductory lines, but also through the translations of the story itself.

Chevrefoil similarly draws attention to the process of translation and transmission that underwrites the text's composition – a process that once again includes a female character. The subject matter of this *lai* is connected to the hugely popular medieval story of Tristan and Yseut: a pair of courtly lovers whose adulterous relationship involves betrayal of King Mark, Tristan's uncle and Yseut's husband as well as the pair's sovereign. Marie's *lai* fixes on a small detail of this vast story matter: an encounter in the Cornish forest that Tristan engineers while in exile from the royal court. Having received news of the court's celebration of Pentecost in Tintagel, Tristan lies in wait near the path he knows the queen will have to take. He carves a message into a piece of wood, which he leaves by the roadside for Yseut to see; recognising this sign from her beloved, the queen leaves the path and the couple enjoy a brief reunion before separating once more. Upon returning to his native Wales, Tristan – possibly at Yseut's behest – composes the *lai* that Marie retells in French, to commemorate the lovers' tryst and the words exchanged between them.

In *Chevrefoil*, Marie once again uses interlinguistic translation to highlight the process that brings the *lai* into being. She translates the *lai*'s title into French and English; this time, however, she makes no explicit mention of the Celtic (Breton? Welsh? Cornish?) term upon which these translations are based, and introduces her bilingual gloss of the title in the text's concluding lines rather than at its opening. In the body of the text, Marie uses the French term 'chevrefoil' (honeysuckle) to refer to the plant and to the *lai* that bears its name. One of the effects of Marie's omission of the Celtic title, when seen alongside her allusion to English and French terms at the end of the *lai*, is to privilege the process of translation over the rendering of a putative source. In contrast to *Laüstic*, what this accentuates is how translation can conceal or suppress what it ostensibly transmits. The absence of Tristan's title is echoed in the construction of this story, which revolves around a message never explicitly communicated by the *lai* itself. Just as the Celtic name remains shrouded in secrecy, so the content of the message that it commemorates is hidden within the French translation that recreates and partially transmits it.

The communication around which the *lai* revolves once again highlights women's collaborative input into the work of literary composition, while leaving the nature of that input ambiguous. The *lai* makes the communication between Tristan and Yseut a central focus without explicitly conveying any of its content.[15] *Chevrefoil*'s epilogue re-emphasises the relationship between the commemorative function of the *lai* and its depiction of a communication partially omitted from the work itself:

> Pur la joie qu'il ot eüe
> De s'amie qu'il ot veüe
> E pur ceo k'il aveit escrit,
> Si cum la reïne l'ot dit,
> Pur les paroles remembrer,
> Tristram, ki bien saveit harper,
> En aveit fet un nuvel lai;
> Asez briefment le numerai:
> Gotelef l'apelent en engleis,
> Chevrefoil le nument Franceis.
> Dit vus en ai la verité,
> Del lai que j'ai ici cunté.   (*Chevrefoil*, ll. 107–18)

(Because of the joy he experienced at seeing his beloved and because of what he had written, just as the queen had said/asked him to/told him, in order to preserve the memory of those words, Tristan, who was an accomplished harpist, composed a new *lai*. I will name it briefly: it is called *Gotelef* in English and *Chevrefoil* by the French. I have [now] told you the truth about the *lai* that I have recounted here.)

If the words exchanged between the lovers are not communicated directly, so too the process of composition mentioned in the text remains opaque. In the context of Tristan's creation of the *lai*, Marie's allusion to what the queen says ('si cum la reïne l'ot dit') makes it difficult to pinpoint the precise nature of Yseut's contribution to this creative endeavour. It is unclear whether the queen dictates the *lai* that Tristan composes, whether she instructs him to compose the work, or whether Tristan simply takes it upon himself to commemorate Yseut's words. In any event, Tristan's *lai* memorialises his communion with the queen while withholding the words exchanged between the lovers from other readers or listeners. This gap between word and referent is echoed by Marie's presentation of her title, which omits the Celtic name of Tristan's original composition but provides French and English glosses for it. As in *Laüstic*, the purpose of interlinguistic translation is not merely functional here, but emphatic. Whereas *Laüstic* translates a Breton term that replaces any French or English equivalents in the text, *Chevrefoil*'s use of such equivalents underscores the absence of the suppressed Celtic title. Thus, in this closing presentation of the *lai*, what Marie's translations underscore is, on the one hand, the absence of the written and spoken words commemorated by her text and, on the other hand, the way translation nonetheless serves to convey the import of those words. The lovers' exchanges, like Tristan's original title, are experienced through a translation that is inevitably incomplete and which folds women's contributions to textual composition and transmission into a collaboration that passes through various written and spoken languages.

Ysopë (after Aesop, translator of the fables) – the work for which Marie was most known in her own time – explores a different kind of relationship between text, language, and translation. As well as emanating from textual traditions that explicitly encompass Greek, Latin, and English, Marie's fable collection bears the marks of Arabic influences that probably emerged from twelfth-century Arabic-European cultural exchange.[16] The first forty fables in *Ysopë* derive from an eleventh-century Latin work known as the *Romulus Nilantii*, which was an important source of Christian didacticism in the twelfth century; the remaining sixty-two can be linked more diffusely to a range of other sources, including Arabic fable collections such as the *Kalilah wa Dimnah*. Though there is no record of the source Marie claims for her work, comparison with the traditions from which these fables are likely to stem suggests her version adapts the material to a twelfth-century feudal context, focusing on ethical, political, and religious values regarded by contemporaries as essential to rulership.[17] Her dedication of the work to an English count suggests such changes were made with a particular target audience in mind. Fables draw upon a broader cast of characters than the *Lais*, including the peasantry as well as non-human creatures; these tales often feature verbal trickery or ruse among animals as well as humans, before offering a moralising gloss that interprets the meaning of the story for readers or listeners. For example, Fable 13 in *Ysopë* recounts how a fox outwits a crow that has stolen a cheese, by flattering the bird's pride. The fox exclaims within earshot of the crow that the bird's unparalleled beauty would be complete if its voice were as beautiful as its looks, prompting the crow to open its beak to sing, thereby dropping the cheese at the fox's feet. Marie's moralising gloss focuses on the pride and stupidity of those who fall for flattery and lies and who dispense their goods unwisely. This tale thus acts as a warning to her aristocratic audience against persuasive uses – and misuses – of language to gain social advantage.

Fables featuring verbal trickery foreground narrative production and translation in a way distinct from the *Lais* and offer a correspondingly different vision of women's roles within those processes. The fables' extraction of moral messages from the stories they recount might be seen as a form of translation, yet these texts do not usually connect moralisation to interlinguistic forms of translation integrated into the work itself. Marie's adaptations in *Ysopë* occasionally diminish the anti-feminist tenor of her sources.[18] Far more so than in the *Lais*, however, the contributions of human, female characters in the fables tend to have a misogynist inflection. Perhaps not coincidentally, many of these women are depicted as lower class rather than aristocratic. Though the morals of the fables in question do not necessarily dwell upon gendered trickery, women's speech – similarly to that of creatures like the fox – has a potency often used to deceive or misguide. In some cases, there is an implicit recognition of women's superior wit, even as their trickery is taken as a negative example. For instance, in Fable 45, a peasant sees his wife disappearing into the forest with her male lover. Instead of denying her behaviour, the wife claims she must be at death's door, as other female relatives of hers were also seen accompanied by a young man shortly before they died. She instructs her husband to summon her family so they can divide up their belongings, whereupon she will immediately retire to a nunnery. In a panic, the peasant begs his wife not to leave him and retracts his accusation. The woman capitalises on her advantage to make her husband swear in church that he has not seen her with any man – and much more besides. The brief moral lesson accompanying this fable focuses first on women's guile and then on those whose trickery exceeds even the devil's cunning. Fable 72 similarly highlights the power of women's speech to shape others' perceptions of reality and thus to determine a course of events, while presenting the consequences of this as far more serious. In this tale, the mutually beneficial relationship between a peasant and a serpent is irreparably damaged by the intervention of the peasant's wife. The (grammatically feminine) serpent in this story is a figure of courtliness, wisdom, and generosity who, much like a feudal lord, enriches the peasant who sustains her: the peasant brings the serpent milk twice a day and is repaid with the know-how to cultivate his land, as well as material wealth. When the peasant repeats to his wife the serpent's declaration that the slightest fault on his part would break their bond, the woman recommends that her husband kill the creature so as to free himself of the worry such a threat entails. Marie's use of free indirect discourse at this juncture communicates the agency of the wife's words on her husband's thought processes, relaying in the third person how the man should go about double-crossing the snake:

> Ele li respunt hastivement,
> S'il en voleit sun conseil feire,
> Qu'il en purreit a bon chef treire:
> Ocie la, si fera mut bien,
> Puis ne la crendra de nule rien;
> En dute en est, ore en sa merci,
> Bien se deit deliverer de li,
> N'avera dute de sun mesfet;
> Le buket li porte plein de leit,
> Puis si l'asie a tere jus,
> Si s'en traië un poi ensus;
> Quant la serpent vendra avant,
> Sa hache tienge bien trenchant,
> Si la fierge si durement
> Que n'i ait mes recovrement. (*Fables*, 72, ll. 30–44)

(She [the wife] hastily replies to him [her husband] that, if he were to follow her advice, he could bring matters to a good conclusion. Kill her [the serpent] – that would be a good thing, then he won't have anything more to fear. He fears her and is currently at her mercy, he should free himself of her; he won't worry about doing something wrong; he should carry the bucket full of milk to her, then put it on the ground, step back a little, and when the serpent comes out, grab his sharp axe and strike her so hard that she will never recover.)

Though the peasant woman's advice to her husband might not appear unreasonable, especially given the medieval associations of serpents who promise to lavish wisdom on humankind in Genesis, the feudal colouring of the reciprocity between *villein* and serpent in Marie's text makes the moral stakes of the wife's counsel crystal clear. Indeed, in a comparable way to the wife's betrayal of her werewolf husband in *Bisclavret* (one of the Harley *Lais*), Marie here presents a course of action that seems understandable in context as a form of treachery that draws the negative associations of the non-human creature in question onto the human, female character.

Rather than telling a story about a deceptive serpent, the fable instead focuses on the wife's deceptively bad advice, which irreversibly unleashes upon the peasant's family the wrath of their former protector. When compared with the moralisation in Latin versions, Marie considerably develops the theme of bad counsel, which is pertinent to the feudal context of her didactic message, while passing through a conventionally misogynist devaluation of women's speech.

Far more so than the *Lais*, *Ysopë*'s depiction of women's involvement in narrative production thus tends to distinguish Marie's literary activity from the stories woven by female characters. If the fables spotlight women's capacity to harness the power of language for themselves, as well as that of men and non-human creatures, the moral interpretations of this potency often warn readers against heeding women's words. In this way, Marie's translations repeat rather than overturn conventional stereotypes about women's speech. Even if her moralisations convert these stories into universal lessons for the ruling classes, they do not explicitly challenge the misogyny of their subject matter. The *Lais* and *Ysopë* consequently position the female writer differently with regard to her material. Marie's self-presentation as the work's translator in the epilogue that concludes her fable collection gestures towards a more positive model for educated noblewomen. The epilogue presents the female writer as learned and shrewd: she is the conduit for the transmission of this text and refuses to be forgotten and have her work appropriated by male clerics (*Fables*, Epilogue, ll. 1–12). Marie's self-portrait here reveals a woman using her linguistic skills for the right purposes, to instruct rather than mislead. This nonetheless implies a contrast with many of the – usually lower class – human women depicted in the collection itself, rather than an identification with them.

In the *Espurgatoire*, Marie uses translation as a mode of writing that not only transmits textual content but that also has the capacity to uncover spiritual truths situated at the limit of what human language can express. In doing so, she again implicitly aligns her work as a female translator with the translational networks depicted in the text she renders in French. Unlike the processes of story-making seen in other works, however, the intradiegetic networks in the *Espurgatoire* pass principally through men. The interest the *Espurgatoire* demonstrates in translation's revelatory capacities is comparable to the uses to which vernacular translation is put in other contemporary religious works, including Anglo-Norman texts by women such as Clemence of Barking. More unusually, Marie's text situates its exploration of translation's revelatory potential in a purgatorial otherworld located in Ireland, at the western limit of the Angevin kingdom and of the known world. Marie's description of purgatory consequently confronts her audience with phenomena that defy description or comprehension, while contextualising this by reference to a linguistic situation on the outskirts of Angevin territories. Translation performs within this setting as a means of opening other spiritual dimensions as well as other texts and languages.

Marie's *Espurgatoire* is a relatively close translation of a Latin source about the discovery of the opening to purgatory. The *Espurgatoire* was the first in a series of vernacular translations of the *Tractatus de Purgatorio Sancti Patricii* (*c.* 1170–85) by Huntingdon monk 'H.' de Saltrey. The *Espurgatoire*'s composition has conventionally been dated to *c.* 1190, though Carla Rossi argues convincingly for an earlier date of 1173.[19] Both the *Tractatus* and the *Espurgatoire* are therefore likely to have been composed in the years following the arrival of the first colonisers in Ireland, in 1169. Indeed, the religious and political conquest of Ireland is arguably the subtext of these retellings of the legend.[20] The *Espurgatoire* recounts two interconnecting stories: that of St Patrick's discovery of the entrance to purgatory, and that of an Irish knight called Owen, who visits purgatory to atone for past sins. In the first section of the text, Patrick travels to Ireland to preach. Shortly afterwards, God shows the saint the opening to purgatory to assist him in converting the Irish, by providing evidence that Patrick's teachings are true. The geography of this event is important. Translation is integral to the saint's communication with the people he aims to convert in Ireland. Indeed, the first confession described in the text requires the use of a *latimer* (interpreter) to translate for the saint (*Espurgatoire*, ll. 229–34). Later, Owen not only mediates between the known world and the purgatorial otherworld but also acts as a linguistic interpreter for a monk from Cîteaux called Gilbert (*Espurgatoire*, ll. 1951–60). Like the *Lais*, the *Espurgatoire* uses proximate experiences of multilingualism to contextualise a more expansive reflection on translation and narrative composition. Ireland is already a terrain where Christian holy men are confronted with cultural and linguistic differences that must be overcome if their evangelising mission is to succeed; the country is additionally home to a portal to purgatory that poses its own translation challenges, by defying adequate description in any known language. Owen is positioned at the intersection of these encounters with difference: as an Irish knight who interprets for Gilbert, and as a witness who has returned from purgatory and lived to tell the tale.

In the prologue, Marie associates her role as translator with that of Owen. In presenting her translation, she invites readers to see God's grace as the inspiration for her work and, a little later, focuses on the limitations of her experience of the subject matter. These are characteristics that Marie's endeavours share with Owen's experiences while in purgatory. The account of Owen's purgatorial adventure often highlights the indescribable nature of what he witnesses, as well as the conceptual limits with which the place confronts him (for example, *Espurgatoire*, ll. 1103–10, 1663–6). Like Owen's experience, Marie's encounter with her material ultimately leads her closer to God, even if it cannot be based on perfect understanding (*Espurgatoire*, ll. 9–30). Marie's epilogue briefly returns to issues of translation and comprehension in emphasising the popularising motivation for her text:

> Joe, Marie, ai mis en memoire
> le livre de l'Espurgatoire,
> en romanz, k'il seit entendables
> a laie genz e covenables. (*Espurgatoire*, ll. 2297–300)

> (I, Marie, have put into memory
> the book of purgatory
> in the romance language, that it might be understandable
> and fitting to laypeople.)

We know from Marie's prologue and dedication, as well as from the way purgatorial experience is represented in the *Espurgatoire*, that the memory and the understanding she mentions in these lines are incomplete. Translation nonetheless offers partial access to the truths which each of these faculties may be used imperfectly to grasp – and thus holds out the promise of spiritual improvement for less educated members of Marie's audience.

Works attributed to Marie bear witness to the historical moment in which they were written in several ways that have a bearing on how we conceptualise their authorship. The forms of composition featured in these texts are connected to the reading or glossing of other works, as well as to practices of translation and adaptation. These texts often locate themselves within a multilingual setting and highlight the role of the female writer-translator within that context. The works identified with Marie are shaped to varying degrees by French, Latin, Breton, English, Arabic, and Irish cultures and languages. Translation suffuses all of these texts as a mode of literary production. It is even actively thematised in some of them. The female writer illuminates the significance of composing in French by reference to other languages, particularly those relevant to Angevin Britain. In the *Lais* and the *Espurgatoire*, this consciousness of the particularity of French translation in an insular setting also goes beyond the framing of the text.

The subtle deployment of translation in these works as a concept as well as a mechanism of textual transmission shows a sophisticated grasp of how the limits of vernacular translation can uncover deeper levels of meaning or understanding for audiences with multilingual awareness.

Even where an explicit focus on interlinguistic translation is less to the fore, the corpus attributed to Marie depicts textual production and translation as collaborative enterprises involving women as well as men. This conception of authorship means that Marie's presentation of herself as the writer responsible for the French work often invites comparison with male and female characters involved in story-making and textual composition within the texts themselves. That comparison is nonetheless modulated differently across this corpus and does not always straightforwardly identify the female writer with female characters. The *Lais*, though occasionally critical of women's speech, offer numerous examples of women's involvement in compositional networks. In this collection Marie's literary activities might be aligned with those of female (as well as male) composers and storytellers. *Ysopë* is more equivocal. In Marie's fables, the misogynist imputations of women's narrative agency suggest a distinction between the aristocratic woman writer and the lower-class women who populate the tales themselves. In the *Espurgatoire*, Marie's role in communicating experiences that defy complete description or comprehension identifies her most notably with Owen, the male intermediary and translator in her text. In all of these works, the writer we have come to identify as 'Marie de France' is positioned within collaborative networks of authorship that pass through translation, as well as oral and written modes of composition. Whoever this Marie was – or these Maries were – the works bearing this name invite us to view them as part of a polyglot textual culture that valued translation, adaptation, and authorship equally. The thematisation of translation and textual production within the works themselves further shows how this could be a source of authority for the female writer, by emphasising her place within medieval textual traditions usually dominated by men and by subtly underscoring her role in perpetuating those traditions.

Notes

1. Marie de France, *Les Fables: Édition critique accompagnée d'une introduction, d'une traduction, de notes et d'un glossaire*, ed. and trans. Charles Brucker (Paris and Louvain: Peeters, 1998). All references to the *Fables/Ysopë* are to this edition. In-text references give the number of the fable or section heading, followed by verse number. Translations from French throughout this chapter are my own.

2. Constance Bullock-Davies, 'Marie, Abbess of Shaftesbury, and her Brothers', *English Historical Review* 80 (1965), 314–22. Jessie Crosland, *Medieval French Literature* (Oxford: Basil Blackwell, 1956), 97. John Charles Fox, 'Mary, Abbess of Shaftesbury', *English Historical Review* 26 (1911), 317–26. Antoinette Knapton, 'A la recherche de Marie de France', *Romance Notes* 19 (1978), 248–53. Ezio Levi, 'Maria di Francia e le abbazie d'Inghilterra', *Archivum Romanicum* 5 (1921), 472–93. Urban T. Holmes, 'New Thoughts on Marie de France', *Studies in Philology* 29 (1932), 1–10. Urban T. Holmes, 'Further on Marie de France', *Symposium* 3 (1949), 335–9. P. N. Flum, 'Additional Thoughts on Marie de France', *Romance Notes* 3 (1961), 53–6. Carla Rossi, *Marie de France et les érudits de Cantorbéry*, Recherches littéraires médiévales, 1 (Paris: Éditions Classiques Garnier, 2009).
3. *La vie Seinte Audrée: poème anglo-normand du XIIIe siècle*, ed. Östen Södergård (Uppsala: A.-B. Lundequistska Bokhandeln, 1955). June Hall McCash, '*La vie seinte Audree*: A Fourth Text by Marie de France?', *Speculum* 77.3 (2002), 744–77. Logan E. Whalen, *Marie de France and the Poetics of Memory* (Washington, DC: Catholic University of America Press, 2008), 159–73. Rossi, *Marie de France*, 151–201. Rupert T. Pickens, 'Marie de France *Translatrix* II: *La Vie Seinte Audree*', in *A Companion to Marie de France*, ed. Logan E. Whalen (Leiden: Brill, 2011), 267–95. Jocelyn Wogan-Browne with an Appendix by Ian Short, 'Recovery and Loss: Women's Writing Around Marie de France', in *Women Intellectuals and Leaders in the Middle Ages*, ed. Kathryn Kerby-Fulton, Katie Ann-Marie Bugyis, and John Van Engen (Cambridge: D. S. Brewer, 2020), 169–89. For discussion of gender and reception in this text, see also Christiania Whitehead, Chapter 12 in this volume.
4. Wogan-Browne with Ian Short, 'Recovery and Loss', 185–9.
5. An overview of this scholarship can be found in Glyn S. Burgess, *Marie de France: An Analytical Bibliography* (London: Grant and Cutler, 1977; Supplement No. 1, 1986; Supplement No. 2, 1997).
6. Examples of work in this vein include Susan Crane, 'Anglo-Norman Cultures in England, 1066–1460', in *The Cambridge History of Medieval English Literature*, ed. David Wallace (Cambridge: Cambridge University Press, 1999), 35–60; Jocelyn Wogan-Browne, *Saints' Lives and Women's Literary Culture, 1150–1300: Virginity and Its Authorizations* (Oxford: Oxford University Press, 2001), 1–3; Sharon Kinoshita and Peggy McCracken, *Marie de France: A Critical Companion* (Cambridge: D. S. Brewer, 2012); Marianne Fisher, 'Culture, Ethnicity, and Assimilation in Anglo-Norman Britain: The Evidence from Marie de France's *Lais*', *Exemplaria* 24.3 (2012), 195–213; Sahar Amer, *Ésope au féminin. Marie de France et la politique de l'interculturalité*, Faux titre, 169 (Amsterdam: Rodopi, 1999); Sif Rikhardsdottir, *Medieval Translations and Cultural Discourse: The Movement of Texts in England, France and Scandinavia* (Cambridge: D. S. Brewer, 2012).
7. *Marie de France, Lais with introduction and bibliography by Glyn S. Burgess*, ed. Alfred Ewert, 2nd ed. (London: Bristol Classical Press, 1995, repr. 2001). In-text references give the title of the *lai* or the prologue in italics, followed by verse numbers.

8. *Marie de France,* Le Purgatoire de saint Patrick *accompagné des autres versions françaises en vers et du* Tractatus de Purgatorio sancti Patricii *de H. de Saltrey*, ed. and trans. Myriam White-Le Goff (Paris: Champion, 2019).
9. For discussion of these two works, see Christiania Whitehead, Chapter 12 in this volume.
10. For example, Anne Paupert, 'Les Femmes et la parole dans les *Lais* de Marie de France', in *Amour et merveille: Les 'Lais' de Marie de France*, ed. Jean Dufournet (Paris: Champion, 1995), 169–87; Robert Sturges, 'Texts and Readers in Marie de France's *Lais*', *Romanic Review* 71 (1980), 244–64; Diana M. Faust, 'Women Narrators in the *Lais* of Marie de France', in *Women in French Literature*, ed. Michel Guggenheim (Saratoga: Anma Libri, 1988), 17–27; Roberta L. Krueger, 'Marie de France', in *The Cambridge Companion to Medieval Women's Writing*, ed. Carolyn Dinshaw and David Wallace (Cambridge: Cambridge University Press, 2003), 172–83; Simon Gaunt, *Retelling the Tale: An Introduction to Medieval French Literature* (London: Duckworth, 2001), 60–69.
11. For example, *Lecheor* and the *Lay of the Beach*. Chrétien's romance *Erec et Enide* also depicts women composing a *lai*. See Amanda Hopkins, 'The "Lay of the Beach" and the Breton Lay Genre', *Nottingham Medieval Studies* 54 (2010), 57–72; E. Jane Burns, *Bodytalk: When Women Speak in Old French Literature* (Philadelphia: University of Pennsylvania Press, 1993), 195–6; Sophie Marnette, 'Gender and Genre in the *Lai du Lecheor*', *Le Cygne* 8 (2021), 29–55.
12. Gaunt, *Retelling the Tale*, 63–6. Robert S. Sturges, *Medieval Interpretation: Models of Reading in Literary Narrative, 1100–1500* (Carbondale and Edwardsville: Southern Illinois University Press, 1991).
13. For more extensive analysis of translation in these texts, see Emma Campbell, *Reinventing Babel in Medieval French: Translation and Untranslatability (c. 1120–c. 1250)* (Oxford: Oxford University Press, 2023).
14. See, for example, Michelle A. Freeman, 'Marie de France's Poetics of Silence: The Implications for a Feminine *Translatio*', *Publications of the Modern Language Association of America* 99.5 (1984), 860–83 (867–71); R. Howard Bloch, *The Anonymous Marie de France* (Chicago: University of Chicago Press, 2003), 72–4; R. Howard Bloch, 'The Voice of the Dead Nightingale: Orality in the Tomb of Old French Literature', *Culture and History* 3 (1988), 63–78; Miranda Griffin, 'Gender and Authority in the Medieval French Lai', *Forum for Modern Language Studies* 35 (1999), 42–56 (45–6); Catherine Brown, 'Glossing the Origin: Lost Wax Poesis in the "Lais" of Marie de France', *Romance Philology* 43.1 (1989), 197–208; Sarah Bernthal, 'Dismemberment and Remembrance in the *Lais* of Marie de France', *Pacific Coast Philology* 54.1 (2019), 20–37; Karlheinz Stierle, 'Légendes de l'amour absolu: remembrance et écriture dans les *Lais* de Marie de France', *Zeitschrift für Französische Sprache und Literatur* 121.1 (2011), 66–79 (73–4).
15. What exactly Tristan may have written on the stick has been much discussed. Reviews of the debate include Anna G. Hatcher, 'Lai du *Chievrefueil*', *Romania* 71 (1950), 330–44; Christine Martineau-Génieys, 'Du *Chievrefoil*, encore et

toujours', *Le Moyen Âge* 78 (1972), 91–114; Pierre Kunstman, 'Symbole et interprétation: le message de Tristan dans le *Chèvrefeuille*', *Tristania* 13 (1988), 35–52.

16. Amer, *Ésope au féminin*. On sources, see also Marie de France, *Les Fables*, ed. and trans. Brucker, 6–9; Kinoshita and McCracken, *Marie de France*, 42–3; Rossi, *Marie de France*, 75–7.

17. Karen K. Jambeck, 'The *Fables* of Marie de France: A Mirror of Princes', in *In Quest of Marie de France, A Twelfth-Century Poet*, ed. Chantal A. Maréchal (Lewiston: Edwin Mellen Press, 1992), 59–106; Charles Brucker, 'The *Fables* of Marie de France and The Mirror of Princes', in *A Companion to Marie de France*, ed. Logan E. Whalen (Leiden: Brill, 2011), 209–35.

18. Amer, *Ésope au féminin*. Harriet Spiegel, 'The Woman's Voice in the *Fables* of Marie de France', in *In Quest of Marie de France, A Twelfth-Century Poet*, ed. Chantal A. Maréchal (Lewiston: Edwin Mellen Press, 1992), 45–58.

19. Arguments for the later date of *c*. 1190 presume the *Tractatus* was composed between 1185 and 1190; Marie's text must therefore have been written in or after 1190. Rossi argues for an earlier date for both works. She proposes that the *Tractatus* dates to 1173, which also provides a *terminus post quem* for Marie's *Espurgatoire*. De Wilde's unpublished doctoral thesis supports an earlier date for the *Tractatus*; he argues it was composed 1170–5. See Rossi, *Marie de France*, 86–8; Peter de Wilde, 'Le Purgatoire de saint Patrice. Origines et naissance d'un genre littéraire au XIIe siècle, avec une édition de la version en vers anglo-normande du manuscrit British Library, Cotton Domitianus A. IV' (unpublished doctoral thesis, University of Antwerp, 2000), cited in Keith Busby, *French in Medieval Ireland, Ireland in Medieval French: The Paradox of Two Worlds* (Turnhout: Brepols, 2017), 62, n. 143. On dating, see also Marie de France, *Le Purgatoire de saint Patrick*, ed. and trans. White-Le Goff, 10–11 and 121; Yolande de Pontfarcy, 'Le *Tractatus de purgatorio sancti Patricii* de H. de Saltrey: sa date et ses sources', *Peritia* 3 (1984), 460–80; Marie de France, *L'Espurgatoire seint Patriz*, ed. and trans. Yolande de Pontfarcy (Louvain: Peeters, 1995), 1–10; Lucien Foulet, 'Marie de France et la legende du Purgatoire de Saint Patrice', *Romanische Forschungen*, 22 (1908), 599–627; Robert Easting, 'The Date and Dedication of the *Tractatus de Purgatorio Sancti Patricii*', *Speculum* 53 (1978), 778–83; Karl Warnke, 'Die Vorlage des Espurgatoire St. Patriz der Marie de France', in *Philologische Studien aus dem romanisch-germanischen Kulturkreise: Karl Voretzsch zum 60. Geburtstage und zum Gedenken an seine erste akademische Berufung vor 35 Jahren*, ed. B. Schädel and W. Mulertt (Halle: Niemeyer, 1927), 135–54.

20. Bloch, *The Anonymous Marie de France*, 272; Myriam White-Le Goff, 'Pour une lecture politique de la légende du Purgatoire de saint Patrick', in *Vérité poétique, vérité politique. Mythes, modèles et idéologies politiques au Moyen Âge*, ed. Jean-Christophe Cassard, Élisabeth Gaucher, and Jean Kerhervé (Brest: CRBC, 2007), 435–45; Laura Ashe, *Fiction and History in England, 1066–1200* (Cambridge: Cambridge University Press, 2007), 194–204. Busby further connects this to the interest in language and interpreting demonstrated by these texts; Busby, *French in Medieval Ireland*, 69–70.

Further Reading

Amer, Sahar (1999). *Ésope au féminin. Marie de France et la politique de l'interculturalité*, Faux titre, 169, Amsterdam: Rodopi.

Baum, Richard (1968). *Recherches sur les œuvres attribuées à Marie de France*, Heidelberg: C. Winter.

Bloch, R. Howard (2003). *The Anonymous Marie de France*, Chicago and London: University of Chicago Press.

Fisher, Marianne (2012). Culture, Ethnicity, and Assimilation in Anglo-Norman Britain: The Evidence from Marie de France's *Lais*. *Exemplaria* 24.3, 195–213.

Freeman, Michelle A. (1984). Marie de France's Poetics of Silence: The Implications for a Feminine *Translatio*. *Publications of the Modern Language Association of America* 99.5, 860–83.

Griffin, Miranda (1999). Gender and Authority in the Medieval French Lai. *Forum for Modern Language Studies* 35, 42–56.

Kinoshita, Sharon, and Peggy McCracken (2012). *Marie de France: A Critical Companion*, Cambridge: D. S. Brewer.

Maréchal, Chantal A., ed. (1992). *In Quest of Marie de France: A Twelfth-Century Poet*, Lewiston, NY: Edwin Mellen Press.

Rikhardsdottir, Sif (2012). *Medieval Translations and Cultural Discourse: The Movement of Texts in England, France and Scandinavia*, Cambridge: D.S. Brewer.

Whalen, Logan E., ed. (2011). *A Companion to Marie de France*, Leiden: Brill.

CHAPTER 19

Julian of Norwich
A Woman's Vision, Book, and Readers

Barry Windeatt

The anchoress Julian of Norwich (1342–after 1416) – the first woman author writing in the English language who can be identified – could hardly be bolder in interpreting her visionary experience to affirm that God is as truly our mother as our father.[1] For Julian, God as our mother is an informing theme that unlocks her revelations. As Julian understands it, motherhood was in the role and nature of the Son as Second Person of the Trinity before time began or any human mothers were created, so it is less that Christ acts like a mother than that mothers at their most maternal share in Christ-like characteristics. Not only did God become flesh in a woman's womb but, as a mother, Christ carries humanity within himself to term and, after the most painful labour (on the cross), gives birth to us into life and to bliss, breastfeeding us with the sacraments (ch. 60, ll. 13–17, 22–4). Moreover, since Julian sees humanity's redemption as always divinely intended from before time – and man's fall as therefore incidental – she never mentions Eve and completely ignores the whole misogynist tradition of blaming women's supposed guilt for human fleshly weakness and temptation. Nor does Julian bother to include conventional recommendations of virginity and chastity, or marriage and widowhood – as if to specify them would delimit women, where Julian's focus is always on humankind itself. Here is the stunningly independent and original testimony of a medieval English woman author.

Julian's motive as an author, and the source of inspiration for her writing, are implicit in her text. Julian becomes an author because she experiences some extraordinary revelations and acknowledges a divine imperative to make them known. Her text, however, is much more reflective about its nature and evolution than a mere report. It embodies in itself Julian's struggles to interpret numinous revelations that provide her authority and subject matter as a woman author but also test troublingly the boundaries of orthodoxy. In the process, Julian becomes the first person of any gender to write serious theology in English. The nature of her text and aspects of its reception history are correspondingly challenging witnesses to how one astonishingly audacious woman author negotiated a role within medieval literary culture.

It is an indication of Julian's contemporary reputation that Margery Kempe records seeking out Julian for her advice on deceptive revelations, 'for the ankres was expert in swech thyngys and good cownsel cowd yevyn'.[2] Julian dates her revelations to May 1373 and says she was thirty-and-a-half (ch. 2, ll. 1–2; ch. 3, l. 1), but otherwise little is known of her circumstances beyond what can be deduced from her texts, which never explicitly acknowledge being authored by an anchoress. Four surviving wills record legacies left to a recluse named Julian in Norwich or at St Julian's Church in Norwich between 1394 (when Julian would have been fifty-two) and 1416.[3] It seems unlikely that Julian was not an anchoress before 1394 – she dates to 1393 her breakthrough in interpreting her revelations (ch. 51, l. 69) – but no record survives. Kempe refers to Julian as 'Dame Jelyan', a customary form of address for nuns, but this is the only indication that Julian might have been a nun before becoming an anchoress. Since there was only one nunnery in Norwich, at Carrow, it is sometimes claimed – plausibly, albeit without evidence – that Julian was educated there. Julian describes herself as a simple unlettered creature (ch. 2, l. 1), and although this may be a claim to ignorance of Latin rather than illiteracy, it was probably prudent at times for Julian as a woman author to claim both. Her characterisations of the alphabet as an elementary level of learning (ch. 51, ll. 209–10; ch. 80, ll. 6–8) imply that she could read and write in English, as do her painstaking revisions of her writings. Where Julian acquired her manifest learning remains unknown, but late-medieval Norwich had a vibrant religious culture, and Kempe's experience witnesses also to an empowering oral culture of holy conversation with clerics and contemplatives in which a woman was a welcome participant.

Julian's text survives in two authentic versions, one four times longer than the other. A single copy of the Short Text (ST) survives in British Library, MS Add 37790 (a Carthusian anthology of contemplative material). This manuscript was copied *c.* 1450 but retains a rubric claiming that this text of the short version preserves one copied during Julian's lifetime: it identifies the text as a vision 'to a devoute woman, and hir name es Julyan, that is a recluse atte Norwyche and yitt ys on lyfe, A.D. 1413'.[4] This Short Text includes various circumstantial details about the revelations as an event and experience which do not appear in the longer version and suggest this is an authentic early version closer to Julian's experience of her revelations. Precisely how early remains a matter of debate, but it is notable that this relatively undeveloped version of Julian's text is still being circulated forty years after the date of the revelations, perhaps because its immediacy kept it very accessible. By contrast, no complete medieval copies of Julian's Long Text are extant and it survives only in post-Reformation copies. This might imply that this profoundly original version was never widely circulated, possibly by design at a time when official anxieties over the spread of heresy would make risky any expression of unorthodox views.

In Julian's Short Text and Long Text, the different perspectives on female authorship that are represented in one woman's two versions of her life's work point to how women authors might negotiate their contemporary literary culture. The short version is open about its authorship by a woman and defiantly rejects being precluded from authorship by her gender, but its content shows, as yet, little of a distinctively female approach to Julian's revelations. The much longer version, audaciously original, is the inverse of this: it suppresses all reference to its author's being female but develops Julian's uniquely woman-centred exposition of her revelations.

The Short Text does not conceal its female authorship, although claiming ignorance and disclaiming intent to teach by writing: 'Botte God forbede that ye schulde saye or take it so that I am a techere, for I meene nought soo ... For I am a woman, leued [ignorant], febille, and freylle' (ST, ch. 6, ll. 34–5). At the same time, Julian sounds almost indignant in the Short Text when querying why she should be precluded by her gender from authoring what she understood God wished her to make known: 'Botte for I am a woman, schulde I therfore leve that I schulde nought telle yowe the goodenes of God, syne that I sawe in that same tyme that it is his wille that it be knawen?' (ST, ch. 6, ll. 39–40). To create space for herself as a woman author, Julian lays strategic claim to an ignorance that is patently belied by her writing and pre-empts potential criticism by disclaiming the male clerical role of writing to instruct. Julian's Short Text also retains tantalising hints that she lived and wrote within a female support network. It records her curiosity to learn about the spiritual progress of a female friend (ST, ch. 16, l. 12). The Short Text also implies a close mother–daughter relationship, telling how Julian's mother was present at Julian's bedside during the supposedly mortal illness when Julian experienced her revelations, and how her mother believed Julian to have died: 'My modere, that stode emangys othere and behelde me, lyftyd uppe hir hande before me face to lokke myn eyen, for sche wenyd I had bene dede' (ST, ch. 10, ll. 26–7).

By contrast, the absence from the Long Text (LT) of any reference to its author's being a woman may be variously interpreted. It may signal prudent caution, mindful of the singularity of female authorship, yet it also leaves behind any explicit defensiveness. This may reflect an increased authorial confidence that makes earlier apologetic uncertainty no longer relevant to include. The passage on Julian's concern about her female friend has been rewritten so as to obscure the friend's gender (ch. 35, ll. 1–4). Reference in the Short Text to her mother being present during Julian's revelatory experience while gravely ill disappears from the Long Text, yet it is the Long Text that includes Julian's extended exposition on the theme of Christ as our mother (chapters 57–63), which is not yet present in the Short Text. With this come references to female bodily experience – childbirth, breastfeeding, and nursing – as channels for spiritual understanding. In this way, a hint in the Short Text of Julian's closeness to her own mother is rewritten by the Long Text into Julian's transformational understanding of Christ as mother to us all.

For Julian, 'this fair lovely word "moder" it is so swete and so kynd of the self that it may ne verily be seid of none but of him' (ch. 60, ll. 34–5). Julian is eloquent about how Christ 'usith the condition of a wise moder' (ch. 61, l. 37). Christ's sustaining and nurturing of humanity resembles a mother's role in first breastfeeding her child, nursing it, and then modifying her maternal role but not her love as the child grows, allowing it to learn from its falls while being always the child's first recourse and constant loving support (ch. 60, ll. 22–44; ch. 61, ll. 24–38). For Julian, humanity achieves 'non heyer stature in this life than childhode' (ch. 63, ll. 32–3), implying that spiritually we remain in a childlike dependence on Christ, like the child on its mother. Yet Julian's sensitive account of this 'moderhede of werkyng' is only the third and least mysterious of her 'three manner of beholdyng of moderhede in God' (ch. 59, ll. 33–7), which also include Julian's understanding of creation and redemption.

As Julian explains it, the higher part (or 'substance') of the souls of all those who will ever be born was created all at once and united with the Second Person of the Trinity ('He made us all at onys', ch. 58, ll. 4). This 'first making' pre-exists the union of substance with the lower part of the soul (the 'sensuality' or our whole sensory consciousness) when the soul descends to earth at an individual's birth. This first making is Julian's first 'manner of beholdyng of moderhede in God', for she sees this initial creation of all our souls as a kind of maternity, just as the second maternity is Christ's assuming of human flesh in his incarnation ('And thus is Jesus our very moder in kynde, of our first makyng, and he is our very moder in grace, be takyng of our kynde made', ch. 59, ll. 29–30). God who 'knew us and lovid us fro aforn any tyme' always intended 'that the second Person shuld becom our moder' and be the fount of all human motherhood ('All the fair werkyng and all the swete kindly office of dereworthy moderhede is impropried [appropriated] to the second Person', ch. 59, ll. 30–1). In taking on human sensuality in his incarnation as fully human, the Second Person restores sensuality to its original relation with the divine substance, but Julian ignores the traditionally gendered view of a masculine higher part of the soul and a fallible, female lower part. Just as a child was believed to derive its physicality from its mother, Christ is our mother in that he has reunited the higher and lower parts of our existence, both substantial and sensual, body and soul. In the whole performance of motherhood by earthly mothers, 'it is he that doth it in the creatures be whom that it is done' (ch. 60, l. 38), and yet in his care and protection of us he surpasses the most caring of earthly mothers (ch. 61, ll. 24–7).

Christ may be our mother, but this mother remains 'he' and 'him': Julian never refers to Christ by other than male pronouns. This is an understanding of Christ's motherhood that coexists with the male gender of the historical Christ made flesh in time. There is something comparable with how Julian sees the identification of Christ with wisdom in the Trinity or with the Church ('He will that we taken us mytyly to the feith of holy church, and fyndyn there our dereworthy moder', ch. 61, ll. 40–1). The Second Person is identified with wisdom, and wisdom is personified as female in the apocryphal book of Wisdom (Wisdom 7:8–14, 22–9). Maternity and wisdom, understood as female, become united in Christ: 'thus in our very moder, Jesus, our life is groundid in the forseing wisdam of himselfe from without begynnyng' (ch. 63, ll. 21–2), because in Christ 'the depe wisdam of the Trinite is our moder' (ch. 58, l. 25). Moreover, Christ is identified with the Church, which traditionally is also characterised in maternal terms, so that the Church's administration of the sacraments becomes identified, in Julian's understanding, with Christ feeding us with himself through the sacraments like a breastfeeding mother (ch. 60, ll. 22–4).

Part of her revelations' challenge for Julian was their combination of Passion-themed visions with other revelations involving mysterious intuitions and the hearing of divine utterances or locutions. In representing Julian's process of interpreting them, her accounts of the revelations present an implicitly autobiographical record of a woman author's struggles with her material. Julian's camera-like observation of her Passion revelations may

Illustration 19.1 Christ before Herod. Panel painting; Norwich, *c.* 1400–1425. © The Fitzwilliam Museum, Cambridge.

respond to the stimulus of what Julian had seen in contemporary visual culture, except that for Julian the paintings now move and stream with blood in a way perhaps alert to women's experience.[5] A fragment of contemporary panel painting from Norwich, showing blood flowing from the crown of thorns over Christ's brow, is broken off at bottom left where the same bleeding face of Christ also appears in an 'Ecce Homo' scene (see Illustration 19.1). In the complete panel Christ's bleeding face apparently featured recurrently in the same plane, not unlike Julian's revelation.

It is only in her Long Text that Julian interprets her perplexing second revelation – of seeing the two halves of Christ's face alternatingly covered with dried blood – by aligning it with the relic of St Veronica's veil ('It made me to thinke of the holy vernacle of Rome', ch. 10, ll. 27–8). This was the image of his face that Christ left imprinted on the veil with which Veronica wiped his face on the way to Calvary.[6] Julian thus equates her revelation with this miraculous likeness of Christ's face uniquely vouchsafed to a woman, but which Julian knows to fluctuate bafflingly in appearance, not unlike her own vision. If Julian comes to authorise her vision of Christ's face by thinking of it in parallel with St Veronica's miraculous image, Julian may thereby identify herself with Veronica, who in turn was commonly identified with the 'Haemorissa' in the Gospels. This was the woman suffering with a twelve-year 'issue of blood' (probably heavy menstrual bleeding), and hence regarded as unclean, whose 'fountain of her blood' Christ heals because she believes she need only touch his garment to be cured (Mark, 5:25–34). Julian later alludes to this miracle ('Touch we him, and we shall be made clene', ch. 77, ll. 36–7), suggesting how much she identifies with this haemorrhaging and suffering woman, in the very chapter where Julian's exclamation 'This place is prison . . . ' has been read as an autobiographical outburst about her own enclosed life as an anchoress, though it may simply refer to all earthly life.

Flows of blood also suffuse Julian's fourth revelation, which has its visual germ in late-medieval devotional images of the Flagellation that depict Christ covered with multiple bleeding wounds (ch. 12, ll. 1–4). Julian's vision far transcends such images, seeing the saving blood streaming through the whole firmament of earth, heaven, and hell. In Julian's revelation it is the blood that performs Christ's missions to harrow hell, to cleanse earth of sin, and to ascend into heaven (ch. 12, ll. 15–23). This is an astonishing vision of the cosmic plenitude and power of Christ's saving blood but, while Julian contemplates this, it occurs to her that, if it were not a vision, the sheer volume of blood would have so saturated her sickbed that it would have flooded and overflowed (ch. 12, ll. 6–8). The cosmic vision of blood's transformative power goes along with the woman visionary's nightmare panic about what would happen if there were some unstaunchable bleeding, presumably because issue of blood and heavily bloodied bedclothes might be a source of horrified shame as well as a sign of pain.

It is notable in some of Julian's other Passion revelations that she later decodes their details as revealing how Christ is our mother. Julian's eighth revelation is a forensic close-up of the dehydrating of Christ's body during the Crucifixion. There was a view that since Christ's fleshliness came only from his mother, his flesh was therefore more sensitive than that of a man with two human parents, with the consequence that Christ's capacity to suffer on the cross was all the greater. Julian's focus on the drying and dying body is responding to Christ's words from the cross – 'I thirst' – which Julian later comes to understand as a ghostly thirst or love-longing in Christ as our mother to give birth to us all into salvation (ch. 63, ll. 17–20), a maternal longing that was in him from without beginning (ch. 31, ll. 27–30). On one level, the revelation's comparison of Christ's torn flesh with a cloth sagging as it hangs is the observation of a woman who had grown up alongside the processes of the local cloth-making industry, such as the cloth-drying on open-air frames in St Giles's parish in Norwich.[7] But later in her text Julian re-envisions all this photographically detailed physicality of Christ's drying flesh in terms of Christ's child-bearing maternal role, for his ghostly thirst will never let him stop 'till all his derworthy children be born and forth browte' (ch. 63, l. 18).

Julian's tenth revelation also develops a cue from visual culture and, after subsequent meditation, comes to interpret what has been revealed as a manifestation of Christ's motherhood. The visual motif behind this revelation is apparently the stylised depiction of the wound in Christ's side, often pictured in close-up, along with the wounded hands and feet, as the focus for devotional contemplation of the Instruments of the Passion or *Arma Christi*. In such pictures, the side-wound is depicted as a long, narrow, vulva-like aperture (see Illustration 19.2).[8] When Christ in Julian's revelation looks into his side and reveals within 'a faire, delectabil place' which is so mysteriously expansive as to be 'large enow for al mankynd that shal be save to resten in pece and in love' (ch. 24, ll. 3–4), Julian may be envisaging not only a vulva-like side-wound but beyond it the womb in which Christ as our mother carries all mankind to rebirth in redemption. Since Julian is also mindful of the blood and water streaming from Christ's side (ch. 24, ll. 4–5), this mysterious inward space sits very much adjacent to bleeding and bodiliness. Meditating on her vision of penetrating Christ's side-wound, Julian understands this mysterious insight inside Christ's body as a mystical transformation, whereby breastfeeding is transcended by illumination within Christ's breast ('The moder may leyn the child tenderly to hir brest, but our tender moder Jesus, he may homley leden us into his blissid brest be his swete open syde, and shewyn therin party of the Godhede', ch. 60, ll. 29–31).

The complexity of Julian's first revelation had introduced these themes by combining a Passion vision – of blood streaming over Christ's brow like

Illustration 19.2 Instruments of the Passion, Bohun Psalter and Hours (*c.* 1380), showing the side-wound bottom centre. Bodleian Library, MS Auct. D.4.4., f. 236 v. Used by permission of Bodleian Libraries, University of Oxford.

rain pouring over the house eaves in a shower (ch. 7, ll. 16–17) – with such arresting visionary insights as seeing 'a littil thing ... in the palme of my hand' and understanding 'it was generally answered thus, "It is all that is made"' (ch. 5, ll. 6–8). When Julian declares that this little thing she is shown in her hand is 'the quantitye of an hesil nutt' (ch. 5, l. 6), she is using the language of medieval English cookery, for the size of a hazel nut was a commonly used measure of quantities to be used in English recipes.[9] When Julian sees in her revelation how 'the grete dropis of blode fel downe from under the garland like pellots' (ch. 7, l. 11) – a comparison by which she seeks to describe the globular droplets ('pellotts, for roundhede, in the comynge out of the blode', ch. 7, ll. 19–20) – Julian is also using a term found in medieval recipes.[10] The everyday measures of a housewife's domestic experience in the kitchen are applied by a woman author to express visionary insights. This first revelation initiates a continuous awareness throughout Julian's text of welling blood and of visions of enclosing and being enclosed that implicitly reference Christ bearing humankind within him like a mother.

The idea of enclosing and being enclosed – of a kind of mutual indwelling – stands at the beginning and end of Julian's revelatory experience, in her first and sixteenth revelations. In the first revelation Julian understands that God enwraps us, so that we are as if enclosed within him (ch. 5, ll. 3–5; ch. 6, ll. 33–4), and this is a revelation of his homeliness with us, the favour of his intimacy, as suggested by a very unusual fifteenth-century Norfolk image of God enfolding his saints within his robe (see Illustration 19.3).[11]

In the climactic sixteenth revelation, which Julian views as the fulfilment of the rest, Julian sees Christ seated in majesty in the city of the human

Illustration 19.3 Saints enfolded in God's robe; historiated initial of All Saints as Crucifix-Trinity. The Ranworth Antiphoner, f. 271 v; Norwich(?), c. 1460–80. By kind permission of the Parochial Church Council, Church of St Helen, Ranworth, Norfolk.

soul, and thus enclosed within us (ch. 67, ll. 1–6). Between these two revelations Julian rings many thematic changes on these ideas, and one of the most liberating is her exposition of the structure of the soul, in which God is present in the soul at the very point where its two parts, substance and sensuality, are conjoined (ch. 55, ll. 19–21). Indeed, by cross-referencing her sixteenth revelation Julian even equates sensuality with the city of God, and sees Jesus enclosed in our sensuality, just as our substance is enclosed in Christ's soul that sits in the Godhead (ch. 56, ll. 18–20). This dazzling play on mutual indwelling characterises Julian's interpretation of what has been revealed to her about Christ's role as our mother in his incarnation, which is to reunite our substance and sensuality. In an extraordinary passage, Julian describes how Christ, enclosed in Mary's womb, took upon him our sensual soul but then – 'in which takyng, he us al haveyng beclosid in him' – he united our sensuality with our substance (ch. 57, ll. 30–4). Himself enclosed in Mary's womb, Christ then encloses us in himself to effect the reunion of our soul's two parts. Citing both her first and sixteenth revelations in support, Julian sees Christ as our mother in a kind of perpetual childbirth, in which his eternally giving birth to us will never alter our enclosure within him: 'And our savior is our very moder, in whom we be endlesly borne and never shall come out of him' (ch. 57, ll. 36–7). Moreover, Julian understands that at the end of time there will be a kind of spiritual returning to the womb, whereby 'al his blissid children which ben comen out of him be kinde shal be browte ageyn into him be grace' (ch. 63, ll. 38–9).

The most significant woman's body is Mary's; the most meaningful enclosure is the Virgin's womb, as suggested by such contemporary artworks as 'vierges ouvrantes', devotional images of Mary where her belly is hinged to open like a cupboard (see Illustration 19.4).[12] As Julian sees it, Mary is also our mother, in whom we are all enclosed and all born of Mary in Christ's birth (ch. 57, ll. 34–6). For Julian, even her revelation of the Annunciation – when Mary learns she will become Christ's mother – signifies Christ's purpose to become our mother (ch. 60, ll. 4–10). Mary consequently makes three appearances in Julian's revelations (ch. 4, ll. 21–31; ch. 18, ll. 1–5; ch. 25, ll. 1–8), but perhaps the most important reference to Mary is a brief passage in Julian's analysis of how she sees 'full mystily a wondirful example of a lord that hath a servant' (ch. 51, ll. 1–2). This 'example' comes in answer to Julian's need to see how God sees the problem of sin's existence (ch. 50, l. 15), and so all normal perspectives of human perception are exploded. The emblematic scene of a lord who sends a willing servant on an errand, in which the servant falls into a ravine, is

Illustration 19.4(a) and (b) Shrine of the Virgin. German, *c.* 1300. (a) Image closed as the Virgin and Child. (b) Image opened to show the Trinity enclosed within the Virgin Mary. God the Father holds a cross (the figure of the crucified Christ and the dove symbolising the Holy Spirit have been lost). The wings depict scenes from Christ's Nativity: (left) Annunciation, Nativity, Adoration of the Magi; (right) Visitation, Presentation in the Temple, Announcement to the Shepherds. Gift of J. Pierpont Morgan, 1917. By courtesy of The Metropolitan Museum of Art, New York: accession no. 17.190.185a, b.

understood to refer concurrently both to God's initiating the incarnation and to the Fall of Adam. Images of Christ and Adam are as if mutually superimposed on the other, because from God's merciful perspective Christ could not but 'fall' with Adam – that is, humankind – and so redeem all. The fall is into the 'slade' or valley of Mary's womb ('Gods Son fell with Adam into the slade of the mayden wombe', ch. 51, ll. 173–4). Julian can ignore the Genesis narrative of a man tempted by a woman, Eve, who is subsequently scapegoated, for since Julian understands the Trinity as always intending to redeem humankind through the motherhood of the Second Person, Adam's fall was incidental not causative. Nor does Julian mention God's punishment of Eve: 'in sorrow thou shalt bring forth children' (Genesis 3:15). In place of this pointedly absent Eve, the focus is on Mary's womb as the enclosure within a woman's body where the future of humankind is resolved.

It is another pointed absence that also underlines Julian's striking independence as a woman author: her text includes no apparatus of references acknowledging the authority of other texts. Julian's work is implicit with learning, but this is now hard to identify with specific reading. Even biblical references tend to be allusive rather than word-for-word citations. Julian simply does not engage with the familiar nervous tic of (overwhelmingly male) medieval authors who recruit the authority of other, more authoritative texts by citing them to bolster their own works – a cultural tic that Chaucer subverts through a woman's voice in the Wife's account of her husband's habit of reading out examples of 'wikked wyves' to her ('Wife of Bath's Prologue', III.669–787). For Julian, authority lies in the locutions and images of her revelations: as a woman author she is her own authority, through authorisation from the revelatory experience vouchsafed to her. Ignoring any male clerical authorities, Julian instead substitutes a reference system whereby what she records herself seeing, hearing, and understanding becomes self-authorising through a system of cross-references that criss-cross her text. Julian's method enables the evidence of one revelation to become a contributory part of Julian's interpretation of another, so that authority is constructed through an overarching system of interconnecting references that work to strengthen each other and the whole. Julian deploys various types of such cross-reference; mostly she relies on quoting or paraphrasing key phrases: 'And this shewid he in these gracious words: "I kepe the ful sekirly"' (ch. 61, ll. 52–3; citing ch. 37, ll. 6–7). Sometimes she references thematic motifs from earlier contexts: 'For he longyth ever to bryng us to the fulhede of joy, as it is afornseid, where he shewith the gostly threst [thirst]' (ch. 40, ll. 17–18; citing ch. 31, ll. 9–14). Some of Julian's cross-referencing cites from her sixteen revelations by their number in the sequence, with or without the citation of the memorable phrase or thematic motif: 'This was shewid in the first and more openly in the iii wher it seyth "I saw God in a poynte"' (ch. 35, ll. 13–14; citing ch. 5, l. 2; ch. 11, l. 1); 'And this was shewid in the xiii, ner at the begynnyng, wher it spekith of pite. For he seith ...' (ch. 77, ll. 23–9; cf. ch. 28, ll. 21–6). All such modes of reference exemplify the problems in ensuring accurate cross-reference within texts in a manuscript culture. They thereby reveal Julian's determination to shape her self-authorisation not by reference to external authority, but in effect by citing herself. This self-referencing system goes back to how Julian develops the authority deriving from her original experience, as recorded in her Short Text, by constructing a commentary on it in her Long Text through an apparatus of interlinking cross-references. Textual format here becomes the outward expression of a remarkable woman author's autonomy.

That same autonomy also lies behind the text's implicitly autobiographical archive: it records severe crises of confidence in her revelations that have evidently been resolved through her own meditation, with never a mention of any clerical adviser's input. Yet if the cross-references suggest a woman author boldly constructing a self-authorising apparatus that dispenses with male clerical authority, her system also implies that the extant Long Text may not be far removed from a private working draft. Cross-references back to already described revelations make sense, but Julian not infrequently cross-refers ahead for authorisation to revelations (particularly the last) that she has not yet reported to the reader. Julian also references her exposition of substance and sensuality (ch. 45, ll. 1–4) before she has provided it (chs. 53–9). All this suggests that, at the time of composing the surviving Long Text, guiding a readership came second to working through the text for her own understanding. This text is still being thought through, and for Julian is her means of thinking through. It is as if the most current state of Julian's text is for her more of a map or chart than a linear narrative, and she moves around it in her mind with a cursor: it is as much spatial and diagrammatic as linear and chronological, which continues to make it exhilarating and inspirational to read.

Julian does not record God instructing her to write a book but reports her understanding that he wanted the content of her revelations known (ST, ch. 6, l. 40). The distinction may explain why, unlike other women contemplatives, Julian nowhere mentions amanuenses or difficulties in getting her book transcribed (which for Kempe makes her dependant on male clerics), perhaps because Julian experienced no great difficulty in a centre like Norwich, but possibly because Julian was unconcerned about transcription. Julian's revelations rarely allude to themselves as a book, once referring to 'the hole revelation . . . that is to sey, of this boke' (ch. 51, ll. 62–3), but the surviving manuscripts of her work represent a history of composition and preserve an archive of developing understanding and interpretation.

This careful editing that is intrinsic to Julian's presentation of her text becomes part of its reception history. Her short text survives in an anthology in British Library, MS Add 37790 alongside some texts definitely not intended for beginners in contemplation. With no surviving medieval copies, the only record of medieval reception of the Long Text rests on selections from it included in a contemplative florilegium of *c.* 1450 (Westminster Cathedral Treasury, MS 4), most probably made for use by nuns.[13] Here, unattributed excerpts from Julian are woven into one continuous sequence, following extracts from the mystical psalm-commentaries *Qui Habitat* and *Bonum Est*, and from Hilton's *Scale of Perfection*. Just once, a brief connecting passage inserted by the compiler refers to the author as 'her' (*Revelations*, 169, l. 149). Ironically, this manuscript's women readers may not have realised that they were reading a woman author, whose work has been silently recruited without acknowledgement to provide the concluding summation of a compilation for advanced practitioners of the contemplative life.

If this Westminster text records fifteenth-century nuns reading Julian, it is also to the later reading of Julian by nuns that we owe the survival of her Long Text, since the three extant manuscript copies of Julian's Long Text were probably made by post-Reformation English nuns exiled on the Continent.[14] The houses of English Benedictine nuns in Cambrai and Paris evidently had access to either medieval manuscripts or later copies. In writing the biography of one such nun, Augustine Baker (1575–1641) – Benedictine monk and spiritual director of the Paris nuns – refers to 'the old manuscript Booke' of Julian's revelations as if this was familiar in the milieu of the Paris nuns. This may refer to the manuscript that is now Paris, Bibliotheque Nationale, MS fonds anglais 40 (P), or perhaps to an earlier, medieval manuscript. It was from another such source that the copy that is now British Library, MS Sloane 2499 (S1) was transcribed, and the transcription has sometimes been attributed to a nun of the Paris house, Anne Clementia Cary (1614–71).[15] These two post-Reformation manuscripts on which modern editions of Julian are based – P and S1 – represent readings that preserve clues to the reception of Julian's medieval content by early modern women, but they may also record some medieval reception of Julian's work. These two texts are curious opposites of each other. In layout and script P has the appearance of a very tidy fake of a medieval manuscript, but the language of Julian's text that it contains has undergone modernisation. By contrast, S1 is written in a seventeenth-century handwriting that makes no attempt to disguise its period but preserves more of the medieval language of Julian's text. Both texts, or their predecessors, have been subject to forms of textualisation that may not derive from Julian. The reference system inbuilt into Julian's text sometimes makes cross-reference by the numbers of the revelations, but Julian only gives numbers to four of her revelations within her text, other than in the list of revelations in the first chapter that might be an editorial addition. Systematic numbering – and hence demarcation of the boundaries between revelations – is provided by the chapter rubrics in P and the chapter summaries in S1. The latter cannot derive from Julian, at least in their present form, since they both reveal her gender, which she has carefully obscured, and talk of her ('this blissid woman') in terms that she would hardly use of herself. Chapter-division is broadly the same in both P and S1, and hence derives from an earlier phase of the text but, if editorial, serves to remind us that for Julian the primary units in her work remained the revelations.

Both manuscripts have features possibly retaining traces of female readership or even of Julian's original perspective as a woman author. In its chapters on Christ our Mother, S1 capitalises the initial 'M' of 'Moder' and 'Moderhede' even while following common medieval scribal practice in not necessarily capitalising 'God' or 'Father' as in modern religious language: 'All our dett that we owen be gods biddyng be faderhede & Moderhede' (ch. 60; S1, f.44 r); 'Our gracious Modere hath browte us up to our faders bliss' (ch. 63; S1, f.46 v). In P there are intriguing occasional contexts that refer to the soul as female, as here: 'And welle I wott the more the soule seeth of god, the more she desyeryth hym by grace ... For whan a soule is temptyd, troblyde, and lefte to her selfe by her unrest, then is it tyme to praye to make her selfe suppull and buxum to god' (ch. 43; P, f. 79 v). But such feminising of the soul soon lapses, to be replaced by the extant manuscripts' more customary reference to the soul as 'it' or 'him', as in the very next sentence: 'But she by no manner of prayer makyth God suppell to hym ... ' where 'hym' replaces 'her'. Such instances perhaps record the occasional response of women copyists to the material being transcribed, unless they represent vestiges of what was once a more consistent reference to the soul as feminine in earlier copies.[16]

Evidence survives both of the nuns' continued reading and copying of Julian – as in the Upholland Anthology – but also of endeavour to live out Julian's example, as in the devotions of Margaret Gascoigne (1608–37), a nun at Cambrai.[17]

The Upholland Anthology is a miscellany of excerpts on the contemplative life including, under the heading of 'Saint Julian', her twelfth revelation (ch. 26) and early sections from the thirteenth (chs. 27, 28, 30, 32). The anthology was probably compiled between the 1640s and 1680s by Cambrai nuns, including Barbara Constable (1617–84), from a source resembling the Paris manuscript. 'Certein Devotions of Dame Margaret Gascoigne ... Found uppon her death, of her owne hande writing' were edited by Augustine Baker, who also provided a spiritual biography of Margaret, interpreting the devotions as her progression towards advanced contemplation. Baker describes how written below the crucifix at which Margaret gazed during her last illness and until her death was an inscription with 'these holy words that had sometime ben spoken by God to the Holie Virgin Julian the ankresse of Norwich, as appeareth by the old manuscript Booke of her Revelations'. These words, as Baker gives them, are 'Intend [attend] to me,

I am enough for thee: rejoice in me thy Saviour, and in thy Salvation' (ch. 5, l. 28; ch. 36, ll. 35–6). Margaret takes these divine words to Julian 'as appeareth by the booke of her revelations' as also spoken to her, and the words are recurrently cited throughout Margaret's devotions, much as Julian cites herself. Indeed, Margaret cites scriptural phrases, especially from Psalms, and then, despite the different literal meanings of the biblical texts, glosses them by invoking these same divine words to Julian. These words embolden Margaret to aspire to the contemplative's unbroken attention to the divine. Margaret's intent dying gaze at a crucifix, to which an inscription of Julian's words has been attached, suggests both a devout emulation of Julian's deathbed experience and also an identification with the words of her text, perhaps from that 'old manuscript Booke of her Revelations'.

It was from such a manuscript – either P or a text very like it – that Serenus Cressy (1605–74), a Roman Catholic convert briefly chaplain at the Paris convent, produced in 1670 the first printed edition of Julian's Long Text, which he entitled *Revelations of Divine Love*. This first appearance of Julian's work in print provoked Edward Stillingfleet, Bishop of Worcester, to include in his *Discourse Concerning the Idolatry Practised in the Church of Rome* (London, 1671) a contemptuous condemnation of the *Revelations* that is strongly gendered. Stillingfleet's rationalist objections to the perceived 'fanaticism' of the Catholic Church include, plural 'the great number of female Revelations approved in the Roman Church' and the way in which 'Private revelations [are] made among them the grounds of believing some points of doctrine'. Stillingfleet repeatedly equates Julian's revelations with fanaticism and madness, referring to 'the Fanatick Revelations of Mother Julian' with 'Some instances of the blasphemous Nonsense contained in them' as also 'the Fanatick Revelations of distempered brains' exemplified by Julian, and 'such Fooleries, which deserve no other name at the best than the efforts of Religious madness'. An observant close reader of Julian, Stillingfleet cites a long list of brief statements culled from her revelations and paraphrased out of context in such a way as to make them sound outlandish to a reader ignorant of Julian's original. His list opens with 'she speaks of our being beclosed in the mid-head of God', and concludes indignantly with 'she discourseth of three properties in the Holy Trinity, of the Fatherhead, of the Motherhood, and of the Lordship, and she further saw that the second person which is our Mother substantially, the same dear worthy person is now become our Mother sensual'. Using 'hysterical' in its old sense, where emotions and intellect are understood to be influenced by disturbances of the uterus, all this and the rest is dismissed as 'the blasphemous and senseless tittle tattle of this *Hysterical* Gossip … the Canting and Enthusiastick expressions, which signifie nothing in Mother Julian's Revelations'. Nonetheless, Julian's 'senseless tittle tattle' continued to be copied by hand, not least because Cressy's edition remained the only one until the nineteenth century. At the French Revolution the English Benedictine nuns of Paris fled home to England, having narrowly escaped the guillotine. They were sheltered by the Marchioness of Buckingham, herself a Catholic convert, and a handwritten copy of Julian's *Revelations* is later found in the Buckinghams' library at Stowe (now British Library, MS Stowe 42).

In closing her work, Julian declares that 'This booke is begunne ... but it is not yet performid [completed]' (ch. 86, l. 1). Unfinished, and perhaps unfinishable, the revelations would never cease yielding understandings for analysis. One characteristic aspect of Julian's analytical method is how alert she is in her revelations to the significance of what she has not been shown. In this, Julian's approach to negative or absent evidence offers a model for how, as a woman author, her text engages with literary culture through the implications of what she does not say explicitly. If Julian does not explain her revelation of St John of Beverley's forgiven but unspecified youthful sinfulness (ch. 38, ll. 19–25), is she thinking of his criminal violence towards women in one version of his legend, where he rapes and murders his sister while drunk? Does Julian's acceptance of incompleteness, of what she does not know, imply that she has not sought (or not been convinced by) any guidance from male clerics to explain, edit, and control? Is not Julian's implicitly positive view of human sensuality – and of unregretted bodily nature – a more independent-minded female approach than clerical group-fear and loathing of the human body, especially female bodies? Julian is shrewdly politic in outwardly disclaiming any intention to teach as a woman author (ST, ch. 6, ll. 34–5), yet her practice is otherwise. Julian's parallels between Christ as our teacher and every mother's teaching role in forming her child morally by correcting and upbringing (ch. 60, ll. 38–44; ch. 61, ll. 24–40) quietly but subversively claims back for the woman author the equality that Julian's understanding of Christ as our mother throughout her revelations so triumphantly affirms.

Notes

1. 'As veryly as God is our fader, as verily God is our moder'; see Barry Windeatt (ed.), *Revelations of Divine Love* (Oxford: Oxford University Press, 2016), ch. 59, l. 9. All reference to Julian's text is to this edition (hereafter *Revelations*), by chapter and line number.

2. Barry Windeatt (ed.), *The Book of Margery Kempe* (Cambridge: D. S. Brewer, 2004), ch. 18.
3. *Revelations*, xiii–xiv, n. 2.
4. *Revelations*, 3, 29.
5. Barry Windeatt, 'Julian of Norwich and Medieval English Visual Culture', in *'Truthe is the beste'*, ed. N. Jacobs and G. Morgan (Bern: Peter Lang, 2014), 185–203.
6. Barry Windeatt, 'True Image? Alternative Veronicas in Late Medieval England', in *Manuscript and Print in Late Medieval and Early Modern Britain*, ed. Tamara Atkins and Jaclyn Rajsic (Cambridge: D. S. Brewer, 2019), 219–40.
7. C. Rawcliffe and Richard Wilson (eds.), *Medieval Norwich* (London: Hambledon, 2004), 215, 387.
8. See Flora Lewis, 'The Wound in Christ's Side and the Instruments of the Passion: Gendered Experience and Response', in *Women and the Book: Assessing the Visual Evidence*, ed. Lesley Smith and Jane H. M. Taylor (London: The British Library, 1996), 204–29.
9. The size of one hazelnut is the measure of quantity in a medicine taken during childbirth: see Alexandra Barratt (ed.), *The Knowing of Woman's Kind in Childing: A Middle English Version of Material Derived from the Trotula and Other Sources* (Turnhout: Brepols, 2001): 'tak of myrre, þe quantite of j hasull not, & ȝyf here to drynk in wynne & with-owtyn fayl sche schall be delyuerd a-noon' (64).
10. See Robina Napier (ed.), *A Noble Boke off Cookry ffor a prynce houssolde or eny other estately houssolde* (London: Elliot Stock, 1882): 'when the potte boileth, put in the peletes like an hassille nott' (93).
11. See Kathleen L. Scott, *Later Gothic Manuscripts 1390–1490*, 2 vols. (London: Harvey Miller, 1996), 2.325: 'an All Saints initial with a conflated subject of a Crucifix-Trinity acting as a 'Schutzmantel' figure (possibly the only such figure in English book illustration)'. It is more usual for the Virgin Mary to be shown enfolding souls in her robe.
12. For a 'vierge ouvrante' once in Durham Cathedral, see Margaret Harvey and Lynda Rollason (eds.), *The Rites of Durham: William Claxton*, Surtees Society, vol. 226, Catholic Record Society, Records Series vol. 88 (Woodbridge: Boydell Press, 2020): 'Over the which alter was a merveylous lyvlye and bewtifull image of the picture of Our Ladie, so called the Ladie of Boulton. Which picture was made to open with gymers [hinges] from her brest downward ... And euery principall day the said image was opened, that eueryman might se pictured within her the Father, the Sonne, and the Holy Ghost, most curiouslie and fynely gilted' (165–6). See also Elina Gertsman, *Worlds Within: Opening the Medieval Shrine Madonna* (University Park: Pennsylvania State University Press, 2015).
13. See *Revelations*, 165–77, and Barry Windeatt, 'Constructing Audiences for Contemplative Texts: The Example of a Mystical Anthology', in *Imagining the Book*, ed. Stephen Kelly and John J. Thompson (Turnhout: Brepols, 2005), 159–71.

14. See Laurence Lux-Sterritt, *English Benedictine Nuns in Exile in the Seventeenth Century: Living Spirituality* (Manchester: Manchester University Press, 2017).
15. A third manuscript, British Library, MS Sloane 3705, derives from S1 but is more modernised.
16. Other instances in P include: 'No sowle is in reste till it is noughted ... when she is wilfully noughted for loue, to haue him that is all, then is she able to receive ghostly reste' (ch. 5; f. 10r); 'And how a sowle shall haue [behave] her in his beholding, he shall teach hym selfe' (ch. 10; f. 23r); 'And the more that the lovyng soule seeth this curtesy of god, that levyr she ys to serve hym all her lyfe' (ch. 14; f. 30v); 'Sodenly is the soule onyd to god when she [corrected from 'it'] is truly peesyd [reconciled] in her selfe' (ch. 49; f. 91r).
17. For the Upholland and Gascoigne texts, see Nicholas Watson and Jacqueline Jenkins (eds.), *The Writings of Julian of Norwich* (Turnhout: Brepols, 2006), 437–48.

Further Reading

Baker, Denise N. (1994). *Julian of Norwich's Showings: From Vision to Book*, Princeton, NJ: Princeton University Press.
Beckwith, Sarah (1993). *Christ's Body: Identity, Culture and Society in Late Medieval Writings*, London: Routledge.
Bynum, Caroline Walker (1982). *Jesus as Mother: Studies in the Spirituality of the High Middle Ages*, Berkeley: University of California Press.
Erler, Mary J. (2002). *Women, Reading, and Piety in Late Medieval England*, Cambridge: Cambridge University Press.
Hill, Carole (2010). *Women and Religion in Late Medieval Norwich*, Woodbridge: Boydell Press.
Lamm, Julia A. (2019). *God's Kinde Love: Julian of Norwich's Vernacular Theology of Grace*, Freiburg: Herder and Herder.
McAvoy, Liz Herbert (2004). *Authority and the Female Body in the Writings of Julian of Norwich and Margery Kempe*, Cambridge: D. S. Brewer.
McAvoy, Liz Herbert, ed. (2008). *A Companion to Julian of Norwich*, Cambridge: D. S. Brewer.
Nelstrop, Louise (2019). *On Deification and Sacred Eloquence: Richard Rolle and Julian of Norwich*, London: Routledge.
Salih, Sarah, and Denise N. Baker, eds. (2009). *Julian of Norwich's Legacy: Medieval Mysticism and Post-Medieval Reception*, Basingstoke: Palgrave Macmillan.
Turner, Denys (2011). *Julian of Norwich, Theologian*, New Haven: Yale University Press.

CHAPTER 20

The Communities of The Book of Margery Kempe

Anthony Bale

Dear Miss Allen – Margery Kempe would have been unbearable in the flesh, but I rather enjoy reading her, though she gets tiresome in spots.[1]

Such was the reaction, in 1943, of one reader of *The Book of Margery Kempe*. This reader sent their reaction to the medievalist Hope Emily Allen, who had identified and co-edited the manuscript telling the story of Kempe's remarkable life. This reaction is not unusual and often attends Kempe today: students and readers enjoy encountering Kempe but at the same time criticise her for being a lonely controversialist, an irritating chatterbox, and a slapdash mystic.[2] On internet social media, Kempe attracts more ire and disapprobation than any other medieval figure. She is frequently upbraided for her failure, as some readers see it, to cleave to her proper community – of being either a correct wife and mother, or a truly dedicated nun, or a thoroughgoing, sober mystic.

Kempe, according to her own account, is not popular and finds it hard to integrate into many of the communities with which she engages: repeatedly, she is mocked, castigated, and many times subject to violent threats of death by burning, a pariah of society. At Hessle in 1417, local men shout out at Kempe, calling her 'Lollard', and the *Book* provides the memorable detail that 'women cam rennyng owt of her howsys wyth her rokkys' (1.3054), demanding that Kempe be burnt for heresy.[3] The women's distaffs, their spindles, exemplify womanly industry in contrast to Kempe's contemplation, and their vocal rage is opposed to Kempe's patience (or obstinacy, depending on how one reads her). *The Book of Margery Kempe* takes pains to show how Kempe is an isolated outsider and scapegoat, whereas the men and women of Hessle are presented as if united as a community. This is one of several examples of how Kempe is not liked by men and she is not like other women. Kempe records that subsequently, during the journey from Hessle to Beverley, local people tell her to abandon her way of life, 'go spynne and carde as other women don' (1.3057–8). The people of Yorkshire in 1417, or perhaps Kempe's scribe some years later, invoked Kempe's gender here as a way of understanding her perceived status as a loner; to the community, she should be safely spinning wool like a 'normal' woman, rather than perverting her gender and religion. As Susan Dickman has commented, 'Margery was inclined to interpret her spiritual experience in social terms'.[4]

Kempe is repeatedly cast as a maverick who both eschews and is eschewed by the wider community. Her own ambivalent adoption of white clothes sets her apart from other women. In a socially legible and performative move, Kempe puts on a highly noticeable outfit that is disruptive: it is 'synguler', says the Bishop of Lincoln, Philip Repyngdon, as he refuses to support her request to wear it (1.798–9). People sneer at the white clothes and Kempe herself worries that they will brand her a hypocrite. In this vein, Carolyn Dinshaw has influentially described Kempe as a 'queer' character, on account of her steadfast disruption to norms of gender, sexuality, and sociability. Kempe's social alterity is also a gendered alterity, and thus Dinshaw states that in calling her 'queer' we can 'focus not only on individual acts of sex/gender manipulation, but on the relationship between such acts and other kinds of social disorder' in *The Book of Margery Kempe*.[5]

In other words, many readers, with either a positive or a negative valency, focus on Kempe's strangeness and her status as an outsider. Yet encrypted in *The Book of Margery Kempe* is an account of a woman who was well able to make friends, find supporters, and build forms of community. In her elegant reading of *The Book of Margery Kempe*, Rebecca Krug emphasises the functions of friendship and solace, fulfilled by the *Book* itself in making Kempe 'no longer lonely'. Krug posits that *The Book of Margery Kempe* is 'the product of a no-longer-lonely reader, that is, one who, as both an individual and a member of a larger community, is both hopeful about the future and critical of the present state of affairs'.[6] In Krug's reading of Kempe, the acts of reading and writing were fundamentally collaborative, enabling Kempe to connect with others in similar situations and with similar experiences. This book-ish collaboration, Krug suggests, was sociable and consoling: Kempe could understand herself, her fears and doubts, through establishing a community of like-minded readers, writers, and interlocutors.

We might read the *Book* as the story of the discovery of two kinds of community – one earthly, the other heavenly – which mark Kempe's transformation and exile from her domestic community in Lynn and her acceptance into other kinds of community. Her worldly communities are repeatedly spiteful and disappointing; the heavenly community promises her a much more agreeable kind of 'dalyaunce' or conversation. One can, however, read the *Book*'s emphasis on the limitations of worldly friendship as a narrative trope, contrasting the impermanence of earthbound relationships with the enduring nature of communion with Christ, Mary, and the saints. As such, I suggest that the *Book* – either in Kempe's voice or in the hands of her amanuenses – masks various kinds of community with which she did successfully engage. Taking as a starting point Krug's argument that the production of the *Book* is itself communal, in this chapter I want to recover three kinds of community with which Kempe 'successfully' engages: Franciscan, Birgittine, and the monastic reception community that attended her *Book*. Each of these communities plays an important role for Kempe, even as her *Book* focuses on her individual rather than communal navigation of them.

Kempe's Franciscan Group Tour

Kempe visited Jerusalem in 1414, during a transformative journey which lasted about eighteen months and encompassed Venice, Assisi, and Rome, as well as a defining stay in the Holy Land. It was at Calvary, inside the Church of the Holy Sepulchre in Jerusalem, that Kempe received her first bout of divinely ordained tears, which became a foundation of her distinctive and disruptive religious style. Readers of Kempe's account of Jerusalem are often struck by its 'emptiness' of local detail and colour, understanding that Kempe, or her scribe, wished to present her pilgrimage as a devotional rather than touristic journey and therefore did not include extraneous or worldly information.[7] What has been largely overlooked in accounts of Kempe's Holy Land experience is its thoroughgoing indebtedness to the Franciscan order and, consequently, her largely successful integration into Franciscan-led pilgrimage community.

Kempe's wider indebtedness to Franciscan spirituality has long been noted; Denise Despres has pointed out how 'Margery's meditations present interesting questions about the nature of lay devotions popularized by the Franciscans, who encouraged imaginative participation and the embellishment of sacred texts and scriptural narrative to mesh personal history with salvation history'.[8] It is clear that Kempe's visual, narrative meditations are profoundly influenced by the Franciscan key-text *The Meditations on the Life of Christ*, then attributed to Bonaventure. This is no surprise as the *Meditations*, in its translation by the Carthusian Nicholas Love, was one of the most popular texts in fifteenth-century England and was the cornerstone of orthodox popular religion for lay people.

More specifically, we can see Kempe's incorporation in a Franciscan spiritual community during her time in the Holy Land. St Francis of Assisi (d. 1226), the founder of the Franciscan order, had visited Jerusalem in 1219 in order to preach to, and convert, the Muslims there; to this end, Francis had an audience with the Ayyubid Sultan, Malik al-Kamil (1177–1238), in Cairo. This interview – in which Francis sought unsuccessfully to spread the Christian faith – became one of the key moments celebrated in Francis's *vita*, although it came to be remembered as Francis's ordeal before the Sultan rather than as an interview. Kempe herself would have seen this episode portrayed in the remarkable frescoes of Francis's life in the Upper Church at Assisi, which she visited later in 1414.[9] Kempe may well have had St Francis in mind as an exemplary figure, as he was described as being blinded not by old age but by the profusion of his holy tears.[10] In the centuries subsequent to Francis' trip to Jerusalem, the Franciscan desire to reconquer the Holy Land through piety was transformed into a new role: that of holy travel agency, in league with the ruling Mamluks (who had conquered the Ayyubid dynasty in 1250).

In the 1320s, Sultan Nasir ad-Din Muhammad granted a number of privileges to the Franciscans, guaranteeing ongoing access to the holy places of the Holy Land and making them the representatives of western Christendom there. The Franciscans established their base at Mount Zion, on the south-west side of Jerusalem, a complex that included a dormitory, a library, what was said to be the tomb of King David, and the Cenacle, the reputed site of the Last Supper. The Franciscans of the Holy Land became known as the *Custodia Terra Sancta*, and by 1350 they had official control, with the Sultan's permission, of the Church of the Nativity in Bethlehem too. The Franciscans were deeply committed to the imitation of Christ and their activities shifted from trying to retake the Holy Land to enabling European travellers like Kempe to visit the scenes of Christ's life and death.[11] They operated throughout the pilgrimage route, from Venice to Jerusalem and beyond, with an effective monopoly on Latin devotional travel in the eastern Mediterranean. The Franciscans of Mount Zion sold the pilgrims short booklets, holy travel-guidebooks called 'processionals', which marked out the prayers, Psalms, and indulgences for all the holy places in Jerusalem and the Holy Land. In this way, the sacred landscape itself became a kind of text, read and experienced through a script.

Moreover, western visitors such as Kempe were by no means free to wander around Jerusalem or the Holy Land to their own itinerary. They were subject to constant regulation from their Mamluk hosts and expected to carry a type of certificate, a precursor of the passport, that gave them safe conduct to the holy places but did not permit them to go off route.[12] Increasingly, visiting pilgrims subjected themselves to a ritual itinerary, the *ordo peregrinationis* – a kind of programmatic route through holy sites. In time, this became the Stations of the Cross and the *via dolorosa* tradition.

Kempe arrived in the Holy Land on a pilgrim galley from Venice in the summer of 1414. The journey between Venice and Jerusalem is barely recorded, other than the 'tribulacyon' (1.1547) Kempe suffered at the hands of her fellow pilgrims. After arguments about the ownership of a sheet and about which boat to sail in, Kempe establishes herself as outside the pilgrim community; she supposes that the other pilgrims 'weryn greyvd wyth hir' and asks them to be charitable towards her as she has been to them. She adds piously, mimicking the language of the Lord's Prayer, 'And, yyf any of yow hath anything trespasyd agens me, God forgeve it yow and I do' (1.1548–51). It is thus part of Kempe's devotional style to present herself as an outsider, walking in Christ's footsteps in her own *via crucis*, as this authorises her own *imitatio Christi* and, as is seen clearly in this example, gives her spiritual authority to speak in God's name and God's voice.

As the pilgrims approach Jerusalem, Kempe again portrays herself as a spiritual outcast: on her first sight of Jerusalem, she departs from the shared vision of 'erdly cyté Jerusalem' and looks towards 'the blysful cité of Jerusalem abovyn, the cyté of hevyn'. This prompts Jesus to answer 'to hyr thowt', in her mind, and causes her almost to fall from her mount (1.1555). Two German pilgrims help her, with reviving, medicinal spices, and on arriving in Jerusalem Kempe once again asks her community not to be displeased by her vocal and disruptive displays of religiosity: 'Serys, I prey yow beth nowt displesyd thow I wepe sore in this holy place wher owyr Lord Jhesu Crist was qwyk and ded' (1.1562–3). In this way, *The Book of Margery Kempe* makes explicit both Kempe's desire to be part of her social grouping and the friction caused by the unusual sincerity and depth of her religious feelings. Such incidents have the effect of spotlighting Kempe whilst pushing the group tour of which she was indubitably a part into the background.

The standard package tour of which Kempe was a member is manifested in the brief description of her entry into the Church of the Holy Sepulchre:

> Than went thei to the tempyl in Jerusalem, and thei wer latyn in on the to day at evynsong tyme and abydyn therin til the next day at evynsong

tyme. Than the frerys lyftyd up a cros and led the pylgrimys abowte fro on place to an other wher owyr Lord had sufferyd hys peynys and hys passyons, every man and woman beryng a wax candel in her hand. And the frerys alwey, as thei went abowte, teld hem what owyr Lord sufferyd in every place (1.1563–8)

This description clearly accords with those of other fifteenth-century Jerusalem pilgrims, as a group tour in which the pilgrims took part in a night-time vigil followed by a solemn, quasi-liturgical procession, narrated by Franciscan friars and emphasising the pilgrims' shared emotional and pious community. Again, Kempe marks herself out as separate from this community not only by weeping and sobbing but by seeing Christ, 'in her soul', with the eye of contemplation which eclipses or surpasses her worldly vision.

Visiting in the 1480s, the Zurich-born friar Felix Fabri describes in detail the thirteen rules for behaviour as stipulated by the friars; these included buying a wax taper that each pilgrim must carry during the procession and the injunction that pilgrims must stay in the procession in an orderly manner.[13] This was an experience of ritualised, group expression, liturgically framed, in which praying and crying were encouraged, and tears were desirable and frequent. Fabri describes the pilgrims' collective singing and chanting, their touching and kissing of stones around the Church, and the movement from psalmody to lamentation at Calvary: here, as for Margery Kempe, 'wailings and groans' replaced the singing of hymns. As Fabri says, 'no one was there who could withhold himself from tears and cries'.[14] But in *The Book of Margery Kempe*, Kempe's amanuensis wrote an excursus on the meaning of Kempe tears as contemplative crying received from God, focusing on the special nature of Kempe's devotion rather than the formulaic nature of her reaction at Calvary.

Kempe's description of where her weeping took place follows a standard Franciscan tour of the Church of the Holy Sepulchre. First, she visits the Holy Sepulchre itself, 'the grave wher owyr Lord was beriid' (1.1646), where 'sche fel down wyth hir candel in hir hand as sche schuld a deyd for sorwe.' This causes her to weep and sob 'as thow sche had seyn owyr Lord beriid even befor hir' (1.1648–9), directly recalling both Franciscan *imitatio* and the successful intellectual movement of placing oneself in the biblical narrative as described in the *Meditations on the Life of Christ*.

Then Kempe visits the Franciscan Chapel of the Nailing to the Cross, where she cries and weeps 'ythowtyn mesur that sche myth not restreyn hirself', suggesting an emotional reaction that was unusually strong even within this context. At the Stone of Unction, the 'ston of marbyl that owyr

Lord was leyd on whan he was takyn down of the cros', she again weeps with compassion, 'havyng mend of owyr Lordys Passyon'. Further crying attended Kempe receiving communion at Calvary, where 'sche wept, sche sobbyd, sche cryed so lowde that it wondyr was to heryn it' (1.1658). She then mentions that she received communion in four places within the Church, each time with plentiful tears and noisy sobbing: at Calvary, at the Holy Sepulchre, at the Slab, and at St Helena's chapel 'ther the holy cros was beriid' (1.1675–6). The last places she describes in the Church are 'the chapel ther owyr blyssed Lord aperyd to hys blysful modyr on Estern Day at morwyn fyrst of alle other' (1.1734–5) – that is, the Franciscan Chapel of the Apparition – and finally, the Chapel of Mary Magdalene.[15]

Kempe's route around the building is similar though not identical to those of other later medieval Latin visitors. Kempe largely avoided Greek, Armenian, and non-Latin sites that were not shared with the Franciscans, and the majority of the chapels she visited were Franciscan (the Latin Calvary, the Chapel of the Nailing, the Chapel of the Apparition, and the Chapel of the Magdalene). It is especially telling that her journey around Jerusalem ends at the Franciscan Chapel of Mary Magdalene within the Church of the Holy Sepulchre. The Chapel of Mary Magdalene was (and remains) a Franciscan space, adjacent to the Franciscan monastery which serves the Church of the Holy Sepulchre. Kempe is described thus: 'sche stode in the same place ther Mary Mawdelyn stode whan Crist seyd to hir, "Mary, why wepyst thu?"' (John 20:15) (1.1736–7).

At the culmination of her tour, a tableau is described in which Kempe styles herself as standing alone like Mary Magdalene;[16] she directly refers to the gospel of John and explicitly invites comparison with Mary Magdalene's crying. By presenting herself as the Magdalene, Kempe strategically authorises not only her weeping, but her own intense perception of her pilgrimage and her own special closeness, like Mary Magdalene's, to Christ. But we become complicit in Kempe's self-promoting stratagem if we do not read her disruptive emotional performance as social, citational, and allusive: in other words, her emotional performance in the Church of the Holy Sepulchre only makes full sense within the framework of a Franciscan-led pilgrimage tour. Kempe was not an independent traveller, but very much part of a group.

The Book of Margery Kempe records that 'the Frerys of the Tempyl mad hir gret cher and govyn hir many gret relykys, desiryng that sche schuld a dwellyd stille amongs hem, yyf sche had wold, for the feyth thei had in hir' (1.1739–41). This detail suggests that the Franciscans invited Kempe to lodge with them at their base at Mount Zion ('Mownt Syon', 1.1667), which Kempe visited after the Church of the Holy Sepulchre. Kempe's account takes care to show her proximity to the friars even as she provokes the ire of the rest of the pilgrimage group. This becomes the key memory of her trip from Jerusalem to Bethlehem:

> Aftyrward sche rood on an asse to Bedlem and whan sche cam to the tempyl and to the crybbe wher owyr Lord was born, sche had gret devocyon, mech spech, and dalyawns in hyr sowle, and hy gostly comfort wyth mech wepyng and sobbyng so that hir felaws wold not latyn hir etyn in her cumpany. And therfor sche ete hir mete be hirselfe alone. And than the Grey Frerys whech had led hir fro place to place receyved hir into hem and sett hir wyth hem at the mete that sche schuld not etyn alone. And on of the frerys askyd on of hir felawshep yyf that wer the woman of Inglond the which thei had herd seyd spak wyth God. And, whan this cam to hir knowlach, sche wist wel that it was trewth that owyr Lord seyd to hir er sche went owt of Inglond, 'Dowtyr, I schal makyn al the werld to wondryn of the, and many man and many woman schal spekyn of me for lofe of the and worshepyng me in the.' (1.1699–709)

Her 'devocyon', manifested in 'mech wepyng and sobbyng', means that 'hir falws' will no longer eat with her: 'cumpany', the literal breaking of bread (*cum pane*) of sociability and commensality, is fractured. But the 'Grey Frerys', the Franciscans, not only eat with her but transmit her devout reputation to the other pilgrims, as a friar asks one of the pilgrim group if Kempe is the Englishwoman who can speak with God. Thus, holy reputation among the friars trumps communal acceptance, and Kempe turns her ejection from the group into an exalted status, warmly welcomed among the Franciscans of the Holy Land.

Kempe's Birgittine Communities

Kempe's crying at Calvary has another saintly intertext alongside that of St Francis: the well-known figure of St Bridget of Sweden, who was moved to tears, 'wepinge and hevi', at Calvary. The influence of Bridget on Kempe is well established and has been fully charted by Susan Dickman, Gunnel Cleve, Naoë Yoshikawa, and others.[17] Bridget (Birgitta Birgersdotter, 1303–73) developed a distinctive and popular mystical voice, as recorded in her widely disseminated *Liber celestis*, her collected revelations, which were certainly known to Kempe. The question of where Kempe first encountered the saintly role model, and the writings, of Bridget of Sweden remains a live one. Bridget's cult was well known in Norfolk prior to Kempe's departure for the Holy Land in 1413; indeed, a Norwich monk, Adam Easton, wrote a *Defensorium Sanctae Birgittae* in favour of Bridget's canonisation in the 1390s. Bridget was known in Kempe's home town of Lynn, as is evinced by the writing of indices to Bridget's *Revelations* by Kempe's confessor, Alan Warnekyn.[18] This provides a more than plausible conduit through which Kempe learned about the Swedish saint's life. However, it is in Rome, during her long stay there in 1414/15, that Kempe seems to deepen and affirm her relationship with Bridget. A further Birgittine community is glimpsed in Kempe's *Book* when she visits the Birgittine community at Syon (Middlesex) much later, in the 1430s, and receives an indulgence there.

As in Jerusalem, so in Rome, Kempe is a spurned outsider. Lodging at the English Hospital of St Thomas of Canterbury, an English priest arrives and through his 'evyl langage' (1.1862) causes Kempe to be ejected. Moreover, Kempe's maidservant, who had apparently travelled with her from England and abandoned her mistress at Venice, reappears at the Hospital, now enjoying 'meche welth and prosperyté' (1.2218–19), working as a wine-keeper there. The difficulties of being part of a group of English fellow-travellers pursue Kempe, but she, in her own account, turns such social isolation into glory: she takes to the streets of Rome, finds favour fortuitously with apparently random wealthy strangers, and, eventually, is welcomed back into the English Hospice (1.2212) with an apology from the Master.

Yet this rejection from the English expatriate community becomes an opportunity for a deep emulation of St Bridget and her central principles of humility, chastity, and poverty. Kempe visited St Bridget's house and death-chamber in Rome, adjacent to the English pilgrims' hostel, and made the acquaintance of the saint's Swedish maid (who described Bridget's 'lawhyng cher', her smiling face) and another man who 'telde hir that he knew [Bridget] hys owyn selfe' (1.2229). Kempe also used the time in Rome to emulate the Swedish saint: she visited the church of St John Lateran, where Bridget had been witnessed levitating (1.2000); she made a mystical marriage with the Godhead, along very similar lines to Bridget's own wedding to the Godhead (1.2005); she deepened her relationship with St Bridget's legacy, including acting as godmother for a Roman woman's daughter christened with the name 'Brigypt'. And, memorably, Kempe voluntarily makes herself poor, as Bridget had done. As a sign of her pious humility, Bridget chose a life of poverty, distributing her wealth to her children, the poor, and the church before leaving Sweden to make Rome her home. Similarly, Kempe is instructed to serve an elderly poor lady (1.1992) and to live in squalor, begging and lice-ridden, for six weeks, as she transforms from mayor's daughter to street beggar, from giver of charity to its recipient.

According to Kempe's account, holiness and charity follow her through Rome; the city is, as Rebecca Krug has suggested, a 'magical space' for Kempe.[19] Fortune repeatedly favours her, as if God is steering her. Wenceslas/Wenzel, a confessor who speaks no English, supports her; Marcello, a local man, gives her money; Richard the Irishman with the broken back befriends her and escorts her to Rome. And Kempe receives the patronage of a crucial if encrypted presence, 'Margaret Florentyne', who, as I have suggested elsewhere, was probably the Florentine magnate and widow, Margherita degli Alberti, at this point in exile in Rome.[20] Margaret, like Wenceslas, also speaks little or no English, and it becomes clear that in being separated from the community of English people, Kempe has instead become part of a more cosmopolitan, international, and rootless group. Richard, Wenceslas, and Margaret were all, like Kempe, non-Roman visitors (from Ireland, Germany or Bohemia, and Florence, respectively). Kempe therefore embraces her alienated identity and presents a model of 'felawschep' that transcends her nation.

This, however, is to read *The Book of Margery Kempe* on its own terms; Kempe's Roman sojourn can be read in a slightly different way, as Kempe becomes the abject object of charity. 'Margaret' gives Kempe a lift from Assisi to Rome and invites her to dine with her each Sunday, serving her meat with her own hands and giving her a hamper and good wine and, sometimes, cash too (eight 'bolendinys'; 1.2189). The patronage received from 'Margaret' is highly fortuitous for Kempe, for whom this is a sign of God's protection; Kempe thanks Christ for her poverty, becoming a 'partynyr' in Christian merit rather than wealth (1.2206). But, from the perspective of 'Margaret Florentyne', we can read this patronage as part of a programme of pious charity that puts Kempe at the heart of Birgittine-Dominican circles in Florence and Rome at the time.

Margherita degli Alberti's brother Antonio had founded, between 1392 and 1397, the first Birgittine monastery in Italy: the Paradiso in Florence.[21] At the time Kempe was in Rome, the preacher and Observant leader Giovanni Dominici (d. 1419), who was said to have cured Catherine of Siena of a speech impediment, was actively promoting the interests of the Paradiso in Florence and was working with the Dominican prioress Chiara Gambacorta to establish Bridget's cult in Pisa. Bartolomea degli Alberti, Margherita's sister-in-law, was Dominici's spiritual daughter, and Dominici dedicated three of his spiritual treatises to her. The most important of these is the *Regola del governo di cura familiare* (1401), a pedagogical work which argues that a woman should keep biblical pictures and sculptures in her house to educate her children, recommending especially the Virgin, the baby Jesus at play, and John the Baptist as suitable subjects. Nirit Ben-Aryeh Debby observes that these suggestions 'show a familiarity with the iconography of his period and a recognition of the utility of art as a teaching tool; children would identify with the painted figures and consequently be instructed along religious lines'.[22] Such an attitude towards imagery, conduct, and a materially inflected mysticism has much in common with Kempe's own devotional style.[23]

On returning to England in the early 1430s, after her long, last pilgrimage to Wilsnack and Aachen, Kempe visits the final pilgrimage site mentioned in the *Book*: the magnificent and prestigious Birgittine priory at Syon, to the west of London. The *Book* refers to Syon as 'Schene', using the name of Sheen Priory, the Carthusian house located just across the River Thames from Syon and part of Henry V's 'Great Work' (his project, commenced in 1413, to build a royal and monastic complex around this bend in the river). We know Kempe went to Syon rather than Sheen because her *Book* foregrounds the indulgence available there on Lammas Day, 'the principal day of pardon' (2.637): this was 1 August, probably 1434, and, in the words of 'The Pardon of the Monastery of Shene, whiche is Syon', the indulgence gave pilgrims like Kempe plenary remission for their sins 'in all casis'.[24]

At Syon, Kempe unintentionally encounters Reynald/Reginald, a hermit of Lynn, who had previously accompanied her as she set off on this journey. Together, they return to Lynn, and the *Book* achieves a kind of narrative circle: Kempe has returned home, receiving a prestigious and desirable Birgittine pardon first, then reconciliation with the Lynn hermit.[25] By this point, Kempe was probably about sixty years old, a venerable age in the fifteenth century, and the Syon pardon thus places a Birgittine imprimatur on her whole life. The narrative of the *Book* effectively ends here, and its attention turns to the form of Kempe's prayers, offering her as an authority for efficacious intercession and prayerfulness.

The Book of Margery Kempe is, understandably, focused on the travails and development of its eponymous heroine. Yet in Rome it encrypts a generous and powerful community, built around the memory and emulation of St Bridget of Sweden. Syon domesticates and nationalises Kempe's experience of Bridget in Rome, both bringing the saint home 'with' Kempe and individualising what was a collective experience of the saint. *The Book of Margery Kempe* is therefore shaped by Kempe's successful

The Communities of The Book of Margery Kempe

interactions with Bridget and her cult, which offered powerful and influential communities that Kempe understood as supportive.

A Textual Community in Norfolk

The elderly Kempe can easily be read as an isolated figure in Norfolk in the 1420s and 1430s. She suffered from a chronic illness (1.3245–52) and removed herself from her husband and her family home in order to dedicate herself to contemplation and to avoid rumours about breaking her vow of celibacy. And yet much of the 1430s, as far as we can establish, was a period of sustained, if frustrated, textual composition for her, as she worked with a number of male scribes and amanuenses to bring *The Book of Margery Kempe* into being. Research into these figures has tended to focus on their identification, in particular the possibility that Robert Springold was the 'scharp' confessor who wrote the bulk of the *Book*.[26] In the final section of this chapter I want to look at this issue in a slightly different way: in terms of a textual community of people – male clerics, mostly – constellated around Kempe in the period from *c.* 1430 to 1520.

Returning to Norfolk in 1417, following perilous arrests and serious interrogations in Leicester, Cawood, and Hessle, Kempe waits at the little port of West Lynn, across the River Great Ouse from her home in Lynn. She is reluctant to enter the town without the approval, via a letter of endorsement, of the Archbishop of Canterbury, given the febrile atmosphere of anti-heretical surveillance and suspicion at this time. She sends out a request that three men sail from Lynn to West Lynn to meet her: her husband John, and her spiritual advisors Alan Warnekyn and Robert Springold (1.3214–18). Kempe has shown her fierce indomitability in the face of powerful adversaries such as the Steward of Leicester and the Duke of Bedford, but here her *Book* foregrounds her need for a network of male figures of authority, spiritual and worldly. She then leaves West Lynn with her husband, and the pair travel to London to find another authority, the Archbishop of Canterbury, to vouch for her. In becoming notorious and continuing to engage in worldly affairs, Kempe finds herself further dependent on the support of men around her. Kempe's stated reliance on clerical amanuenses and scribes to write down her *Book* similarly shows how independence was brokered through her power to make useful allies.

In her lifetime, Kempe had dealings with most of the major monastic and fraternal orders: Augustinians, Benedictines, Birgittines, Carmelites, Carthusians, Dominicans, and Franciscans all feature within the *Book*'s pages, as well as various hermits, recluses, and anchorites. It is clear, through the *Book*'s own account, that several male clerics were instrumental to the writing of it, especially the 'good priest' with spectacles who transformed the bulk of the text into something like what we have today. Furthermore, Richard Salthouse, the scribe of the surviving manuscript, was a monk at Norwich's wealthy and influential Benedictine priory, whilst it was among Carthusians in Yorkshire that Kempe's reputation was cherished in the generations after her death. Thus, Kempe's spiritual health, her reputation, and her written testament were maintained by male, clerical communities. Once again, this is at odds with Kempe's disputatious, maverick persona as presented in the *Book*, but it is clear that Kempe was well able to harness clerical support.

Many of the people encountered by Kempe as confessors and spiritual counsellors were themselves involved in scribal crafts or textual composition. Kempe's first miracle, of the falling beam at Lynn, sees her holding a book in her hand, whilst another minor miracle involves a monastic book, a 'portose, a good lytyl boke' (1.1312), that a monk from the nearby Augustinian house at Pentney (Norfolk) is nearly cheated over. Alan of Lynn was a Carmelite friar, born in Lynn to an 'esterling' family (that is, an immigrant family from Flanders, the Hanse, or Prussia).[27] He wrote a large number of theological texts, mostly lost, although two manuscripts of his theological indices, including his *tabula* of St Bridget, survive. Richard Caistor (d. 1420), whom Kempe had met in Norwich and at whose grave she cried extravagantly, was said to have written various religious books, although only one of his lyrics, the widely circulated 'Jesu, Lord, that madest me', now survives. Julian of Norwich, with whom Kempe enjoyed several days of 'dallyaunce' in her Norwich anchorhold, was evidently known to Kempe as a spiritual authority rather than an *auctrix*, although Julian's writing soon made her a celebrated mystic.

Kempe's clerical community is absolutely parallel with other East Anglian literary communities of the times. We know from the patrons and readers of cleric-poet figures such as John Lydgate (Benedictine, Bury St Edmunds), Osbern Bokenham (Augustinian, Clare Priory), and John Capgrave (Augustinian, Lynn) that the gentry and aristocracy of Norfolk and Suffolk were part of a vibrant literary world, configured around orthodox religiosity and high-value book production.[28]

Clerical community persists within the manuscript of the *Book*, in the form of the marginalia that was written in its one surviving manuscript (London, British Library, Add. MS 61823) in the later fifteenth century at the Carthusian house at Mount Grace (Yorkshire). In particular, Kempe's *Book* was clearly read and adduced as a model for the ecstatic mysticism of

Richard Methley (d. 1527/8), the former prior of Mount Grace. As Laura Saetveit Miles has recently written, 'Kempe's precedent helped to authorize Methley's similar spirituality many decades later', with her *Book* being used as a prooftext for Methley's contemplation, mystical experience, and 'groaning and weeping.'[29] Methley's own writings, from the 1480s, have much in common with Kempe's register: for instance, the 'healing sickness' of loving God, the 'outbursts' of joyful tears, the interplay of weariness and ecstasy, the melting of the soul in a fire of love.[30] The annotations in the manuscript of *The Book of Margery Kempe* referring to Methley and to Prior John Norton (d. 1522), also a former prior of Mount Grace, were written by the 'Red Ink Annotator', almost certainly a Carthusian monk who enthusiastically endorsed Kempe's spirituality. This annotator was probably writing in the 1530s (after Methley's death) and far removed from Kempe herself; nonetheless, Kempe's example proved desirable to a clerical community interested in the various and sincere experiences of the mystical perception of God.

In sum, four to six people annotated the manuscript of *The Book of Margery Kempe*, and it is clear that elements of Kempe's persona were amenable to various kinds of religious community and that her disruptive social activity was not mirrored in the reception of *The Book of Margery Kempe*. This reception was orthodox and established. The kinds of annotations made include corrections, deletions, and amplifications; others trace themes, imagery, and textual authorities corroborated in the text. The annotations also attest, as several scholars have shown, to the making of a saintly reputation for Kempe, marking key moments in her life that map onto a saintly *vita*.[31] Moreover, Katie Bugyis has persuasively argued that the 'Red Ink Annotator' corrected the text of the manuscript in order for Kempe to become 'a model not only of affective devotion for laywomen readers but also of perfect contemplation for Carthusians'.[32] The reading and reception of Kempe's *Book* at Mount Grace placed it in a Carthusian library that included canonical works of mysticism: an English *Mirror of the Life of Christ* (now Cambridge University Library, MS Add. 6578), the *Speculum spiritualium* (now York Minster, MS XVI.I.9), *The Cloud of Unknowing* (British Library, Harley MS 2373), and a translation by Mount Grace's Richard Methley of Marguerite Porete's *Mirror of Simple Souls* (Cambridge, Trinity College, MS O.2.56). Kempe thus seems to have been successfully absorbed into the Carthusian community at Mount Grace, at least in terms of the one surviving manuscript of her *Book*.

Can we extrapolate from the reception of this manuscript a larger incorporation or clerical acceptance of Kempe in the generations after her death? The absence of surviving books and manuscripts is not, I contend, necessarily a sign of Kempe's reputational oblivion; after all, only minute textual fragments survive of the 'Maid of Kent' (Elizabeth Barton, d. 1534), yet we know that manuscript and printed accounts of her mystical visions circulated widely.[33] Writings about Barton were explicitly censored, but Kempe's life too was precisely the kind of material that was hidden, destroyed, and dis-esteemed during the English Reformation. More pertinently, we might recall the published versions of Kempe's life produced by Wynkyn de Worde (*c.* 1500) and Henry Pepwell (1521) which, albeit heavily edited, suggest the lively relevance of Kempe in the early sixteenth century. These printed editions would have been produced in runs of hundreds, and would only have been published because de Worde and Pepwell believed there was a market for her life. That said, this life was much more heavily edited in print than in manuscript. Kempe was incorporated into (masculine) clerical models of reading, shown most clearly in de Worde and Pepwell's versions of her: she becomes a 'devout ancres', almost all her biography removed, retaining only her contemplative prayerfulness and mystical revelations.

It is undoubtedly true that, in this way, *The Book of Margery Kempe* was effectively censored, constrained, in its afterlives. At the same time, we should not consider Kempe as a curiosity or outlier, but as a canonical figure in the devotional marketplace of pre-Reformation England. The Kempian strategy is to present its protagonist as a unique maverick, an eccentric and controversialist even. But this is a strategy towards spiritual exceptionalism and thence to sanctity.

The Book ends with a bold articulation of heavenly rather than earthly community. Kempe's first-person voice appears in an extended sequence of prayers. The prayers address God, then the Virgin and the whole court of heaven. They then extend to all of human society through a long series of intercessory prayers, repeating the opening formula, 'I crye yow mercy', to Jesus. These intercessions end by appealing to Kempe's audience: 'for alle tho that feithyn and trustyn er schul feithyn and trustyn in my prayerys into the worldys ende, sweche grace as thei desiryn, gostly er bodily, to the profite of her sowlys, I pray the, Lord, grawnt hem for the multitude of thi mercy. Amen' (2.798–800). So, the *Book* concludes with a model of universal prayerfulness and a strong assertion of Kempe's exemplary and authoritative role as an intercessor on behalf of the Christian community. We are asked to emulate and trust her, for future salvation, and to join and follow her devotional community, just as Kempe herself was successfully incorporated into the communities of her *Book*.

Notes

1. Bryn Mawr College, H. E. Allen collection 16, box 6.
2. See George Burns, 'Margery Kempe reviewed', *The Month* 171 (1938), 238–44; Marea Mitchell, The Book of Margery Kempe*: Scholarship, Community, and Criticism* (New York: Peter Lang Publishing, 2005), 55–67.
3. References to *The Book of Margery Kempe* are taken from *The Book of Margery Kempe*, ed. Lynn Staley (Kalamazoo, MI: Medieval Institute Publications, 1996), online edition at d.lib.rochester.edu/teams/publication/staley-the-book-of-margery-kempe. Subsequent references are given within the text to this edition.
4. Susan Dickman, 'Margery Kempe and the Continental Tradition of the Pious Woman', in *The Medieval Mystical Tradition in England* 3, ed. Marion Glasscoe (Cambridge: D.S. Brewer, 1984), 150–68 (167).
5. Carolyn Dinshaw, *Getting Medieval: Sexualities and Communities, Pre- and Postmodern* (Durham, NC: Duke University Press, 1999), 152.
6. Rebecca Krug, *Margery Kempe and the Lonely Reader* (Ithaca, NY: Cornell University Press, 2017), 12.
7. Sylvia Schein, 'Bridget of Sweden, Margery Kempe and Women's Jerusalem Pilgrimages in the Middle Ages', *Mediterranean Historical Review* 14 (1999), 44–58.
8. Denise Despres, 'Franciscan Spirituality: Margery Kempe and Visual Meditation', *Mystics Quarterly* 11 (1985), 12–18 (13).
9. Alexandra Dodson, 'Trial by Fire: St. Francis and the Sultan in Italian Art', in *The World of St Francis of Assisi*, ed. Bradley Franco and Beth Mulvaney (Leiden: Brill, 2015), 60–79.
10. Diane Apostolos-Cappadona, 'Pray with Tears and your Request will find a Hearing: On the Iconology of the Magdalene's Tears', in *Holy Tears: Weeping in the Religious Imagination*, ed. Kimberley Patton and John Hawley (Princeton, NJ: Princeton University Press, 2005), 201–28 (206).
11. Michele Campopiano, *Writing the Holy Land: The Franciscans of Mount Zion and the Construction of a Cultural Memory, 1300–1550*, The New Middle Ages (Basingstoke: Palgrave Macmillan, 2020).
12. See Nicole Chareyron, *Pilgrims to Jerusalem in the Middle Ages*, ed. and trans. Donald Wilson (New York: Columbia University Press, 2005); Zrinka Stahuljak, 'The Pilgrim Translation Market and the Meaning of Courtoisie', in *The French of Outremer: Communities and Communications in the Crusading Mediterranean*, ed. Laura Morreale and Nicholas Paul (New York: Fordham University Press, 2018), 201–20.
13. Felix Fabri, *Wanderings in the Holy Lands*, ed. and trans. Aubrey Stewart, 2 vols. (London: Committee of the Palestine Exploration Fund, 1897), 2.346.
14. Fabri, *Wanderings*, ed. and trans. Stewart, 2.364.
15. I explore Kempe's tearful itinerary in greater detail in 'Where did Margery Kempe cry?' in *Fluid Bodies and Bodily Fluids in Premodern Europe*, ed. Anne

M. Scott and Michael David Barbezat (Amsterdam: Arc Humanities Press, 2019), 15–30.
16. See further Suzanne L. Craymer, 'Margery Kempe's Imitation of Mary Magdalene and the "Digby Plays"', *Mystics Quarterly* 19 (1993), 173–81.
17. Susan Dickman, 'Margery Kempe and the Continental Tradition of the Pious Woman', in *The Medieval Mystical Tradition in England* 3, ed. Glasscoe, 150–68; Gunnel Cleve, 'Margery Kempe: A Scandinavian Influence on Medieval England', in *The Medieval Mystical Tradition in England* 4, ed. Marion Glasscoe (Woodbridge: D. S. Brewer, 1992), 163–78; Naoë K. Yoshikawa, 'Margery Kempe's Mystical Marriage and Roman Sojourn: Influence of St Bridget of Sweden', *Reading Medieval Studies*, 28 (2002), 39–57.
18. Susan Maddock, 'Margery Kempe's Home Town and Worthy Kin', in *Encountering* The Book of Margery Kempe, ed. Laura Kalas and Laura Varnam (Manchester: Manchester University Press, 2021), 163–84.
19. Krug, *Margery Kempe*, 185.
20. Anthony Bale and Daniela Giosuè, 'A Women's Network in Fifteenth-Century Rome: Margery Kempe Encounters "Margaret Florentyne"', in *Encountering* The Book of Margery Kempe, ed. Laura Kalas and Laura Varnam (Manchester: Manchester University Press, 2021), 185–204.
21. Giovanni da Prato, *Il Paradiso degli Alberti, 1389*, ed. Alessandro Wesselofsky (Bologna, 1867).
22. Nirit Ben-Aryeh Debby, 'The Images of Saint Birgitta of Sweden in Santa Maria Novella in Florence', *Renaissance Studies* 18 (2004), 509–26 (516–17).
23. On the materiality of Kempe's idiom, see Sarah Beckwith, 'A Very Material Mysticism: The Medieval Mysticism of Margery Kempe', in *Medieval Literature: Criticism, Ideology and History*, ed. David Aers (Brighton, Sussex: Harvester Press, 1986), 34–57; on Kempe's maternal imagery, see Tara Williams, 'Manipulating Mary: Maternal, Sexual, and Textual Authority in The Book of Margery Kempe', *Modern Philology* 107.201, 528–55.
24. George James Aungier, *The History and Antiquities of Syon Monastery* (London: J.B. Nichols & Son, 1840), 425.
25. A similar point is developed by Ann M. Hutchison, 'Reflections on Aspects of the Spiritual Impact of St Birgitta, the Revelations, and the Bridgettine Order in Late Medieval England', in *The Medieval Mystical Tradition in England* 7, ed. E. A. Jones (Cambridge: D.S. Brewer, 2004), 69–82 (72).
26. See A. C. Spearing, 'Margery Kempe', in *A Companion to Middle English Prose*, ed. A. S. G. Edwards (Cambridge: D.S. Brewer, 2004), 83–99.
27. Maddock, 'Margery Kempe's home town'.
28. See Anthony Bale, 'A Norfolk Gentlewoman and Lydgatian Patronage: Lady Sibylle Boys and her Cultural Environment', *Medium Ævum* 78 (2009), 261–80.
29. Laura Saetveit Miles, 'Introduction', in *The Works of Richard Methley*, trans. Barbara Newman (Collegeville: Liturgical Press, 2021), xlviii.
30. *The Works of Richard Methley*, trans. by Newman, 12, 19.

31. Katie Bugyis, 'Handling the Book of Margery Kempe', in *New Directions in Medieval Manuscript Studies and Reading Practices*, ed. Kathryn Kerby-Fulton, John Thompson, and Sarah Baechle (Notre Dame, IN: University of Notre Dame Press, 2014), 138–58. See also Joel Fredell, 'Design and Authorship in The Book of Margery Kempe', *Journal of the Early Book Society* 12 (2009), 1–28; and Kelly Parsons, 'The Red Ink Annotator of The Book of Margery Kempe and His Lay Audience', in *The Medieval Professional Reader at Work*, ed. Kathryn Kerby-Fulton and Maidie Hilmo (Victoria, BC: English Literary Studies, 2001), 217–38.
32. Bugyis, 'Handling', 139.
33. See Diane Watt, 'The Posthumous Reputation of the Holy Maid of Kent', *Recusant History* 23 (1996), 148–58; and Genelle Gertz and Pasquale Toscano, 'The Lost Network of Elizabeth Barton', *Reformation* 26 (2021), 105–28.

Further Reading

Bale, Anthony and Daniela Giosuè (2021). A Women's Network in Fifteenth-Century Rome: Margery Kempe Encounters 'Margaret Florentyne'. In Laura Kalas and Laura Varnam, eds., *Encountering* The Book of Margery Kempe. Manchester: Manchester University Press, 185–204.

Bugyis, Katie (2014). Handling *The Book of Margery Kempe*. In Kathryn Kerby-Fulton, John Thompson, and Sarah Baechle, eds., *New Directions in Medieval Manuscript Studies and Reading Practices*. Notre Dame, IN: University of Notre Dame Press, 138–58.

Craymer, Suzanne L. (1993). Margery Kempe's Imitation of Mary Magdalene and the 'Digby Plays'. *Mystics Quarterly* 19, 173–81.

Despres, Denise (1985). Franciscan Spirituality: Margery Kempe and Visual Meditation. *Mystics Quarterly* 11, 12–18.

Dickman, Susan (1984). Margery Kempe and the Continental Tradition of the Pious Woman. In Marion Glasscoe, ed., *The Medieval Mystical Tradition in England* 3, Cambridge: D.S. Brewer, 150–68.

Dinshaw, Carolyn (1999). *Getting Medieval: Sexualities and Communities, Pre- and Postmodern*, Durham, NC: Duke University Press.

Krug, Rebecca (2017). *Margery Kempe and the Lonely Reader*, Ithaca, NY: Cornell University Press.

Schein, Sylvia (1999). Bridget of Sweden, Margery Kempe, and Women's Jerusalem Pilgrimages in the Middle Ages. *Mediterranean Historical Review* 14, 44–58.

Spearing, A. C. (2004). Margery Kempe. In A. S. G. Edwards, ed., *A Companion to Middle English Prose*. Cambridge: D.S. Brewer, 83–99.

Yoshikawa, Naoë K. (2002). Margery Kempe's Mystical Marriage and Roman Sojourn: Influence of St Bridget of Sweden. *Reading Medieval Studies* 28, 39–57.

CHAPTER 21

Christine de Pizan
Women's Literary Culture and Anglo-French Politics

Nancy Bradley Warren

From early in her career as a writer, Christine de Pizan herself, as well as the texts she produced, was imbricated in Anglo-French political affairs. The receptions of both Christine as an authorial figure and her writings were shaped by the fortunes of politically powerful English men throughout her texts' circulation in England and changed along with those men's fortunes. Though scholars differ on the precise timing of the event, Christine de Pizan's son, Jean de Castel, travelled to England at some point in 1398 to reside in the household of John Montagu, Earl of Salisbury, to be educated to serve as a companion for the earl's son, Thomas.[1] In her autobiographical *L'Avision Christine* (*The Vision of Christine de Pizan*), Christine de Pizan writes:

> Around this time as the daughter of the King of France was married to King Richard of England, there came from there for this reason a certain noble count of Salisbury. And this gracious knight loved poems and was himself a courteous poet, after what he had seen, some of my poems, he begged me through various important people so that I agreed – albeit unwillingly – that the older of my sons, a very clever and good singer of thirteen years of age, might go with him to England to be the companion to one of his own sons of the same age.[2]

This arrangement, in which the son of a poet of the French court is educated in the household of an English magnate on the basis of an appreciation for poetry, highlights the close relationships between literary and political cultures in France and England alike during the late fourteenth century.

In addition to being fond of the French literature that was fashionable at the Ricardian court, John Montagu, third Earl of Salisbury, was one of the so-called Lollard knights in the court of Richard II, though presumably Christine was unaware of his interest in heterodox religion.[3] Significantly, he was also a stalwart Ricardian loyalist. After Henry IV deposed Richard

II, the earl was summoned to Henry's first parliament and was accused for his involvement in the prosecutions of 1397.[4] John Montagu was imprisoned in the Tower of London and tried before parliament, though, as Anthony Goodman points out, the earl was not sentenced but released on surety because he had been challenged to combat by Lord Morely as a result of his (Montagu's) involvement in the Duke of Gloucester's death.[5] After his release, John Montagu engaged in plotting with John Holland, Earl of Huntington; Thomas Holland, Earl of Kent; and Edward, Earl of Rutland to murder Henry IV and restore Richard II to the throne. The plot failed, and the earl was executed, probably on 8 January 1400. Upon the earl's execution, Henry IV acquired his manuscripts, including Christine's 'dittiez' that she had sent to John Montagu.[6]

I began with this somewhat extended account of John Montagu's affairs to emphasise, first, the extraordinarily fraught political environment in which Christine was engaged and from which she found herself needing to extricate her son after Henry IV deposed Richard II. The process of extrication reveals her considerable political astuteness and her own awareness of the political value of her writing. I also start with this account of John Montagu's political fortune because he and his son Thomas, to whom Jean de Castel served as a companion, demonstrate how much changed in the space of a generation to alter the reception and use of the figure of Christine and her writings. Thomas Montagu petitioned for and received restoration of his father's earldom, a return to royal favour enabled by Thomas Montagu's extensive military service fighting in France during the Hundred Years' War. Thomas Montagu was killed in battle in October 1428, laying siege to Orléans – the very siege in which Joan of Arc, who is the subject of the final poem Christine de Pizan wrote, would eventually achieve her great victory. The figure of Joan of Arc, the legacies of her victories, and the association of Joan of Arc with Henry VI's queen, Margaret of Anjou, are vital pieces of the textual environment that shifted reception and use of Christine's texts in England between the late fourteenth century and the mid-sixteenth century.

The years between 1445 and 1540 witnessed not only Margaret of Anjou's arrival in England as Henry VI's queen and Joan of Arc's official rehabilitation by the Church, but also the height of Christine de Pizan's popularity in England. This popularity might initially seem rather surprising, since Christine, though Italian by birth and supported by Burgundian as well as Valois patrons, identified strongly with France and the French royal cause. Indeed, she exhibited particularly strong animosity towards the English, who, as she claims in the *Lamentacion sur les maux de la France*, were the 'natural enemies' of the French.[7] Given Christine's sympathies, and given that in this era of English history France and the status of the English claim to France were extremely difficult issues, Christine's work would seem unlikely to be attractive to English audiences. Furthermore, her most popular texts – *L'Epistre d'Othéa*, *Le Livre de fais d'armes et de chevalerie*, and *Le Livre de la cité des dames* – emphasise many of the most troubling problems facing the English monarchy during the later medieval and early modern periods: military training, the conduct of war, proper governance, and – crucially, for the ever-fraught issue of royal succession, the catalyst for so much of the domestic and international conflict in this period – women's place in lineages as well as the proper parameters of female authority.

The *Epistre au dieu d'amours* (1399) – which Thomas Hoccleve, as is well known, used as the basis for his 1402 adaptation *Letter to Cupid* – and the *Epistre d'Othéa* (1400) were sent to England during the time Jean de Castel was there.[8] They were thus the first long-format works of Christine's to be read in England. I have therefore chosen to use the reception history of the *Othéa* to illustrate the shifts in reception of Christine as an author and her writing over the course of the later medieval and early modern periods. This text's reception mirrors trends also visible in the reception of her *Fais d'armes* and *Cité des dames*, which were, along with her *Othéa*, her most popular works in England.

Many scholars believe Christine wrote the *Othéa* for her son, or at least with him in mind, since he was at the time of the text's composition near in age to the fictional addressee of Othéa, Hector. This work consists of 100 verse texts accompanied with prose glosses providing wisdom and advice in the *speculum princeps* tradition. Dedicatory evidence in a fifteenth-century copy of the *Othéa*, as well as information from Christine's *Vision*, indicate that she sent a copy of the text to Henry IV, with a personalised dedication, as part of her negotiations to get her son safely back to France. In the *Vision*, Christine says that after the Earl of Salisbury was executed:

> King Henry, who still reigns and who had stolen the crown, saw these aforementioned books and poems – several of which I had already sent being eager to please the said count. Then he most joyfully brought my child to his court and held him in high favor and a very high situation. In fact ... he asked me [to come], beseeching me and promising great benefits if I might go there.[9]

Christine confesses that she was not tempted by Henry IV's offer but 'concealed my feelings until I might have my son, expressing my thanks profusely and saying that I was fully at his command'. Finally, Christine reports that it was 'with great effort and by means of my books that I obtained leave for my said son to come and fetch me to a place I have yet to see'.[10]

The presentation copy that Christine sent to Henry IV has not been found, but British Library, MS Harley 219 is, as Stephanie Downes argues, 'almost certainly descended from the manuscript Christine sent to Henry to bargain for her son's return to France'.[11] In her recent identification of Hoccleve as one of the scribes/annotators of Harley 219, Misty Schieberle puts in place another link between this and the royal presentation copy, noting that Hoccleve's proximity to the king as a Clerk of the Privy Seal and of the Exchequer helps explain his early access to the *Epistre au dieu d'amours* and *Othéa*, which, she argues, seems to have influenced some of Hoccleve's other works.[12] MS Harley 219 is dedicated to a 'prince excellent de haute renomee' and a 'roy noble'. This version of the dedication only exists, as Schieberle notes, in one other manuscript: Stockholm, Kungliga Biblioteket, MS Vu 22.[13] It is the only instance of Christine dedicating her work to a non-French monarch.

The *Epistre Othéa* gained significant popularity in fifteenth- and sixteenth-century England in both French and English language versions. Downes notes that three English translations – two in manuscript and one in print – were made of the *Othéa* during this period, and numerous manuscript versions in French circulated in England alongside the translations. She continues: 'Five of the eight French language manuscripts of the *Othéa* currently held in libraries in England reached their English audiences no later than 1535, and at least three were produced by scribes and illustrators working in England or on the continent for English patrons.'[14] I turn now to two versions of the *Othéa* in circulation in England – the early fifteenth-century version in Harley 219 and Stephen Scrope's 1450 translation – to illustrate how the political significance and use of this influential text, and of Christine as an author, shifted with changes in Anglo-French relations and English court culture.

The version of the *Othéa* in MS Harley 219 is characteristic of the early fifteenth-century reception of the text as a didactic work providing instruction on chivalry, virtue, and morality[15]. As Downes notes, the manuscript as a whole 'appears to be a didactic treatise for a young English noble … with a specific emphasis on the fine-tuning of contemporary French language skills'.[16] Alongside the *Othéa*, MS Harley 219 contains a wide variety of French and Latin texts, but the core of the manuscript, of which the *Othéa* is part, appears to have been gathered purposefully.[17] In addition to the *Othéa*, this core consists of the *Livre du gouvernement des roys et princes* (a French version of the pseudo-Aristotelian epistolary *speculum princeps* the *Secretum secretorum*, purportedly written for Alexander the Great), a collection of animal fables by Odo de Cheriton in Latin, and a collection of excerpts from the *Gesta romanorum*, also in Latin.[18] Interestingly, there is also a trilingual wordlist/dictionary that begins on the final folio of the *Othéa*, consisting of words and phrases in French with their equivalents in Latin or English, reinforcing the sense that the collection has an educational purpose.

Schieberle has convincingly made a case that the manuscript may have been Hoccleve's personal copy or, if not his own, one written for one of his fellow clerical colleagues rather than for an English nobleman. She observes that the text's didacticism would probably have been appealing 'for the author of the *Regiment* and the formulary', and points out that the addition of the list of Treasurer offices to the manuscript suggests it may have served as a reference work for clerks. She also comments that the manuscript need not be seen purely as a didactic tool, noting that Hoccleve and other clerks may have used the manuscript for the pleasure and cachet of reading French literature.[19]

Thus, the version of the *Othéa* in Harley 219 indicates how the text participated in a cultural environment in which French literature, as well as writers and readers of it, had cultural capital. Christine realised this value in sending the *Othéa* to Henry IV to ensure Jean de Castel's protection. Henry IV himself realised that value in his invitation to Christine to join the English court. As Paul Strohm observes, Henry IV's invitation may have been prompted by his hope of acquiring the 'adherence of established figures' to his kingship and the literary celebration of his accession by poets, a move certainly characteristic of later Lancastrian monarchs.[20] Henry IV valued Christine as a literary authority figure. Her active role as an author and textual creator had worth for his political agenda, as did the texts themselves that she produced. Harley 219 also perhaps represents, if Schieberle is correct about its audience of clerical bureaucrats, the expansion of access to the symbolic as well as practical benefits of knowing the French language and a sort of democratisation of the cultural prestige of French literature.

By the time Stephen Scrope made his translation of the *Othéa*, the text still had didactic appeal as an instructional work on chivalry.[21] However, the contours of what constituted English chivalric masculinity had changed, as had English perceptions of French literary culture and of

Christine de Pizan as a French female writer. Stephen Scrope seems to have written his translation of the *Othéa* around 1450, and one possibility for mid-fifteenth-century interest in the text has to do with the *Othéa*'s politically useful celebrations of women's position in lineages and of female virtue. These were subjects of concern to Lancastrian monarchs, especially Henry V and VI, as they attempted to legitimise the English claim to the throne of France, which depended on, and was contested on, the basis of the English monarchs' descent from Edward III's mother.

Christine de Pizan played an interesting role in the French project of crafting a model of succession that excluded women from opportunities to rule, a project prompted in part by English claims. Sarah Hanley points out that Christine's *City of Ladies* circulated at the French court, its readers including 'Queen Isabelle of Bavaria (regent intermittently for the ill Charles VI) and men and women of the high nobility; jurists, *parlementaires*, academics, and royal officials', spreading the idea that women have ruled successfully in the past, currently do so in the present, and can readily do so again in the future.[22] Hanley notes that in response to the *City*, Jean de Montreuil, with whom Christine had been engaged in the debate about women and the *Romance of the Rose*, wrote *To All the Knighthood* (1409) and the *Treatise Against the English* (1413). These texts refuted Pizan's political arguments, arguing instead for the exclusion of women from royal succession. As Hanley observes,

> In those works he introduced, for the first time, textual renditions of a Salic Law [a law prohibiting women from succeeding to the throne or transmitting the right to succeed to the throne] .... In order to thwart Pizan's influential *City of Ladies*, refurbish his reputation tarnished by the earlier exchanges, and defend his own political agenda, Montreuil fabricated a Salic Law.[23]

The Lancastrians therefore needed to validate the role of women to pass on the right of succession but not, crucially, to inherit that right themselves. These Lancastrian celebrations of virtuous women as conduits in support of the English claim to the throne of France seemingly take place within the boundaries of a perceived masculine hierarchy and, at least superficially, focus on a passive female role. For example, Lancastrian propaganda often brings to bear the example of the Incarnation as a case in which a virtuous woman legitimately transmits a divine inheritance to her son.[24]

An association of Christine and her work with passive rather than active roles for women established itself in English reception of the *Othéa* as a result of English losses in France and the cultural connections of Christine with two other French women who were powerful presences in the Lancastrian political landscape: Joan of Arc, whose legacy lived on after her death, and Margaret of Anjou, the politically active French queen of Henry VI. The careers of these women intersect in significant ways. Among the most obvious (although not the only) connections are the facts that Margaret owned a copy of Christine's *Fais d'armes* (in London, British Library, MS Royal E VI, given to the queen as a wedding present by John Talbot) and that Joan became the subject of Christine's celebratory *Ditié de Jehanne d'Arc*.

The *Ditié* is replete with accounts of Joan that foreground the resonances between matters of gender and Anglo-French politics. Not content merely to celebrate English losses on the battlefield, Christine highlights Joan's symbolic emasculation of the English as well. Explicitly emphasising the anxiety-provoking spectacle of a woman in armour, Christine calls Joan a 'fillete' (young girl) of just sixteen years '[a] qui armes ne sont pesans' (on whom arms do not weigh heavily).[25] Christine also draws attention to Joan's power over men as their military commander when she says 'Et de noz gens preux et abiles / Elle est principal chevetaine.' (She is the principal commander of our brave and able men).[26] If Joan surpasses even noble, capable, and brave French men, just think of the implications for the defeated English! Furthermore, Joan outdoes even that paragon of chivalry embraced as progenitor by the English (as well as by the French) monarch, Hector; Christine exults of Joan, 'tel force n'ot Hector n'Achilles!' (neither Hector nor Achilles had such strength).[27]

John Talbot, who gave British Library, MS Royal E VI containing Christine's *Fais* to Margaret of Anjou, would have had an especially personal knowledge of – and probably a particular animosity towards – Joan of Arc. Indeed, both he and John Fastolf may have encountered Christine's profoundly anti-English celebration of Joan's success while they were in France. Both of these men knew other texts of Christine's, and they both imported some of her works into England. Although we cannot definitively prove these English men's knowledge of Christine's *Ditié*, Christine, as a French woman claiming both expertise in military matters and the right to voice strong political opinions against the English, still had a suggestive connection with Joan. Talbot, for example, was one of the chief commanders at the battle of Patay, where he was captured when the French army, inspired by Joan, crushed the English forces. Many manuscripts of Christine's texts came to England via John Fastolf, who may well have become acquainted with her work during his service in

France to the Lancastrian regime.[28] In addition to making Christine's work on chivalry, good governance, and military theory known to later generations of translators and disseminators, including Anthony Woodville, Lord Rivers; Stephen Scrope; and William Worcester (who used the *Fais d'armes* in his *Boke of Noblesse*),[29] Fastolf, like John Talbot, would have had plenty of experience of Joan of Arc to pass on to these men as well. Fastolf was also one of the commanders at Patay, where Talbot was taken prisoner. In fact, in the autumn of 1441 or the spring of 1442, Fastolf had to 'rebut a charge, laid before the king and his peers by the aggrieved Lord Talbot, of conduct unbecoming a knight of the Garter at the battle of Patay'.[30]

Joan of Arc is a sort of 'missing link' connecting Margaret and Christine. Joan, that source of ongoing anxieties about gender and English national identity, hovers on the scene like a returning manifestation of that which has been culturally repressed. Her afterlife thus colours fifteenth- and sixteenth-century perceptions of women's participation in the realms of war and government. Margaret of Anjou is, in fifteenth-century historical sources, explicitly linked to Joan of Arc.[31] In fact, according to a commentary of Pope Pius II, Margaret even compared *herself* to Joan in a speech to her troops. She reportedly declared, 'I have often broken their [the English] battle line. I have mowed down ranks far more stubborn than theirs are now. You who once followed a peasant girl, follow now a queen.'[32] Given these connections, I contend that, consciously or unconsciously, the legacy of Joan of Arc shapes the way in which Christine's work, at once so problematic and so useful, is redacted in England from the middle of the fifteenth century onwards.

English interest in Christine and her work in this particular textual environment is no mere accident of history. Although Christine's works foreground politically difficult matters, the English found value in these texts in their efforts to advance their political causes. The *Livre de fais d'armes et de chevalerie* has, for instance, an ironic history of being used to justify English efforts to take French territories. This text, although written to educate a French prince to fight against the English, provided advantageous arguments for the English to use in pressing their claim to French territories. In her explication of just causes of war, for example, Christine says that among the lawful grounds for military action is the need to recover 'lands, lordships, and other things stolen or usurped for an unjust cause'.[33] In the *Boke of Noblesse*, written about 1450 and then revised in 1475, William Worcester cites precisely this passage to justify a new English invasion of France.[34] Furthermore, Henry VII later found the *Fais* to be a similarly useful tool for supporting his own renewed interest in the

English claim to France, as William Caxton's epilogue to his printed translation of the *Fais* reveals.[35]

In confronting the challenges that female lineages and politically active French women presented to English nationhood and English chivalric manhood, English redactors of Christine's works seized the chance to make a virtue of necessity, engaging in elaborate containment strategies that turned threats into assets. Strategic manipulations of the figure of Christine, combined with targeted transformations of her works, provided opportunities for retroactive revisions of the very things Christine and her countrywomen Joan of Arc and Margaret of Anjou destabilised. Scrope's translation of the *Othéa* achieves this metamorphosis through a dynamic of simultaneous celebration and minimisation of women's political roles, joined with valorisations of male heroism and masculine authority. In the end, his translation of the *Othéa* stabilises the mutually informing gender boundaries and national boundaries that the originals so often disturb.[36]

Christine's *Othéa* presents the goddess of prudence, Othéa, instructing the fifteen-year-old Hector of Troy in 'those things which are necessary / To great valor and contrary / To the opposite of Prowess'.[37] In doing so, she is an ideal manifestation of virtuous female behaviour because she enacts just the sort of transmissive function envisioned as appropriate for women. The opening lines of the text position Othéa as one who 'addresses hearts great in valor', as she declares to Hector, 'I desire / Your great profit.' She adds, 'By my letter I wish to counsel / You.'[38] She thus passes on her knowledge to the 'prototype of the ... chivalric hero'[39] who will be the one to put the theories she expounds actively into practice. One of Scrope's three dedications for his translation of the *Othéa*, found in MS M. 775 in the Pierpont Morgan Library, is to a 'hye princesse' – a dedication that suggests Scrope too may have envisioned such a role for an English noblewoman.[40]

Furthermore, in many of its glosses and allegories, the *Othéa* transforms the feminine, even the potentially threatening figure of the politically and militarily active woman, into something securely under the control of the masculine, thus making it 'safe' to praise. For instance, in the gloss on the verse concerning Minerva, a text which focuses on her invention of armour, that invention is transferred firmly into Hector's hands. He is called son of Minerva because he, in Scrope's Middle English, 'couthe sette armure wel a-werke'; according to Scrope, 'it was *his ryghte crafte*.'[41] The craft of arms, though it originates with Minerva, belongs properly, rightly, to the male hero who actually performs deeds of arms, setting 'armure wel a-werke'.

The text's treatments of women's place in lineages, their virtue, and their passively transmissive roles prove, however, to be problematically double-edged, working in some ways against the political agenda the text is mobilised to serve. The *Othéa* as a text and Christine as a female author prove to be as difficult to contain within a masculinist political and ideological framework as Joan of Arc and Margaret of Anjou were. For instance, the treatment of female lineage in the *Othéa* is not as straightforwardly useful for the English monarchical cause as it might initially seem. On one level, the text helpfully portrays Hector, called son of Minerva, as the legitimate masculine heir to the divine qualities she, and her fellow goddess Othéa, his instructor, pass on. On another level, though, the text celebrates not only women's transmissive functions but also assertively independent female figures. For instance, as Jane Chance has observed, in the *Othéa* Christine 'rewrite[s] the genealogy of the gods from a female perspective'.[42] This rewriting famously includes a series of allegories that 'feminizes' the masculine Christian trinity using the goddesses Diana ('we shall take for Diana God of Paradise'), Ceres ('we shall take for Ceres, whom the good knight should resemble, the blessed Son of God'), and Isis ('There where it says that the good spirit ought to resemble Isis, who is a planter, we may understand the holy conception of Jesus Christ by the Holy Spirit in the holy Virgin Mary').[43] Here is a version of women's place in a divine genealogy different from a merely passive one.

That the *Othéa* begins and ends with accounts of the value, even the necessity, of specifically female knowledge and wisdom heightens the work's disquieting suggestions that women may capably take on active roles. The first passage is Othéa's initial address to Hector, and the gloss on this text begins 'Othéa in Greek can be taken from the wisdom of woman.'[44] The accompanying allegory opens thus: 'As prudence and wisdom are mother and conductress of all virtues, without which the others could not be well-governed, it is necessary to the chivalrous spirit that it be adorned with prudence.'[45] The final text concerns the instruction of Caesar Augustus by the Cumaean Sibyl, and here the gloss explains that Caesar 'learned to know God and belief from a woman'.[46] The last word of the allegory for this text is, as Chance notes, *sapiencia*,[47] which is, as she points out, 'wisdom written by a woman'.[48]

Strikingly, the 'most powerful figures' in the *Othéa* are 'mothers, female warriors, and female scholars'.[49] Immediately after being described as Minerva's son, Hector is told to embrace the goddess Pallas and so 'reap with your prowess'. Othéa further advises that 'All will go well for you if you have her; / Minerva sits well with Pallas.'[50] The gloss elaborates, 'So she is named Minerva in that which appertains to chivalry, and Pallas in all things which appertain to wisdom',[51] demonstrating in a single sentence the superlative skills of women in the martial and intellectual spheres. Such descriptions foreground the very things that Scrope's translation would evidently rather strategically minimise: women's powerful maternal roles in lineages, their military abilities, and their intellectual capacity.

In the 1450s, Margaret was beginning to adopt the sorts of political authority that the *Othéa* suggests women can successfully wield, and such figures as Pallas and Minerva emphasise precisely the 'Joan-like' roles that Margaret was starting to embrace. When Scrope's translation was first circulating, Henry VI experienced his initial period of incapacitating disability. At this juncture, Margaret 'attempted to conceal his condition and then tried to prevent a council or regent from taking power by securing it for herself'. Reports also came to light, in January of 1454, 'that she had "made a bille of five articles, desiryng those articles to be graunted [by parliament]"'. This bill would have given her 'the whole ruele of this land' and would have enabled her to name various high officers of state, including the treasurer, normally chosen by the king himself.[52]

The difficulties raised by women's participation in political affairs in the *Othéa* make Scrope's representation of Christine as a cloistered woman religious and a patron of scholarly male clerics who are said to be the text's real authors particularly significant. After dedicating the translation to John Fastolf, Scrope writes: 'And this seyde boke, at the instaunce & praer off a fulle wyse gentyl-woman of Frawnce called Dame Christine, was compiled & grounded by the famous doctours of the most excellent clerge the nobyl Vniuersyte off Paris.'[53] Because both Scrope and Worcester are closely linked with Fastolf, P. G. C. Campbell's assertion, made long ago, that Fastolf may be behind the transformation of Christine de Pizan into a lifelong nun – a claim present in Scrope's *Othéa* and Worcester's *Boke of Noblesse* (as I discuss later in the chapter) – has special political relevance.[54] Jennifer Summit points out that the depiction of Christine as a nun gains popularity 'because it upholds a gendered model of authorship that makes masculine communities into centers of authorized textual production and displaces literate women into the margins'.[55] A similar argument can be made for this cloistered representation of Christine in relation to a gendered model of political power, particularly since the exclusion of active women from this sphere was perceived as critical in later medieval and early modern England. As a nun and patron of male scholars, Christine performs the only role that women should take on in this 'properly' masculine arena – that of enabling male action and supporting male authority.

'Cloistered' Christine the patron rather than Christine de Pizan the author appears both in William Worcester's *Boke of Noblesse* (mentioned previously) and in Henry Pepwell's preface to Brian Anslay's translation of the *Cité des dames* (1521).[56] In a move following a venerable tradition of use to neutralise politically problematic women (note the monk of Canterbury's desire to shut Margery Kempe in a cloister[57]), Christine is put into the secure enclosure of a religious foundation, thereby conveniently removing her from the role of active, knowledgeable participant in literary and political affairs.[58] Witness a Latin note about Christine de Pizan written in the margin of the *Boke*. When her *Fais d'armes* is invoked, we are told that the 'dame Cristyn', previously quoted as the apparent author of the so-called *Tree of Batailles*, is in fact 'domina praeclara natu et moribus, et manebat in domo religiosarum apud Pasaye prope Parys' (a woman distinguished by both birth and manners, and she lived in a house of religious women at Poissy near Paris) and that she sponsored the compilation of 'plures libros virtuosos, utpote *Liber Arboris Bellorum*' (a number of virtuous books, particularly the *Tree of Battles*) by 'plures clericos studentes in universitate Parisiensi' (several clerks studying at the University of Paris).[59] Not only are Christine's authorship and her authority to speak on military matters reassigned to men, but, having purportedly been a lifelong resident of the nunnery of Poissy, she is firmly excluded from active participation. Christine's text is still politically useful; she herself as an authority figure, however, requires careful containment.

Brian Anslay's translation makes no effort to hide Christine's authorship, but Pepwell's prologue describes the book as being 'by Bryan Anslay, / Yoman of the seller / with the eyght kynge Henry'.[60] This description minimises the female authorial role and female political authority. Pepwell's edition also continues the tradition of 'cloistering' Christine. In the woodcut depicting Christine in her study, she is dressed in traditional widow's garb. This attire, with its barb and veil, presents a portrait that 'closely resembles the iconography of religious women from woodcuts that Pepwell had previously printed of Saints Bridget and Catherine of Siena'.[61] The depiction of Christine illustrates the ways in which Pepwell's text uses iconography to suggest a model of proper feminine conduct. The woodcut of the 'cloistered' Christine (See Illustration 21.1) points to what women like Joan of Arc and Margaret of Anjou *should* have been doing rather than meddling in public affairs. The woodcut, like the earlier textual constructions of Christine as a religious woman, functions to remove an active, knowledgeable woman from the political and literary realms.[62] This understanding of Christine de Pizan's value represents a shift from the time of Henry IV, when he invited Christine to the English court *because* of her value as an activity literary authority figure.

Hope Johnston's exploration of the 1521 translation suggests Anslay may also have had political motivations in relating his translation to the subject of female lineages, that topic so relevant to earlier Lancastrian monarchs.

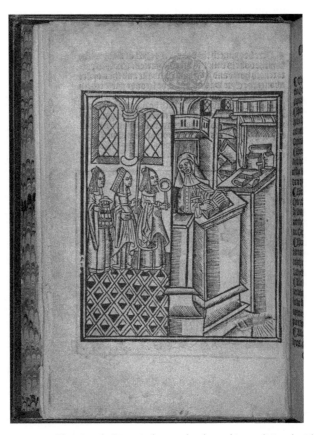

Illustration 21.1 Christine de Pizan in her study, dressed in traditional widow's clothing which closely resembles the monastic attire of St Birgitta of Sweden and St Catherine of Siena in contemporary woodcuts. From Henry Pepwell's 1521 edition of *The Book of the City of Ladies* STC (second edn)/7271. Reproduced by kind permission of the British Library.

She notes that Anslay was not just a yeoman of the king but rather one specifically associated with Queen Catherine of Aragon's household. By 1521, Henry VIII was seriously concerned about the issue of succession, since his heirs included a legitimate daughter and illegitimate son. The daughter, Mary, was five years old in 1521, and Catherine of Aragon was working to begin educating her as a future monarch. As Johnston observes,

> [T]he political circumstances were ripe for the publication of *The Cyte of Ladies* in 1521: the book's support for the education of women and its stories about women who were capable leaders made it a topical choice consistent with Catherine's interest, for, if Mary were confirmed as the king's true heir, a divorce would be unnecessary for purposes of succession.[63]

Johnston also calls attention to Henry Pepwell's use of Catherine of Aragon's pomegranate badge as indication of his support for Catherine of Aragon and the Catholic faith[64]. In light of these political attachments, the facts that Pepwell chooses visually to 'cloister' Christine and to assign authorship to Anslay suggest that, here again, while female descent may be politically desirable, ruling women ought to attend carefully to traditional gendered expectations and religious limitations on their power. Placing Christine in the cloister enables Scrope, Worcester, and Pepwell alike to fulfil the desire to contain female literary authority and political agency in defined bounds.

Scrope takes the additional step of moving beyond 'cloistering' Christine further to emphasise the necessity of denying women independent roles in literary and political spheres by listing at some length in his preface the male classical and patristic sources for the text's material: 'Vyrgyl, Ouyde, Omer … Hermes, Plato, Salomon, Aristitles, Socrates, Ptholome … Austyn, Jerom, Gregorie, Ambrose … the Holy Ewaunngelistes and Epistollys and othyr holy doctours'. To much the same end, he tellingly changes the title from the *Epistle of Othéa to Hector* to the *Book off Knyghthode* or the *Boke off Cheuallry*.[65] The retitling, like Pepwell's assertion of Anslay's authorship, effaces female authority; the removal of Othéa and her authorship of the epistle from the title mirrors the displacements of Christine to the nunnery and the role of textual patron. At the same time, Scrope's introduction of references to knighthood and chivalry further occlude female knowledge in matters of arms and policy in favour of masculine military and political skill.

Scrope's preface contains another detail that reveals his need to contain the possibilities for female power suggested by the text of the *Othéa*. After describing 'Dame Christine' as the patron of the text, he goes on, somewhat oddly, to celebrate at length the career of the Frenchman John, Duke of Berry, for whom he supposes Christine wrote the work. Scrope praises his 'victories, dedis of cheualrie and of armys', his skill in 'grete police vsyng', and his 'spirytuell and gostly dedys'. The duke's success is, furthermore, hyperbolically increased when he is said to have lived 'C yeers' in which time he 'flowrid and rengnyd in grete worchip and renovnne of cheualrie'.[66] For Scrope, it seems, it is better to praise the successes of a French man in arms and diplomacy than to admit a French woman's skill in such matters. Scrope's juxtaposition of Christine, turned into a religious woman and patron of clerics, with the politically and militarily successful French duke serves to reinforce gender roles deemed culturally appropriate, an agenda that did significant work to transform the reception of Christine as an author and of her texts from the late fourteenth through the sixteenth centuries.

Notes

1. See J. C. Laidlaw, 'Christine de Pizan, the Earl of Salisbury and Henry IV', *French Studies* 36.2 (1982), 129–43.
2. Christine de Pizan, *The Vision of Christine de Pizan*, ed. and trans. Glenda McLeod and Charity Cannon Willard (Woodbridge: Boydell), 106.
3. Anthony Goodman, 'Montagu [Montacute], John, third earl of Salisbury (c. 1350–1400), magnate and courtier', *Oxford Dictionary of National Biography*, 23 Sep. 2004: https://doi.org/10.1093/ref:odnb/18995.
4. Goodman, 'Montagu, John', *ONDB* online.
5. Goodman, 'Montagu, John', *ONDB* online.
6. Stephanie Downes, 'A "French booke called the Pistill of Othéa": Christine de Pizan's French in England', in *Language and Culture in Medieval England: The French of England c.1100–c.1500*, ed. Jocelyn Wogan-Browne (Woodbridge: Boydell and Brewer/York Medieval Press, 2013), 458. Further on Christine's conduct writing, see Kathleen Ashley, Chapter 8 in this volume.
7. Earl Jeffrey Richards, 'French Cultural Nationalism and Christian Universalism in the Works of Christine de Pizan', in *Politics, Gender, and Genre: The Political Thought of Christine de Pizan*, ed. Margaret Brabant (Boulder, CO: Westview, 1992), 75.
8. For a comparison of the reception of Christine de Pizan's and Hoccleve's version, see Rory G. Critten, 'Imagining the Author in Late Medieval England and France: The Transmission and Reception of Christine de Pizan's *Epistre au dieu d'amours* and Thomas Hoccleve's *Letter of Cupid*', *Studies in Philology* 112.4 (2015), 680–97. For a fascinating analysis of reception of the *Epistre au dieu d'amours*, see Elizaveta Strakhov and Sarah Wilma Watson, 'Behind Every Man(uscript) Is a Woman: Social Networks, Christine de Pizan, and Westminster Abbey Library, MS 21', *Studies in the Age of Chaucer* 43 (2021), 151–80.

Christine de Pizan 453

9. Christine de Pizan, *Vision*, trans. McLeod and Willard, 106–7.
10. Christine de Pizan, *Vision*, trans. McLeod and Willard, 107.
11. Downes, 'French booke', 462.
12. Misty Schieberle, 'A New Hoccleve Literary Manuscript: The Trilingual Miscellany in London, British Library. MS Harley 219', *The Review of English Studies* 70 (2019), 799–822.
13. Christine de Pizan, *Epistre Othéa*, ed. Gabriella Parussa, *Textes littéraires français* 517 (Geneva: Droz, 1999), Introduction, 107.
14. Downes, 'French booke', 457–58. Bühler points out that '[n]ot many French contributions of so early a date aroused sufficient interest to call forth three separate English translations within the space of a hundred years' – C. F. Bühler (ed.), *The Epistle of Othéa Translated from the French Text of Christine de Pisan by Stephen Scrope*, Early English Text Society O.S. 264 (London: Oxford University Press, 1970), xii–xiii.
15. See Sandra L. Hindman, *Christine de Pizan's Epistre Othéa: Paintings and Politics at the Court of Charles VI* (Toronto: University of Toronto Press, 1986), 138–42.
16. Downes, 'French booke', 461.
17. Downes, 'French booke', 462.
18. For an account of the full contents of MS Harley 219, see Schieberle, 'New Hoccleve Literary Manuscript', 800.
19. Schieberle, 'A New Hoccleve Literary Manuscript', 822.
20. Paul Strohm, 'Saving the Appearances: Chaucer's Power of the Purse and the Fabrication of the Lancastrian Claim', in *Chaucer's England: Literature in Historical Context*, ed. Barbara Hanawalt (Minneapolis: University of Minnesota Press), 35.
21. For an expanded and somewhat differently pointed reading of Scrope's translation of the *Othéa* in which this text is put in extended conversation with English translations of the *Fais d'armes* and the *Cité des dames*, see ch. 3 of Nancy B. Warren. *Women of God and Arms: Female Spirituality and Political Conflict, 1380–1600* (Philadelphia: University of Pennsylvania Press, 2005).
22. Sarah Hanley, 'Mapping Rulership of the French Body Politic: Political Identity, Public Law and the King's One Body', *Historical Reflections/ Reflexions Historiques* 23 (1997), 131, emphasis in original.
23. Hanley, 'Mapping Rulership', 131–32.
24. For a detailed discussion of such Lancastrian representational strategies, and of Lancastrian and Yorkist techniques for representing their claims to the thrones of England and France more generally, see ch. 5 of Nancy B. Warren, *Spiritual Economies: Female Monasticism in Later Medieval England* (Philadelphia: University of Pennsylvania Press, 2001). Another likely, and not mutually exclusive, possibility is that discussed by Jennifer Summit, who notes the ways in which the *Othéa*, like the *Fais d'armes*, 'works to dislodge chivalry from its medieval associations with courtly love' and to demonstrate that 'study and learning are . . . as strenuous and demanding as the arts of war'. The text thus participates in the process of 'redefining the knight as a figure of learning

and prudence'; Jennifer Summit, *Lost Property: The Woman Writer and English Literary History, 1380–1589* (Chicago: University of Chicago Press, 2000), 67.
25. Angus J. Kennedy and Kenneth Varty (eds.), *Ditié de Jehanne d'Arc*, Medium Ævum Monographs N.S. 9 (Oxford: Society for the Study of Mediaeval Languages and Literatures, 1977), ll. 273–75. Translations are my own unless otherwise noted.
26. Kennedy and Varty (eds), *Ditié*, ll. 285–6.
27. Kennedy and Varty (eds), *Ditié*, l. 287.
28. Dhira B. Mahoney, 'Middle English Regenderings of Christine de Pizan', in *The Medieval Opus: Imitation, Rewriting, and Transmission in the French Tradition*, Faux Titre: Etudes de la langue et littérature françaises 116, ed. Douglas Kelly (Amsterdam: Rodopi, 1996), 407–8. Fastolf also served as John, Duke of Bedford's master of the household, and Bedford too brought many manuscripts of Christine's texts (including the famous London, British Library, MS Harley 4431 presented to Isabeau of Bavaria) back to England from France as spoils of victory.
29. On this 'genealogy' of textual transmission, see Summit, *Lost Property*, 68–81.
30. K. B. McFarlane, 'William Worcester: A Preliminary Survey', in *Studies Presented to Sir Hilary Jenkinson*, ed. J. Conway Davies (London: Oxford University Press, 1957), 200. Fastolf was, significantly, assisted in this case by none other than William Worcester, who had in turn his own disquieting experience with the French when he was captured at Dieppe and only managed to escape by bribing some French seamen (McFarlane, 'William Worcester', 200, n. 7).
31. On this connection, see Ann W. Astell, *Political Allegory in Late Medieval England* (Ithaca, NY: Cornell University Press, 1999), 139.
32. Florence Alden Gragg, trans., *The Commentaries of Pius II, Book IX*, Smith College Studies in History 25 (Northampton, MA: Department of History, Smith College, 1939–40), 580. On Margaret's self-identification with Joan, see also Astell, *Political Allegory*, 147, and Patricia-Ann Lee, 'Reflections of Power: Margaret of Anjou and the Dark Side of Queenship', *Renaissance Quarterly* 39.2 (1986), 198–9.
33. Charity Cannon Willard (ed.), *Christine de Pizan, The Book of Deeds of Arms and of Chivalry*, trans. Sumner Willard (University Park: Pennsylvania State University Press, 1999), 16.
34. See William Worcester, *The Boke of Noblesse Addressed to King Edward the Fourth on his Invasion of France in 1475, with an Introduction by John Gough Nichols* (1860; repr. New York: Burt Franklin, 1972), 6–7.
35. See Frances Teague, 'Christine de Pizan's *Book of War*', in *The Reception of Christine de Pizan from the Fifteenth through the Nineteenth Centuries: Visitors to the City*, Medieval and Renaissance Series 9, ed. Glenda K. McCleod (Lewiston, NY: Edwin Mellen, 1991), 36–7; and Wogan-Browne's head note to 'William Caxton, Translation of Christine de Pizan's *Book of Fayttes of Armes and of Chyvalrye*: Prologue', in *The Idea of the Vernacular: An Anthology of Middle English Literary Theory, 1280–1520*, ed. Jocelyn Wogan-Browne, Nicholas Watson, Andrew Taylor, and Ruth Evans (University Park:

Pennsylvania State University Press, 1999), 169. The epilogue appears in A. T. P. Byles, ed., *The Book of Fayttes of Arms and of Chyvalrye* (Oxford: Oxford University Press, 1937).

36. Summit makes a somewhat parallel argument in *Lost Property*, in which she argues that the figure and writings of Christine de Pizan paradoxically enable English recastings of aristocratic masculinity and authorship in the literary sphere (61–107).
37. Jane Chance (trans.), *Christine de Pizan's Letter of Othéa to Hector* (Newburyport, MA: Focus, 1990), 35.
38. Chance (trans.), *Othéa to Hector*, 35.
39. Chance (trans.), *Othéa to Hector*, Introduction, 26.
40. For a discussion of this introduction, and possible identifications of the 'hye princesse', see Bühler (ed.), *Epistle*, xix–xxi as well as A. I. Doyle's Appendix B to this edition, 125–7.
41. Bühler (ed.), *Epistle*, 23, emphasis added.
42. Chance (trans.), *Othéa to Hector*, Introduction, 8.
43. Chance (trans.), *Othéa to Hector*, 59–60.
44. Chance (trans.), *Othéa to Hector*, 36.
45. Chance (trans.), *Othéa to Hector*, 38.
46. Chance (trans.), *Othéa to Hector*, 120.
47. Chance (trans.), *Othéa to Hector*, 120, n. 1.
48. Chance (trans.), 'Christine's Minerva, the Mother Valorized', *Othéa to Hector*, 133.
49. Chance (trans.), 'Christine's Minerva, the Mother Valorized', *Othéa to Hector*, 125.
50. Chance (trans.), *Othéa to Hector*, 51.
51. Chance (trans.), *Othéa to Hector*, 51.
52. Lee, 'Reflections of Power', 191, brackets and ellipses in original. As Lee indicates, such queenly machinations were regarded with extreme disfavour, and 'one of the motives for establishing the regency was the desire to prevent her from gaining power' ('Reflections of Power', 191). Helen E. Maurer's excellent study *Margaret of Anjou: Queenship and Power in Late Medieval England* (Woodbridge: Boydell, 2003) provides a valuable account of Margaret's power and opposition to it; see especially ch. 9, 'Conditions and Means'.
53. Bühler (ed.), *Epistle*, Appendix A, 122–3. The preface is printed from MS Longleat 253.
54. P. G. C. Campbell, 'Christine de Pisan en Angleterre', *Revue de littérature comparée* 5 (1925), 669.
55. Summit, *Lost Property*, 68.
56. As Hope Johnston points out, the *Cité* circulated in England in manuscript prior to the publication of Anslay's translation in 1521. John of Lancaster, Duke of Bedford, owned a copy (London, MS BL 4431), which he acquired when he purchased Charles VI's library. Richard, Duke of York, and his wife Cecily Neville owned a copy which they acquired prior to 1460, as did Alice Chaucer, according to her 1466 inventory; 'How *Le Livre de la cité des dames* first came to

be printed in England', in *Desireuse de plus avant enquerre . . . : Actes du VI colloque international sur Christine de Pizan*, ed. Liliane Dulac, Anne Paupert, Christine Reno, and Bernard Ribémont (Paris: Champion, 2008), 385–86.
57. See Margery Kempe, *The Book of Margery Kempe*, ed. Lynn Staley (Kalamazoo, MI: Western Michigan University Press, 1996), 41.
58. Jennifer Summit similarly argues that Christine's 'cloistering" denies her a role as an active participant in 'the communities of men who are imagined to be the true creators of her books' (*Lost Property*, 81).
59. Worcester, *Boke of Noblesse*, 54–5, note b.
60. 'Brian Anslay, Translation of Christine de Pizan's *Book of the City of Ladies*', in *The Idea of the Vernacular*, ed. Wogan-Browne et al., 306, ll. 9–10.
61. Summit, *Lost Property*, 101. Summit cites Martha Driver on this point; see 'Christine de Pisan and Robert Wyer: The C Historyes of Troye or L'Epistre d'Othea Englished', *Sonderdruk aus Gutenberg-Jahrbuch* (1997), 137.
62. Summit additionally observes that the woodcut removes Christine 'from the scene of gentlemanly reading and textual exchange that Pepwell invokes in his prologue' (*Lost Property*, 101).
63. Johnston, 'How *Le Livre de la cite des dames*', 388–9.
64. Johnston, 'How *Le Livre de la cite des dames*', 391.
65. Bühler (ed.), *Epistle*, Appendix A, 122–4.
66. Bühler (ed.), *Epistle*, Appendix A, 122–3.

Further Reading

Campbell, P. G .C. (1925). Christine de Pisan en Angleterre. *Revue de littérature comparée* 5, 659–70.
Hindman, Sarah L. (1986). *Christine de Pizan's Epistre Othéa: Painting and Politics at the Court of Charles VI*, Toronto: University of Toronto Press.
Johnston, Hope (2008). How *Le Livre de la cité des dames* first came to be printed in England. In *Desireuse de plus avant enquerre . . . .: Actes du VI colloque international sur Christine de Pizan*, ed. Liliane Dulac, Anne Paupert, Christine Reno, and Bernard Ribémont. Paris: Champion, 385–86.
McCleod, Glenda K., ed. (1991). *The Reception of Christine de Pizan from the Fifteenth through the Nineteenth Centuries: Visitors to the City*, Medieval and Renaissance Series 9, Lewiston, NY: Edwin Mellen.
Schieberle, Misty (2019). A New Hoccleve Literary Manuscript: The Trilingual Miscellany in London, British Library, MS Harley 219. *Review of English Studies*, N.S. 70, 799–822.
Strakhov, Elizaveta, and Sarah Wilma Watson (2021). Behind Every Man(uscript) is a Woman: Social Networks, Christine de Pizan, and Westminster Abbey Library, MS 21. *Studies in the Age of Chaucer* 43, 151–80.
Summit, Jennifer (2000). *Lost Property: The Woman Writer and English Literary History, 1380–1589*, Chicago: University of Chicago Press.

CHAPTER 22

Beyond Borders
Women Poets in Ireland, Scotland, and Wales up to c. 1500

Cathryn A. Charnell-White

This chapter speaks to the devolutionary and cross-border impulse of 'Women's Poetry in Ireland, Scotland, and Wales 1400–1800'.[1] This project is a response to what Kate Chedgzoy calls the 'casual anglocentricity' of feminist recovery activity, as well as theoretical paradigms that have tended to marginalise the poetry of Celtic-speaking and anglophone women poets of Ireland, Scotland, and Wales.[2] Late medieval women poets, however, are doubly marginalised, for they occupy a liminal position within the mainstream poetic traditions of their respective national canons, as well as in relation to the mainstream anglophone or British female canon uncovered by second-wave feminist scholarship.[3] A collaborative enterprise between experts in the literatures of the three nations, the project draws on archival research to produce an innovative devolved female canon, both geographically and linguistically. With its devolutionary focus on both the Celtic-language and anglophone poetry of the three nations, the project's approach is a synthesis of feminist literary study and archipelagic literary study, nicely articulated by Sarah Prescott with the term 'archipelagic feminism'.[4] As well as expanding the borders of the canon of women poets from the wider British archipelago, Prescott shows that the project's 'devolved attention to the geographically marginal' also reappraises that 'perceived marginality' and leads to different conclusions as to the status of particular poets, the significance of their poetry, and that of individual poems'.[5]

In keeping with the broader project's devolved aims, this chapter draws from the geographic, linguistic, and canonical borders that define the cultural and poetic contexts of late medieval women poets from Ireland, Scotland, and Wales, and foregrounds some of those previously doubly marginalised poets. Borders also stimulate questions of belonging: through the poetry of close contemporaries from Wales and Scotland – Welsh poet

Gwerful Mechain (*c.* 1460–*c.* 1502) and Scottish Gaelic poets, mother and daughter Iseabal Campbell, Countess of Argyll (1427–1510), and Iseabal ní Mheic Cailéin (1459–*c.* 1493) – I discuss how these women poets' high social status afforded them the agency to overcome the professional and generic boundaries of the male-dominated bardic cultures within which they practised. Since their privileged status also afforded them poetic agency through bardic circles and coterie activity, this chapter explores the peformativity of their poems, in terms of bardic or poetic discourse and identity.

Women's Canons in Ireland, Scotland, and Wales

Grass roots scholarship and second-wave feminist scholarship in Ireland, Scotland, and Wales can achieve only a partial reconstruction of the poetry that was produced by women between 1400 and 1800. Given common features across the three nations – women's predominantly amateur status, the mutability of oral transmission, and the vicissitudes of manuscript culture – medieval women poets are less well attested in the surviving female canons of Ireland, Scotland, and Wales than their early modern successors.[6] Different patterns of survival emerge across the three nations which underline the instability of the female canons and any putative female traditions.

Ireland's Irish-language female canon before 1800 comprises approximately forty poems by around fifteen individuals.[7] The earliest extant Irish poem reliably attributed to a woman poet, 'A mhacaoimh dhealbhas an dán' (Oh young man who composes the poem) by Brighid Fitzgerald (*c.* 1589–1682), falls beyond the scope of this volume. Approximately 200 Scottish Gaelic poems survive by around 25 named women poets and many anonymous poets. Only individuals from the latter part of the eighteenth century have multiple surviving poems to their names, or even a modest canon. The earliest surviving Scottish Gaelic poem attributed to a named woman is an elegy to her husband by Aithbhreac Inghean Coirceadail (*c.* 1470s), and others who fall within the compass of this book include the women discussed here as case studies: Iseabal Campbell and her daughter (and namesake), Iseabal ní Mheic Cailéin.[8] Wales's female canon up to 1800 also comprises approximately 200 Welsh-language poems.[9] However, the Welsh poems are attributed to about 80 named individuals and very few anonymous poets. This higher ratio of women to poems reflects the fact that as many as half the named women poets have only one surviving poem to their name. The earliest surviving Welsh-language poems by women belong to the fifteenth century, a high point for Welsh-language strict-metre poetry known as 'y ganrif fawr' (the great century).[10] Gwerful Mechain is the only medieval Welsh-language female poet by whom a significant body of work survives, and she is also the most well-attested Welsh-language woman poet before 1700. A renowned *ymryson* (discursive) and religious poet in her day, she is the most recognised of a small number of Welsh medieval gentlewomen poets who include Gwerful Fychan (b. *c.* 1430) and her daughter Gwenllïan ferch Rhirid Flaidd (Gwenllïan, daughter of Rhirid Flaidd; *fl.* 1460s).[11]

Women and Bardic Culture in Ireland, Scotland, and Wales

Medieval Ireland, Scotland, and Wales's professional bardic cultures were essentially courtly and panegyric and served the ruling classes. Scotland and Ireland had a shared Gaelic bardic culture (*c.* 1200–*c.* 1600) in which professional poets, following a shift from ecclesiastic to lay patronage in the twelfth century, held strong affiliations with particular families and clan chieftains.[12] Wales's poets served native princes until the end of the thirteenth century, when the Edwardian Conquest of 1282 brought an end to Welsh political autonomy and instigated a patronage vacuum that was filled by Wales's gentry classes until the mid-seventeenth century.[13] Elite and professionalised, Irish, Scottish Gaelic, and Welsh bardic cultures share general features and demonstrate some striking parallels with regard to women poets. Foremost among these is a stylised form of diction or versification. A complex patterning of consonance, alliteration, and internal rhyme was employed in syllabic strict-metres to achieve a satisfying aural effect that is evoked in the names of these forms of diction: *dán díreach* (strict metre) in the Gaelic traditions and *cynghanedd* (harmony) in the Welsh tradition.[14] Other common features are of a generic and thematic nature, and include eulogy and elegy (genres embedded in the panegyric tradition), religious, love and occasional verse, as well as a traditional body of tropes and imagery.[15]

As befits a prestigious profession, poetry for the medieval Welsh *bardd* (plural *beirdd*) and the Irish and Scottish *file* (plural *filí*) had a hereditary dimension,[16] and poetry's elite professional status meant that conservative poetic guilds, especially in Wales, were largely closed to amateurs, whether women or low-born men. Aspiring women poets in Ireland, Scotland, and Wales, therefore, could not receive the requisite training that ensured both the professional standard of strict-metre poetry and the stability of the classical rules that underpinned the profession. In medieval Wales and

Ireland, bardic training occurred alongside a professional poet or Ollamh (for Irish and Scottish Gaelic poets).[17] Professional training involved initiation, accordingly, into *cynghanedd* or *dán díreach*, as well as their classical, syllabic strict metres and conventions, and trainee poets also learned the pedigrees of elite families and gained a wealth of traditional and historical knowledge.

Biographical information about known women poets, however, shows that in practice the tension between professionalism and amateurism did not impede individual, albeit high-status, women from acquiring poetic knowledge and practicing strict-metre poetry, sometimes in its looser forms. The existence of a recognised nomenclature for women poets, as well as an authentic female canon, indicates that women poets in medieval Ireland, Scotland, and Wales were recognised. *Prydyddes* (poetess), the feminine form of *prydydd*, a prestigious variant of the term *bardd* (poet), was used both literally and figuratively in medieval Wales,[18] and *banfile* (female poet) was in use in early medieval Ireland.[19] Few medieval women poets adopted bardic names, and Wales's Gwenllïan ferch Rhirid Flaidd and Gwerful Mechain are notable exceptions. Bardic names are significant emblems of self-identification for poets, and that both Gwenllïan and Gwerful are recognised by their bardic names in contemporary amateur and professional networks also points to a degree of sanction by the profession, albeit in acknowledgement of the women's high social status.

Known medieval women poets such as those discussed here were privileged, and were generally the wives or daughters of Scottish chiefs and Welsh gentry. Gender may have precluded women from formal bardic training, but high social status afforded them access to professional poets and bardic poetry in a courtly and performative context. Courtly, bardic poetry and its performance formed part of native polite culture in Ireland, Scotland, and Wales, and was either performed by the poets themselves or by professional declaimers (W. *datgeiniaid*; G. *reacairí*), to live audiences that included women.[20] Medieval Welsh law identifies discrete male and female spheres, namely the elite strict metres for men and the informal and less prestigious free metres for women.[21] In practice, however medieval courtly audiences comprised women, for bardic poetry praises women in medieval Ireland, Scotland, and Wales for their hospitality and generosity to poets, and sometimes recognises them as patrons.

Gaelic and Welsh bardic poetry was performative in nature and refined audiences would have been attuned to the aural aesthetic of *cynghanedd* and *dán díreach*, even if they did not fully comprehend the metrical nuances. Women's presence at court performances, and their appreciation of the classical or bardic poetry declaimed there, surely encouraged women's own amateur strict-metre compositions in the same way that Gaelic and Welsh noblemen acquired the craft. Indeed, the case studies used here show that this was the case in Scotland, and, for Wales, Nia Powell has argued that hearing poetry performed was a pathway to participation in strict-metre Welsh poetry for cultured individuals: 'It is likely, however, that some knowledge of poetic skill could be gleaned aurally by listening to declamation, and gentlemen poets not formally trained as bards themselves relied on this to acquire knowledge of the art.'[22] Evidence of women's involvement in poetic coteries is as unstable and partial as the Irish, Scottish Gaelic, and Welsh female canon itself. Yet the poems discussed here highlight the intellectual and creative stimulation born of the intimate, sociable, and often situation-bound performative context of bardic culture and activity. This is particularly salient when we consider the erotic and proto-feminist tenor of the poetry produced by Gwerful Mechain, Iseabal Campbell, and Iseabal ní Mheic Cailéin – three noblewomen for whom *cynghanedd* and *dán díreach*, and the elite and courtly strict-metre poetry they sustained, lay at the heart of their respective cultural heritage and native elite culture.

Biographies and Bardic Circles

Gwerful Mechain's father was Hywel Fychan of Llanfechain, Powys. She was related through marriage to the poet Llywelyn ab y Moel, and her closely intertwined family networks included patrons of Wales's professional bardic guild.[23] In terms of metre, Gwerful Mechain composed mainly *cywyddau* and *englynion*, the chosen form of professional and amateur poets alike.[24] The religious, prognostic, occasional, and erotic themes and genres of her poetry reflect both her amateur status and also the collective activity of amateur poets alongside whom she trained, under the tutelage of the gentleman poet Dafydd Llwyd of Mathafarn (*fl. c.* 1400–90): Ieuan Dyfi, Llywelyn ap Gutun, and others.[25] It is clear from Gwerful Mechain's proto-feminist poems and erotic discourses with Dafydd Llwyd that she cut a commanding figure in the amateur bardic circle, and was accepted by her fellow poets. Textual evidence also locates her in a broader bardic network that includes professional poets such as Guto'r Glyn, Dafydd ab Edmwnd, and Tudur Aled, where she commanded less respect and was satirised by Tudur Aled in what went beyond the routine ribbing of fellow poets.[26] Through the process of textual recovery, nineteen of the forty poems attributed to Gwerful Mechain have been deemed authentic by Nerys A. Howells.[27] That her *cywydd* 'Dioddefaint Crist' (Christ's Passion) survives in sixty-nine manuscript witnesses, and that 'Cywydd y Gal' (*Cywydd* to the penis) by the iconic poet Dafydd ap Gwilym (*fl.* 1320–70) is also attributed to her, indicates that Gwerful's work was held in high esteem.[28] She has also gained renown with new audiences for her strident poems that include counter-strokes against male violence and engagement with the European *querelle des femmes*, as well as ripostes to the male gaze that are both erotic and satiric.[29]

Gwerful Mechain's close contemporaries in the Scottish Gàidhealtachd, Iseabal Campbell, Countess of Argyll, and Iseabal ní Mheic Cailéin, had greater aristocratic and political standing. Iseabal the Elder, a member of the royal Stewart line, was married to Cailein Campbell (d. 1493), first Earl of Argyll (acc. 1457), and their daughter, Iseabal ní Mheic Cailéin, may have been married to William, Master of Drummond or Aonghas Óg Mac Domhnaill (d. 1490), son of the last hereditary Lord of the Isles.[30] As a result of the manuscript context in which their poetry is preserved, mother and daughter have been largely undifferentiated by scholars until recently.[31] Such conflation of poets and concomitant problems of attribution pose methodological problems for scholars undertaking textual recovery – similarly, Gwerful Mechain was conflated in Wales's oral tradition with near-contemporary Gwerful Fychan (b. *c*. 1430) – and are a practical illustration of the fragililty of medieval women poets' reputations and poetic legacies.[32] Only one poem survives by Iseabal the Elder, in the form of an erotic satire on the family priest's penis, and two poems attributed to her daughter and namesake engage with the motifs and generic conventions of courtly love.

Their small combined canon of three poems is preserved in *The Book of the Dean of Lismore*, the most culturally and linguistically important manuscript to have survived from the late medieval Scottish Gàidhealtachd, compiled at the behest of Seumas (James) MacGregor between 1512 and 1542.[33] MacGregor, the eponymous Dean of Lismore, was patronised by the Campbells of Glen Orchy; his eclectic repository of poems reflects the circle of professional and amateur poets known as the Inveraray circle that centred on Fortingall and included Earl Cailein and Iseabal Campbell, his Countess; their daughter, Iseabal; Cailein's cousin, noted poet Donnchadh Campbell of Glen Orchy (d. 1513); as well as other professional poets and clerics known to the Dean. The poems of this 'Inveraray circle',[34] then, are the product of coterie activity, characterised, according to William Gillies, by a strong sense of 'literary *jeu d'esprit*' or 'running debate' concerning anti-clerical and misogynist themes,[35] in a way that, according to Wilson McLeod and Meg Bateman, also constitutes a backlash against the 'studied manner' of the genre of courtly love.[36] These qualities replicated the way in which intelligentsia in other parts of the anglophone British archipelago regarded 'the rhetorical formulae of misogyny as a game' that allowed them to exercise their own discursive skills as well as engage those of their readers or audiences.[37]

The Poems

The poems of Gwerful Mechain, Iseabal Campbell, and Iseabal ní Mheic Cailéin had their genesis in a coterie or bardic circle, and consequently bear the hallmarks of coterie activity, production, and performance. The dominant themes of Dafydd Llwyd's bardic circle and the Inveraray circle play out the rhetorical formulae of misogyny characteristic of late medieval Welsh and Scottish Gaelic professional and amateur verse: the *querelles des femmes* and wicked women, jealous husbands, *malmariées*, and bawdy anticlerical satire. Reading the texts of Gwerful and the two Iseabals alongside each other in the context of a devolved female canon not only allows us to look beyond the solitary or lone text,[38] but also foregrounds the extent to which their poems articulate the performative context of their respective bardic cultures.

Although we cannot recapture the paralinguistic features of a performative context – tone of voice, physical gestures, and facial expressions – these are partially conveyed through other aspects that relay the texts' performativity.[39] Recognised inscribed 'performative features' indicate that the poems were composed to be performed to a specific audience: acknowledging the physical location of the performance; addressing or engaging the implied audience; specific references to time, place, and people; including direct or indirect quotation.[40] To this list we can add placing the self within the narrative, as well as intertextual and discrete cultural and bardic references that the implied audience would understand. In this, and in the way in which these poets' work is situated in relation to their bardic traditions, their poems also perform a self-consciously gendered (bardic) identity. On the surface, their poems are highly entertaining and ludic, but their poems also engage meaningfully – and, in Gwerful Mechain's case, unforgivingly – with bardic discourse: genres, conventions, and motifs. Such latitude towards professional bardic conventions is a common feature of amateur practice, and so it is not unusual for women poets, who occupied a liminal position in relation to the professional bardic guild, to appropriate bardic conventions for subjective ends.[41] What is striking, however, is the way in which these women's engagement with bardic discourse simultaneously speaks to their native bardic traditions and also creates, reflexively, female discourse, if not female bardic models of identity, through what Judith Butler might call the performativity of their texts.[42]

Gwerful Mechain's *cywydd* 'I wragedd eiddigus' (To jealous wives) is a good example of how women's poetry appropriates conventions whilst also refracting the texts and ideas, if not poetic performances, of fellow male poets. Read in isolation, this *cywydd* is a feisty parody of the 'jealous husband' (*gŵr eiddig*), a staple motif of Welsh love poetry borrowed from the courtly love repertoire.[43] Read in context, it is also an engaging response to a satricial poem to jealous wives by Gwerful's bardic tutor, Dafydd Llwyd,[44] whose poem focuses on the jealous wife of a man called Iago and has the satisfaction of male sexual desire at its heart. In her own poem, Gwerful Mechain inverts both the motif of the husband who jealously controls his wife's sexuality and Dafydd Llwyd's satire. Her stance is initially surprising, for she concurs with Dafydd Llwyd's premise that men should be allowed to love freely. However, as her poem unfolds, it is clear that her attitude is based on parity, for she promotes the satisfaction of female sexual desire. She further enfranchises women by berating those jealous wives who seek to prevent other women from enjoying the pleasures of the flesh with their husbands. In so doing, she invokes the authority of a female bardic predecessor, Gwenllïan ferch Rhirid Flaidd:

> Meddai i mi Wenllïan,
> Bu anllad gynt benllwyd gân,
> Nid cariad, anllad curiaw,
> Yr awr a dry ar aur draw.
> Cariad gwragedd bonheddig
> Ar galiau da, argoel dig!
> Pe'm credid, edlid adlais,
> Pob erchog caliog a'm cais:
> Ni rydd un wraig rinweddawl,
> Fursen, ei phiden a'i phawl,
> O dilid gont ar dalwrn,
> Nid âi un fodfedd o'i dwrn,
> Nac yn rhad, nis caniadai,
> Nac yn serth, er gwerth a gâi.[45]

(Gwenllïan said to me / (the ancient song of yore was wanton) / that it is not love (wanton pining) / that turns the hour yonder golden. / The love of noble wives / is for good penises – a bitter omen! / If I am believed (angry cry), / every seeker with a big penis pursues me: / no virtuous wife (the coquette!) / gives her penis and her pole / if it follows a cunt in an open field; / it wouldn't get an inch [away] from her fist, / not freely (she would not allow it), / nor vulgarly – not for any price she could get!)

Key words in her poem, such as 'eiddigedd' (jealousy), and the notion that a penis can steal a woman's sense provide a knowing intertextual nod to Dafydd Llwyd's poem, the significance of which could also have been reinforced by tone of voice or gesture in performance. Her *cywydd* is also uproariously self-referential: Gwerful Mechain owns her poem with a first-person perspective and discursive asides to her implied audience that expose its performative dimension: 'Meddai i mi' ([she] told me), 'Pe'm credid' (were I to be believed).[46] The poem's irreverent closing lines are also a good example of these performative narrative techniques:

> Ni chenais 'y nychanon,
> Gwir Dduw hynt, ddim o'r gerdd hon,
> I neb o ffurfeidd-deb y ffydd
> A fyn gala fwy no'i gilydd.[47]

(I did not sing my satire / (the course of the true God), [nor] any of this poem, / to anyone of formal faith / who desires a bigger penis than the rest.)

As well as responding to a particular literary motif, Gwerful Mechain also critiques the conservative nature of poetry that objectified woman and privileged male needs. She reprises these themes in 'Cywydd y gont' (*Cywydd* to the cunt), in which she parodies *descriptio pulchritudinis*, the convention of describing a woman formulaically, starting with the hair, eyebrows, and facial features, then moving to the smooth breast, arms, hands, and elegant feet.[48] In its systematic objectification of a woman's body, this standard convention of medieval poetry, and of fifteenth-century Welsh love poetry in particular, perfectly projects the male gaze and the unequal power relations between the male viewer and the female object. Dafydd Johnston nicely sums up the genre: 'the act of seeing and of gazing is the foundation of fifteenth-century [Welsh] love poems'.[49] Gwerful Mechain introduces her case without demurring, rooting her argument firmly in a bardic context. The praise of vain and drunken poets is inadequate, specifically *descriptio pulchritudinis* and its practised avoidance of a woman's best physical feature, her vagina:

> Moli gwallt, cwnsallt ceinserch,
> A phob cyfryw fyw o ferch,
> Ac obry moli heb wg
> Yr aeliau uwch yr olwg.

> Moli hefyd, hyfryd tew,
> Foelder dwyfron feddaldew,
> A moli gwen, len loywlun,
> Dylai barch, a dwylaw bun ...
> Gado'r canol heb foliant
> A'r plas lle'r enillir plant,
> A'r cedor clyd, hyder claer,
> Tynerdeg, cylch twn eurdaer,
> Lle carwn i, cywrain iach,
> Y cedor dan y cadach.[50]

([Poets] praise the hair (gown of fair love) / and every sort of living girl, / and, below, praise genially / the brows above the eyes. / [Poets] also praise (lovely [and] fat) / the smoothness of the soft [and] plump breasts; / and praise [the] girl / and her arms (bright drape) ... / [Poets] leave the middle without praise, / [that is] the place where children are conceived, / and the snug quim (clear excellence), / tender and plump, golden [and] ardent broken circle / (where I would love), in good health / the pubic hair beneath the clothing.)

In this direct challenge to her fellow poets, and to the male gaze, Gwerful Mechain deftly employs the poets' own generic conventions against them: she dissects the convention of *descriptio pulchritudinis* in order to question its legitimacy, and offers an alternative female gaze and female bardic model. Urging male poets to circulate poems that do not ignore a woman's most glorious part (ll. 39–42), Gwerful amplifies her scorn for the poets' 'diffrwyth wawd' (fruitless praise) in a fruitfully descriptive celebration of the female genitals:

> Sawden awdl, sidan ydiw,
> Sêm fach, len ar gont wen wiw,
> Lleiniau mewn man ymannerch,
> Y llwyn sur, llawn yw o serch,
> Fforest falch iawn, ddawn ddifreg,
> Ffris ffraill, ffwrwr ddwygaill deg,
> Breisglwyn merch, drud annerch dro,
> Berth addwyn, Duw'n borth iddo.[51]

(The Sultan [=chief] of an *awdl*,[52] it is silk, / [it is] a little seam, a curtain on a fine bright cunt, / flaps in a place of greeting, / [it is] the sharp-tasting grove (it is full of love), / a very proud forest (a faultless gift),/ tender frieze,[53] the fur for two fair testicles, / a girl's untidy bush (circle of dear greeting): / lovely bush, [may] God keep it!)

Here she uses the bardic convention of *dyfalu*, a feat of proliferating imaginative metaphors and images, whose opening metaphor, 'Sawden awdl' (Sultan [=chief] of the *awdl* [=ode]), asserts the vagina's merit as a bardic subject.

The ideal woman of medieval love poetry, including courtly love, was pious, obedient, and quiet,[54] but the intelligent and articulate personas performed in their poems by Gwerful Mechain and the two Iseabals challenge this very passive ideal. Not only do they acknowledge female sexual desire but also, by appropriating mysogynist bardic genres and reorienting bardic conventions and motifs such as *descriptio pulchritudinis*, *dyfalu*, and courtly love, they assert female sexual agency. Iseabal Campbell, Countess of Argyll's four short verses express heterosexual desire for the priest's penis: 're scél na mbod bríoghmhar, / do shanntaich mo chridghe-sa' (the vigorous prick / that has made my heart hunger).[55] Like Gwerful Mechain, she conveys a female gaze, albeit in a cursory description of the priest's penis. Unlike Gwerful Mechain, whose explicit descriptions of Dafydd Llwyd's penis place her as an active agent in her satire, Iseabal Campbell maintains a playful distance with her implied audience. Other performative features include self-reflexivity, for Iseabal never promises to tell more than 'some of this tale' ('cuid dana scéalaibh do sgríobhadh', l. 4) and implies – 'scéal breácach' (a likely tale; l. 14) – that the proportions of the priest's penis, as well as her own knowledge of it, are perhaps exaggerated:

> Atá a riabh ro-reamhar
> An sin 's ni h-e scéal breácach
> Nocha chuala cho-reamhar
> Mhotha bhod arís.[56]

(It's that plump tool of his / – a likely tale! – / of whose like you'll never hear again / for bulk or breadth.)

Iseabal's poem also has an intertextual dimension, because hers is not the only poem to the chaplain's penis preserved in *The Book of the Dean of Lismore* and seems to have been composed in deliberate response.[57]

The two poems attributed to Iseabal the Younger belong to the same family circle at Inveraray, yet have a slightly different dynamic. 'Is mairg dá ngalar an grádh' (Alas for the one whose affliction is love) and 'Atá fleasgach arm o thí' (There is a youth intent upon me) are 'short and effective' examples of courtly love, a rare genre that reached Gaelic Scotland via Ireland,[58] and demonstrate European influence on the Scottish Gaelic tradition. These poems are more overtly courtly in nature than Iseabal's mother's poem.[59] Furthermore, McLeod and Bateman argue that Scottish Gaelic examples of the genre are more playful and impressionistic, and convey motifs and the general tone of courtly love rather than its comprehensive philosophy.[60] This is certainly true of Iseabal ní Mheic

Cailéin's inversions of the male gaze that emphasise lovesickness and the pain of love, and present a more restrained erotic yearning than that adopted by Gwerful Mechain and, indeed, the early medieval *trobairitz*, in relation to the same themes.[61] Iseabal ní Mheic Cailéin's more tempered tone may reflect her youth in relation to other members of the Inveraray circle, or if indeed the man addressed is her future husband, the political and social complexities around brokering her marriage.[62] It may also reject the casual poetic misogyny of the circle and the prevalence elsewhere of women as, according to W. J. Watson, 'the subject of love-lyric or as the objects of satire',[63] in poems that address male subjects and reprise motifs of the *querelle des femmes*. Both of Iseabal ní Mheic Cailéin's poems express the courtly motifs of an aloof, if not entirely cold, mistress wounded by unreciprocated love and incompatibility. They also have a satirical edge, in the self-deprecation which, along with the first-person position and awareness of the implied audience, speaks to their performative context:

> Atá fleasgach ar mo thí,
> A Rí ba ríogh go rí leis!
> A bheith sínte ré mo bhroinn
> Agus a chium ré mo chneis![64]

(There is a youth intent upon me, / O King of kings, may fortune favour him! / May he be stretched out beside me / with his chest against my heart!)

Gwerful Mechain's most performative poem – and, indeed, her most personal – is 'I ateb Ieuan Dyfi' (To answer the poet Ieuan Dyfi). It is a riposte to a suite of *cywyddau* by Ieuan Dyfi, an amateur poet who was also part of Dafydd Llwyd's bardic circle, in which he sings of his former lover, Anni Goch (Red Annie). Ieuan Dyfi's most direct poem to her, and the one which Gwerful Mechain specifically answers, is 'I Anni Goch' (To Red Annie). In it he recounts his disappointment in love and evokes popular antifeminist motifs of the European tradition of the *querelle des femmes*. As such, the pair of poems represent the earliest examples in Welsh of the *querelle des femmes*, and are unique in medieval Welsh poetry for presenting the views of both male and female poets.[65] Whilst the poems by Ieuan Dyfi and Gwerful Mechain are not kept together in any single manuscript, that the *cywyddau* speak to each other in theme and structure, and have complementary performative qualities too, suggests that they are, indeed, part of a poetic discourse which likely had its genesis in Dafydd Llwyd's bardic circle.

In his poem Ieuan Dyfi employs familiar examples of men who have been deceived: Sampson, Solomon, Alexander the Great, and Achilles. Gwerful Mechain's riposte is a strident defence of women in which Anni

Goch is alluded to with devastating effect. Gwerful Mechain matches Ieuan Dyfi's male exemplars with an equal number of praiseworthy women – 'Mwy no rhai o'r rhianedd, / Gwell no gwŷr eu gallu a'u gwedd' (bigger than some women, / [and] better than men in their authority and manner) – who not only vouch for Anni Goch, but also reveal the depth of Gwerful's learning and knowledge of bibilical, Classical, and native Welsh traditions, including sources such as Welsh-language material derived from *Historia Regum Britanniae* (1136).[66] Her roll-call begins with the most well-known of deceived women, Dido, and continues with women who demonstrate leadership (Gwenddolen), peaceable mediation (Tonwen and Genuissa), upholding the law (Marsia), exemplary piety and charity (Judas Iscariot's mother, Pontius Pilot's wife, Elen (Helen) wife of Constantine, the widow of Zaraphath), veracity (Aelfthryth, Susannah), and wisdom (the Sibyl).[67] The Sibyl, renowned for wisdom and for foreseeing the Last Judgement, is a pointed final exemplar who legitimates Gwerful Mechain's closing lines, which call Ieuan Dyfi to account for his ill-use of Anni Goch. Her words do so with a series of questions and direct advice to him in the imperative mood:

> Dywed Ifan, rwy'n d'ofyn,
> Yn gywir hardd, ai gwir hyn?
> Ni allodd merch, gordderchwr,
> Diras ei gwaith, dreisio gŵr.
> Dig aflan, o dôi gyfle,
> Ymdynnu a wnâi, nid am ne'.
> Gad yn wib, godinebwr,
> Galw dyn hardd gledren hŵr.
> Efô fu'n pechu bob pen,
> Ac o'i galon pe gwelen',
> Dywed Ifan, ar dafawd,
> Rhodiog ŵr, cyn rhydu gwawd,
> Ai da i ferch golli'i pherchen,
> A'i phrynt a'i helynt yn hen?
> Yr un ffŵl a neidio wrth ffon
> Neu neidio wrth lw anudon,
> Aed ffeilsion ddynion yn ddig,
> Duw a fyddo dy feddyg.[68]

([Do] tell, Ifan, I ask you, / truly and beautifully, is this true? / A girl could not, you adulterer / (wicked work [and] morally corrupt), rape a man. / Angry, unclean, if an opportunity arose, / he would not strive for heaven. / Adulterer, desist in haste from / calling a beautiful girl a whore's pale protector. / He who sinned against everyone / from his heart, if [only] we could see it. / [Do] say frankly, Ifan, [you] liar, / before poetry rusts, / is it acceptable for a woman to lose her rights / and her looks, and to lose her way when she is old? / The same fool jumps to a stick / or a false oath, / may false men be angered, / [and] may God be your healer.)

Gwerful Mechain's accusations and angry asides in this passage prompt her contemporary audience to recall the complex case outlined against Ieuan Dyfi and Anni Goch in consistory court records of 1502. The pair had been accused of adultery by Anni's husband, John Lippard, in July of that year; Ieuan Dyfi confessed to adultery in August and was whipped eight times around Presteigne Church. By October, Anni Goch ('Agneta Goze *alias* Lippard') denied the accusation and, in Ieuan Dyfi's absence, she claimed that he had raped her.[69] Like the biblical Susannah, pointedly referenced by Gwerful Mechain, Anni Goch was found innocent in the face of sexual defamation, and so Gwerful's poem is a powerful counter to the self-pity expressed by Ieuan Dyfi in this and other poems to Anni Goch. However, had Gwerful Mechain lived to learn of the plot twist that emerged in consistory court proceedings in 1517, she may well have revisited her poem, for Anni Goch, when accused by her husband of plotting his death, admitted to having committed adultery years earlier with Ieuan Dyfi and two other men, and noted that her husband had sold her to the poet.[70]

Conclusions

An archipelagic feminist approach yields several new insights. By reading the poems of our Welsh and Scottish Gaelic case studies alongside each other, this chapter demonstrates how a cross-border focus on the geographically, linguistically, and canonically marginalised can add new layers of interest to both the native Celtic-speaking canons and so-called mainstream anglophone canon. Although medieval Wales and Scotland's bardic cultures have some shared features, notably the liminal and amateur position of women poets, the patterns of participation and engagement represented by Gwerful Mechain, Iseabal Campbell, and Iseabal ní Mheic Cailéin (and indeed other contemporaries) show that social status (and concomitant familial literary connections) conferred more creative poetic agency on medieval women than gender or the dynamics of nation. As cultured high-status women they were steeped in their respective bardic traditions yet, even from the supposed geographic and cultural margins, they drew on broader European cultural and literary influences to enrich their home-grown poetic range.

All three women composed erotic and satirical poems through which they validated female sexuality and also challenged the patriarchal ideal of the feminine that was embedded in late medieval society and encoded in the bardic genres, conventions, and motifs of Wales's fifteenth-century love poetry and in the conventions of European courtly love also current in Gaelic Scotland and Wales. All three are, as a result, remembered by posterity principally as erotic, transgressive poets, with all the opprobrium that entails. Despite their resolutely satiric tone, the erotic dialogues of Gwerful Mechain and Dafydd Llwyd fuelled an oral tradition that they were lovers; Gwerful Mechain's first editor, Leslie Harries, dismissed her as little more than a whore ('namyn putain') and excluded her poems from the published version of his MA thesis.[71] However, close reading of the genre, conventions, motifs, and language employed in the women's poems reorient their marginal position, for they demonstrate how the very poetic genres and tropes that diminish women, and deny them agency, could also be employed to empower women. In this, they not only present an alternative female gaze, but also a self-reflective female bardic discourse that engages with and subverts accepted genres and conventions. That they achieved this in a bardic and performative coterie context shows a level of acceptance for women poets and their participation in bardic circles and dialogue, as well as the way in which private or closed aristocratic coterie sensibility provided a safe creative space for female members to practise.

Devolved attention also leads to new conclusions as to the significance of individual women poets and their poems and, in this respect, this chapter shows that the coterie context is more important to the production, performance, and transmission of women's poets than previously assumed. The discussion of individual poems foregrounds the performative features of the texts and the ways in which the women poets engage their implied audiences through various narrative techniques and informed poetic, cultural, and intertextual allusion. Going forward, there is certainly more to be said about the performative dimension of women's poetry. In addition to external evidence for coterie activity, internal textual evidence of performativity could be used to identify performative elements in the texts of other women poets from the three nations, thus revealing further coterie and collaborative practice that is not documented elsewhere.

Notes

1. The project's homepage is located at Aberystwyth University: womenspoetry.aber.ac.uk/en; Sarah Prescott (gen. ed.), *Women's Poetry from Ireland, Scotland, and Wales: An Anthology 1400–1800* (Cambridge: Cambridge University Press, forthcoming).
2. Kate Chedgzoy, *Women's Writing in the British Atlantic World: Memory, Place and History, 1550–1700* (Cambridge: Cambridge University Press, 2007), 124; see also J. Stevenson and P. Davidson (eds.), *Early Modern Women Poets (1520–1700): An Anthology* (Oxford: Oxford University Press, 2001) as a model for a more inclusive and multilingual female canon.
3. Sarah Dunnigan, 'Introduction', in *Woman and the Feminine in Medieval and Early Modern Scottish Writing*, ed. C. Marie Harker and Evelyn S. Newlyn (Basingstoke: Palgrave Macmillan, 2004), xv.
4. Sarah Prescott, 'Archipelagic Feminism: Anglophone Poetry from Ireland, Scotland and Wales', in *The Oxford Handbook of Early Modern Women's Writing in English, 1540–1700*, ed. Elizabeth Scott-Baumann, Danielle Clarke, and Sarah C. E. Ross (Oxford: Oxford University Press, 2022), 377–91; Sarah Prescott, 'Archipelagic Literary History: Eighteenth-Century Poetry from Ireland, Scotland and Wales', in *Women's Writing, 1660–1830: Feminisms and Futures*, ed. Jennie Batchelor and Gillian Dow (London: Palgrave Macmillan, 2016), 179–201. For archipelagic theory, see J. G. A. Pocock, *The Discovery of Islands: Essays in British History* (Cambridge: Cambridge University Press, 2005), 4–43; John Kerrigan, *Archipelagic English: Literature, History, and Politics 1603–1707* (Oxford: Oxford University Press, 2008).
5. Prescott, 'Archipelagic Feminism'.
6. Ceridwen Lloyd-Morgan has made a case for women's greater reliance on oral composition and transmission, and hence greater likelihood of their poems being lost. See Ceridwen Lloyd-Morgan, 'Women and Their Poetry in Medieval Wales', in *Women and Literature in Britain, 1150–1500*, ed. Carol M. Meale (Cambridge: Cambridge University Press, 1993), 183–201; Ceridwen Lloyd-Morgan, 'Oral Composition and Written Transmission: Welsh Women's Poetry from the Middle Ages and Beyond', *Trivium* 26 (1991), 87–102.
7. A selection of these poems, along with English translations, can be found in *The Field Day Anthology of Irish Writing. Volume IV: Irish Women's Writing and Traditions*, ed. Angela Bourke (Cork: Cork University Press, 2002), an anthology that was itself borne of omissions in the preceding three volumes of the canon-forming Field Day series. Thomas Owen Clancy has argued that a corpus of anonymous, female persona poems dated before 1600 may well include poems composed by women; see 'Women Poets in Early Medieval Ireland: Stating the Case', in '*The fragility of her sex'? Medieval Irish Women in their Medieval Context*, ed. C. E Meek and M. K. Simms (Blackrock: Four Courts Press, 1996), 43–72.

8. Catherine Kerrigan, *Anthology of Scottish Women Poets* (Edinburgh: Edinburgh University Press, 1991). Gaelic poems by women have also been published in mainstream anthologies: Wilson McLeod and Meg Bateman (eds.), *Duanaire Na Sracaire / Songbook of the Pillagers: An Anthology of Scotland's Gaelic Verse to 1600* (Edinburgh: Birlinn, 2007); and Ronald Black (ed.), *An Lasair: Anthology of 18th Century Scottish Gaelic Verse* (Edinburgh: Birlinn, 2001).
9. For a chronological overview of the canon and its main features, see Cathryn A. Charnell-White and Sarah Prescott, 'Early Modern Welsh Women Writers', in *The Palgrave Encyclopedia of Early Modern Women's Writing*, ed. P. Pender and R. Smith (Springer Nature Switzerland, 2021): doi.org/10.1007/978-3-030-01537-4_11-1.
10. Ceri W. Lewis, 'The Court Poets: Their Function, Status and Craft', in *A Guide to Welsh Literature*, vol. 1, ed. A. O. H. Jarman and G. R. Hughes (Swansea: Christopher Davies, 1976), 123–56.
11. Kate Gramich and Catherine Brennan (eds), *Welsh Women's Poetry 1460–2001* (Dinas Powys: Honno Welsh Women's Press, 2003); Cathryn A. Charnell-White, *Beirdd Ceridwen: Blodeugerdd Barddas o ganu menywod hyd tua 1800* (Treforys: Cyhoeddiadau Barddas, 2005).
12. William Gillies, 'Gaelic Literature in the Later Middle Ages: The Book of the Dean and Beyond', in *The Edinburgh History of Scottish Literature: From Columba to the Union (1707)*, ed. Thomas O. Clancy and Murray Pittock (Edinburgh: Edinburgh University Press, 2007), 219; Wilson McLeod, *Divided Gaels: Gaelic Cultural Identities in Scotland and Ireland c. 1200–c. 1650* (Oxford: Oxford University Press, 1999), 5.
13. Ceri W. Lewis, 'The Decline of Professional Poetry', in *A Guide to Welsh Literature c. 1530–1700*, vol. 3, ed. R. Geraint Gruffydd (Cardiff: University of Wales Press, 1997), 29–74.
14. Mererid Hopwood, *Singing in Chains: Listening to Welsh Verse* (Llandysul: Gomer, 2004); Eleanor Knott, *An Introduction to Irish Syllabic Poetry for the Period 1200–1600* (Dublin: Dublin Institute for Advanced Studies, 1934; 1966); William Gillies, 'The form of Scottish Gaelic poetry', *The International Companion to Scottish Poetry*, ed. Carla Sassi (Glasgow: Scottish Literature International, 2015), 105–8.
15. J. E. Caerwyn Williams, 'The Development of Poetry', in *The Irish Literary Tradition*, ed. J. E. Caerwyn Williams and Patrick K. Ford (Cardiff: University of Wales Press, 1992), 159; John MacInnes, 'The Panegyric Code in Gaelic Poetry and its Historical Background', *Transactions of the Gaelic Society of Inverness* 50 (1976–78), 435–98; M. Pía Coira, *By Poetic Authority: The Rhetoric of Panegyric in Gaelic poetry of Scotland to c. 1700* (Edinburgh: Dunedin Academic Press, 2012); *A Guide to Welsh Literature*, vol. 2, ed. A. O. H. Jarman and G. R. Hughes (Swansea: Christopher Davies, 1979).
16. Osborn Bergin, *Irish Bardic Poetry*, ed. David Greene and Fergus Kelly (Dublin: Dublin Institute for Advanced Studies, 1970); Marc Caball, 'The Literature of Medieval Ireland 1200–1600: From the Normans to the Tudors',

The Cambridge History of Irish Literature, ed. Margaret Kelleher and Philip O'Leary, vol. 1 (Cambridge: Cambridge University Press, 2008), 78.

17. Damian McManus, 'The Bardic Poet as Teacher, Student and Critic: A Context for the Grammatical Tracts', in *Unity in Diversity: Studies in Irish and Scottish Gaelic Language, Literature and History*, ed. Cathal G. Ó Háinle and Donald E. Meek (Dublin: School of Irish, Trinity College, 2004), 97.
18. See Charnell-White, *Beirdd Ceridwen*, 29–30, for examples from the fourteenth and fifteenth centuries.
19. Máirín Ní Dhonnchada, 'Travelers and Settled Folk: Women, Honor, and Shame in Medieval Ireland', in *Constructing Gender in Medieval Ireland*, ed. Sarah Sheehan and Ann Dooley (New York: Palgrave Macmillan, 2013), 17–38, and Clancy, 'Women Poets in Early Medieval Ireland', 43–72. For Scotland, see Colm Ó Baoill, '"Neither Out nor In": Scottish Gaelic Women Poets 1650–1750', in *Woman and the Feminine in Medieval and Early Modern Scottish Writing*, 136–52.
20. Bergin, *Irish Bardic Poetry*.
21. Nia M. W. Powell, 'Women and Strict-Metre Poetry in Wales', in *Women and Gender in Early Modern Wales*, ed. Michael Roberts and Simone Clarke (Cardiff: University of Wales Press, 2000), 130.
22. Powell, 'Women and Strict-Metre Poetry', 130. Gentleman poets in Scotland held amateur status and unofficial training; Martin MacGregor, 'Creation and Compilation: The Book of the Dean of Lismore and Literary Culture in late Medieval Gaelic Scotland', in *The Edinburgh History of Scottish Literature*, ed. Clancy and Pittock, 213.
23. Nerys Ann Howells (ed.), *Gwaith Gwerful Mechain ac Eraill* (Aberystwyth: University of Wales Centre for Advanced Welsh and Celtic Studies, 2001), 4, 48.
24. The *cywydd* is structured around rhyming couplets that pair stressed and unstressed rhymes, while the shorter *englyn* is a unit of four lines that stands independently or in a series. See Hopwood, *Singing in Chains*, 65–73.
25. Howells, *Gwaith Gwerful Mechain ac Eraill*, 4–16.
26. For Gwerful Mechain's ill-treatment by fellow bards at the court of Richard Cyffin, Bishop of Bangor, see Howells, *Gwaith Gwerful Mechain ac Eraill*, 8–16; Cathryn A. Charnell-White, 'Problems of Authorship and Attribution: The Welsh-Language Women's Canon Before 1800', *Women's Writing*, 24.4 (2017), 409–10. doi.org/10.1080/09699082.2016.1268336.
27. Howells, *Gwaith Gwerful Mechain ac Eraill*, passim.
28. Dafydd ap Gwilym's text is edited and translated in *Medieval Welsh Erotic Poetry*, ed. Dafydd Johnston (Cardiff: Tafol, 1991), 28–31.
29. The poems have been translated by Katie Gramich in *The Works of Gwerful Mechain* (Peterborough, Ontario: Broadview Press, 2018).
30. Details of the marriages of Earl Cailein's children differ in contemporary sources; another daughter, Catherine, may have been Aonghas Óg's wife, which lends a stronger courtly dimension to the poem that is addressed to him

yet attributed to Iseabal the Younger. See *Highland Papers*, vol. 2, ed. J. R. N. MacPhail (Edinburgh: Scottish History Society, 1916), 989.
31. See Martin MacGregor, '"Surely one of the greatest poems ever made in Britain": The Lament for Griogair Ruadh MacGregor of Glen Strae and its Historical Background', in *The Polar Twins*, ed. Edward J. Cowan and Douglas Gifford (Edinburgh: John Donald, 1999), 138). Wilson McLeod and Meg Bateman (eds.), *Duanaire Na Sracaire*, 514.
32. Charnell-White, 'Problems of Authorship and Attribution, 398–417.
33. MacGregor, 'Creation and Compilation', 210.
34. Martin MacGregor, 'The View from Fortingall: The Worlds of the *Book of the Dean of Lismore*', *Scottish Gaelic Studies* 22 (2006), 35–85; Gilles, 'Gaelic Literature of the Later Middle Ages', 221, 224.
35. William Gillies, 'Courtly and Satiric Poems in the Book of the Dean of Lismore', *Scottish Studies*, 21 (1977), 46; Gillies, 'Gaelic Literature in the later Middle Ages', 224; William Gillies, 'The Book of the Dean of Lismore: The Literary Perspective', in *Fresche Fontanis: Studies in the Bulture of Medieval and Early Modern Scotland*, ed. Janet Hadley Williams and J. Derrick McClure (Cambridge: Cambridge Scholars Publishing, 2013), 179–216.
36. McLeod and Bateman, *Duanaire Na Sracaire*, 287.
37. Alcuin Blamires, *The Case for Women in Medieval Culture* (Oxford: Clarendon Press, 1997), 12.
38. Marie-Louise Coolahan, *Women, Writing and Language in Early Modern Ireland* (Oxford: Oxford University Press, 2010), *passim*.
39. Paralinguistic features of oral poetry are discussed by J. Niles, *Homo Narrans: The Poetics and Anthropology of Oral Literature* (Philadelphia: University of Philadelphia Press, 1999), 33–65.
40. Evelyn Birge Vitz, Nancy Freeman Regaldo, and Marilyn Lawrence (eds.), 'Introduction', in *Performing Medieval Narrative* (Cambridge: D. S. Brewer, 2005), 4–5.
41. For Wales, see Charnell-White and Prescott, 'Early Modern Welsh Women Writers', 3; Charnell-White, 'Problems of Authorship and Attribution', 14. For Scotland, see MacGregor, 'Creation and Compilation', 214.
42. Judith Butler, *Gender Trouble: Feminism and the Subversion of Identity* (rev. ed., New York and London: Routledge, 2007), 34, 185–93; Judith Butler, *Excitable Speech: A Politics of the Performative* (London: Routledge, 1997), 185–93.
43. Huw M. Edwards, *Dafydd ap Gwilym: Influences and Analogues* (Oxford: Clarendon Press, 1996), 57–59, 73, 77–78.
44. W. Leslie Richards, *Gwaith Dafydd Llwyd o Fathafarn* (Caerdydd: University of Wales Press, 1964), 'Cywydd dychan i'r eiddiges a moliant i'r wraig fonheddigaidd oedd eiddigus' (A satirical *cywydd* to the jealous wife and praise to the noblewoman who was not jealous, no. 80), 173–4.
45. Charnell-White, *Beirdd Ceridwen*, no. 12, ll. 9–18.
46. Charnell-White, *Beirdd Ceridwen*, no. 12, ll. 9, 15.

47. Charnell-White, *Beirdd Ceridwen*, no. 12, ll. 55–8.
48. Ann Matonis, 'Nodiadau ar Rethreg y Cywyddwr: y *descriptio pulchritudinis* a'r Technegau Helaethu', *Y Traethodydd CXXXIII* (1798), 155–67; Edwards, *Dafydd ap Gwilym*, 252.
49. Dafydd Johnston, *Llên yr Uchelwyr: Hanes Beirniadol Llenyddiaeth Gymraeg 1300–1525* (Cardiff: University of Wales Press, 2014), 104.
50. Charnell-White, *Beirdd Ceridwen*, no. 11, ll. 13–16, 21–6.
51. Charnell-White, *Beirdd Ceridwen*, no. 11, ll. 27–34.
52. *Awdl*: an extended strict-metre form that represented the accomplishment of a professional poet. See Hopwood, *Singing in Chains*, 73–80.
53. Frieze: heavy and course woollen cloth.
54. Sioned Davies, 'Y Ferch yng Nghymru'r Oesoedd Canol', in *Cof Cenedl: Ysgrifau ar Hanes Cymru 9*, ed. Geraint H. Jenkins (Llandysul: Gomer, 1994), 1–32.
55. Translated by Kate Mathis in *Women's Poetry from Ireland, Scotland, and Wales: An Anthology 1400–1800*.
56. Prescott, *Women's Poetry from Ireland, Scotland, and Wales: An Anthology 1400–1800*.
57. Gillies, 'Courtly and Satiric Poems in the *Book of the Dean of Lismore*', 41.
58. Domhnall Uilleam Stiùbhart, 'Women and Gender in the Early Modern Western Gàidhealtachd', in *Women in Scotland: c.1100–c.1750*, ed. Elizabeth Ewen and Maureen M. Meikle (East Linton: Tuckwell Press, 1999), 233–4. See also William Gillies, 'The dánta grá and the Book of the Dean of Lismore', in *Ollam: Studies in Gaelic and Related Traditions in Honor of Tomás Ó Cathasaigh*, ed. Matthieu Boyd (Madison, NJ: Fairleigh Dickinson University Press, 2016), 257–69.
59. McLeod, *Divided Gaels*, 23.
60. McLeod and Bateman, *Duanaire Na Sracaire*, 262–5.
61. Howells, *Gwaith Gwerful Mechain ac Eraill*, 45; Meg Bogin, *The Women Troubadours* (New York and London: Paddington Press, 1980).
62. Kate Louise Mathis, 'Women's Poetry in the Gàidhealtachd 1400–1660: The Earliest Women Poets in the Book of the Dean of Lismore' in *The Edinburgh Biographical Dictionary of Scottish Writers*, ed. Alan Riach, Caroline E. McCracken-Flesher, and Ronald Black (Edinburgh: Edinburgh University Press, forthcoming).
63. Gillies, 'Courtly and Satiric Poems in the *Book of the Dean of Lismore*', 39–48.
64. Prescott, *Women's Poetry in Ireland, Scotland, and Wales: An Anthology 1400–1800*.
65. Marged Haycock, 'Merched drwg a merched da: Gwerful Mechain v. Ieuan Dyfi', in *Ysgrifau Beirniadol XVII*, ed. J. E. Caerwyn Williams (Dinbych: Gwasg Gee, 1990), 97–110.
66. Howells, *Gwaith Gwerful Mechain ac Eraill*, 138–47; see Charnell-White, *Beirdd Ceridwen*, no. 9, ll. 55–6.
67. See Haycock, 'Merched drwg a merched da'.
68. Charnell-White, *Beirdd Ceridwen*, no. 9, ll. 63–80.

69. Llinos Beverley Smith, 'Olrhain Anni Goch', in *Ysgrifau Beirniadol XIX*, ed. J. E. Caerwyn Williams (Dinbych: Gwasg Gee, 1993), 115.
70. Smith, 'Olrhain Anni Goch', 115–16, 119.
71. Leslie Harries, 'Barddoniaeth Huw Cae Llwyd, Ieuan ap Huw Cae Llwyd, Ieuan Dyfi, a Gwerful Mechain' (unpublished MA thesis, University College of Wales, Swansea, 1933), 26.

Further Reading

Charnell-White, Cathryn A. (2017). Problems of Authorship and Attribution: The Welsh-Language Women's Canon Before 1800. *Women's Writing* 24.4, 398–417. doi.org/10.1080/09699082.2016.1268336.

Gillies, William (1977). Courtly and Satiric Poems in the Book of the Dean of Lismore. *Scottish Studies* 21, 35–53.

Gillies, William (2007). Gaelic Literature in the Later Middle Ages: The Book of the Dean and Beyond. In *The Edinburgh History of Scottish Literature: From Columba to the Union (1707)*, ed. Thomas O. Clancy and Murray Pittock (Edinburgh: Edinburgh University Press), 219–25.

Gillies, William (2016). The *dánta grá* and the Book of the Dean of Lismore. In *Ollam: Studies in Gaelic and Related Traditions in Honor of Tomás Ó Cathasaigh*, ed. Matthieu Boyd (Madison, NJ: Fairleigh Dickinson University Press), 257–69.

Lloyd-Morgan, Ceridwen (1991). Oral Composition and Written Transmission: Welsh Women's Poetry from the Middle Ages and Beyond. *Trivium* 26, 87–102.

MacGregor, Martin (2006). The View from Fortingall: The Worlds of the *Book of the Dean of Lismore*. *Scottish Gaelic Studies* 22, 35–85.

Powell, Nia M. W. (2000). Women and Strict-Metre Poetry in Wales. In *Women and Gender in Early Modern Wales*, ed. Michael Roberts and Simone Clarke (Cardiff: University of Wales Press), 129–58.

Prescott, Sarah, gen. ed. (in production). *Women's Poetry from Ireland, Scotland, and Wales: An Anthology 1400–1800* (Cambridge: Cambridge University Press).

Prescott, Sarah (2016). Archipelagic Literary History: Eighteenth-Century Poetry from Ireland, Scotland and Wales. In *Women's Writing, 1660–1830: Feminisms and Futures*, ed. Jennie Batchelor and Gillian Dow (London: Palgrave Macmillan), 179–201.

Stiùbhart, Domhnall Uilleam (1999). Women and Gender in the Early Modern Western Gaidhealtachd. In *Women in Scotland: c.1100–c.1750*, ed. Elizabeth Ewen and Maureen M. Meikle (East Linton: Tuckwell Press), 233–49.

General Index

Abbey of the Holy Ghost, The, 98, 130
   copy in possession of Paston family, 129
Adela of Normandy, 57
Adeliza of Louvain (queen), 56
Adgar, Guillaume, *Gracial, Le*, 31
Ælfric, *Catholic Homilies*, 32
Ælred of Rievaulx (abbot), 257
   Rule for a Recluse, 87
Æthelburga, Abbess of Barking, 251, 255, 288
Æthelflæd ('Lady of the Mercians'), 51
Æthelthryth, Abbess of Ely, 251, 256–7, 259, 260, 261, 263
Aithbhreac Inghean Coirceadail (poet), 458
Alan of Lynn (theologian), 428, 432
Alberti, Margherita degli, patron of Margery Kempe, 429
Albertus Magnus (theologian), 144
Alfred (king), 381
   childhood reading contest, 51
Alice of France, 309
Alighieri, Dante, *Commedia*, 275
Alphonse of Jaen, *Epistola solitarii ad reges*, 110
Amesbury (priory), 5, 133, 316
Amphelisa, Prioress of Lillechurch, 41
anchoritic literature, 83–99
   Ancrene Wisse, 259
   Ancrene Wisse Group, 84, 86
   Hali Meidenhad, 85, 210, 259
   Katherine Group, 84, 85, 86, 259
   Sawles Warde, 85, 259
   Wooing Group, 84, 86, 213
ancilla/scribe, 32
   scribal hand, 34
Ancrene Riwle. *See Ancrene Wisse*
Ancrene Wisse, 83, 211, 213, 259, 277, *See also* anchoritic literature
   adapted for male readership, 93
   and affective spirituality, 95
   audience of, 92
   and beguine movement, 98
   Early English Text Society editions of, 91
   editions and criticism, 89–95
   extant manuscripts, 88
   and other devotional works, 96–9
Andreas II of Hungary (king), 272
Andrewe, Alice, Prioress of St Michael's, Stamford, 69
animals, collective terms for, 193
Anna of Württemberg, love spell, 188
Anne (saint), 262
Anne of Brittany (queen), 167–8
Anne of France, *Lessons*, 164–5
Anslay, Brian, translation of *Cité des dames*, 449, 450
Anthony of Egypt (saint), 83

Baker, Augustine, 414, 415
Barking (abbey), 31, 33, 257, 258, 259, 287, 288
   Ordinale, 287, 288
Barton, Elizabeth ('Maid of Kent'), 115–16, 434
Baudri, abbot of Bourgueil, 'Adelae Comitissae' (poem), 57
Beatrice de Planisolles, potions, 188
Beauchamp, Margaret, Book of Hours, 186
Beaufort, Lady Margaret, 111, 112
   book commissioning, 112
   literary patronage, 300
   translations of devotional texts, 60
Beauvale Charterhouse, 279
Becket, Mary, Abbess of Barking, 33, 258, 379
Becket, Thomas (saint), prayer to, written by *ancilla*, 32–3
Bede, *Historia ecclesiastica*, 57, 251–2, 255
Benedictine Rule, 66, 69, 71
Benoît de Sainte-Maure, *Roman de Troie*, 348
Bergson, Henri, on humour, 325
Bernard (saint), *Liber de modo bene vivendi* attributed to, 67
Bernard of Clairvaux, 277
Berners, Dame Juliana (Julian)

478

as compiler of her *Book*, 192
Book of Hawking, Hunting and Blasing of Arms, The, 189–90
Bey, Matilda, 28–31
  'Directions for the Troubled', 28–30
  scribal hand, 34
  'Seisine, La' (poem), 28, 31
Birgitta (saint). *See* Bridget of Sweden (saint)
Birgittine Rule. *See* Bridgettine Rule
birthing girdle, 144, 181–6
Boccaccio, Giovanni
  Decameron, 275
  Filostrato, Il, 348
Bokenham, Osbern, 261–3, 432
  Life of St Anne, 263
Bonde, William, *Directory of Conscience*, 72, 113
Book of St Albans, The. *See* Berners, Dame Juliana (Julian), *Book of Hawking*
Book of the Dean of Lismore, The, 462, 467
Book of Vices and Virtues, The, 98
Bordesley (abbey), 213
Boyd, Thomas, Earl of Arran, 133
Bridget of Sweden (saint), 72, 104, 109–11, 218, 449
  affect, displays of, 427
  copy of *Liber de modo bene vivendi*, 67
  Fifteen Oes, The, attributed to, 112
  Revelations, 71, 106, 110, 218, 278, 427
  Sermo angelicus, 107, 111
  vision of the Visitation, 107
Bridgettine Rule, 66–7
  Additions to the Rule, 107
Bruyant, Jacques, 'Chemin de Pauvrete et de Richesse' (poem), 172
Burton, Agnes, 293
Byrkenhed, Dame Margery, 285

Campbell, Iseabal (poet), 458
  biography, 462–3
  poem on a priest's penis, 467
Campsey Ash (priory), 73, 259
canon of women poets (Irish-language, Scottish-Gaelic, and Welsh-language), 458
Capgrave, John, 262, 432
Carneburgh, Betrice, 73
Cary, Anne Clementia, transcription, of Julian of Norwich, 414
Catherine of Aragon (queen), 451
Catherine of Siena (saint), 115, 218, 449
  Dialogo, Il, 108
  Orchard of Syon, The, 108
Caxton, William, 60, 112, 167, 170, 446
  Fayt of Armes and of Chyualrye, 188
  Malory's *Morte Darthur*, 311
  prologue to *Blanchardyn and Eglantine*, 300

Centurio, Grace, 73
Charlotte de Savoie, 164, 166
charms, 180–8
  abortifacients, 186
  against theft of cattle, 27
  for childbirth, 144, 181–6, 187
  mandrake roots, 188
  sator-arepo formula, 181, 185
Chatteris (abbey), 256
Chaucer, Geoffrey, 342, 370
  Book of the Duchess, The, 351
  books owned by Paston family, 131
  Canterbury Tales, portrayals of women in, 344–8
  Ceyx and Alcyone, story of, 367–8
  Constance, story of, 364–5
  Dido, story of, 360–2
  dream visions, 350–4
  Franklin's Tale, The, 311
  House of Fame, The, 352–3
  Knight's Tale, The, 133
  Legend of Good Women, The, 262, 359–68
  Marriage Group, 346
  Medea, story of, 362–4
  Nun's Priest's Tale, The, 301
  Parliament of Fowls, The, 192, 353–4
  Prioress, 345–6
  reference to the *Trotula*, 145
  St Cecilia, 347
  'The Complaint of Venus' (poem), 241
  translatio, 350
  Troilus and Criseyde, 250, 301, 348–50
  Wife of Bath, 344
  Wife of Bath's Prologue, The, 193, 412
  Wife of Bath's Tale, The, 366–7
  women as subjects in, 346–50
Chichele, Henry, archbishop of Canterbury, pontifical by, 66
Chrétien de Troyes
  Chevalier de la Charrete, Le, 300
  Yvain, 305
Christina Mirabilis (saint), 263
Christine de Pizan, 144, 438–52
  Avision Christine, 166, 438
  Book of the Duke of True Lovers, The, 169
  Cité des dames, 443, 451
  conduct literature, 166–9
  dedication written to Henry IV, 440
  Ditié de Jehanne d'Arc, 444
  English reception of *Othéa*, 443
  Enseignemens moraux, 167
  Epistre au dieu d'amours, 440, 441
  Epistre d'Othéa, 167, 440–3
  female version of Christian trinity, 447

Christine de Pizan (cont.)
  image recast as cloistered nun, 452
  Jean de Castel (son), trip to England, 438, 439, 442
  Lamentacion sur les maux de la France, 440
  Livre de fais d'armes et de chevalerie, Le, 167, 188, 440, 444–5
  Livre de la cité des dames, Le, 440
  Livre des faits et bonnes moeurs du sage Roy Charles V, Le, 167
  Livre des trois vertus, Le, 167
  reactions to *L'Epistre d'Othéa*, 446–9
Chubbes, William, master of Jesus College Cambridge, 72
Clemence of Barking, 392
  criticism of Henry II, 258
  Vie de sainte Catherine, 257–8, 382
Cloud of Unknowing, The, 95, 433
Comnena, Anna, *Alexiad*, 58
compilations, devotional, 110, 206
  authority of female visionaries in, 108
  Book to a Mother, 207, 216
  Chastising of God's Children, The, 73, 97, 110, 214
  dialogic model, 214, 215, 216, 217
  Disce mori, 97, 207, 212, 214–16, 218
  Good Remedy Against Spiritual Temptations, A, 207
  Ignorancia sacerdotum, 215
  Life of Soul, The, 208
  Little Treatise Against Fleshly Affections, A, 207, 216
  Mirror to Devout People, A, 109, 110, 207, 217, 218
  Pore Caitif, 208–10
  Speculum devotorum, 217
  Talking of the Love of God, A, 212
  Treatise of Love, The, 97, 210–13
  use of women authors, 218
conduct literature, 160
  for aristocratic children, 161–5
  and bourgeois values, 172–3
  circulation of, 166
  Griselda, story of, 172
  hunting, 188–93
  Ménagier de Paris, Le, 172–3, 180, 188, 192
  Miroir des bonnes femmes, 170
  Miroir des dames, 166
  mirror for princes, 161, 167
  mirror for princesses, 167
  Speculum dominarum, 166
Constantinus Africanus
  Pantegni, 146
  Viaticum, 147
Copland, Robert, 196

Cressy, Serenus, printing of Julian of Norwich's Long Text, 416
Cupper, Robert, will of, 124

Darcy, Elizabeth, 301
Darker, William (scribe), 67
Dartford (priory), 73
David of Augsburg, *Formula novitiorum*, 68
de Clare, Matilda, Countess of Gloucester, 92
De doctrina cordis, 89
de Vere, Elizabeth, Countess of Oxford, 262
de Vere, Lucy, Prioress of Castle Hedingham, 41
de Worde, Wynkyn, 97, 112, 196, 211, 434
Dhuoda, *Liber manualis* (*Handbook for William*), 161–2
Dominici, Giovanni, *Regola del governo di cura familiare*, 429
Donizo of Canossa, *Vita Mathildis* (*Song of the Princes of Canossa*), 57
drama, medieval, and role of women, 285
  Chester 'Assumption', 292
  Chester Innkeepers Guild, 293
  costuming, 287, 293
  Coventry Cycle, 293
  Coventry Smiths' Guild, 293
  Digby *Mary Magdalene*, 293
  mystery plays, performance and production, 291–4
  performers in liturgical dramas, Barking Abbey, 287
  Processional of the Priory of the Blessed Virgin Mary, 285
  tableaux vivantes, participating in, 295–6
  terminology, 286
  Visitatio Sepulchri, 287–9
  York Drapers' Guild, 293
Durand of Champagne, 166
Dyfi, Ieuan (poet), 468
  confession of adultery, 470

Ealhswith (saint), and ownership of 'Book of Nunnaminster', 51
Easton, Adam, *Defensorium sanctae Birgittae*, 428
Edith of Wessex (queen), patron of *Vita Edwardi Regis*, 52–3
Edward, Duke of York, *Master of the Game*, 191
Edwardian Conquest, 459
Ela, Countess of Salisbury, Abbess of Lacock Abbey, 43
  profession of obedience, 44
Eleanor of Aquitaine (queen), 300
  literary patronage, 57
Elizabeth of Hungary (saint), 71, 262
  and misattributed *Revelations*, 272
Elizabeth of Naples, 272

General Index

Elizabeth of Spalbeek (saint), 263, 264
Elizabeth of Töss, 272
Elizabeth of York (queen), 42
   copy of Prose *Tristan*, 301
Emma of Normandy (queen), and *Encomium Emmae*, 52
emotion and affect, of women, 240, 271, 273, 274
   affective devotion, 271
   in the *Alexiad*, 59
   dramatic, 288
English lyrics, medieval, 229–43
   'A wayle whyte as whales bon', 237
   'As I went on Yol Day', 236
   authorship by women, 242–3
   'Come home, dere herte, from tarieng', 241, 242
   and gender ambiguity, 237
   'Goe, lytyll byll', 233
   'I syng of a myden that is makeles', 232
   'Litel wot it any man / How derne love may stonde', 237
   'Maiden in the mor lay', 234–6
   misogyny in, 236, 238
   'My deth y love, my lyf ich hate', 237
   'O Wicket wemen, wilfull, and variable', 238
   'Of wimmen cometh this worldes welle', 239
   romance and eroticism in, 234
   satirical views of women, 238
   'Stond wel, moder, under rod', 231
   'The man that I loued al ther best', 237
   'Weping haueth myn wonges wet', 238
   'What-so men seyn', 242
   'Where Y haue chosyn, steadfast woll Y be', 242
   'Yit wulde I nat the causer faryd amysse', 242

fabliaux 1,
   audience of, 336
   baise honteuse, 328, 332
   Berengier au long cul, 327–31
   Chevalier qui fist les cons parler, Le, 334
   Gageure, La, 332–3
   gender relations, caricaturing of, 325–7, 335
   humiliation in, 324–5
   misogyny in, 329, 332
   sex and gender in, 329, 335
   Trois dames qui troverent un vit, Les, 333
Fabri, Felix, rules for Church of Holy Sepulchre pilgrims, 425
Fastolf, John, 444, 448
Feasts and the Passion of Our Lord Jesus Christ, The, 74
Fewterer, John, *Mirror or Glass of Christ's Passion, The*, 115
Fickonis, Anna, Abbess of Vadstena, 71
fin amor, 170, 240

Findern manuscript, authorship of, 239–42, 301,
   See also English lyrics, medieval
Fishbourne, Thomas, 278
Fitzalan, Joan, 59
Fitzgerald, Brighid (poet), 458
Flete, William, *Remedies against Temptations*, 277
Fox, Richard, edition of *Rule of seynt Benet*, 68
Francis of Assisi (saint), audience with sultan, 423
Franciscan community, in Holy Land, 423

Gambacorta, Chiara, Prioress of San Domenico, 429
Gaston III, Count of Foix, *Livre de la chasse*, 191
gender and character construction, in medieval English literature, 342
Geoffrey de Beaulieu, 163
Geoffrey of Monmouth, *Historia Regum Britanniae*, 469
Gerberga II, Abbess of Gandersheim, 289
Gertrude the Great, *Legatus divinae pietatis*, 273
Gesta romanorum, excerpted in Harley 219, 442
Gibbs, Elizabeth, Abbess of Syon, 67, 68, 70, 111
   book commissioning, 112
Gilbertus Anglicus (physician), 144
   Compendium medicinae, 148, 151
Gordon, Bernard (physician), 144
Gower, John, 342, 354–9, 370
   Ceyx and Alcyone, story of, 367–8
   Cinkante Balades, 357–8
   Confessio amantis, 355–6, 359–68
   Constance, story of, 364–5
   Dido, story of, 360–2
   Medea, story of, 362–4
   Mirour de l'Omme, 358–9
   Tale of Florent, 366–7
   Vox clamantis, 356
Greenhalgh, James, 216
Grey, Richard, benefactor of Syon Abbey, 70
Guernes de Pont-Sainte-Maxence, *Life of St Thomas Becket*, 258
Gulbadan Banu Begum, *Humayunnama*, 60
Gwenllïan ferch Rhirid Flaidd (poet), 459, 464
Gwerful Fychan (poet), 459, 462
Gwerful Mechain (poet), 458, 459
   biography, 461–2
   'Cywydd y gont' (poem), 465–6
   descriptio pulchritudinis, parody of, 465
   'I ateb Ieuan Dyfi' (poem), 468–70
   'I wragedd eiddigus' (poem), 464–5

hagiography, 265
   and anchoritic literature, 259–60
   Anglo-Norman audiences of, 256
   Anglo-Saxon abbessial model, 255, 261
   and aristocratic patronage, 262

hagiography (cont.)
  and Chaucer, 345, 347, 360
  influence on romance, 306
  insular saints, women, in 260–5
  for married readership, 263
  staging of physical suffering in, 264
  women exemplars, Irish and Welsh in, 255
Hampole, Richard, 215
Handon, Christine, 293
Helfta (convent), 143, 273
Henry II (king), 300, 381
Henry III (king), 259
Henryson, Robert, *Testament of Cressid*, 348
Herrad of Hohenburg, *Hortus deliciarum*, 275
Hilda, Abbess of Whitby, 251
Hildebert, Bishop of Lavardin, 56, 85
Hildegard of Bingen (saint), 289
  Book of Divine Works, The, 146
  Causes and Cures, The, 143, 146
  on human reproduction, 146
  medical texts, 146–7
  on menstruation, 146
  Ordo Virtutum, 290–1
  Physica, 146, 186
  theology of *viriditas*, 275–6
Hildelith, Abbess of Barking, 255, 288
Hilton, Walter, 70, 96
  Scale of Perfection, The, 95, 112, 219, 414
historical analysis, 'exceptional woman' model of, 50
Hoccleve, Thomas, 441
  Letter to Cupid, 440
  Regiment of Princes, 133
Holland, Margaret, Duchess of Clarence
  book gifting, 111
  copy of *Life of St Jerome*, 111
Honest Bede, An, 212
Horwode, Elizabeth, Abbess of Minoresses of London, 70
Hrotsvitha of Gandersheim (dramatist/poet), 254
  Ducitius, 255
  Latin plays, 289–91
Hugeburc, 253–4
  Life of Willibald, 253
Hugh of Fleury, 57
Hull, Dame Eleanor, 59, 190, 207
  Meditations Upon the Seven Days of the Week, 219

Inveraray circle, 462, 463, 468
Isabel de Warenne, Countess of Arundel, 259
Isabel, Duchess of York, book gifting, 301
Isabella of France (queen), literary patronage, 59
Isabelle of Bavaria (queen), 443
Iseabal ní Mheic Cailéin (poet), 458

'Atá fleasgach arm o thí' (poem), 467
biography, 462–3
'Is mairg dá ngalar an grádh' (poem), 467

Jacob of Voragine, *Golden Legend*, 71, 128
Jan de Wael (Johannes Gallicus), *Manual for the Young Ones*, 68, 73
Jean de Montreuil
  To All the Knighthood, 443
  Treatise Against the English, 443
Joan of Arc, 444
John of Thoresby, Archbishop of York, 208
John of Tynemouth, *Sanctilogium*, 261
Jordan, Agnes, Abbess of Syon, 70, 113, 115
Judith of Flanders
  donor portraits, 53
  literary patronage, 53–5
Julian of Norwich, 96, 97, 400–17
  Christ, maternal qualities of, 400, 403
  meeting with Margery Kempe, 269, 401
  Passion-themed visions, 409
  references to authorship as woman, 402
  Revelation of Love, A, 207, 218, 277
  self-authorisation as visionary, 412–13
  Vision Shewed be the Goodenes of God to a Devoute Woman, A, 279
  use of womb imagery, 412

Kalender of Shepherds, The, 198–9
  astrology in, 196
  health advice in, 196
  'Of an assaute agaynst a Snayle' (poem), 197
  physiognomy in, 197
  reprint history, 194–5
Kalilah wa Dimnah, 389
Katherine Group. *See* anchoritic literature
Katherine of Sutton, Abbess of Barking, 287, 288
Kempe, Margery, 265
  accusations of heresy, 279
  affect, displays of, 274, 422, 425, 427
  annotators of her *Book*, 433
  Book of Margery Kempe, 269, 274, 279
  and clerical community, 432
  influence of Bridget of Sweden, 427, 428
  interrogations for heresy, 431
  life in Norfolk, 431
  meeting with Julian of Norwich, 269, 401
  queerness of self-portrayal, 421
  Red Ink Annotator, 433
  tour of Holy Land, 422–7
  trip to Rome, 427–30
  visit to Syon Abbey, 112, 430–1

General Index

Lacock (abbey), foundation of, 44
Langland, John, bishop of Lincoln, 69
Leoba (saint), 252–3
Leonor of Portugal (queen), 168
Liber Eliensis, 256
Livre du gouvernement des roys et princes, Le, 442
Llwyd, Dafydd (poet), 461, 463, 464
lore (instruction and folk belief), of women, 179–205
Louis IX (king), *Enseignemenz (Teachings)*, 162–3
Love, Nicholas
  Mirror of the Blessed Life of Christ, 71, 72, 97, 422, 433
Lydgate, John, 262, 432
  'Life of St Margaret' (poem), 133
  lyrics attributed to, 239
  Siege of Thebes, The, 133, 302
  Troy Book, 302
Lyston, Isabel, book ownership, 310

MacGregor, Seumas (James), dean of Lismore, 462
Malik al-Kamil, al- (sultan), audience with St Francis, 423
Malory, Thomas, *Morte Darthur*, 315–17
Manner of Good Living, The, 67
Marchant, Guy (printer), 194
Margaret of Anjou (queen), 167, 439, 444, 448
  comparison to Joan of Arc, 445
  entry into Coventry, 294
Margaret of Nevers, 167
Margaret of Provence (queen), 163
Margaret of Scotland (queen and saint), 54–6
  gospel book, 55
Marian lyrics. *See* Virgin Mary
Marie d'Oignies (saint), 115, 263, 270
  affect, displays of, 274
  Life, 279
Marie de Champagne, 300
Marie de France, 300, 379–95
  Chaitivel, 384
  Chevrefoil, 385, 387–9
  Espurgatoire Seint Patriz, 33, 392–5
  Lais, 303, 383–92
  Lanval, 309
  Laüstic, 385–7
  Milun, 384
  misogyny in fables, 390–2
  and polyglot literary culture, 380–2
  suggested identity of, 33, 379
  use of translation, 385–9
  visionary experience and translation, 393
  Yonec, 383
  Ysopë, 389
Marie, Countess of Ponthieu, literary patronage, 59

Mary de Bohun, 59
Mary Magdalene, 262
Matilda (empress), 57
  dedicatee of *Gesta Regum Anglorum*, 56
Matilda of Canossa, Countess of Tuscany, 57
Matilda of England, 59
Matilda of Scotland (queen), literary patronage, 56
Maud (Matilda) de Leveland, 31
Maud (Matilda), Abbess of Barking, 31
Mechthild of Hackeborn (saint), 218
  affect, displays of, 274
  Book of Gostlye Grace, The, 108
  Liber specialis gratiae, 108, 143, 273
  literary influence, 275
  Revelations, 71
  use of imagery and analogy, 278
  vision of union with Christ, 143, 276
Mechtild of Magdeburg
  Das fließende Licht der Gottheit, 273
medical texts, medieval
  Bald's Leechbook, 180
  Bien sachies femmes, 149
  Book called 'Trotela', The, 150
  De curis mulierum, 142, 147
  De ornatu mulierum, 142, 147
  De passionibus mulierum B, 145
  Genicia Cleopatrae ad Theodotam, 150
  Knowing of Woman's Kind in Childing, The, 145, 150–1, 182–5, 186
  Lacnunga, 180
  Liber de sinthomatibus mulierum, 142, 147
  Non omnes quidem, 145, 150
  Quant Dex nostre Seignor, 149, 150
  Secrés dé femmes, 148
  Secreta mulierum, 144
  Sickness of Women, The, 151–3
  Tractatus de egritudinibus mulierum, 148
  Trotula ensemble, 147–50
medicine, medieval, 141
  Arabic tradition, 147
  conception of venous system, 143
  Hippocratic tradition, 141–6
  infertility, 148
  menstruation, 142, 146, 147, 150
  reproduction and shame topos, 148, 149, 151
  role of uterus, 142
  Soranic tradition, 145
  women practitioners of, 142
Meditationes vitae Christi, 71, 109
Melton, William, 270
Methley, Richard, 433
  affect, displays of, 433
minoresses of London, 73
molestiae nuptiarum (tribulations of marriage), 87

Montagu, John, 3rd Earl of Salisbury, 438
Montagu, Thomas, service in Hundred Years'
    War, 439
Morepath, Edyth, 73
mortuary rolls
    and women scribes, 41–3
Muscio (physician), *Gynaecology*, 145

Nasir ad-Din Muhammad, al- (sultan), 423
Norton, John, prior of Mount Grace, 433
Nun of Barking, *Vie d'Edouard le confesseur*,
    257–8, 382

Odo de Cheriton, 442

Palmer, Kathryn, 73
Paston family, 124–34, 143
    Agnes Paston, 124–7
    Anne Paston, 128
    John Paston II, library inventory, 129–31
    Margaret Paston, 128–31
    Margery Brews Paston, 128, 132
    William Paston I, 125
Pater Noster of Richard Ermyte, The, 210
Paul the Hermit (saint), 71
Pearl (poem), 217, 275
Peckham, John, Archbishop of Canterbury, 208
Pepwell, Henry (printer), 434, 449, 451
Percy, Eleanor, Duchess of Buckingham, 239
Peter the Venerable, 71
Philip of Clairvaux, 264
Pikerell, Agnes, 287
Piramus, Denis, on women and *lais*, 300
poetic diction, Gaelic
    dán díreach (strict metre), 459
poetic diction, Welsh
    cynghanedd (harmony), 459
Pole, William de la, 1st Duke of Suffolk, 133
Porete, Marguerite
    burning as heretic, 280
    Mirror of Simple Souls, The, 279, 433
Prick of Conscience
    copy loaned to Agnes Paston, 124–7
    extant manuscripts, 89
Priory of the Blessed Virgin Mary, Chester,
    285, 286
Psalms, 190, 219
    apotropaic power of, 28–30

Records of Early English Drama, 285
Revelation of Purgatory, A, 278
Rolle, Richard, 95, 96, 114, 215
    Commandment, The, 213
    Ego dormio, 213
    Form of Living, The, 209, 214

romance literature, medieval, 5
    agency of women portrayed in, 303
    Auchinleck manuscript, 301
    critical perspectives, 299
    Emaré, 307
    Erle of Tolous, The, 307
    exemplary suffering in, 306
    French Arthurian romance, 301
    Havelok the Dane, 303
    issues of consent in, 305
    King Horn, 303
    magic and otherworlds, 308–11, 315
    Mort Artu, 317
    Partonope of Blois, 309
    reader response to, 302
    Sir Beves of Hamtoun, 304–5
    Sir Degaré, 308
    Sir Degrevant, 301
    Sir Gawain and the Green Knight, 311
    Sir Gowther, 308
    Sir Launfal, 309
    Sir Orfeo, 308
    Sir Tryamowre, 306
    Stanzaic *Morte Darthur*, 317
    William of Palerne, 310
    and women readers, 300
    Ywain and Gawain, 305
Romulus Nilantii, 389
Rudolf of Fulda, *Life of Leoba*, 252
Rule of St Saviour. See Bridgettine Rule
Rustaveli, Shota, *The Knight in the Panther Skin*, 58

Salisbury Psalter
    glossator of, post-Conquest, 39
    role of women in production of, 35–9
Salthouse, Richard, 432
Scrope, Stephen, 445
    representation of Christine de Pizan, 452
    translation of *Othéa*, 441, 442, 446
Secretum secretorum, 442
Sewell, Joanna, 216
Shaftesbury (abbey), 36
Sheen Charterhouse, 279
Sir Gawain and the Green Knight, 190, 192
Smaragdus, *Diadema monachorum*, copied by
    nun, 40
Sopwell (abbey), 190
Soranus of Ephesus (physician), 145
Speculum spiritualium, 433
Springold, Robert, 270–431, 431
St Augustine's (abbey), 73
St Sepulchre, Canterbury (priory), 114
St Werberg's (abbey), 292
Stanburne, Margaret, Prioress of St Michael's,
    Stamford, 68–70

Stanley, Sir George, 292
Stillingfleet, Edward, bishop of Worcester, *Discourse Concerning the Idolatry Practised in the Church of Rome*, 416
Stixwould (priory), 69
Suso, Henry, *Horologium divinae sapientiae*, 71
Suzanne de Bourbon, printing of *Lesson*s, 164
Symonde, Catherine, 73
Syon (abbey), 66–8, 70, 73, 74, 104–16, 212, 214, 216, 278
  Additions for the Sisters, 72
  Dyetary of ghostly helthe, 66, 75
  library, 105, 133
  Mirror of Our Lady, The, 108, 109, 110, 113, 278
  profession day, 72
  readings of *Sermo angelicus*, 107–8
  Sandre, Stephen, confessor general, 72
  Swedish motherhouse (Vadstena), 71, 105, 114
  Thomas Prestius, 68
  visit by Bishop of London and the Confessor General, 72
  visit by Margery Kempe, 112

Talbot, John, 1st Earl of Shrewsbury, 167, 444–5
Tamar of Georgia (queen), 58
Thomas à Kempis, *Imitatio Christi*, 60, 67
Tour Landry, Geoffrey de la, *Livre du Chevalier de la Tour, Le*, 169–71
Tractatus de Purgatorio Sancti Patricii, 393
translatio studii, 342
Troon, Maria, 114
Trota, *Trotula*, 142, 145, 181, 186, *See also* medical texts, medieval
Twici (Twiti), Guillaume, *L'art de venerie*, 190

Upholland Anthology, 415

Vérard, Antoine (publisher), 194
Vie seinte Audrée, 33, 256–7, 382
Virgin Mary
  prayer to, written by *ancilla*, 32
  as subject of lyrics, 229
  in vernacular theology, 229

  womb of, in Julian of Norwich's *Revelation*, 412
Voyage of St Brendan, 56

Whitford, Richard
  Daily Exercise and Experience of Death, A, 112, 115
  Pype or tun of Perfection, 113
William of Malmesbury, *Gesta Regum Anglorum*, 56
William of Saint-Pathus, 163
Witham Charterhouse, 279
women poets, medieval, in Ireland, Scotland, and Wales, 457
  and bardic culture, 459–61
  and female sexual agency, as subject, 467
  nomenclature for, 460
  poems and performance style, 463–70
women, aristocratic
  and literary/cultural patronage, 50
  book gifting, 111, 301
  patrons of hagiography, 262
women, religious
  acquisition of books, 70–1
  as authors and scribes, 44–5
  book gifting, 73–4, 92, 97
  book ownership, Syon nuns, 105
  books commissioned by, 67–70
  intellectual/spiritual formation of, 67–9
  marginalia by, 25–39, 68–9
  modes of learning, 65
  multilingual literacy, 87
women, visionary, 269–80, *See also* Kempe, Margery; Julian of Norwich, Mechthild of Hackeborn
  as literary community, 269
  and role as author, 110
  as subjects of attacks and accusations, 109, 270, 279, 416, 431
  conversational theology of, 274
  shared imagery, 275
Woodford, Elizabeth, 74
Woodville, Anthony, 2nd Earl Rivers, 445
Woodville, Elizabeth (queen), 42
Wooing Group. *See* anchoritic literature
Worcester, William, *Boke of Noblesse*, 445, 448, 449
Wulfhilda, Abbess of Barking, 288
Wyllowby [Willughby], Elizabeth, 73

Index of Manuscripts

Aberdeen, University of Aberdeen Library, MS 25, 186
Aberystwyth, National Library of Wales, MS Brogynton II. 1, 153

Cambridge, Cambridge University Library, Additional MS 3035, 358
Cambridge, Cambridge University Library, MS Additional 2604, 261
Cambridge, Cambridge University Library, MS Dd.ii. 33, 68
Cambridge, Cambridge University Library, MS Ff. 6.33, 107
Cambridge, Cambridge University Library, MS Ff.i. 6, 239
Cambridge, Cambridge University Library, MS Kk 1.6, 219
Cambridge, Corpus Christi College, MS 383, 33–4
Cambridge, Corpus Christi College, MS 402, 91
Cambridge, Gonville and Caius, MS 234/120, 93
Cambridge, Magdalene College, Pepys Library MS 1047, 190
Cambridge, St John's College, MS N. 24, 60
Cambridge, St John's College, MS N. 31, 41–3
Cambridge, Trinity College, MS O.2.56, 433
Cambridge, Trinity College, MS O.5.2, 133
Cambridge, Trinity College, MS R.14.52, 152
Cambridge, University Library, MS Additional 6578, 433

Dublin, Trinity College Dublin, MS 301, 232

Glasgow, Glasgow University Library, MS Hunter 341, 148
Glasgow, Glasgow University Library, MS Hunter 136 (T.6.18), 67

Kew, The National Archives C1/579/15, 70

London, British Library, MS Additional 12195, 150
London, British Library, MS Additional 18632, 133
London, British Library, MS Additional 29729, 239
London, British Library, MS Additional 37790, 279, 401, 413
London, British Library, MS Additional 61823, 432
London, British Library, MS Additional 70513, 258
London, British Library, MS Arundel 119, 133
London, British Library, MS Arundel 286, 208
London, British Library, MS Arundel 327, 261
London, British Library, MS Egerton 2849, 41–3
London, British Library, MS Harley 219, 440–3
London, British Library, MS Harley 2253, 231–2, 331
London, British Library, MS Harley 2340, 190
London, British Library, MS Harley 2373, 433
London, British Library, MS Harley 2397, 70
London, British Library, MS Harley 2965, 51
London, British Library, MS Harley 585, 180
London, British Library, MS Harley 612, 106
London, British Library, MS Harley 978, 381
London, British Library, MS Lansdowne 285, 132
London, British Library, MS Lansdowne 436, 261
London, British Library, MS Or. 166, 60
London, British Library MS Royal 12 D.xvii, 180
London, British Library, MS Royal 12 E.i, 232
London, British Library, MS Royal 17 A.xxvii, 86
London, British Library, MS Royal 2 A.xviii, 60, 186
London, British Library, MS Royal E.vi, 444
London, British Library, MS Sloane 2463, 152
London, British Library, MS Sloane 249, 152
London, British Library, MS Sloane 2499, 414
London, British Library, MS Stowe 42, 417

Index of Manuscripts

London, British Library, Cotton MS Claudius B. i, 106
London, British Library, Cotton MS Cleopatra CVI, 92
London, British Library, Cotton MS Galba A. xiv, 41
London, British Library, Cotton MS Julius F. ii, 106
London, British Library, Cotton MS Nero A. xiv, 89
London, British Library, Cotton MS Titus D. xviii, 94
London, British Library, Cotton MS Vespasian D.xiv, 34–5
London, British Library, Cotton MS Vitellius E.vii, 90
London, British Library, Cotton MS Vitellius F.vii, 90, 91, 220
London, British Library, MS Nero A.xiv, 86
London, British Library, MS Titus D.xviii, 86
London, British Museum, MS Royal 15 E.vi, 167
London, Lambeth Palace Library, MŞ 546, 74
London, Royal College of Surgeons, MS 129, 152
London, Wellcome Library, MS 632, 182
London, Wellcome Library, MS 5650, 152
London, Westminster Cathedral Treasury, MS 4, 207, 218, 414

New Haven, Beinecke Rare Book & Manuscript Library, Takamiya MS 56, 182
New Haven, Yale Medical Library, MS 47, 151
New York, Morgan Library, MS Glazier 39, 182
New York, Morgan Library, MS Glazier 9, 186
New York, Morgan Library, MS M 492, 57
New York, Morgan Library, MS M. 775, 446
Notre Dame, Indiana, University of Notre Dame, MS 67, 217

Oxford, Bodleian Library, MS Ashmole 59, 239
Oxford, Bodleian Library, MS Bodley 240, 261
Oxford, Bodleian Library, MS Bodley 451, 40
Oxford, Bodleian Library, MS Digby 133, 293
Oxford, Bodleian Library, MS Digby 86, 231, 238
Oxford, Bodleian Library, MS Douce 114, 263
Oxford, Bodleian Library, MS Egerton 3277, 59
Oxford, Bodleian Library, MS Lat. Liturg. f. 5, 55
Oxford, Bodleian Library, MS Lat. Liturg. F 9, 186
Oxford, Bodleian Library, MS Laud Misc. 210, 208
Oxford, Bodleian Library, MS Laud Misc. 416, 133
Oxford, Bodleian Library, MS Laud Misc. 517, 67
Oxford, Bodleian Library, MS Rawlinson D 913, 56
Oxford, Jesus College, MS 39 (J), 214
Oxford, Magdalen College, MS Latin 67, 90
Oxford, St John's College, MS 182, 279
Oxford, St John's College, MS Douce 114, 279

Paris, Bibliotheque Nationale, MS fonds anglais 40 (P), 414
Princeton, Princeton University Library, MS 138.44, 186

Salisbury, Salisbury Cathedral Library, MS 150, 35–9
San Marino, Huntington Library, MS HM. 502, 208
Stanford, Stanford University Libraries Special Collections, Codex MS 0877, 42
Stockholm, Kungliga Biblioteket, MS Vu 22, 441

Wiltshire, Longleat House, MS 14, 72

York, York Minster, MS XVI.I. 9, 433